HUMAN RIGHTS WATCH

WORLD REPORT
2023
EVENTS OF 2022

Copyright © 2023 Human Rights Watch
All rights reserved.
Printed in the United States of America
ISBN 978-1-64421-240-0

Cover photo: Children from Mariupol, Ukraine, look out the window of their family's car, marked with the word "children," after arriving at an evacuation point for people fleeing areas under Russian control, May 2, 2022.
© 2022 Chris McGrath/Getty Images

Cover and book design by Rafael Jiménez

www.hrw.org

Human Rights Watch defends the rights of people worldwide.

We scrupulously investigate abuses, expose facts widely, and pressure those with power to respect rights and secure justice.

Human Rights Watch is an independent, international organization that works as part of a vibrant movement to uphold human dignity and advance the cause of human rights for all.

Human Rights Watch began in 1978 with the founding of its Europe and Central Asia division (then known as Helsinki Watch). Today it also includes divisions covering Africa, the Americas, Asia, Europe and Central Asia, the Middle East and North Africa, and the United States. There are thematic divisions or programs on arms; business and human rights; children's rights; crisis and conflict; disability rights; the environment and human rights; international justice; lesbian, gay, bisexual, and transgender rights; refugee rights; and women's rights.

The organization maintains offices in Amman, Amsterdam, Beirut, Berlin, Bishkek, Brussels, Chicago, Geneva, Goma, Hong Kong, Johannesburg, Kiev, Kinshasa, London, Los Angeles, Miami, Moscow, Nairobi, New York, Paris, San Francisco, São Paulo, Seoul, Silicon Valley, Stockholm, Sydney, Tokyo, Toronto, Tunis, Washington DC, and Zurich, and field presences in more than 50 other locations globally.

Human Rights Watch is an independent, nongovernmental organization, supported by contributions from private individuals and foundations worldwide. It accepts no government funds, directly or indirectly.

WORLD REPORT 2023

Table of Contents

A New Model for Global Leadership on Human Rights — 1
by Tirana Hassan

COUNTRIES — 15

Afghanistan	17
Algeria	24
Angola	29
Argentina	34
Armenia	40
Australia	47
Azerbaijan	54
Bahrain	61
Bangladesh	67
Belarus	73
Bolivia	80
Bosnia and Herzegovina	86
Brazil	91
Burkina Faso	101
Burundi	106
Cambodia	111
Cameroon	117
Canada	125
Central African Republic	132
Chad	138
Chile	142
China	149
Colombia	162
Cuba	171

TABLE OF CONTENTS

Democratic Republic of Congo	180
Ecuador	185
Egypt	191
El Salvador	199
Eritrea	208
Eswatini	213
Ethiopia	217
European Union	224
France	236
Georgia	244
Germany	250
Greece	259
Guatemala	265
Haiti	272
Honduras	280
Hungary	287
India	291
Indonesia	300
Iran	306
Iraq	315
Israel and Palestine	324
Italy	334
Japan	340
Jordan	345
Kazakhstan	351
Kenya	357
Kosovo	362
Kuwait	366
Kyrgyzstan	371
Lebanon	377
Libya	385
Malaysia	393

Maldives	400
Mali	405
Mexico	411
Morocco and Western Sahara	420
Mozambique	427
Myanmar	432
Nepal	440
Nicaragua	444
Nigeria	451
North Korea	460
Pakistan	466
Papua New Guinea	473
Peru	478
Philippines	485
Poland	490
Qatar	495
Russian Federation	500
Rwanda	513
Saudi Arabia	518
Serbia	525
Singapore	529
Somalia	533
South Africa	538
South Korea	545
South Sudan	550
Spain	555
Sri Lanka	561
Sudan	569
Syria	575
Tajikistan	585
Tanzania	590

TABLE OF CONTENTS

Thailand 593
Tunisia 600
Turkey 606
Turkmenistan 617
Uganda 623
Ukraine 629
United Arab Emirates 646
United Kingdom 651
United States 661
Uzbekistan 677
Venezuela 683
Vietnam 693
Yemen 700
Zimbabwe 706

WORLD REPORT 2023

… HUMAN RIGHTS WATCH

A New Model for Global Leadership on Human Rights

By Tirana Hassan, *Acting Executive Director*

The obvious conclusion to draw from the litany of human rights crises in 2022—from Russian President Vladimir Putin's deliberate attacks on civilians in Ukraine and Xi Jinping's open-air prison for the Uyghurs in China to the Taliban's putting millions of Afghans at risk of starvation—is that unchecked authoritarian power leaves behind a sea of human suffering. But 2022 also revealed a fundamental shift in power in the world that opens the way for all concerned governments to push back against these abuses by protecting and strengthening the global human rights system, especially when the actions of the major powers fall short or are problematic.

We have witnessed world leaders cynically trading away human rights obligations and accountability for human rights abusers in exchange for seeming short-term political wins. US presidential candidate Joe Biden's principled pledge to make Saudi Arabia a "pariah state" over its human rights record was eviscerated once he was in office and facing high gas prices by his bro-like fist bump with Saudi Arabia's Mohammed Bin Salman. And the Biden administration, despite its rhetoric about prioritizing democracy and human rights in Asia, has tempered criticism of abuses and increasing authoritarianism in India, Thailand, the Philippines, and elsewhere in the region for security and economic reasons, instead of recognizing that all are linked.

Of course, these kinds of double standards are not solely the purview of global superpowers. Pakistan has supported the United Nations high commissioner for human rights' monitoring of abuses in Muslim-majority Kashmir, but owing to its close relationship with China, has turned its back on possible crimes against humanity against Uyghur and other Turkic Muslims in Xinjiang. Pakistan's hypocrisy is especially glaring given its coordinator role of the 57-member Organisation of Islamic Cooperation.

Human rights crises do not arise from nowhere. Governments that fail to live up to their legal obligations to protect human rights at home sow the seeds of discontent, instability, and ultimately crisis. Left unchecked, the egregious actions of abusive governments escalate, cementing the belief that corruption, censorship, impunity, and violence are the most effective tools to achieve their aims. Ignoring human rights violations carries a heavy cost, and the ripple effects should not be underestimated.

But in a world of shifting power, we also found opportunity in preparing our 2023 World Report, which examines the state of human rights in nearly 100 countries. Each issue needs to be understood and addressed on its own merits, and each requires leadership. Any state that recognizes the power that comes from working in concert with others to affect human rights change can provide that leadership. There is more space, not less, for governments to stand up and adopt rights-respecting plans of action.

New coalitions and new voices of leadership have emerged that can shape and further this trend. Finland, Norway, and Sweden have taken a principled approach to holding Saudi Arabia accountable for war crimes in Yemen. South Africa, Namibia, and Indonesia have paved the way for more governments to recognize that Israeli authorities are committing the crime against humanity of apartheid against Palestinians.

Pacific Island nations as a bloc have demanded more ambitious emissions reductions from those countries that are polluting the most, while Vanuatu leads an effort to put the adverse effects of climate change before the International Court of Justice for their own sake—and ours.

And while the US Supreme Court struck down 50 years of federal protection for reproductive rights, the "green wave" of abortion-rights expansions in Latin America—notably Argentina, Colombia, and Mexico—offers a compelling counternarrative.

This is the overarching lesson of our ever-more disrupted world: we need to reimagine how power in the world is exercised, and that all governments not only have the opportunity but the responsibility to take action to protect human rights within and beyond their borders.

Ukraine: Beacon and Rebuke

Vladimir Putin's full-scale invasion of Ukraine in February and ensuing atrocities quickly rose to the top of the world's human rights agenda in 2022. After Ukrainian troops forced the Russian military's withdrawal from Bucha, north of the capital, Kyiv, the UN found that at least 70 civilians had been the victims of unlawful killings, including summary executions, which are war crimes. This pattern of Russian atrocity has been repeated countless times.

At the Drama Theater in Mariupol, hundreds of displaced residents took refuge, painting the Russian word "DETI" (children) on the ground outside in letters so large they could be seen in satellite imagery. This alert was meant to protect the civilians, including many children, sheltering inside. Instead, it seemed only to serve as an inducement for Russian forces whose bombs destroyed the building and killed at least a dozen, and likely more, of its occupants. Inflicting civilian suffering, such as the repeated strikes on the energy infrastructure that Ukrainians depend on for electricity, water, and heat, seems to be a central part of the Kremlin's strategy.

Putin's brazenness has been made possible largely because of his longstanding free hand to operate with impunity. The loss of civilian life in Ukraine comes as no surprise to Syrians who suffered grave abuses from airstrikes following Russia's intervention to support Syrian forces under Bashar al-Assad in 2015. Putin tapped prominent military commanders from that campaign to lead the war effort in Ukraine, with predictable—and devastating—consequences for Ukrainian civilians. Russia has accompanied its brutal military actions in Ukraine with a crackdown on human rights and anti-war activists in Russia, throttling dissent and any criticism of Putin's rule.

But one positive outcome of Russia's actions has been to activate the full global human rights system created to deal with crises like this. The UN Human Rights Council promptly opened an investigation to document and preserve evidence of human rights violations in the war, and later created a special rapporteur to monitor the human rights situation inside Russia. The UN General Assembly four times condemned—mostly by wide margins—both Russia's invasion and its human rights violations. The General Assembly also suspended Russia from the UN Human Rights Council, blunting its spoiler capacity on Ukraine and other serious human rights crises on the council's docket.

European countries welcomed millions of Ukrainian refugees, a commendable response that also exposed the double standards of most European Union member countries in their ongoing treatment of countless Syrians, Afghans, Palestinians, Somalis, and others seeking asylum. The prosecutor of the International Criminal Court (ICC) in The Hague opened a Ukraine investigation following a referral of the situation by an unprecedented number of the court's member countries. Governments have also mobilized to weaken Putin's global influence and military power, with the European Union, the United States, the United Kingdom, Canada, and others imposing targeted international sanctions against Russian individuals, companies, and other entities.

This extraordinary response showed what is possible for accountability, for refugee protection, and for safeguarding the human rights of some of the world's most vulnerable people. At the same time, the attacks on civilians and horrendous abuses in Ukraine should be a reminder that this consolidated support, critical as it is, should not be confused with a quick fix.

Rather, governments should reflect on where the situation would be if the international community had made a concerted effort to hold Putin to account much earlier—in 2014, at the onset of the war in eastern Ukraine; in 2015, for abuses in Syria; or for the escalating human rights crackdown within Russia over the last decade. The challenge going forward is for governments to replicate the best of the international response in Ukraine and scale up the political will to address other crises around the world until there is meaningful human rights improvement.

Achieving Accountability in Ethiopia

The armed conflict in northern Ethiopia has received only a tiny fraction of the global attention focused on Ukraine, despite two years of atrocities, including a number of massacres, by the warring parties.

In 2020, tensions between Ethiopia's federal government and Tigray's regional authorities, the Tigray People's Liberation Front (TPLF), boiled over into conflict in the Tigray region, with Amhara regional forces and Eritrea's military supporting the Ethiopian armed forces. The government has heavily restricted access to conflict-affected areas for independent rights investigators and journalists ever since, making scrutiny of abuses as they unfold difficult, even as the conflict spread to the neighboring Amhara and Afar regions.

Governments and the UN have condemned the summary killings, widespread sexual violence, and pillage, but have done little else. An ethnic cleansing campaign against the Tigrayan population in Western Tigray resulted in many deaths, sexual violence, mass detention, and the forced displacement of thousands. The government's effective siege of the Tigray region continued through 2022, denying the civilian population access to food, medicine, and life-saving humanitarian aid, as well as electricity, banking, and communication, in violation of international law.

The three elected African members of the UN Security Council—Gabon, Ghana, and Kenya—as well as Russia and China, have blocked even placing Ethiopia on its formal agenda for discussion, despite the council's mandate to maintain and restore international peace and security.

Governments have also hesitated to adopt targeted sanctions against Ethiopian entities and individuals responsible for abuses. International scrutiny has instead rested with the UN Human Rights Council, which narrowly renewed the mandate of the mechanism it created in December 2021 to investigate and preserve evidence of grave abuses and identify those responsible. However, Ethiopian federal authorities continue to block its work fiercely.

A 10-day African Union-led peace process culminated in November in a truce between the Ethiopian federal government and Tigrayan authorities, which offers an opportunity for outside states to play a leadership role in supporting solutions that can break deadly cycles of violence and impunity. With pathways for domestic accountability elusive, international monitoring of the agreement is needed, along with credible efforts to hold accountable those responsible for wartime abuses.

The agreement's key backers and observers, including the AU, UN, and US, should signal and maintain pressure to ensure that independent investigative organizations can access conflict areas, and document and preserve evidence. Accountability for these crimes needs to remain a priority so victims and their families can obtain a measure of justice and reparations.

A Brighter Spotlight on Beijing

Chinese President Xi Jinping secured a precedent-breaking third term as head of the Chinese Communist Party in October, setting himself up as a "leader for life," and all but ensuring the Chinese government's unrelenting hostility to human rights protections will continue. Xi has surrounded himself with loyalists and doubled down on building a security state, deepening rights violations across the country.

In the Xinjiang region, Beijing's mass detention of an estimated one million Uyghurs and other Turkic Muslims—who are subject to torture, political indoctrination, and forced labor—and severe restrictions on rights to religion, expression, and culture for the general population, stand out for their gravity, scale, and cruelty. The UN found that violations in Xinjiang could amount to crimes against humanity, echoing the findings of Human Rights Watch and other human rights groups.

The rigorous report of the then-UN high commissioner for human rights, Michelle Bachelet, based on years of investigation and the Chinese government's internal documents, laws, policies, data, and policy statements, created a critical common reference point from which governments should act. That the report was released only in the final minutes of Bachelet's term is indicative of Beijing's intense pressure to bury it.

The report sparked notable diplomatic mobilization. A resolution to open a debate about the report was introduced in the Human Rights Council and fell short by only two votes. The result reflected Beijing's pressure on governments like Indonesia—which said we "must not close our eyes" to the plight of Uyghurs and then voted "no"—as well as its influence on the actions of those states that abstained, including Argentina, India, Mexico, and Brazil. But the "yes" votes of Somalia, Honduras, and Paraguay, and the co-sponsorship support of Turkey and Albania, together with 24 mostly Western countries, show the potential in cross-regional alliances and fresh coalitions to come together to challenge the Chinese government's expectation of impunity.

The collective spotlight on the dismal human rights situation in Xinjiang has put Beijing on the defensive, and the Chinese government is working hard to explain away its heinous behavior. The outcome in Geneva heightens the responsibility of the UN leadership to throw its full political weight behind the report and to continue to monitor, document, and report on the situation in Xinjiang, and more broadly in China. Anything less would be an abdication of the human rights pillar of the UN system's responsibility to protect Turkic Muslims in Xinjiang.

Meanwhile, as discomfort around the Chinese government's repressive ambitions has grown, governments, including those of Australia, Japan, Canada, the UK, EU, and US have looked to cultivate trade and security alliances with India, taking cover behind its brand as the "world's largest democracy." But Prime Minister Narendra Modi's Hindu-nationalist Bharatiya Janata Party has mimicked many of the same abuses that have enabled Chinese state repression—systematic discrimination against religious minorities, stifling of peaceful dissent, and use of technology to suppress free expression—to tighten its grip on power.

The seemingly careless trade-off on human rights that world leaders make, justified as the cost of doing business, ignores the longer-term implications of their compromises. Deepening ties with the Modi government while avoiding its troubling rights record squanders valuable leverage to protect the precious, but increasingly endangered, civic space on which India's democracy relies.

Respect for Rights as a Prescription for Stability

Autocrats benefit from the illusion they project as being indispensable to maintaining stability, which in turn seemingly justifies their oppression and widespread human-rights violations committed toward achieving that end.

But this "stability," driven by the endless quest for power and control, infects and erodes every pillar needed for a functional society based on the rule of law. The result is frequently massive corruption, a broken economy, and a hopelessly partisan judiciary. Vital civic space is dismantled, with activists and independent journalists in jail, in hiding, or fearing retaliation.

The months-long protests in Iran in 2022 underline the grave risks for autocracies of imagining that repression is a shortcut to stability. Protests erupted across the country in response to the death of the 22-year-old Kurdish-Iranian woman Mahsa (Jina) Amini in September, following her arrest by "morality police" for wearing an "improper hijab." But protest against the mandatory use of the hijab is just the most visible symbol of repression. The new generation of protesters across the country echoes the frustrations of generations past: people tired of living without fundamental rights, and of being ruled by those who callously disregard the welfare of their people.

The demand for equality triggered by women and schoolgirls has morphed into a nationwide movement by the Iranian people against a government that has systematically denied them their rights, mismanaged the economy, and driven people into poverty. Iranian authorities have ruthlessly cracked down on what became widespread anti-government protests with excessive and lethal force, followed by sham trials and death sentences for those who dare challenge the government's authority. Hints that authorities may disband the morality police fall well short of the demand to abolish the discriminatory compulsory hijab laws, and even further from the fundamental structural reforms the protesters are demanding to make the government more accountable.

The link between impunity for abuses and mismanaged governance can be seen elsewhere. Shortages in fuel, food, and other essentials, including medicine, sparked massive protests in Sri Lanka, forcing Prime Minister Mahinda Rajapaksa, and then his brother, President Gotabaya Rajapaksa, to resign. Unfortunately, the man who parliament chose to replace them, Ranil Wickremasinghe, has walked away from commitments to justice and accountability for egregious violations committed during the country's 26-year civil war, which ended in 2009. President Wickremasinghe, instead of focusing on the economic crisis and ensuring social justice, cracked down on protests, even using the notorious Prevention of Terrorism Act to detain student activists.

Cracks have also emerged in the foundations of seemingly impenetrable countries. In November, mounting frustration over Beijing's strict lockdown measures as part of its "zero Covid" strategy spilled over into the streets, with protesters in cities across the country denouncing the Communist Party's draconian measures and, in some cases, Xi's rule. These remarkable shows of defiance, led mostly by young people and young women, demonstrate that desires for human rights cannot be erased despite the enormous resources the Chinese government has devoted to repressing them.

It is easy to celebrate the protesters who take the fight for human rights to the streets. But we cannot expect the protesters to diagnose the problems—which they do at great risk to themselves and their families—and to hold those responsible for the deprivations they have suffered to account by themselves. Rights-respecting governments need to lend their political stamina and attention to ensure that needed human rights change comes to fruition. Governments should live up to their global human rights responsibilities, not just ponder and posture about them.

Consider Sudan, whose people's revolution of 2018-19 challenged the abusive power structure that repressed the country for decades. The two-year joint civilian-military transition that led the country was sabotaged by a military coup in late 2021, putting Sudanese autocrats and military commanders implicated in serious abuses—some of whom are once again committing abuses—in charge of the country's future.

But Sudanese grassroots Resistance Committees—pro-democracy civilian groups created out of the 2018 revolution—persist, despite deadly crackdowns. These groups insist on a civilian-only transition and want those responsible for abuses to be held to account. In December, political actors reached a preliminary agreement with the military coup leaders, postponing discussions on justice and security sector reforms to a later stage, but protesters and victims' groups have rejected the deal.

If Sudan is to move toward a more rights-respecting future, the demands of these groups, including calls for justice and an end to impunity for those in command, should be a priority of the US, UN, EU, and regional partners in engaging with Sudan's military leadership. Those who staged a coup to obtain power will not give it up without deterrents or financial costs.

Similarly, centering the demands of the millions of people pressing for human rights and democratic civilian rule in Myanmar remains critical to addressing the ongoing crisis. In February 2021, Myanmar's military staged a coup and has brutally suppressed widespread opposition ever since. For two years, the military junta has carried out systematic abuses, including extrajudicial killings, torture, and sexual violence, that amount to crimes against humanity and war crimes.

The Association of Southeast Asian Nations (ASEAN) produced a "Five Point Consensus"—negotiated between the bloc and Myanmar's junta—to address the crisis in the country. It has failed, with several ASEAN countries, including Malaysia, Indonesia, and Singapore acknowledging the junta's refusal to comply. Since the coup, ASEAN has barred Myanmar junta representatives from the bloc's high-level meetings. Beyond that, ASEAN has imposed minimal pressure on Myanmar, while other powerful governments, including those of the US and UK, hide behind regional deference to justify their own limited action.

To achieve a different result, ASEAN needs to adopt a different approach. In September, Malaysia's then-Foreign Minister Saifuddin Abdullah was the first ASEAN official to meet openly with representatives of Myanmar's opposition National Unity Government, formed by elected lawmakers, ethnic minority representatives, and civil society activists after the coup. The bloc should follow suit and extend its engagement to representatives of civil society.

ASEAN should also intensify pressure on Myanmar by aligning with international efforts to cut off the junta's foreign currency revenue and weapons purchases, which would in turn weaken Myanmar's military. As ASEAN chair in 2023, Indonesia should lead a review of the junta's human rights record and failure to comply with the Five-Point Consensus and consider suspending Myanmar to uphold the bloc's commitment to a "people-oriented, people-centered ASEAN."

Human Rights Can Define—and Design—the Path Ahead

Another year of shrinking real and virtual civic space around the world brings the recognition that attacks on the human rights system are due in part to its effectiveness—because by exposing the abuses and elevating the voices of survivors and those at risk, the human rights movement makes it harder for abusive governments to succeed.

In 2022, six weeks into the full-scale invasion of Ukraine, Russian authorities summarily shuttered the Human Rights Watch office in Moscow after 30 years of continuous operation, together with those of more than a dozen foreign nongovernmental organizations. The closures followed a decade of repressive laws and measures that the Russian government adopted to decimate civil society and force hundreds of activists, journalists, human rights lawyers, and other critics into exile. The Kremlin has gone to such great lengths to extinguish dissent because dissent threatens it. And therein lies a fundamental truth: those who work assiduously to repress human rights show their weakness, not their strength.

Time and again, human rights prove to be a powerful lens through which to view the most existential threats we face, like climate change. From Pakistan to Nigeria to Australia, every corner of the world faces a nearly nonstop cycle of catastrophic weather events that will intensify because of climate change, alongside slow onset changes like sea-level rise. In simple terms, we are seeing the cost of government inaction, a continued assault by big polluters, and the toll on communities, with those already marginalized paying the highest price.

The unbreakable link between people and nature has been recognized by the UN General Assembly, which last year confirmed the universality of the human right to a clean, healthy, and sustainable environment. With the destructive effects of climate change intensifying around the world, there is a legal and moral imperative for government officials to regulate the industries whose business models are incompatible with protecting basic rights.

To stave off the worst effects of climate change and confront the human rights toll at all stages of their operations, governments need to urgently work to implement a just transition to phase out fossil fuels and prevent agribusiness from continuing to raze the world's forests. At the same time, governments should act with urgency in upholding human rights in their responses to climate extremes and slow-onset changes that are already inevitable, protecting those populations most at risk, including Indigenous peoples, women, children, older people, people with disabilities, and people living in poverty.

Many of these communities are also leading the charge to protect their ways of life and their homes against coal, oil, and gas operations that pollute the water they rely on to cook, clean, and drink, and result in the rising of the seas that engulf the lands where they live. Centering frontline communities and environmental defenders is one of the most powerful ways to push back against corporate and government activities that harm the environment and protect critical ecosystems needed to address the climate crisis.

Indigenous forest defenders are critical to the protection of the Brazilian Amazon, an ecosystem vital for slowing climate change by storing carbon. Rather than supporting them, the administration of then-President Jair Bolsonaro enabled illegal deforestation and weakened Indigenous rights protections. The spectacular environmental destruction during his four-year term went hand-in-hand with serious rights violations, including violence and intimidation against those who tried to stop it.

Brazil's newly elected president, Luiz Inácio Lula da Silva, has pledged to reduce Amazon deforestation to zero and defend Indigenous rights. During his previous two terms from 2003 to 2010, deforestation dropped dramatically, but his administration also promoted dams and other infrastructure projects with high environmental and social impacts in the Amazon. President Lula's ability to deliver on his climate and human rights commitments are critical for Brazil and the world.

A New International Embrace of Human Rights

The magnitude, scale, and frequency of human rights crises across the globe show the urgency of a new framing and new model for action. Viewing our greatest challenges and threats to the modern world through a human rights lens reveals not only the root causes of disruption but also offers guidance to address them.

Every government has the obligation to protect and promote respect for human rights. After years of piecemeal and often half-hearted efforts on behalf of civilians under threat in places including Yemen, Afghanistan, and South Sudan, the world's mobilization around Ukraine reminds us of the extraordinary potential when governments realize their human rights responsibilities on a global scale. All governments should bring the same spirit of solidarity to the multitude of human rights crises around the globe, and not just when it suits their interests.

HUMAN RIGHTS WATCH

HUMAN RIGHTS WATCH

LEAVE NO ONE BEHIND
People with Disabilities and Older People
in Climate-Related Disasters

WORLD REPORT
2023

COUNTRIES

WORLD REPORT 2023

"Even If You Go to the Skies, We'll Find You"
LGBT People in Afghanistan After the Taliban Takeover

Afghanistan

The Taliban, which took power in August 2021, continued to impose numerous rules and policies violating a wide range of fundamental rights of women and girls, including freedom of movement, right to work and a livelihood, and access to education and health care. Authorities also repressed or threatened the media and critics of Taliban rule, forced the closure of civil society organizations, and dismantled government offices meant to promote or uphold human rights.

Taliban security forces throughout the year carried out arbitrary detentions, torture, and summary executions of former security officers and perceived enemies, including security personnel in the former government or alleged members or supporters of the armed group Islamic State of Khorasan Province (the Afghan affiliate of the Islamic State, known as ISKP). ISKP carried out attacks on schools and mosques, mostly targeting ethnic Hazara Shia Muslims. Afghanistan's criminal code makes same-sex conduct a criminal offense, and the Taliban have echoed the previous government's support for the criminalization of same-sex relations, with some of their leaders vowing to take a hard line against the rights of lesbian, gay, bisexual, and transgender (LGBT) people.

A deepening economic crisis continued in 2022, underpinned by several factors, including massive cutoffs in donor assistance in 2021 and corresponding cuts to wages of essential workers; a massive liquidity crisis; spiking prices for essential goods like food; and restrictions by outside governments impacting the banking sector. Millions of children continued to face acute malnutrition. More than 90 percent of Afghans were food insecure throughout the year. Women and girls were particularly hard hit by the economic crisis for reasons, including Taliban actions pushing many women out of paid work and blocking female aid workers from being able to do their jobs.

Women's and Girls' Rights

Since taking power, the Taliban have imposed a long and growing list of rules and policies that comprehensively prevent women and girls from exercising their fundamental rights, including to expression, movement, work, and education affecting virtually all their rights, including to life, livelihood, shelter, health care, food, and water.

In March 2022, the Taliban announced that women and girls would continue to be barred from secondary education, a decision that drew widespread criticism and statements of concern from around the world, including from the entire membership of the United Nations Security Council, the Organisation of Islamic Cooperation, and almost all members of the G7 and G20.

The Taliban's leadership, which is entirely comprised of men, has not permitted women to participate in governance at any level or hold any senior positions in the civil service, including as judges. Authorities announced and frequently enforced rules prohibiting women from traveling or leaving their homes, including to go to the workplace without a male family member accompanying them—an impossible requirement for almost all families—and barred women from holding most types of jobs. Authorities also announced rules requiring women's faces be covered in public—including women TV newscasters—and stipulated that male family members will be punished when a women violate rules regarding movement and dress.

Taliban forces in several instances used excessive force to disperse women engaged in public protests against Taliban policies or rules, arbitrarily detained some protesters and their family members, and allegedly subjected some to torture or beatings.

Economic and Humanitarian Crises

Afghanistan's humanitarian crisis worsened in 2022, largely because of the country's enduring economic collapse in the wake of the Taliban takeover. Over 90 percent of the population remained food insecure through the year, including tens of millions forced to skip meals daily or endure whole days without eating. Persistent malnutrition has caused increased starvation deaths and longer-term health problems in children.

Multiple causes underpin the economic crisis. In 2022, most donor countries maintained cutoffs to income assistance and wages for essential workers providing health care, education, and other vital services. Resulting widespread wage losses coincided with increasing prices of food, fuel, and other essential goods.

Agricultural output also decreased during 2022 due to a major drought and lack of affordable access to fertilizer, fuel, and other agricultural inputs.

US restrictions on the Central Bank of Afghanistan, also known as Da Afghanistan Bank (DAB), have continued to prevent the bank from carrying out essential central banking services, essentially keeping the entire economy in a state of collapse. DAB's incapacities have caused a massive and enduring liquidity crisis, as well as shortages of banknotes in both US dollars and Afghan currency, severely restricting legitimate financial activities by businesses, humanitarian agencies, and ordinary Afghans.

Women and girls are disproportionately affected by the crisis and face greater obstacles to obtaining food, health care, and financial resources. Taliban policies barring women from most paid jobs made the situation worse, especially for households in which women were the sole or main wage earners. Where the Taliban has allowed women to work, doing so was rendered almost impossible by oppressive requirements such as having a male family member escort women to work and even remain there throughout the workday.

World Food Program surveys revealed that for most of 2022, nearly 100 percent of female-headed households lacked adequate food and almost all are taking "drastic measures" to obtain it, including selling vital household items, sending children to work, or marrying off young girls for dowry.

On September 14, 2022, the US government announced the creation of "The Afghan Fund," a Swiss-based financial mechanism intended to act as a trustee for Afghanistan's foreign currency reserves and conduct limited transactions and other activities in the place of DAB. However, several essential central banking services can still only be carried out by DAB, and economic impacts will continue until the US reaches an agreement with Taliban authorities about DAB's status. Serious concerns remained about the Afghan Fund's viability as a longer-term approach to address Afghanistan's economic problems, and the delay in taking steps to stabilize the collapsed economy came at a steep human cost.

Extrajudicial Killings, Enforced Disappearances, Torture, and War Crimes

Taliban forces have carried out revenge killings and enforced disappearances of former government officials and security force personnel. They have also summarily executed people they claim are members of the Islamic State of Khorasan Province (ISKP). The United Nations Assistance Mission in Afghanistan (UNAMA) issued a report in August 2022 detailing numerous cases of killings or disappearances committed by Taliban forces since August 2021. It is not always possible to discern those killed were former government personnel or alleged ISKP.

In numerous cases over the year, Taliban forces conducted military operations and night raids targeting residents they accuse of harboring or providing support for ISKP members. During many operations, soldiers assaulted civilians and detained people without due process. Detainees were forcibly disappeared or killed, in some cases by beheading. In some provinces, Taliban authorities dumped bodies in public areas or hung bodies on streets or intersections as warnings.

In late 2021 and into 2022, residents in Nangarhar exhumed a mass grave in a canal that contained at least 45 bodies in various stages of decomposition, many with signs of torture or brutal executions: some had missing limbs, ropes around their necks, or had been beheaded.

In Panjshir province, the Taliban carried out search operations targeting communities they alleged were supporting the armed opposition group National Resistance Front (NRF), detaining and torturing local residents. Authorities also imposed collective punishment and disregarded protections to which detainees are entitled.

Attacks by Islamic State of Khorasan Province (ISKP)

The ISKP claimed responsibility for numerous bombings and armed attacks against Hazaras in 2022, which killed and injured at least 700 people. On April 19, ISKP claimed responsibility for a suicide bombing at a high school in Dasht-e Barchi, west Kabul, a predominantly Hazara and Shia area, which killed or injured 20 students, teachers, and staff.

ISKP also claimed responsibility for an attack two days later at Seh Dokan Mosque in Mazar e Sharif that killed 31 people and wounded 87 others. On April 27, unidentified gunmen killed five Hazara men on their way to the Dare-Suf coal mine in Samangan. On September 30, an attack on an educational center in west Kabul, again a Hazara dominated area, killed 53 and injured 100 students, mostly women and girls.

The Taliban's failure to provide security to at-risk populations and medical and other assistance to survivors and affected families exacerbated the harm caused by the attacks.

Beyond their immediate devastation, the attacks exacted a severe long-term toll, depriving survivors and families of victims of breadwinners, often imposing severe medical burdens, and restricting their access to daily life.

Freedom of Media, Speech

Taliban authorities carried out extensive censorship and violence against Afghan media in Kabul and provinces. Hundreds of media outlets were shut down and an estimated 80 percent of women journalists across Afghanistan lost their jobs or left the profession since the Taliban takeover in August 2021.

The Taliban's Directorate of Intelligence engaged in a pattern of threats, intimidation, and violence against members of the media, and were responsible for targeted killings of journalists. Authorities also banned outlets in Afghanistan from broadcasting international news programs, including Voice of America and the BBC, in Dari, Pashto, and Uzbek languages. Journalists covering women's rights protests faced particular abuse. The Taliban also shut down websites of two media outlets.

Access to information has become very limited in Afghanistan and in many provinces, The Taliban ordered journalists to not report on a wide range of issues. Several journalists were beaten for trying to report on anti-Taliban protests, arbitrary detention, rising food prices, and other subjects the Taliban authorities deem too critical.

On June 7, the General Directorate of Intelligence (GDI) released a video of Afghan blogger Ajmal Haqiqi—well-known on YouTube—with bruises on his face and ostensibly under duress, apologizing for encouraging "prostitution" online and "insulting verses of the Quran."

On May 24, Taliban authorities detained Mirza Hassani, director of Radio Sedai Aftab, at a checkpoint in Herat city, accusing him of supporting opposition groups. On May 10, GDI officials detained Khan Mohamad Sayal, a TV journalist in Urzugan, without explanation.

The Taliban have used various measures to silence media in Afghanistan, ranging from establishing restrictive guidelines to sending intelligence officials to meet with media staff and forcing media workers to confess to crimes.

The Taliban's media restrictions have been particularly devastating for women journalists, who typically have had to work harder than their male counterparts to establish their careers in media in the face of sexism and security risks.

Key International Actors

The United Nations Security Council passed a resolution in March 2022 extending the United Nations Assistance Mission for Afghanistan (UNAMA) and its mandate to report on human rights conditions. The UN Human Rights Council in Geneva renewed and strengthened the mandate of the UN special rapporteur on Afghanistan in October.

The Security Council held numerous debates on Afghanistan and extended several sanctions and removed exemptions that had been granted to some Taliban officials who are under travel bans.

Key donors, including the United States, European Union, United Kingdom, and Japan continued to maintain restrictions on donor assistance and took inadequate steps to ensure that legitimate banking transactions involving Afghanistan are not restricted by UN or bilateral sanctions on Taliban officials. Like-minded governments with concerns about Taliban human rights abuses—including those that have committed to having a feminist foreign policy—failed to adopt a common and sustained multilateral position and strategy for pressuring the Taliban to change its conduct.

The prosecutor of the International Criminal Court (ICC) continued to request permission from the court's judges to resume an investigation into war crimes and crimes against humanity, following a 2020 request from the former Afghan government to defer to their own investigations. As the ICC is a court of last resort, the ICC prosecutor can only override a deferral request of this kind by petitioning the judges. In an August 2022 submission, the prosecutor argued that the Taliban, which now controls the country, "are not continuing, cannot continue and will not continue" relevant national justice efforts.

Algeria

Algerian authorities continued their crackdown on dissent despite a lull in anti-government protests through restrictions on freedoms of expression, association, assembly, and movement. Activists, human rights defenders, journalists, and lawyers have been prosecuted for their peaceful activism, opinions, or in connection to their professions. Around 250 individuals were being held in prison for their participation in peaceful protest, activism, or expression as of October, of which one-third were in pre-trial detention, according to national rights groups.

Authorities have increasingly used charges related to terrorism, after expanding an already overly broad definition of the crime in June 2021, to prosecute human rights defenders, activists, and other critics. They have also taken legal action to dissolve or else restrict the activities of civil society organizations and opposition political parties.

Political Rights and Freedom of Expression

On February 19, Faleh Hammoudi, head of the Tlemcen office of the Algerian League for the Defense of Human Rights (LADDH), was arrested. He was sentenced to three years in prison for "offending public bodies," "spreading fake news" that might harm public safety, and "running an unregistered association," according to the National Committee for the Liberation of Detainees (CNLD). Hammoudi was provisionally released on March 30. Upon appeal, he was sentenced on May 15 to a one-year suspended prison term.

Authorities are prosecuting eight members of LADDH for their activism or expression, including four—Kaddour Chouicha, Djamila Loukil, Saïd Bouddour, and Hassan Bouras —on unsubstantiated terrorism-related charges. Bouras has been in pretrial detention since September 12, 2021.

Zaki Hannache, a human rights defender known for his activism in the Hirak pro-reform movement and for his monitoring of arrests and trials of other activists, was arrested on January 18. As of November, Hannache was under investigation for unsubstantiated charges of "apology for terrorism," "spreading false news," "obtaining funds in order to undermine national unity," and "undermining the security of the state." He was granted provisional release on March 30.

On April 24, Hakim Debbazi, a Hirak activist, died in custody in unclear circumstances. Debbazi was arrested on February 20 and held in pretrial detention in connection to a Facebook post related to the Hirak protest movement. He was charged with "inciting an unarmed gathering," "offending public officials" and "publishing content that might "harm the national interest." His family filed a legal suit against the Algerian state for manslaughter after his death. Algerian authorities said Debbazi died of natural causes, citing a government autopsy report.

Two lawyers, Abdelkadir Chohra and Yacine Khlifi, have been imprisoned for denouncing Debbazi's suspicious death in custody. Authorities arrested Chohra on May 14 and Khlifi on May 30 in connection to a video published on Facebook about the activist's death and detention conditions in Algerian prisons. Both lawyers were charged with "spreading fake news" among others. On August 15, they were sentenced to six-month suspended prison terms and released, according to the CNLD.

In an effort to crush dissenting voices, authorities also targeted activists and critics in Algeria's diaspora. Between January and April, they imposed arbitrary travel bans on at least three Algerian-Canadian activists. The dual nationals were blocked for months from leaving Algeria.

On March 24, Mohamed Benhalima, a former military officer and activist who fled to Spain in 2019 fearing reprisals for his participation in the Hirak movement, was deported to Algeria. Spain twice rejected Benhalima's asylum application despite the UN Refugee Agency's opinion that he faced a credible risk of torture and that Algeria's criminalization of peaceful opposition was recognized internationally.

In May, Benhalima was notified that he had been sentenced to death in absentia by a military court. Prosecuted in dozens of cases on terrorism-related charges and espionage among others, Benhalima was jailed and tried for his videos posted on social media related to alleged state corruption. On June 19, he declared in court that he had been subjected to torture. On September 4, he was sentenced to a total of 12 years in prison in connection with three separate cases, according to El Watan newspaper. In 2021, a court sentenced Benhalima to 10 years in prison in absentia for his online publications related to the army.

Freedom of Association and Assembly

On September 1, authorities closed the headquarters of Santé Sidi El Houari, a group focused on preserving the cultural and historical heritage of the city of Oran. The governor of Oran had filed a complaint against the association in May, alleging "foreign funding without the approval of the competent authorities." The administrative court of Oran has not yet issued a judgment, but the authorities have frozen the group's activities.

An Algiers court dissolved Rassemblement Action Jeunesse (RAJ), a prominent civic association, on October 13, 2021, after an Interior Ministry complaint that its activities were contrary to the objectives of Law 12-06 related to associations and the group's bylaws. In April, RAJ activists appealed the decision to the highest administrative court in Algeria. RAJ has openly supported the Hirak movement and authorities have since prosecuted 13 of its members, imprisoning at least 10.

In April 2021, another association known for its support of the Hirak protest movement, SOS Beb El Oued, was shut down by the authorities after 21 years of activity, and its president Nacer Meghnine imprisoned for his activism.

The Algerian legal framework related to associations is restrictive and breaches the right to freedom of association. Under law 12-06, the authorities have broad discretion to withhold legal recognition from nongovernmental associations, requiring groups to obtain a registration receipt before they can legally operate. The law also forbids associations from receiving any foreign funding, cooperating with, or seeking membership in foreign organizations without the government's agreement and empowers the government to suspend an association if it "interferes with the internal affairs of the state or violates national sovereignty."

Women and Girls' Rights
Algeria's Family Code contains discriminatory provisions against women and restricts women's rights. The code allows men to divorce their spouses unilaterally without explanation but requires women to apply to courts for a divorce on specified grounds.

Féminicides Algérie, a civil society initiative monitoring femicides, reported that by October, 34 women and girls were killed in 2022 by their husbands, ex-husbands, neighbors, brothers, fathers, sons, or other family members.

Algeria's laws allow men to escape punishment for violence against women. Article 326 of the penal code, a colonial-era relic, allows a man who abducts a minor to escape prosecution if he marries his victim. A 2015 law amended the penal code to make assault of a spouse punishable by up to 20 years in prison and a life sentence for injuries resulting in death. However, it contains loopholes that allow convictions to be dropped or sentences reduced if victims pardon their perpetrators. The law also does not set out any measures to prevent abuse or protect survivors, such as protection orders.

There were no laws to ensure unmarried pregnant girls and adolescent mothers, who are exposed to threats of criminal punishment, can remain in school. Corporal punishment of children is prohibited in schools but not in the home and remains common.

Migrants and Refugees

During 2022, Algerian authorities continued arbitrary and collective expulsions to Niger and Mali of migrants of multiple nationalities, including children, often without individual screenings or due process. Migrants reported cases of violence, theft of their belongings, arbitrary detention, poor treatment in detention, and other mistreatment by Algerian authorities during arrests, detention, and expulsions to land borders. Algerian authorities expelled at least 14,000 migrants to Niger between January and May 2022, according to Doctors Without Borders.

The collective expulsions were carried out in inhumane conditions, and in violation of Algeria's obligations under international and regional refugee and human rights law. As in prior years, most expelled migrants, including some who had suffered serious mistreatment, were abandoned in the desert at the Algeria-Niger border.

Though a party to the African and UN refugee conventions, Algeria lacks a national asylum law and protection framework.

Sexual Orientation and Gender Identity

Same-sex relations are punishable under Article 338 of the penal code by up to two years in prison. Article 333 increases the penalty up to three years in prison for public indecency if it involves "acts against nature with a member of the same sex," whether between men or women.

Restrictions on freedom of assembly, and association under Law 12-06 hinder the work of lesbian, gay, bisexual, and transgender (LGBT) groups. This law poses risks to those who want to form or become active in LGBT groups, as well as to human rights organizations that otherwise might support such activities.

According to a 2019 analysis by the International Lesbian, Gay, Bisexual, Transgender, and Intersex Association, laws regulating nongovernmental organizations in Algeria make it virtually impossible for organizations working on issues of sexual orientation and gender identity to register legally.

Angola

President João Lourenço was elected for a second term in highly disputed elections held on August 24. The ruling People's Movement for the Liberation of Angola (MPLA) extended its five-decade long rule but lost its two-thirds majority in parliament. The coalition led by the National Union for the Total Independence of Angola (UNITA), for the first time received more votes in the capital, Luanda, than the ruling party.

Voting was largely peaceful but marred with severe restrictions on freedom of expression and assembly, and limited access to information due to government repression and censorship in state media and in private media outlets controlled by ruling party officials.

The president pledged to prioritize the creation of jobs for the youth and to respect human rights, especially those of minorities and marginalized groups, such as children and older people.

Security forces continued to use excessive force, intimidation, and arbitrary detention against peaceful protesters with impunity. The press was under attack on several occasions throughout 2022.

In July, Angola's long-term former President José Eduardo Dos Santos died in Barcelona, Spain, at age 79, after years of prolonged illness.

Abuses by State Security Forces

Angolan state security forces continued to be implicated in serious human rights abuses, including excessive and unnecessary use of force against peaceful protesters, as well as intimidation and arbitrary detentions of activists.

On January 10, police arbitrarily arrested, at least 17 people in Luanda, among them peaceful taxi drivers who had gathered for an announced nationwide strike to protest Covid-19 regulations, which limited the number of passengers allowed on public and private transportation. The Covid-19 restrictions, according to the taxi drivers association, negatively impacted the income and livelihoods of their members. A police spokesman claimed that the taxi drivers had attacked an office of the ruling MPLA and set a bus on fire. Yet various taxi drivers told Human

Rights Watch the attack on the bus and office was started by local residents, before the strike began.

On April 9 in Luanda, police arrested and charged 22 people who were peacefully protesting the detention of political prisoners and calling for free and fair elections in August. Those detained included Laurinda Gouveia and her 6-month-old baby boy. Both mother and son were kept in a crowded cell without food or water for more than 48 hours. On April 14, a judge at the Luanda provincial court ordered the release of 20 of the 22 protesters for lack of evidence linking them to the crimes of rioting and disobeying an order to disperse. The other two were sentenced for civil disobedience and ordered to pay the equivalent of $135 in fines.

On July 31, police used batons and sticks to prevent a group of peaceful activists from gathering to protest the detention of political prisoners in Luanda. Police also detained at least 10 activists, who were later released at the police station.

On August 17, police arrested dozens of protesters and civil society activists who had gathered near the Santa Ana cemetery to protest alleged election irregularities. Among those arrested was the Voice of America (VOA) correspondent Coque Mokuta.

On August 29, Angolan rights group Friends of Angola denounced acts of police intimidation against members of the civic movement "Mudei" (I changed). In a letter to the Office of the Ombudsman, the Commission for Human Rights, and to the Ministry of Justice and Human Rights, the group demanded the unconditional release of six activists, among them two women, who were arbitrarily detained while trying to protest elections, in Uije province, on August 25 and 26.

On September 14, a day before the president's inauguration, police prevented a protest against the election results near the Santa Ana cemetery, and arbitrarily arrested three political activists during a radio interview at the local of the protest. Friends and family of Zola Mandela, a political activist, told Human Rights Watch that on the same day, he was forcibly taken from his house by men who identified themselves as police officers.

Freedom of the Media

The press was under attack on several occasions throughout 2022. In some cases, members of the public and security forces were implicated in cases of intimidation, physical and verbal attacks as well as arbitrary detention of reporters.

On January 10, six journalists working for news outlets TV Zimbo and TV Palanca were assaulted by unidentified people and forced to flee to safety while reporting on a nationwide strike by taxi drivers in Luanda. The secretary-general of the Journalists Union, Teixeira Cândido, told the Committee to Protect Journalists that public media journalists in Angola are increasingly becoming the targets of people's anger because of the perceived bias against the government and ruling party.

On February 10, a correspondent for the German outlet Deutsche Welle (DW) in Cuanza Norte, was brutally assaulted by private security guards of a major regional supermarket, while investigating a case of food poisoning. The security guards also seized the equipment of the DW reporter and of two others working for the local radio station Eclesia.

On August 17, the Voice of America (VOA) correspondent in Luanda, Coque Mokuta, was arbitrarily detained by police while filming a protest. He told Human Rights Watch that he was kept inside a car that drove around Luanda for several hours while he was being questioned. He was later released without charges and was allowed to take his equipment.

On August 25, DW submitted an official complaint to the Ministry of Social Communications, after one of its reporters was arbitrarily arrested and questioned for an hour by police officers in Malange, for filming proceedings at a voting station during the August 24 elections.

Millions of Angolans across the country remained without access to free, diverse, and impartial information. This is because Angola remained the only southern African country without community radio stations. The Angolan broadcasting act, currently under review, stipulates license fees of over $100,000 for local and community stations, an amount that local media rights groups consider prohibitive.

Ahead of the August 24 general elections, activists and media rights groups accused the state sponsored media, which has the largest coverage of Angolan territory, of bias toward the ruling party and its candidates. The representative of media rights group Misa-Angola, Andre Mussano, said in some cases, "90 percent of the airtime [during the election campaign] was dedicated to one side [the ruling party]."

Women's and Girls' Rights

Widespread gender inequalities, especially at the highest levels of political power, persisted in Angola. However, the country registered significant progress in the number of women holding ministerial portfolios and positions of relevance, following the August 24 election. The top state positions, including vice-president and speaker of parliament will be occupied by women. At government level, women will control 10 out of 28 ministerial positions.

In May, Angola launched its national chapter of the African Women Leaders Network (AWLN), a movement of African women leaders implemented with the support of the Office of the African Union Special Envoy on Women, Peace, and Security, and of the United Nations Entity for Gender Equality and the Empowerment of Women (UN Women). This national chapter aims to enhance the leadership of women in the transformation of Africa.

Angola lacks a reentry or continuation policy that protects a pregnant girl's right to education. This has led to uneven enforcement of education rights, where school officials can decide what happens to girls' education, or where discriminatory attitudes and social barriers pressure girls to drop out altogether.

Key International Actors

Several countries and international bodies, including the African Union (AU), Southern African Development Community (SADC), the European Union (EU), and the United States (US) congratulated Angolans for the "peaceful environment" during elections in August. The EU also urged Angolan authorities to respond to the complaints of the opposition.

In his inaugural speech, Angolan President Joao Lourenco reiterated his government's commitment to peace resolutions in the SADC region and the Central African Republic, as well as in the borders between the Democratic Republic of Congo (DRC), Rwanda, and Uganda.

Earlier in July, President Felix Tshisekedi of the Democratic Republic of Congo (DRC) and his Rwandan counterpart, Paul Kagame, agreed at a summit organized by Angola to de-escalate tensions from a rebel insurgency at the border of the two countries.

In August, while in Kinshasa, US Secretary of State Antony Blinken expressed his support for the mediation efforts between the DRC and Rwanda, which were led in part by Angola.

Argentina

Human rights problems in Argentina include police abuse, poor prison conditions, and endemic violence against women. A longstanding economic crisis has particularly impacted people living in poverty.

President Alberto Fernández, Vice President Cristina Fernández de Kirchner, and members of the cabinet used hostile rhetoric against the judiciary, the Attorney General's Office, and the independent press.

A political crisis fueled by economic problems and polarization has created a challenging environment for human rights progress. An investigation into a man's attempt, in September 2022, to kill Fernández de Kirchner by triggering his gun twice near the vice president's head, was ongoing at time of writing.

Judicial and Prosecutorial Independence

High-level authorities have used hostile rhetoric against judges and prosecutors who rule against the government or investigate the vice president's alleged involvement in corruption.

In August 2022, a prosecutor asked that Fernández de Kirchner be sentenced to 12 years in prison for her alleged participation in a corruption scheme concerning the construction of roads in Santa Cruz province. The vice president denied the allegations, accused the prosecutor of conducting an abusive and politically motivated investigation, and mobilized her supporters to the streets.

The Fernández administration and its allies introduced several judicial reforms that could undermine the independence of courts and prosecutors. In September, pro-administration and other legislators passed a bill in the Senate expanding the Supreme Court from 5 to 15 justices, a move that prior administrations have used to pack the court. The bill had not been discussed in the House of Representatives at time of writing.

An interim attorney general has served since 2018, as the Senate cannot muster the two-thirds majority required to appoint an attorney general. In 2020, the Senate passed an administration-promoted bill to reduce the required majority, but the House had not discussed it at time of writing.

The Supreme Court ruled in 2015 that delays in appointments, which leave temporary judges serving for years, undermine judicial independence. As of September 2022, 257 federal and national judgeships remained vacant.

In April, the Council of the Judiciary, which selects candidates for federal and national courts, changed structure, following a 2021 Supreme Court ruling: The Supreme Court president joined and presides; representatives of Congress, the Bar Association, academia, and the national judges were added. The Fernández administration criticized the structure and urged Congress to pass an administration-promoted bill changing it. The bill was approved by the Senate in April but, as of October, it had not been discussed by the House of Representatives.

Economic Rights

A longstanding economic crisis, which deepened during the Covid-19 pandemic, has disproportionately impacted low-income people and severely limited people's ability to realize their economic rights.

The government reported that 36.5 percent of the population lived in poverty as of June 2022, a 0.8 percent reduction from December 2021. People living in extreme poverty—i.e., unable to afford their most basic food needs—amounted to 8.8 percent of the population, a 0.6 percent increase from December 2021. Children were particularly affected: More than half of children under 14 were living in poverty and more than one in ten in extreme poverty. The central bank projected that inflation could exceed 100 percent in 2022, making it even harder for people to afford to realize their essential needs.

Freedom of Expression

High-level authorities, including President Fernández, have used hostile rhetoric against independent journalists and media.

In November 2021, a group of people threw explosives into the Buenos Aires headquarters of the Clarín Group—Argentina's largest media conglomerate. Nobody has been held to account for this crime.

A federal court continued investigating a former director and deputy director of Argentina's Federal Intelligence Agency on conspiracy charges for the illegal surveillance of journalists, union members, and politicians under former President Mauricio Macri.

Some provinces and municipalities lack freedom of information laws, undermining transparency.

Prison Conditions and Abuses by Security Forces

The National Penitentiary Office reported 233 cases of alleged torture or ill-treatment in federal prisons in 2021; and 117 from January through June 2022. The Attorney General's Office reported 43 detainee deaths in federal prisons in 2021, including 9 violent deaths and 9 from Covid-19.

Almost half of the 11,280 federal prison detainees are awaiting trial, the government reports.

Security forces occasionally participate in abuses and employ excessive force. In June, a woman died in a police station in Laprida, Buenos Aires province. Five police officers were arrested for allegedly killing her and portraying her death as a suicide.

Confronting Past Abuses

The Supreme Court and federal judges, in the early 2000s, annulled pardons and amnesty laws shielding officials implicated in the 1976-1983 dictatorship's crimes. As of September 2022, the Attorney General's Office reported 3,631 people charged, 1,088 convicted, and 165 acquitted of crimes against humanity.

As of September, 130 people illegally taken from their parents as children during the dictatorship had been identified and many had been reunited with their families, according to the Abuelas de Plaza de Mayo, a human rights group.

The large number of victims, suspects, and cases makes it difficult for prosecutors and judges to bring those responsible to justice while respecting their due process rights.

Impunity for the AMIA Bombing

Twenty-eight years after 85 people died and more than 300 were injured in the bombing of the AMIA Jewish Center, court battles continue. Nobody has been convicted.

In February 2019, a court convicted a former intelligence chief and a judge of interference in the initial investigation but acquitted former President Carlos Menem. An appeal of the judge's conviction remained pending as of October 2022.

In 2015, prosecutor Alberto Nisman, who had accused then-President Fernández de Kirchner of covering up Iran's role in the attack, was found dead. In 2018, a court of appeal said that he appeared to have been murdered. As of writing, nobody has been convicted in connection with his death.

A federal court, in 2021, dismissed Nisman's accusation against Fernández de Kirchner, saying her actions did not constitute a crime.

In August 2022, President Fernández said Nisman had committed suicide and that he hoped that a prosecutor who charged Vice President Fernández de Kirchner with corruption would not do the same.

The Ombudsperson's Office

The Ombudsperson's Office, which is structurally independent from and can investigate the executive for human rights violations, remains vacant. Congress has failed to appoint an ombudsperson since 2009. The office's ability to protect rights has been hamstrung since 2013, when a deputy ombudsperson's term ended.

Women's and Girls' Rights

A landmark 2020 law legalized abortion until the 14th week of pregnancy, and longer in cases of rape or risk to the life or health of the pregnant person.

Authorities reported over 64,000 legal abortions during 2021. Obstacles to accessing legal abortion reportedly included lack of access to information about the law, lack of technical training, and undue delays.

Women with disabilities who have been declared legally incompetent or who are under court orders restricting their capacity to exercise their reproductive rights must have assistance from a legal representative or relative in consenting to abortions. This impedes their exercise of the right.

In August, a court released a woman who had been detained since November 2021, in Corrientes province, accused of aggravated homicide, after an obstetric emergency.

Despite a 2009 law detailing comprehensive measures to prevent and prosecute violence against women, their unpunished killing remains a serious concern. The National Registry of Femicides reported 231 femicides—the murder of women based on their gender—and only six convictions in 2021.

In an important step in 2021, Argentina became one of the first ten countries to ratify the International Labour Organization's Convention 190, which establishes state obligations to protect women from violence and harassment in the workforce.

Sexual Orientation and Gender Identity

In September, Argentina reached a friendly settlement with the Inter-American Commission on Human Rights in the 2011 violent killing of a navy officer, Octavio Romero, that was not properly investigated and in which sexual orientation could have been a motivating factor. Argentina recognized its responsibility for the lack of an effective investigation and committed to undertake public policies that promote the prevention, punishment, and eradication of gender-based violence, broadly defined. This sets an important precedent for Latin America, where authorities often fail to carry out effective investigations into crimes perpetrated against LGBT people.

Children's Right to Education

Educ.ar, a website built and offered by Argentina's National Ministry of Education for children's education during the pandemic, collected and transmitted children's personal data to advertising technology companies, enabling these companies to track and target children across the internet for advertising purposes.

Indigenous Rights

Indigenous people face obstacles to accessing justice, land, education, health care, and basic services.

The Argentine Constitution protects Indigenous communal ownership of traditional lands. In 2020, the Inter-American Court of Human Rights ordered Argentina to adopt legislative measures to guarantee those rights. Yet debates on a law to concretize protections are continually postponed.

Key International Actors and Foreign Policy

In 2022, Argentina assumed the presidency of the United Nations Human Rights Council. It supported the council's scrutiny of rights violations in Afghanistan, Belarus, Eritrea, Nicaragua, Russia, and Ukraine. However, Argentina abstained from voting resolutions extending the mandate of a group of UN experts investigating systematic rights violations in Venezuela and proposing a debate on the human rights situation in the Xinjiang Uyghur Autonomous Region of China.

Argentina assumed the 2022 presidency of the Community of Latin American and Caribbean States (CELAC), which serves as a space for regional integration and cooperation with other countries, such as China and India. In a CELAC meeting in August, President Fernández said that the CELAC should replace the Organization of American States (OAS) which, in his view, "no longer represents" Latin America and the Caribbean.

Argentina voted in favor of resolutions passed by the OAS in 2022 condemning Russia's invasion of Ukraine, suspending Russia's OAS permanent-observer status, and urging the Nicaraguan government to release political prisoners.

In October, a federal court in Argentina opened a criminal investigation into Nicaragua's President Daniel Ortega and Vice President Rosario María Murillo for alleged crimes against humanity. The court applied the principle of universal jurisdiction, which allows authorities to prosecute certain grave crimes, regardless of where they occur and the nationality of victims and perpetrators.

Armenia

Political tensions and growing insecurity from the unresolved conflict over Nagorno-Karabakh dominated events in Armenia.

Authorities pursued ambitious judicial, police, and constitutional reforms. Human rights problems included ill-treatment by law enforcement, interference with freedom of assembly, domestic violence, discrimination against people with disabilities, and violence and discrimination based on sexual orientation and gender identity.

The Russia-brokered truce broke down several times as Azerbaijan made incursions in Nagorno-Karabakh and Armenia. The political opposition blamed Prime Minister Nikol Pashinyan, held ongoing protests, and demanded his resignation.

Armenian authorities reported that the fighting temporarily displaced more than 7,600 civilians, mostly women and children, from three regions of Armenia that border Azerbaijan and damaged or destroyed numerous residential buildings. Sporadic incidents of military hostilities continued to threaten the safety and livelihoods of civilians residing in villages in Nagorno-Karabakh and along the Armenia-Azerbaijan border.

Aftermath of the Nagorno Karabakh Conflict

The Russia-brokered 2020 truce broke down several times as Azerbaijan made incursions into Armenia. Sporadic incidents of military hostilities continued to threaten the safety and livelihoods of civilians residing in villages in Nagorno-Karabakh and in several surrounding districts and along the Armenia-Azerbaijan border

Armenian authorities reported that the September 2022 fighting killed at least three civilians and temporarily displaced more than 7,600 civilians, mostly women and children, from three regions of Armenia that border Azerbaijan, and damaged or destroyed numerous residential buildings. Three ethnic Armenian civilians were also killed in Nagorno Karabakh in earlier conflict-related incidents.

A video authenticated by Human Rights Watch showed the extrajudicial execution of at least seven Armenian soldiers, apparently by Azerbaijani forces, during the September 2022 fighting.

According to Armenian lawyers, at least 30 Armenian prisoners of war (POWs) and three civilians remain captured in relation to the 2020 hostilities remain in Azerbaijani custody by October 2022. Azerbaijani authorities do not recognize any of these individuals as POWs (see Azerbaijan chapter).

According to the Ombudswoman's office, as of late August, 303 people, a mix of civilians and military, remain missing from the 2020 hostilities. Lawyers and human rights groups in Armenia allege that some were last seen alive in the custody of Azerbaijani forces.

In October 2022 the Azerbaijani Prosecutor General's Office stated that since the 2020 ceasefire, through mid-October 2022, 34 civilians were killed and another 80 wounded by landmines in Nagorno Karabakh and the surrounding area.

Neither Azerbaijan nor Armenia is a party to the international treaty prohibiting anti-personnel landmines.

Ill-Treatment in Custody

Torture and ill-treatment in custody persists and is often perpetrated with impunity. Even when criminal investigations are launched in response to allegations of torture, they are mostly closed based on findings that no crime was committed or suspended for failure to identify a suspect.

Seven years after torture became a specific criminal offense in Armenia, in March a court delivered its first ruling on such charges, sentencing a former prison official to seven years and six months. Previously, officials held accountable for physical abuse faced general "abuse of office" offenses.

Freedoms of Speech and Assembly, Protection of Human Rights Defenders

Law enforcement interfered with freedom of assembly during protests throughout the year. The Armenian Helsinki Committee, a non-governmental group, documented disproportionate use of force during opposition protests in May and June.

In August, police in Yerevan briefly detained without explanation some 20 people protesting Russia's war in Ukraine. In September, police outlawed a protest in front of the Russian embassy, briefly detaining two activists.

The Committee to Protect Freedom of Expression (CPFE), a local group, noted an increase in violence against journalists. Through June 2022, they documented 12 incidents with 13 victims, perpetrated by both public officials and private individuals. Most happened during various opposition protests. CPFE reported 23 cases of other types of pressure during the same period.

In a positive move, Armenia decriminalized "severe insult," removing the offence from the criminal code.

Armenia increased fines for failure to provide official information upon request, but CPFE reported 69 cases of violation of the right to receive and disseminate information.

Authorities continued to press spurious criminal incitement charges against Sashik Sultanyan, chairperson of the nongovernmental Yezidi Center for Human Rights. The charges stem from Sultanyan's public interview alleging discrimination of the Yezidi minority in Armenia.

Disability Rights

Children with disabilities remain segregated in orphanages, special schools, or at home, with little or no education.

In 2022, there were 475 children with disabilities living in five state orphanages; only 230 attended school. The government has not announced comprehensive plans to relocate children with disabilities from state institutions to birth or foster families. The government continued to invest in the three remaining state orphanages for children with disabilities, instead of investing in community-based services and support, in line with international obligations. An unknown number of children with disabilities also continued to live in six private orphanages, with minimal government oversight.

Children who live in orphanages have the right to apply for state financial support to buy a home when they turn 18. In October 2021, the government adopted a discriminatory decree effectively stripping people without "self-care skills" who live in institutions of this right.

The authorities have not yet fulfilled their commitment to introduce legislation for supported decision-making mechanisms. Adults with psychosocial or intellectual disabilities can be deprived of legal capacity and placed under full guardianship, in violation of international obligations. Authorities lack comprehensive plans to introduce community-based services for people with psychosocial disabilities, and instead continue to invest in institutions and institutional care.

In August, the government adopted two regulations on personal assistance services and reasonable accommodation for people with disabilities. However, according to two disability rights groups—the Coalition on Inclusive Legal Reforms and Disability Rights Agenda—the regulations on personal assistance services are available only to people with disabilities from socially and economically marginalized families, and they will have no say over when and how they receive it.

In November 2022, Armenia ratified the Optional Protocol to the Convention on the Rights of Persons with Disabilities, making it possible for individuals to file complaints with the Committee on the Rights of Persons with Disabilities, which oversees states parties' compliance with the convention.

Violence against Women and Children

Domestic violence cases remain largely underreported. A 2021 survey in Armenia showed that almost 36 percent of women interviewed who were ever in a partnership experienced at least one form of physical, sexual, or psychological violence by a current or former intimate partners; only 5 percent of those who experienced physical or sexual violence by a partner sought help from police and only 4.8 percent sought help from a health provider. sought help from police and only 4.8 percent sought help from a health provider.

The authorities investigated 391 criminal domestic violence complaints through June, bringing charges against 128 persons. In 85 of those cases, husbands were alleged perpetrators. Authorities initiated 21 cases against perpetrators for failing to fulfill or observe protective measures.

Eight women had been killed by partners, former partners or family members as of August 31. In March, a man killed himself and his ex-wife. According to their son, the man repeatedly violated police-imposed protective measures and kept threatening and harassing his ex-wife. Police were aware of the threats but failed to take further steps.

Law enforcement bodies lack adequate awareness and training on protection mechanisms required by law to prevent domestic violence, such as protection orders, and do not adequately apply or enforce them.

Authorities opened support centers providing psychological and other support to domestic violence survivors in all regions of Armenia, but state funding for them, according to women's rights groups, is inadequate.

There are only two domestic violence shelters; both are in Yerevan and are run by a nongovernmental organization.

The ratification of the Council of Europe Convention on Preventing and Combating Violence against Women and Domestic Violence (Istanbul Convention) remained stalled following misinformation campaigns in previous years claiming that the convention threatens traditional values and families.

The new criminal code identifies domestic violence as an aggravating circumstance in a number of crimes, but domestic violence is not a stand-alone criminal offense.

Sexual Orientation and Gender Identity

Lesbian, gay, bisexual, and transgender (LGBT) people in Armenia continue to face harassment, discrimination, and violence. The criminal code does not recognize animus due to sexual orientation or gender identity as aggravating criminal circumstances in hate crimes.

In March a criminal court delivered the first verdict in which violence against a person was committed based on a homophobic motive.

In its May judgement, the European Court of Human Rights found that Armenia violated the prohibition against torture and anti-discrimination in the case of Oganezova v. Armenia. Oganezova was a well-known LGBT activist whose club was attacked and set on fire in 2012. The court also found that Armenian authorities failed to discharge their positive obligation to effectively investigate the arson attack, which was committed with a homophobic motive.

Fear of discrimination and humiliation due to public disclosure of their sexual orientation or gender identity continue to prevent many LGBT people from reporting crimes against them, even when they are clearly motivated by anti-LGBT bias. When reported, investigations into such crimes are often inconclusive or ineffective.

In August, a man used anti-trans slurs while approaching a trans woman standing on a street and slapped her hard with a ring on his finger, causing an injury. A local group with homophobic and transphobic bias handed him a certificate for "carrying out patriotic acts." There was no effective investigation at time of writing.

New Generation and PINK, two LGBT rights groups, documented 27 incidents of physical attacks based on sexual orientation or gender identity through September. Authorities initiated criminal investigation in 12 cases. Armenia lacks comprehensive anti-discrimination legislation.

Key International Actors

The European Union sought a greater proactive role in conflict resolution efforts between Armenia and Azerbaijan. European Council President Charles Michel hosted several rounds of trilateral meetings with the Armenian and Azerbaijani leaders, discussing issues related to border delimitations, transport links, and peace agreement that would also address the rights and security of Nagorno-Karabakh's ethnic Armenian population.

In October 2022, the Council of the European Union announced the deployment of up to 40 EU monitors along the Armenian side of the international border with Azerbaijan to "facilitate[e] the restoration of peace and security… , the building of confidence and the delimitation of the international border between the two states."

Also in October, by invitation of the Armenian government, the Organization for Security and Co-operation in Europe (OSCE) announced it would send a team to Armenia to "assess the situation in certain border areas."

In its November 2021 Concluding Observations the United Nations Human Rights Committee, *inter alia*, urged Armenia to amend legislation to ensure equality and non-discrimination on all grounds, including on sexual orientation and gender identity, and to ensure access to effective and appropriate remedies for victims of discrimination. It also urged Armenia to criminalize acts of hate speech and hate crime on all prohibited grounds. It further recommended revising the law on domestic violence to ensure "a victim-centered approach that guarantees access to immediate means of redress and protection."

The committee also urged prompt, impartial, thorough and effective investigations into all allegations of torture and ill-treatment, and for perpetrators to be prosecuted, and victims provided with full reparation.

The EU-Armenia Partnership Council meeting in May reiterated that of democracy, good governance, rule of law, fight against corruption, human rights and gender equality remained the cornerstone of the Eastern Partnership policy framework. In April, the EU encouraged Armenia to make further progress towards greater freedom of the media.

In its January resolution, the Council of Europe Parliamentary Assembly called on Armenia, *inter alia*, to adopt anti-discrimination legislation, adding sexual orientation, gender identity, gender expression and sexual characteristics to the prohibited grounds for discrimination.

In May the US Secretary of State Antony J. Blinken and Armenian minister of foreign affairs launched the US-Armenia strategic dialogue, that includes discussion on programs, *inter alia*, to support human rights, media literacy, social protection, and justice sector reforms.

Australia

Following Anthony Albanese's election as prime minister, Australia's first change of government in nine years led to some improvement in human rights, including more ambitious greenhouse gas emission targets to address climate change. However, many rights concerns remain, such as the significant overrepresentation of First Nations people in the criminal justice system and mandatory offshore processing and "turn-backs" of asylum seekers who arrive by boat.

In the wake of devastating floods and heatwaves, climate change was a key concern for many Australians in the 2022 election, with a record number of politicians elected on ambitious climate justice platforms. The Albanese government's continued support for the expansion of fossil fuel industries contributes to the global climate crisis and undermines the right to a healthy environment. In 2022, several Australian states introduced new laws targeting peaceful climate and environmental protesters with disproportionate punishments and excessive bail conditions.

Asylum Seekers and Refugees

2022 marked ten years since the Australian government reintroduced offshore processing of asylum seekers who arrive by boat. At time of writing, approximately 200 refugees and asylum seekers remained in abroad in Papua New Guinea and Nauru, with more than 1,045 people admitted to the United States under an Australia-US resettlement deal.

In March, the Australian and New Zealand governments announced an arrangement to allow refugees currently in Nauru or who were transferred from Nauru or Papua New Guinea to Australia temporarily, to resettle in New Zealand, covering up to 150 people per year over three years.

By turning back a boat carrying asylum seekers just days after the election, the Albanese government signaled its intention to continue the "turn-back" policy of interdicting boats and summarily turning them to the high seas or returning individuals to countries of departure or origin. The new government has since confirmed that it has no plans to end the policy of offshore processing of asylum seekers.

In January, authorities detained tennis star Novak Djokovic at the Park Hotel in Melbourne after cancelling his visa, bringing international attention to the plight of approximately 30 asylum seekers and refugees held in the same hotel, many of whom had faced more than eight years of detention and uncertainty under Australia's offshore processing policy. In April, authorities released the remaining asylum seekers and refugees held at the hotel.

The Albanese government fulfilled its pledge to allow an ethnic Tamil family, asylum seekers who had been detained on Christmas Island, to return home to the town of Biloela and granted them permanent residency.

More than 4,000 Ukrainian asylum seekers arrived in Australia since Russia invaded Ukraine in February. The government allocated 31,500 humanitarian and family visa places to Afghan nationals over five years, with nearly 6,000 visas granted.

Indigenous Rights

Indigenous people are significantly overrepresented in the criminal justice system, with Aboriginal and Torres Strait Islander people comprising 29 percent of Australia's adult prison population, but just 3 percent of the national population.

At least 15 Indigenous people died in custody in Australia in 2022. An inquest into the death in custody of Indigenous woman Veronica Nelson in Victoria uncovered that she allegedly screamed for help for hours, but authorities did not send her to a hospital for medical treatment, and then found her dead in her cell.

The state government in Western Australia refused to install air conditioning in residential cells at Roebourne Regional Prison, despite temperatures reaching a record high of 50.5 degrees Celsius (123 degrees Fahrenheit) and the prison inspector saying the conditions posed a significant risk to prisoner health. Ninety percent of the prisoner population at Roebourne are First Nations people. In November, following public pressure from the Aboriginal Legal Service, Human Rights Watch, and others, the state government backtracked and said it would install air conditioning, but not until next summer.

In October, the United Nations Subcommittee on Prevention of Torture suspended its visit to Australia due to obstructions it encountered in visiting several detention sites in Australia and accessing requested documentation.

The Albanese government has committed to holding a referendum to enshrine in the Australian constitution a body to advise the parliament on Indigenous issues, to be known as the Aboriginal and Torres Strait Islander Voice. First Nations people are currently not recognized in the Australian Constitution.

Children's Rights

Indigenous children are 20 times more likely to be incarcerated than non-Indigenous children.

In Australia, the minimum age of criminal responsibility is 10, lower than the internationally accepted age of 14. An estimated 444 children under the age of 14 were imprisoned in the past year across Australia. The Australian Labor Party has pledged to support the review of the minimum age of criminal responsibility. The Australian Capital Territory has committed to raise the age from 10 to 14. In November, the Northern Territory government passed legislation to raise the age to 12. Tasmania has committed to raise the minimum age of detention from 10 to 14 years.

The Western Australia prison inspector concluded that the conditions in Banksia Hill Juvenile Detention Centre did not meet international standards and "breached human rights," with children not receiving the minimum time out of cell required. Prison authorities then moved 17 children from Banksia Hill to a maximum-security adult prison. Multiple incidents of self-harm and suicide attempts were reported after the transfer.

In May, Human Rights Watch reported that the education ministry of New South Wales had violated children's right to privacy and other rights through eight education technology products it had authorized for children's education during the pandemic. All products, except one, surveilled or had the capacity to surveil children online, outside school hours, and deep into their private lives.

Disability Rights

The Royal Commission into Violence, Abuse, Neglect and Exploitation of People with a Disability continued its hearings in 2022, with Human Rights Watch giving evidence to the commission on how prisoners with disabilities are disproportionately held in solitary confinement for 22 hours a day, for weeks, months, and sometimes even years. People with disabilities often fall prey to violence or resort to self-harm because proper support is lacking.

Western Australia's prisons remain damaging and at times deadly for people with disabilities. A Human Rights Watch analysis of deaths in those prisons from 2010-2020 found that about 60 percent of adult prisoners who died in jail had a disability. In 2022, there have been two reported suicides of Aboriginal men in Western Australian prisons. Due to limited resources, mental health services in prisons remain inadequate.

Rights of Older People

Staff working in Australian nursing homes warned that staffing shortages during the Omicron Covid-19 wave saw lower standards of care that risked the survival of frail residents.

Many Australian nursing homes continue to use dangerous drugs, often without informed consent, to control the behavior of older people with dementia, known as "chemical restraint." A Human Rights Watch analysis in March found some aged care facilities did not meet compliance standards and failed to regularly monitor the use of drugs that are administered for chemical restraint, failed to provide individual care plans with ways to manage behavior without the use of chemical restraints, and did not provide alternative strategies to ensure that chemical restraint is a last resort.

Freedom of Expression

In April, the state of New South Wales introduced new laws and penalties specifically targeting climate protesters, punishing them with hefty fines and up to two years prison for protesting without permission.

Human Rights Watch research found authorities in New South Wales were disproportionately punishing climate protesters, and that magistrates were imposing harsh disproportionate penalties and bail conditions on climate protesters in violation of their rights. New anti-protest laws passed in the states of Victoria and Tasmania also invoke severe penalties for non-violent protest.

In March, the Australian Parliament's Joint Committee on Intelligence and Security released a report examining foreign interference at Australian universities, highlighting concerns over Chinese government supporters threatening and intimidating pro-democracy students from China as well as university staff. It recommended mechanisms to report incidents of foreign interference, deterrence for students who report on activities of fellow students to foreign governments, and closer scrutiny of student associations linked to authoritarian governments.

Terrorism and Counterterrorism

The Albanese government repatriated 17 Australian citizens — 13 children and 4 women — who had been arbitrarily detained in harsh conditions in camps and prisons in northeast Syria, as suspected members of the Islamic State (ISIS) and their relatives. At time of writing, approximately 60 Australians, including 30 children and 16 women, still await repatriation.

In July, one of the detainees, an Australian teenager forced as a child to live under the Islamic State, was reported to have died earlier that year in a prison in Northeast Syria.

Climate Change Policy and Impacts

Australia is among the top 20 emitters and one of the world's biggest per capita emitters of greenhouse gases responsible for the climate crisis.

Australia is one of the world's largest exporters of coal and gas and Australian fossil fuel companies benefit from significant tax breaks. In the 2021-22 budget period, Australian federal and state governments' total fossil fuel subsidies are estimated to have cost A$11.6 billion (US$7.4 billion), up A$1.3 billion (US$830 million) compared to the previous year.

Prime Minister Albanese pledged in May to end divisive political "climate wars" and make Australia a "renewable energy superpower."

In September, Australia's parliament passed a bill legislating a 43 percent emissions reduction target by 2030. The Labor government gave strong support to renewable energy projects, and for the first time, an Australian environmental minister said she would reject a new coal mine because of its possible impact on the nearby Great Barrier Reef.

However, the Albanese government is still actively supporting the expansion of fossil fuels industries, denying responsibility for emissions created by the vast amounts of coal and gas Australia exports overseas and flatly ruling out any discussion on banning new fossil fuel projects.

In September, in a ground-breaking decision, the United Nations Human Rights Committee found that the Australian government had violated the rights of Indigenous Torres Strait Islanders by failing to adequately protect them against the adverse impacts of climate change. This failure violated their rights to enjoy their culture and be free from arbitrary interferences with their private life, family, and home. The committee ordered the government to pay adequate compensation to the claimants and secure the communities continued safe existence on the islands, as well as avoiding similar violations in the future.

Foreign Policy

Australia's relationship with the Chinese government remained strained, while the country refocuses its trade and diplomatic relationships with members of the Quad, (Australia, Japan, India, the United States) and Southeast Asian and Pacific nations as part of an effort to counter Beijing's influence in the region. With the Association of Southeast Asian Nations (ASEAN) countries, the Australian government has deferred to principles of ASEAN centrality and "maintaining a region which is peaceful, stable and prosperous, in which sovereignty is respected." It avoids public discussion of rights concerns with the ASEAN member governments of Vietnam, Philippines, Cambodia, and Thailand. The same reluctance to publicly discuss human rights issues is also evident in Canberra's relationship with the Modi government in India.

Australia used its "Magnitsky-style" sanctions legislation for the first time in March, targeting Russian individuals responsible for the mistreatment and death of Russian lawyer Sergei Magnitsky. Since then, the government has enacted no new targeted sanctions under the regime.

Unlike the United Kingdom, United States, Canada, and the European Union, the Australian government has not imposed targeted sanctions on senior military leaders and entities in Myanmar responsible for the February 2021 coup and ensuing rights violations.

Australia joined other UN member countries in condemning China's serious abuses in Xinjiang, following the groundbreaking report by UN High Commissioner for Human Rights Michelle Bachelet.

However, the Australian government has not joined the EU, UK, US, and Canada in imposing targeted sanctions on senior Chinese officials who have been accused of serious human rights violations against Uyghurs and other Turkic Muslim communities in Xinjiang.

In opposition, the Australian Labor Party pledged to strengthen Australia's Modern Slavery Act to address forced labor around the world, including in Xinjiang. The current legislation under review does not respond to calls to introduce stand-alone legislation similar to the US that blocks the import of goods made with forced labor, both from Xinjiang and other locations inside and outside of China.

Australia has not endorsed the Safe Schools Declaration, an intergovernmental pledge now supported by 112 countries to protect education in times of conflict.

Azerbaijan

Azerbaijan's human rights record did not improve in 2022. In May, authorities released more than 20 individuals imprisoned on politically motivated and bogus charges. But at least 30 others remained wrongfully imprisoned while authorities continued to target its critics and other dissenting voices.

Restrictive laws continued to impede nongovernmental organizations (NGOs) from operating independently. Other persistent human rights problems included systemic torture and ill-treatment in custody and restrictions on media freedoms.

In July, amid an energy crisis spurred by Russia's invasion of Ukraine and its manipulation of the country's hydrocarbon supplies, the European Union signed a deal with Azerbaijan aimed at increasing the country's gas exports to Europe. The EU did not use ongoing negotiations on a broad bilateral agreement to secure human rights improvements.

Fighting between Armenian and Azerbaijani forces broke out in mid-September when Azerbaijan made incursions into Armenia. The fighting marked one of several breakdowns of the Russia-brokered 2020 truce that ended hostilities over the unresolved Nagorno-Karabakh war. A video authenticated by Human Rights Watch showed the extrajudicial execution of at least seven Armenian soldiers, apparently by Azerbaijani forces, during this fighting.

Sporadic incidents of military hostilities continued to threaten the safety and livelihoods of civilians residing in villages in Nagorno-Karabakh and along the Armenia-Azerbaijan border.

Aftermath of the Nagorno Karabakh Conflict

Fighting between Armenian and Azerbaijani forces broke out in mid-September when Azerbaijan made incursions into Armenia. The fighting, which killed three civilians in Armenia, marked one of several breakdowns of the Russia-brokered 2020 truce that ended hostilities over the unresolved Nagorno-Karabakh war. Sporadic incidents of military hostilities continued to threaten the safety and livelihoods of civilians residing or working in villages in Nagorno-Karabakh and several surrounding districts, and along the Armenia-Azerbaijan border, leaving at least three ethnic Armenian civilians dead in Nagorno-Karabakh.

A video authenticated by Human Rights Watch showed the extrajudicial execution of at least seven Armenian soldiers, apparently by Azerbaijani forces, during this fighting.

According to Armenian lawyers, at least 30 Armenian prisoners of war (POWs) and three civilians captured in relation to the 2020 hostilities remained in Azerbaijani custody by October 2022. Azerbaijani authorities do not recognize any of these individuals as POWs and have charged them with such crimes as terrorism, illegal weapons possession, illegal border crossing and torture of Azerbaijani prisoners during the 1990s war.

In October 2022 the Azerbaijani Prosecutor General's Office stated that since the 2020 ceasefire, through mid-October 2022, 34 civilians were killed and another 80 were wounded due to landmines in Nagorno Karabakh and the surrounding areas.

Neither Azerbaijan nor Armenia is a party to the international treaty prohibiting anti-personnel landmines.

Prosecuting Political Opposition and Other Critics

Some political activists were among those freed in May under presidential pardon. They included prominent members of the opposition Azerbaijani Popular Front Party (APFP), Saleh Rustamli, sentenced in 2019 to seven years in prison on spurious money-laundering charges, and Pasha Umudov, sentenced in 2020 to four years and five months on bogus drug charges.

Also in May, APFP activist, Agil Maharramov, Rustamli's co-defendant, was released after completing a four-year prison sentence on bogus money-laundering charges. In January, APFP senior politician Alizamin Salayev, convicted on defamation charges in 2020, was granted amnesty and released.

Authorities continued to use spurious drug charges to lock up political activists critical of the government. In many cases, the detainees reported ill-treatment in police custody, allegations that the authorities dismissed.

In May, authorities arrested Rashad Ramazanov, a blogger and former political prisoner, and remanded him to pre-trial detention on bogus drug charges. Police allegedly beat Ramazanov in custody, attempting to secure a drug possession confession. There was no effective investigation into the beating. Ramazanov had previously served six years in prison on bogus drug charges, before being pardoned and released in 2019. Ramazanov had actively criticized on social media police arbitrariness and government corruption.

In May, authorities arrested and sent to pretrial custody APFP member Razi Alishov on bogus drug charges. They failed to effectively investigate his allegations of torture in police custody.

In March, a court sentenced APFP activist Shahin Hajiyev to six years in prison on spurious drug trafficking charges. Hajiyev, in custody since November 2021, had often criticized the government on Facebook. He made police abuse allegations in custody. After police pressured Hajiyev to tell investigators that injuries inflicted by the beating were from a fall days before his arrest, prosecutors refused to investigate Hajiyev's allegations of abuse.

Authorities brought spurious drug charges against several individuals who were deported to Azerbaijan in 2021 after failing to gain asylum in Germany and, in some cases, publicly criticizing Azerbaijani authorities. These included Punhan Karimli and Jafar Mirzayev, deported in November 2021, and arrested in January 2022. Malik Rzayev and Mutallim Orujov were similarly arrested and charged in 2021. Authorities claimed to have found narcotics on each of these men at the time of arrest. In April, police detained Samir Ashurov on charges of assault with a knife, weeks after he was deported home. Their lawyers alleged that police questioned them about their activities in Germany.

In September, the chief editor of Xural TV, an online channel, journalist Avaz Zeynalli and, Elchin Sadigov, a lawyer who defended many government critics, were remanded to four months' pretrial detention on allegations of bribery that both deny. The allegations were made following a pro-government media story accusing Zeynalli of accepting a bribe from an imprisoned Azerbaijani businessman facing criminal charges in exchange for ending critical reporting about him. The story alleged that Sadigov, the businessman's lawyer, was the intermediary. A court released Sadigov to house arrest upon appeal.

Authorities also held several government critics in jail for up to 30 days following pro-forma court hearings on bogus misdemeanor hooliganism or disobedience charges. These included, in March, APFP member, Elkhan Aliyev, and in July, opposition Musavat Party member, Alikram Khurshidov. Both men were harshly critical of authorities on social media.

Freedom of Assembly

Azerbaijan effectively imposes a blanket ban on protests in the central areas of the capital, Baku. In May, a group of civic activists held an unsanctioned rally in downtown Baku, demanding an end to impunity for abuse and violence against government critics. Police briefly detained at least 25 protesters. Hours before the protest, police detained three of the protest organizers, drove them in some cases several hundred kilometers from Baku and abandoned them there, apparently to prevent them from participating in the rally.

In July, authorities briefly detained more than 40 protestors after attempting to hold an unsanctioned protest, demanding the opening of land borders that have remained closed since the start of the Covid-19 pandemic. Police detained Aziz Mamiyev, a Musavat member, on his way to the rally and a court sentenced him to 30 days' detention on disobedience charges. Mamiyev reported that police beat him during apprehension and at the police station. A court sentenced another activist, Gulmira Rahimova, to 460 hours of community service on slander charges for having posted on social media a photo of the officer who struck Mamiyev.

Freedom of Expression

All mainstream media remained under tight government control. People who publicly criticized the government faced threats aimed at silencing them.

In February, President Ilham Aliyev signed a law on media that limits media independence by, among other things, barring non-residents from owning media and requiring journalists to have higher education, a formal contract, and three years' experience to obtain accreditation. The Council of Europe (CoE) commissioner for human rights, Dunja Mijatović, said the law "overregulates the media … and grants discretionary powers to authorities … including through licensing, excessively restricting journalists' work, and introducing several limitations to media companies and entities."

In May, an unknown man threatened prominent journalist Aytan Mammadova with a knife in the elevator of her apartment building. Mammadova believes the threat aimed at stopping her ongoing reporting on a high-profile child murder trial. At time of writing, the criminal investigation had not identified the suspect.

The authorities use criminal defamation to silence government critics. According to the Media Rights Institute (MRI), an independent media monitoring group, in 2022, prosecutors demanded imprisonment in 11 defamation cases filed under private prosecution procedures. The lawsuits resulted in the conviction of at least four individuals, some of whom, MRI said, had been "targeted for their opinions or articles on matters of public interest."

In January, a court sentenced Ali Aliyev, the chairman of the Citizen and Development Party (VİP), to five months' imprisonment in a slander lawsuit filed by one of the two border guards who survived a helicopter crash in November 2021. Aliyev had commented to the media that he doubted that the border guards had in fact survived. Aliyev also argued that the crash was a provocation by Russia. In April, a court increased the sentence by another month, satisfying the complaint by the second survivor. In June, a court extended Aliyev's sentence to one year in prison on unrelated charges of insult, based on a complaint filed by a former official of the ruling party.

In March, a regional court sentenced journalist Jamil Mammadli to a year and six months of correctional labor on slander and insult charges for corruption allegations he made against the head of a district official.

In June, a regional court sentenced lawyer Ilham Aslanoglu to six months in prison for insult related to a video he posted in which he accused an officer of torture in the Terter case (see below). It was Aslanoglu's second conviction in a year on the same charges.

Torture and Ill-Treatment in Detention

Authorities routinely dismiss complaints of torture and other ill-treatment in custody, especially those filed by government critics.

For instance, in January, the prosecutor's office refused to launch a probe into the severe beating of leading opposition politician Tofiq Yaqublu while in detention in December 2021, which resulted in multiple injuries. The prosecutor's office refused to investigate, claiming Yaqublu's injuries were "self-inflicted."

In April, masked men kidnapped prominent opposition activist Bakhtiyar Hajiyev and took him to an undisclosed location, blindfolded, beat, and threatened to kill him if he continued to publicly criticize the interior minister. After Hajiyev publicized the incident, the interior minister met with him and a criminal investigation was launched, but at time of writing, the authorities had not identified any suspects. According to Hajiyev, investigators claimed the CCTV cameras from the crime scene were "out of order" at the time of the kidnapping. In August, police briefly detained Hajiyev, and a senior police official allegedly threatened him with reprisals if he continued criticizing the minister.

In an exception to the pattern of impunity for torture, throughout 2022, authorities continued a new investigation, begun in December 2021, into the torture in 2017 of military officers in Terter region accused of allegedly spying for Armenia. The new investigation followed public outrage about the case, which prompted the chief military prosecutor in November 2021 to publicly acknowledge that more than a hundred officers had been subjected to physical violence.

According to NGOs, at least 10 had died of torture, four of whom were posthumously acquitted. In September, authorities announced that 405 victims had been identified in Terter and two other regions, of whom several hundred had been tortured. Authorities prosecuted 17 high-ranking military officers for abuse and torture. In September, the prosecutor's office announced that an army general and a military lawyer had been arrested on charges of unlawful imprisonment, torture and inhumane treatment, and abuse of power.

Key International Actors

In a January letter, CoE Commissioner for Human Rights Dunja Mijatović urged President Aliyev to return the media bill to parliament for substantial revisions to bring it in line with freedom of expression and media standards. In June, the Venice Commission, an expert body of the Council of Europe, concluded that the law has "a problematic focus on restricting the activities of the media rather than creating the necessary conditions enabling the media to fulfil their 'public watchdog' role."

In May, the British Embassy in Azerbaijan condemned incidents of police violence during the May 14 rally. The Azerbaijani Interior Ministry called on the British Embassy to refute its statement.

In May, the US government welcomed the presidential pardon of persons "incarcerated for exercising their fundamental freedoms" and called on the government to also release others arrested "for exercising those same rights." In September, US Secretary of State Antony Blinken brought together the foreign ministers of Armenia and Azerbaijan on the sidelines of the UN General Assembly in New York in the wake of the breakdown of the truce between the two countries and Azerbaijan's incursions into Armenia. The meeting came one week after shelling killed more than 200 troops.

The EU has been more actively engaged on talks between Armenia and Azerbaijan. In July, the European Commission President Ursula von der Leyen and President Aliyev signed a memorandum of understanding to more than double gas purchases from Azerbaijan. Following the signing ceremony, von der Leyen referred to the negotiations of a comprehensive bilateral agreement that would vastly expand EU investment in Azerbaijan. She noted the importance to investor confidence of "greater involvement of civil society, and a free and independent media" without meeting with civil society organizations during her visit. Later in July, the EU top diplomat Josep Borrell stated that decisive progress was needed to create an enabling environment for an active civil society in Azerbaijan.

Bahrain

Bahrain's 2022 parliamentary elections, held in November, were neither free nor fair. All members of previously dissolved political groups were barred from running in the elections. Authorities also have sought to restrict former opposition members from participating in civil society organizations. Independent media has been banned since 2017.

Twenty-six Bahrainis remain on death row. At least eight of these men were convicted and sentenced following manifestly unfair trials based primarily, or in some instances solely, on coerced confessions.

Prominent opposition figures and human rights defenders, including Abdulhadi al-Khawaja and Abdel-Jalil al-Singace, remained in prison without access to adequate medical care. Authorities failed to hold officials accountable for torture and ill-treatment in detention.

Closure of Political Space and Freedom of Association

Bahrain's November 2022 parliamentary and municipal elections took place amid serious restrictions on political and civil rights, free speech, and assembly.

Political isolation laws, passed in June 2018, explicitly ban members of previously dissolved political parties from running for parliament and from sitting as members on the boards of directors of civil society organizations. The laws also ban formerly convicted felons, even if pardoned or convicted on abusive speech or assembly-related charges, and those previously deemed to have "disrupted" constitutional life in Bahrain. In 2016 and 2017, Bahrain's judiciary dissolved the country's two major opposition parties, Al Wifaq and Waad.

On January 31, 2022, the Bahrain Human Rights Society (BHRS), one of Bahrain's oldest human rights organizations, learned that three candidates nominated to run in the society's board of directors' election—Abdul-Jalil Yousef, the organization's secretary-general, Issa Ebrahim, and Mohsin Matar—were banned from the board because of the political isolation laws. All three are former members of Bahrain's now-dissolved National Democratic Action Society (Waad).

WORLD REPORT 2023

The government also expanded practices that limit economic opportunities for former opposition members and political prisoners through the routine delay or denial of "good conduct certificates," a document required for Bahraini citizens and residents to obtain employment, apply for university, or even join a sports or social club.

Death Penalty

Bahraini courts have convicted and sentenced defendants to death following manifestly unfair trials, based solely or primarily on confessions allegedly coerced through torture and ill-treatment.

Since 2017, Bahrain has executed six people and, as of June 2022, 26 others are on death row with their appeals exhausted. Human Rights Watch and the Bahrain Institute for Rights and Democracy (BIRD) examined the cases of eight men facing the death penalty, based primarily on court records and other official documents. The defendants were convicted and sentenced following manifestly unfair trials based primarily, or in some instances, solely on coerced confessions. The trial and appeal courts in these cases dismissed credible allegations of torture during interrogation, relied on secretly sourced documents, and denied or failed to protect fundamental fair trial and due process rights, including the rights to counsel during interrogation and to cross-examine prosecution witnesses. Bahraini authorities also violated their obligations to investigate allegations of torture and abuse.

Freedom of Expression and Peaceful Assembly

Thirteen prominent opposition leaders have remained behind bars for more than a decade for their roles in the 2011 pro-democracy protests. They include Hassan Mushaima, the head of the unlicensed opposition group Al-Haq; Abdulwahab Hussain, an opposition leader; Abdulhadi al-Khawaja, a prominent human rights defender; and Abdel-Jalil al-Singace, the spokesman for Al-Haq. All four are serving life terms following manifestly unfair trials.

No independent media has operated in Bahrain since the Information Affairs Ministry suspended Al Wasat, the country's only independent newspaper, in

2017. Foreign journalists rarely have access to Bahrain, and Human Rights Watch and other international rights groups are routinely denied access.

Security Forces and Prisons

Authorities continue to deny Bahraini prisoners adequate medical care, causing unnecessary suffering and endangering the health of prisoners with chronic medical conditions. In May, prison authorities did not respond adequately to a tuberculosis outbreak in Jau prison. Two prisoners with symptoms of tuberculosis were ignored by prison authorities for more than a week. Prison authorities failed to provide hospital care to a prisoner, Ahmed Jaber, for 11 months. Jaber became sick in prison in April 2021 but was not transferred to a hospital until March 2022.

Abdel-Jalil al-Singace began a hunger strike in July 2021 that continued throughout 2022. In 2022, Bahraini authorities delayed or denied the delivery of multiple necessary medicines to al-Singace, including medications necessary for his nervous system and bodily functions, and eye drops. Abdulhadi Al-Khawaja has been denied adequate medical care since he chanted solidarity slogans with Palestinians in the prison yard in February 2022.

Authorities have failed to credibly investigate and prosecute officials and police officers who allegedly committed serious violations, including torture, since the 2011 protests.

Children's Rights

Bahrain authorities arbitrarily detained six boys, ages 14 and 15, in an orphanage in Seef district, after summoning and arresting them in December 2021 and January 2022. Authorities did not provide the boys or their families with any written justification for their detention and they first learned about the alleged legal basis from a public statement issued in February by the Office of the Public Prosecution that accused them of throwing a Molotov cocktail. Authorities also denied parents' requests to be present during their sons' interrogations and to visit them. The children's alleged offenses appear to have occurred in December 2020 or January 2021, when they were 13 and 14.

Bahrain's 2021 Restorative Justice Law for Children sets the minimum age of criminal responsibility at 15 but permits authorities to "place the child in a social welfare institution" for renewable weekly periods "if the circumstances require." The law fails to guarantee children access to a lawyer and their parents during interrogations and provides that children may be detained if they participate in unlicensed protests.

Online Surveillance and Censorship

The Bahraini government continued its use of NSO Group's Pegasus spyware to target activists and human rights defenders in Bahrain. In February 2022, a joint investigation by Red Line 4 Gulf, Amnesty International, and Citizen Lab found that critics of the Bahraini government, including Mohammed Al-Tajer, a prominent Bahraini lawyer, Dr. Sharifa Siwar, a mental health counselor, and an online journalist were targeted with the spyware between June and September 2021.

Bahrain has purchased spyware to target government critics and human rights defenders for over a decade.

Migrant Workers

Bahrain continues to **enforce** the *kafala* (sponsorship) system that ties migrant workers' visas to their employers, which means if they leave their employer without their employer's consent, they lose their residency status and can face arrest, fines, and deportation for "absconding." In 2009, Bahrain allowed migrant workers to **terminate** their employment contracts after one year with their first employer if they give reasonable notice to their employer of at least 30 days. However, in January 2022, the parliament **voted** to extend this to two years. The workers are also expected to bear their own fees for the two-year work permit, which has been too onerous for many, resulting in little up-take.

Bahrain's Labor Law includes domestic workers but excludes them from protections within it such as weekly rest days, a minimum wage, and limits on working hours.

Women's Rights, Gender Identity, and Sexual Orientation

Bahrain passed a unified family law in July 2017, but it continues to discriminate against women's rights to marry, divorce, and inherit on an equal basis to men. Women are required to obey their husbands as the head of the household. The 1963 Citizenship Act prohibits women from conferring their nationality to their children from a non-Bahraini father.

Although no law explicitly criminalizes same-sex relations, authorities have used vague penal code provisions against "indecency" and "immorality" to target sexual and gender minorities.

In December 2018, Bahrain amended its labor law to ban discrimination based on sex, origin, language, or creed, and sexual harassment in the workplace, but the law does not refer to sexual orientation, gender identity, disability, or age.

Key International Actors

In July, US President Joe Biden met Bahrain's King Hamad in Jeddah and underscored "the United States' appreciation for the longstanding strategic partnership with Bahrain, including its hosting of the US Navy Forces Central Command/5th Fleet."

The United Kingdom government funded Bahrain-led and owned reform and capacity-building programs involved in egregious human rights violations through the Gulf Strategy Fund (GSF). The GSF has supported Bahrain's Ministry of Interior and the Special Investigations Unit and other security bodies implicated in the abuses of at least eight men currently on death row.

The European Union's Joint Communication on a partnership with the Gulf failed to highlight the poor human rights situation in Bahrain and made no attempt to link progress in bilateral relations to specific human rights benchmarks.

Serbia extradited a Bahraini political dissident to Bahrain on January 24 despite an order by the European Court of Human Rights that specifically prohibited his extradition pending more information. Bahraini authorities had previously subjected the dissident, Ahmed Jaffer Muhammad, 48, to torture and ill-treatment. Serbia initiated extradition proceedings after Interpol, the international police body, issued a Red Notice alert at Bahrain's request.

Bangladesh

Following the US Global Magnitsky human rights sanctions against Bangladesh's Rapid Action Battalion (RAB) and some of its top commanders in December 2021, extrajudicial killings and enforced disappearances dropped dramatically, indicating that authorities have the ability to bring security force abuses under control. However, instead of taking steps toward reform, authorities launched a campaign of threats and intimidation against human rights defenders and families of victims of enforced disappearances. campaign of threats and intimidation against human rights defenders and families of victims of enforced disappearances.

Bangladesh continues to host about 1 million Rohingya refugees, but authorities have intensified restrictions on their livelihoods, movement, and education. International attention has waned and the 2022 Joint Response Plan for the Rohingya humanitarian crisis remained severely underfunded at time of writing.

Starting in August, there were increasing attacks against political opposition members, raising concerns about violence and repression ahead of upcoming parliamentary elections. elections.

In March, Bangladesh ratified International Labour Organization (ILO) Convention 138 on child labor, making Bangladesh party to all ILO Fundamental Instruments.

Attacks on Human Rights Defenders

Following the US sanctions, victims' families reported that officers came to their homes, threatened them, and forced them to sign false statements that their relative was not forcibly disappeared and that they had intentionally misled the police. Security forces also ramped up surveillance of human rights activists and harassment of human rights organizations. United Nations rights experts urged the government to end reprisals.

The Foreign Ministry reportedly prepared a list of dissidents abroad who are committing "anti-state" activities, and authorities increasingly targeted relatives of expat dissidents. In September, officers from the Detective Branch arrested the brother of London-based news editor Shamsul Alam Liton after he published an editorial critical of the ruling party and organized protests in Britain against disappearances. The same month, police arrested Abdul Muktadir Manu, the brother of another London-based correspondent for the same newspaper. Nusrat Shahrin Raka, sister of US-based journalist Kanak Sarwar, received bail after nearly six months in detention.

The government also increasingly targeted human rights organizations. A leaked government circular signed on January 25 appeared to show that the Finance Ministry and the Prime Minister's Office were tasked in response to the US sanctions with monitoring foreign funding to several human rights organizations.

On June 5, the Non-Governmental Organization Affairs Bureau sent a letter to Odhikar, one of the country's most prominent human rights organizations, denying the group's renewal of registration. The decision was upheld by the Prime Minister's Office on September 1. Odhikar's secretary, Adilur Rahman Khan, and director, ASM Nasruddin Elan, were additionally facing ongoing trials as part of longstanding harassment to punish the organization for reporting extrajudicial killings by Bangladesh security forces in 2013. reporting extrajudicial killings by Bangladesh security forces in 2013.

Disappearances and Extrajudicial Killings

Despite a temporary drop in abuses following the announcement of US sanctions, security forces showed signs of returning to old practices, targeting the ruling Awami League's political opponents and critics. The government dismissed the allegations that led to sanctions, saying they were "false and fabricated." In January, Prime Minister Sheikh Hasina awarded two sanctioned RAB officials prestigious police medals for their "bravery and service to the country."

On August 14, Netra news—which is blocked in Bangladesh—published a whistleblower report revealing that Bangladesh officials were allegedly holding and torturing victims of enforced disappearance at a secret detention site.revealing that Bangladesh officials were allegedly holding and torturing victims of enforced disappearance at a secret detention site.

The torture and death in custody of Indigenous activist Nabayan Chakma Milon shed light on security force abuses in the Chittagong Hill Tracts, including extrajudicial killings, enforced disappearances, sexual violence, and land-grabbing, with little redress.

Freedom of Expression

Authorities continued to arrest critics under the draconian Digital Security Act. The government ignored pleas from the UN and international partners to suspend and reform the abusive law. In July, the government released the draft Data Protection Act, which experts say could increase surveillance and violate the rights to privacy.

Covid-19

At time of writing, Bangladesh reported over 440,000 new confirmed cases of Covid-19 and 1,300 deaths in 2022. However, at time of writing, the positive test rate was above 27 percent, indicating that transmission rates are likely higher than is reported. Schools fully reopened in July after almost 18 months of Covid-19-related school closure, one of the longest in the world. Children's rights advocates raised concerns that tens of thousands of students were not returning to school and instead that many of these children were pushed into child labor amid the economic fallout during the pandemic.

Women and Girls' Rights

According to Bangladeshi human rights organization Ain o Salish Kendra, as of October 1, 193 women and girls were reportedly murdered by their husband or husband's family in 2022. Women in Bangladesh continue to have little recourse to seek protection, services, or access justice in case of domestic violence. Bangladesh continues to have one of the highest rates of child marriage in the world..

Following widespread protests and advocacy by women's rights activists, the cabinet approved a draft amendment to section 155(4) of the Evidence Act, removing aspects that allowed the defense to denigrate the character of women if they pursue criminal charges for sexual violence.

Sexual Orientation and Gender Identity

Same-sex conduct is criminalized in Bangladesh with penalties from 10 years to life in prison. Lesbian, gay, bisexual, and transgender people and advocates faced violence and threats without adequate protection from the police.

Disability Rights

In September, the Committee on the Rights of Persons with Disabilities published concluding observations in its review of Bangladesh, expressing concern over discrimination that creates barriers to education, health care, and justice, especially for women and girls with disabilities.

In September, Human Rights Watch interviewed people with disabilities and their families following the flash floods in Sylhet in May that displaced almost 9 million people and killed hundreds. Interviewees described a lack of warning systems that would have enabled them to prepare and seek shelter. After the floods, people with disabilities faced additional hurdles accessing toilets, food, water, and medicines, putting their lives and health at increased risk.

Rohingya Refugees

In the Rohingya refugee camps, Bangladesh officials closed community-led schools, arbitrarily destroyed shops, and imposed new obstacles on movement, including threats, frequent curfews, and harassment at checkpoints. The government allowed humanitarian actors in the camps to begin teaching the Myanmar curriculum but continues to deny refugee children any accredited education.

Authorities moved about 8,000 Rohingya refugees to Bhasan Char, bringing the total to around 28,000 refugees living on the remote silt island where they face severe movement restrictions, food, and medicine shortages, and abuses by security forces. Despite the involvement of the United Nations High Commissioner for Refugees (UNHCR), many continue to be transferred without full, informed consent, and have been prevented from returning to the mainland.

In January, the Bangladesh government and Myanmar junta announced joint plans to "expeditiously complete the verification process" for repatriation, even though conditions do not exist for voluntary, safe, and dignified returns.

Increased fighting between the Myanmar military and Arakan Army ethnic armed group in Rakhine State has spilled across the border, endangering Rohingya refugees and Bangladesh civilians.

Climate Change Policies and Actions

Bangladesh is among the countries most vulnerable to the impacts of climate change, despite having contributed little to the greenhouse gas emissions causing rising temperatures. Due to climate change, cyclones will become more intense and frequent, posing a growing threat to tens of millions of people living along the country's low-lying coastline. In June, an estimated 7.2 million people in Bangladesh were affected by record level flooding in the northeast.

An ongoing buildout of coal and gas projects in Chattogram, if constructed, will emit greenhouse gases equivalent to five years of Bangladesh's annual greenhouse gas emissions, as well as air pollution that threatens the health of local populations and biodiversity. In June, the government announced that it cancelled plans to build the controversial Matarbari 2 coal plant, following the loss of Japanese investment. But the government now plans build a liquified natural gas (LNG) power plant instead, continuing to lock Bangladesh into decades of greenhouse gas emissions.

Key International Actors

United Nations High Commissioner for Human Rights Michelle Bachelet, during her three-day visit to Bangladesh in August, called on the government to protect rights and establish an independent mechanism to "investigate allegations of enforced disappearances and extrajudicial killings". She offered her office's support to create a special mechanism in line with international standards. She also warned that as "the biggest contributor of uniformed personnel to UN peacekeeping missions, Bangladesh should ensure it has a robust system in place for the careful human rights screening of security personnel."

On March 3, the UN urged the Bangladesh government to provide information on the implementation of the recommendations regarding allegations of torture reported during a 2019 review of its obligations under the Convention against Torture, which it has ignored for over two years.

In March, a European Union monitoring mission travelled to Bangladesh to assess the human rights situation, and urged progress in the context of the enhanced engagement process under the Everything But Arms (EBA) scheme. Further talks were held in May. Also in March, undersecretary for political affairs at the US Department of State, Victoria Nuland, met with Bangladesh officials during the US-Bangladesh Partnership Dialogue, during which she called for accountability for security force abuses.

Bangladesh attempted to balance a strategic relationship between China and India, and both failed to publicly back calls from the US, UK, and Japan to ensure free and fair elections.

Belarus

In 2022, Belarusian authorities continued to purge independent voices, including through bogus prosecutions and harassment of human rights defenders, journalists, lawyers, opposition politicians, and activists. At time of writing, at least 1,340 people were behind bars on politically motivated charges and not a single human rights organization could operate in Belarus legally.

As of February 24, the Belarusian government has been letting Russian forces use the country's territory in Russia's full-scale invasion of Ukraine. Belarusian authorities prosecuted critics of the Russia-Ukraine war and brutally dispersed anti-war protests.

Authorities failed to conduct effective investigations into the widespread allegations of torture and other ill-treatment of peaceful protesters by law enforcement officers in August 2020 following the manipulated presidential vote.

Governmental Crackdown on Peaceful Protests and Dissent

According to the prominent Belarusian human rights organization Viasna, at least 3,458 people faced criminal prosecution in connection with the 2020 mass protests between November 2021 and October 2022, and more than 3,148 people faced administrative sanctions.

Authorities increasingly used charges of "dissemination of extremist materials" to prosecute people for sharing publications from independent news outlets and Telegram channels the government designated "extremist."

On February 27, the Belarusian authorities held a referendum on constitutional amendments which, among other things, cancelled Belarus's nuclear weapon free status and exempted former presidents from accountability for actions committed during their term in office. Human rights defenders deemed the referendum non-transparent and illegitimate.

On the day of the referendum, peaceful demonstrations took place across the country protesting Russia's military invasion of Ukraine. Police detained hundreds of protesters and subjected them to beatings and other ill-treatment.

In the following months, police routinely detained people for anti-war placards and inscriptions. Authorities opened dozens of criminal cases for "aiding extremist activity" against people who shared photos and videos of Russian troops' movement.

Human Rights Defenders, Civil Society Groups, and Lawyers

At time of writing, three members of Viasna, which had been particularly hard hit by the authorities, remained behind bars on bogus "smuggling" and "financing group actions that disrupted public order" charges, including its leader and Nobel Peace Prize winner Ales Bialiatski, vice-chair Valentin Stefanovich, and lawyer Uladzimir Labkovich. Three other members of Viasna, namely, Maria (Marfa) Rabkova, Andrey Chapiuk, and Leanid Sudalenka were serving their sentences of 15, 6, and 3 years, respectively. Viasna reported inhumane prison conditions, including refusal of medical care and restrictions on correspondence.

In December, a court in Homiel designated Viasna's website and social media pages as "extremist," which led to their blocking. Authorities also blocked the websites of other civil society organizations, including another leading rights group Human Constanta, after either designating them "extremist" or finding them in violation of mass media laws.

In April, the prosecutor general announced the blocking of Human Rights Watch's website. The decision came days after the organization published a report on war crimes by Russian forces in Ukraine.

In April, authorities raided offices of several independent trade unions, detaining at least 14 of their leaders and members on charges of "organization of activities gravely violating public order." In July, the Supreme Court of Belarus shut down four major independent trade unions and the Belarusian Congress of Democratic Trade Unions.

By October, authorities had moved to shut down 653 civil society organizations. In January, amendments into the Criminal Code entered into force, reintroducing criminal liability for participation in activities of unregistered organizations, punishable with up to two years in prison.

Authorities continued repression against lawyers in retaliation for expressing views on rights issues, representing clients in politically motivated cases, and speaking out against the war in Ukraine. Since August 2020, at least 70 attorneys lost their licenses following arbitrary decisions of the Justice Ministry or politically motivated disbarment procedures. At time of writing, seven attorneys faced politically motivated criminal charges, ranging from "calls for actions damaging to Belarus's national interests" to "organizing mass riots." Lawyers also continued to face administrative charges, detentions, searches, and harassment.

Freedom of Expression, Attacks on Journalists

From January to October, the Belarusian Association of Journalists documented 93 cases of arbitrary detention, raids, fines, and administrative arrests of journalists. At time of writing, 28 journalists and media workers were behind bars on bogus criminal charges ranging from "insulting the president" to "treason" and "conspiracy to seize state power."

By October, at least 29 independent media outlets had been designated "extremist" and blocked by the authorities.

In June, the Supreme Court designated TUT.BY media "an extremist organization." At time of writing, three TUT.BY's staff, including the editor-in-chief Maryna Zolatava, were behind bars on bogus criminal charges; nine more were placed under their own recognizance pending trial.

On July 13, a court in Homiel found Katsiaryna Andreyeva (Bakhvalova), a journalist from a Poland-based broadcaster Belsat, guilty of high treason. At time of sentencing, she was already serving another sentence. After this second verdict, the length of her jail time was increased to eight years and three months.

Prosecution of Political Opposition Members and Supporters

In December, a court in Homiel delivered judgement in the case against former presidential contender Siarhei Tsikhanouski and his five alleged supporters charged with "organizing mass protests." Tsikhanouski, who is married to the Belarusian opposition leader in exile Sviatlana Tsikhanouskaya, was sentenced

WORLD REPORT 2023

to 18 years in prison. The other defendants, including opposition politician, Mikalay Statkevich, and Radio Free Europe consultant, Ihar Losik, were sentenced to between 14 and 16 years in prison.

In August, authorities transferred Tsikhaunouski from a penal colony to prison with harsher detention conditions.

Humanitarian Crisis and Violence at Belarus-Poland Border

Starting in August 2021, Belarusian authorities orchestrated a humanitarian crisis by facilitating tourist visas to thousands of migrants, mainly from the Middle East, to encourage them to travel to the European Union borders. Pushed back to Belarus at the EU borders, migrants suffered serious abuses, including beatings and at least one instance of rape by Belarusian border guards and other security agents. Belarusian authorities prevented them from leaving the border areas and forced them to repeatedly attempt crossing into the EU. This resulted in hundreds of people stuck in limbo for weeks and months in circumstances that put their lives at risk.

Death Penalty

Belarus remains the only country in Europe and Central Asia to carry out the death penalty. Authorities take months to inform families of an execution and refuse to disclose the place of burial, causing additional suffering.

In November 2021, the family of Viktar Paulau, who had been sentenced to death following his conviction for murder and larceny, finally received official confirmation of his death on May 13, 2021. Authorities executed Paulau despite the UN Human Rights Committee's order to suspend his capital punishment while the committee considered his case.

The fate of Viktar Syarhel, convicted of murder and put on death row in 2021, is unknown. The family of Viktar Skrundzik, sentenced to death for murder and attempted murder, has yet to receive any official confirmation of his death, although in September 2021 the state broadcaster referred to Skrundzik's execution.

In May, amendments to the Criminal Code entered into force, introducing the death penalty for vaguely defined non-lethal "attempted acts of terrorism."

Key International Actors

In November 2021, 35 OSCE states invoked the Vienna Human Dimension Mechanism, highlighting the failure of Belarusian authorities to investigate and remedy gross human rights violations.

Between December 2021 and September 2022, the United States, Canada, the European Union, and the United Kingdom introduced further sanctions against Belarus in response to continuing attacks on human rights, including sanctions against individuals and entities, and actions to expand and tighten export controls to Belarus.

The UN Human Rights Committee issued three decisions on capital punishment cases in Belarus. In September 2021, the committee found violations of the right to life and the right to fair trial in the case of Aliaksei Mikhalenia, who had been executed in 2018. In March 2022, the committee condemned the execution of Viktar Paulau. In May 2022, the UN body found that Belarusian authorities ill-treated the mother of Pavel Sialiun as they mailed her son's death row clothes to her and refused to reveal the place of his burial.

In February, the Venice Commission, an advisory body of the Council of Europe, issued an urgent interim opinion on the constitutional reform in Belarus, stressing that it "fails to correct the strong imbalance of powers [...] and indeed may even aggravate it."

In March, the office of the UN High Commissioner for Human Rights presented a new report under its mandate relating to examination of the human rights situation in Belarus in the run-up to the 2020 presidential election and in its aftermath, documenting rights abuses and lack of effective investigation. In April, the UN Human Rights Council renewed this mandate for one year. In July, the UN special rapporteur on the human rights situation in Belarus presented her annual report documenting the continuous deterioration of the human rights situation; the mandate of the special rapporteur was renewed by the Human Rights Council in June.

In May, the European Parliament issued a resolution condemning the crackdown on trade unionists. In August, the Council of the EU reiterated its support for the democratic aspirations of Belarusian people.

On July 21, the UN Economic and Social Council (ECOSOC) voted in favor of granting UN consultative status to the Belarusian Helsinki Committee, whose application had been unfairly blocked for years by Russia and China.

In November, the UN Human Rights Committee expressed "profound regret" that Belarus had denounced the First Optional Protocol to the International Covenant on Civil and Political Rights, blocking the UN Human Rights Committee's mandate to review individual complaints from Belarus.

In November, the European Parliament adopted a resolution, calling on Belarusian authorities to cease the continuing repression and reiterating support for Belarusian democratic opposition and civil society.

Bolivia

Political interference plagued Bolivia's justice system during the governments of former President Evo Morales (January 2006-November 2019) and former Interim President Jeanine Áñez (November 2019-2020). President Luis Arce, who took office in November 2020, has failed to spur justice reform.

The Arce administration supports unsubstantiated and excessive charges of terrorism and genocide against former President Áñez. In June 2022, a judge sentenced her to 10 years in prison on charges of dereliction of duty and contravening the law, which are defined very broadly in Bolivia. She was not allowed to attend her trial in person.

Nobody has been held accountable for 37 killings in the context of election-related protests in 2019, including of 20 people in two massacres during which state security forces opened fire on protesters, according to witnesses.

Women and girls remain at high risk of violence. Prison overcrowding—and excessive pretrial detention—continues. Indigenous communities face obstacles to exercising their right, under international law, to free, prior, and informed consent to measures that may affect them.

Judicial Independence and Due Process

The Morales and Áñez governments pursued what appeared to be politically motivated charges against political rivals.

After winning the October 2020 presidential election, President Arce said the justice system should be independent from politics, but his government has failed to take concrete steps to reform it.

In a May 2022 report, the United Nations special rapporteur on the independence of judges and lawyers said external interference in the justice system is a long-standing, continuing problem. Almost 50 percent of judges and 70 percent of prosecutors in Bolivia remained "temporary" as of February, the report noted. Officials who lack security of tenure may be vulnerable to reprisals, including arbitrary dismissal, if they make decisions that displease those in power.

In March 2021, police detained former Interim President Áñez and two of her former ministers on terrorism and other charges. The attorney general later accused Áñez of genocide in connection with two massacres during her government. Human Rights Watch reviewed the charging documents and found the terrorism and genocide charges unsubstantiated and grossly disproportionate. The definition of those crimes is overly broad under Bolivian law. As of October 2022, the two former ministers remained in pretrial detention.

In June 2022, in a separate case, a tribunal sentenced Áñez to ten years of prison for dereliction of duty and taking decisions contrary to the law—crimes that are also very broadly defined in Bolivian law—for her actions as she took office as interim president in November 2019. Áñez was not allowed to attend her own trial in person, as judges argued that they could not guarantee her health or security in the courthouse. That prevented Áñez from conferring with her lawyers during the hearings.

In April, Marco Aramayo died in his seventh year of detention amid serious allegations of inadequate health care and ill-treatment. In 2015, after he became the director of the state Indigenous development fund, he reported several corruption schemes allegedly involving prominent supporters of the Morales government. Instead of properly investigating those allegations, prosecutors had him detained and charged with corruption, according to ITEI, a Bolivian nonprofit.

Responding to criticism by Human Rights Watch and others, police said in June they would stop presenting people they had arrested to the press, a practice that risked violating the presumption of innocence. Yet, the minister of the interior continued to post photos of suspects on social media.

Protest-Related Violence and Abuses

The Interdisciplinary Group of Independent Experts (GIEI, in Spanish), established under a government agreement with the Inter-American Commission on Human Rights (IACHR), issued a report in August 2021 documenting the deaths of 37 people in the context of protests over contested October 2019 elections.

It documented acts of violence "instigated" by the Morales administration, including injuries, abductions, and torture of anti-Morales protesters. It asserted that police failed to protect people from violence by both pro- and anti-Morales supporters, and in some locations encouraged and collaborated with violent groups of anti-Morales supporters acting as "para-police."

It also concluded that, during the Áñez government, security forces killed 20 pro-Morales protesters and injured more than 170 people in massacres in Sacaba, a city in Cochabamba, and Senkata, a neighborhood of El Alto. The report provided robust evidence of other abuses throughout the country, including illegal detentions, sexual violence, and "systematic" torture by police in the predominantly Indigenous city of El Alto.

The GIEI highlighted major flaws in probes of the abuses and called on the Attorney General's Office to reopen cases it had closed without crucial investigative steps. As of October 2022, no one had been held responsible for the crimes; Congress and the government were discussing a bill and policy to provide reparation to victims.

In March, the government signed an agreement with the IACHR for creation of an international mechanism to monitor implementation of the GIEI's recommendations, but it failed to create a national-level mechanism for which the GIEI had also called.

Freedom of Expression and Access to Information

The National Press Association, which represents the country's main print media, reported several cases of violence by police or demonstrators against reporters in 2022.

In August, the Attorney General's Office announced an investigation of two journalists, a newscaster and other individuals who worked for a state TV channel during the Áñez administration, for allegedly paying the former newscaster a salary that was higher than the allowable rate. The crimes they were accused of carry a maximum penalty of ten years in prison. The president of the La Paz Press Association viewed the investigation as an attempt by the Arce administration, working with prosecutors, to intimidate Bolivian journalists.

Bolivia lacks a law regulating the allocation of paid advertising by the state. From January through August, 80 percent of the advertising contracts by the state with print media had gone to only two pro-government newspapers, several media reported.

Bolivia also lacks a law to implement the right of access to information enshrined in its constitution. In May 2022, the Arce administration said journalists' associations—not the government—should draft an access to information bill.

Accountability for Past Abuses

Bolivian authorities have made insufficient efforts to hold accountable officials responsible for human rights violations under authoritarian governments between 1964 and 1982. Only a handful have been prosecuted. The armed forces have generally refused to share information.

After camping outside the Justice Ministry for more than a decade, several victims' associations signed an agreement with the government in August, in which the Arce administration committed itself to reparation payments to victims or family members of various authoritarian-era abuses.

Detention Conditions

Detention centers in Bolivia hold more than 2.5 times more detainees than they were built to accommodate. The prison population grew 12 percent between November 2021 and March 2022, to 20,864 people, official data obtained by Fundación Construir, a Bolivian nongovernmental organization (NGO), showed.

Bolivia's justice system continues to use pretrial detention excessively. As of March 2022, 65 percent of male detainees and 71 percent of female detainees were awaiting trial, Fundación Construir said.

Indigenous Rights

The 2009 constitution includes comprehensive guarantees of Indigenous peoples' rights to collective land titling; intercultural education; protection of Indigenous justice systems; and free, prior, and informed consent on development projects. Yet, Indigenous peoples face barriers in exercising those rights.

The Documentation and Information Center of Bolivia (CEDIB), an NGO, and the United Nations special rapporteur on toxics and human rights reported that growing, illegal use of mercury in mining is damaging the health of Indigenous communities.

Women's and Girls' Rights

Women and girls remain at high risk of violence, despite a 2013 law establishing comprehensive measures to prevent and prosecute gender-based violence. The law created the crime of "femicide," defining it as the killing of a woman under certain circumstances, including domestic violence.

The attorney general reported 108 femicides in 2021 and 69 from January through September 2022.

A study published in The Lancet in February 2022 estimated, using data from 2000 to 2018, that 42 percent of Bolivian girls and women between 15 and 49 years old have suffered violence by a partner or former partner, the highest percentage in Latin America and the Caribbean.

Under Bolivian law, abortion is not a crime when pregnancy results from rape or when necessary to protect the life or health of a pregnant person. However, women and girls seeking such legal abortions are likely to encounter stigma, mistreatment, and revictimization.

Sexual Orientation and Gender Identity

In December 2020, Bolivia's civil registry abided by a court order and registered a gay couple's relationship as a "free union," Bolivia's first same-sex union. In May 2022, after delaying a year, the registry also registered a lesbian couple's relationship.

The case brought by the first gay couple is pending before the Constitutional Court, which is expected to determine whether all same-sex couples can join in "free unions."

Key International Actors

Throughout 2022, Bolivia has consistently opposed scrutiny on certain states' human rights records and failed to protect victims' rights in international forums. In the United Nations General Assembly and the UN Human Rights Council, it abstained or voted against multiple resolutions condemning Russia's rights violations in Ukraine and voted against renewing the mandate of the UN fact-finding mission in Venezuela and holding a debate on the human rights situation in the

Xinjiang Uyghur Autonomous Region of China. In the Organization of American States, it abstained from a resolution calling on the Nicaraguan government to release political prisoners and cease persecution of media.

In March, the UN Human Rights Committee urged Bolivia to guarantee judges' and prosecutors' independence and impartiality; allow same-sex couples to enter into free unions; and protect journalists from threats and violence.

In July, the Committee on the Elimination of Discrimination against Women expressed its concern over high levels of gender-based violence in Bolivia and called on the government to ensure thorough investigations. It also urged Bolivia to remove barriers to legal abortion, and to decriminalize abortion.

Bosnia and Herzegovina

Authorities failed to prioritize human rights protections in Bosnia and Herzegovina (BiH) in 2022. Discrimination against minorities remains a serious concern. Progress in war crimes prosecutions remains slow. A court handed down a landmark ruling upholding a complaint about discrimination against lesbian, gay, bisexual, and transgender (LGBT) people.

In October, the European Commission published its annual progress report on BiH, granting European Union candidate status to the country, even though "significant reforms are still needed to ensure that all citizens are able to exercise their political rights" and a lack of progress on rule of law and election reform.

Discrimination and Intolerance

The Organization for Security and Co-operation in Europe (OSCE) recorded 91 hate crimes based on ethnicity or religion between January and June, four involving physical violence. At time of writing, 13 hate crime trials were ongoing and 1 person was convicted in 2022.

After her visit to BiH in June, United Nations High Commissioner for Human Rights Michelle Bachelet highlighted discrimination based on ethnicity, gender, and sexual orientation and expressed concerns about access to education, social protection, and the rights of Roma and people with disabilities.

The Office of the High Representative (OHR) in July proposed controversial changes to the election law, including reducing representation from the country's three main groups in the upper house of Federation BiH Parliament if a group makes up less than 3 percent of the population in a particular area. The measure was withdrawn following protests while others were maintained.

After polls closed on election day, October 2, the OHR imposed further election changes, provoking widespread criticism, including of the timing. The measures fail to address long-standing political discrimination against Jews, Roma, and other minorities who are barred from standing for the Presidency, notwithstanding the modest increase in the number of seats for such minorities in the upper house of the Federation Parliament.

A report on the impact of Covid-19 in BiH published by UNICEF and UNDP in June found that the pandemic increased poverty and food deprivation and worsened social and economic inequalities, especially among already disadvantaged groups and those at risk of deprivation or deemed "vulnerable."

Roma people face obstacles to the enjoyment of their rights. According to a 2022 study by the Romani Early Years Network (REYN), many Roma children face discrimination when accessing public services, including education and health care.

Accountability for War Crimes

The pace of war crimes prosecutions remains slow. The OSCE concluded in June that authorities were unlikely to meet a deadline to process all remaining war crime cases by the end of 2023.

At the end of July, 237 war crime cases against 502 defendants were pending before courts in BiH, according to the OSCE. Almost 500 war crimes cases involving 4,000 suspects have yet to reach the courts. In the first six months of 2022, courts in BiH rendered first instance judgments in 20 cases and final judgements in 14 cases.

As of August 2022, there were 51 pending cases involving allegations of conflict-related sexual violence. In the first six months of 2022, courts reached 4 first instance judgments and 5 final judgements.

A March report published by TRIAL International, Vive žene, and the Global Survivors Fund found that BiH has not yet provided adequate and effective reparations to survivors of conflict-related sexual violence due to an inadequate legal framework. Only about 1,000 of an estimated 20,000 survivors have received some form of reparations.

In July, the Constitutional Court of BiH found unconstitutional an attempt by Republika Sprska to limit a 2021 genocide denial law on its territory. The issue continues to be politicized 27 years after the genocide in Srebrenica.

In July, authorities in the district of Brcko approved a draft law to provide civilian victims of the 1992-95 war with reparations and recognize the rights of children born as a result of conflict-rated sexual violence. The UN called on other authorities in BiH to follow suit. Later the same month, the parliament of the Federation of BiH approved a draft law aiming to provide similar reparations.

Asylum Seekers and Migrants

Although the Service for Foreigners' Affairs registered 11,881 persons between January and August expressing an intention to seek asylum, the UN Refugee Agency (UNHCR) reported that only 90 people submitted asylum applications in the first six months of 2022. Bosnian authorities issued 35 decisions. Of these, none were granted refugee status and 12 were granted subsidiary protection.

By June, the Service for Foreigner's Affairs recorded 363 Ukrainians in BiH, 102 of whom expressed intention to apply for asylum. Ukrainians are granted temporary residence on humanitarian grounds.

A survey of child migrants, predominantly unaccompanied children, found widespread abuse by police, smugglers, and others, including sexual violence and pushbacks. Reports of pushbacks and abuses at the Croatian border continued.

Domestic and Other Gender-Based Violence

A January submission by the Institution of Human Rights Ombudsman of Bosnia and Herzegovina to the UN Special Rapporteur on the right to health concluded that domestic violence in BiH, especially violence against women, is among the country's most serious human rights violations.

According to the women's rights organization Kvinna till Kvinna, progress in addressing gender-based violence is hindered by many issues, including ineffective coordination among judiciary, law enforcement, and centers for social work.

In July, the House of Peoples adopted the Draft Law on Protection from Domestic Violence, aiming to harmonize national legislation with the Convention on Preventing and Combating Violence against Women and Domestic Violence, known as the Istanbul Convention, which Bosnia ratified in 2013. The Federation BiH Parliament also amended the criminal code to align it more closely with the Convention.

Sexual Orientation and Gender Identity

Between January and August 2022, the Sarajevo Open Center recorded eight hate incidents against LGBTQ+ people, all of which were physical attacks.

Sarajevo Pride took place in June 2022. Ahead of the parade, monitoring showed an increase in anti-LGBT speech on social media including by politicians.

In April, a municipal court in Sarajevo ruled in favor of two activists who sued a former assembly woman for encouraging state institutions to discriminate against LBGT people. It was the first ever verdict in a BiH court against discrimination based on sexual orientation or gender identity.

Freedom of Media

In April, the national public radio and TV broadcaster BHRT faced risk of closure, after RTRS, the public broadcaster in Republika Srpska, refused to pass on millions of Euros of shared revenue from the national license fee despite its obligation to do so, a move described by Reporters Without Borders as an attack on media pluralism. BHRT's accounts were unfrozen following the intervention of the BiH Federation Parliament.

Pollution and Human Rights

Authorities failed to tackle the country's horrific air pollution, which kills thousands of people prematurely each year and is detrimental to the health of thousands more. The country's reliance on coal and wood for heat and coal for electricity generation makes cities in BiH some of the world's most polluted during winter months. Despite health and climate impacts, authorities remain committed to coal, particularly for electricity.

WORLD REPORT 2023

Brazil

Luiz Inácio Lula da Silva won the presidential elections in October at a critical time for Brazil's democracy.

Throughout his term, former President Jair Bolsonaro harassed and insulted Supreme Court justices and journalists. He tried to undermine trust in the electoral system, making unproven claims of electoral fraud. Political violence rose during the campaign season.

Eighty-four percent of the 6,145 people police killed in 2021 were Black, the latest available data show.

Deforestation and human-caused fires ravaged the Amazon rainforest. Indigenous people, community leaders, and others who defended it suffered threats and attacks.

Democratic Rule

Lula won the October election by a narrow margin. Bolsonaro did not explicitly recognize defeat but allowed the transition, as of November.

Ahead of the October elections, then-President Bolsonaro insulted and tried to intimidate Supreme Court justices and repeated unproven claims of electoral fraud. He said it "appears" that election winners would be those "who have friends" in the Superior Electoral Court. He told dozens of ambassadors in July that Brazil's electoral system was unreliable. In September, he said that if he did not get 60 percent of the vote, "something wrong would have happened" at the electoral court.

In August, more than one million Brazilians, including prominent businesspeople, former Supreme Court justices, politicians, and artists, co-signed a manifesto defending democracy and the rule of law.

Political violence marred the electoral contest. Four people were killed during the electoral campaign season in circumstances suggesting they were targeted for their political views.

The Observatory of Political and Electoral Violence at Rio de Janeiro's Federal University compiled 426 cases of threats and violence against individuals engaged in politics—or their relatives—from January through September 2022. Women candidates, especially Black and trans women, were particularly targeted for threats and online harassment, civil society organizations reported.

The Superior Electoral Court prohibited carrying guns in a 100-meter area around polling places on and immediately before and after election day. The Supreme Court also temporarily suspended portions of presidential decrees that had made it easier to buy and carry guns.

Corruption

Despite running on an anti-corruption platform, the Bolsonaro government faced corruption investigations, including into misuse of public resources in the Education Ministry and in the response to the Covid-19 pandemic.

In 2019, then-President Bolsonaro broke with the tradition of selecting an attorney general from a list of three candidates elected by prosecutors across the country and appointed one not on the list. Transparency International said that former President Bolsonaro weakened the fight against corruption by also supporting the creation of the so-called secret budget, a special budgetary provision that redirected billions of dollars to congressional spending projects with virtually no transparency, among other factors.

Freedom of Expression, Access to Information

The nongovernmental organization Reporters without Borders and the Federal University of Espírito Santo identified more than 2.8 million social media posts with insults, threats, and other offensive content against journalists and the media during the first month of the election season, which officially started August 16. The study found that supporters of former President Bolsonaro targeted reporters, particularly women, after he publicly insulted them.

A court in São Paulo, in June, ordered Bolsonaro to pay 100,000 Brazilian reais (US$18,760), in collective damages to Brazilian media for harassing it.

The former president routinely blocked critics on social media accounts he used to discuss matters of public interest, violating their free speech rights. As of August, he had blocked 95 journalists and 10 media outlets, the Brazilian Association of Investigative Journalism reported.

During 2021 and 2022, a working group of government officials—created without participation of Congress, the justice system, or civil society—reviewed national human rights policy. Authorities refused to share information about the discussions.

Detention Conditions

More than 679,500 people were incarcerated in Brazil as of December 2021, exceeding prison capacity by 45 percent, the Justice Ministry reported. Another 156,000 were under house arrest.

The number of children and young adults in juvenile detention—13,684 in 2021—has significantly decreased in recent years, the organization Brazilian Public Security Forum (FBSP) reported. Yet Rio de Janeiro and Rio Grande do Sul states retained occupation rates above capacity, according to official data.

In July, a court found personnel at a detention center in São Paulo had tortured and mistreated children between 2013 and 2015 and ordered the state government to pay 3 million reais (about US$570,000) in damages to a municipal fund supporting projects advancing children's rights in São Paulo.

Public Security and Police Conduct

Homicides fell 5 percent from January through June 2022, compared to the same period a year earlier. Fewer than 40 percent of homicides result in criminal charges, the group Sou da Paz reported.

Police killed 6,145 people nationwide in 2021—a 4 percent drop from 2020, driven by declining killings in São Paulo state, FBSP reported.

While some police killings are in self-defense, many result from illegal use of force. Police abuses contribute to a cycle of violence that undermines public security and endangers the lives of civilians and police alike. In 2021, 190 police were killed—77 percent while off duty, the FBSP reported.

Rio state police killed 1,011 people from January through October 2022.

Police conducted three of the five deadliest operations in Rio state's history in 2021 and 2022, despite a Supreme Court ruling prohibiting raids in low-income Rio neighborhoods during the Covid-19 pandemic, except in "absolutely exceptional cases." The deadliest raid ever left an officer and 27 residents dead in the Jacarezinho neighborhood of Rio city in May 2021. Prosecutors charged two alleged drug dealers with the killing of the officer and filed evidence tampering and, in some cases, homicide charges against four police officers in connection with three other killings. They closed all other cases. Removal of bodies by police to destroy evidence, inadequate forensic analysis, and failure to interview witnesses contributed to botched investigations. Prosecutors never opened an investigation into command responsibility for the deadly raid.

To comply with a Supreme Court order—but without consulting any civil society organization—Rio state drafted a plan to curb killings by police in March 2022. The plan lacked timelines, a budget, or proper accountability measures. The court ordered the state to draft a new plan.

The Rio attorney general, in 2021, eliminated a unit specialized in preventing and investigating police abuse. In contrast, the São Paulo attorney general created a new unit in August 2022 with a strong mandate to oversee police conduct.

In Sergipe, a Black man with a psychosocial disability choked to death, on May 25, after Federal Highway Police officers detained him in the back of a patrol vehicle and threw in what seemed to be a teargas grenade. Three officers were charged with abuse of power, torture, and homicide.

In August, the Supreme Court reversed an appeals court decision and upheld the conviction of 73 police officers in the 1991 killing of 111 inmates at Carandiru prison.

Military-Era Abuses

Former President Bolsonaro and members of his cabinet repeatedly praised the military dictatorship of 1964-1985, which was marked by widespread torture and killings.

A 1979 amnesty law has shielded perpetrators from justice. The Supreme Court upheld the law in 2010, but the Inter-American Court of Human Rights (IACHR) ruled that it violated Brazil's international legal obligations.

Since 2012, federal prosecutors have filed charges in more than 50 cases against former agents of the dictatorship. Courts have dismissed most, citing the amnesty law or the statute of limitations. In only one case, in June 2021, did a judge issue a criminal conviction; the ruling was overturned in February 2022.

Women's and Girls' Rights

Implementation of the 2006 "Maria da Penha" law against gender-based violence lags. Authorities told Human Rights Watch in September that, in a country of more than 215 million people, only 77 shelters for survivors were operating. The Bolsonaro administration reduced the federal budget to fight violence against women by 90 percent in 2022, compared to 2020.

Between January 2020 and May 2022, judges received almost 600,000 requests for protective orders, which typically require suspected abusers to stay away from targeted women, the National Council of Justice (CNJ) reported. Courts granted nine out of ten requests; 30 percent took longer than the 48-hour deadline established by law.

Police stations registered more than 230,000 reports of physical violence against women, in 2021, the FBSP reported, and a police hotline received 619,353 complaints of domestic violence.

More than one million cases of domestic violence and nearly 6,300 cases of femicide—defined under Brazilian law as the killing of women "on account of being persons of the female sex"—were pending before the courts in 2021.

Abortion is legal in Brazil only in cases of rape, to save a woman's life, or when the fetus has anencephaly.

The Bolsonaro administration tried to restrict access to abortions. In 2020, it required health professionals to report to police rape survivors seeking to terminate pregnancies.

The Health Ministry approved telemedicine in the context of the Covid-19 pandemic, in 2020, but later clarified exclusion of abortion, because that "can cause irreversible damage to the woman." The World Health Organization (WHO) recommends telemedicine as an option for accessing abortion.

Just 73 hospitals in the whole country carried out legal abortions, the organization Article 19 reported in September.

Women and girls who have illegal abortions not only risk injury and death but face up to three years in prison. People who perform illegal abortions face up to four years in prison.

From 2018 through 2022, trial and appeals courts heard an average of 400 criminal abortion cases a year, São Paulo University and Columbia Law School's Human Rights Institute reported. Black women are more likely to face prosecution, which often happens after health professionals inform on them, in violation of their right to privacy, the report showed.

Brazilian law mandates house arrest instead of pretrial detention for pregnant women, mothers of people with disabilities, and mothers of children under 12, except for those accused of violent crimes or crimes against their dependents. Yet in 2021, judges ordered pretrial detention of more than a third of pregnant women at their first hearing after arrest, CNJ and the United Nations Development Program (UNDP) showed.

Disability Rights

Thousands of adults and children with disabilities are confined in institutions, where they may face neglect and abuse, sometimes for life. Brazil lacks a comprehensive plan for progressive deinstitutionalization of adults and children with disabilities.

In April 2021, the National Council of Prosecutors' Offices, a government body, passed a resolution requiring prosecutors to oversee and inspect institutions for adults with disabilities yearly and take legal action in cases of abuse.

Education

The federal government failed to address the huge impact of the Covid-19 pandemic on education, particularly for Black and Indigenous children and those from lower income households, resulting in significant learning losses. For instance, fifth-grade public-school math test results indicated loss of the equivalent of a whole year of learning, a government assessment showed.

The percentage of students dropping out of public high school more than doubled, from 2.3 in 2020 to 5.6 in 2021, government data show.

Minas Gerais and São Paulo states authorized unsafe online learning products during the pandemic, Human Rights Watch found. Nine products surveilled children online, outside school hours, and transmitted their data to advertising technology companies, enabling them to track and target children across the internet. As of October, neither state had acted to protect children's privacy.

Lawmakers have introduced over 200 bills at local and federal levels, since 2014, to ban "indoctrination" or "gender ideology" in schools. The Supreme Court struck down eight of these in 2020. Several teachers told Human Rights Watch that teaching gender or sexuality issues resulted in harassment, police requests for statements, or administrative proceedings.

Environment and Indigenous Rights

The Bolsonaro administration severely weakened environmental law enforcement, effectively encouraging the criminal networks driving deforestation, which have used threats and violence against forest defenders.

The government adopted policies that facilitated encroachment and removed experienced personnel from leadership positions at the agency tasked with protecting Indigenous rights. Illegal logging, mining, poaching, and land grabbing in Indigenous territories were 180 percent higher in 2021 than in 2018, the year before former President Bolsonaro took office, the non-profit Indigenist Missionary Council reported.

The number of environmental fines was 33 percent lower in the first half of 2022 when compared to the same period in 2018, the non-profit Climate Observatory reported. In March, the Bolsonaro-appointed director of the main federal environmental enforcement agency published a decision that could result in the cancelation of about 60 percent of fines for environmental infractions issued between 2008 and 2019, amounting to approximately R$16.2 billion (US$3 billion), news outlet UOL reported.

Official data show 11,568 square kilometers of Amazon rainforest were cleared from August 2021 through July 2022.

After extracting valuable timber, criminal groups frequently burn remaining vegetation to prepare the land for pasture or speculation. The number of fire hotspots in the Amazon for the first nine months of 2022 surpassed those for all of 2021.

As of November, Brazil's Congress was examining bills that would ease environmental licensing, open Indigenous territories to mining and other high-environmental-impact activities, and provide an amnesty for land grabbing,

Amazon forest defenders continued to suffer threats and attacks. A family of three environmentalists were killed in Pará in January; an Indigenous rights advocate and a British journalist were killed in Amazonas in June; and an Indigenous forest defender was killed in Maranhão in September.

More than 60 people were killed in conflicts over land and resources in the Amazon between January 2020 and early July 2022, the organization Pastoral Land Commission (CPT) reported.

Climate Change Policy and Impacts

As one of the world's top ten emitters of greenhouse gases, Brazil contributes to the climate-crisis toll on human rights.

In the 2016 Paris Agreement, Brazil committed to scaling up greenhouse gas reductions in relation to its initial plan. The update it submitted in April 2022 failed to meet that commitment. An annex re-stated Brazil's commitment to eliminating illegal deforestation by 2028.

The Climate Action Tracker, which provides independent scientific analysis, rated Brazil's 2022 climate action plan as "insufficient" for meeting the Paris Agreement goal of limiting global warming to 1.5°C above pre-industrial levels.

Increased deforestation in the Amazon under President Bolsonaro drove up overall emissions. If continued, it may turn vast portions of the rainforest into dry savannah in coming years, releasing billions of tons of stored carbon. Large areas of the Amazon have already been logged and degraded, reducing the forest's capacity to regenerate, a study led by the Amazon Network of Georeferenced Socio-Environmental Information showed.

Climate change may have contributed to intense rainfall that led to floods and landslides in the northeastern states in the first half of 2022, scientists from the World Weather Attribution initiative found. The events displaced an estimated 25,000 people and resulted in 133 deaths.

Migrants, Refugees, and Asylum Seekers

Thousands of Venezuelans, including unaccompanied children, have crossed the border into Brazil in recent years, fleeing hunger, lack of basic health care, or persecution.

About 388,000 Venezuelans lived in Brazil as of October 2022.

Brazil has facilitated asylum for Venezuelans by recognizing a "serious and widespread violation of human rights" in their country. It granted refugee status to 51,618 Venezuelans, including 2,829 between January and August 2022. Venezuelans can also apply for residency. Brazil granted asylum to about 940 people of other nationalities from January through August.

The government has granted humanitarian visas to Afghans and Ukrainians.

Key International Actors

Eight UN rapporteurs, the Office of the UN High Commissioner for Human Rights (OHCHR), and the Inter-American Commission on Human Rights (IACHR) expressed concern about political violence during the electoral season, calling on authorities to ensure peaceful elections.

The IACHR and OHCHR expressed concern, in 2022, about attacks on environmental defenders and Indigenous people. The European Parliament approved a resolution, in July, urging Brazil to "prevent human rights violations and protect environmental and indigenous defenders."

The Inter-American Court of Human Rights (IACtHR) granted provisional measures, in July, requiring Brazil to protect the rights of the Yanomami, Ye'kwana, and Munduruku Indigenous peoples.

The Organisation for Economic Co-operation and Development (OECD) adopted a roadmap for the accession process of Brazil that required government action in halting illegal deforestation, enforcing environmental laws, investigating violence against forest defenders, and protecting Indigenous rights.

UN special rapporteurs urged Brazil's Senate to reject a bill that would ease approval and use of dangerous pesticides. The bill was pending as of August.

In April, more than 140 international and Brazilian organizations co-signed a letter urging the government to invite a fact-finding mission from the UN's new mechanism to advance racial justice and equality in law enforcement. The government said it would consider the visit only in 2023.

UN rapporteurs and the IACHR denounced Brazil's "systemic" police violence. In September, the UN high commissioner for human rights praised Brazil's Supreme Court intervention to curb police abuse in Rio de Janeiro.

Foreign Policy

The Bolsonaro administration led efforts by a group of governments, including several authoritarian regimes, seeking to restrict access to abortion worldwide.

The administration's position regarding the war in Ukraine was inconsistent. A few days before Russia's full-scale invasion, then President Bolsonaro said, in Moscow, that Brazil stood "in solidarity with Russia." Over the following months, Brazil voted for a UN resolution establishing a commission to investigate war crimes in Ukraine but abstained on one suspending Russia's membership on the UN Human Rights Council and opposed a World Trade Organization declaration on the war's devastating impact on Ukraine's ability to export and import.

In October, Brazil abstained on a resolution that would have allowed the Human Rights Council to discuss crimes against humanity in China. It voted in favor of extending the mandate of a fact-finding mission on Venezuela

Burkina Faso

Burkina Faso's human rights situation seriously deteriorated in 2022 as deadly attacks by Islamist armed groups against civilians surged, military forces and pro-government militias committed violations during counterterrorism operations, and political instability deepened as a result of two military coups.

The mounting civilian and military casualties and the loss of government-held territory to Islamist armed groups, which reportedly control about 40 percent of the country, spurred anti-government protests and two military coups, the first of which, in January, overthrew President Roch Marc Christian Kaboré, who was re-elected in 2020.

Hundreds of attacks on civilians and military targets by armed groups in 10 of Burkina Faso's 13 regions markedly intensified a humanitarian crisis and brought the total number of people internally displaced since 2016 to nearly 2 million, or just under 10 percent of the population.

There was scant progress toward providing justice for the alleged killings of hundreds of suspects during past security forces operations. Rule-of-law institutions remained weak; however, the government denounced social media posts that were inciting violence against a minority group and took steps to reduce the numbers of suspects in pretrial detention.

The African Union (AU) and the Economic Community of West African States (ECOWAS), as well as Burkina Faso's international partners including the European Union, France, the United Nations, and the United States denounced both coups and abuses by Islamist armed groups but were largely reluctant to denounce or push for investigations into allegations of abuse by the military and pro-government militias.

Political Developments

In late 2021 and January 2022, protesters demonstrated against the government's inability to stem the worsening violence, prompting government protest bans and internet shutdowns. On January 24, military officers from the Patriotic Movement for Safeguard and Restoration (*Mouvement patriotique pour la sauve-*

garde et la restauration, MPSR), citing the worsening security situation, overthrew President Kaboré in a coup that left at least seven security force members dead.

On February 16, the coup leader, Lt.-Col. Paul Henri Damiba, was sworn in as president, and on March 5, appointed a transitional government. Damiba said he was committed to a return to legislative and presidential elections in 2024.

On September 30, Damiba was himself overthrown in the second military coup in a year. The coup leader and new transitional president, Capt. Ibrahim Traore, said he was committed to respecting the February 2024 deadline for elections set by his predecessor.

Abuses by Islamist Armed Groups

Islamist armed groups allied to Al-Qaeda and the Islamic State in the Greater Sahara (ISGS) killed hundreds of civilians during attacks on villages and convoys and at water points and gold mines. Many attacks targeted communities that had formed local civil defense groups.

On May 25, Islamist fighters allegedly killed 50 civilians trying to flee an armed Islamist blockade of Madjoari village in eastern Burkina Faso, and on June 22, killed 86 people during an attack on Seytenga village, near the Niger border, in the year's worst atrocity.

Other lethal attacks by Islamist armed groups included the January 5 attack on Ankouna village that killed 14; the January 15 attack on Namsiguia killing nine; the June 26 attack on a baptism ceremony in Sandiaga killing eight; the July 3 and 4 attacks on Bourasso killing 22; and the August 18 attack in Kossi province, near the Mali border killing 22. Attacks in March, April, and August on artisanal gold mining sites and a convoy of miners killed 48.

Dozens of people were killed by improvised explosive devices (IEDs), allegedly planted by Islamist armed groups, including 35 people who died when their convoy, escorted by the security forces, hit an IED on September 5 near Djibo.

Across the country, Islamist fighters raped dozens of girls and women who were foraging for wood, traveling to and from market and fleeing the violence. They also burned and looted villages, markets, and businesses; and commandeered ambulances and looted health centers. The fighters prevented farmers from accessing their fields; destroyed bridges, water sources, and telecommunications and electricity infrastructure; and engaged in widespread pillage, acutely exacerbating the humanitarian crisis.

Islamist armed groups abducted numerous civilians including 50 traders during a September 27 ambush on a convoy bringing supplies to the embattled northern town of Djibo and in April, an American nun who was released five months later.

Abuses by State Security Forces and Pro-Government Militia

Pro-government forces including soldiers and militiamen from the Volunteers for the Defense of the Homeland (VDP), a state-sponsored self-defense group, allegedly unlawfully killed or forcibly disappeared dozens of suspects during counterterrorism operations, at times coordinating operations.

On November 23, soldiers allegedly executed 18 men near Djigoue, close to the border with Côte d'Ivoire. Six of 15 men arrested on February 21 by soldiers in Todiame, Nord region, were forcibly disappeared. In August, over 50 men allegedly detained by members of the security forces in and around Tougouri commune, Centre-Nord region, were found dead, most along local roads.

On February 17, eight men were found dead after being detained by VDP militia in Fada N'Gourma. The VDP allegedly executed over 15 men in several incidents between late 2021 and April 2022 in the Est, Sahel, Cascades and Sud-Ouest regions. VDP and soldiers working together allegedly unlawfully killed two men in February and March.

Accountability for Abuses

There was little progress with investigations into past atrocities by the security services—notably the 2018 and 2019 killings of scores of suspects in Burkina Faso's Sahel region; the deaths of over 200 men in Djibo in 2020; and the deaths of 12 men in gendarme custody in Tanwalbougou in 2020.

The military justice directorate, mandated to investigate incidents involving the security forces, continued to be underfunded. Progress on the government's pledged investigation into several of these incidents was scant.

An immunity provision in a 2021 decree creating a counterterrorism special force, providing that special force members "may not be prosecuted for acts committed in the exercise of their functions," undermined accountability.

The high-security prison for terrorism-related offenses remained overcrowded. The vast majority had been detained far beyond the legal time limit. The government took steps to address the backlog and to ensure due process by releasing numerous suspects accused of terrorism-related offenses against whom they had insufficient evidence. Very few detainees had access to defense lawyers.

On April 6, a military tribunal convicted 11 men including the former president, Blaise Compaoré, for the 1987 assassination of President Thomas Sankara and 12 others. Compaoré was tried in absentia and remains in Côte d'Ivoire, where he has lived since being ousted in a popular uprising in 2014. In September, three soldiers were convicted for the 1990 murder of a student.

Hate Speech and Incitement

The Burkinabè government strongly denounced an uptick in social media posts that incited violence against ethnic Peuhl, perceived to support Islamist armed groups. In July, the police arrested and charged at least two men for incitement including a man who had, in June, threatened journalist Newton Ahmed Barry, a Peuhl, apparently for his reporting on counterterrorism.

Children's Rights and Attacks on Education

Armed groups, notably armed Islamists, increased their recruitment and use of children.

The United Nations verified attacks on 46 schools, primarily by armed Islamist groups. As of September 2022, 4,258 schools across the country were closed due to insecurity. Access to education is particularly concerning for forcibly displaced children who make up more than half of the country's internally displaced.

Key International Actors

Burkina Faso's key partners, notably France, the US, the EU, and the UN, expressed concern about the January coup and pressed for a prompt return to constitutional order. The EU and UN condemned the September coup.

International partners roundly denounced abuses by Islamist armed groups, but were reluctant to condemn abuses by the military and pro-government militias.

The UN Office of the High Commissioner for Human Rights maintained a country office mandated to monitor and report on human rights abuses, and support civil society, but, during 2022, did not publish any reports.

Following the January coup, the Economic Community of West African States (ECOWAS) and the AU suspended Burkina Faso from all governing bodies, pending the restoration of constitutional order.

The US suspended US$160 million in foreign assistance to Burkina Faso as a result of the January 2022 coup, as stipulated by US law. The US-funded Millennium Challenge Corporation similarly paused support related to an agreement signed in August 2020 for $450 million.

The EU provided €52.4 million (around US$ 53.9 million) in 2022 in humanitarian assistance to Burkina Faso. Since 2018, the EU has allocated €265 million (around US$272 million) in support for the G5 Sahel joint counterterrorism force of Burkina Faso, Chad, Mali, Mauritania, and Niger, which includes logistics, equipment and infrastructure, as well support for the promotion of human rights.

France, Burkina Faso's leading bilateral donor, provided military training to its troops and to the military justice directorate.

In response to the gravity and number of attacks on schools and the killing and maiming of children, the UN secretary-general included Burkina Faso as a situation of concern for the UN's monitoring and reporting mechanism on grave violations against children during armed conflict.

In September, transitional authorities signed a handover protocol with the UN to ensure the transfer of children apprehended by military forces during armed conflict to civilian authorities for reintegration.

Burundi

The authorities lifted some restrictions on media and civil society but promises by President Évariste Ndayishimiye's administration to rein in the ruling party's youth league, the Imbonerakure, remained unfulfilled. The ruling party strengthened its grip on power, including by encouraging youth league's members to carry out official activities and entrenching the party's control at the local level. Burundian armed forces and Imbonerakure members took part in armed combat in neighboring Democratic Republic of Congo.

Killings, disappearances, torture, ill-treatment, arbitrary arrests, and detention of real or suspected opponents were documented by international and Burundian rights groups throughout 2022. Unidentified bodies, often mutilated or tied up, were regularly found in different parts of the country, often buried by local authorities, Imbonerakure members, or police, without investigation.

Abuses by Security Forces and Ruling Party Youths

Burundi's national intelligence services, police, and ruling party youth members killed, arbitrarily detained, tortured, and harassed people suspected of belonging to opposition parties or of working with armed opposition groups.

Authorities continued to crack down on suspected opponents in response to attacks on both civilians and state agents by armed assailants or suspected rebel group members in various parts of the country in 2020 and 2021. They showed little regard for credible investigations, objective evidence, or due process needed to hold those responsible to account. Instead, they targeted perceived opponents of the ruling National Council for the Defense of Democracy-Forces for the Defense of Democracy (*Conseil national pour la défense de la démocratie-Forces pour la défense de la démocratie*, CNDD-FDD).

After he took power in 2020, Ndayishimiye made some efforts to rein in members of the Imbonerakure and their involvement in human rights abuse was less visibly apparent. However, in 2022, government and ruling party officials explicitly encouraged them to perform "law enforcement" duties, ensuring the ruling party remains in control. Imbonerakure members, some of whom are armed, have arrested, ill-treated, and killed suspected opponents, sometimes in collaboration with or with the support of local administrative officials, police, or intelligence agents.

Révérien Ndikuriyo, secretary general of the CNDD-FDD and a hardliner within the party, made several incendiary speeches during gatherings of CNDD-FDD members and Imbonerakure. In August, he attacked international human rights organizations and called on the Imbonerakure to continue night patrols and to kill any "troublemakers." Imbonerakure members took part in training programs on "patriotism" across the country.

On June 22, the National Assembly enacted a law on the Burundian national defense forces, which created a new reserve force (*Force de réserve et d'appui au développement*, FRAD). Its duties include organizing paramilitary trainings, "supporting other components in protecting the integrity of the national territory," but also conceiving and implementing development projects, and operationalizing national and international partnerships. It is open to all Burundians who can be mobilized for the "defense" and the "development" of the country, following a military training.

Military Operations in Eastern DR Congo

Throughout 2022, the Burundian army conducted operations targeting RED-Tabara (Resistance Movement for the Rule of Law-Tabara, *Mouvement de la résistance pour un État de droit-Tabara*), an armed group that has launched attacks in Burundi in recent years, in the neighboring Congo. Civilian members of the Imbonerakure, who have mostly not received formal military training, supported the operations. According to rights groups and media reports, little or no explanation was given to the families of those who die on the battlefield. In August, Burundian troops officially entered Congo as the first deployment of an East African regional force agreed upon by the East African Community (EAC) in April.

Judiciary and Rule of Law

The judiciary in Burundi is not independent. Despite calls by Ndayishimiye for the judiciary to be reformed, no substantive steps were taken to end political interference and release political prisoners.

On April 28, Pierre Nkurikiye, the spokesperson for the Interior, Public Security and Community Development Ministry, told media that in cases of alleged disappearances, family members should make a complaint to judicial or administrative authorities so that they can investigate. However, in many cases documented by Human Rights Watch, family members feared reprisals from authorities for reporting disappearances or other human rights violations.

Six former Burundian refugees, part of a group of eight who were detained incommunicado and tortured in Tanzania before being forcibly returned to Burundi, remained in jail. Burundi's authorities put them on trial for participation in armed groups, and despite a Burundian judge saying the case was political, and the court acquitting them of all charges in August 2021, then again on appeal in March 2022, prison and judicial authorities failed to release them.

The authorities failed to conduct a transparent, credible, and impartial investigation into a prison fire that broke out in Gitega, the country's political capital, on December 7, 2021. According to Human Rights Watch's research at the time, scores—maybe hundreds—of prisoners died in the fire. Authorities did not communicate findings transparently, including the names of the dead and the injured, or fairly prosecute anyone who may be held responsible.

There are no independent institutions providing scrutiny of the government's actions. The Independent National Commission on Human Rights (*Commission Nationale Indépendante des Droits de l'Homme*, CNIDH), despite having recovered its "A" status in 2021, does not report on the most sensitive and political human rights violations taking place. Its annual reports largely fail to address killings; torture; ill-treatment and arbitrary arrests of opposition members; political detentions and prosecutions; and restrictions on public freedoms.

Civil Society and Freedom of Media

Despite some steps taken by authorities to lift suspensions of civil society organizations and media, most of the restrictions introduced under Pierre Nkurunziza's presidency (2005-2020) remain in place. The conviction in absentia of 12 human rights defenders and journalists in exile has not been overturned.

Human rights organizations in Burundi are restricted in their ability to work freely or independently, particularly outside Bujumbura. On March 14, police suspended a joint press conference organized by OLUCOME (*Observatoire de Lutte contre la Corruption et les Malversations Economiques*) and PARCEM (*Parole et Action pour le Réveil des Consciences et l'Évolution des Mentalités*), two anti-corruption organizations, claiming they did not have permission to hold such a meeting.

Lawyer and former human rights defender Tony Germain Nkina remained in jail following the decision of the Court of Appeal of Ngozi on September 29, 2021, to uphold his conviction and five-year prison sentence following an unfair trial. Despite no credible evidence presented by the prosecution, he was convicted of collaborating with RED-Tabara.

Burundi's media authority announced in March that it would lift its ban on the BBC, nearly three years after the National Communication Council withdrew its operating license in 2019, accusing it of violating press laws and unprofessional conduct.

Humanitarian Situation

The humanitarian situation in Burundi is dire. The country has been impacted by the war in Ukraine, the Covid-19 pandemic, and inflation, which have contributed to soaring prices of basic food and goods in the first half of the year. Fuel shortages have also driven inflation, notably for necessities. Food insecurity levels remain high with 52 percent of children under 5 stunted and high levels of malnutrition among rural communities, according to the World Food Program.

Refugees

As of September 2022, there were over 250,000 Burundian refugees living in Tanzania, Rwanda, Congo and Uganda. According to the UN High Commissioner for Refugees, around 200,000 refugees have been repatriated to Burundi since 2017, including 16,621 in 2022, under its "voluntary repatriation" programs. The repatriations primarily took place from Tanzania, Uganda, Congo and Rwanda, where refugees face worsening conditions, and authorities encouraged refugees to repatriate.

Sexual Orientation and Gender Identity

Burundi punishes consensual same-sex sexual relations between adults with up to two years in prison under Article 567 of the penal code. Article 29 of the Constitution of Burundi explicitly bans same-sex marriage.

Key International Actors

Despite overwhelming evidence of persistent and serious abuses in Burundi, the European Union, the United States, and other international partners have pursued a policy of rapprochement with the authorities, lifting restrictive measures and sanctions since Ndayishimiye came to power in 2020. The EU resumed its political dialogue with the Burundian government in May.

The UN special rapporteur on Burundi, appointed in April, presented his first report in September. The special rapporteur called on Burundi to "engage more effectively in the rule of law and the fight against impunity" and found that "despite commitments and measures taken by the government, the human rights situation in Burundi has not changed in a substantial and sustainable way." The government of Burundi has repeatedly rejected the special rapporteur's requests for access to the country to carry out his work. The UN Human Rights Council extended the special rapporteur's mandate for a year in October.

In September, Ndayishimiye replaced Prime Minister Alain Guillaume Bunyoni, who was until last year under US sanctions, with Gervais Ndirakobuca, a hardliner within the party. Following his appointment, the EU lifted sanctions on Ndirakobuca and two others.

Cambodia

During the year, Prime Minister Hun Sen intensified his crackdown on the political opposition, as well as land activists, trade union leaders, civil society activists, and critical media outlets.

Cambodia's politicized courts pursued a series of mass trials against more than 100 political opposition members and dozens of human rights defenders. Prosecutors claimed the defendants engaged in "incitement to commit a felony" simply by exercising their rights to freedom of expression, association, and peaceful public assembly. Cambodia currently has more than 50 political prisoners behind bars.

In the lead-up to the June 2022 commune elections, the government obstructed and harassed members of the revived Candlelight Party, the largest opposition party contesting against the ruling Cambodia People's Party (CPP). The National Election Commission and the CPP filed defamation charges against Candlelight Party Vice-President Son Chhay for criticizing the conduct of the election.

New Rights-Abusing Laws and Bills

Under the guise of combatting the Covid-19 pandemic, the government used the 2021 Law on Measures to Prevent the Spread of Covid-19 and other Serious, Dangerous and Contagious Diseases to interfere with activists' right to peaceful assembly. The law provided officials with unfettered powers to punish so-called offenders of Covid-19 measures with up to 20-year prison sentences. The law contains overly broad provisions and lacks independent oversight or procedural safeguards. In March 2022, the United Nations Human Rights Committee reviewed Cambodia's compliance with the International Covenant on Civil and Political Rights and noted that over 700 arrests were made between March and October 2021 based on the law.

In February 2021, authorities adopted the Sub-Decree on the Establishment of the National Internet Gateway, which will enhance the government's powers to monitor all internet activities and block and disconnect internet connections. However, authorities have yet to formally implement the decree as scheduled, starting in February 2022, leaving the decree looming over Cambodian internet

WORLD REPORT 2023

users. Other laws such as the Telecommunications Law of 2016 already empower the government to conduct intrusive online surveillance.

In January 2022, the Ministry of Interior stated its intention to draft a foreign interference law modelled on Singapore's oppressive Foreign Interference Act, but no draft had been publicly released at time of writing.

During the year, authorities provided several public updates on their efforts to draft a law to establish a national human rights institution. However, they did not release a draft of the law, nor indicate whether it would conform with the Paris Principles to ensure the body will be independent, impartial, and effective. to ensure the body will be independent, impartial, and effective.

Freedom of Association and Assembly

In 2022, the government enforced a de facto ban on peaceful assembly. Authorities used public health measures to end peaceful, legitimate strikes. The government also stepped up its crackdown on independent unions and their rights to freedom of association, peaceful assembly, and to strike.

The government used the Covid-19 public health crisis as an excuse to forcibly break up the peaceful strike of the Labor Rights Supported Union of Khmer Employees of NagaWorld (LRSU), who were protesting in central Phnom Penh to demand the reinstatement of dismissed workers and fair compensation in their protracted labor dispute with NagaWorld casino. Uniformed police and plainclothes officers used excessive force to shove strikers onto city buses and transport them to sub-par quarantine centers in remote areas on the outskirts of Phnom Penh where they were then stranded.

In December 2021, authorities arrested, detained, and prosecuted dozens of union activists based on allegations that the strike was "illegal". On February 5, police arrested six activist union members at Phnom Penh's NagaWorld casino as they left a Covid-19 testing site and baselessly charged three of them with obstructing the government's Covid-19 efforts. This followed the jailing of eight LRSU unionists, including the union president, Chhim Sithar, on "incitement" charges. While all were eventually released on bail, charges remained pending against them, meaning they can be detained again at any time.

Attacks Against the Political Opposition

Prior to the commune elections on June 5, 2022, authorities violated the rights of opposition Candlelight Party members by removing as many as 150 candidates from Cambodia's National Election Committee lists, arresting party activists, threatening candidates to withdraw their candidacies or face spurious criminal charges and prosecution, and interfering in the election campaign. Despite these obstacles, the Candlelight Party won 18 percent of the national vote—but that translated into only 4 commune chief positions out of a total of 1,652 commune chief seats being elected. seats being elected.

Starting with court summons issued in November 2020, prosecutors launched mass trials in 2021 that continued into 2022 against more than 100 people connected with the dissolved Cambodian National Rescue Party (CNRP), as well as civil society activists.

On March 17, a Phnom Penh court convicted 20 opposition politicians and activists, plus one defendant's relative, and sentenced them to between 5 and 10 years in prison. The court also convicted in absentia a total of seven persons abroad and sentenced them to 10-year prison sentences based on three counts of unsubstantiated charges of "incitement," "inciting military personnel to disobedience," and "conspiracy." These charges allegedly were connected to the formation of the overseas opposition Cambodia National Rescue Movement (CNRM) in 2018, and social media comments criticizing the government.

On June 14, a Phnom Penh court convicted at least 51 CNRP members and political activists on unsupported charges of "incitement" and "conspiracy." Twelve defendants received eight-year prison sentences while another 19 defendants got six years in prison. Another 20 defendants received five-year suspended sentences. A total of 27 defendants are currently in exile and were tried in absentia. The case related to the support for Sam Rainsy's attempted return to Cambodia in November 2019, and the activities of the dissolved CNRP and overseas CNRM.

The co-leader of the CNRP, Kem Sokha, continued to face trumped-up treason charges and onerous restrictions on his political rights, and the court slow-walked the ongoing conduct of his trial, claiming prosecutors no longer deemed his case a "priority."

Freedom of Media

On August 16, 2022, officers from the Prime Minister's Bodyguard Unit (BHQ) arbitrarily detained five journalists affiliated with the independent news outlet, Voice of Democracy (VOD News), and four environmental defenders affiliated with the Khmer Thavrak group. The journalists and environmental defenders were reporting on forest clearing activities in Phnom Tamao forest in southern Cambodia, where up to 500 hectares of forest are believed to have been cut down in a week at the beginning of August. The authorities forcibly confiscated the reporters' equipment and accused them of spreading false information.

International Justice

In September, the Extraordinary Chambers in the Court of Cambodia (ECCC) ruled to deny the appeal of Khmer Rouge head of state Khieu Samphan and upheld his conviction for genocide and crimes against humanity. His sentence of life imprisonment remained the same. With this action, the work of the ECCC was completed, having convicted three persons at a cost of approximately US$330 million since the court was established in 1997.

Key International Actors

The Chinese government is the country's primary economic and political partner, investing US$1.29 billion during the first half of 2022. On January 1, the China-Cambodia Free Trade Agreement (CCFTA) came into effect, under which "China and Cambodia agree to impose zero tariffs on over 90 percent of products and commit to an open market in services". The agreement also commits to boost cooperation under China's "Belt and Road Initiative," despite concerns about human rights violations in those projects.

During the 11th Cambodia-EU Joint Committee Meeting in March, the European Union reiterated its call on the government to uphold "democratic pluralism, human rights and fundamental freedoms, labor rights, and the rule of law." Hun Sen's failure to backtrack on its human rights crackdown continues to cost the country the partial withdrawal of its "Everything But Arms" (EBA) trade benefits with the EU. Arms" (EBA) trade benefits with the EU.

In May, the European Parliament condemned the Cambodian government's continuing abuses and reiterated its call on the EU Council to adopt targeted sanctions against Cambodia's political leadership and leaders of the security forces responsible for the crackdown in the country. It urged the EU to consider a full withdrawal of Cambodia's EBA privileges.

In May, the United States hosted Prime Minister Hun Sen at a United States-Association of Southeast Asian Nations (ASEAN) Special Summit at the White House ahead of the ASEAN Summit chaired and hosted by Cambodia, in an effort to strengthen engagement and shore up alliances with ASEAN countries.

A French court issued arrest warrants against two senior Cambodian generals for the grenade attack on an opposition political rally in Phnom Penh on March 30, 1997, which killed 16 people and injured more than 150. The court stated that it also issued a summons for Prime Minister Hun Sen for his role in the attack, but the French government blocked its delivery, citing head of state immunity.

Cameroon

In 2022, armed groups and government forces committed human rights abuses, including unlawful killings, across Cameroon's Anglophone regions and in the Far North region.

As the crisis in the Anglophone regions continued for the sixth year 598,000 people were internally displaced as of August and at least 2 million people needed humanitarian aid in the North-West and South-West.

Separatists, who have violently enforced a boycott on education since 2017, continued to attack schools, students and education professionals, destroying buildings and depriving hundreds of thousands of children of their fundamental right to education.

The Islamist armed groups Boko Haram and Islamic State in West Africa Province (ISWAP) continued attacks in the Far North region from January to April, killing scores of civilians and contributing to the internal displacement of over 378,000 people as of July. Government forces violated applicable international humanitarian and human rights law by failing to fairly prosecute suspected members of the Islamist groups who committed serious crimes. The government has fallen short on its promises to assist former members of Boko Haram and ISWAP who voluntarily left as part of a disarmament program. The authorities have also failed to assist and protect women and children linked to these groups.

Restrictions against freedoms of expression and association continued as did persecution of lesbian, gay, bisexual, and transgender (LGBT) people. Mob attacks against members of the LGBT community intensified.

Government forces subjected Cameroonian asylum seekers deported from the United States in 2020 and 2021 to serious human rights violations following their return, including physical assault and abuse, arbitrary arrest and detention, extortion, and confiscation of identity documents, thus impeding freedom of movement, ability to work, and access to public services.

In April, Cameroon took an important step to protect the right to education of students who are pregnant and adolescent mothers. The government's new re-entry policy prescribes that pregnant students will be able to stay in school until the 26th week of their pregnancy and will be allowed back in school after delivery, subject to a number of conditions.

Anglophone Crisis

At least 6,000 civilians have been killed by both government forces and armed separatist fighters since late 2016 in the North-West and South-West regions, as armed separatist groups seek independence for the country's minority Anglophone regions.

Violations by Government Forces

Security forces responded to separatist attacks with a heavy hand, often targeting civilians across the Anglophone regions.

On April 24, in Ndop, North-West region, soldiers from the Rapid Intervention Battalion (*Bataillon d'intervention rapide*, BIR) stopped, severely beat, and detained between 30 and 40 motorbike riders who were part of a funeral convoy, allegedly because they suspected the bikers of being separatist fighters. Up to 17 of those detained are presumed forcibly disappeared. As of September, their whereabouts remained unknown.

On June 1, soldiers from the 53rd Motorized Infantry Battalion (*Bataillon d'infanterie motorisée*, BIM) killed nine people, including four women and an 18-month-old girl, in Missong village, North-West region, in a reprisal operation against a community suspected of harboring separatist fighters.

On June 8, soldiers conducted a military operation in Chomba, North-West region, burning a home and looting the local health center. They also arrested a woman along with her 11-year-old foster child and held them for 24 days at the BIR barracks in Bafut, North-West region.

From June 9 to 11, in Belo, North-West region, security forces killed one man, injured another, burned at least 12 homes, destroyed a community health center, and looted at least 10 shops.

Abuses by Armed Separatists

Separatist fighters continued to kill, torture, assault, and kidnap civilians. They also continued their attacks against pupils, teachers, and education, depriving thousands of students of the right to education.

On June 12, separatist fighters physically assaulted, threatened, and humiliated a group of 11 students, aged from 14 to 18, walking to the Bokova high school, in Buea, South-West region. They shot one of the students in the right leg and seized or destroyed the students' school material.

On January 19, separatist fighters attacked the government high school in Weh, North-West region, abducting five teachers, and injuring two students for not complying with a school boycott and for not contributing financially to their struggle for independence. The teachers were released on January 24 following a ransom payment.

Separatist fighters, vowing to disrupt the Africa Cup of Nations soccer tournament, which was held in Cameroon between January 9 and February 6, carried out a series of attacks in the town of Buea on January 12. They declared a lockdown and punished people who did not observe it. They shot and killed a 30-year-old male taxi driver and another man at Bwitingi market area and shot a man in both his legs and stomach at the checkpoint area in the same area of the city.

On January 13, separatist fighters attacked a rubber estate plantation of the Cameroon Development Corporation (CDC), a public agribusiness company, in Tiko, South-West region, abducted nine workers, six of whom were women, and set a tractor ablaze. The workers were all released on January 25 following a ransom payment.

On February 11, separatist fighters set fire to three dormitories of the all-girls boarding secondary school Queen of the Rosary College, in Okoyong, South-West Region.

On April 5, separatists stormed the campus of the Bamenda university, North-West region, shooting in the air, causing panic among students and teachers, leading to a stampede that injured at least five people. The fighters attacked the university for not observing a "lockdown," or stay-at-home order, that they had declared across the area.

On April 28, separatist fighters attacked the taxi and bus station in Mamfe, South-West region. They burned at least five cars and killed three men, accusing station workers of operating during their declared lockdown.

On May 30, suspected separatist fighters kidnapped and killed Lukong Francis, a retired teacher at the government high school in Jakiri, North-West region, and a member of the ruling party, in retaliation for his participation in the May 20 public celebrations for Cameroon's Unity Day, which separatist groups oppose.

On June 10, suspected separatist fighters burned down the district hospital in Mamfe, South-West region, depriving 85,000 people of access to health care.

On September 16, armed militants attacked and set fire to St. Mary's Church in Nchang, diocese of Mamfe, and kidnapped nine people – including five priests. Pope Francis joined an appeal by bishops from Bamenda Provincial Episcopal Conference to release those abducted. The nine abducted people were all released on October 23.

Restrictions on Humanitarian Access and Abuses against Aid Workers

Humanitarian access was restricted in the Anglophone and Far-North regions and humanitarian workers have been victims of attacks by both government forces and armed groups. According to the United Nations Office for the Coordination of Humanitarian Affairs (UNOCHA), humanitarian actors continued to operate under severe constraints including repeated lockdowns, harassment at checkpoints, and the risk of improvised explosive devices by armed separatist fighters in the Anglophone regions.

In April, Médecins Sans Frontières (Doctors Without Borders, MSF) suspended all its activities in the South-West region following the "unjust detention" of four of its workers. In December 2020, Cameroonian authorities had suspended MSF activities in the North-West region, accusing the organization of being too close to Anglophone separatists, leaving tens of thousands of people in the region without access to health care.

Separatist fighters and Islamist armed groups have hindered aid agencies' access in the areas under their control.

On February 25, unidentified armed men kidnapped five MSF workers from their residence in Fotokol, Far-North region, an area where Boko Haram operates. They were released a month later.

On February 26, separatist fighters stopped two vehicles from the Cameroon Baptist Convention Health Services (CBCHS), a nonprofit medical organization, at a checkpoint in Mile 90, North-West region. They fired at one vehicle, killing a 46-year-old nurse, and injuring another nurse and a doctor.

On July 2, in the Far-North region, suspected Boko Haram fighters attacked the Mada hospital in the Logone-et-Chari division, killing one civilian, leading to the temporary closure of the health facility, and leaving thousands without essential healthcare.

Attacks by Boko Haram and ISWAP

Attacks and raids by the Islamist armed groups Boko Haram and ISWAP continued in the Far North region.

The UN Department of Safety and Security (UNDSS) reported an escalation of violence with 23 attacks by both Boko Haram and ISWAP, leading to 13 civilians killed, including 2 children and one woman; 12 injured, 10 kidnapped, and an additional 7, 600 internally displaced. In response to this resurgence of attacks, Cameron has deployed hundreds of additional troops to the Far North region.

Crackdown on Political Opposition, Dissent

The government continued to limit the ability of the political opposition and civil society to function freely.

On April 22, four UN special rapporteurs focusing on human rights defenders, extrajudicial executions, the right to freedom of expression and the right to association, addressed a letter to Cameroon's President Paul Biya raising concern over repeated death threats sent since 2015 to the president of Organic Farming for Gorillas, a Cameroonian civil-society organization which has exposed abuses by businesses in the North-West regions.

On August 11, soldiers arrested Abdul Karim Ali, a prominent Cameroonian Anglophone peace activist, in Bamenda, North-West region. While there are no official charges against Ali, he was told he is accused of "apology for terrorism" for possessing a video on his phone showing alleged human rights abuses committed by a Cameroonian soldier against civilians in the country's English-speaking regions. As of September, Ali remained in detention awaiting trial.

At least 105 opposition party members and supporters arrested in September 2020 for defying a ban on protests remain in detention as they have been sentenced by military courts to prison terms ranging from two to five years on politically motivated charges. They include Olivier Bibou Nissack and Alain Fogué Tedom, two prominent members of the Cameroon Renaissance Movement.

Some detainees died in appalling detention conditions in the country's prisons, including Rodrigue Ndagueho Koufet, one of six detainees in Douala prison who died of cholera between February and April. Koufet had been held arbitrarily since September 2020 for taking part in peaceful assemblies.

In an October opinion adopted at its 94th session, the UN Working Group on Arbitrary Detention qualified the 2018 arrest and detention of 10 Cameroonian activists in Abuja, Nigeria, as arbitrary and called for their immediate release. The group observed that the individuals were forcibly returned from Nigeria to Cameroon in 2018, in violation of the principle of non-refoulement, and concluded that the overall proceedings of the court did not meet international standards.

Sexual Orientation and Gender Identity

Cameroon's penal code punishes "sexual relations between persons of the same sex" with up to five years in prison. There was an uptick in violence and abuse against LGBTI people in Cameroon in 2022.

From March to May, security forces arbitrarily arrested at least 6 people and detained 11, for alleged consensual same-sex conduct and gender nonconformity. In April, a crowd of about eight men armed with machetes, knives, sticks, and wooden planks, attacked a group of at least 10 LGBTI people. Gendarmes detained and beat at least two of the victims.

Justice and Accountability

Between January and August, eight hearings were held in the trial of three security force members accused of involvement in the killings of 21 civilians in Ngarbuh village, North-West region. The trial is being held before a military court in Yaoundé and at time of writing had lasted 21 months. Senior officers who could have command responsibility have not been arrested or charged, and there are limited opportunities for access by victims' families.

In June 2020, the French ambassador to Cameroon told the media that President Biya had assured him that an investigation would be opened into the death in custody of journalist Samuel Wazizi in August 2019. However, as of September, there has not been any progress on the investigation.

In a June 7 press release, Cameroon's army spokesperson Col. Cyrille Serge Atonfack Guemo acknowledged the military's responsibility for the killing of nine people in Missong village, North-West region, on June 1. He said that four soldiers have been arrested and an investigation has been opened. As of September, there has not been any progress on the investigation.

In a September 21 press release, the Ministry of Defense acknowledged the responsibility for the killing of 2 civilians in Momo division, North-West region, on September 19. The communique indicates that elements of the Defence and Security Forces acted in violation of the instructions.

Key International Actors

On March 21, the European Union expressed concerns over "the ongoing crisis in the North-West and South-West regions" and called for "immediate end to the violence, respect of human rights and humanitarian principles, unimpeded humanitarian access and a safe environment for humanitarian work."

On April 15, the United States Department of Homeland Security announced the designation of Cameroon for Temporary Protected Status (TPS) for 18 months. Cameroonian nationals residing in the US as of April 1, and who cannot safely return due to the conditions in their home country—including violence by government forces and armed groups, destruction of civilian infrastructure, economic instability, and food insecurity—will be able to remain in the US until conditions improve.

On July 25 and 26, French President Emmanuel Macron visited Cameroon and met with President Biya. The visit focused on strengthening political and economic ties between Paris and Yaoundé. Macron did not publicly express concerns on the human rights situation in the country.

Canada

In September 2021, Prime Minister Justin Trudeau was elected for a third term following a snap election. In office since 2015, his government has championed human rights, but longstanding challenges remain across Canada. These include widespread violations of the rights of marginalized groups including Indigenous peoples, immigration detainees, people with disabilities, and older people.

The Trudeau government has also failed to address serious human rights concerns beyond Canada's border, including impunity for abuses by Canadian mining companies overseas. Canada also continues to ignore the need to adopt and implement robust climate mitigation policies. For over three years, the government has also rebuffed calls by Canada-based family members and top United Nations officials to repatriate dozens of Canadians, most of them children, unlawfully detained in life-threatening conditions in northeast Syria.

Rights of Indigenous Peoples

Decades of structural and systemic discrimination against Indigenous peoples has led to widespread abuses that persist across Canada.

Inadequate access to clean, safe drinking water continues to pose a major public health concern in many Indigenous communities and impede efforts to advance Indigenous rights in Canada, one of the world's most water-rich countries.

The government of Prime Minister Trudeau committed to end all drinking water advisories on First Nations reserves by 2021 but, as of September, 28 First Nations communities across Canada remained subject to long-term water advisories, which alert communities when their water is not safe to drink.

In July, Canada signed a US$14 billion final settlement agreement to compensate First Nations children and families unnecessarily taken into government care due to its failure to provide funding for child and family services in Indigenous communities.

Violence against Indigenous Women

In May, a Statistics Canada report found that 81 percent of Indigenous women who had been in the child-welfare system had been physically or sexually assaulted in their lifetime.

In June 2021, the federal government published a report promising a series of "transformative changes" to address persistent discrimination and violence against Indigenous women and gender-diverse people. That year, the Trudeau government released a National Action Plan in response to the National Inquiry into Missing and Murdered Indigenous Women and Girls' findings and recommendations. In June, an assessment by the Native Women's Association of Canada on the government's performance deemed it to be a "failure."

Immigration Detention

People in immigration detention, including persons with disabilities and those seeking refugee protection in Canada, continue to be regularly handcuffed and shackled, and at risk of being held indefinitely. With no time limits on immigration detention, they can be detained for months or years. Many are held in provincial jails alongside people detained on criminal charges or convictions, and they are also sometimes subjected to solitary confinement.

The Canada Border Services Agency (CBSA) remains the only major law enforcement agency in Canada without independent civilian oversight. The federal government has introduced oversight legislation, but it has yet to pass. CBSA's unchecked exercise of its broad mandate and enforcement powers has repeatedly resulted in serious human rights violations in the context of immigration detention.

CBSA has the sole authority to decide where immigration detainees are held: immigration holding centers, provincial jails, or other facilities. Following the launch of a joint Human Rights Watch and Amnesty International campaign, #WelcomeToCanada, the governments of British Columbia, Nova Scotia, Alberta and Manitoba gave notice of termination of their immigration detention contracts with the federal government. This means CBSA will no longer have the power to detain refugee claimants and migrants in those provinces' jails solely on immigration grounds.

Corporate Accountability

Canada is home to more than half of the world's mining companies, with Canadian companies operating in nearly 100 countries and holding foreign mining assets estimated at US$130 billion. The government of Prime Minister Trudeau has not taken adequate steps to ensure that Canadian authorities exercise meaningful oversight of Canadian extractive companies operating abroad.

The Canadian Ombudsperson for Responsible Enterprise (CORE), appointed in April 2019 to address corporate human rights challenges and receive complaints about Canadian garment, mining, oil and gas companies' conduct abroad, still does not have the authority or independence required to effectively investigate claims of wrongdoing or compel documents and witness testimony.

In March, two private members bills were tabled in the House of Commons aimed at advancing accountability for human rights abuses linked to Canadian companies' operations or supply chains abroad. Bill C-262 would require companies to identify, prevent, and mitigate human rights abuses throughout their global operations and supply chains, including violations to the right to a healthy environment. The bill provides affected communities with a statutory right to bring a civil lawsuit against a company in a Canadian court to seek justice and remedy for causing harm or failing to undertake human rights due diligence. Bill C-263 seeks to establish an Office of the Commissioner for Responsible Business Conduct Abroad, essentially transforming the CORE into a corporate watchdog able to independently investigate allegations of abuse.

In June, Canada's parliament unanimously consented to a second reading of a bill that would expand an existing prohibition on importing goods produced with forced labor to include goods produced with child labour. Bill S-211, would require government and private entities to submit annual reports on any measures taken to prevent and reduce the risk of forced or child labor in their supply chains.

In April, a coalition of Canadian civil society organizations filed a complaint with the CORE urging the body to investigate allegations that products sold by 14 Canadian companies are made in whole or in part with forced labor in China.

Right to Education

The education ministries of Ontario and Quebec failed to act following reports that they had recommended unsafe online learning products for children during the Covid-19 pandemic. Five products surveilled or had the capacity to surveil children online, outside of school hours, and deep into their private lives, and transmitted children's personal data to advertising technology companies.

Counterterrorism

Since February and March 2019, the Kurdish-led authorities in northeast Syria have arbitrarily detained an estimated four dozen Canadians in locked desert camps and prisons for Islamic State (ISIS) suspects and their families. Despite being held in appalling and life-threatening conditions, the government of Prime Minister Trudeau continues to fail to take adequate steps to assist and repatriate these nationals. To date, none of the Canadians have been charged with a crime or brought before a judge to review the legality and necessity of their detention. More than half of the Canadian detainees are children.

In January 2021, Global Affairs Canada adopted a consular policy framework specifically for this group of citizens that makes it near-impossible for them to return home. The policy, made public in February 2022, was not shared with the detainees or their family members seeking assistance for nearly a year.

In February, more than a dozen UN independent experts called on Canada to urgently repatriate a gravely ill Canadian woman, Kimberly Polman. Despite offers of assistance by a former US ambassador, Canada prevented her and an unrelated young Canadian child from coming home for life-saving medical care that month. Polman remained in detention until late October, when she was repatriated with another Canadian woman and two children.

In June, UN experts sent an urgent appeal to Canada relating to the plight of a detained Canadian man expressing serious concern about his continued detention in northeast Syria. The appeal called for the repatriation of all Canadian citizens. UN officials including Secretary-General António Guterres have repeatedly called on all countries with nationals held in northeast Syria to repatriate their citizens for rehabilitation, reintegration, and prosecution as warranted.

Climate Change Policy and Impacts

As a top 10 global greenhouse gas emitter, and one of the highest per capita emitters in the world, Canada is contributing to the climate crisis, and taking a growing toll on human rights around the globe. Since being re-elected in 2021, the Trudeau government has repeated its pledges to pursue ambitious action to reduce greenhouse gas emissions. In March, the government released a new Emissions Reduction Plan (ERP), setting out how it intends to meet its commitment to cut greenhouse gas emissions 40-45 percent below 2005 levels by 2030. According to Climate Action Tracker, Canada's climate goals are not sufficient to meet the Paris Agreement goal to limit global warming to 1.5°C above pre-industrial levels.

Canada is the top public financier of fossil fuels among G20 nations and projects increased oil and gas production through 2050. Canadian oil sands are among the most carbon intensive and polluting oil production methods globally. The government continues to permit oil and gas pipeline expansions, including on First Nations' lands. Plans to increase fossil fuel production disregard the government's human rights obligation to adopt and implement robust climate mitigation policies.

Federal and provincial climate change policies have failed to put in place adequate measures to support First Nations in adapting to current and anticipated impacts of climate change and have largely ignored the impacts of climate change on First Nations' right to food. A 2022 report by the Canadian Climate Institute found that the climate crisis, especially permafrost thaw, is widening the Northern infrastructure gap and putting communities at risk. Much more government action is needed to address the impact of the climate crisis on First Nations and to ensure that appropriate food subsidies and health resources are available to all who need them.

The British Columbia's Coroner's report from June 2022 confirmed there was inadequate government response during the June 2021 "heat dome" that resulted in 619 deaths— mostly among older people and people with disabilities. In March, the province hosted small, limited engagements with heat-sensitive populations, including people with disabilities and older people. It remains unclear how the recommendations from people with lived experience will inform government policy. In July, the BC government released its new climate adaptation strategy which includes steps to prepare for and address heat risks but fails to discuss how these can be applied to at-risk populations.

Sexual Orientation and Gender Identity

Prime Minister Trudeau's government has taken significant steps domestically and internationally to advance the rights of lesbian, gay, bisexual, and transgender (LGBT) people. In August, the federal government launched its first national action plan to advance and strengthen LGBT rights at home and abroad, committing US$72 million over five years to develop and implement the plan.

Key International Actors

In March, the UN Committee on the Elimination of Discrimination against Women (CEDAW) called on Canada to address long-standing gender-based discrimination in the country's Indian Act, which continues to discriminate against Indigenous women.

In April, the UN Committee on the Elimination of Racial Discrimination (CERD) expressed concerns about the "escalated use of force, surveillance, and criminalization against land defenders and peaceful protesters." The committee urged Canada to stop construction on two natural gas and oil projects until the government obtains consent from affected Indigenous communities.

In June, the UN Committee on the Rights of the Child called on Canada to "take immediate measures to repatriate Canadian children" from northeast Syria and "provide them with appropriate assistance for their full physical and psychological recovery and social reintegration."

Foreign Policy

Since Russia's full-scale invasion of Ukraine in February, Canada imposed a series of targeted sanctions on more than 1,150 individuals and entities complicit in human rights abuses. Canadian sanctions also targeted Russia's oil, gas and chemical industries, defense sector and officials and entities involved in disinformation efforts. In March, Canada referred the situation in Ukraine to the International Criminal Court (ICC) in coordination with other ICC states parties.

In March, Canada, in coordination with the United Kingdom and the United States, imposed targeted sanctions against individuals and entities "responsible for procuring and supplying arms and military equipment" to the Myanmar military, including the commander of the Air Force.

At the March session of the UN Human Rights Council, Canada and seven Latin American states presented a resolution to create a group of experts charged with investigating human rights violations in Nicaragua. The resolution passed by a vote of 20 to 7.

In September, Canada co-led the resolution with a group of Latin American states to renew the mandate of the UN Fact-Finding Mission on Venezuela, charged with investigating grave human rights violations committed by all parties in Venezuela since 2014. The resolution was approved by 19 votes in favour.

In July, following a decision of the International Court of Justice (ICJ) declaring the admissibility of the case, Canada reaffirmed its intention to intervene, together with the Netherlands, in proceedings relating to Gambia's case before the court alleging that Myanmar's atrocities against the Rohingya violated the Genocide Convention.

At this session, Canada also supported a resolution renewing the mandate of the Sri Lanka Accountability Project tasked with collecting evidence of international crimes during and following the civil war.

Canada, together with 46 other countries, also supported a joint statement at the UN Human Rights Council on the human rights situation in China calling on authorities to end the arbitrary detention of Muslim Uyghurs and other communities in Xinjiang.

In October, following the widespread outcry over the death of an Iranian woman in the custody of Tehran's "morality police," Canada imposed targeted sanctions on Iranian officials, including the Iranian Revolutionary Guard Corp (IRGC)'s top leadership, rendering them inadmissible to Canada for life.

Central African Republic

Despite a unilateral ceasefire declared by President Faustin Archange Touadéra in October 2021, ongoing conflicts in the Central African Republic continued to seriously affect civilians in 2022. Fighting between the national army, alongside Russian mercenaries and Rwandan forces, and elements of the Coalition of Patriots for Change (*Coalition des patriotes pour le changement*, CPC) was at times intense, with dozens of civilians killed in some attacks.

Security conditions hampered humanitarian relief and grave violations of human rights and international humanitarian law have resulted in high numbers of refugees and internally displaced people.

Russian mercenaries from Wagner—a Russian private military security contractor with apparent links to the Russian government—are deployed in the country. Rumors around Wagner's official presence circulated for years, which government officials have denied. But in June, Fidèle Gouandjika, minister special advisor to the president, suggested to international media that forces were indeed from Wagner.

The group's control over some road checkpoints makes travel difficult outside the capital, Bangui. While officially in the country to serve as military instructors, in the past the United Nations had reported several instances in which these mercenaries participated in active fighting and were implicated in human rights abuses and violations of international humanitarian law.

Russian speaking forces, possibly from Wagner, carried out an attack in Ouham province, outside Bossangoa, killing at least 12 people in July 2021. The government committed to investigate the crime via a special commission of inquiry that at time of writing had yet to publish any findings. The UN reported that foreign forces, possibly from Russia, recruited anti-balaka militia to fight other armed groups.

The country remained dangerous for humanitarian actors, with over 87 attacks on them registered between January and July.

Attacks on Civilians

From December 6 to 13, 2021, anti-balaka fighters carried out an attack on the village of Boyo in Ouaka province, according to the UN. Over the course of the eight days, at least 20 civilians were killed, 5 women and girls raped, at least 547 houses burned and looted, and more than 1,000 villagers forced to flee.

In March, the rebel group Return, Reclamation and Rehabilitation (3R) launched attacks against civilians in Ouham-Pendé province, including at Nzakoundou where at least four civilians were killed.

In May, the Union for Peace in Central Africa (UPC) attacked a village and killed at least 10 civilians in Bokolobo, Ouaka province, according to the UN. The UPC's military leader Ali Darassa, who is also the chief of staff for the CPC, claimed the attacks were carried out by the national army and its allies.

In a February meeting at the UN security council, the United States accused fighters from Wagner of committing serious human rights abuses, including the summary execution of 30 people in Aïgbando, Haute Kotto province, in January. Russia said the accusations were not verified.

Media and other sources have made allegations about Russian mercenaries carrying out attacks on artisanal miners in the border zones between Central African Republic and Sudan from March to May.

Constitutional Referendum

In March, Touadéra's party, the United Hearts Movement (*Mouvement Cœurs unis*, MCU), attempted to introduce a constitutional amendment that would remove the two-term limit and allow the president to run for a third term. Touadéra was first elected in 2016 and was re-elected in 2020 amid a military offensive by the CPC. The changes were first proposed during a "republican dialogue"—promised by Touadéra after his re-election in 2020—which was boycotted by most of the opposition. The proposals sparked an outcry from civil society and the opposition. Nonetheless, in May, political allies of President Touadéra again proposed changes to the constitution that would let him keep running for office, prompting opposition protests.

In August, Touadéra announced a constitutional referendum. Later that month he created a committee responsible for drafting a new constitution to propose changes to enable him to run for a third term.

In September, the Constitutional Court ruled in response to a petition filed by a civil society group that the decree setting up the committee "was not in compliance with the country's constitution."

On October 17, the minister in charge of the general secretariat of the government and relations with institutions, Maxime Balalou, announced the retirement of the president of the Constitutional Court, Danièle Darlan, and instructed the government to take steps to replace her. On October 19, Darlan wrote to Balalou stating that the minister's decision to dismiss a judge from the court is unconstitutional and reiterated her intentions to finish her term, set to expire in March 2024. Danièle Darlan was dismissed on October 24 by presidential decree.

The next presidential vote is scheduled for 2025.

Justice for Serious Crimes

In March 2022, Chad surrendered a former anti-balaka military coordinator, Maxime Mokom, to the International Criminal Court (ICC). Mokom had fled to Chad after having taken part in the CPC's unsuccessful bid to take Bangui in 2020. Mokom had previously been one of the highest ranked anti-balaka leaders in the country and in 2019 was appointed minister for disarmament, de-mobilization, re-integration, and repatriation under a failed peace deal. The ICC had issued his arrest warrant under seal in 2018 on charges of war crimes and crimes against humanity committed between December 5, 2013, and at least December 2014.

In April, the Special Criminal Court (SCC)—part of the domestic justice system but which has both national and international staff and benefits from extensive UN and other international assistance—opened its first trial. The case is against three suspects from the 3R rebel group, Issa Sallet Adoum, Ousman Yaouba, and Tahir Mahamat, who are accused of being responsible for war crimes and crimes against humanity committed in May 2019 in Koundjili and Lemouna in Ouham Pende province. On October 31, the court convicted the three men of war crimes and crimes against humanity.

In August, the ICC made public an arrest warrant for Noureddine Adam, the former number two of the Seleka. The warrant, which dates to January 2019, states that Adam is wanted on charges of war crimes and crimes against humanity, including torture. He is reportedly currently in Sudan. Adam oversaw Seleka fighters, and Human Rights Watch documented how fighters under his command likely committed atrocities in Bangui and nearby areas since 2013. After he fled Bangui in 2014, Adam took command of other armed groups in the northeast of the country.

In September, the ICC trial of Seleka commander Mahamat Said Abdel Kani began in The Hague. Said is accused of war crimes and crimes against humanity committed in Bangui in 2013 and was an "immediate subordinate" of Adam, according to the court. He is the first Seleka leader to face charges before the ICC.

The trials of anti-balaka leaders Patrice-Edouard Ngaïssona and Alfred Yékatom continued at the ICC. The charges against both include war crimes and crimes against humanity committed between December 2013 and December 2014. Ngaïssona was arrested in France and transferred to the ICC in December 2018. Yékatom was transferred to the ICC by Central African Republic authorities in November 2018.

Hassan Bouba, a government minister, who faces charges for war crimes and crimes against humanity at the SCC remained a fugitive. Bouba was a leader of the UPC and in 2017, he was named a special councilor to the president, and later became the minister of livestock and animal health. The UPC started committing serious abuses in the Ouaka province in 2014. Bouba was expelled from the group in January 2021. In late November 2021, national gendarmes released Bouba from detention in defiance of SCC orders and escorted him home. He was scheduled to appear before the SCC that day for a custody hearing but did not do so.

Displacement and Humanitarian Needs

The number of internally displaced persons (IDPs) remained high due to fighting. Over 1.3 million Central Africans, according to the UN, were either refugees in neighboring countries (735,000) or internally displaced (654,000) as of September 2022. Conditions for IDPs and refugees, many of whom stay in camps, remained harsh. Assistance to IDPs was seriously hampered by attacks on humanitarians and general insecurity in the country.

About 3.1 million people, out of a population of 4.9 million, needed humanitarian assistance. The humanitarian response plan was underfunded, with a budget gap of around US$136 million as of September 2022.

Women and Girls' Rights

Insecurity and ongoing violence created a hostile environment for women and girls. Sexual violence remains a threat for women and girls, particularly for those who are internally displaced. According to the 2021 Human Development Report, the country ranks 159 out of 162 countries with a gender inequality index of 0.680. Women are underrepresented in decision-making and suffer one of the highest maternal mortality rates in the world.

Girls are severely affected by unwanted pregnancies and child marriage: 229 per 1,000 adolescent girls and women ages 15 to 19 gave birth; and 68 percent of girls are married before turning 18. The country has the second highest prevalence of child marriage globally.

Children's Rights

The UN verified that at least 329 children, some as young as age 7, were recruited by parties to the conflict in 2021, including by national armed forces. At least 104 children were killed or maimed, primarily from gunshots and crossfire. The UN verified 211 cases of rape or other sexual violence against girls. At least 52 schools were attacked, including 26 by government or pro-government forces, and an additional 55 schools were used for military purposes, primarily by government forces.

Key International Actors

The UN Security Council and the United States imposed sanctions on Ali Darassa, the leader of the UPC, in December 2021. As the group's founder and leader, he was implicated in serious human rights abuses, including the killing of civilians, torture, rape and causing displacement.

Under the Child Soldier Prevention Act, the US added the Central African Republic to its list of governments using child soldiers for the first time since 2014. The designation entails sanctions on military assistance, in the absence of a presidential waiver.

The UN peacekeeping mission, MINUSCA, deployed 11,598 military peacekeepers and 2,085 police across many parts of the country. Under Chapter VII of the UN Charter, the mission is authorized to take all necessary means to protect the civilian population from the threat of physical violence and to "implement a mission-wide protection strategy." In November 2021, the UN Security Council extended the mandate of the mission for an additional year.

In April, the governments of Cameroon, the Central African Republic, Chad, the Republic of Congo, the Democratic Republic of the Congo, the Sudan, and South Sudan adopted a declaration aimed at creating regional action to help displaced Central Africans.

Chad

April 2022 marked one year since Mahamat Idriss Déby Itno seized power and declared himself head of the Transitional Military Council (*Conseil militaire de transition*, CMT) following the sudden death of his father Idriss Deby Itno, president since 1990. Security forces used excessive force, including live ammunition and tear gas, to disperse opposition-led demonstrations across the country, and arbitrarily arrested demonstrators, many of whom reported torture and other ill-treatment in detention.

Free, fair, and credible elections by October 2022, as promised by Mahamat Déby, did not happen and were postponed.

On August 8, the transitional military council and more than 40 rebel groups signed a peace accord in Doha, Qatar, to end a decades long conflict and initiate a broader national dialogue. The accord was welcomed by the United Nations and the African Union Commission chief Moussa Faki Mahamat. However, nine armed factions, including the Front for Change and Concord in Chad (*Front pour l'alternance et la concorde au Tchad* - FACT), the Libya-based group whose fighting led to the death of the former president in April 2021, rejected the deal, saying it did not consider their demands.

On August 20, the national dialogue—a series of talks to be attended by all segments of Chadian society and aimed at defining a timeline and rules for presidential elections— opened in the capital, N'Djamena. Some members and supporters of opposition parties and civil society organizations have refused to participate in the dialogue, deeming it "not inclusive."

On October 1, the national dialogue adopted a measure to extend the transition for a maximum of 24 months and delegates decided that Mahamat Déby would remain as interim head of state, despite warnings from international partners that transitional authorities should not monopolize power. The forum further allowed him to run for president when elections are held.

On October 20, security forces fired on protesters in several cities across the country killing at least 50 people and injuring dozens of others. The protests, which were banned the previous day, marked the date the military administration had initially promised to hand over power to a civilian government.

Crackdown on Political Opposition, Dissent

The military junta harassed, intimidated, and occasionally prosecuted opposition political parties and supporters. Security forces continued to enjoy widespread impunity for the excessive use of force against demonstrators.

Security forces killed at least 13 people—including a 12-year-old child—and injured over 80 people in Abéché, Ouaddaï province on January 24 and 25. Security forces violently dispersed a demonstration there against plans to appoint a new traditional chief from the ethnic Bani Halba community, killing three protestors. The following day, security forces opened fire at the funeral for those killed, killing an additional 10 people and injuring at least 40 others.

In May, Chadian authorities arrested six members and supporters of Wakit Tamma, a coalition of Chadian opposition parties and civil society organizations, for participating in a May 14 demonstration and charged them with "disturbing the public order, harm to property, and physical assault." In the days following the arrests, the Chadian bar association announced a strike in protest of the politically motivated charges.

Wakit Tamma led demonstrations across the country the week of May 14 denouncing France's military presence in Chad and its perceived support for the military junta. Three months later, authorities barred Wakit Tamma outright from protesting ahead of the opening of the National Inclusive Dialogue.

Political repression continued to escalate after the official launch of the national dialogue.

Security forces used excessive force, including tear gas, in N'Djamena on September 2, 3, and 9, injuring scores of protesters and arresting over 220 people, mostly members and supporters of the opposition party The Transformers (*Les Transformateurs*), several of whom reported being held in detention in inhuman conditions, including lack of space, hygiene, ventilation, and light. On September 3, security forces also beat four Chadian journalists, including Aristide Djimalde, a 25-year-old female reporter working for Chadian media Alwihda Info, and arrested three of them for covering the security forces' crackdown on opposition.

In the aftermath of the October 20 protests, officers from the army, gendarmes, and police beat and arrested hundreds of people, many apparently arbitrarily. Following the crackdown, the Prime Minister announced that government would create a "judicial commission" to establish responsibility for the abuses. On October 21, the justice minister ordered several courts across the country to open cases on the protests and the security forces response.

Abuses by Armed Groups

The Islamist armed groups Boko Haram and the Islamic State in West Africa Province (ISWAP) continued to carry out unlawful attacks against civilians as well as against security forces in the Lake Chad area.

In the Sahel, Chad has been providing substantial military contributions to regional counterterrorism operations for years. Operation Barkhane, the French-led counterinsurgency operation against armed Islamist groups in the Sahel, is headquartered in N'Djamena, and the country currently contributes the third-highest number of troops to the United Nations Multidimensional Integrated Stabilization Mission in Mali (MINUSMA).

Chad is a member of the G5 Sahel, a joint force for fighting terror in the region which also comprises Burkina Faso, Mauritania, Niger, and until recently, Mali.

International and National Justice

Former Chadian President Hissène Habré died of Covid-19 on August 24, 2021, while serving a life sentence. Habré was convicted of crimes against humanity, war crimes and torture on May 30, 2016, by an African Union-backed court in Dakar, Senegal. He was also convicted of sexual crimes, including rape and the sexual slavery of women to serve his soldiers.

On September 19, the Chadian government announced it had released 10 billion FCFA (USD $14.8 million) to compensate victims and survivors of Habré era abuses, many of whom have been waiting since the 2016 conviction to receive their court-ordered compensation.

On December 24, the transitional government granted amnesty to nearly 300 rebels and political dissidents who had been convicted of grave offenses including recruiting child soldiers.

Sexual Orientation and Gender Identity

Article 354 of the 2017 Penal Code prohibits "sexual relations with a person of one's own sex." Under the code, individuals convicted of same-sex relations face up to two years' imprisonment and a fine between 50,000 à 500,000 CFA francs (roughly US$75-750).

Women's Rights

In July, the Chadian government banned young girls from leaving the country without parental permission allegedly in response to concerns over "a migratory flow of young girls" leaving for the "purpose of exploitation." Chad has the highest rate of child marriage in the world, with 70 percent of girls being married before the age of 18. In August, an Islamic High Court in the northeastern region of Mangalmé ruled that people who refuse a marriage proposal must pay a fine known as "amchilini". Women's rights groups have denounced the "amchilini" fine and the ban on young girls from leaving the country, noting that it is discriminatory and violates girls' right to freedom of movement.

Social and Economic Rights

According to the World Food Programme, Chad has one of the highest levels of hunger in the world and an estimated 42 percent of the population live in poverty. For decades, the country has underinvested in social protection while climate change and desertification have negatively impacted agricultural yields.

In June, Mahamat Déby declared a national food emergency as international grain prices dramatically increased following the onset of the Russia-Ukraine war. Since the beginning of the Covid-19 pandemic, the number of people estimated to be experiencing acute food insecurity in the country increased by nearly 70 percent. Between June and September, during the year's lean season, 2.1 million people were estimated to require humanitarian food assistance.

Chile

Gabriel Boric won the December 2021 presidential election and, despite a highly polarized campaign, his opponent rapidly recognized the results.

In 2020, Chileans overwhelmingly supported writing a new constitution, but in September 2022 rejected the draft written by a constitutional convention. As of October, political parties were in negotiations to initiate a new constituent process.

Both the presidential election and the constitutional process respected democratic principles, which stood out in a hemisphere where political leaders have tried to undermine democracy in recent years.

Authorities have taken initial steps to reform the national police but have yet to make crucial changes to the disciplinary system and protocols.

Chile faces important human rights challenges regarding migrants, refugees, women, children, Indigenous people, and lesbian, gay, bisexual, and transgender (LGBT) people.

The Boric administration has consistently promoted human rights abroad, regardless of the ideology of the government committing the abuses.

Constituent Process

Massive protests over deficiencies in the provision of public services, an increase in the price of public transportation, and economic inequality erupted across Chile in October 2019. Police used excessive force against demonstrators and bystanders.

As an "institutional exit" from the crisis, political parties then agreed to consult the citizenry on a constituent process.

In 2020, an overwhelming majority of Chileans voted to establish a convention to write a new constitution; in May 2021, under a unique convention framework set by Congress that included gender parity and almost 10 percent of reserved seats for Indigenous people, voters selected representatives.

In July 2022, the convention presented the draft of a new constitution, which included protection for many rights. It also made important changes to the justice system and presidential powers, and restructured the legislative branch.

On September 4, almost 62 percent of voters rejected the draft constitution. That night, President Boric called on Congress and civil society to agree on a new constituent process. As of October, political parties were in negotiations to initiate a new constituent process

Police Reform

Hundreds of complaints of use of excessive force against protesters and ill-treatment of detainees since 2019 prompted calls for police reform but have not yet led to structural changes.

Chile's national police, the Carabineros, have updated various public-order protocols, including on use of anti-riot shotguns. However, deficiencies remain, leaving ample room for abuse.

Chile's laws granting the Carabineros broad powers of detention, which they exercise with very little oversight, have not been amended. Studies based on official data show that carabineros may have used these powers in a discriminatory way for years, targeting migrants, women, and people living in poverty.

A legal reform that went into effect in February 2022 included some measures of transparency and civilian oversight but did not overhaul the Carabineros' disciplinary regime, which fails to guarantee independent and impartial investigations.

In August, the Boric administration established a police reform commission—made up of cabinet members, undersecretaries, and carabineros—and a reform advisory unit—made up of congresspeople, governors, mayors, nongovernmental organizations, and experts. The objective is to advance efficiency, transparency and probity, a gender and human rights approach to policing, and full subordination of police to civilian authorities.

As of July 2021, 1,433 administrative investigations of carabineros for involvement in "acts of violence" had resulted in 158 disciplinary sanctions, including the firing of 22 police.

By April 2022, the Attorney General's Office had reported only 16 convictions from 8,581 investigations of police abuses allegedly committed from October 2019 through March 2020.

Migrants and Asylum Seekers' Rights

Chile hosts some 1.4 million migrants, particularly Venezuelans, Peruvians, and Haitians.

Between 2010 and 2021, authorities reported granting only 701 of almost 22,000 applications for refugee status and rejecting around 7,000. Migration policies since 2019 have made it increasingly difficult for many people to obtain visas or asylum. A series of 2021 rulings by the Supreme Court and appeals courts exposed violations of due process in hundreds of deportations and ordered those deportations to be stopped.

Under an immigration law that took effect in February 2022, illegal entry is not a crime. Yet the law allows immediate expulsion of migrants who cross or attempt to cross the border, raising due process concerns.

Collective expulsions of people already living in Chile, carried out during the administration of former President Sebastián Piñera (2018-22), stopped during Boric's administration. The National Migration Service said it continues to deport individuals "who have committed a crime and have a criminal record."

In February, then-President Piñera declared a state of emergency in four northern provinces to control irregular immigration, stationing troops near the border with Bolivia and Perú. At President Boric's request, Congress approved an extension of the state of emergency but Boric let it expire in April, while maintaining heavy military presence in the border areas.

Also in March, President Boric called for a regional plan to respond to Venezuelan migration, proposing a quota system.

Seven migrants died crossing the high-altitude border from Bolivia to Chile from January through July.

Anti-migrant protests and xenophobic attacks continued during 2022, forcing some migrants out of Chile.

Women's and Girls' Rights

Chile's 28-year total abortion ban ended in 2017, when the Constitutional Court upheld a law decriminalizing abortion when the life of a pregnant person is at risk, the fetus is non-viable, or a pregnancy results from rape. As of September 5, official statistics showed 320 people had received legal abortions in 2022.

Health facilities impose unnecessary hurdles, including restrictive and discretionary interpretations of exceptions to the ban. Around 50 percent of public health obstetricians have registered as conscientious objectors and refuse to perform abortions in cases of rape. Private hospitals and clinics can also register as conscientious objectors.

The rejected draft of a new constitution established that the state should ensure access to abortion. An Ipsos survey in 2021 showed over 70 percent of Chileans support legalizing abortion in some or all circumstances.

The group Women's Network Against Violence Against Women reported 35 victims of femicide from January through early September 2022, compared to 29 reported by the government. Since 2020, the law no longer requires a relationship between the perpetrator and victim for a killing to be considered femicide.

One of President Boric's first initiatives was to introduce a gender-balanced cabinet.

Indigenous Rights

Long-standing conflict between the government and certain Mapuche Indigenous activists continues. Activists told Human Rights Watch that no government, including the Boric administration so far, has properly addressed core complaints regarding land rights, political representation, and security.

A state of emergency declared by former President Piñera in four southern provinces in 2021 expired in March 2022. President Boric declared a state of emergency, in May, in the same provinces, citing increasing violence and road blockades. As of October, the state of emergency remained.

Sexual Orientation and Gender Identity

In March, a law came into effect recognizing same-sex couples' right to civil marriage, joint adoption, and assisted reproductive technology, among other rights. Data obtained by Fundación Iguales, a Chilean organization, indicates that 170 same-sex couples married during the law's first month. As of September, the Civil Registry had registered 395 children of same-sex couples. Fundación Iguales cited problems with the implementation of the law, especially in the registration of children of same-sex couples, as well as with the excessive delay in the delivery of birth and marriage certificates.

Children's Rights

After complaints of sexual exploitation and human rights violations in shelters for children separated from their families, the National Service for Minors (SENAME) underwent structural reforms. In 2021, a new National Specialized Protection Service for Children and Adolescents took over SENAME's child protection programs. Passage, in September 2022, of a bill creating a National Youth Social Reintegration Service—to reintegrate into society children in conflict with the law—will allow closure of SENAME once the president signs it into law. The bill also requires Chile to create a specialized juvenile justice system, with expert prosecutors, judges, and defenders.

Human Rights Watch found that *Aprendo en Línea*, an online learning product used by the Education Ministry during the Covid-19 pandemic, used an invasive technique that captured information and transmitted children's personal data to an advertising technology company. As of September, the Education Ministry had failed to stop the children's violation of privacy.

Disability Rights

Chile's laws strip many people with disabilities of their legal capacity, including by providing for full guardianship, and use derogatory language. In August, members of the Chamber of Deputies presented a bill to replace "crazy and insane," in the Criminal Code, with "people with psychosocial disability," but failed to address restrictions on legal capacity.

The rejected draft constitution included provisions protecting rights of people with disabilities, including to enjoy legal capacity.

Prison Conditions and Pretrial Detention

The prison population increased more than 10 percent in a year, surpassing 43,000 people as of August 2022, about 3 percent above the facilities' capacity.

Thirty-seven percent of detainees awaited trial, as of August. Chile's criminal code allows broad use of pretrial detention and does not establish a maximum period for it.

As of April 2021, the Attorney General's Office had identified 570 criminal gangs operating inside prisons, which it considered a threat to other detainees. The office pledged, in September 2022, to work with the government and prison police to address crimes inside Chilean prisons.

Confronting Past Abuses

Chilean courts continue to try agents of Augusto Pinochet's dictatorship (1973-1990) for human rights abuses.

In June, former military officer Miguel Krassnoff and two former police officers were convicted in the 1975 homicide of a teacher. It was the 80th conviction for Krassnoff, who participated in the assault on the presidential house during the coup against former President Salvador Allende, and it raised his prison sentence to 900 years for crimes against humanity.

Key International Actors

President Boric has consistently criticized human rights abuses in other countries—including El Salvador, Venezuela, Nicaragua, and Cuba—regardless of the political ideology of the government committing those abuses. He called the imprisonment of opposition candidates for Nicaragua's 2021 elections "unacceptable."

Chile signed the Los Angeles Declaration on Migration and Protection, committing to strengthen and expand paths toward safe legal migration and asylum.

In June, Chile ratified the Escazú Agreement, an international treaty protecting environmental defenders and guaranteeing rights related to the environment.

Chile and five other Latin American countries led the renewal of the mandate for the UN Independent International Fact-Finding Mission on Venezuela in October.

The same month, Chile was elected as a member of the UN Human Rights Council for the 2023-2025 term.

China

Repression deepened across China in 2022. Xi Jinping secured an unprecedented third term as the general secretary of the Chinese Communist Party, making him the country's most powerful leader since Mao Zedong. In October, a man draped two banners over a bridge in Beijing, calling for the "dictatorial traitor" Xi to be removed, and for freedoms and universal suffrage for people in China. The lone protestor inspired solidarity protests around the world.

The Chinese government tightened its Covid-19 restrictions, imposing repeated, unpredictable lockdowns on hundreds of millions of people. In some cases, officials used barbed wire, metal bars, and large barriers to prevent people from leaving their homes. In Sichuan province, residents were unable to leave buildings even during an earthquake. During these lockdowns—which lasted from days to weeks—people reported difficulties accessing food and medical care, in some cases leading to deaths. Others reported privacy violations, censorship, disruptions to their livelihoods, and government brutality as police and health officials kicked and shoved people who resisted Covid restrictions. In Tibet and Xinjiang, residents reported even more draconian Covid-19 controls imposed by local authorities already severely limiting rights.

China suffered its most severe heat wave ever recorded, causing widespread power shortages that prompted authorities to revert to using coal, and underscoring the urgency of a transition to clean energy.

Beijing and Hong Kong authorities continued their assault on human rights in the territory, a downward trajectory that is expected to continue as Beijing appointed an abusive former police official, John Lee, as the city's chief executive.

International attention to Chinese government human rights violations grew. Eight governments engaged in a diplomatic boycott of the 2022 Beijing Winter Olympics in protest. In June, entry into force of the United States Uyghur Forced Labor Prevention Act established a presumption that goods from Xinjiang are made from forced labor and cannot be imported. In August, the former United Nations high commissioner for human rights released her report on Xinjiang, concluding that the abuses in the region "may constitute crimes against humanity."

Hong Kong

Hong Kong authorities attacked press freedom. National security police raided the office of influential media outlet Stand News on December 29, 2021, charged its editors with sedition, and effectively forced it to close; this prompted seven other outlets to close within two weeks. In April, police arrested the ex-Stand News columnist and veteran journalist, Allen Au, on baseless charges of sedition. Later that month, the Hong Kong Foreign Correspondents' Club canceled the Human Rights Press Awards, citing fear of arrest. In September, police charged Hong Kong Journalists Association chair Ronson Chan with "obstructing police officers" during a reporting assignment.

In August, the High Court ruled that journalistic materials are not legally protected under the draconian National Security Law (NSL). The decision affirmed the legality of police searches of the phones of media tycoon Jimmy Lai, who faces three NSL charges and one sedition charge, along with six other executives of Hong Kong's former leading pro-democracy paper *Apple Daily*.

At least 231 people have been arrested for allegedly violating the NSL since it was imposed on June 30, 2020, and for "sedition," a colonial-era law the authorities have revived to crush dissent. The NSL imposes a presumption against bail, a rule inconsistent with the presumption of innocence. Among the 138 individuals charged, most had been under pretrial detention for nearly a year or more.

In May, police charged 90-year-old pro-democracy advocate Cardinal Joseph Zen and five others for failing to properly register the legal aid group 612 Humanitarian Relief Fund. Under police pressure, in July, the Bar Association opened inquiries into the professional conduct of at least 35 barristers who represented the fund's beneficiaries.

After police arrested unionists and effectively forced many unions to disband, in September the government further restricted union activities by requiring founders of new unions to pledge that they will not threaten "national security."

Censorship is now commonplace in Hong Kong. In May, a government-run book fair banned several publishers of political books from participating. Public libraries, commercial bookstore chains, and some school libraries continue to pull from their shelves politically "sensitive" titles.

Several films portraying Hong Kong political issues were banned under the new censorship regime, which prohibits movies that may "endanger national security." In August, a film festival dropped an award-winning film after its director refused to yield to authorities' demand to remove a scene depicting the 2014 pro-democracy Umbrella Movement.

Universities were complicit in the authorities' repression of students, who have been central to the city's pro-democracy movement. After four universities removed artwork about the 1989 Tiananmen Massacre in late 2021, in January 2022, the University of Hong Kong further covered up Tiananmen-related slogans painted on university pavement. All eight public universities have obstructed their student unions' operations, including by ceasing to recognize them and refusing to help them collect membership dues. Universities introduced mandatory national security law courses while the Chinese University of Hong Kong began hosting weekly Chinese flag-raising ceremonies.

Police intensified surveillance of Hong Kong society. In June, police set up a "counter-terrorism" hotline in addition to an existing "anti-violence" hotline for reporting national security violations. In August, the police said it would "dispel misinformation" about the force through a "round-the-clock public opinion tracking system."

Hong Kong people continued to risk arrests to protest. On June 4, many people commemorated the 1989 Tiananmen Massacre in public; police made six arrests that day. In September, as hundreds gathered outside the British consulate to mourn the passing of the British Queen Elizabeth II, some sang the banned protest song "Glory to Hong Kong." Police arrested a man for sedition for playing the protest tune on a harmonica. Over 150,000 people have left Hong Kong since the NSL was imposed; many have continued their activism abroad.

Xinjiang

In December 2021, authorities replaced Xinjiang's party secretary, Chen Quanguo, who oversaw the region's repressive "Strike Hard Campaign against Violent Terrorism," with Ma Xingrui, a technocrat experienced in governing wealthier coastal regions. In July, President Xi visited Xinjiang, and said that while the region must "maintain a firm grip on stability," it should also "move towards prosperity."

Despite government propaganda portraying its policies in the region as successful efforts to counter terrorism, international scrutiny of crimes against humanity in the region grew. In May, an anonymous source released hacked police files from the region, which included nearly 3,000 photos of Uyghur detainees, along with key policy documents outlining harsh policies from China's top leadership. As many as a million people were wrongfully detained in political education camps, pretrial detention centers, and prisons at the height of the Strike Hard Campaign. While some have been released, the Chinese authorities have also sentenced an estimated half-million people, many of whom remain imprisoned, Human Rights Watch found in a September report.

Tibet

Authorities in Tibetan areas continue to enforce severe restrictions on freedoms of religion, expression, movement, and assembly. Popular concerns over issues such as mass relocation, environmental degradation, or the phasing out of the Tibetan language in primary education were met with repression. Local officials are required to educate the public in "obeying the law," and cash rewards are offered to citizens prepared to inform on others.

Under intense censorship, Tibetans continue to be detained for online offenses, such as having banned content on their phones or "spreading rumors." Authorities introduced a ban on posting religious teaching and other content online, intended to enforce tight official control over religious institutions and teachers. In a Tibetan area of Sichuan province, regional authorities ordered the demolition of outdoor statues and temples, the construction of which had initially been approved.

Reports emerged of the arrest and sentencing of Tibetan religious and cultural figures suspected of dissent, and of their mistreatment in detention—notably the writers Go Sherab Gyatso, Rongwo Gendun Lhundrup, and Tubten Lodro (alias Sabuchey). In March, the popular young pop singer Tsewang Norbu staged a self-immolation protest in front of the Potala Palace, the first by a Tibetan from an urban background.

Freedom of Religion

State control over religion has increased since 2016, when Xi called for "Sinicization" of religions. Going beyond controlling religion by dictating what constitutes "normal," and therefore legal, religious activity, authorities now seek to comprehensively reshape religions such that they are consistent with the party's ideology and that they help promote allegiance to the party and to Xi.

Police continue to harass, arrest, and imprison leaders and members of "house churches," congregations that refuse to join official Catholic and Protestant churches. Authorities also disrupt their peaceful activities and ban them outright. In September, dozens of members of a Shenzhen church fled to Thailand to seek refuge after having left China three years ago due to escalating police harassment and after they failed to secure refugee status in South Korea. The group reported being monitored by Chinese government agents in Thailand.

The new Measures on the Administration of Internet Religious Information Services came into effect in March, prohibiting individuals or groups from teaching or otherwise propagating religion online without official approval. A widely used Catholic app, CathAssist, shut down in August because it was unable to obtain a license. The regulations have reportedly severely disrupted people's religious life as many have increasingly relied on online religious gatherings and information especially during the Covid-19 pandemic.

In October 2022, the Vatican and the Chinese government renewed an agreement signed in 2018. It was renewed despite the Chinese government's arrest of Cardinal Joseph Zen and the continued detentions of Bishops Zhang Weizhu and Cui Tai, among others.

Covid-19

Authorities maintained a strict "Zero Covid" policy, viewing even a single infection as unacceptable, even though effective vaccines and medication are widely available.

In Ruili, a border city in Yunnan province, residents endured seven separate lockdowns from March 2021 to April 2022, spending 119 days confined to their homes except for mandatory Covid testing. In Shanghai, a commercial hub of 25 million people, residents endured a similarly strict lockdown from March to May. Chengdu, a city of 21 million people, was locked down for two weeks in September.

While such draconian measures prevented Covid-related deaths and illnesses, they significantly impeded people's access to health care, food, and other necessities. An unknown number of people died after being denied medical treatment for their non-Covid-related illnesses. In some cases, residents had to resort to threats of self-harm or violence to have their family members admitted to hospitals. In Shanghai, authorities separated small children from their parents after positive Covid tests, which required those testing positive to isolate in a hospital or designated facility, reversing the policy only after public outcry. Numerous people reported that they faced severe shortages of food, medicines, menstrual hygiene products, and other essential items. People in mandatory quarantine facilities also took to social media to expose crowded and unsanitary conditions there.

While authorities apologized for "shortcomings and deficiencies" in their Covid responses, they continued to control the flow of information regarding the pandemic. Censors removed numerous social media posts criticizing the government, such as a viral video that protested the lockdown in Shanghai and angry comments after a bus carrying dozens to a quarantine center crashed and killed 27 in the middle of the night, while police across the country detained netizens who complained about the government's Covid response.

The lockdowns and other Covid control measures also forced factories, restaurants, and businesses to cut jobs and wages, or to close altogether. Videos posted on social media showed people begging officials to release them from lockdown so they could go to work and feed their families.

Human Rights Defenders

Authorities continued to harass, detain, and prosecute human right defenders. In December 2021, authorities in Jilin province forcibly disappeared human rights lawyer Tang Jitian. Before his disappearance, authorities stopped Tang from traveling to Japan to visit his daughter, who was in a coma due to illness.

In June, a court in Shandong province held secret trials of prominent legal scholar Xu Zhiyong and human rights lawyer Ding Jiaxi for "subversion." Their verdicts were unknown at time of writing. The men were detained in 2020 and 2019 respectively after organizing a small gathering to discuss human rights and democracy issues. Li Qiaochu, a women's rights activist and Xu's partner, has also been detained since February 2021.

In September, Dong Jianbiao, the father of Dong Yaoqiong, who authorities disappeared for splashing ink on a poster of President Xi Jinping in 2018, died in a prison in Hunan province. Family members said his body showed signs of injuries. Dong had protested his daughter's disappearance and was imprisoned for a domestic dispute. Also in September, Shanghai police detained Ji Xiaolong, an activist who had called on Shanghai Party Secretary Li Qiang to resign for Covid mismanagement.

Huang Xueqin, a journalist and leading voice in China's #MeToo movement who was disappeared by Guangdong authorities in September 2021, was reportedly in poor health. Authorities dismissed Huang's family-appointed lawyer, and instead forced her to use a government-appointed lawyer.

Shenyang-based human rights lawyer Li Yuhan, who had been detained since 2017, was reportedly ill-treated by detention center authorities and was seriously ill. Li was tried in 2021 but no verdict had been issued at time of writing. The whereabouts of human rights lawyer Gao Zhisheng, who went missing in August 2017, remained unclear. Gao's family had continued to call on the Chinese government to disclose whether he was still alive.

Freedom of Expression

Authorities continue to harass, detain, and prosecute people for their online posts and private chat messages critical of the government, bringing trumped-up charges of "spreading rumors," "picking quarrels and provoking trouble," and "insulting the country's leaders." In May, a court in Hainan province sentenced former journalist Luo Changping to seven months in prison for a Weibo post that questioned China's justification for its involvement in the Korean War.

Authorities continued to suppress online content deemed politically sensitive. In early 2022, after Russia invaded Ukraine, censors removed social media posts critical of the Russian government or those that advocated peace. In June, prominent live streamer Li Jiaqi went offline for three months after he showed off a tank-shaped cake ahead of the 33rd anniversary of the Tiananmen Square Massacre, even though he was likely unaware of the tank's symbolism. In August, the Cyberspace Administration announced that it "dealt with" 1.34 billion social media accounts, "cleaned up" 22 million illegal messages, and closed 3,200 websites.

Despite Beijing's sophisticated censorship apparatus, netizens continued to develop creative ways to evade control. In Guangzhou, residents used vernacular Cantonese terms, instead of standard Mandarin, to express their frustrations with the government's draconian Covid policy.

Women's and Girls' Rights

China's #MeToo movement continued to gain traction, despite online censorship and repression of women's rights activists. Chinese tennis star Peng Shuai's November 2021 Weibo post, which alleged that she was sexually assaulted by a retired senior party official, took #MeToo accusations to the top echelons of the CCP. While her Weibo post, along with discussions around it, was quickly censored within the country, it generated enormous interest outside the country as the Chinese government prepared to host the Winter Olympics in February. Peng was not seen in public for weeks after making the post. Her subsequent appearances in videos and photos were widely believed to have been stage-managed by the authorities.

In August, a Beijing court rejected the appeal of Zhou Xiaoxuan, who filed a sexual harassment lawsuit against a prominent TV host at the state broadcaster CCTV, ruling the evidence submitted "insufficient." The landmark sexual harassment case had inspired many others to share their stories of sexual assault.

In September, Chinese police detained Du Yingzhe, a prominent Chinese film director, for sexual abuse. Twenty-one women and girls accused him of coercing students and staff members into having sex with him over a period of 15 years. In October, Richard Liu, a Chinese tech billionaire, settled a civil rape case in Minnesota, after Jingyao Liu, a former University of Minnesota student, sued him in 2018.

Two cases involving sexual violence generated nationwide outrage in 2022. In January, a video showing a woman chained around her neck in a hut in rural Jiangsu province went viral. A government investigation found that the woman was trafficked and sold as a bride twice in the late 1990s. Authorities censored the video and discussions, detained activists who tried to visit the woman's village, threatened people who did their own online research, and questioned the official findings.

In June, CCTV footage circulated online showed four women being viciously attacked after one of them rejected a man's sexual advance in a restaurant in the northeastern city of Tangshan. The video sparked heated debates around gender-based violence. Twenty-eight people were later charged in relation to the incident.

Sexual Orientation and Gender Identity

China decriminalized same-sex conduct in 1997. It does not have laws protecting people from discrimination on the basis of sexual orientation or gender identity, and same-sex partnerships are not recognized.

Authorities continued to ban depictions of same-sex relationships from film and television. In February, the popular American sitcom "Friends" returned to several Chinese streaming sites, but scenes featuring lesbian characters were cut. In April, references to a gay relationship in Warner Brothers' movie "Fantastic Beasts 3" were edited out. In June, authorities banned Disney's animation "Lightyear" after the company refused to cut out a scene featuring a same-sex couple kissing.

Disability Rights

In China, people with real or perceived psychosocial disabilities can be shackled—chained or locked in confined spaces—due to inadequate support and mental health services as well as widespread beliefs that stigmatize people with psychosocial disabilities.

In September, the UN Committee on the Rights of Persons with Disabilities recommended that the Chinese government "repeal provisions and practices that allow for the deprivation of liberty of adults and children with disabilities on the basis of actual or perceived impairment."

Belt and Road Initiative

The Belt and Road Initiative (BRI), announced in 2013, is the government's trillion-dollar infrastructure and investment program stretching across some 100 countries. Some BRI projects have since been criticized for lack of transparency, disregard of community concerns, and negative environmental impacts, prompting widespread protests.

In August, Chinese authorities announced they would waive 23 interest-free loans for 17 African countries, covering about 1 percent of total loans, according to a study by Boston University. A study by the Pretoria-based Institute for Security Studies on Chinese companies' labor practices in six African countries found widespread labor rights violations, including unpaid wages, physical violence, instant dismissal in the event of injury or sickness and the lack of workplace safety.

In August, protesters in Pakistan's port city Gwadar, a signature project of the China-Pakistan Economic Corridor, took to the street demanding water and electricity and a stop to Chinese trawlers' illegal fishing in the area. Local fishermen had raised concerns about the lack of transparency and consultations, and potential impacts on their livelihoods. This was seen as part of a growing backlash against the BRI in Pakistan.

Climate Change Policies and Actions

China remains the largest emitter of greenhouse gases, although its per capita emissions put it only in the top 40 countries. Much of the considerable energy that has fueled economic growth comes from coal, driving these emissions. It produces half of the world's coal and is also its largest importer of oil, gas, and coal.

The Chinese government announced in 2021 it would reach carbon neutrality before 2060 and reach peak carbon emissions before 2030. Despite these improved targets, the Climate Action Tracker rates the domestic target as "highly insufficient" to meet the Paris Agreement goal to limit global warming to 1.5°C above pre-industrial levels.

China also leads the world in renewable energy production and is the largest funder of overseas renewable projects, some of which, however, have been linked to human rights abuses. Much of the global production capacity for the minerals and materials needed for renewable energy technologies, including wind turbines, solar panels, and electric car batteries, is in China. Some of these minerals are produced in Xinjiang, raising concerns about the use of forced labor.

Chinese companies' operations abroad frequently caused or contributed to human rights abuses and environmental damage. In Guinea, Human Rights Watch documented the involvement of a Chinese company in a bauxite (aluminum) mining joint venture that has exploited farmers land without adequate compensation and destroyed local water sources.

China's imports of agricultural commodities drive more deforestation globally than those of any other market. This deforestation is largely illegal. In November, the US and China jointly committed to eliminating global illegal deforestation by enforcing their respective laws that ban illegal imports of timber. China has yet to enforce a restriction on illegal timber imports it adopted in 2019.

Key International Actors

In May, Michelle Bachelet made the first visit to China by a United Nations high commissioner for human rights in 17 years; authorities closely controlled her activities. In August, Bachelet released a report substantiating the widespread human rights violations in Xinjiang, concluding that the abuses "may amount to crimes against humanity."

The Chinese government repeatedly sought to stop the release of the report. Following the report's publication, more than 40 UN independent experts released a joint statement supporting its findings. In September, the US, Australia, Canada, Denmark, Finland, Iceland, Lithuania, Norway, Sweden, and the United Kingdom launched an initiative at the UN Human Rights Council to hold a discussion on the report during its March 2023 session. The effort fell short by a close vote of 17-19, with support from all UN regional groups: Ukraine subsequently expressed support, narrowing the margin to a single vote. However, the number of UN delegations willing to publicly condemn the government's abuses in Xinjiang keeps growing. In October, a record 50 UN member countries joined a Canadian-led joint statement calling on Beijing to end human rights violations in Xinjiang and implement the recommendations in Bachelet's report.

Governments increasingly took steps to ensure commercial activity does not fuel repression across China. In addition to the entry into force of the US Uyghur Forced Labor Prevention Act, the European Union was reportedly deliberating a ban on the import and export of all forced labor products, prompted in part by concerns over Xinjiang abuses. The EU introduced draft legislation to establish global standards for human rights due diligence for companies. The International Olympic Committee and its lead sponsors did not publish their human rights due diligence assessments ahead of the 2022 Winter Games in China.

In March, the US Justice Department announced cases against five people for harassing critics of the Chinese government in the US, reflecting growing concern about threats to diaspora communities. In Australia, the University of Technology Sydney campus took a step towards better protecting academic freedom for students wanting to offer views critical of the Chinese government by adding to orientation materials a new warning informing students of their right to be free from any form of state-backed harassment or political intimidation.

Foreign Policy

In February, Russian President Vladimir Putin visited China, where he and Xi published a statement pledging the two governments' "no-limits friendship." The Chinese government has not condemned Russia's invasion of Ukraine or the numerous violations of the laws of war committed by Russian forces in the conflict.

The Chinese government continues to provide direct assistance and military aid to several highly abusive governments, including the Taliban in Afghanistan and the military junta in Myanmar.

In October, the Chinese consul-general in Manchester, England, and other consulate staff dragged a pro-Hong Kong democracy protester into the compound and struck him; the consul-general justified his conduct as his "duty."

Chinese diplomats also attacked the mandates of UN human rights bodies in response to their increasingly vocal concern about violations inside China. Beijing dismissed the high commissioner's report on Xinjiang as a "farce," and efforts to advance a debate on the situation as "illegal and invalid."

Colombia

Abuses by armed groups, limited access to justice, and high levels of poverty, especially among Indigenous and Afro-descendant communities, remain serious human rights concerns in Colombia.

The 2016 peace accord between the Revolutionary Armed Forces of Colombia (FARC) and the government ended a five-decade-long conflict and brought an initial decline in violence. But violence took new forms and abuses by armed groups increased in many remote areas in later years, reaching similar levels in 2022 to those that existed immediately before the peace process.

Human rights defenders, journalists, demobilized FARC fighters, Indigenous and Afro-descendant leaders, and other activists face pervasive death threats and violence.

President Gustavo Petro took office in August and Francia Marquez, an environmental leader, became Colombia's first Afro-Colombian vice president. The new government vowed to fight climate change, implement the 2016 peace accord, and prioritize a "total peace" policy that would seek an accord with the National Liberation Army (ELN) guerrillas and the negotiated disarmament of other armed groups, including criminal gangs.

In February, the Constitutional Court decriminalized abortion in all circumstances up to the 24th week of pregnancy.

Abuses by Armed Groups

Numerous armed groups operate in Colombia fueled by illegal economies, including drug trafficking and illegal mining. These include the ELN guerrillas, which was formed in the 1960s; over 30 "dissident" groups that emerged from the 2017 demobilization of the FARC; and the Gaitanist Self-Defense Forces of Colombia (AGC), which emerged from the demobilization of paramilitary groups in the mid-2000s and are also known as "Gulf Clan." Many of these groups have fluid and complex links to each other and some are parties to non-international armed conflicts.

Armed groups continue to commit serious abuses against civilians, including killings, child recruitment, and rape, especially in rural areas of the Pacific region and along the Venezuelan and Ecuadorian borders. Security forces and judicial authorities have failed to effectively protect the population, ensure victims' access to justice, and prosecute and dismantle the groups.

In May, the AGC ordered an "armed strike," imposing movement restrictions on civilians in over 170 municipalities in 11 states. The restrictions suggested an alarming geographical expansion, compared to its 2012 armed strike, affecting 26 municipalities. The strike came in response to the extradition to the United States of its top commander, Darío Antonio Úsuga David, alias "Otoniel." The group also killed 36 police from June through August 2022.

Fears of antipersonnel landmines, threats by armed groups, and the hazards of crossfire prevented 96,000 people from leaving their communities between January and October a situation known as "confinement."

The Office of the High Commissioner for Human Rights (OHCHR) reported 60 "massacres," defined as the intentional killing of three or more civilians in a single incident, in 2022, as of October.

In the southern state of Nariño, fighting among FARC dissident groups has displaced thousands, mainly Afro-descendants and Awá Indigenous people, who also suffer threats, confinement, kidnappings, and killings.

In neighboring Cauca, the ELN and FARC dissident groups have recruited over 500 mostly Indigenous children since 2021, according to local groups. Nasa Indigenous people who oppose abuses by armed groups have been threatened and killed. Fighting by armed groups, mainly in Argelia municipality, left more than 2,600 people displaced and confined.

In the border areas of Colombia's Arauca and Venezuela's Apure state, fighting between the ELN and a coalition of FARC dissident groups have caused a dramatic increase in violence, including a spike in killings. Over 12,000 people were displaced or confined. In Apure, ELN fighters conducted joint operations with members of the Venezuelan security forces, which were complicit in their abuses.

In Putumayo state, on the Ecuadorian border, Comandos de la Frontera and the Carolina Ramírez Front, two groups that emerged from the FARC, control the population, imposing dress codes and curfews and threatening to kill those who fail to comply.

Violations by Public Security Forces

Security force abuses remain a serious concern.

On March 28, 2022, 11 people died in a controversial army operation in El Remanso, Putumayo state, in southern Colombia. The army claimed it complied with international humanitarian law, saying the operation had targeted Comandos de Frontera. At least four civilians died, including one Indigenous and one community leaders. Criminal investigations into whether the army used excessive force continued as of October.

Police have committed serious human rights violations in response to largely peaceful protests across Colombia since 2019. Efforts to investigate and prosecute them have been limited.

In 2021, Human Rights Watch reviewed evidence linking police to 25 killings of protesters and bystanders, as well as dozens of injuries and arbitrary arrests, in the context of peaceful demonstrations. As of October, four officers had been charged and five others indicted in connection with homicides. Nobody had been charged for the injuries or arbitrary arrests.

There have been limited reforms to improve accountability and prevent future violations.

In August, President Petro appointed Iván Velásquez, a widely respected former judge and anti-corruption prosecutor, as the minister of defense. Velásquez said the government would pursue further police reform, including by transferring the police out of the Ministry of Defense, where the line between its functions and the military's have often been blurred.

Violence Against Human Rights Defenders, Other Community Leaders

More than 1.000 human rights defenders and social leaders have been killed in Colombia since 2016, according to the Human Rights Ombudsperson's Office.

Colombian law includes a broad range of policies, mechanisms, and laws to prevent abuses against human rights defenders and protect former FARC fighters. But implementation, especially of measures established under the 2016 peace accord, has often been poor.

The Human Rights Ombudsperson's Office reported 182 killings of human rights defenders between January and October 2022.

In February 2022, in San Martín municipality, Cesar state, armed men killed Teófilo Acuña and Jorge Tafur, prominent peasant leaders who, for decades, led small-farmer and small-scale miner communities. As of October, one person had been charged in connection with their killings.

Peace Negotiations, Negotiated Disarmament, and Accountability

The 2016 peace agreement created a truth commission; the Special Jurisdiction for Peace (JEP), charged with trying abuses committed during the conflict; and an agency to seek the bodies of those disappeared during the conflict.

The Truth Commission presented its findings in June 2022 and established a committee to monitor, for seven years, implementation of its recommendations to the government, including creating an "anti-violence policy," re-starting peace negotiations with the ELN, and reforming security and drug policies. The report included comprehensive analysis of violence committed against women, LGBT people, children, Afro-descendants and Indigenous people.

The JEP has made significant strides in investigating and prosecuting war crimes and crimes against humanity, charging top former FARC commanders with hostage-taking and several army officers with extrajudicial executions, known as "false positive" killings.

In July, the JEP said it would initiate a nation-wide "macro-case" into sexual violence and other crimes based on prejudice committed by the FARC and security forces, which will encompass crimes motivated by gender, sex, sexual orientation, and gender identity.

In late October, the JEP issued its first indictment, accusing 11 army officers and one civilian of extrajudicial executions committed in North Santander in 2007 and 2008.

In November, the JEP indicted former FARC top commanders for their responsibility in hostage-taking. The commanders had acknowledged their role in these crimes in a June hearing, and the JEP said they should be sentenced to between five and eight years of "special sanctions."

In early December, the JEP indicted 14 other army officers for their role in "false positive" killings committed on the Caribbean Coast between 2002 and 2005. The judges said that 12 of the officers had fully acknowledged their responsibility and confessed to their crimes, but that two others had not and should stand trial.

Defendants who fully cooperate with the JEP and confess to their crimes are subject to up to eight years of "special sanctions," including restrictions on liberty but no prison time. Because the language in the existing legislation on these sanctions is vague and no punishments have been imposed, it remains unclear how the "special sanctions" will operate in practice.

In early November, Congress passed a Petro administration-sponsored law that allows it to negotiate a peace accord, including new transitional justice mechanisms, with some armed groups, such as the ELN. On November 21, the peace talks with the ELN re-started in Venezuela. Authorities said that they would also introduce a bill to offer reduced sentences for other armed groups. As of November, it remained unclear how authorities would ensure victims' access to justice and to what extent the government would treat gangs and armed groups that are parties to the conflict differently.

Internal Displacement, Reparations, and Land Restitution

Conflict-related violence has displaced almost 8.4 million Colombians since 1985, government figures show.

The United Nations Office for the Coordination of Humanitarian Affairs (OCHA) reported 70,000 people displaced between January and October 2022, in "mass displacements" of 50 or more people or 10 or more families.

Municipalities and state governments often lack sufficient funding to assist displaced people, and national government assistance has often been slow and insufficient.

In 2011, Congress passed a Victims' Law to ensure redress for victims and restore millions of hectares left behind or stolen from Colombians displaced during the conflict. As of October 2022, courts had issued rulings on only 13,507 of over 142,000 claims filed. Under 14 percent of over 9 million registered victims of the armed conflict had received reparations, as of October.

Refugees, Asylum Seekers, and Migrants

Colombia has received by far the largest number of refugees, asylum seekers, and migrants fleeing the human rights and humanitarian crises in Venezuela. As of February, more than 2.5 million Venezuelans lived in Colombia.

In 2021, then-President Iván Duque announced temporary protection for Venezuelans, granting them 10 years of legal status. As of October 2022, authorities had granted temporary protection to over 1.4 million Venezuelans, out of more than 2.4 million who had requested it.

More than 3,000 people, including Venezuelans and Colombians who had been living in Venezuela's Apure state, fled to Colombia's Arauca and Vichada states in early 2022, escaping fighting and abuses by armed groups. Aid has been very limited.

Hundreds of thousands of migrants—mostly Venezuelan—crossed Colombia's Darien gap into Panama in 2022, believed to be heading in most cases to the US. The number of people crossing the gap increased significantly, in large part driven by the flow of Venezuelans. During their days-long walk across the gap, migrants of all nationalities are frequently victims of robbery and serious abuses, including rape. They receive little security, aid, or access to justice.

Gender, Sexuality, and Gender-Based Violence

Gender-based violence, including by armed groups, is widespread. Lack of training and poor implementation of treatment protocols impede timely access to medical services and create obstacles for women and girls seeking post-violence care and justice. Perpetrators of violent, gender-based crimes are rarely held accountable.

Despite many legal protections based on sexual orientation and gender identity, lesbian, gay, bisexual, and transgender people in Colombia continue to face high levels of violence and discrimination. In 2021, the organization Colombia Diversa registered attacks against 405 LGBT people in the country, including 103 cases of police violence and 205 homicides attributed to other actors. Between January and late-October 2022, the Attorney General's Office registered homicides against 111 LGBT persons.

In February, the Constitutional Court decriminalized abortion in all circumstances up to the 24th week of pregnancy, and maintained access beyond that time in cases of rape, a non-viable pregnancy, or risk to a pregnant person's health or life.

In February, the court also recognized a non-binary gender marker, the first such ruling issued by a supreme or constitutional court in the region.

Economic and Social Rights

High levels of poverty especially among Indigenous and Afro-descendant communities remain a serious human rights concern.

The 2016 peace accord established "Territorial Development Programs" (PDET) to increase the presence of state institutions in 170 municipalities highly affected by the armed conflict, poverty, and illegal economies. In 2020, the multidimensional poverty rate (32.9 percent) in these areas was nearly double the national rate (18.1 percent). Efforts to implement the PDET have been limited.

Between January and November 2022, at least 65 children under age five—the majority Indigenous Wayuu—died in La Guajira state of causes associated with malnutrition and limited access to safe drinking water.

Technology and Rights

The Education Ministry failed to act following reports that it had recommended unsafe online learning products for children during the Covid-19 pandemic. All eight products surveilled or had the capacity to surveil children online, outside of school hours, and deep into their private lives.

Climate Policy and Impacts

Colombia's national plan to reduce greenhouse gas emissions is "highly insufficient" to meet the Paris Agreement goal of limiting global warming to 1.5°C above pre-industrial levels, according to the Climate Action Tracker. The plan commits Colombia to reducing deforestation to 50,000 hectares per year by 2030. Colombia subsequently joined the Glasgow Declaration, which commits it to "halt and reverse forest loss and land degradation by 2030."

Government figures registered 174,000 hectares deforested in 2021, a 1.5 percent increase over 2020, and figures for the first trimester of 2022 show deforestation increased 10 percent compared to the same trimester in 2021. More than 9,000 hectares were razed on land officially held by Indigenous peoples, in some cases leading to their forced displacement. Roughly two-thirds of deforestation occurs in the Amazon region.

Cattle ranchers and FARC dissident groups primarily drive deforestation, pressuring residents to fell trees, extorting farmers, promoting coca crops to produce cocaine, and threatening people who defend conservation.

The former Duque government's flagship initiative to combat deforestation, Operation Artemisa, achieved limited results.

In September, the environment minister announced that, as part of a new forest conservation strategy, the government would work with communities to prevent logging and seek criminal prosecutions against people and armed groups who promote it.

Key International Actors

The US, the most influential foreign actor in Colombia, approved US$471 million in assistance for fiscal year 2022. In October, Secretary of State Antony Blinken met President Petro in Bogota and expressed his support for implementing the 2016 peace accord.

In 2016, the UN Security Council established a political mission to monitor and verify implementation of the FARC peace accord, which was succeeded in 2017 by the UN Verification Mission in Colombia. In 2022, the Security Council extended the mission's mandate until October 2023, including the verification of compliance with JEP sanctions.

President Petro and Venezuelan President Nicolás Maduro re-established diplomatic relations in August and reopened the border on September 26. President Maduro agreed in September to take part in peace negotiations between the National Liberation Army (ELN) and the Colombian government.

In early August, Colombia did not support a resolution in the Organization of Americas States (OAS) to condemn human rights violations in Nicaragua. Foreign Minister Alvaro Leyva later said that the decision was part of an effort to seek the negotiated release of political prisoners, but the Daniel Ortega government in Nicaragua seemingly rejected the request; the detainees remained behind bars, as of writing.

In September, Colombia withdrew from a "core group" of governments from across the political spectrum—Brazil, Canada, Chile, Ecuador, Guatemala, and Paraguay—that led the initiative to extend the mandate of the United Nations Fact Finding Mission on Venezuela.

Also in September, President Petro rightly criticized the "war against drugs," calling for it to end to during his speech in the United Nations General Assembly.

Cuba

The government continues to repress and punish virtually all forms of dissent and public criticism, as Cubans endure a dire economic crisis affecting their rights.

Authorities responded with brutal, systematic repression and censorship when thousands of Cubans took to the streets in July 2021 to protest the Covid-19 response, scarcity of food and medicines, and long-standing restrictions on rights. Trials of hundreds of such protesters in 2022 often violated basic due process guarantees and resulted in disproportionate prison terms.

Demonstrations across the country continued in 2022, triggered by blackouts, shortages, and deterioration of living conditions.

The government's repression and apparent unwillingness to address the underlying causes that took people to the streets have forced Cubans to leave the country in unprecedent numbers.

The United States continued a failed policy of isolation towards Cuba, including a decades-long embargo on trade with Cuba.

Arbitrary Detention and Prosecution

The government continued to employ arbitrary detention to harass and intimidate critics, independent activists, political opponents, and others.

Security officers rarely presented arrest warrants when detaining critics. Officers prevented people from attending protests, arresting critics and journalists on their way—or keeping them from leaving home.

On July 11, 2021, thousands took to the streets in the largest nationwide demonstrations against the government since the Cuban revolution. One protester, Diubis Laurencio Tejeda, a 36-year-old singer, died, seemingly at the hands of police.

Cuban rights groups counted more than 1,500 people, mostly peaceful demonstrators or bystanders, detained; more than 660 remained behind bars as of Oc-

WORLD REPORT 2023

HUMAN RIGHTS WATCH

Prison or Exile
Cuba's Systematic Repression of July 2021 Demonstrators

tober 2022. Many were periodically held incommunicado. Some suffered ill-treatment—in some cases, torture.

The government acknowledged convicting over 380 detainees, including several children, of a broad range of public order offences. Many were prosecuted in summary trials on vaguely defined charges such as "public disorder" or "contempt." Others were charged in ordinary trials with "sedition"—accused of violence such as rock-throwing—and received disproportionate prison terms of up to 25 years. Some trials were carried out in military courts, contravening international law.

Prosecutors framed as criminal behavior such actions as protesting peacefully, signing songs that criticize the government or insulting the president or police—lawful exercises of freedom of expression and association. Prosecutors and judges used unreliable or uncorroborated evidence to prosecute and convict demonstrators, including statements solely from security officers or supposed "traces" of protesters' "odor" on rocks they were accused of throwing.

Some victims and their relatives, repeatedly harassed by security forces, left Cuba.

Migration

The number of Cubans leaving their country dramatically increased in 2022, surpassing historic peaks in the 80s and 90s.

The US Border Patrol apprehended over 203,000 Cubans between January and September 2022—a dramatic increase over the 33,000 Cubans apprehended during the same period of 2021. The US Coast Guard interdicted over 6,182 Cubans at sea from October 2021 through September 2022, by far the most in five years.

Cubans who journey to the US face abuses by gangs and security forces throughout the route, particularly in the Darien Gap—at the Colombia-Panama border—and at Mexico's southern border.

After Nicaragua waived visa requirements for Cubans in late 2021, many Cubans now begin their journey there.

Travel Restrictions

Since reforms in 2013, many people previously denied permission to travel to and from Cuba have been able to do so, including human rights defenders and bloggers. The reforms, however, give the government broad discretionary power to restrict travel on grounds of "defense and national security" or "other reasons of public interest." Authorities selectively deny dissidents the ability to exit or return to the country.

On February 16, 2022, Cuban authorities denied entry to Anamely Ramos, a Cuban art curator and activist. Ramos was in the US for personal business when she decided to return to Cuba. An airline employee in Miami informed her that the Cuban government was refusing her admission. She remains in the US.

Economic, Social, and Cultural Rights

The economic crisis in Cuba, which deepened during the Covid-19 pandemic, severely impacts peoples' enjoyment of social and economic rights, including through blackouts, and acute shortages of food, medicines and other basic items.

In January 2022, authorities recognized that medicine shortages had worsened, and blamed the US embargo. The head of the state-run pharmaceutical industry group said that 88 of the 262 most needed medicines were "unavailable."

In May, authorities said that the country's energy service was in a "complex situation" that "paralyzed an important part of the economy." There were blackouts in parts of Cuba during 29 of the 31 days of July, according to official information reviewed by the news organization EFE.

In August, the Inter-American Commission on Human Rights said that Cubans were suffering a "collapse of the public healthcare system" and a "widespread rise in poverty and inequality."

Political Prisoners

Cuba was holding over 1,020 people who met the definition of political prisoners as of September, Prisoners Defenders, a Madrid-based organization said. These included 235 under house arrest or on conditional release.

Cubans who criticize the government risk prosecution. They are not guaranteed due process or a fair trial by a competent, independent, and impartial tribunal. In practice, courts are subordinate to the executive branch.

José Daniel Ferrer, leader of the Cuban Patriotic Union, the main opposition party, remained in prison as of October. In April 2020, a court in Santiago de Cuba sentenced him to four-and-a-half years of "restrictions on freedom" for alleged "assault." In July 2021, officers arrested Ferrer as he was heading to a demonstration. Charged with "public disorder" for "deciding to join" the demonstrations, he was held in pretrial detention. A Santiago de Cuba court ruled in August 2021, that Ferrer had failed to comply with the "restrictions on freedom" and sent him to prison.

In June 2022, a court in Havana convicted activists Luis Manuel Otero Alcántara and Maykel Castillo Pérez, who performed in the 2021 music video for "Motherland and Life," which repurposes the government's old slogan, "Motherland or Death" (*patria o muerte*), to criticize repression. They were prosecuted for exercising their freedom of expression, for example, by posting a meme of President Díaz Canel, and were sentenced to five-year and nine-year prison sentences, respectively.

Prison Conditions

Prisons are often overcrowded. Detainees have no effective mechanism to seek redress for abuses. Those who criticize the government or engage in hunger strikes often endure extended solitary confinement, beatings, restriction of family visits, and denial of medical care.

The government continues to deny Cuban and international human rights groups access to prisons.

In April 2020, to reduce Covid-19 risks, authorities suspended family visits. This, coupled with their refusal to allow detainees to call their families, left many people incommunicado for days, sometimes weeks.

In June 2022, the nongovernmental organizations 11J and Cubalex—citing findings of poor sanitary conditions, lack of food and medical attention, and degrading conditions—launched the campaign "Look at Cuba's prisons" to press authorities to authorize visits by international organizations and United Nations experts.

Freedom of Expression

The government controls virtually all media in Cuba, restricts access to outside information, and periodically censors critics and independent journalists.

In February and August 2021, authorities expanded the number of permitted private economic activities, yet independent journalism remained forbidden.

Journalists, bloggers, social media influencers, artists, and academics who publish information considered critical of authorities are routinely subject to harassment, violence, smear campaigns, travel restrictions, internet cuts, raids on homes and offices, confiscation of working materials, and arbitrary arrests.

Starting in 2019, authorities allowed importation of routers and other equipment, and connection of private wired and Wi-Fi internet in homes and businesses. Increased access has enabled activists to communicate, report on abuses, and organize protests. Some journalists and bloggers publish articles, videos, and news on websites and social media, including Twitter and Facebook. Yet high costs and limited access prevent most of Cubans from reading independent news.

Authorities routinely block access to many news websites within Cuba and have repeatedly imposed targeted and at times widespread restrictions on critics' access to mobile phone data. When the July 11, 2021, protests began, several organizations reported countrywide internet outages, followed by erratic connectivity, including restricted social media and messaging platforms.

In August 2021, authorities published Decree Law 35, regulating use of telecommunications and severely restricting freedom of expression online.

In May 2022, the National Assembly passed a criminal code that, among many broadly defined restrictions, includes a provision punishing with up to 10 years in prison whoever provides, receives, or has funds intended to pay for "activities against the State and its constitutional order." Such broad language opens the door to prosecutions that would undermine Cubans' right to mobilize and peacefully question government abuse.

Authorities continue to use Decree Law 370/2018—prohibiting dissemination of information "contrary to" people's "social interest, morals, good manners and integrity"—to interrogate and fine journalists and critics and confiscate their materials.

Labor Rights

Cuba has ratified International Labour Organization treaties protecting workers' rights on freedom of association and collective bargaining, yet its Labor Code, updated in 2014, violates them. While Cuba allows formation of independent unions, in practice, authorities only allow one confederation of state-controlled unions, the Workers' Central Union of Cuba.

Thousands of Cuban health workers deployed abroad provide valuable services, including in response to the Covid-19 pandemic. But the government imposes rules on them that violate their basic rights, including to privacy, liberty, movement, and freedom of expression and association.

Human Rights Defenders

The government refuses to recognize human rights monitoring as a legitimate activity and denies legal status to Cuban rights groups. Authorities have harassed, assaulted, and imprisoned human rights defenders documenting abuses.

In May, the UN Committee against Torture urged Cuba to adopt measures to prevent or stop arbitrary detentions, harassment, intimidation, threats, and discrediting of human rights defenders.

Sexual Orientation and Gender Identity

The 2019 constitution explicitly prohibits discrimination based on sexual orientation and gender identity. However, many lesbian, gay, bisexual, and transgender (LGBT) people suffer violence and discrimination, particularly in Cuba's interior.

Structural discrimination affects in different ways women, Afro-Cuban, and lesbian, gay, LGBT people, the special rapporteur on economic, social, cultural, and environmental rights of the Inter-American Commission on Human Rights said in August 2022.

In September, a new family code that included a gender-neutral definition of marriage, opening the door to same-sex marriage, was approved by referendum.

Women's Rights

Cuba decriminalized abortion in 1965. It is available and free at public hospitals.

The new family code strengthens women's and girls' rights, reinforcing sexual and reproductive rights, including the right to assisted reproduction, prohibiting domestic violence and all forms of physical punishment, and recognizing the right to equitable distribution of domestic and caretaking work among all family members.

Key International Actors

The international community has, for decades, been unable to secure sustained progress on human rights in Cuba.

The US embargo gives the Cuban government an excuse for problems, a pretext for abuses, and sympathy from governments that might otherwise condemn repressive practices. In May, the EU welcomed the US government's lifting of some restrictions.

US President Joe Biden has not lifted former President Donald Trump's re-designation of Cuba as a state sponsor of terrorism. He has repeatedly condemned abuses against protesters and imposed targeted sanctions on several officials credibly linked to repression. In May 2022, the US announced it would increase visa processing in Havana; expand authorization of professional and educational travel; increase support for Cuban entrepreneurs and remove the limit on family remittances.

During its third review of Cuba, in June, the UN Committee on the Rights of the Child expressed concerns over reports of mistreatment and arbitrary detention of children who participated in the 2021 protests.

In July, the newly elected government of Colombian President Gustavo Petro and the National Liberation Army (ELN) guerrillas announced in Havana their intention to re-start peace talks. In early October, the ELN delegation left for Venezuela and announced that negotiations would restart in November.

In November, the UN General Assembly voted overwhelmingly—185 countries in favor; the US and Israel opposed; and Brazil and Ukraine abstaining— to condemn the embargo.

Since being elected to the UN Human Rights Council in 2020—its fifth term in the past 15 years—Cuba has consistently opposed resolutions spotlighting human rights abuses, including in Russia, Ethiopia, Syria, and Nicaragua.

The European Union continued its policy of "critical engagement" with Cuba, and issued statements of concern around human rights violations by the government. Frustrated by the lack of progress on Cuba's human rights record, in December 2021 the European Parliament adopted a resolution condemning "systematic abuses" against dissidents and critics and urged the EU to consider suspending the bilateral Political Dialogue and Cooperation Agreement on human rights grounds.

Democratic Republic of Congo

The human rights and security situation in the Democratic Republic of Congo continued to deteriorate, particularly in eastern provinces. President Félix Tshisekedi's administration made little progress on promised systemic reforms to break the cycles of violence, abuse, corruption, and impunity that have plagued the country for decades.

In an atmosphere of growing intolerance for dissenting voices, repression against journalists, activists, government critics, and peaceful protesters continued.

In eastern Congo, the military rule imposed a year earlier in North Kivu and Ituri failed to curb widespread violence and atrocities by numerous armed groups against civilians. Armed groups and government forces killed more than 2,000 people between January and late October across both provinces.

Resurgent M23 rebels, backed by Rwanda, launched their biggest offensive against state forces in a decade, seizing portions of territory in North Kivu, which worsened the dire humanitarian situation in the region.

Nearly 5.6 million people were displaced across the country as of July, with more than 1.7 million in Ituri and more than 1.8 million in North-Kivu provinces alone, according to the United Nations.

An East African military force started deploying in eastern Congo in August amid regional tensions; the UN peacekeeping mission, MONUSCO, was repeatedly accused of failing to protect civilians, triggering violence and the looting of several MONUSCO bases.

Freedom of Expression, Peaceful Assembly, and Media

Freedoms of expression and association have drastically deteriorated in two eastern provinces under martial law. Initially imposed to address insecurity in the region, military authorities used it to quash peaceful demonstrations with lethal force, arbitrarily detain and prosecute activists, journalists, and political opposition members.

In January, security forces killed Mumbere Ushindi, a 22-year-old member of Lucha (*Lutte pour le changement* or Struggle for Change), a citizens' movement, during a protest against martial law in Beni. In August, 13 Lucha activists were released after nine months in detention in Beni for opposing martial law.

In April, police used excessive force to disperse a sit-in at the parliament in Kinshasa organized by political opposition supporters calling for a consensus around the electoral law, injuring at least 20 protesters.

In September, security forces used excessive force to break up a peaceful demonstration by a medical union in Kinshasa, injuring several people.

Attacks on Civilians by Armed Groups and Government Forces

Some 120 armed groups were active in eastern Congo's Ituri, North Kivu, South Kivu, and Tanganyika provinces, including several groups with fighters from neighboring Rwanda, Uganda and Burundi. Many of their commanders have been implicated in war crimes, including massacres, sexual violence, recruiting children, pillaging, and attacks on schools and hospitals.

Various armed actors, some unidentified, killed at least 2,446 civilians in South Kivu, North Kivu, and Ituri provinces, between January and late October, according to data collected by the Kivu Security Tracker, which documents violence in eastern Congo. This includes at least 155 civilians killed by Congolese security forces.

Congolese and Ugandan joint military operations against the Allied Democratic Forces (ADF), a Ugandan-led armed group with ties to the extremist armed group Islamic State (also known as ISIS), did not stop deadly attacks by the ADF against civilians in North Kivu and Ituri.

In North Kivu, the M23 rebel group attacked the positions of government troops near Goma. Responsible for widespread abuses in 2012 and 2013, including war crimes and crimes against humanity, M23 rebels deliberately killed at least 29 civilians in areas under their control in June and July, and dozens more by the end of the year.

In a confidential report to the UN Security Council that leaked to the media in August, the UN Group of Experts on Congo found "solid evidence" of Rwandan forces providing direct support to M23 fighters. Rwanda denied these accusations.

Countries of the East African Community (EAC), which Congo joined in April, agreed to set up a regional force to fight armed groups in eastern Congo.

In late April and in early December, Kenya hosted talks between the Congolese government and several armed groups aimed at securing the surrender and demobilization of fighters. The authorities failed to take several thousand surrendered fighters from various armed groups through its demobilization program, prompting many to return to armed groups.

Tensions remained high in South Kivu's highlands, with fighting involving several armed groups, some backed by neighboring countries. Burundian troops, which were conducting secret incursions since late 2021, entered South Kivu as the first deployment of the EAC force in August.

In July, violence broke out in Kwamouth in the western province of Mai-Ndombe between ethnic Teke and Yaka communities over land and customary rights. Dozens of people were reportedly killed, and thousands displaced. A high-profile government delegation visited the area in August, and Congolese soldiers were deployed to reinforce security.

Justice and Accountability

A four-year trial failed to uncover the full truth about the 2017 murders of two UN investigators, Zaida Catalán and Michael Sharp, and the fate of their Congolese interpreter, Betu Tshintela; motorbike driver, Isaac Kabuayi; and two other unidentified motorbike drivers.

On January 29, a military court in Kananga sentenced to death 49 defendants, many in absentia, on various charges including terrorism, murder, and the war crime of mutilation. An army officer, Col. Jean de Dieu Mambweni, was sentenced to 10 years in prison for disobeying orders. A local immigration officer, Thomas Nkashama, was among those sentenced to death. The prosecution failed to examine who planned and ordered the killings, ignoring information pointing to the involvement of senior Congolese officials.

In March, the government launched national consultations on a new transitional justice initiative and reaffirmed its commitment to accountability for serious crimes committed across the country. But these consultations made little progress and Tshisekedi's administration has not taken concrete steps to end impunity.

On May 11, the High Military court upheld the guilty verdicts of two senior Congolese police officers involved in the 2010 assassination of prominent human rights defender Floribert Chebeya and his driver Fidèle Bazana. Former Col. Christian Ngoy Kenga Kenga was sentenced to death—commuted to life imprisonment—and former Lt. Jacques Mugabo was sentenced to 12 years in prison. The court acquitted former Maj. Paul Mwilambwe. Although the trial represents a positive step toward justice and accountability in Congo, several individuals believed to be implicated in the assassination have yet to be prosecuted. Suspect and former head of police, Gen. John Numbi, fled the country in 2021 and was still at large at time of writing.

Little progress was made in a trial to establish culpability for the December 2018 massacres in Yumbi territory in the country's northwest in which at least 535 people were killed. The trial started in 2021.

In June, former presidential Chief of Staff Vital Kamerhe was acquitted by an appeals court after being sentenced to 20 years' imprisonment in 2020 for the embezzlement of nearly US$50 million.

In August, former staunch Tshisekedi ally and head of his political party Jean-Marc Kabund was arrested on charges of contempt of head of state. Kabund was evicted from the presidential party in July and formed his own opposition party.

Also in August, Tshisekedi's former security advisor Francois Beya was granted conditional release on health grounds. He was arrested in early February, charged with plotting against the president, and put on trial in June.

Gédéon Kyungu, a warlord responsible for atrocities in the southern region of Katanga who escaped from house arrest in Lubumbashi in March 2020, remained at large at time of writing.

Militia leader Guidon Shimiray Mwissa, wanted by Congolese authorities for serious crimes, including child recruitment and rape, remained active in North Kivu, commanding a faction of the Nduma Defense of Congo-Rénové. In May, Guidon joined a coalition of armed groups, some of them rivals, that fought alongside Congolese forces against the M23.

Environment and Human Rights

Congo's territory contains most of the world's second largest rainforest, which holds billions of tons of carbon underground and is home to Indigenous peoples.

In April, the Environment Ministry released an audit by the General Inspectorate of Finance, dated May 2021, that revealed at least six former ministers had granted illegal logging permits in violation of a nationwide moratorium. The audit also showed widespread tax avoidance by concession holders. The government suspended 12 concessions but fell short of cancelling all illegal permits.

In November, Tshisekedi signed a new law on the Protection and Promotion of the Rights of Indigenous Pygmy Peoples.

In July, the government launched an auction for licensing rights to 27 oil and 3 gas blocks, opening an estimated 11 million hectares of the rainforest to drilling. Drilling in these blocks could release up to 5.8 billion tons of carbon, more than 14 percent of the world's total greenhouse gas emissions in 2021.

Key International Actors

In June, King Philippe of Belgium visited Congo for the first time and reaffirmed his "deepest regrets" for colonial-era abuses but did not offer an apology or raise the issue of reparations. Belgian authorities returned a tooth of the murdered Congolese independence hero Patrice Lumumba to his family. The relic from the country's first prime minister was taken around Congo ahead of a funeral in Kinshasa.

In August, United States Secretary of State Antony Blinken met with President Tshisekedi in Kinshasa and pledged an additional $10 million to promote peaceful political participation and transparent elections.

In December, the European Union added eight individuals to its targeted sanctions list (freezing of financial assets and travel bans), bringing to 17 the number of people, including senior officials, subjected to restrictive measures. The same month, the UN Security Council extended MONUSCO's mandate for one year.

Ecuador

Insecurity is a top concern for many Ecuadorians. The homicide rate had increased to nearly 16 per 100,000 citizens, as of October. In response to gang violence, the government in August declared the fourth state of emergency since October 2021.

Overcrowding and lack of state control in Ecuador's prisons have enabled detained gang members to commit several massacres nationwide since 2021, killing around 400 detainees.

Anti-government protests in June highlighted longstanding structural problems impacting Indigenous communities and households in poverty. Demonstrators protested inadequate access to health care, education, and employment, and removal of fuel subsidies. Security forces responded with abuses at times, and violence by protesters—or infiltrators—erupted.

Weak rule of law, alleged corruption, lack of enforcement of Indigenous peoples' rights, restrictions on access to abortion, and limited protection of children and lesbian, gay, bisexual, and transgender (LGBT) people remained serious concerns.

Prison Conditions and Killings

Poor prison conditions, including overcrowding, contributed to a string of gang-related mass killings. Between February 2021 and October 2022, nine massacres left approximately 400 detainees dead and dozens injured. Human Rights Watch documented insufficient steps to stop the killings, including an eight-hour delay before police entered a Guayaquil prison during a November 12, 2021, massacre.

As of August, nobody had been convicted for participating in any of the 2022 massacres.

Overcrowding appears to be rooted in excessive use of pretrial detention, harsh drug policies and delays in granting benefits. Prison guards are poorly trained and insufficient to contain violence.

In February, the government adopted a policy to improve prison conditions and detainees' access to basic services. In April, it initiated a process to hire and train 1,400 guards.

In June, a commission of experts convened by the president to reform the prison system released its final report, concluding that Ecuador's prisons are "punishment warehouses" rather than centers for rehabilitation.

Ecuador's government has not kept accurate data on the number and identity of detainees. A census to collect socio-demographic information on the prison population started on August 22.

Use of Force by Security Forces

In Quito and Guayaquil, police responded to peaceful demonstrations commemorating International Women's Day, March 8, with excessive force, including indiscriminate use of teargas and pepper spray.

During anti-government protests starting June 13, police responded several times with excessive force, shooting teargas canisters directly at demonstrators or close to areas sheltering children and injured people. Protests began peacefully but turned violent. Demonstrators blamed provocateurs for vandalism, looting, and blocking medical deliveries to hospitals. Six civilians and one member of the military died, and over 300 people suffered injuries, Ecuadorian human rights groups and media reported. In one case, the government confirmed a death by teargas canister impact.

On August 22, a law took effect prohibiting security forces from using excessive, arbitrary, or illegitimate force, and stressing that the use of force should follow principles of legality, necessity, proportionality, precaution, humanity, non-discrimination and accountability. The law allows use of lethal weapons only under threat of severe injury or death.

Rule of Law and Anti-Corruption Efforts

Democratic institutions damaged under former President Rafael Correa (2007-2017) remain fragile, amid allegations of corruption, interference in the appointment of authorities, and politically motivated removal of authorities prior to the end of their term. Several reforms improved the independence of key judicial institutions. But reports of trial delays, lack of due process and improper pressure on courts continued.

Rights of Indigenous Peoples

On June 30, officials and Indigenous leaders reached an agreement to stop the protests organized in response to authorities' perceived unwillingness to address structural problems. Protesters' demands included guaranteeing Indigenous peoples' collective rights and access to health, education, and employment; lowering the prices of food and other essential goods; and repairing the social and environmental impacts of mining and oil extraction in Indigenous territories.

The 90-day dialogue between government and Indigenous groups to discuss the issues that prompted the protests concluded on October 14 with over 120 agreements.

Many Indigenous communities have long-opposed oil development in the Amazon. In January, the Heavy Crude Oil Pipeline ruptured, affecting areas of the Cayambe Coca National Park. Contaminated water reached dozens of Indigenous Kichwa communities. The company and government started a cleanup, and authorities began an investigation into the cause and environmental impact.

That same month, the Constitutional Court ruled Indigenous communities must be consulted on extractive projects that could affect their lands, and that only in exceptional circumstances can officials authorize projects without the community's consent.

In September, the government declared a temporary moratorium on 15 extraction areas and said it will grant no further mining concessions until a law regulating consultation processes is approved.

At time of writing, the Inter-American Court of Human Rights was considering its first case on Indigenous communities in voluntary isolation. The Tagaeri and Taromenane ethnic groups sued Ecuador for harming their territories, natural resources, and way of life, and for failing to prevent violent deaths of community members. Ecuador has accepted partial responsibility, including for failing to investigate the deaths.

Women's Rights

A Constitutional Court ruling in 2021 decriminalized abortion in rape cases, setting in motion an effort to amend legislation accordingly.

President Guillermo Lasso, in March, partially vetoed an abortion bill. Legislators accepted his proposed restrictions on access, including short deadlines, broad conscientious objection, and unreasonable requirements like first reporting rapes to authorities. The amended law entered into force in April.

The Constitutional Court provisionally suspended measures requiring raped girls to obtain a legal representative's authorization for abortion. At time of writing, a final decision was pending.

Stigmatization, mistreatment, fear of criminal prosecution, and a narrow interpretation of the health exception to the general abortion ban remain barriers to access.

The Attorney General's Office reported 53 femicides—murders of women deemed gender related—between January and August. Civil society organizations reported an increase in all killings of women compared to previous years; over 200 as of September.

Disability Rights

On September 16, complying with an Inter-American Court of Human Rights ruling, Ecuador publicly recognized its responsibility for the disappearance of Luis Eduardo Guachalá Chimbo, a 23-year-old with a mental health condition. Guachalá disappeared from a hospital in 2004, and Ecuador did not fulfill its obligation to search for him, the court found. The ruling established standards on informed consent, legal capacity and supported decision making for people with disabilities.

Children's Rights

Sexual violence is a longstanding problem in public and private schools. Nearly 30 percent of over 14,000 reports of sexual violence that Ecuador's Ministry of Education registered between January 2014 and April 2022 happened in schools. Publicly reported cases probably represent only a fraction of cases. Many survivors face re-traumatization at school and barriers to accessing justice.

Human Rights Watch research found that Educa Contigo, an Education Ministry website launched during the Covid-19 pandemic, collected and transmitted children's personal data to third-party companies, enabling them to track and target children for advertising purposes.

Sexual Orientation and Gender Identity

The National Assembly has yet to comply with Constitutional Court orders to revise civil marriage provisions to include same-sex couples; to allow self-determination in gender recognition procedures; to regulate assisted reproduction methods; and to allow same-sex couples to register children with their surnames.

The constitution discriminates against same-sex couples by excluding them from access to adoption.

Refugees, Asylum Seekers, and Migrants

From January to July 2022, Ecuador recognized 1,857 people as refugees. As of September, the country was sheltering more than 500,000 Venezuelan migrants and refugees. Most asylum seekers are Venezuelan.

President Lasso decreed a year-long regularization process for Venezuelans, starting September 1. Those with irregular status who entered through official border checkpoints before June 1 can receive temporary visas lasting two years, with an option to extend for a third.

Freedom of Expression

During June protests, the non-governmental organization Fundamedios documented physical and verbal attacks by, mainly, protesters against 114 journalists, 40 cameramen and 80 media outlets.

On October 3, the Constitutional Court ruled some provisions of a communications bill restricted the right to freedom of expression, partially agreeing with an August veto by Lasso. At time of writing, the bill has not entered into force.

Key International Actors and Foreign Policy

The Inter-American Commission on Human Rights (IACHR) released a report, in March, describing longstanding government abandonment of the prison system. In May, a spokesperson for the United Nations High Commissioner for Human Rights reiterated deep alarm at recurring prison violence.

On June 9, Ecuador was elected as a non-permanent member of the UN Security Council starting in January 2023.

On June 10, Ecuador signed the Los Angeles Declaration on Migration and Protection, committing to strengthening and expanding paths toward safe, legal migration and asylum.

During the June protests, the IACHR and its special rapporteur for freedom of expression expressed concern about attacks against journalists and violence. The UN Committee on the Rights of the Child expressed concern over security force violence against children, including indiscriminate use of tear gas.

Ecuador condemned Russia's invasion of Ukraine and human rights violations in Venezuela. After sham elections in Nicaragua, it did not send a delegation to Daniel Ortega's inauguration.

Ecuador and five other countries in the region led the renewal, in October, of the UN Independent International Fact-Finding Mission on Venezuela.

Egypt

September 2022 marked one year since the Egyptian government launched the national human rights strategy, but authorities took few if any steps to ease the wholesale campaign of repression against critics or repeal any of the numerous laws that are routinely used to curtail basic freedoms. While authorities released hundreds of detainees in a piecemeal manner, they arrested many others and re-arrested some of those released. Thousands remain unjustly detained for their peaceful activism.

President Abdel Fattah al-Sisi declared 2022 the "year of civil society," but key members of civil society continued to face arbitrary travel bans, asset freezes, and criminal investigations in retaliation for their peaceful activism or criticism.

Egypt faced an intensifying economic crisis in 2022, which increasingly impacted access to food and other socioeconomic rights, while the government negotiated yet another loan agreement with the International Monetary Fund.

Abuses by Police and Security Forces

Interior Ministry police and National Security agents continued to forcibly disappear opponents in unofficial detention places where detainees are subjected to torture and forced confessions.

On January 12, security forces disappeared Hossam Menoufy, a supporter of the Muslim Brotherhood, after a plane carrying him from Khartoum to Istanbul made an unscheduled landing in Luxor. Although Egypt's Interior Ministry said in a January 15 statement that Menoufy was detained and under investigation, authorities refused to respond to questions about his whereabouts.

Authorities failed to investigate incidents of torture and mistreatment, which remained widespread. In May 2022, Egypt's Supreme State Security head prosecutor, Khaled Diaa, referred for mass trial a group of detainees who had appeared in two leaked videos, published by the *Guardian,* showing them in a Cairo police station with wounds that appeared to be the result of torture. The alleged police perpetrators faced no serious investigation.

On April 10, police informed economist Ayman Hadhoud's family that he had died in custody after being forcibly disappeared in February 2022. Egyptian authorities failed to conduct an independent, effective, and transparent investigation into Hadhoud's suspicious death in custody and ignored mounting evidence that the authorities forcibly disappeared, tortured, and otherwise ill-treated him, and denied him access to timely and adequate health care.

War in North Sinai

In April, President al-Sisi indicated in a public speech that the ongoing military operations in North Sinai, involving mainly the army against the local extremist armed group Islamic State (also known as ISIS) affiliate Wilayat Sina,' were drawing to a close, stating, "The issue has ended."

But in July and August, videos and photographs circulated on social media by groups representing army-affiliated militias showed three extrajudicial executions of shackled or wounded men in custody in North Sinai. A Human Rights Watch analysis of these videos verified their authenticity. The analysis indicated that members of both the militias and the army itself were responsible for the killings.

According to media and human rights reports, army-affiliated militias comprised of members of local clans trained and supported by the army were increasingly involved in fighting in North Sinai in 2022.

The government allowed some families to return to their lands in late 2021 and early 2022. The Egyptian army has led a massive demolitions campaign that included destroying over 12,300 buildings from 2013 to July 2020 without upholding its human rights obligations on forced evictions. Many of these demolitions lacked evidence of "absolute" military necessity, likely making them war crimes. Hundreds of families remain uncompensated.

Prison Conditions and Deaths in Custody

The dire conditions in Egyptian prisons and detention centers remained shielded from independent oversight or monitoring in 2022, despite government public relations campaigns touting the opening of new prisons.

In February, prison officials refused multiple requests by prominent dissident Salah Soltan to see an independent doctor and to obtain the necessary medication and medical equipment. Authorities' denial of health care and other ill-treatment appears to be in retaliation for his son Mohamed's advocacy in the US. In September, Soltan was moved from the notorious Scorpion prison to the new Badr Complex in eastern Cairo. He told his family that authorities continued to hold him in solitary confinement and that an officer told him he would only leave prison as a "dead body." Like many other inmates of Badr prison, he is exposed to fluorescent lights 24 hours a day and has CCTV surveillance cameras inside his cell.

Authorities continued to deny unjustly detained Egyptian-British blogger and political activist Alaa Abdel Fattah consular access and visits by his lawyer. Abdel Fattah ended his hunger strike in mid-November.

According to a joint report released in April by the Egyptian Front for Human Rights and the Freedom Initiative, Egyptian security forces and prison staff were found to employ systematic sexual violence to degrade and torture detainees including men, women, transmen, and transwomen.

At National Security Agency sites, detainees, who are usually victims of enforced disappearances, could be raped, molested, electrocuted on their genitals, or threatened with sexual violence against them or their relatives to coerce confessions. Female prisoners were particularly subject to sexual violence in prisons, where guards would often assault them while carrying out "cavity searches."

Denial of Fair Trials, Due Process

In February 2022, the president confirmed prison sentences imposed on activist Alaa Abd al Fattah, Mohamed al-Baqer, a human rights lawyer, and Mohamed "Oxygen" Ibrahim, a blogger. The decisions were handed down by extraordinary Emergency State Security Courts and are not subject to appeal.

Judges and prosecutors routinely remanded thousands of detainees in custody without presenting evidence. Three Egyptian activists began hunger strikes on February 10 and 11, 2022, to protest their indefinite pretrial detention. When judges issued release orders for the three, prosecutors "recycled" them to different cases to circumvent the two-year limit on pretrial detention in Egyptian law.

Freedom of Association, Attacks on Human Rights Defenders

President al-Sisi has called for a national dialogue with elements of the country's political opposition in May for the first time since he assumed power in 2014. However, the dialogue at time of writing had produced no concrete policies to improve in the human rights situation in Egypt.

Authorities continued to use arbitrary travel bans to target key members of civil society for their peaceful work, including rights lawyers, journalists, feminists, and researchers. The virtually indefinite bans, which authorities usually do not formally announce and provide no clear way to challenge them in court, have separated families, damaged careers, and harmed the mental health of those subjected to them. Some of those civil society members faced asset freezes that have locked them out of the banking system.

In January 2022, The Arab Network for Human Rights Information (ANHRI), one of Egypt's leading independent human rights organizations, announced that it was ending operations after nearly 18 years. The group was forced to close due to a series of threats, violent attacks, and arrests by the National Security Agency, as well as the looming deadline requiring all nongovernmental organizations (NGOs) to register under the draconian associations law.

Authorities worked to utilize the hosting of the United Nations Climate Change Conference (COP27) to whitewash the country's human rights abuses, even though the government has imposed arbitrary funding, research, and registration obstacles that have debilitated local environmental groups, forcing some activists into exile and others to steer clear of important work.

As a result, environmental groups' ability to carry out independent policy, advocacy, and field work was largely restricted. They are barred from studying the impact on local communities and the environmental toll of fossil fuel operations. They are also barred from determining the impact of Egypt's vast and opaque military business activity, such as destructive forms of quarrying, water bottling plants, and some cement factories, as well as "national" infrastructure projects (such as a new administrative capital) associated with the president's office or the military.

Freedom of Expression and Assembly

In April 2022, authorities arrested TV presenter Hala Fahmy and journalist Safaa al-Korbagy apparently in response to their criticism of the National Broadcasting Authority. Both remained in pretrial detention at time of writing.

On March 28, a court sentenced two singers to a year in prison and fines on vague charges of "violating family values in Egyptian society and profiting from a video including dancing and singing." The charges stemmed from an October 2020 video showing the two men singing and dancing along with a female Brazilian belly dancer.

In September, prosecutors summoned three *Mada Masr* journalists, as well as the chief editor, and charged them with "spreading false news" over a news article about the Nation's Future Party, the pro-government party that holds a majority in parliament. The chief editor was also charged with operating unlicensed news site.

Authorities continued to block access to hundreds of news and human rights websites without judicial orders.

Refugees and Asylum Seekers

During 2022, Egyptian authorities and security forces subjected refugees and asylum seekers to arbitrary detention, physical abuse, and refoulement—forced returns to a country where individuals may face threats to their lives or freedom, torture, or other serious harm. Egypt is a party to the 1951 UN and 1969 African (OAU) refugee conventions and the 1984 Convention against Torture, which prohibit refoulement.

In December 2021 and January 2022, Egyptian police arbitrarily detained at least 30 Sudanese refugees and asylum seekers during raids, subjecting some to forced physical labor and beatings. Detained refugees and asylum seekers were kept in overcrowded rooms and denied adequate food and medical care.

In March, authorities deported 31 Eritreans, including 8 children, after detaining them in poor conditions and denying them access to the UN High Commissioner for Refugees (UNHCR) to lodge asylum claims, according to the Refugees Platform in Egypt. These summary deportations of Eritrean asylum seekers, which followed similar prior deportations during late 2021, violated the international legal prohibition on refoulement.

Women's Rights, Gender Identity, Sexual Orientation

In 2022, Egypt witnessed a spate of heinous killings of women by men including a judge who killed his second wife and mutilated her body before secretly burying her, and a male student who stabbed to death a female fellow student in front of Mansoura University when she refused his marriage proposal. The government has failed for years to enact laws and policies to seriously address violence against women.

Sexual violence remains a pervasive problem in Cairo and other cities. Refugees and asylum seekers, particularly black Africans, live in vulnerable communities where they face assault and rape and the authorities fail to provide them protection, and impede access to justice as police refuse to register survivors' complaints or pursue investigations.

In Egypt, married students who are pregnant or are mothers are reportedly only able to continue their education through homeschooling. Students who become pregnant outside of marriage do not generally receive the same support and encouragement to continue their education at home.

Authorities in Egypt have undermined lesbian, gay, bisexual, and transgender (LGBT) people's right to privacy with digital targeting, namely entrapment on social media and dating applications, online harassment and "outing," online extortion, monitoring social media, and reliance on illegitimately obtained digital evidence in prosecutions.

Human Rights Watch documented cases where security forces have used digital targeting, based on "debauchery" provisions and the Cybercrime Law, to entrap LGBT people, arbitrarily arrest and detain them based on digital evidence found on their personal devices, and ill-treat them in police custody.

Social and Economic Rights

Russia's full-scale invasion of Ukraine had serious impacts on the already-deteriorating economic situation in Egypt, where nearly one-third of the population lives under the national poverty line. Egypt is among the world's largest importers of wheat, 80 percent of which comes from Russia and Ukraine. Egypt also imports over half of its sunflower oil from Ukraine, and the government had already reduced subsidies for sunflower and soybean oil by 20 percent in June 2021 in response to an increase in prices. Trade disruptions caused by the war have increased prices for these basic commodities, limiting access to food for the nation's poorest and most vulnerable populations.

In March, Egyptian authorities requested support from the International Monetary Fund to help mitigate the economic fallout related to Russia's invasion of Ukraine. After months of negotiations, a six-month, US$3 billion program was announced in October. Rights groups have voiced strong concerns in previous years around the lack of emphasis on the need for the Egyptian government to expand social protection, strengthen judicial independence, and address corruption and the need for transparency.

Key International Actors

On September 15, the United States withheld US$130 million of $300 million in Fiscal Year 2021 Foreign Military Financing to Egypt that was conditioned on human rights progress, out of a total of $1.3 billion in annual US security assistance. Congress withheld an additional $75 million in October.

The European Union presented a joint bid with Egypt in early 2022 to co-lead the Global Counter-Terrorism Forum (GCTF), a multilateral platform with far-reaching influence on global counterterrorism policy, despite Egypt's abhorrent record of human rights violations in the name of counterterrorism. In April 2022, GCTF approved the chairmanship of Egypt and the EU of the forum.

In August, the European Commission confirmed that the EU planned to allocate €80 million (around $82.3 million) in 2022 and 2023 to provide equipment and services to Egyptian authorities "in support of border management," including "search and rescue and border surveillance at land and sea borders," despite the country's dire human rights record and the impact the EU funding would have in impeding Egyptians' right to leave.

Many European countries such as France and Italy continued to export weapons to Egypt, despite the country's rights record.

In February, President al-Sisi attended the EU-AU summit in Brussels, receiving little if any public criticism by European leaders. In June, the EU and Egypt endorsed their 2021-27 partnership priorities at the bilateral Association Council meeting. The document refers to an allegedly "shared commitment to the universal values of democracy, the rule of law and the respect of human rights," but fails to acknowledge the deep human rights crisis in Egypt. In November, the European Parliament adopted a damning resolution on human rights in Egypt reiterating its call for a "profound and comprehensive review" of the EU's relations with the country.

In September, two NGOs filed complaints in France urging judicial authorities to investigate France's alleged involvement in a secret Egyptian military operation on the Libyan border on the basis that it involved acts amounting to crimes against humanity.

El Salvador

President Nayib Bukele and his majority in the Legislative Assembly have systematically dismantled democratic checks and balances. In September, he announced he would seek re-election in 2024, despite a constitutional prohibition on immediate re-election.

In March, the National Assembly declared a state of emergency and suspended basic rights in response to gang violence. Authorities committed widespread human rights violations, including mass arbitrary detention, enforced disappearances, ill-treatment in detention, and due process violations.

Gangs continue to exercise control over some neighborhoods and extort residents. They forcibly recruit children and sexually abuse women, girls, and lesbian, gay, bisexual, and transgender (LGBT) people. They kill, disappear, rape, or displace those who resist.

Judicial Independence

Since taking office in 2019, President Bukele and his allies have taken steps to effectively co-opt democratic institutions.

In May 2021, Bukele's two-thirds majority in the Assembly summarily removed and replaced all five judges on the Supreme Court's Constitutional Chamber and the attorney general.

In June 2021, the Assembly appointed five new judges to the Supreme Court for a total of 10 out of 15 Supreme Court judges, although under the law each newly elected legislature is allowed to appoint only five judges to the court.

In September 2021, lawmakers passed laws allowing the Supreme Court and the attorney general to dismiss judges and prosecutors over 60 years of age and expanding their power to transfer judges and prosecutors to new posts. The laws have been used to abusively dismiss or transfer independent judges or prosecutors.

Also in September, the Supreme Court's Constitutional Chamber ruled that the constitution allowed for immediate presidential re-election, although it had been consistently interpreted to forbid immediate re-election.

A Bukele administration-sponsored overhaul to the constitution, which would reform the courts and other bodies, remained pending at time of writing.

Gang Violence

Gangs continued to forcibly recruit children and sexually assault, kill, abduct, rape, and displace people. For decades, the response by authorities has oscillated between obscure negotiations with gangs and iron fist security policies that have led to rights violations.

Violence in areas controlled by gangs drives internal displacement. The Office of the United Nations High Commissioner for Refugees in 2021 reported 71,500 internally displaced people. More than 153,000 Salvadorans sought asylum in other countries, mostly the US, in 2021.

El Faro, a prestigious digital news outlet, reported that, before being fired in 2021, former Attorney General Raúl Melara had been investigating negotiations between the Bukele administration and the country's three largest gangs. According to El Faro, the government offered members prison privileges and employment opportunities in exchange for lowering the homicide rate.

Between March 24 and 27, 92 people were killed in El Salvador, seemingly by gangs; the highest homicide number in years, which led to authorities' state of emergency declaration. According to El Faro, the wave of violence in March was triggered by the collapse of government negotiations with the MS-13 gang. Nobody had been convicted of the killings as of September.

The government reported that there were no homicides during many days of 2022, but authorities have told journalists that the aggregated data on homicides is "classified." The official homicide rate declined from about 36 per 100,000 in 2019 to 17 per 100,000 in 2021. In July 2019, the government changed the way killings are counted, excluding cases in which police officers were reported to have killed alleged gang members in confrontations.

HUMAN RIGHTS WATCH

"We Can Arrest Anyone We Want"
Widespread Human Rights Violations Under El Salvador's "State of Emergency"

Abuses During the State of Emergency

In March 2022, the Legislative Assembly adopted for 30 days a state of emergency that suspends some basic rights. Legislators had extended the measure six times and it remained in place at time of writing.

Also in March, legislators approved gang-related legislation that allows authorities to imprison children as young as 12 and expands the use of pretrial detention.

Over 55,000 people were detained under the state of emergency between late March and mid-October, authorities report. Many arrests appear to have been based on the appearance or social background of the detainees, and local human rights groups have documented that hundreds of people with no connection to gangs have been detained.

Human rights organizations, including Cristosal and Human Rights Watch, have documented serious abuses by security forces during the state of emergency, including arbitrary arrests, enforced disappearances, torture and other forms of ill-treatment, and due process violations.

Cristosal reported over 2,900 cases of human rights violations during the state of emergency.

Over 45,000 people arrested during the state of emergency went into pre-trial detention, contributing to prison populations increasing to an estimated 84,000 detainees, over three times official capacity. Historically poor conditions in detention—overcrowding, violence, and poor access to such services as food and drinking water—worsened.

Over 80 detainees died in prison, local rights groups reported. In some cases, authorities have failed to conduct autopsies or else follow internationally accepted medical and legal standards.

Disappearances

The Attorney General's Office registered more than 28,000 complaints of missing people between January 2005 and August 2021. This is more than the estimated 8,000 to 10,000 disappeared during the 12-year civil war that ended in 1992. Between January and May 2022, Foundation Studies for the Application of Law (FESPAD), a local nongovernmental organization, counted 500 disappearances registered by the National Civil Police. Perpetrators include gangs and security forces. Accountability in these cases is rare.

Transparency and Anti-Corruption

At the time of his removal, in May 2021, Attorney General Melara was investigating six government officials for alleged corruption regarding funds allocated for Covid-19.

In June 2021, the new Attorney General, Rodolfo Delgado, ended a cooperation agreement with the International Commission Against Impunity in El Salvador (CICIES), a body backed by the Organization of American States (OAS) to fight corruption.

In January 2022, the Attorney General's Office raided the offices of prosecutors who had, under Melara, been investigating allegations of corruption and officials' negotiations with gangs. Four prosecutors fled the country, fearing persecution.

The Bukele administration has weakened the role of the Access to Public Information Agency including by changing the agency's regulations in ways that undermine its autonomy and by dismissing one of its members.

Prosecutors in 2017 charged former President Mauricio Funes (2009-2014), living in Nicaragua since 2016, with offenses involving corruption, embezzlement, and money laundering. Nicaraguan President Daniel Ortega granted Funes Nicaraguan citizenship in 2021.

Freedom of Expression

The government has created a hostile environment for the media.

The Association of Journalists of El Salvador (APES) reported 421 "press freedom violations" between 2019 and 2021, including physical attacks, digital harassment, and restrictions on journalists' work and access to public information. APES also reported that nine journalists fled the country fearing harassment and arbitrary arrests.

In January 2022, Citizen Lab and Access Now reported that Pegasus spyware had been used to hack the mobile phones of at least 35 Salvadoran journalists and civil society members, including 22 reporters from El Faro.

In April, the Legislative Assembly passed an overly broad law establishing new criminal offenses carrying prison sentences of up to 15 years for journalists who reproduce messages by gangs.

The Bukele administration proposed a "foreign agents" law, in November 2021, requiring individuals and organizations that "directly or indirectly" receive funding from abroad to register as "foreign agents." In August 2022, the speaker of the government's party, Christian Guevara, said authorities would use it, once passed, to punish El Faro.

Accountability for Past Abuses

Impunity for abuses committed during the country's civil war (1980-1992) remains the norm.

Nobody has been sentenced for the 1981 massacre in El Mozote village, in which a US-trained battalion killed 978 civilians, including 553 children, and raped and tortured many victims. A trial of former military commanders accused in the massacre started in 2016. In 2021, Jorge Guzmán, the judge in the criminal case against the alleged perpetrators of the massacre, was ousted and the trial stalled.

Women and Girls' Sexual and Reproductive Rights

Abortion is illegal under all circumstances.

Many women have been convicted, and in some cases sentenced to decades, in prison, on related charges, including after miscarriages or obstetric emergencies. In June 2022, a court sentenced a woman who suffered an obstetric emergency to 50 years in prison for "aggravated homicide."

Between September 2021 and September 2022, courts released six women who had served 6 to 13 years in prison on charges of abortion, homicide, or aggravated homicide.

El Salvador officially ratified the International Labour Organization Convention on Violence and Harassment (C190), after the Legislative Assembly ratified it in May 2022. The treaty obligates El Salvador to provide comprehensive protections to ensure a world of work free from violence and harassment, including gender-based violence and sexual harassment."

Disability Rights

El Salvador's legislative framework remains inconsistent with international disability rights law, with restrictions on legal capacity for people with intellectual and psychosocial disabilities—and insufficient measures to improve physical and communications access.

Sexual Orientation and Gender Identity

Lesbian, gay, bisexual, and transgender (LGBT) people remain targets of homophobic and transphobic violence by police, gangs, and the general public. In many cases, LGBT people are forced to flee the country, and often seek safety in the United States.

In February 2022, the Supreme Court ordered the Legislative Assembly to create, within one year, a procedure for transgender people to change their names on identity documents. Legislators had not begun discussions as of September 2022. Meanwhile, transgender people continue to experience discrimination due to a mismatch between their gender and their identity documents, including in the ambits of health, employment, voting, and banking.

Key International Actors

For fiscal year 2022, the US appropriated over US$66 million in bilateral aid to El Salvador, particularly to reduce extreme violence and strengthen state institutions. The US Congress prohibited Foreign Military Financing to El Salvador and, in 2021, the United States Agency for International Development redirected assistance away from the National Police and the Institute for Access to Public Information and towards civil society groups.

WORLD REPORT 2023

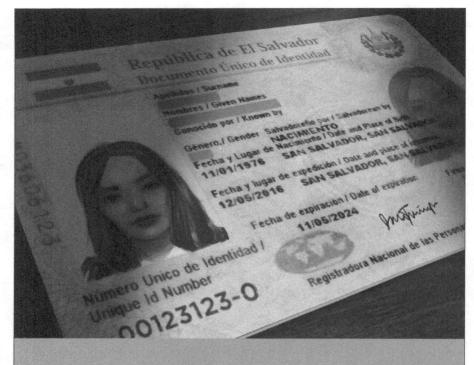

"We Just Want to Live Our Lives"
El Salvador's Need for Legal Gender Recognition

In July 2022, the administration of US President Joe Biden added six Salvadorans to the 19 already on the "Engel List" of individuals engaged in "significant corruption" or acts that "undermine democratic processes." They included President Bukele's legal advisor and press secretary, and the speaker of his party.

In March 2022, UN Secretary-General Antonio Guterres expressed concern about soaring violence in El Salvador and asked authorities to address it with measures "in line with international human rights law and standards."

In April 2022, the Office of the UN High Commissioner for Human Rights expressed concern over the Salvadoran government's response to gang violence, including arrests without warrants, reports of ill-treatment, and amendments to the criminal code.

In June, six United Nations experts expressed "serious concerns" over allegations of abuses committed during the state of emergency, including enforced disappearances and a "pattern" of arbitrary arrests.

In March 2021, El Salvador announced it was re-negotiating a US$1.3 billion loan with the International Monetary Fund (IMF). Negotiations have been stalled, apparently due to El Salvador's adoption in September 2021 of bitcoin as legal tender and concerns over the weakening of judicial independence and the reduction of transparency and accountability. The Inter-American Development Bank approved $1.3 billion in funds for El Salvador for 2021-2024 and, in 2021, the Central American Bank of Economic Integration approved an $8,884.7 million loan—its largest to any country in the region.

Eritrea

Eritrea's government continued to severely repress its population, imposing restrictions on freedom of expression, opinion, and faith, and restricting independent scrutiny by international monitors. Eritrea continued to negatively impact the rights environment in the Horn of Africa region.

Eritrea is a one-man dictatorship under unelected President Isaias Afewerki, with no legislature, no independent civil society organizations or media outlets, and no independent judiciary. In 2001, Isaias closed all independent newspapers and arrested 10 journalists held incommunicado to date. Elections have never been held in the country since it gained independence in 1993, and the government has never implemented the 1997 constitution guaranteeing civil rights and limiting executive power.

The government has taken no steps to end its widespread forced labor and conscription, instead, reports of mass roundups (*giffas* in Tigrinya) and forced conscription to fill the army's ranks increased in the second half of the year as fighting resumed in Ethiopia's Tigray region. In September, it reportedly recalled reservists (up to the age of 55) in anticipation of renewed fighting alongside Ethiopian security forces in Tigray.

Eritrean forces remained in parts of Ethiopia's Tigray region where they have continued to commit serious violations, including mass arbitrary detentions, and pillage and rape of Tigrayans in Western Tigray zone.

The Africa Centres for Disease Control and Prevention (CDC) did not report any information on vaccination campaigns in Eritrea.

Eritrea was re-elected, in late 2021 to the United Nations Human Rights Council on an African group non-competitive slate. However, this did not result in reforms of its oppressive policies, according to the UN special rapporteur on the situation of human rights in Eritrea.

Eritrea continued to refuse to cooperate with key UN and African Union rights mechanisms, including by denying access to the UN special rapporteur. In December 2021, it opposed the establishment of a commission of human rights experts on Ethiopia (ICHREE) to investigate abuses by all parties in the Tigray conflict.

Eritrea's 2015 penal code punishes homosexual conduct with five to seven years in prison.

Indefinite Military Conscription and Forced Labor

The government continued to conscript Eritreans, mostly men and unmarried women, indefinitely into military or civil service for low pay and with no say in their profession or work location. Conscientious objection is not recognized; it is punished. Discharge from national service is arbitrary and procedures opaque. Conscripts are often subjected to inhuman and degrading punishment, including torture, without recourse.

Since Eritrea joined the war in Ethiopia's Tigray region, new waves of mass roundups of Eritreans believed to be evading service to fill the army's ranks have been regularly reported, which have included child recruitment according to the UN special rapporteur on Eritrea. Roundups increased in August and September as fighting resumed in Ethiopia; families of draft evaders also faced reprisals, including arbitrary detentions and evictions from their homes. In September, the media said that reservists, men 55 years old and below who had been discharged from the army but were still expected to undergo guard duties, were also being called up. Families are not given official information about the fate of their loved ones sent to fight in Tigray.

Conscription begins at the Sawa military camp where students, some as young as 16, are forced to attend their final year of secondary school while undergoing compulsory military training. Students in the camp are under military command, with harsh military punishments and discipline, and female students have reported sexual harassment and exploitation. Dormitories are crowded and health facilities very limited.

Unlawful, Prolonged, and Abusive Detentions

There continued to be widespread mass roundups and prolonged arbitrary arrests and detentions without access to legal counsel, judicial review, or family visits, some for decades, targeting perceived government's opponents, including draft evaders.

Countless prisoners languish in the country's extensive formal and informal prison network, held in overcrowded places of detention with inadequate food, water, and medical care.

Many detainees, including top government officials and journalists arrested in 2001 after they questioned Isaias's leadership, are held incommunicado. Some are believed to have died in detention. An additional 16 journalists were also arrested at the time. Ciham Ali Abdu, daughter of a former information minister, has been held for 10 years since her arrest at age 15. Former finance minister and critic of the president, Berhane Abrehe, has been in incommunicado detention since September 2018.

Freedom of Religion

For over two decades, the government has denied religious liberty to anyone whose religious affiliation does not match the four denominations that the government "recognizes": Sunni Islam, Eritrean Orthodox, Roman Catholic, and Evangelical (Lutheran) churches. People affiliated with "unrecognized" faiths continue to be imprisoned, and torture has been used to force them to renounce their religion.

The trend of releases that took place in 2020 and 2021 was reversed. People continue to be detained purely because of their religious beliefs. In March, 29 Christians were reportedly detained during a prayer meeting in Asmara and taken to the Mai Serwa prison. Twenty Jehovah Witnesses remained in detention since at least 2014, including Tesfazion Gebremichael, 80, detained since 2011.

Between October 11 and 15, the Eritrean government detained three Catholic priests, Abba Abraham Habtom Gebremariam, Father Mihretab Stefanos, and Bishop Abune Fikremariam Hagos. Abune Hagos who was arrested as he returned to Eritrea from Italy, had in 2019 penned, along with three other bishops, a pastoral letter obliquely calling for justice and reform. In February, Abune Antonios, the deposed Eritrean Orthodox Church patriarch, died while under house arrest, to which he had been subjected since 2006.

The government continued to take control of schools and other institutions run by the Catholic church. In August, media reported that the government planned to take over two Catholic-run vocational training centers. Some peaceful protesters arrested in 2017 and early 2018 for protesting the government takeover of Al Diaa Islamic school, remained in detention.

Refugees and Returnees

Eritrea is not a party to the 1951 UN Refugee Convention and has not ratified the 1969 African Refugee Convention.

There were over 580,000 Eritrean refugees and asylum seekers abroad as of the end 2021, and "the overwhelming majority cited the indefinite national service as the principal reason they fled the country," according to the May 2022 report of the UN special rapporteur on the situation of human rights in Eritrea.

Eritreans seeking protection abroad have been targeted for abuses by Eritrean authorities and security forces, both while abroad (in Ethiopia), and after forced returns from other countries, such as Egypt.

Since the outbreak of conflict in Tigray in November 2020, warring parties, including Eritrean forces, have subjected Eritrean refugees to serious abuses.

In January, the UN reported that a January air strike near the Mai Aini camp in Tigray region killed three Eritrean refugees, two of them children. Humanitarian access and basic services to the 25,000 Eritrean refugees living in two remaining camps in Tigray has been affected by fighting, an uptick in drone strikes, and the Ethiopian government's effective siege on the Tigray region.

In January, the UN reported 20 preventable deaths there due to lack of medicine and health services. Nongovernmental organizations and UN rights experts raised concerns that the effective siege and impunity for conflict-related abuses was contributing to Eritrean refugee women's vulnerability to sexual violence and exploitation.

In March 2022, Egypt forcibly returned 31 Eritrean refugees and threatened additional repatriations; in December 2021 it had deported 24 Eritrean refugees, including children. In Sudan's capital, Khartoum, for several months, undocumented Eritreans were reportedly arbitrarily detained and released after paying significant sums.

In April, UN human rights experts cited "patterns of human rights violations against Eritreans who have been forcibly returned" to Eritrea, including torture, ill-treatment, enforced disappearance, and arbitrary detention. They stated that some Eritreans, deported by Egypt in October 2021, had not been seen or heard from since and were believed to be held in incommunicado detention by Eritrean authorities.

Key International Actors

In January, the UN launched a new development cooperation framework with Eritrea, sending a high-level delegation to Asmara.

In March, Eritrea voted against a UN general assembly resolution condemning Russia's invasion of Ukraine, one of only five countries (including Russia) to do so. President Isaias later defended Russia in an annual Independence Day speech. He reportedly invited Russia to establish a naval base on its Red Sea Coast.

In its concluding observations on Eritrea, in April, the African Committee of Experts on the Rights and Welfare of the Child (ACERWC) noted that by not affording children the right to freedom of religion, Eritrea had violated the provisions of the African Charter on the Rights and Welfare of the Child.

The committee recommended that Eritrea, referring to the final year of schooling in the Sawa military camp, should ensure that children are not educated in a militaristic environment, revise its policy recognizing only four religions, the law prohibiting independent local media platforms, take legislative measures to explicitly outlaw the use of corporal punishment, and authorize the committee to conduct a fact-finding mission to investigate allegations of child military training in the Sawa camp.

In September, US President Joe Biden extended, for one year, the ability to sanction Eritrean officials for committing serious human rights abuses in Tigray. The European Union maintained individual sanctions on Maj. Gen. Abraha Kassa, head of Eritrea's national security agency, which it rolled out in March 2021, for serious human rights abuses in Eritrea including killings, arbitrary arrests, enforced disappearances, and torture. In September, the US condemned Eritrea's re-entry into the conflict.

In July, Somalia's new president visited Somali troops being trained in Eritrea, reversing his predecessor's denials that any were there.

Eswatini

In 2022, the absolute monarchy in Eswatini, ruled by King Mswati III since 1986, continued to face waves of demonstrations that began in June 2021 against the drastically deteriorating human rights situation in the country, and the lack of democratic reforms. Intervention in November 2021 by South Africa's President Cyril Ramaphosa, then-chairperson of the Organ on Politics, Defense and Security Cooperation, of the Southern African Development Community (SADC), resulted in King Mswati agreeing to a national dialogue facilitated by SADC. There has been no progress toward instituting the Sibaya or "people's parliament" dialogue format proposed by the king. The dialogue format has been rejected as undemocratic by the Multi Stakeholder Forum, an umbrella body of political parties, churches, local businesses, student groups and civil society organizations.

Conduct of Security Forces

Following the series of protests that began in June 2021, authorities continued to use excessive force and the threat of violence against activists and critics, some of whom were assaulted and harassed.

Members of parliament (MPs) who voiced support for the protests have also been targeted. MPs Mduduzi Bacede Mabuza and Mthandeni Dubehave remained in custody since they were arrested in July 2021, after calling for democracy. They are facing trumped-up charges of terrorism under the Suppression of Terrorism Act, and for the alleged murder of Siphosethu Mntshali and Thando Shongwe, who were knocked down and killed by a car in Mbabane during the June 2021 protests. Another MP, Mduduzi Simelane, fled to South Africa, following weeks in hiding, after the police issued a warrant for his arrest in July 2021.

According to media reports, a militarized police unit of the king, the Operation Support Service Unit, has repeatedly used excessive force, including firing live bullets into crowds, to break up sunset rallies. The rallies are a part of an anti-monarchy campaign tagged "Turn Up the Heat" organized since March by the Communist Party of Swaziland.

In February, the authorities detained, and allegedly tortured student union leaders, according to media reports, following protests by university students demanding scholarships and refund of hostels fees unused during the Covid-19 lockdowns. Riot police in April fired teargas and evicted protesting students from university campuses in Mbabane and Manzini.

Freedom of Association and Assembly

The Public Order Act of 2017 protects the rights to freedom of expression, association, and peaceful assembly, but with limitations, which the government has been using to restrict freedoms.

In a setback for the rights of lesbian, gay, bisexual, and transgender (LGBT) people, the High Court of Eswatini decided on April 29, in the case of *Melusi Simelane and Others versus the Minister of Commerce and Industry and Others,* that while LGBT people are entitled to all the relevant rights conferred under the Constitution because they are human beings, those rights are subject to other laws of Eswatini. The court went on to uphold the refusal of the Registrar of Companies to register an LGBT organization, Eswatini Sexual and Gender Minorities, because the criminalization of sodomy under the Criminal Procedure and Evidence Act rendered the purpose of the organization unlawful.

During its Universal Periodic Review (UPR) at the United Nations Human Rights Council (UNHRC), several states made recommendations that Eswatini should take steps to decriminalize same-sex conduct, and to adopt legislation to give effect to LGBT rights.

Rule of Law, Freedom of Media

Despite repeated calls by protesters, Eswatini's international partners, and other actors for rights reforms, there has been no progress on the removal of legislative and other restrictions to the free exercise of civil and political rights. This includes the repeal or amendment of laws that obstruct the freedom of association and expression, removal of the ban on the registration and operation of political parties; ensuring greater political freedoms through free, fair, and transparent democratic elections; implementing measures to increase women's participation at decision-making levels, ensuring the right to health without discrimination; abolition of the death penalty; and decriminalization of same-sex relations and prevention of discrimination based on marital status and sexual orientation.

Reporters Without Borders in its 2022 world press freedom index ranked Eswatini 131 out of 180 countries, stating that the country prevents journalists from working freely and independently by maintaining total control over the broadcast media, infiltrating the newsroom, and spying on, arresting and harassing journalists.

In July, Prime Minister Cleopas Sipho Dlamini published an order declaring South African based online publication, Swaziland News, and its editor, Zweli Martin Dlamini, 'terrorist entities'. He made the order on the recommendation of the Attorney General, Sifiso Khumalo, who accused Dlamini of publishing articles "that instigate violence, the burning of public and state property, the seizure of state power and the overthrow of lawful government."

Women's Rights

Women continue to be under-represented in leadership and decision-making positions in both public and private sectors, despite the provisions of the 2018 Election of Women Act, and the constitutional requirement of 30 percent representation quotas for women and marginalized groups in parliament.

Eswatini has yet to ratify the Protocol to the African Charter on Human and Peoples' Rights on the Rights of Women in Africa, which provides, among other things, for the protection of women from harmful practices. Eswatini has a dual legal system, whereby the common law, based on Roman Dutch law, operates side by side with unwritten customary laws under which women are treated as dependents of their fathers, husbands, and traditional chiefs.

The government proposed two notable bills to parliament, in May, the Marriages Bill and the Matrimonial Properties Bill which seek to address some of these inconsistencies. The proposed bills include provisions to abolish marital power held by husbands over their wives' ability to contract and to litigate, as well as provisions for the equitable distribution and equal access of spouses to matrimonial property

Key International Actors

Following the SADC fact-finding missions to Eswatini in 2021, King Mswati had agreed to hold a national dialogue, which has yet to take place. In April, the King removed Eswatini from the agenda of the SADC Organ's Troika meeting where the national dialogue was supposed to be discussed. The July SADC extraordinary summit was postponed without further notice, due to the unavailability of Eswatini, which was on the agenda, according to media reports.

In March, the UNHRC adopted the outcomes of Eswatini's UPR process, including recommendations to modify, repeal or amend the Public Order Act; the Suppression of Terrorism Act, and the Seditious and Subversive Activities Act; including recommendations to revoke the decree banning political parties; establish an independent human rights institution; adopt laws on prosecuting and investigating cases of torture and ill-treatment; abolish the death penalty; take all measures to combat arbitrary arrests and detentions, as well as to ensure fair trials.

In August, the Southern African Human Rights Defenders Network, the Zimbabwe Human Rights NGO Forum, the Zimbabwe Lawyers for Human Rights, and the Southern African People's Solidarity Network (SAPSN), among others, raised concerns about the King's decree barring citizens from delivering petitions to parliamentarians, which has further worsened the country's political and security situation. The organizations urged the government of Eswatini to create a conducive environment for comprehensive and genuine political dialogue.

Ethiopia

The two-year armed conflict in northern Ethiopia, which began in November 2020, continued to inflict a terrible toll on civilians. A truce was reached by the main warring parties in November. State security forces and armed groups committed serious abuses, in other regions, notably Oromia. Authorities sporadically cut internet and telecommunication services in conflict-affected areas, with internet and other forms of communications cut in Tigray since June 2021.

Conflict and unrest in several regions, followed by drought also exacerbated one of the world's largest humanitarian catastrophes. Over 20 million people required humanitarian assistance in 2022.

In western Oromia, fighting between government forces and armed groups resulted in serious abuses committed by all sides.

Journalists, civil society organizations, and outspoken public figures in the country faced an increasingly hostile and restrictive reporting environment.

Consensual same-sex relationships are outlawed and carry a penalty of up to 15 years in prison.

Despite mounting evidence of international law violations by warring parties in northern Ethiopia, as well as in Oromia, government efforts toward accountability for past and present abuses have been inadequate, and lacked transparency and independent oversight.

Conflict in Northern Ethiopia

The conflict in northern Ethiopia persisted for the second year amid limited global pressure.

In Western Tigray Zone, an ethnic cleansing campaign, amounting to crimes against humanity, against the Tigrayan population by newly appointed officials and Amhara regional security forces and militias, continued.

On January 7, a government drone strike hit a school compound in Dedebit hosting thousands of Tigrayans displaced from Western Tigray, killing at least 57 civilians and wounding more than 42.

Ethiopian authorities maintained an effective siege on Tigray throughout the year that violated international humanitarian law. From mid-December 2021 to April 1, 2022, and also from late August to November 16, no humanitarian convoys entered the region. On March 24, the federal government declared an "indefinite humanitarian truce" and finally let aid reach Tigray as it was obligated to do, but the response did not match the scale of needs.

Basic services, key to people's basic survival, notably banking, electricity, and communications remained shut off. An August report by the United Nations highlighted dire food crisis in Tigray, finding food insecurity in 89 percent of areas surveyed and one out of three children under the age of five acutely malnourished.

In Afar, clashes along the border with Tigray, between Tigrayan forces and Afar forces, starting in late December 2021, intensified in early 2022, with reports of killings, shelling, and looting by Tigrayan forces.

Afar forces also rounded up around 9,000 Tigrayans in detention sites in Afar's regional capital, Semera, in late December 2021 and held them for months. Detainees received limited assistance with reports that several dozen died as a result of conditions there.

Fighting between Ethiopian forces and its allies against Tigrayan forces resumed on August 24. Aid into Tigray by road and air was suspended. Tigrayan forces seized fuel stored at a UN warehouse in Tigray's capital, Mekelle. Fighting also intensified with reports of Eritrean armed forces taking part in offensives and increased airstrikes in the Tigray region.

A September 27 airstrike on a residential area in Adi Daero town killed eight people and injured 13. Attacks continued near Adi Daero with an airstrike on October 4 killing over 50 displaced people. Intensifying Ethiopian and Eritrean operations around Shire town led to killings, property destruction, and further displacement. On October 14, an airstrike on Shire town killed two civilians and an International Rescue Committee aid worker delivering life-saving assistance.

Fighting in the Amhara and Afar regions in September resulted in further displacement, humanitarian access constraints, as well as reports of extrajudicial killing of Amhara residents by Tigrayan fighters, looting, and property destruction in Kobo town during their control.

On November 2, the Ethiopian federal government and Tigrayan authorities reached a cessation of hostilities agreement in South Africa following 10-days of African-Union led negotiations.

Security Force Abuses, Attacks by Armed Groups

Extrajudicial killings, mass arrests, arbitrary detentions, and violence against civilians occurred in other regions facing unrest, insecurity, and conflict.

On June 14, government forces clashed with Oromo Liberation Army (OLA) and Gambella Liberation Front armed groups in the Gambella regional capital. After controlling the town, government forces conducted house-to-house searches and summarily executed residents suspected of collaborating with the armed groups.

Parts of Oromia experienced protracted fighting due to government operations against the OLA. On June 18, heavily armed gunmen killed about 400 Amhara civilians, many women and children and destroyed homes and businesses in villages in West Wellega Zone, in Oromia, and in neighboring Benishangul-Gumuz region. Two weeks later, on July 4, assailants attacked Amhara civilians in Kellem Wellega Zone in Oromia, killing scores.

Fighting intensified between Ethiopian government forces and the OLA in early November, with civilian casualties reported due to fighting and airstrikes. In western Oromia there were reports of fighters from the Amhara region operating in Zone. The UN reported that the violence in the area led to a drastic increase in internal displacement and the destruction of infrastructure.

In late July, the armed group Al-Shabab carried out incursions on three towns hosting regional special forces in Ethiopia's Somali region, the first such attack on Ethiopian territory in over a decade.

Freedom of Expression, Media, and Association

Authorities arrested several journalists, holding them without charge for several weeks despite court orders for their release. In November 2021, authorities arrested Oromia News Network journalists Dessu Dulla and Bikila Amenu, who covered the conflicts in Tigray and Oromia. Dessu and Bikilia were held without formal charges until April, when prosecutors charged them with offenses against the constitution and sought the death penalty. Authorities released both Dessu and Bikila in mid-November.

Journalists and individuals offering a critical or different narrative to that of the federal government faced threats, arrests, and expulsion. In May, security forces arrested Solomon Shumye, an Addis Ababa-based talk show host who has been critical of the government and the war in northern Ethiopia. Solomon was among 19 journalists, including Gobeze Sisay and Meaza Mohammed, detained between May 19 and early July as part of broader government crackdown in which over 4,500 people were arrested in the Amhara region alone. Gobeze and Meaza were both subsequently released, and then rearrested by authorities in September.

In May, federal authorities withdrew the accreditation of Tom Gardner, The Economist's Addis Ababa correspondent, and expelled him from the country.

On September 6, security forces broke up a peace conference organized by a group of 35 local civil society organizations in Addis Ababa. The event was later held online, and the group subsequently issued a joint statement calling for peace. Two days later, a federal official intimidated the group to get them to retract their statement.

Federal authorities maintained their internet and telecommunications shutdown in Tigray since June 2021, and sporadically cut services in parts of Oromia facing insecurity, hampering real-time reporting.

Due Process and Fair Trial Rights

In January, the government dropped charges against several high-profile political opposition figures, including Jawar Mohammed, Bekele Gerba, and Eskinder Nega, whom authorities detained in June 2020 after the assassination of Oromo singer Hachalu Hundessa.

Opposition politicians from the Oromo Liberation Front (OLF), detained since 2020, remain in detention despite multiple judicial orders instructing that they be released on bail. Though Col. Gemechu Ayana was released on May 25, after almost two years in detention, other OLF figures continue to face serious due process violations in detention with some becoming ill, reportedly due to a lack of adequate medical care.

On February 15, Ethiopian lawmakers ended a sweeping nationwide state of emergency declared in November 2021 that led to mass arrests of ordinary Tigrayans. Tigrayans remained detained for several months without charge and were subject to ill-treatment after the lifting of the emergency declaration, including Tigrayans deported from Saudi Arabia.

Federal security forces also rearrested Kibrom Berhe in July, and Hailu Kebede in August, Tigrayan opposition figures and vocal critics of the conflict in Tigray. By October, authorities released Kibrom and Hailu.

Internally Displaced Persons and Refugees

Ethiopia continued to face large-scale internal displacement due in large part to armed conflict, followed by drought and other natural hazards. Figures shifted throughout the year, with 5.6 million internally displaced persons (IDPs) nationally as of March 2022, in addition to 2.8 million returnees (former IDPs).

Refugees were also impacted by conflict and unrest in the country. On January 18, a camp hosting more than 10,000 refugees from Sudan and South Sudan in the Benishangul Gumuz region was looted and burned after fighting broke out between unidentified groups and federal forces.

A January 5 airstrike on Mai Aini refugee camp in Tigray killed three Eritrean refugees, including two children. On February 3, armed men entered the Berahle refugee camp hosting Eritrean refugees in Afar, looted belongings, killed five refugees, and kidnapped several women. The attack caused thousands of refugees to flee. At various points in September, the UN High Commissioner for Refugees lost access to several refugee camps and IDP sites in northern Ethiopia due to renewed fighting. In October, UN human rights experts cited reports of abductions of refugees and internally displaced women and girls fleeing conflict in northern Ethiopia.

Key International Actors

International efforts to support a cessation of hostilities and commence formal talks, between the Ethiopian government and Tigrayan authorities, yielded little results for most of 2022. Directly involved were special envoys on the Horn, including the African Union (AU), United States, European Union, and United Nations. The cessation of hostilities agreement reached by the two main warring parties on November 2 did not immediately lead to a resumption of humanitarian assistance and basic services to Tigray, and lacked formal details on accountability, highlighting the need for robust rights monitoring by key international backers of the truce.

The UN Security Council remained largely paralyzed on Ethiopia with Gabon, Ghana, and Kenya (the three elected members representing the AU on the Security Council until the end of 2022) repeatedly blocking any public discussion of Ethiopia at the council, though they were open to closed-door discussions of the conflict. On October 21, the African members on the council called a closed-door Security Council meeting on Ethiopia given the deteriorating situation and attempted to release a statement that was blocked by Russia and China.

In January 2022, the US suspended Ethiopia's trade privileges under the African Growth Opportunity Act (AGOA) due to concerns about human rights abuses by the Ethiopian government and warring parties in the conflict in northern Ethiopia. In September, US President Joe Biden renewed a 2021 executive order that established a sanctions regime on individuals and entities responsible for human rights abuses in northern Ethiopia, but it has only sanctioned Eritrean entities and individuals.

In December 2021, the UN Human Rights Council established an independent international commission to investigate allegations of international law violations by all parties since November 2020. Ethiopian authorities rejected the commission's mandate, and in March introduced a resolution at the UN General Assembly's budget committee to cut its funding. The budget committee rejected the resolution.

The commission published its first report in September, finding that all parties to the conflict had carried out war crimes, and that Ethiopian federal forces and allied forces committed crimes against humanity against the Tigrayan population.

Ethiopia rejected the findings and opposed the renewal of the commission's mandate. On October 7, council members voted to renew the commission's mandate for one year.

The EU remained a vocal critic of the abuses committed by warring parties in northern Ethiopia and repeatedly called for lifting the effective siege on humanitarian access. On October 6, the European Parliament adopted a resolution on the rights situation in Tigray, finding the use of starvation as a weapon of war. The European Union also played a leading role on Ethiopia at the Human Rights Council, though divisions among EU member states prevented the adoption of other measures, such as an arms embargo.

Though several of Ethiopia's international partners suspended non-humanitarian assistance to the country since the outbreak of conflict, in April the World Bank approved a US$300 million grant to support the response and recovery efforts in conflict-affected areas, including in Tigray, despite concerns surrounding the project's implementation.

European Union

The European Union and most member states espouse a commitment to human rights and democratic values, and on some occasions, such as the response to refugees coming from Ukraine, it lived up to those values in 2022. Too often, however, the policies and actions of the union and member states fell short, leaving the most marginalized and vulnerable exposed to abuse.

Migrants, Refugees and Asylum Seekers

The positive response of the EU to the mass displacement of Ukrainians following Russia's invasion of Ukraine in February contrasted starkly with abusive treatment of migrants and asylum seekers from other regions of the world.

By September, more than 4 million refugees from Ukraine—approximately 90 percent of them women and children—had registered in EU countries following the unprecedented activation of the 2001 Temporary Protection Directive (TPD) in response to the war in Ukraine. There were concerns about the risk of trafficking, gender-based violence, and other forms of exploitation of people arriving from Ukraine, especially women and girls, arising from inadequate protection measures in countries like Poland.

Over one year after the Taliban takeover, Afghan asylum seekers faced pushbacks at EU borders and decreasing refugee recognition rates across the EU. EU countries largely stopped evacuating local staff and Afghans at risk from Afghanistan.

EU member states, including Bulgaria, Croatia, Cyprus, Greece, Poland, and Spain, continued to engage in unlawful pushbacks and violence at their borders.

In April, Fabrice Leggeri resigned as director of the EU border agency Frontex following investigations by the EU Anti-Fraud Office (OLAF) into numerous reports that Frontex was implicated in illegal pushbacks in the Aegean Sea. The OLAF report, leaked in October, provides evidence of Frontex complicity in Greek pushbacks.

In June, the EU Court of Justice found that automatic detention and denial of the right to seek asylum to people irregularly entering Lithuania via Belarus violates

EU law. Rights groups denounced pushbacks, abusive detention as well as racially motivated harassment in Lithuania and similar abuses against people entering Poland via Belarus. In August, Estonia authorized pushbacks at its borders.

According to the UN refugee agency UNHCR, more than 100,700 people arrived irregularly at the EU's southern borders by mid-September, most by sea, while at least 1,207 died or went missing in the Mediterranean Sea.

Reception conditions for asylum seekers remained substandard in several EU countries. Council of Europe Commissioner for Human Rights Dunja Mijatovic noted in August structural shortcomings, conditions in and around the Ter Apel center in the Netherlands, that posed a risk to the right to health, and "stark differences" between treatment of Ukrainians and people from other countries. The intervention followed the death of a baby in the center the same month.

The EU and its member states continued to provide support to Libya to facilitate interceptions of asylum seekers and migrants at sea and disembarkation in Libya, despite known risks of arbitrary detention, torture, and other abuses. UNHCR said at least 18,600 people were intercepted or rescued at sea and disembarked in Libya by the end of October.

The European Commission confirmed it was considering allocating €80 million (around US$83 million) to Egypt in 2022 and 2023 to support land and sea "border management," despite the country's abysmal human rights record. The EU and its member states also continued or increased funding, cooperation, and support to migration control in other African countries, such as Morocco, Mauritania, Senegal, and Niger, despite the negative repercussions for migrants and asylum seekers in the region—including reduced freedom of movement, arbitrary arrests and detention, physical abuse, extortion, and arbitrary expulsions.

In July, the Netherlands' Council of State ruled that Denmark could not be automatically assumed safe for Syrian asylum seekers for the purposes of "Dublin returns" because of the risk of forced return to Damascus and its environs. In September, Denmark and Rwanda announced a "common ambition" to create a mechanism to transfer asylum seekers from Denmark to Rwanda, despite serious concerns for their rights and safety.

Progress on EU asylum reforms remained mired in political divisions, particularly over improvements to responsibility-sharing among member states. In June, 18 EU members and 3 non-EU states agreed on a voluntary solidarity mechanism to share responsibility for some of the asylum seekers rescued at sea, with 112 people relocated from Italy by mid-October.

There was little movement towards creating independent border monitoring mechanisms in EU member states, while national efforts in Croatia and Greece fell short of standards needed to ensure effectiveness, despite European Commission involvement.

EU member states did agree on measures that would undermine fundamental rights, such as a proposed "instrumentalization" regulation that would allow states to derogate from key obligations, including ensuring the right to seek asylum at external borders, and amendments to the Schengen Borders Code that rights groups argue would exacerbate racial and ethnic profiling to facilitate border rejections and expand the use of surveillance technologies at internal borders.

Discrimination and Intolerance

Non-Ukrainians fleeing the conflict in Ukraine faced discrimination and unequal treatment at and inside EU borders. In a March resolution, the European Parliament called on EU countries to admit non-Ukrainian nationals fleeing the conflict, irrespective of nationalities. Roma refugees fleeing Ukraine also reportedly faced discrimination and prejudice in several EU countries.

In March, the council of the EU spoke out against the rise in racist and antisemitic incidents in EU countries and called on member states to develop action plans and strategies by the end of 2022 and to implement the 2020 EU anti-racism action plan and the 2021 EU strategy on combating antisemitism.

In response to increasing anti-Muslim racism and discrimination in many parts of Europe, including through hate speech and hate crimes, the European Commission against Racism and Intolerance (ECRI) issued a General Policy Recommendation in March calling on European countries including EU states to tackle the issue.

Racism in policing, particularly ethnic profiling in identity checks, the use of racist language and excessive use of force against individuals, continues to be an issue in European countries, according to ECRI's annual report published in June. The report also noted that Covid-related restrictions imposed on schools negatively impacted those children who already faced the most difficulties, such as migrant children and Roma. The ECRI report does not mention specific states.

In its 2022 fundamental rights report published in June, the EU's Fundamental Rights Agency (FRA) noted that the pandemic further fueled discrimination, hate crimes, and particularly online hate speech towards migrants and ethnic minorities, and called on EU countries to penalize hate crime, encourage reporting, and better support victims.

Several EU countries, including Hungary, Poland, Romania, and Italy saw strong political rhetoric against a purported "gender ideology," which they amplified in the media and public discourse as well as through efforts to adopt laws specifically targeting LGBT people, and in case of Hungary women's rights.

A Council of Europe (CoE) report published in July acknowledged advances in legislation, practices and public attitudes in guaranteeing legal recognition for trans and non-binary people in all areas of life but noted slow progress and an increase in discrimination experienced by transgender people over the last decade. According to the study, all EU countries except Hungary have some measures in place to recognize a change in gender, but 15 require a compulsory medical intervention and 7 compulsory sterilization.

The CoE's Committee of Ministers issued a recommendation in May on protecting the rights of migrant, refugee, and asylum-seeking women and girls, calling on European countries including EU states to take measures to prevent discrimination against such women, including by promoting access to employment, sexual and reproductive health care, and facilitating access to services and justice for survivors of gender-based violence.

In June, the European Parliament passed a resolution calling on member states to decriminalize abortion and guarantee access to safe and legal abortion and other sexual and reproductive health care without discrimination. In July, MEPs called for an amendment to the EU Charter of Fundamental Rights to include the right to safe and legal abortion.

A July study by the European Institute of Gender Equality (EIGE) reported that one in two women in the EU have experienced psychological violence. The numbers were even higher for women who are seeking asylum or refugees, women of migrant background, women with disabilities or health conditions, women under age 30, and LBTQ women. At time of writing, six member states and the EU itself had yet to ratify the CoE Istanbul Convention on combatting and preventing violence against women.

In its 2021 Conclusions published in March, CoE's European Committee of Social Rights (ECSR) found that discrimination based on age is not prohibited outside employment in certain EU states and that older persons lack adequate resources enabling them to lead a decent life and play an active role in the community in six EU member states (the Czech Republic, Denmark, Malta, the Netherlands, Slovakia, and Spain). The ECSR also noted the devastating effects of Covid-19 on older persons and emphasized the importance of moving away from institutionalization towards community-based care and independent living for older persons.

Poverty and Inequality

Rapidly increasing inflation during the year, particularly in relation to food and energy prices, and the long-term economic consequences of the Covid-19 pandemic impacted the rights of people living on low incomes or in poverty, including to an adequate standard of living, to food, to health, to housing, and to social security.

EU data from September 2022 showed that 95.4 million people (21.7 percent of the population) were at risk of poverty or social exclusion, with women at higher risk than men, and households (particularly those headed by a single parent) with dependent children also at elevated risk. Poverty rates in Romania and Bulgaria exceeded 30 percent. In June, member states presented national poverty reduction targets to the European Commission, committing to reduce by 15.6 million the number of people at risk of poverty or social exclusion by 2030.

In September, the European Commission issued guidelines to its member states, encouraging them to reform existing minimum income programs or establish new ones to ensure that their social security systems provide cash payments to households who need support to live in dignity. Anti-poverty groups welcomed the proposal, and called on the commission to take a binding, rights-based approach in addition to these guidelines.

Official data in January showed that energy price inflation across the EU stood at 27 percent, with rates of over 40 percent in five countries, an upward trend exacerbated by the war in Ukraine and subsequent sanctions. Most EU governments adopted policies to regulate energy prices, including in many cases targeted support meeting energy costs for low-income households.

The Russian invasion of Ukraine in February exacerbated food supply problems, in particular staples such as wheat and sunflower oil. Although EU countries did not face food shortages, affordability remained a concern, particularly for households with low incomes, impacting the right to food. By September, bread prices had risen by a fifth across the region compared to the previous year.

The EU's REACT fund, part of a Covid-19 recovery package, disbursed significant additional focused funding to at least 18 member states to help address pandemic recovery or to support new arrivals displaced by the conflict in Ukraine. The European Social Fund also increased funding provided to member states to deal with the added costs and support for people displaced by the conflict in Ukraine.

In June, the EU Council unanimously approved the European Child Guarantee, requiring member states to ensure children receive one healthy school meal a day, access to learning material, transport to school, and access to decent housing. Children from deprived backgrounds face difficulties with these issues in many EU states, undermining their basic rights. Most member states failed to meet the commission's March deadline to submit national action plans to deliver these recommendations. At time of writing, only 15 states had done so. The deadline for implementing the recommendations is 2030.

In June, the European Parliament and EU member states reached agreement in principle on the EU Commission's proposed directive on adequate minimum wages, a key principle of the European Pillar of Social Rights and factor in determining the right to an adequate standard of living. The European Parliament approved legislation in September, giving member states two years to ensure that their domestic national minimum wage legislation guarantees a decent standard of living.

A June report by the UN special rapporteur on extreme poverty highlighted gaps in social security systems in EU member states. The rapporteur found in most of the social assistance programs it examined that the take-up rate was lower than 60 percent, with illustrative examples from Slovakia, Czechia, Slovenia, Finland, and France suggesting that significant portions of the population were facing barriers accessing needed support.

Rule of Law

EU institutions maintained their scrutiny on rule of law concerns in several EU member states but failed to take decisive action.

A hearing at EU ministers' level under Article 7—the EU treaty procedure to scrutinize threats to rights and rule of law—took place on Hungary in May and November. A hearing was also held on Poland in February, with an update discussion in October. More than four years after the Article 7 procedure was initiated against Hungary (and five since it was initiated against Poland), EU member states continued to shy away from adopting rule of law recommendations or of voting to determine a risk of breach to the rule of law in either country.

In May, the European Parliament criticized the lack of progress by the Commission and Council on Article 7 proceedings on Hungary and Poland and urged the Council to adopt rule of law recommendations. In September, the European Parliament adopted an update to its September 2018 decision to activate article 7 over the situation in Hungary, pressing member states to take responsibility and concluding that Hungary is "no longer a democracy."

The European Parliament monitoring group on the rule of law continued to scrutinize concerns in Bulgaria, Slovakia, Malta, and stepped up its activities on media freedom in Greece. In March, the European Parliament set up an inquiry committee on the use of surveillance spyware, including in Hungary, Poland, and Greece.

In February, the Court of the Justice of the EU dismissed the complaint filed by Hungary and Poland against the EU regulation that established a new rule of law conditionality mechanism for access to EU funding. In March and May, the European Parliament criticized the Commission for dragging its feet in using this mechanism.

In September, the European Commission proposed for the very first time to the Council to suspend some EU funds to Hungary under the rule-of-law conditionality mechanism because of breaches to the rule of law in the country; member states were expected to take a decision on the commission's proposal in December.

Poland's economic plan under the Covid recovery funds was endorsed by the European Commission in June, but the commission continued to retain the actual funds at time of writing because of concerns about the rule of law. At time of writing, the commission had not yet endorsed Hungary's Covid recovery plan because of similar concerns. concerns.

The commission continued to use legal infringement procedures in response to the backsliding on the rule of law in Hungary and Poland but did not take new decisive action to address the lack of implementation of EU Court of Justice rulings by those two governments. In July, the commission addressed a formal request to the Polish government to comply with EU law in the case on the lack of independence and impartiality of the Constitutional Tribunal and its failure to apply EU law. It also transmitted to the EU Court of Justice cases against Hungary on the decision to take an independent radio station off air and on a June 2021 anti-LGBT law.

For the third year, the European Commission released its rule of law report, which included detailed chapters on all 27 members of the EU. It was the first time this report included recommendations to member states. Civil society observers criticized the recommendations as vague, unspecific, and failing to articulate policy consequences for non-implementation.

There remains little or no accountability for the killing of media professionals in EU countries. In July, one of the accused in the murder of journalist Daphne Caruana Galizia in Malta confessed his role in the killing; the court case against him and others accused is ongoing. In February, the Specialized Criminal Court opened the re-trial of those allegedly behind the 2018 assassination of journalist Ján Kuciak and his fiancée. The re-trial was ongoing at time of writing. There has been no significant progress in the investigation into the April 2021 murder of journalist Giorgos Karaivaz in Athens. The trial of two men linked to organized crime and accused of the July 2021 murder of journalist Peter de Vries in Amsterdam was ongoing at time of writing.

In January, the European Commission announced plans for a European Media Freedom Act aimed at protecting media independence and pluralism in the EU. Following a request by the European Parliament, the commission opened in August a consultation on a new EU law on the rights of associations in the EU.

Climate Change Policy and Impacts

The 27 member states of the European Union are among the top 10 greenhouse gas emitters globally, making a major contribution to the climate crisis that is taking a mounting toll on human rights around the globe.

In May, the European Commission launched the REPower EU Plan, intended to reduce its reliance on fossil fuels following the Russia invasion of Ukraine. The plan increases the share of renewable energy but also includes a proposal for new investments in LNG and fossil gas infrastructure, undermining emission reduction efforts.

In July, the European Parliament backed a commission proposal to classify fossil gas and nuclear power as "sustainable" investments. In September, environmental groups launched a legal challenge against the European Commission over this decision, arguing that it undermines the EU's emission reduction efforts and its obligations under the Paris Agreement.

Thousands of people have died as 21 countries across Europe endured unusually high temperatures amid an unprecedented and prolonged yet predictable heatwave during summer months. Older people and those with underlying medical conditions, such as respiratory and cardiovascular diseases, were particularly affected. Data from Spain and Portugal show most people who died were over age 65.

Foreign Policy

Russia's invasion of Ukraine and its effects on European security, economy, and stability dominated the EU's diplomatic efforts in 2022. The EU and its member states put in place unprecedented and coordinated efforts to secure global support ahead of a series of UN votes condemning Russia's aggression and to combat impunity for serious international crimes committed in the conflict.

At the same time, the need to secure energy supplies and markets alternative to Russia's exacerbated pre-existing trends of strengthening ties with others authoritarian governments. In February, shortly before the conflict erupted, the EU hosted the EU-AU summit, welcoming abusive leaders such as Egypt's Abdel Fattah al-Sisi to Brussels.

In June, EU member states approved the commission's joint communication on a strategic partnership with the Gulf, nearly exclusively focused on laying out investment and cooperation opportunities, largely overlooking the Gulf countries' grim human rights records. Similarly, the EU sealed energy deals with Israel, Egypt, and Azerbaijan, and relaunched negotiations for a free trade agreement with India, raising concerns that its already quiet or muted response to these governments' abuses may persist.

In October, the EU resumed its Association Council meeting with Israel after a 10-year stalemate. Human rights groups and several members of the European Parliament harshly criticized the holding of the meeting amid escalating repression of Palestinian civil society by Israeli authorities and growing international consensus that Israeli authorities' severe repression of Palestinians constitutes apartheid.

Also in October, leaders of 44 EU and neighboring countries, including abusive governments such as Turkey and Azerbaijan, gathered for the first meeting of the European Political Community. Discussions focused mainly on the conflict in Ukraine and the energy crisis.

Relations with China remained cold following tit-for-tat sanctions in 2020 and Beijing's "pro-Russia neutrality" over the Ukraine conflict. While all EU member states unanimously supported the bloc's damning statements on China's abuses at the UN Human Rights Council (HRC), Cyprus, Greece, Hungary, and Malta continued to refrain from signing cross-regional statements on Xinjiang.

Lack of unanimity also prevented the EU from supporting the adoption of a resolution to put China on the HRC agenda following the publication of the UN High Commissioner's report on Xinjiang. The EU's 2019 multifaceted strategy on China was confirmed by member states in October, although amid growing awareness that the "systemic rivalry" component is overshadowing its remaining pillars.

In October, the EU lifted targeted sanctions against some Burundian officials, despite acknowledging that "major [human rights] challenges remain unaddressed and unresolved." Strained relations between the EU and Mali over rights abuses and Mali's partnership with the Wagner Group led to a significant reduction in the EU Training Mission in Mali (EUTM) and the EU Capacity Building Mission (EUCAP).

In October, the European Union announced the deployment of up to 40 EU monitors along the Armenian side of the international border with Azerbaijan to "facilitate the restoration of peace and security ... the building of confidence and the delimitation of the international border between the two states."

High Representative Josep Borrell made a series of visits to Latin America, in preparation for a region-to-region summit expected to be held during the second half of 2023.

In February, the European Commission announced a long-awaited legislative proposal on a binding human rights and environmental due diligence mechanism for businesses throughout their value chains. In September, the commission also announced a legislative proposal to ban goods made through forced labor from entering the EU market. Both proposals, while welcome, carry significant weaknesses and need to be further amended to hold corporations accountable for human rights and environmental abuses.

In May, the European Parliament's Trade Committee proposed numerous amendments with the goal of strengthening the transparency, predictability, and ultimately influence the effectiveness of the EU's Generalised Scheme of Preferences (GSP), which grants preferential access to the EU market to low and middle-income countries against varying degrees of human rights conditionality. The new scheme would replace the existing one as of 2024. At time of writing, the council had yet to reach a position on the reform. Current GSP beneficiaries include countries with abusive governments that have failed to meet their human rights obligations under the scheme, such as Pakistan, Sri Lanka, the Philippines, Bangladesh, Myanmar, Cambodia, Kyrgyzstan, and Uzbekistan.

The unanimity requirement remained a major obstacle for the swift adoption of principled EU foreign policy statements, decisions, and measures. The EU's global human rights sanctions regime remained largely underused, with attempts to adopt targeted sanctions against those responsible for atrocities related to the conflict in northern Ethiopia frustrated by the opposition of some member states. Hungary repeatedly blocked EU leadership for an initiative to create a UN HRC monitoring mechanism on the human rights situation in Russia, but a special rapporteur on Russia was eventually established in October through leadership by the other 26 EU member states.

Despite these limitations, the EU has played a leading role on UN General Assembly resolutions on human rights in North Korea and Myanmar, while supporting efforts in the assembly to pressure Syria and Iran over their human rights abuses. The EU has also backed multiple UN General Assembly condemnations of Russia over its invasion of Ukraine and atrocities against civilians there.

At the UN Human Rights Council, the EU played a leading role on important resolutions on Burundi, Belarus, Ethiopia, Eritrea, North Korea, Myanmar, and Afghanistan. However, it failed to support a resolution on racism, racial discrimination, and xenophobia, and continued to express concerns about the mandate of the Commission of Inquiry on the Occupied Palestinian territory, including East Jerusalem and Israel.

France

President Emmanuel Macron was re-elected in April in elections that saw historic gains for the far right, and campaigns marred by xenophobic and intolerant discourse by some candidates The government put in place a series of purchasing power measures to mitigate the effects of inflation but its impact on the most vulnerable remained a major concern. Despite significant efforts to help people fleeing Ukraine, asylum seekers from other crises and conflicts faced abuse. Child protection authorities often failed to provide unaccompanied migrant children with appropriate care and services. Racist violence and discrimination remained a concern. A law against "separatism" threatens freedom of association. Reproductive rights have seen significant progress but deaths of women due to domestic violence increased.

Rule of Law

In its July 2022 Rule of Law report, the European Commission noted the concerns raised by civil society and independent authorities with respect to the law on "separatism" that entered into force in early 2022, and its potential impact on civic space, particularly on freedoms of association and expression. The law extends the list of grounds for dissolution of associations by executive decree and is widely viewed to risk particularly impacting Muslims.

In March and May, the Council of State suspended the dissolution by decree of two pro-Palestinian associations and an anti-fascist group.

Reporters Without Borders moved France up from 34th to 26th place in the press freedom index, citing a positive legal and regulatory framework for press freedom and editorial independence, while alerting about media concentration in the hands of a few owners. In its rule of law report, the European Commission recommended that France enhance transparency of media ownership.

The controller general of places of deprivation of liberty (CGLPL) and the French National Consultative Commission for Human Rights (CNCDH) continued to denounce the persistence of prison overcrowding, a major cause of violation of the rights of prisoners.

The state of health emergency introduced in March 2020 in response to Covid-19 was lifted on August 1.

Poverty and Inequality

In July, the government put in place a series of purchasing power protection measures to mitigate the effects of the cost-of-living crisis, but the crisis' impact on the most vulnerable remained a major concern. A survey published in September by Secours Populaire and Ipsos found that 65 percent of those surveyed said they know at least one person who is experiencing poverty, up from 55 percent in 2021. Of those surveyed, 45 percent said they have difficulty paying for their transportation costs, an increase of 15 points compared to 2021, and 41 percent struggle to pay their energy bills.

According to the French National Institute for Statistics and Economic Studies (INSEE), extreme poverty in France disproportionately affects residents in the overseas departments, particularly single-parent households, people who are unemployed, and pensioners, and results in deprivation of fundamental needs such as food and clothing.

Discrimination and Intolerance

According to official data released in March, reported racially motivated crimes and offenses increased in 2021 by 7.3 percent compared to 2019. Anti-Muslim acts increased by 38 percent and antisemitic acts decreased by 14 percent. Hate speech, including antisemitic and racist conspiracy speech, increased on social networks. The European Commission against Racism and Intolerance (ECRI) raised concerns in its 6th periodic report on France about hate speech becoming more widespread, especially in politics, the media, and social networks. ECRI also noted that Roma people experienced discrimination in all aspects of life.

In June, the Council of State suspended city regulations in Grenoble that allowed burkinis—full-body swimsuits worn largely by Muslim women, in many cases to uphold their faith—in public swimming pools.

A survey published by the International Labour Organization and the Defender of Rights in December 2021 found that more than 1 out of 3 young workers (18 to 24 years old) report having experienced discrimination or discriminatory harassment in their job search or career, particularly because of their origin, ethnicity or nationality, physical appearance, gender identity, or sexual orientation.

In May, SOS Homophobia, a nongovernmental organization, reporting on events from 2021, said that discrimination against LGBT people in the workplace increased, and attacks in schools against LGBT children were more frequent and violent.

In its annual report, the CGLPL denounced the serious violations of the rights of incarcerated transgender people. It noted that transgender people are most often placed in isolation solely because of their gender identity or assigned to quarters that do not correspond to the gender felt and expressed.

A law prohibiting "conversion therapies" aimed at changing a person's sexual orientation or gender identity was enacted in January.

Parliament adopted in February a bill enabling the Harkis—Muslim Algerians who fought alongside colonial France during the Algerian war of independence—and their families to receive compensation for France's abandonment and for the inhuman and degrading living conditions many of them endured in camps in France after the war ended in 1962.

Counterterrorism

In June, a Paris court sentenced the sole surviving perpetrator of the November 2015 Paris attacks to life in prison after a months-long trial that included groundbreaking participation by hundreds of victim-survivors and families of the dead. The court also convicted 19 other men for their involvement in the attacks, which killed 137 people and were claimed by the Islamic State.

The trial of eight suspects for links to the July 2016 Nice attack, which killed 86 people and injured 458, took place from September to December. The suspects were convicted and given prison sentences ranging from two to eighteen years..

Migrants and Asylum Seekers

According to the United Nations refugee agency, by the end of August 101,369 people fleeing Ukraine had registered for temporary protection in France, with access to employment, housing, health, and education. More than 18,000 Ukrainian children have attended school in France, according to official data.

French authorities have continued their policy of systematically dismantling informal encampments in Northern France, confiscating tents and tarps and often personal belongings, according to humanitarian and human rights organizations. The latter have denounced the difference in treatment between Ukrainians and people fleeing other crisis or conflict zones.

Between January and November, the number of irregular crossings of the English Channel exceeded 40,000, according to the British Ministry of Defence. French civil society groups blamed hostile policies, including lack of adequate reception conditions for asylum seekers, that encourage people to try dangerous routes to England.

Although France has provided significant support to Afghan evacuees fleeing the August 2021 Taliban takeover of Afghanistan, evacuees face trauma and psychological distress upon arrival in France aggravated by a significant gap in urgent and adequate psychosocial support.

In April, the CGLPL denounced the undignified and inhumane conditions that persist in some migrant waiting zones and administrative detention centers.

Children's Rights

Unaccompanied migrant children, especially those whose underage status was rejected by the authorities, are often denied the protection to which they are entitled and live in extremely precarious conditions.

In March, the European Court of Human Rights (ECtHR) condemned France for inhuman and degrading treatment of a Georgian child locked in an administrative detention center for 14 days.

In February, the UN Committee on the Rights of the Child found that France's refusal to repatriate French children detained in camps in northeast Syria violates their right to life and their right not to be subjected to inhuman and degrading treatment. In September, the ECtHR ruled that France violated the rights of five French women and children detained in those camps by refusing to repatriate them without any formal review or official decision. France repatriated 77 children and 32 women from northeast Syria between July and October, but around 150 children, 60 women, and an estimated 60 French men remain arbitrarily detained in the region.

Following reports that the government had built and offered two online learning products for children in English and German during the Covid-19 pandemic that were transmitting children's data to advertising technology companies, the Education Ministry removed all data surveillance from its products.

In July, the Defender of Rights expressed concern about lack of access to education for children in overseas territories, aggravated, as elsewhere in France, by the health crisis and noted that children with disabilities continue to face barriers to education.

Women's Rights

A law enacted in March increased the legal timeframe for an abortion from 12 to 14 weeks. A February decree prolonged the legal timeframe for and increased access to medication abortion, a safe alternative to invasive surgical procedures.

According to the High Council for Equality between Women and Men, wage gaps continue to widen, and women are disproportionately represented in low-wage, less secure jobs, exposing them to in-work poverty. Telecommuting and part-time work, often linked to childcare responsibilities, reinforce women's "invisibility" in the workplace and underrepresentation in senior positions, and has a disproportionately negative impact on women's health. Nearly half of French women surveyed (46 percent) have been victims of sexist acts or comments at work. France has not yet ratified the International Labour Organization convention on violence and harassment in employment.

According to the Interior Ministry, the number of deaths of women due to domestic violence increased by 20 percent between 2020 and 2021. In a survey by the feminist group NousToutes, which advocates for action on violence against women, 66 percent of respondents reported poor police response when reporting sexual violence between 2019 and 2021, including dismissive attitudes, victim-blaming, and refusal to take complaints. This increased to 81 percent of non-binary respondents. While the government announced new measures to fight against such violence and protect survivors, including the creation of

11,000 emergency accommodation places in 2023, associations criticized insufficient government efforts.

Disability Rights

In July, Parliament voted to remove consideration of a spouse's income for the purposes of calculating disability benefits.

After a journalistic investigation in January exposed neglect and abuse in nursing homes for older people run by the company Orpea, an administrative investigation and a Senate commission of inquiry found shortcomings in the control of these establishments and insufficient resources allocated to them. A criminal investigation was ongoing at time of writing.

International Justice

In response to a November 2021 Court of Cassation decision to quash the indictment of a Syrian accused of crimes against humanity, civil society organizations highlighted the limitations of France's universal jurisdiction law. The Public Prosecutor's office called for a legislative change, and in June, a French member of parliament, with the support of a Syrian victims group, filed a bill proposing the removal of limitations in the law.

In July, the Paris Assize Court sentenced a former Rwandan prefect to 20 years in prison for complicity in genocide. On November 2, the Court of Assizes in Paris sentenced a former Liberian rebel commander to life imprisonment for wartime atrocities in Liberia.

Climate Change Policy and Impacts

As one of the EU's biggest greenhouse gas emitters, France is contributing to the climate crisis taking a growing toll on human rights around the globe. In a June report, the High Council for the Climate said that, while progress has been made, the government's efforts remain too slow to achieve the current 2030 target to reduce emissions by 40 percent. Following the release of the report the government has pledged to make the target more ambitious. France has already warmed by 1.7 degrees and severe climate impacts such as heat waves and forest fires continue to become more frequent and intense.

Some measures of the purchasing power package put in place to fight inflation have been strongly criticized by deputies and environmental groups because they would harm the environment by promoting the development of fossil fuels.

Foreign Policy

During its six-month European Union Council presidency, France organized hearings on the rule of law situation in Hungary and Poland. But France failed to use its Presidency to take meaningful steps to address serious abuses against migrants and asylum seekers at the EU's external borders.

France contributed to the international response to Russia's full-scale invasion of Ukraine and in the fight against impunity for serious violations committed in Ukraine. France has notably supported the opening of an International Criminal Court investigation into crimes committed in Ukraine and supported the UN General Assembly resolution suspending Russia from the UN Human Rights Council (HRC). France and Mexico drafted a General Assembly resolution adopted in April that demanded Russia allow humanitarian aid access across Ukraine. It also supported other UN Security Council and General Assembly resolutions and initiatives condemning Russia's invasion and atrocities.

At the September session of the HRC, France supported a resolution establishing a Special Rapporteur on Russia to monitor and report on the human rights crisis in the country.

But France's proclaimed commitment to the universal values of human rights and the fight against impunity has been missing in other situations of serious violations of human rights crises. France's unconditional support and arms sales to Egypt, the United Arab Emirates (UAE), and Saudi Arabia continued despite their deplorable human rights records. With a total order intake of €4.5 billion in 2021, Egypt is France's largest arms customer. In December 2021, a reportedly historic €17 billion contract for the sale of 80 Rafale fighter aircrafts was signed between France and the United Arab Emirates. Saudi Arabia is reportedly among the top five largest buyers of French arms, despite the war crimes committed by the Saudi-UAE military coalition in Yemen. On July 19, President Macron awarded the Grand Cross of the Legion of Honor, France's highest honor, to UAE President Mohammed bin Zayed al-Nahyan during a state visit to Paris. On July 28, the French president welcomed Saudi Crown Prince and de facto ruler Mohammed bin Salman to the Elysee Palace, contributing to the latter's rehabilitation on the international scene despite the escalation of domestic repression and the crown prince's approving the murder of journalist Jamal Khashoggi, according to a United States intelligence report.

Despite President Macron's promises to the Lebanese people in the aftermath of the catastrophic Beirut port explosion in August 2020, France failed to take action at the UN Human Rights Council to establish an international investigation mechanism into the blast.

France has deepened its political and economic ties with India while failing to raise public concerns about the escalating crackdown on civil society and discriminatory policies against religious minorities, particularly Muslims, under India's Prime Minister Narendra Modi.

In August, France completed the withdrawal of its Barkhane counterterrorism forces from Mali, prompted by deteriorating relations with Malian authorities and the presence of forces from the private Russian military security company Wagner. The pullout took place amid rising violence against civilians by Islamist armed groups and Malian security forces and their auxiliaries. The French journalist Olivier Dubois, kidnapped in Gao region on April 8, 2021, is still held hostage by Al-Qaeda affiliated Jamaa Nusrat al-Islam wal-Muslimin (JNIM).

Georgia

Freedom of the media suffered setbacks, with numerous attacks against media professionals and the jailing of a critical TV director. Other areas of concern included lack of accountability for law enforcement abuses, illegal surveillance, unfair labor conditions, and violence against women and lesbian, gay, bisexual, and transgender (LGBT) people.

The European Union stated that it was conditioning Georgia's candidacy for membership on progress on 12 issues, many connected to human rights.

Lack of Accountability for Law Enforcement Abuses

Impunity for abuses by law enforcement persisted. In December 2021, parliament hastily abolished the State Inspector's Service, an independent body investigating abuses by law enforcement, instead establishing two new separate bodies tasked with probing abuse of power by law enforcement and monitoring data privacy, respectively.

The sudden decision followed the opening of an investigation by the state inspector into possible ill-treatment and violations of data protection laws regarding jailed ex-President Mikheil Saakashvili. The Council of Europe commissioner for human rights, Dunja Mijatović, called on parliament to reject the bill as it lacked "proper consultation with the relevant stakeholders [and] undermined the independent functioning of the body."

By October, the Ombudswoman's Office received 70 complaints of ill-treatment by prison staff or police. The authorities have been investigating 61 of them. The office petitioned the investigative body to launch investigations into the remaining cases. None had resulted in criminal prosecution at time of writing.

In January, local TV networks broadcasted video footage showing a police officer beating a 17-year-old boy with hearing disability in a metro station. One officer slapped and punched the boy several times, while another stood nearby without interfering. The state inspector's office investigated, and a court sentenced the policeman to five years in prison in July.

In May, Giorgi Mzhavanadze, one of the leaders of Shame Movement, a youth protest group, alleged that policemen at a Tbilisi police station handcuffed and physically and verbally abused him after he arrived to collect a fine notice. The Special Investigation Service, which investigates instances of abuse of office, opened an investigation, while the Interior Ministry claimed it had detained Mzhavanadze for disobedience.

In June, parliament hastily adopted a controversial surveillance bill. Sponsored by the ruling party, the bill authorizes indefinite wiretapping and other surveillance against individuals, without notifying them, in relation to 77 offenses, which now include trafficking, inhuman or degrading treatment and drug-related crimes.

In August, the Venice Commission, an advisory body to the Council of Europe on constitutional matters, urged authorities to re-examine the legislation, stating that "covert surveillance should be seen as an exception" and should be "cautiously worded and narrowly interpreted by the state." Georgia's president vetoed the bill, but in September the ruling party overrode the veto.

In September, an opposition-leaning television station, TV Pirveli, published leaked materials allegedly documenting the State Security Service's massive surveillance of opposition parties for the benefit of the ruling party. The materials show the surveillance of leading politicians in public and private settings.

Freedom of Media

In May, a court sentenced Nika Gvaramia, director of Mtavari Arkhi TV—a leading critical TV channel—to three years and six months in prison for abuse of power over managerial decisions while he was director of another private TV company. The authorities claimed that his managerial decisions brought less profit to the company. The decision was largely criticized by Georgian civil society as unlawful and politically motivated. Georgia's public defender argued that a decision by the director of an enterprise, even a harmful one, cannot be subject to criminal liability, and called for the case to be dismissed. In November, the appeals court upheld the decision.

There were numerous attacks against journalists and instances of interference in their work. In March, several assailants attacked Ema Gogokhia, a reporter for

Mtavari Arkhi, and her cameraman in Zugdidi, as they were filming municipal employees removing a drawing of the Ukrainian flag from the façade of a political party's office. The Special Investigation Service (SIS) launched an investigation into the interference.

In June, two assailants attacked TV Pirveli cameraman Murman Zoidze in Batumi. SIS arrested two people in connection with the incident.

In July, the Prosecutor's Office launched an investigation into an incident in which an MP allegedly physically attacked TV Pirveli's founder, Vakhtang Tsereteli.

In May, three journalists fired by Georgian Public Broadcasting, the national broadcaster, accused the station's management of censorship and "gross interference" in editorial policy, particularly over materials critical of Russia. Days later, another former journalist from the station made similar accusations.

Labor Rights

Despite recent legislative improvements, fair labor conditions remain a concern in Georgia. Overtime regulations are weak, social protections are minimal, unions lack legal guarantees that would allow them to effectively bargain for systemic changes, and shortage of resources hamper the Labor Inspectorate's effectiveness.

Wages are effectively unregulated, leaving workers vulnerable to exploitation. The minimum monthly wage of 20 GEL (approximately US$7) is 12 times lower than the subsistence minimum and has not been updated since 1999. Low wages are compounded by a workplace culture that normalizes wage theft. A report by the Georgia Fair Labor Platform, a coalition of labor unions and nongovernmental groups, found that 88 percent of workers had experienced at least one form of wage theft.

Healthcare workers, already overworked due to the Covid-19 pandemic, have been severely impacted by wage theft. In 2022, the Labor Inspectorate found that 86 private clinics that received special funding to supplement nurses' wages had used the funds for other purposes. In a positive move, the government raised the minimum wage for nurses in public clinics.

Workplace safety also remains a problem. According to the Labor Inspectorate, 23 workers died and 230 were injured in work-related accidents from January through September.

Sexual Orientation and Gender Identity

Lesbian, gay, bisexual, and transgender (LGBT) people in Georgia continue to face harassment, discrimination, and violence. In May, a group of some 30 men attacked five transgender women in their home in Tbilisi. The attackers, armed with stones and bricks, assaulted the women and their landlord, damaged their house, and made death threats. An investigation was pending at time of writing.

In July, the Tbilisi City Court fined three people for raiding the offices of Tbilisi Pride, an LGBT rights group, during mass anti-LGBT attacks in July 2021 that led to dozens of injuries and cancellation of the Pride March. The court acquitted the defendants on more serious charges of persecution and organized group violence. In total, police detained 31 people over the violence. Courts handed prison sentences to 26 people for violence against journalists covering the events. But they failed to identify and prosecute the organizers of the mass violence.

In December 2021, the European Court of Human Rights found that in 2013, Georgia violated freedom of association and prohibitions on inhuman and degrading treatment and discrimination when authorities failed to protect peaceful demonstrators from homophobic and transphobic violence. Violent mobs attacked a group of activists trying to mark the international day against homophobia on May 17, 2013, injuring dozens.

Women's Rights

The prosecutor's office reported 13 cases of femicide and 11 attempted murders of women by family members from January through August. Human Rights Center, a local rights group, said that courts often release on bail abusive partners, who continue to threaten the survivors.

In November 2021, the UN Committee on the Elimination of Discrimination against Women (CEDAW) found that Georgia breached several articles of the

Convention on the Elimination of All Forms of Discrimination against Women regarding the case of Khanum Jeiranova. Jeiranova died in 2014 after experiencing public humiliation and violence by her community. CEDAW found that Georgia, *inter alia*, failed to investigate and punish those responsible for Jeiranova's ill-treatment and death, and failed to protect her from gender-based discrimination.

Key International Actors

In June, in response to Georgia's membership application, the European Council stated its intent to grant candidate status once Georgia fulfills the 12 priorities identified by the European Commission. These include, inter alia, addressing political polarization, strengthening independence and accountability of all state institutions, ensuring an independent judiciary, guaranteeing media independence and pluralism, protecting the rights of vulnerable groups, and enhancing gender equality rights of vulnerable groups, and enhancing gender equality.

In June the European Parliament adopted a resolution deploring the "significant deterioration" of media freedoms in Georgia, including intimidation, violence, and "politically motivated criminal investigations into media workers and owners," and condemned Gvaramia's imprisonment.

Also in June, the International Criminal Court (ICC) issued three arrests warrants for war crimes committed during the 2008 conflict between Georgia and Russia over South Ossetia. The warrants are against three members of the de facto South Ossetia administration on charges of unlawful confinement, torture and inhuman treatment, outrages upon personal dignity, hostage taking, and unlawful transfer. The suspects have not been apprehended and are believed to be currently in territory controlled by South Ossetian or Russian authorities. In 2023, the ICC prosecutor's office anticipates downsizing the investigation in Georgia and focusing efforts on the execution of the three arrest warrants.

In September, the UN Human Rights Committee urged the government to investigate human rights violations and hold perpetrators accountable, step up efforts to combat violence against women, and protect people from discrimination and violence based on sexual orientation and gender identity.

In June, US officials expressed support for the country's democratic aspirations but also "deep concern about Georgia's democratic trajectory."

Following her February visit, Dunja Mijatović, published a report urging Georgian authorities to ensure effective implementation of the anti-discrimination legislation and better protection of labor and environmental rights.

Germany

Right-wing extremism, antisemitism, and racism appeared to be on the rise. A court in Koblenz convicted a former Syrian intelligence officer for crimes against humanity. Despite progress on rights of transgender people through the proposed Self-Determination Law governing legal gender recognition, trans people continue to suffer violence and discrimination. Climate change is taking an increasing toll on the protection of rights.

Discrimination and Intolerance

Official statistics published in May showed a significant increase in politically motivated crimes from 44,692 in 2020 to 55,048 in 2021. Politically motivated violence increased by almost 16 percent. The Ministry of Interior recorded 9,167 right-wing motivated crimes during the first half 2022, including 418 acts of violence. Antisemitic hate crimes increased by roughly 29 percent from 2020 to 2021; the Federal Criminal Police Office (BKA) recorded 965 antisemitic cases of offences in the first half of 2022.

In April, the Federal Office for the Protection of the Constitution (Verfassungsschutz) warned of the spread of antisemitic ideas to mainstream political discourse. In July, vandals chopped down the trees at the memorial for victims of the Buchenwald concentration camp. German chancellor Olaf Scholz was strongly criticized for failing to immediately condemn a statement by Palestinian President Mahmoud Abbas perceived to equate Israeli actions to the Holocaust.

According to a study by Mediendienst Integration, an online information platform for journalists, police are doing too little to prevent racism and antisemitism inside the police, with police trainings in only 5 out of 16 federal states addressing the issue of police racism and antisemitism. Independent bodies handling complaints against the police exist in only seven federal states.

On August 8, police in the city of Dortmund fatally shot a 16-year-old unaccompanied Senegalese asylum seeker six times, claiming he had a knife. According to media reports, he experienced mental health distress. At time of writing, the attack was being investigated.

In August, the Federal Anti-Discrimination Agency said it received more than 5,600 consultation requests in 2021, with 37 percent about racial discrimination and 32 percent about discrimination on the basis of disability.

In May, the first Federal Government Commissioner against Antiziganism (antigypsyism) and for the Life of Sinti and Roma in Germany took office.

Following Russia's invasion of Ukraine in February, the BKA reported more than 1,700 offenses "in relation to the war" by mid-April. The offenses, including insults, threats, physical assaults, and damage to property, targeted Russians, Ukrainians, and Belarussians.

In March, a Cologne court allowed Germany's domestic intelligence agency to formally monitor the Alternative für Deutschland (AfD) party for unconstitutional tendencies.

In April, the Frankfurt public prosecutor's office charged five police officers for sharing racist, antisemitic, and right-wing extremist contents in chat groups between 2014 and 2018. In a separate case, the Frankfurt police chief ordered disciplinary proceedings against five police officers in connection with the sharing of Nazi-symbols in chatrooms. As of July, eight police officers in Münster were under investigation for right-wing extremist and sexist content and glorifying violence in chatrooms.

The Federal Government Commissioner for Disabled Persons and the German Institute for Human Rights announced in May recommendations for the protection of people with disabilities in institutions after repeated cases of violence that include amendments to the legal framework on violence protection.

International Justice

In January, a Koblenz court sentenced a former Syrian intelligence officer to life in prison for overseeing the torture, murder, and rape of detainees in a Syrian prison. The same month, judges in Frankfurt began hearing evidence in a trial involving allegations of torture and murder by state agents during Syria's armed conflict. The accused in the case allegedly worked as a physician in two military hospitals in the cities of Damascus and Homs, Syria.

In April, the trial of a Gambian citizen commenced in the city of Celle for crimes against humanity for his alleged role in the "death squad" created by former Gambian President Yahya Jammeh.

These trials are possible because Germany's laws recognize universal jurisdiction over certain of the most serious crimes under international law.

A regional court in Neuruppin in July sentenced a 101-year-old man who worked as a Nazi concentration camp guard during World War II to five years in prison for complicity in war crimes. The man will likely not be imprisoned due to his age.

In July, Germany returned artifacts it had looted from Tanzania, Cameroon, and Namibia during its colonial period. Germany also signed an agreement with Nigeria to return looted Benin Bronzes.

In March, Germany's federal prosecution office in Karlsruhe opened a structural investigation into possible war crimes in Ukraine.

Business and Human Rights

In April, the president of the German Football Association (Deutscher Fußball-Bund) endorsed the idea of a reparations fund for families of migrant workers who died while building and servicing infrastructure for the 2022 World Cup in Qatar.

The Federal Office for Economic Affairs and Export Control expanded, albeit too slowly, to take on its role as supervisory authority for the 2021 supply chains law, which will enter into force in 2023.

Migrants and Asylum Seekers

In the first nine months of 2022, 134,908 people applied for asylum in Germany, an increase of 34.5 percent compared to the same period last year. Most applicants came from Syria, Afghanistan, and Iraq. By the end of August, 101,380 applications were pending.

The European Court of Justice ruled in August that Germany cannot deny family reunification just because an unaccompanied minor becomes an adult while their application is being processed.

Following Russia's invasion of Ukraine, the Central Register of Foreign Nationals counted more than one million refugees from Ukraine entering Germany between February and October 10, with minors constituting 35 percent. While Ukrainians can apply for a two-year residence permit under Germany's implementation of the European Union temporary directive, allowing them to work, study, and receive social benefits, thousands of third-country nationals who fled Ukraine were not eligible.

A spokesperson for the Interior Ministry said that 222 people from Russia applied for asylum in Germany in April. In May, Germany announced easier and faster visa procedures for Russian human rights activists, employees of non-governmental organziations (NGOs), and civil society groups.

The Interior Ministry announced in June plans to give foreigners who have been living in Germany for at least five years under the "tolerated" status ("Duldung") the possibility of long-term lawful residence. The move could benefit an estimated 105,000 people.

In August, the government reported that in the first half of 2022, 29 out of 43 attacks in or on refugee housing and 349 out of 424 attacks on asylum seekers and refugees were motivated by right-wing extremism. During the same period, there were five offenses against aid organizations and seven offenses against volunteers, almost all of them motivated by right-wing extremist politics. In August, an arson attack was carried out on a refugee center in Leipzig.

Gender Identity and Sexual Orientation

In June, the Ministry of Justice and the Ministry for Family Affairs, Senior Citizens, Women and Youth presented the parameters of a new Self-Determination Law ("Selbstbestimmungsgesetz") that would allow transgender, intersex, and non-binary people to change their name and gender on official documents to reflect their gender identity via a simple administrative procedure and without need for "expert reports." A draft law had not been presented to parliament at the time of writing.

In August, a man brutally attacked a 25-year-old trans man at a pride parade in Münster. He died a week later from his injuries. The alleged assailant remained in custody at time of writing.

In September, a 57-year-old trans woman suffered serious injuries after being assaulted by a group of youths on a tram in Bremen. Authorities were investigating the case as a hate crime at time of writing.

In September, a 16-year-old boy in Berlin was arrested for verbal harassment and attempted assault after he allegedly attacked a 49-year-old trans woman working in a hair salon. The suspect was released from police custody, but authorities were still investigating the case at time of writing.

Freedom of Expression and Association

In May, Berlin police banned several Nakba Day protests citing "immediate danger" of "inflammatory, anti-Semitic exclamations," and responded with force to people who protested despite the ban. Although organizers challenged the ban, a Berlin administrative court and a German appellate court upheld it.

Women's Rights

In June, the Bundestag amended the criminal code to remove the so-called "ban on advertising abortions," allowing doctors to legally inform patients about the procedure without facing charges.

In August, the Berlin senate approved measures to counter violence against women including expanding support and protection services, increasing training of different professional groups, and improving collaboration between institutions. The Senate is also developing a national action plan for the implementation of the Istanbul Convention on violence against women. The feminicide rate in Germany is among the highest in Europe.

Terrorism and Counterterrorism

In March, the government repatriated 37 more nationals—27 children and 10 women—from northeast Syria, where they were held in dire conditions in locked camps for Islamic State (ISIS) suspects and family members. Four of the women were arrested upon arrival on terrorism-related charges, including one accused of enslaving a Yezidi woman. In October, the government repatriated an additional 4 women, 7 children, and a 20-year-old young man, and stated that nearly all German nationals in the camps who wanted to return to Germany had been repatriated. Repatriated children were provided with psycho-social and other support, and when possible, placed in the care of family members.

Economic Justice

Official data published in August found that 15.8 percent of Germany's population, or about 13 million people, were at risk of poverty in 2021, with single-parent households and older women at greater risk than the average. Since then, increasing price inflation for basic goods and services essential to rights has raised concerns about food security and a cost-of-living crisis in the country.

Food prices in Germany increased by 18.7 percent between September 2021 and September 2022. In July, an organization representing nearly 1000 German food banks made an urgent appeal for government assistance, as food bank use reached recorded highs.

Climate Change and Policy Impacts

As the EU's biggest greenhouse gas emitter, Germany is contributing to the climate crisis which is taking a growing toll on human rights around the globe. Greenhouse emissions increased by 4.5 percent in 2021 after a decrease in the previous year. In January 2022, nine children and young adults supported by Environmental Action Germany (Deutsche Umwelthilfe, DUH) filed a case with the constitutional court claiming that the 2021 climate change law does not adequately regulate emission reductions and violates the government's obligation to protect rights.

The government had revised the law after the court found it to be unconstitutional in 2021, following a similar complaint by children and youth. Since the ruling, the government pledged to accelerate climate action to reach its goals of reducing emissions by 65 percent by 2030 compared to 1990 levels and net zero by 2045. According to the Climate Action Tracker, the government has to do more to achieve this target and be consistent with the Paris Agreement goal to stay below 1.5°C of warming, necessary to limit the most catastrophic climate outcomes.

Continued government support for fossil fuels will make it difficult to meet these targets. Due to the energy crisis caused by decreasing gas supply from Russia, the government decided to increase use of coal-fired power stations despite its commitment to phase out coal by 2030. Germany is still among the world's top 10 coal producers.

A report published in August by the Expert Council on Climate Issues found that the measures in the transportation and building sectors fall short of achieving Germany's climate goals.

The 2022 European heat wave impacted Germany greatly and in June, a month with high temperatures, deaths increased compared to last years. Older people and people with medical conditions are at particular risk in heatwaves. Forest fires in Germany have reached record highs.

Foreign Policy

While Germany's foreign policy has focused on the war in Ukraine, German Chancellor Olaf Scholz and Economics Minister Robert Habeck also publicly voiced criticism of the Chinese government's human rights record. German Foreign Minister Annalena Baerbock expressed concern following UN High Commissioner for Human Rights Michelle Bachelet's visit to China, as the trip did not "transparently clarify the serious allegations of grave human rights violations in Xinjiang."

In May, the German Economy Ministry declined to provide guarantees to Volkswagen for new investments in China, stating that it would not offer guarantees for projects in China that are in Xinjiang or have business ties to entities operating there. Volkswagen, in a joint venture with Chinese state company Saic, operates a factory in Xinjiang. Volkswagen reacted by stating that none of its factory workers were subjected to forced labor.

The German government decided to develop a new China strategy, which seeks to diversify economic relations towards the Middle East and other Asian countries to reduce Germany's economic dependence on China.

At the end of July, Baerbock criticized the Turkish government for its human rights violations during her visit to Istanbul, Turkey. She addressed Turkey's threats to launch a new military offensive in northern Syria, the case of jailed human rights defender Osman Kavala, and the reignited dispute between Turkey and Greece over the Greek islands in the east Aegean.

In August, the Federal Foreign Office, announced that the German government would intervene in an International Court of Justice case concerning Myanmar's alleged violations of the Genocide Convention against the ethnic Rohingya population.

In September, Germany, together with all European Union members minus Hungary, put forward a resolution that created a new special rapporteur on Russia at the UN Human Rights Council. In March, it supported the establishment of a commission of inquiry into human rights violations committed in Ukraine following the beginning of the armed conflict, and in April the suspension by the UN General Assembly of Russian membership of the Council.

Germany continued to oppose the waiver of intellectual property and trade rules by the World Trade Organization to speed up the production of Covid-19 vaccines and other health products in other countries.

WORLD REPORT 2023

Greece

Greece welcomed tens of thousands of Ukrainian refugees but failed to protect the rights of other asylum seekers and migrants, including by pushing new arrivals back to Turkey. The crackdown on nongovernmental groups and criminalization of solidarity continued. Curbs on media freedom and a surveillance scandal raised concerns about the state of rule of law. Law enforcement abuse remains widespread. Law enforcement officials failed adequately to respond to hate crimes and in some cases were complicit in them.

Migrants and Asylum Seekers

Greece initiated in April temporary protection for Ukrainian refugees. According to authorities, by July 31 Greece hosted a total of 70,676 Ukrainian refugees while by September 11, 10,139 non-Ukrainians had arrived in Greece in 2022—5,742 by sea and 4,397 by land.

Greece's migration minister, Notis Mitarachi, told parliament in March that Ukrainians are "real refugees," while those arriving from Syria or Afghanistan are "irregular migrants," even though many Syrians and Afghans have valid refugee claims.

While the Greek government continued to deny it engages in illegal pushbacks, it reported in early September "averting" 150,000 irregular arrivals in 2022.

In its annual report published in March, the Greek ombudsman criticized Greek authorities' investigations of pushbacks. An April investigation by Greece's National Transparency Authority—tasked by the government as the independent body to investigate border abuses—found no basis for reports of migrant pushbacks by Greek authorities.

In February, Filippo Grandi, the UN high commissioner for refugees, singled out Greece over pushbacks and rights violations at borders. "We are alarmed by recurrent and consistent reports coming from Greece's land and sea borders with Turkey, where UNHCR has recorded almost 540 reported incidents of informal returns by Greece since the beginning of 2020," he said. Ylva Johansson, European commissioner for home affairs, warned in July that "violent and illegal deportations of migrants must stop, now". The commissioner noted that the European

Commission's "funding is linked to EU fundamental rights being correctly applied".

The European Court of Human Rights (ECtHR) issued a landmark judgment in July concerning Greek authorities' role in the deaths of 11 women and children, including infants, off the Greek island of Farmakonisi in January 2014, in what survivors describe as a pushback operation.

Greece regularly ignores an increased number of emergency orders issued by the ECtHR to prevent the summary return of asylum seekers stranded along the borders with Turkey, and at imminent risk of pushback.

Despite lack of returns to Turkey since March 2020, Greece continued to use the inadmissibility procedures on the basis that Turkey is a "safe third country" for asylum seekers from Syria, Afghanistan, Somalia, Pakistan, and Bangladesh.

A June report by nongovernmental group (NGO) Refugee Support Aegean revealed persisting systematic detention of asylum seekers in Greece. In September, 22 NGOs denounced the "prison-like" conditions at the first EU-funded Closed Controlled Access Centre (CCAC) in Samos, established a year before. Greek courts continued to convict migrants of being "human smugglers," sentencing some to more than 100 years in prison, on dubious evidence.

By mid-September, 1,261 unaccompanied migrant children and 3,700 others deemed vulnerable had been relocated from Greece to other EU and associated countries, including 2,812 to Germany.

Members of the European Parliament sent written questions to the European Commission in September about the EU-funded surveillance systems deployed in migrant reception areas in Greece, which the MEPs believe pose an unacceptable risk to fundamental rights.

Attacks on Civil Society

In June, United Nations special rapporteur on human rights defenders, Mary Lawlor, while presenting her preliminary findings at the end of a 10-day mission in Greece, described an environment of fear and insecurity for human rights defenders in the country, particularly those working on migration. Judicial review applications challenging the legal framework are pending before the Council of State—Greece's highest administrative court.

In its Rule of Law report published in July, the European Commission noted the narrowing space for groups working with migrants and asylum seekers and recommended that Greece ensure registration requirements for civil society organizations are proportionate.

Greek authorities accused NGOs of coordinating with human smugglers to circumvent border controls by making appeals to the ECtHR to prevent pushbacks in the Evros region, with authorities reportedly initiating an "investigation" into organizations active in the region.

After facing two years of "obstacles and hurdles" the NGO Mare Liberum announced in February that it is unable to continue its monitoring of the Aegean Sea, leaving the strait without civilian monitoring. Mare Liberum faced new rules for registration of NGOs that are incompatible with international law.

Nongovernmental groups criticized the conviction in February of two Greek Helsinki Monitor staff by an Athens Court to a 12-month prison sentence suspended for three years on the charge of "falsely accusing" an Orthodox bishop of racist hate speech. Their appeal trial was scheduled for March 2023.

Freedom of Media

Greece fell 38 positions within a year in Reporters Without Borders' 2022 report on the Press Freedom Index, with the organization marking it the lowest-ranked European Union country, reflecting the gravity of concerns about media freedom in the country.

An ongoing surveillance scandal—described by some media as the Greek Watergate—continued during the year. It began with revelations in November 2021 that Greece's intelligence service (EYP) had spied on Stavros Malichoudis, an independent reporter. It emerged in April 2022 that the mobile phone of Thanasis Koukakis, a freelance journalist investigating banking and business stories, was infected by spyware by unknown persons. Days later, it was also revealed that Koukakis was also surveilled by EYP. At the end of July and in early August, it was reported that the leader of the opposition party PASOK and Member of the European Parliament, Nikos Androulakis, was also surveilled by EYP and that there had been an attempt to hack his phone using the same spyware as Koukakis' phone.

A parliamentary inquiry into the surveillance opened in September, but the ruling party blocked dozens of witnesses proposed by opposition parties, including journalists whose phones have been wiretapped. In addition, MPs decided that all inquiry meetings would be held behind closed doors and remain confidential, raising transparency concerns.

In September, the government threatened Der Spiegel Greece correspondent Giorgos Christides with legal action over his reporting of the prolonged failure of the authorities to rescue a child and others stuck on an islet in Evros, despite interim measures from the European Court of Human Rights (ECtHR) ordering it to do so.

In its Rule of Law Report published in July, the commission warned that attacks and threats against journalists persist, and journalists' professional environment has deteriorated further. These include physical attacks, threats, arbitrary detention, criminal lawsuits, and surveillance. It recommended Greece to establish legislative and other safeguards to improve the physical safety and working environment of journalists.

United Nations special rapporteur on human rights defenders, Mary Lawlor, said in June that "Journalists who counter the government's narrative on the management of migration flows are often under pressure and lack access to mainstream media outlets. ... Journalists reporting on corruption are sometimes facing threats and even charges."

The Judicial Council of the Supreme Court ruled out allegations made by authorities against four Greek journalists and publishers that led to criminal charges linked to their investigative reporting into the bribery of state officials and doctors allegedly to grant preferential market access to a pharmaceutical company. The Judicial Council said allegations against the journalists were baseless and declined to send them to trial.

Ingeborg Beugel, a Dutch correspondent in Greece, faced trial on June 1 in the Piraeus Court charged with "facilitating the illegal stay of a third-country national" for hosting in her home in Hydra an Afghan national who had been a rejected asylum seeker. The trial was postponed and is pending at this writing. Beugel experienced online and physical harassment in November 2021 following a heated dialogue with Greek Prime Minister Kyriakos Mitsotakis during a press conference where she questioned him about pushbacks.

There has been no significant progress in the investigation into the April 2021 murder of journalist Giorgos Karaivaz in Athens.

Racism and Intolerance

Statistics on hate crimes for 2021, released in May by the nongovernmental Racist Violence Recording Network (RVNR), showed a decrease in incidents of organized violence. However, in most of the incidents recorded by RVNR and involving refugees and migrants, the victims identify law enforcement officials among the perpetrators. The report identifies racially motivated police violence as a growing trend since 2018, especially during the pandemic.

RVRN also found that lesbian, gay, bisexual, and transgender (LGBT) individuals were targeted by a wide range of perpetrators, including ordinary citizens, public officials, law enforcement officials, and even family members. Reports of incidents of violence against LGBT people intensified amidst the pandemic, including domestic violence and harassing behaviors during periods of restricted movement to control the spread of Covid-19.

In a September report, the European Commission against Racism and Intolerance welcomed Greece's anti-racism action plan and national lesbian, gay, bisexual, transgender, and intersex equality strategy, but warned of continued discrimination against LGBTI pupils in schools, racist and anti-LGBTI police abuse, and forced evictions of Roma.

A Greek court acquitted four police officers over the 2018 killing of 33-year-old queer activist and human rights defender Zak Kostopoulos. Two other men were found guilty of assault and sentenced to 10 years, in one case to be served at home.

The results of an investigation by the Hellenic Data Protection Authority initiated in August 2020 into the lawfulness of a "smart policing" program to scan people's faces and fingerprints were still pending. The program is inconsistent with international human rights standards on privacy and likely to amplify ongoing discrimination, including ethnic profiling resulting from the government's targeted sweep operations against migrants.

Women's Rights

The government came under increasing pressure to combat domestic violence, including by making femicide a standalone crime, as the murders of two women in one day in August sparked public outrage and protests. The killing of a woman set on fire by her husband in September and of another woman and her 10-month-old baby brought the total to at least 17 women murdered so far this year.

Guatemala

President Alejandro Giammattei and his allies deepened the democratic backsliding in Guatemala in an apparent effort to avoid accountability for widespread high-level corruption.

Authorities appointed two key figures in 2022: the attorney general and the human rights ombudsperson in selection processes that were neither fair nor transparent. In May, Giammattei reappointed attorney general Consuelo Porras. Porras has blocked investigations into corruption and brought arbitrary proceedings against independent journalists, prosecutors, and judges.

Harassment and violence against journalists and human rights defenders and challenges in protecting the rights of women and girls, lesbian, gay, bisexual, and transgender (LGBT) people, and migrants remain major concerns.

Corruption

Investigations by the United Nations-backed International Commission against Impunity in Guatemala (CICIG), which operated from 2007 to 2019, and by the Attorney General's Office exposed more than 120 corruption schemes in all three branches of government.

In 2019, then-President Jimmy Morales terminated the CICIG's mandate and forced its head to leave the country. Since then, Attorney General Consuelo Porras has weakened the Office of the Special Prosecutor against Impunity (FECI), responsible for investigating corruption, and progress on the cases has come to a standstill.

The Americas Society and Council of the Americas ranked Guatemala 13th out of 15 Latin American countries in their ability to detect, punish, and prevent corruption, experiencing the sharpest decline in the index from 2021.

Years of investigations have shown that businesspeople have acted in coordination with corrupt officials. Money obtained through corruption and criminal activity is often used to finance electoral campaigns.

Judicial Independence and Checks on Executive Power

Measures adopted recently by Congress, the Attorney General's Office, and other authorities have impeded accountability for corruption and abuses, undermined the rule of law, and weakened human rights guarantees.

As of September, Congress had yet to comply with a 2020 Constitutional Court ruling ordering it to appoint judges and magistrates to fill vacant seats on the Supreme Court and appeals courts for the period 2019-2024. The selection process has been marred by delays and influence peddling allegations.

On May 16, President Giammattei appointed Consuelo Porras as attorney general for a second term, after a selection process marred by several attempts by government authorities and others to undermine the fairness and independence of the process.

During her initial four years in office, Porras undermined investigations into corruption and human rights abuses. She transferred, fired, or, in some cases, promoted spurious criminal proceedings against independent judges, prosecutors, and journalists.

In January 2022, the Attorney General's Office opened seemingly arbitrary investigations into Judge Erika Aifán, who had presided over high-level corruption cases reportedly involving President Giammattei. Aifán fled Guatemala in March.

In February, Virginia Laparra, an anti-corruption prosecutor, was imprisoned on spurious grounds. She remained behind bars as of September.

In late June and early July, Porras abruptly removed eight prosecutors, including Hilda Pineda, who in 2013 prosecuted former President Efraín Ríos Montt for "genocide" and "crimes against humanity" in connection with his alleged role in massacres committed during the country's 1960-1996 civil war.

In July, Congress appointed a new ombudsperson, José Alejandro Cordova, a Giammattei administration ally, through a process that lacked transparency.

In November, Congress appointed the new comptroller general, Frank Bode. The comptroller plays a key role in preventing corruption and the office's work is crucial to ensure free and fair elections presidential elections in June 2023.

Freedom of Expression

The Giammattei administration and Attorney General Consuelo Porras have created a hostile environment for independent journalists and media outlets, including with verbal attacks, restrictions on the press, and abusive criminal proceedings.

The Journalists' Association of Guatemala reported 66 incidents of attacks, persecution, and criminalization of media workers during the first six months of 2022.

In some cases, government officials have used a 2008 anti-gender-based violence law to harass journalists who write about them, claiming that their reporting is a form of "psychological violence" against officials or their female relatives.

On March 8, journalist Orlando Villanueva from *Noticias del Puerto* was shot dead by unidentified individuals in Puerto Barrios, the capital of Izabal department. Other journalists in that department have faced attacks and official harassment, particularly for covering issues related to a mining project in the Indigenous community of El Estor. In September, a judge acquitted journalist Carlos Choc from *Prensa Comunitaria*, who had been accused without evidence of "incitement to commit crime" for his coverage of an October 2021 protest related to the mining project.

In April, journalist Juan Luis Font fled Guatemala. Font has been subject to apparently spurious criminal investigations related to his reporting on corruption allegations against former infrastructure minister Alejandro Sinibaldi, who is under investigation for taking bribes.

In July, prosecutors arrested Jose Rubén Zamora, the owner of the well-respected media outlet El Periódico, which has uncovered several incidents of corruption in the country. He is accused of "money laundering," "blackmail," and "influence peddling".

Accountability for Past Human Rights Violations

The limited progress that Guatemala was making in adjudicating crimes committed during the armed conflict (1960-1996) seems to have come to a standstill in recent years, particularly because of attacks and spurious prosecutions against prosecutors and judges working on such cases.

Challenges persist in searching for and identifying the disappeared during the armed conflict, mainly Indigenous Mayans.

In January, a court in Guatemala sentenced five former members of a paramilitary unit to 30 years in prison for crimes against humanity after finding them responsible for raping and enslaving 36 Mayan women between 1981 and 1985.

In July, legislators introduced a bill that would grant amnesty to security forces for "actions or omissions" they committed during the armed conflict. It was the third time such a bill has been introduced in recent years. It had yet to be discussed as of writing.

Human Rights Defenders

Abuses against human rights defenders and social leaders increased in the last five years, according to the non-profit Unidad de Protección a Defensoras y Defensores de Derechos Humanos de Guatemala (Udefegua), which recorded 11 killings and 1,002 incidents of defamation, harassment or spurious judicial complaints directed mainly at justice operators, journalists, peasants, and land defenders in 2021.

In June 2021, a law limiting the work of nongovernmental organizations (NGOs) took effect. It includes overly broad provisions that could be used by the executive branch to cancel the legal status of organizations that undertake activities "against public order."

Women's and Girls' Rights

The Observatory for Sexual and Reproductive Rights reported over 60,000 pregnancies among adolescents and girls as of July, including 1,323 in girls between 10 and 14 years old.

Abortion is legal only when a pregnant person's life is at risk. On March 8, lawmakers passed a bill increasing penalties and broadening the circumstances under which people could be prosecuted for accessing abortion—broadly defined as the "natural or provoked death" of an embryo or fetus. Congress shelved the bill, after President Giammattei threatened to veto it.

Sexual Orientation and Gender Identity

Guatemala has no comprehensive civil legislation protecting people from discrimination on the grounds of sexual orientation and gender identity, nor a legal gender recognition procedure for transgender people. Authorities have failed to adequately protect LGBT people from violence and discrimination.

In January, a commission in Congress passed a bill that would stigmatize transgender people and curtail children's and adolescents' rights to education, information, and health. The bill remained pending in Congress as of September.

In March, Congress passed—but then shelved at the president's request—a bill that would have banned same-sex marriage and unions and appeared aimed at legally protecting discrimination on the basis of sexual orientation.

Guatemalan civil society organizations reported that, as of October, at least 25 LGBT people had been killed in 2022.

Disability Rights

Children with disabilities with high support requirements are forced to live in institutions in Guatemala. There are few if any policies that would enable them to live in a family household. Reports of abuses against children with disabilities living in institutions are not properly investigated or resolved.

Children's Rights

According to data shared by the Ombudsperson's Office in June, almost half of the children under 5 years old in Guatemala suffer chronic malnutrition—a situation that worsened during the Covid-19 pandemic. According to government data, there were 15,862 cases of severe malnutrition of children under 5, and 42 had died as of September.

Human Rights Watch found that Mineduc Digital, an online learning product used by the Education Ministry during the Covid-19 pandemic, transmitted children's personal data to advertising technology companies, enabling them to track and target children across the internet. As of September, the ministry had failed to stop children's privacy violations.

Migrants and Asylum Seekers

In cooperation with the administration of US President Joe Biden, President Giammattei has increased efforts to prevent non-Guatemalan migrants and asylum seekers from reaching the United States. From January through October 2022, police detained and expelled more than 13,000 people to Honduras, mostly Venezuelans without a visa.

President Giammattei has deployed police and soldiers to Guatemala's southern border to prevent migrants from entering the country. In October, they clashed violently with a migrant caravan attempting to cross the border from Honduras.

In September 2021, after an increase in the number of Ecuadorians arriving at the US border, and a decision by Mexico to end visa-free travel for Ecuadorians, Guatemala did the same.

Key International Actors

In March, the United Nations High Commissioner for Human Rights said that Guatemala faced "systemic and structural challenges," including regarding the "the fight against impunity, democratic spaces and citizen participation."

Between February and May, the European Union issued four statements expressing concern over deteriorating rule of law, threats to judicial independence, and the reappointment of Attorney General Consuelo Porras.

In April, the European Parliament adopted a resolution expressing concern for the rule of law in Guatemala, condemning the criminalization, detention, and harassment against judicial operators, human rights defenders, and journalists, and urging to respect the separation of powers between branches of government.

In June, the Inter-American Commission on Human Rights included Guatemala, along with Venezuela, Cuba, and Nicaragua, in the chapter of its annual report reserved for states with grave, massive, or systematic violations of human rights and serious attacks to democratic institutions.

In the same month, Guatemala signed the Los Angeles Declaration on Migration and Protection, committing to strengthening and expanding paths toward safe, legal migration and asylum.

In July 2022, the US Department of State released its Corrupt and Undemocratic Actors Report for 2021. It includes several current and former Guatemalan public officials, as well as five Guatemalan businesspeople.

President Giammattei did not attend the Ninth Summit of the Americas in Los Angeles following criticism by the Biden administration of Guatemala's decision to reappoint Attorney General Consuelo Porras. Shortly before the summit, the US placed sanctions on Porras, citing involvement in significant corruption.

Guatemala and five other countries led the renewal of the mandate for the UN Independent International Fact-Finding Mission on Venezuela in October.

Haiti

In 2022, Haiti remained in a long-standing political, security and humanitarian crisis that has left all government branches inoperative, compounding overwhelming impunity for human rights abuses.

Armed gangs intensified their control of strategic areas increasing violence, including at the main fuel terminal in Port-au-Prince, and preventing the distribution of fuel. The lack of access to fuel has harshly impacted businesses, schools, and hospitals and created shortages of basic goods including water and telecommunications.

More than 42 percent of Haiti´s population needs humanitarian assistance and up to 40 percent of the country experiences acute food insecurity, according to the United Nations Office for the Coordination of Humanitarian Affairs (OCHA).

Despite dire conditions, the United States and other countries repatriated almost 41,000 Haitians by air and sea from January 2021 to September 2022, and the Dominican Republic expelled almost 59,000 people to Haiti by land between February and October 2022, including people born in the Dominican Republic but considered by Dominican authorities to be Haitian, available data show.

Starting in late August, thousands of Haitians took to the streets in nationwide demonstrations against the government and to protest increasing gang violence, widespread hunger, a lack of basic public services, runaway inflation and fuel price increases triggered by Prime Minister Ariel Henry's removal of subsidies.

An outbreak of cholera caused at least 223 deaths as of November 27.

Constitutional Crisis

Since the assassination of President Jovenel Moïse in July 2021, Prime Minister Henry has led the government without a constitutional mandate, as he did not receive parliamentary approval.

Parliament stopped functioning in January 2020, when former President Moïse refused to organize legislative elections. Prime Minister Henry rules by decree.

In September 2021, the prime minister signed a political agreement with several civil society groups and political parties—organized as the Commission for a Haitian Solution to the Crisis (known as the Montana Group)—to co-establish a new transitional government to organize elections.

On January 31, 2022, the Montana Group elected Fritz Jean, former head of Haiti's central bank, as interim president. Neither the international community nor the Henry government recognized him.

In July, Henry said he would hold general elections, but he did not appoint any members to the Provisional Electoral Council, the body tasked with organizing elections, which is not now functioning. Negotiations on a transitional government continued as of October.

Dysfunctional Justice System

Haiti's justice system barely functioned. Only 3 of 12 justices of the Supreme Court of Justice continued working—meaning the court lacks a quorum to hear cases and issue rulings. Without an elected president and functioning Senate, the appointment of additional justices stalled.

In the first half of 2022, the Council of Ministers, which is made up of the cabinet members, appointed 113 lower-level judges, increasing the capacity of the judicial system. But in June, a gang took control of Port-au-Prince's Palace of Justice, the main justice complex in the country. It appears to have stolen or destroyed evidence that may be impossible to recover, as Haitian courts do not have digital copies of files.

Four people had been detained for more than a year, without formal charges, as of October, in connection with the August 2020 killing of Monferrier Dorval, Port-au-Prince Bar Association president. As of October, no judge had been appointed to the case after the previous judge's February resignation.

Only 200 criminal trials were held from October 2021 through September 2022, the nongovernmental organization National Human Rights Defense Network (RNDDH) reported. In some jurisdictions, courts had held no hearings on criminal cases for three years, the Office of the United Nations High Commissioner for Human Rights (OHCHR) reported.

As of September, Haiti's prisons held almost three times more detainees than for which they were built. Many of the more than 11,700 detainees—84 percent of whom were awaiting trial— are living in inhumane conditions. The Ombudsperson's Office, UN agencies, and Haitian rights groups have reported cases of torture by prison guards, of rape by other detainees, and scores of deaths related to malnutrition.

The entry into force of new criminal procedure and penal codes providing alternatives to pretrial detention was postponed from June 2022 to June 2024 to allow a government commission to organize their implementation.

In early November, prime minister Henry appointed a new president of Haiti´s Supreme Court.

Investigation of President Moïse's Assassination

President Moïse was assassinated on July 7, 2021. In response, security forces killed 3 people and arrested 47 in Haiti, including former Colombian military officers, the RNDDH reported. One detainee died, four were released, and 42 remained imprisoned, as of October. None have been charged.

Four judicial officials who conducted initial proceedings in the Moïse case said they were threatened. Three investigating judges later resigned, citing personal reasons linked to security problems. One faced a corruption accusation. A fourth resigned in April, complaining he had no access to the case file. In May, a fifth judge was appointed to the case.

Chief Prosecutor Bedford Claude asked a judge, in September 2021, to approve charges against Prime Minister Henry, arguing he had made phone contact, hours after the assassination, with one of the main suspects. Prime Minister Henry denied the allegation and fired Claude. A judicial decision regarding Claude's request to indict Prime Minister Henry remained pending as of October 2022.

The Colombian suspects continued complaining, in 2022, that they had not had any hearings, lacked legal assistance, and suffered inhumane detention conditions. Some said police had tortured them.

The related investigation in the US made some progress. A convicted drug trafficker and former DEA informant, a former Colombian military officer, and former Haitian senator were charged in early 2022 with various offenses, including conspiring to commit murder offenses.

Gang Violence

Violence escalated, mainly in the Port-au-Prince metropolitan area, as the 92 gangs operating there fought for territory, the NGO Fondasyon Je Klere (FJKL) reported. Several officials told Human Rights Watch that gangs had links with politicians and police officers.

Nationwide, BINUH reported 1,349 homicides, from January through August 2022 and 877 kidnappings.

The Institute for Justice & Democracy in Haiti (IJDH), the RNDDH, and the FJKL have documented 20 massacres in Port-au-Prince since 2018, with at least 1,000 victims. There are no charges in these killings.

Gangs reportedly used sexual violence to terrorize and control neighborhoods. From January through March 2022, BINUH registered an average of 98 victims of sexual violence a month in gang-controlled areas of Port-au-Prince. The real number is very likely much higher, as sexual violence remains chronically underreported.

The wave of brutality displaced 96,000 people in the metropolitan area of Port-au-Prince as of October 2022, BINUH reported.

Human Rights Defenders and Journalists

Civil society groups documented several incidents of attacks, threats, and intimidation against human rights defenders, journalists, and judges from January through October 2022.

In January, gangs killed two journalists investigating the murder of a police inspector. A third journalist survived the attack, but fled Haiti after receiving death threats. In February, a journalist was shot dead while covering a demonstration. In September, gangs killed two journalists while they reported gang violence. No progress has been made in investigations of these or the killings of two other journalists in June 2021.

RNDDH reported that an influential political figure and others held meetings in March, including with a gang leader, to plan the killing of its director. The organization said a person present in one of the meetings revealed the plan.

In 2019, Charlot Jeudy, president of Kouraj, an organization advancing the rights of lesbian, gay, bisexual, and transgender (LGBT) people, was found dead in his home. No progress has been reported in the investigation.

Abuses by Security Forces

Police responded to anti-government protests with excessive force. A journalist was killed and two injured after police allegedly opened fire with live ammunition on demonstrators in February. The RNDDH reported that several demonstrators were injured, allegedly after inappropriate use of teargas by police.

The police internal affairs office was investigating 50 cases of alleged human rights violations by police from January through October, BINUH reported.

Rights to Health, Water, and Food

More than half of Haitians are chronically food insecure, and 22 percent of children are chronically malnourished.

Exacerbating Haiti's hunger crisis, food prices were 23 percent higher in June 2022, compared to June 2021. Dramatic floods and soil erosion triggered by deforestation and watershed degradation have also undermined agricultural production in some areas.

The 2021 earthquake affected 800,000 people. Insecurity and insufficient funds stalled aid delivery to areas affected by a devastating earthquake in 2021. Those in need of humanitarian assistance, including shelter and access to health, education, and other essential services, increased from 4.4 million in 2021 to 4.9 million in 2022.

Over a third of the population lacks access to clean water and two-thirds have limited or no sanitation service. Only 1 percent of the population had been fully vaccinated against Covid-19, as of October.

The first case of cholera was confirmed in early October and the outbreak has spread rapidly. Haiti's Health Ministry reported more than 11.800— nearly half of them children under 14— suspected cases and at least 223 deaths as of November 27. The real number of cases is likely much higher, because of under-reporting, UN agencies warned.

Right to Education

Nearly half of Haitians aged 15 and older are illiterate. The quality of public education is generally poor, and 85 percent of schools are private, charging fees that exclude most children from low-income families.

The 2021 earthquake destroyed or heavily damaged 1,250 schools. Insecurity and insufficient funds kept most from being rebuilt. More than 250,000 children lacked access to adequate school buildings, UNICEF estimated.

Gang violence and the cholera outbreak may keep over 2.4 million children out of classrooms, UNICEF warned.

Women's and Girls' Rights

Gender-based violence is common, exacerbated by the 2021 earthquake and escalating gang violence.

In 2020, the International Federation of Football Association (FIFA) Ethics Committee banned Haitian Football Federation (FHF) President Yves Jean-Bart for life, after finding evidence of systematic sexual abuse of female players. FIFA later banned another FHF official for life and suspended another four in connection with the abuses, but did not remove other officials also implicated. In July 2022, Evans Lescouflair, a former sports minister, was arrested in Puerto Rico and sent to Haiti, in connection with child sexual abuse cases filed by survivors.

The new penal code, scheduled to enter into force in 2024, lists sexual harassment and gender-based violence as punishable offenses.

Haiti has a total ban on abortion. The new code will legalize it in all circumstances until the twelfth week of pregnancy, and at any time in cases of rape or incest or when the mental or physical health of the pregnant person is in danger.

Disability Rights

Although Haiti ratified the Convention on the Rights of Persons with Disabilities, its legislative framework has not been harmonized and includes offensive and discriminatory provisions. People with disabilities experience discrimination in access to health, education, and justice, and significant stigma places them at heightened risk of violence.

The pending penal code prohibits violence or incitement against people with disabilities.

Sexual Orientation and Gender Identity

Lesbian, gay, bisexual, and transgender (LGBT) people are particularly exposed to violence. Haitian law does not currently protect LGBT people. The pending penal code provides some protections based on sexual orientation by, for example, imposing higher penalties for crimes motivated by a victim's real or perceived sexual orientation.

Migration

Between January and September 2022, several countries in the region sent more than 21,000 people back to Haiti by flight or boat, compared to 10,152 in the same period of 2021, the International Organization for Migration (IOM) reported. Of those repatriated in 2022, 69 percent were returned by the US, which inappropriately used a health policy known as Title 42. The recent returnees comprised more than 4,000 children, including hundreds of children born in Chile and Brazil of Haitian parents.

The Dominican Republic expelled almost 59,000 people to Haiti by land between February and October 2022, including people born in the Dominican Republic but considered by Dominican authorities to be Haitian, according to the nonprofit Support Group for Refugees and Returnees (GARR).

The US Coast Guard interdicted 7,137 Haitians at sea from October 2021 through September 2022, by far the most in five years.

Most of those the US returned had settled in South America years ago, escaping an already difficult economic and security situation in Haiti. Some suffered discrimination and violence on their way north, as well as lack of access to health care and adequate food and hygiene products in US detention centers. Some returnees said they wanted to ask for asylum in the US but were not given a chance to do so.

As of October, there was no reintegration program to help returnees in Haiti or human rights monitoring mechanisms to assess whether any were persecuted or otherwise harmed upon return.

Key International Actors

The United Nations Security Council extended BINUH's mandate until July 15, 2023.

After the 2021 earthquake, the UN appealed for US$187 million for immediate emergency relief in the area affected, and received about 40 percent from donors. The UN asked for $373 million for nationwide humanitarian response for 2022. By June, it had raised less than 30 percent.

In October, the UN Security Council approved sanctions against gang leaders involved in violence, including freezing of assets, travel bans, and arms embargoes. In November, the United Stated and Canada sanctioned the president of the Haitian Senate and a former Haitian senator, whom they accused of involvement in drug trafficking.

Honduras

In January 2022, Xiomara Castro became the first female president of Honduras, after winning the elections by a wide margin, promising to defend human rights. In April, former President Juan Orlando Hernández (2014-2022) was extradited to the United States on drug trafficking and gun charges.

Honduras' justice system has suffered political interference for years. As of October, the Castro administration and the United Nations were negotiating to establish an international commission to investigate corruption. Congress repealed an overly broad secrecy law but has not revoked other laws that pose major barriers to corruption investigations.

Gang violence and human rights violations cause internal displacement and migration. Women, human rights defenders, Indigenous, Afro-Honduran, and lesbian, gay, bisexual, and transgender (LGBT) people are at particular risk of violence.

Judicial Independence and the Fight Against Corruption

President Castro campaigned on a promise to work for independent and impartial justice. The justice system's weak response to corruption, a structural problem in Honduras, and a series of laws hindering prosecutors' capacity to investigate have enabled impunity for corrupt acts that contribute to human rights violations.

In February, Congress passed a government-supported amnesty for people charged, on "political grounds," for protesting or defending rights, including to land, as well as for former public officials during the administration of Manuel Zelaya (2006-June 2009), President Castro's husband. While human rights organizations applauded the amnesty for defenders and protesters, anti-corruption organizations warned that overbroad language—amnesty for authorities charged or convicted for "actions related to the exercise of their public function"—could shield corrupt former officials.

In July, Congress passed a law regulating the committee in charge of nominating candidates for the 15 Supreme Court vacancies that will open in January 2023.

The law specifies evaluation standards for the committee; requires that sessions and interviews be public; allows civil society, media, and UN agencies to participate as observers; and reserves at least seven seats on the new Supreme Court for women. The committee started working in September.

But the law did not set any criteria for Congress as a whole to choose the new justices from the list of at least 45 candidates sent by the committee. In the past, parties have split the vacancies among them, according to the proportion of seats they held in Congress.

Lack of transparency and clear criteria also plague the selection of lower-court judges and decisions over their careers. The Supreme Court president has ultimate power over selection, promotion, transfer, and discipline of lower-court judges.

Congress took a positive step by repealing the so-called official secrets law in March. Previous governments had abused it, classifying, for up to 25 years, budgets, expenses, and other documents having nothing to do with national security. But, as of October, the Castro administration had not informed the public about the use of a fund, previously considered secret, that collected a tax from any financial transaction. Congress has not repealed other laws that drastically curtail prosecutors' power to conduct anti-corruption investigations.

President Castro's negotiations with the UN to implement an international commission against impunity and corruption continued, as of October.

Human Rights Defenders

The UN special rapporteur on the situation of human rights defenders called Honduras, in 2019, one of Latin America's most dangerous countries for defenders. From January through August 2022, the Office of the High Commissioner for Human Rights (OHCHR) reported attacks on 120 human rights defenders, including 78 environment and land defenders. Such defenders are frequently unfairly charged with misappropriation, theft, or other crimes—or sued—to impede their work, the OHCHR said.

In February, a court annulled, because of due process violations, a trial against eight Guapinol River defenders who protested opening an iron oxide mine inside a national park. It ordered the release of six who remained in pretrial detention and had spent more than 29 months in jail. In 2020, the UN Working Group on Arbitrary Detention had found their detentions arbitrary.

In June, David Castillo was sentenced to more than 22 years in prison as a co-conspirator in the killing of environmental and Indigenous rights activist Berta Cáceres, in 2016. The tribunal said Castillo targeted Cáceres for her opposition to a private hydroelectric dam project he directed. Cáceres' family and the organization she led, the Consejo Cívico de Organizaciones Populares e Indígenas de Honduras (COPINH), say prosecutors are not thoroughly investigating others who helped orchestrate the killing.

The mechanism Honduras created in 2015 to protect journalists, human rights defenders, and justice system professionals has serious flaws. In January, its then-director told Human Rights Watch that it suffered from staff shortages, lack of financial autonomy, and prioritization of reactive measures rather than root causes. Naming a new director in July, the Castro administration vowed to coordinate with civil society to make the mechanism more effective, transparent, and accountable.

Attacks on Journalists

Honduras is one of Latin Americas' deadliest countries for journalists, Reporters Without Borders noted in 2022. From 2001 to October 2022, 98 journalists were killed—5 in 2022—C-Libre, a Honduran free-speech NGO reported. In only 10 cases—about 10 percent—were killers tried and found guilty, C-Libre said.

Migration, Asylum, and Internal Displacement

Violence, lack of opportunity, unemployment, and climate-related disasters contribute to push thousands of Hondurans to flee, studies by the United Nations High Commissioner for Refugees (UNHCR), the International Organization for Migration (IOM), and the Migration Policy Institute (MPI) show.

From January through September, 23,146 Hondurans—more than any other nationality—requested asylum in Mexico, Mexico's refugee agency reported. Many more continue to the United States. Migrants face serious risks—including kidnapping, robbery, and discrimination—throughout the journey.

From January through September, 72,111 Hondurans were forcibly returned—more than throughout 2021—the government reported, almost all from Mexico and the US, evenly divided.

As they transit Honduras, heading north, Haitians, Nicaraguans, Cubans, Venezuelans, and other migrants risk being targeted for serious crimes such as robbery, sexual abuse, and murder.

Gang violence and human rights violations caused the internal displacement of some 191,000 people between 2004 and 2018, the latest comprehensive government data shows. Those most affected are children fleeing forced gang recruitment, professionals and business owners facing extortion, domestic violence survivors, and LGBT people and members of ethnic minorities enduring discrimination and violence, the Inter-American Commission on Human Rights (IACHR) reports.

Prison Conditions

The military took control of prisons in 2019, but in August, President Castro ordered national police to take charge for a year, calling for a plan to gradually transfer their oversight to other civilian authorities.

As of September, almost 20,000 detainees occupied prisons with capacity for under 11,000. Almost half of male and more than half of female detainees were in pretrial detention, official statistics show.

Women's and Girls' Rights

Honduras has the highest rate of femicide—defined as "the killing of a woman by a man in the context of unequal power relations between men and women based on gender"—in Latin America, the UN Economic Commission for Latin America and the Caribbean reports. The *Centro de Derechos de Mujeres*, a Honduran NGO that monitors media reports, counted 211 femicides from January through September 2022. In January, UN Women estimated that 90 percent of Honduran femicides go unpunished.

Abortion is illegal in Honduras under all circumstances, with prison sentences of up to six years for people who have abortions and their providers. Emergency contraception—the "morning-after pill"—to prevent pregnancy after rape, unprotected sex, or contraceptive failure, is prohibited.

Sexual Orientation and Gender Identity

LGBT people in Honduras continue to suffer high levels of violence and discrimination in all areas of life, pushing some to flee the country.

In May, President Castro committed to implement a 2021 Inter-American Court of Human Rights ruling finding Honduras responsible for the killing of Vicky Hernández, a transgender woman, during the 2009 military coup. Among other measures, the ruling ordered the creation of a simple and accessible procedure through which trans people can change their name and gender on official documents to reflect their gender identity. As of October, it had not been established.

Indigenous Rights

Honduras has no national legislation implementing Indigenous people's right under international law to free, prior, and informed consent to legislative or administrative measures affecting them.

In April, Congress revoked a law that had created so-called ZEDEs (Areas of Employment and Economic Development, in Spanish), geographic areas in which private companies were granted extensive operational autonomy, including the power to establish their own courts. Indigenous and *garifuna*—Afro-Indigenous—organizations say authorities created zones within their traditional territories without proper consultation. As of October, they reported that ZEDEs that had been established before the April law repeal were still operating.

Indigenous and Afro-Honduran communities report enormous obstacles to obtaining title to traditional lands, which the National Agrarian Institute administers.

Children's Rights

Honduras' fragile institutions fail to protect children's—including adolescents'—rights and access to education and health care, the IACHR reported in 2019.

More than 256,000 children ages 5 through 17 work, the National Statistics Unit reported in 2021, and almost a third of those under 17 do not attend school.

Child recruitment by gangs has caused many children to flee, abandoning school. The average age of first contact with gangs is 13, the UN Development Programme reported in 2020.

Key International Actors

Under President Castro, Honduras maintained a hesitant stance on human rights in its foreign policy. It voted in favor of multiple UN resolutions condemning Russia's rights violations in Ukraine. It abstained from UN Human Rights Council resolutions renewing the mandate of the UN fact-finding mission in Venezuela and initially voted against, but then clarified its intention to abstain on, a resolution establishing a group of experts to investigate human rights violations in Nicaragua.

Honduras also abstained on a vote to create a new special rapporteur on Russia but was one of only two countries in the region to vote in favor of a decision to discuss a report by the High Commissioner for Human Rights on violations against Uyghurs and other predominantly Muslim communities in the Xinjiang region of China. In the Organization of American States, it abstained from a resolution urging Nicaragua to release political prisoners and cease media persecution.

WORLD REPORT 2023

Hungary

The ruling party, Fidesz-KDNP, won another two-thirds majority in the April national elections. The government continued its attacks on rule of law and democratic institutions. It replaced a previous Covid-19-related state of danger with a state of danger due to the war in Ukraine, giving the government extraordinary powers to rule by decree and sidestep parliamentary process.

Independent journalists, media outlets, and civil society organizations were vilified by high-ranking public officials and in pro-government media outlets. Discrimination persisted against lesbian, gay, bisexual, and transgender (LGBT) people, women, and the Roma. Unlawful pushbacks of migrants and asylum seekers to Serbia continued and access to asylum procedures was close to impossible. Hungary continues to face scrutiny by European Union institutions under the Article 7 procedure—the EU treaty mechanism that holds to account governments in breach of the rule of law.

Attacks on Rule of Law and Public Institutions

Following national elections in April, the government declared a new "state of danger"—a special legal order giving the executive extraordinary power to rule by decree—due to the war in Ukraine. The "state of danger" declaration stemmed from an April 10 constitutional amendment allowing the government to declare a "state of danger" in case of "armed conflict, war, or humanitarian disaster in a neighboring country." A subsequent April amendment to the Disaster Management Act gives the government a carte blanche to override any acts of parliament in any area during such "state of danger."

The new special legal order is a nearly verbatim copy of a previous special legal order declared in March 2020, and extended several times, related to the Covid-19 pandemic. In June, parliament passed a law, which entered into force the same day, authorizing the government to extend the effect of emergency government decrees until the state of danger is terminated by the government. The amendments were passed without public consultation.

The Hungarian Helsinki Committee in a September report raised serious concerns about several unlawful appointments of judges to the Kuria, Hungary's Supreme Court.

In May, the Global Alliance of National Human Rights Institutions downgraded the Hungarian Commissioner for Fundamental Rights from category "A" to "B" for failing to adequately address human rights concerns, including on refugees and migrants, LGBT people, and ethnic minorities. The downgrading means the loss of voting rights in the Global Alliance, participation limited to observer status, and no active participation in the work of the Alliance at the UN Human Rights Council.

In a flagrant example of casual abuse of power to interfere with independent institutions, the government fired the chiefs of the National Weather Service without explanation when fireworks for Hungary's national holiday celebrating the foundation of the state were cancelled based on what turned out to be an incorrect forecast of inclement weather.

The July European Commission rule of law report expressed concerns about the independence of the judiciary, the system of checks and balances, pressure on civil society organizations, and continued concerns with media pluralism and challenges for media professionals to conduct their work, including surveillance of journalists.

Freedom of Media

Most media outlets remain directly or indirectly controlled by the government, creating a hostile climate for independent journalism. Journalists and media outlets critical of the government continued to be harassed and smeared in government-aligned media and by government officials.

In July, the European Commission referred Hungary to the Court of Justice of the European Union because its Media Council refused to extend independent radio station Klubradio's broadcasting license "on highly questionable grounds," effectively forcing the station off the airwaves. It now broadcasts only online. A group with close links to the government subsequently was awarded Klubradio's former frequency.

The election observation commission of the Organization for Security and Co-operation in Europe (OSCE) in its preliminary April conclusions raised concerns that bias and lack of balance in news coverage considerably limited voters' opportunity to make informed choices.

Sexual Orientation and Gender Identity

The government continued its attacks on the rights of LGBT people. In April, on national election day, the government held a hostile referendum about limiting children's access to information on LGBT issues. The referendum was declared void as insufficient valid votes were cast, in part due to a civil society campaign urging citizens to cast invalid votes. As a result of the campaign, the National Election Commission fined 16 human rights organizations for encouraging invalid votes, citing interference with the electoral process. The Supreme Court in April largely overturned the fines except against Hatter Tarsasag, an LGBT rights group, and Amnesty International Hungary.

In July, the European Commission referred Hungary to the Court of Justice of the EU for its 2021 amendments to the Child Protection Law, which included unjustified restrictions on LGBT content, with the excuse of protecting children. The commission argued that the law violates human dignity, freedom of expression and information, the right to privacy, and the right to data protection.

Women's Rights

In September, the Ministry of Health issued a decree making it mandatory for women seeking abortions to listen to the fetal heartbeat prior to terminating the pregnancy, creating another barrier to safe abortions and restricting women's reproductive rights.

Discrimination Against Roma

Discrimination against Roma remained a serious problem, particularly in educational institutions, state care homes, and workplaces.

In February, a Budapest lower court found that the Ministry of Human Capacities had violated the right to equal treatment of children, the majority Romani, who had been removed from their families and often placed under state care on grounds of child endangerment when families are unable to afford basic needs. The ruling stated that the families had been discriminated against on socio-economic and poverty grounds and because of their Romani ethnicity.

In July, the European Court of Human Rights ruled that Hungary had violated Article 3—prohibition of torture and inhumane and degrading treatment—of the European Convention on Human Rights in a 2014 incident when a Romani man was subjected to police brutality during an arrest. The Court awarded the Romani applicant €19,500 (around US$19,400) in damages.

Migration and Asylum

Access to Hungary's asylum system remained virtually impossible. Pushbacks to Serbia, sometimes violent, continued. According to official police statistics between January and August, border officials had carried out over 90,000 unlawful pushbacks.

According to police data cited by the UN Refugee Agency, 28,289 people fleeing the conflict in Ukraine had registered for Temporary Protection as of August 1.

Council of Europe Commissioner for Human Rights Dunja Mijatovic, in a June letter to the Hungarian government, raised concerns about the long-term prospects for protection for third country nationals and stateless persons from Ukraine who are excluded from the Temporary Protection scheme and have no possibility to apply for asylum in the country.

The Court of Justice of the EU in November 2021 ruled that Hungary's law criminalizing aid to asylum seekers and restricting the right to seek asylum violates EU law. The case refers to a 2018 amendment to the Asylum Act, dubbed the "Stop Soros" law, which prevented people from applying for asylum in Hungary if they arrived from a country of origin or transit country where their life and freedom were not a risk. The bill also criminalized individuals and organizations for providing support and aid to migrants and asylum seekers.

In December 2021, Prime Minister Viktor Orban stated that "[w]e will not do anything to change the system of border protection… We will maintain the existing regime, even if the European court ordered us to change it."

India

The Bharatiya Janata Party (BJP)-led government continued its systematic discrimination and stigmatization of religious and other minorities, particularly Muslims. BJP supporters increasingly committed violent attacks against targeted groups. The government's Hindu majoritarian ideology was reflected in bias in institutions, including the justice system and constitutional authorities like the National Human Rights Commission.

Authorities intensified efforts to silence civil society activists and independent journalists by using politically motivated criminal charges, including terrorism, to jail those exposing or criticizing government abuses. The government used foreign funding regulations and allegations of financial irregularities to harass rights groups, political opponents, and others.

Indian authorities intensified restrictions on free expression and peaceful assembly in Jammu and Kashmir.

In May, the Supreme Court effectively halted all use of the colonial-era sedition law in an interim ruling, a law repeatedly used by the authorities to arrest peaceful critics of the government.

The Indian government has supported humanitarian efforts in Sri Lanka, Afghanistan, and Ukraine.

Jammu and Kashmir

Three years after the government revoked Jammu and Kashmir's constitutional autonomous status and split it into two federally governed territories, violence continued with 229 reported deaths as of October, including 28 civilians, 29 security force personnel, and 172 suspected militants. Although local Kashmiris complained that some of those described as militants killed in gunfights were in fact civilians, no independent investigation was made public.

Minority Hindu and Sikh communities in the Muslim-majority Kashmir Valley came under attack. There were seven targeted killings in Ma, four of them of Kashmiri Hindus, known as Pandits. The other three were Muslim police officials. After gunmen shot Rahul Bhat, a Kashmiri Pandit government employee on May

12, Kashmiri Pandits employed in government jobs in Kashmir Valley went on an indefinite strike, demanding relocation.

On June 1, the Kashmiri Pandit Sangharsh Samiti, a group representing religious minorities in the province, wrote to the region's chief justice raising concerns for their safety. In September, Jammu and Kashmir administration passed orders to withhold salaries of employees still on strike in the valley. In October, militants killed a Kashmiri Pandit and two migrant workers.

In January, journalists aligned with the government and police forcibly took over the Kashmir Press Club, an independent media body, which authorities later shut.

In January, police arrested Sajad Gul, a journalist at the Kashmir-based digital news site The Kashmir Walla, on charges of criminal conspiracy after he reported a public protest. A month later, authorities arrested editor-in-chief Fahad Shah on sedition and terrorism charges after his site reported contradictory claims after a shootout in which security forces killed four people who they said were militants. Authorities rearrested both Shah and Gul under the Public Safety Act after they had been granted bail separately in cases filed against them, continuing their arbitrary detention at time of writing.

Since August 2019, at least 35 journalists in Kashmir have faced police interrogation, raids, threats, physical assault, restrictions on freedom of movement, or fabricated criminal cases for their reporting.

Impunity for Security Forces

Allegations of torture and extrajudicial killings persisted, with the National Human Rights Commission registering 147 deaths in police custody, 1,882 deaths in judicial custody, and 119 alleged extrajudicial killings in the first nine months in 2022.

In March, the Indian government reduced the number of districts under the Armed Forces (Special Powers) Act (AFSPA) in some northeast states. However, it remained in effect in Jammu and Kashmir and 43 of 90 districts in four northeastern states, providing effective immunity from prosecution to security force personnel, even for serious human rights violations.

The Border Security Force frequently used excessive force along the Bangladeshi border, targeting Indian residents and irregular immigrants and cattle traders from Bangladesh.

Dalits, Tribal Groups, and Religious Minorities

In October, police in Gujarat publicly flogged Muslim men accused of disrupting a Hindu festival in a form of abusive punishment while authorities in Madhya Pradesh demolished the homes of three men accused of throwing stones at a Hindu ceremonial dance, without any legal authorization. In April, authorities in Madhya Pradesh, Gujarat, and Delhi summarily demolished property mostly owned by Muslims in response to communal clashes. Although they tried to justify the demolitions by claiming the structures were illegal, the destruction appeared intended to be collective punishment for Muslims. "Houses that were involved in stone pelting will be turned into rubble," the BJP home minister in Madhya Pradesh state warned.

In June, a BJP politician's remarks against the Prophet Mohammed led to widespread protests by Muslims across the country. Police in Jharkhand allegedly used excessive force against protesters, killing two people, while authorities in Uttar Pradesh illegally demolished homes of Muslims suspected of being "key conspirators" behind protest violence.

In June, three United Nations special rapporteurs wrote to the Indian government raising serious concerns over the arbitrary home demolitions against Muslim communities and other low-income groups for alleged participation in inter-communal violence. They said that "authorities reportedly failed to investigate these incidents, including incitement to violence and acts of intimidation that contributed to the outbreak of the violence."

In August, the BJP government approved the early release of 11 men sentenced to life in prison for gang rape and murder during the 2002 anti-Muslim riots, which BJP affiliates celebrated publicly. The men were convicted after a Muslim woman, Bilkis Bano, testified in court. Opposition lawmaker Mahua Moitra filed a petition in the Supreme Court challenging the early release, which is not usually permitted in gang rape cases, saying, "This nation had better decide whether Bilkis Bano is a woman or a Muslim."

In January, photographs of over 100 Muslim women, including journalists and activists, were displayed on an app saying they were for sale, to humiliate and intimidate them.

Laws forbidding forced religious conversion were misused to target Christians, especially from Dalit and Adivasi communities. In July, six Dalit Christian women were arrested on charges of forced conversion in Uttar Pradesh, based on a complaint by a Hindu nationalist organization.

In August, the National Crime Records Bureau reported 50,900 cases of crimes against Dalits in 2021, an increase of 1.2 percent over the previous year. Crimes against Adivasi communities increased by 6.4 percent, at 8,802 cases. In September, two Dalit teenage girls were raped and killed in Uttar Pradesh, once again spotlighting that Dalit and Adivasi women and girls are at heightened risk of sexual violence.

Civil Society and Freedom of Association

Authorities harassed and threatened activists and rights groups through politically motivated prosecutions, tax raids, allegations of financial irregularities, and use of the Foreign Contribution Regulation Act (FCRA), the law regulating foreign funding for nongovernmental organizations.

In September, income tax officials raided the offices of Oxfam India, Delhi-based think tank Centre for Policy Research, and Bengaluru-based Independent and Public Spirited Media Foundation, alleging FCRA violations. In January, India's national investigative agency, the Central Bureau of Investigation, searched the offices of prominent human rights organization Centre for Promotion of Social Concerns in Tamil Nadu state alleging fraud and financial irregularities under the FCRA.

In June, authorities arrested prominent human rights activist Teesta Setalvad, as well as police officers R.B. Sreekumar and Sanjeev Bhatt, in apparent reprisal for pursuing accountability for the 2002 mob violence targeting Muslims in Gujarat state. In September, police filed charges accusing them of "false and malicious criminal proceedings against innocent people," including Prime Minister Narendra Modi, who was chief minister of Gujarat during the riots.

Delhi police arrested Mohammed Zubair, co-founder of an independent fact-checking website Alt News in June, accusing him of hurting Hindu sentiments in a 2018 Twitter post. Zubair's arrest appeared to be reprisal for exposing a television news network that aired controversial remarks of a BJP politician about the Prophet Mohammed, leading to criticism by several Muslim governments.

Freedom of Expression

Authorities arrested journalists critical of the government on politically motivated charges. In July, police in Jharkhand arrested independent journalist Rupesh Kumar Singh, who reports on the rights of Adivasi communities, on various charges, including under the Unlawful Activities Prevention Act (UAPA), a draconian counterterrorism law. Singh and his wife were petitioners in the Supreme Court on the government's alleged use of Israeli-produced spyware Pegasu to target journalists and activists, after their phone numbers were included on a list of potential targets.

In September, the Supreme Court chief justice granted bail to journalist Siddique Kappan after being held for two years on baseless charges of terrorism, sedition, and other offenses. Kappan, who was arrested in October 2020 while on his way to report on the gang rape and murder of a Dalit girl in Uttar Pradesh, remained in custody on other charges.

Authorities also continued to stop activists and journalists critical of the government, from traveling abroad.

In August, the committee of experts constituted by the Supreme Court to investigate the use of Pegasus spyware on Indian citizens submitted its report, which revealed that 5 out of 29 phones examined had malware on them, but failed to determine whether it was Pegasus. The Supreme Court noted that the government did not cooperate with the committee's investigation but did not make the report public.

In July, Meta, formerly Facebook, decided not to publish the pending Human Rights Impact Assessment on India, meant to independently evaluate the company's role in spreading hate speech and incitement to violence on its services in India, which led to severe criticism from civil society in India. Meta merely published some snippets from the report as part of its first annual human rights report, an abdication of its human rights responsibilities. Meta asserted it withheld publication out of safety concerns.

Women's and Girls' Rights

Violence against women and girls continued at alarming rates, with 31,677 cases of rape registered in 2021, an average of 86 cases daily.

In September, the Supreme Court failed to deliver a verdict on whether Muslim female students can wear hijab, a headscarf, in educational institutions in BJP-led Karnataka state with two judges expressing opposing views. In February, the state government had issued a directive backing discriminatory bans at several government-run educational institutions on students wearing the hijab inside classrooms and a month later, the state high court upheld the government order.

In September, the Supreme Court delivered a progressive ruling on abortion rights, expanding access to legal abortion to all women regardless of marital status and to persons other than cisgender women. It also expanded access to rape survivors, including victims of marital rape.

Right to Education

By February, educational institutions across the country began to resume in-school classes after multiple reopening and closures since the Covid-19 pandemic struck in March 2020. The school closures caused massive disruption in the education of millions of children, disproportionately affecting girls and children from poor and marginalized communities who did not have access to online learning, putting them at increased risk of dropping out, loss of learning, child marriage, and child labor.

Sexual Orientation and Gender Identity

In August, in an important ruling toward advancing the rights of lesbian, gay, bisexual, and transgender (LGBT) communities and women, the Supreme Court widened the definition of family to include same-sex couples, single parent, and other households considered "atypical," saying family benefits under the law should be extended to them.

Refugee Rights

Rohingya Muslim refugees in India face tightened restrictions, arbitrary detention, violent attacks often incited by political leaders, and a heightened risk of forced returns. In March, the Indian government forcibly returned a Rohingya woman to Myanmar despite an order by the Manipur State Human Rights Commission putting the deportation on hold.

India also failed to adequately protect the rights of refugees from Myanmar fleeing renewed fighting between the Myanmar military and armed groups.

Climate Change Policies and Impacts

India is currently the world's third-largest greenhouse gas emitter, after China and the United States. In August, the federal cabinet approved the country's updated Nationally Determined Contribution (NDC) to the Paris Agreement, which commits to reaching net-zero emissions by 2070, meet half of the country's energy needs from renewable sources by 2030, and reduce emissions intensity of the economy by 45 percent by 2030.

Climate change is expected to have a significant impact on India due to more frequent and intense heatwaves, sea level rise, drought, glacial melt, and changes in rainfall. India experienced an unusually early heatwave, beginning in March, recording the highest temperature in the month in over a century. The March heatwave was made 30 times more likely due to climate change, according to a study by the World Weather Attribution Network.

Key International Actors

The European Union and its member states held numerous high-level meetings with Indian authorities but continued to refrain from publicly expressing concerns over the Indian government's growing abuses. Rare exceptions were a tweet by the EU special representative for human rights and a statement by German Foreign Office in July.

In April, the EU and India launched a bilateral Trade and Technology Council, and in June, they officially resumed negotiations for a free trade agreement. In July, the EU held its tenth, and largely fruitless, local human rights dialogue with India.

In April, US Secretary of State Antony Blinken publicly referred to "concerning developments in India, including a rise in human rights abuses by some government, police and prison officials." The US Commission on International Religious Freedom stated that "religious freedom conditions in India significantly worsened" in the last year and recommended that the State Department designate India a "country of particular concern."

The UK rushed to finalize a free trade agreement with India despite concerns raised by the House of Lords International Agreements Committee that the UK government's negotiating objectives did not provide enough information on the importance it would give to "human, environmental and other rights and protections."

Foreign Policy

India did not speak out against serious human rights violations in South Asia, including in Myanmar and Bangladesh. In July, India abstained on a UN Human Rights Council resolution on Syria but supported a HRC resolution in October, to renew the mandate of the special rapporteur to monitor and report on the human rights situation in Afghanistan.

Throughout the year, India abstained during votes on resolutions at the United Nations related to Russia's invasion of Ukraine, including a UN General Assembly resolution adopted in March censuring Russia for its military actions and calling on Moscow to unconditionally withdraw its troops.

India's unwillingness to criticize Russia's actions or join the sanctions against Russian oil and defense purchases drew criticism in the United States and EU. The Indian government defended its decision to import Russian oil, saying it must source oil from where it is cheapest. Prime Minister Modi privately and publicly criticized the war when engaging directly with Russian President Vladimir Putin.

India was the biggest provider of aid to Sri Lanka, extending nearly US$4 billion, including credit lines for essentials such as food, fuel, and medicines, as the country faced its worst economic crisis in decades. India also supported Sri Lanka in obtaining aid from the International Monetary Fund.

India extended aid to Afghanistan, including wheat and medical supplies, amid the ongoing humanitarian crisis, exacerbated after the Taliban takeover in August 2021.

Following clashes between British Hindus and Muslims in September in Leicester city in the UK, the Indian High Commission one-sidedly condemned the "vandalisation of premises and symbols of the Hindu religion."

In September, India and China started pulling back troops from a disputed area along the Himalayan border to de-escalate tensions since the standoff in May 2020.

Indonesia

Indonesia was in the spotlight during the year, hosting the G20 summit on November 17-18 in Bali amid international tensions caused by the war in Ukraine, and friction in the region between the US and China.

The Indonesian government frequently violated basic civil and political rights, especially of disadvantaged groups, based on religious, ethnic, social, gender, and sexual orientation grounds. Military and police abused rights across the country with impunity, and especially in Papua and West Papua provinces where diplomats, foreign rights monitors, and international media are largely excluded.

Islamist groups committed numerous abuses against religious minorities, women and girls, and lesbian, gay, bisexual, and transgender (LGBT) people while authorities looked the other way.

President Joko "Jokowi" Widodo, whose term runs until 2024, did little to stand up for rights during the year. His government was distracted as it struggles to finance a US$30-billion mega project to move the flood-ridden and congested national capital from Jakarta to a remote area in Kalimantan.

Proposed Criminal Code

Indonesia is currently revising its criminal code, and the current draft in the parliament is focused on the recognition of "any living law" in Indonesia. These "living laws" could be interpreted to include customary criminal law and Sharia (Islamic law) regulations at the local level, which include hundreds of ordinances and regulations that discriminate against women, religious minorities, and LGBT people. As there is no official list of "living laws" in Indonesia, this provision opens the door to widespread rights abuses through possible prosecutions under these discriminatory local regulations.

At time of writing, the Indonesian parliament was still considering passage of the criminal code, which is widely expected before the end of the year. Indonesian civil society groups and communities are mobilizing opposition against the proposed legislation.

Women's and Girls' Rights

Most of Indonesia's provinces, and dozens of cities and regencies, impose discriminatory and abusive dress codes on women and girls. Human Rights Watch documented widespread bullying of girls and women into wearing a jilbab, and the deep psychological distress it causes to girls and women, and their families. Girls who do not comply have been ejected from schools, including state schools, or forced to withdraw under pressure, while female civil servants, including teachers and university lecturers, have lost their jobs or resigned. Many Christian, Hindu, Buddhist, and other non-Muslim students and teachers have also been forced to wear the jilbab. Human Rights Watch has documented these negative impacts caused by at least 64 mandatory jilbab regulations in Indonesia.

In a major victory for women's rights, Indonesia's armed forces ended all so-called "virginity tests" as part of the recruitment process for women. Maj. Gen. Budiman, the armed forces surgeon general, announced in April 2022 that all three branches of the military—Army, Navy, and Air Force—had "effectively ended virginity tests" for recruitment.

Violations of Right to Freedom of Religion and Belief

The 1965 blasphemy law and the so-called religious harmony regulation caused serious problems by making it easier for people to weaponize the toxic regulations against religious minorities in this predominantly Sunni Muslim country.

The harmony regulations, which give religious majorities in a community the veto power over activities of minority religions, make it virtually impossible for recognized religious minorities (Christians, Hindus, Buddhists, Confucians, and other smaller religions and beliefs) to construct houses of worship.

Worship and other religious activities face serious discrimination and sometimes criminalization for Islamic minorities in the country (Ahmadiyah, Shia) as well as adherents of small religions such as Jehovah's Witnesses, and local faiths like Kejawen, Sunda Wiwitan. The government also did little to stop attacks by militant Islamic groups against religious minorities or hold such attackers accountable for rights abuses and destruction of houses of worship.

In April, authorities in Ciamis, West Java, prosecuted Muhammad Kace, a former Muslim cleric who converted to Christianity in 2014 and sentenced him to 10 years in prison for blasphemy against Islam. Kace's alleged crime was making YouTube videos that criticized his former faith.

In Jakarta, a court sentenced Ferdinand Hutahaean, a Christian who converted to Islam, to five months in prison in April for simply replying to a tweet that "Your Allah is weak."

Religious Affairs Minister Yaqut Cholil Qoumas became the target of an angry campaign after he had issued a February decree to regulate the volume on loudspeakers at mosques around the country. He asked mosques to use loudspeakers indoors and to limit the volume to 100 decibels when using them outside for the call to prayer. Two politicians reported him to the police for blasphemy against Islam after he had compared noisy mosques with barking dogs.

A politician named Roy Suryo, a former national cabinet member, became a blasphemy suspect after he had tweeted the picture of a Borobudur stupa, an image of which had been photoshopped to resemble President Jokowi. Kevin Wu, a leader of Dharmapala Nusantara, a Buddhist group in Jakarta, reported Suryo to the police in June; he has been detained since August for investigation and trial.

In March 2021, a state school in Tarakan, North Kalimantan province, allowed three Jehovah's Witness students to move grades after denying them for three years due to their faith, despite their good marks. A court ordered the school to stop considering them "committing blasphemy." A total of 22 children have faced similar problems elsewhere in Indonesia since 2016 but most parents sought to move their children to other schools that did not discriminate against them.

In September, Cilegon Mayor Helldy Agustian, in response to a Muslim group demonstration, banned the proposed construction of Maranatha church. The new church is designated to be part of the Batak Protestant Christian Church (Huria Kristen Batak Protestan, HKBP). The Ministry of Religious Affairs stated that Cilegon, a major steel production town, does not have a single church despite having nearly 9,000 Christians.

Sexual Orientation and Gender Identity

Officials continued to target lesbian, gay, bisexual, and transgender (LGBT) people. For example, on August 1, the Makassar police forced the cancellation of a gathering of more than 30 transgender women. Police in Sambas, West Kalimantan, disbanded a transgender fashion week gathering on September 7. Abdul Muthalib, the Sambas police chief, said that it had a request to close the fashion show from the Indonesian Ulama Council.

Rodrigo Ventocilla Ventosilla, a transgender man from Peru who travelled to Bali as a tourist, died on August 11 while in police custody after he was allegedly mistreated and discriminated against by police.

Indonesia has also increasingly used other laws to target and prosecute LGBT people, including the 2008 Anti-Pornography law.

In September, a Jakarta military tribunal dismissed two sergeants and a sailor for same-sex conduct. One of them was sentenced to six months in jail for having sex with two other male civilians.

Land Rights

The Indonesian government is failing to protect the rights of communities living on or near land allotted to commercial agriculture. Human Rights Watch documented the upheaval wrought on affected communities by long-running conflicts between companies and rural communities, and the Indonesian government's failure to protect the rights of these communities, and ensure they have access to land to sustain their livelihoods.

Indonesia allowed a moratorium on new plantations permits to lapse that had been in place and continuously renewed since 2011. The government still maintains a permanent ban on granting new permits to clear primary forests and peatlands for plantations or logging. However, Human Rights Watch research showed that ongoing monitoring and oversight by relevant government agencies is poor, the plethora of existing regulations creates ambiguity, and private entities take advantage of these gaps to circumvent or not comply with the law.

Due to minimal ongoing monitoring and oversight, some of these plantations degrade the environment in which they operate, in some cases causing almost irreparable damage to peatlands, one of the world's most important carbon sinks.

Rights Abuses in West Papua

Military police arrested six soldiers in September suspected in the killing of four Indigenous Papuans in Timika, Papua province. The mutilated bodies of the four men were discovered outside the mining town of Timika, in sacks floating down the Pigapu River. The victims were identified as Irian Nirigi, a local village leader; Arnold Lokbere; Atis Tini; and Kelemanus Nirigi.

A rarely used Indonesian human rights court put Maj. (ret.) Isak Sattu on trial for alleged crimes committed during a 2014 massacre in Papua. Sattu alone is charged with crimes against humanity for the killing of five Papuans, including four teenagers, on December 8, 2014, in the town of Enarotali, in Papua province. At least another 17 people were injured in the massacre, during which soldiers opened fire with live ammunition against peaceful protesters. On December 8, 2022, the court acquitted Sattu on all charges.

Expressing views in support of Papuan self-determination continues to be severely restricted and punished in West Papua and in other parts of Indonesia.

Climate Change Policy and Impact

Indonesia, one of the world's top 10 emitters of greenhouse gases, is contributing to the climate crisis taking a mounting toll on human rights around the globe.

Estimates by Global Forest Watch (GFW) indicate a downward trend in forest loss in 2021, the most recent available data. Despite an official ban on primary forest clearing in force since 2011, the latest GFW data indicates Indonesia lost 203,000 hectares in 2021.

Disability Rights

In Indonesia, people with real or perceived psychosocial disabilities continue to be shackled—chained or locked in confined spaces—due to social stigma, as well as inadequate support and mental health services.

In September, the UN Committee on the Rights of Persons with Disabilities expressed grave concern about "the prolonged use of harmful and forced practices against persons with psychosocial disabilities such as shackling, seclusion and restraints," and recommended that the Indonesian government prohibit these, as well as forced medical interventions of people with disabilities, and develop non-coercive, community-based mental health supports and services.

Key International Actors

President Jokowi sought to balance Indonesian relations with global powers. He became the first Asian leader to visit Kyiv and to meet with Ukraine's President Volodymyr Zelensky, urging Russian ends to blockages of Ukrainian wheat exports to the world. Jokowi also met Russian leader Vladimir Putin in Moscow on July 1. Indonesia hosted the Group of 20 leaders in November in Bali, having all of them but Putin.

ASEAN (the Association of Southeast Asian Nations) failed to make any sort of progress on the Five Point Consensus roadmap that Myanmar junta head Sr. Gen. Min Aung Hlaing had agreed on in April 2021. Indonesia will become ASEAN chair in January 2023. Next steps to implement the ASEAN decision in principle to admit Timor Leste as the 11th member of the bloc will also likely be on the new chair's agenda.

In October, at the UN Human Rights Council, Indonesia voted against a motion to discuss the human rights situation in China's Xinjiang region. Indonesia's vote against the motion, which failed 19 votes to 17, was crucial. Ukraine later announced its support for the motion, narrowing the final margin to one.

Iran

Authorities brutally repressed widespread protests in 2022 demanding fundamental rights, with security forces unlawfully using excessive and lethal force against protesters.

Iran's government arrested and sentenced scores of peaceful human rights activists on vague national security charges, while failing to investigate reports of abuse or torture by police and security forces.

Security agencies targeted ethnic and religious minorities and violently enforced discriminatory dress codes for women.

Freedom of Assembly and Expression, Right to Participate in the Conduct of Public Affairs

Iranian authorities have severely restricted freedoms of assembly and expression. During the year, security forces responded to widespread protests with excessive and lethal force and arrested thousands of protesters.

The death on September 16 of Mahsa (Jina) Amini, a 22-year-old Kurdish woman from Sanandaj in western Iran, in the custody of the morality police after being arrested for wearing an "improper" *hijab* sparked demonstrations across the country, including in schools and universities. Authorities claimed Amini died because of a medical condition that led to her going into a coma within a couple of hours of her arrest, a claim her family denied.

Human Rights Watch documented security forces using shotguns, assault rifles, and handguns against protesters, in largely peaceful and often crowded settings. On September 30, security forces opened fire on demonstrators in the town of Zahedan (Sistan and Baluchistan province), killing and injuring dozens. As of November 14, human rights groups were investigating the reported deaths of 341 protestors, including 52 children.

Earlier in 2022, labor union strikes and ongoing protests against rising prices escalated and were also met with force. According to Human Rights Activists News Agency (HRANA), between May 2021 and 2022, over 69 workers' rights activists had been arrested, dozens more summoned for interrogations, and many subjected to violence and torture. Authorities have shown no willingness to investigate serious human rights violations committed under their control.

In December 2021, thousands of teachers protested in the streets across hundreds of cities and towns demanding fair wages, better healthcare, and the release of jailed teachers. A video circulated on Twitter showed security forces attempting to violently disperse the protesters in front of the parliament.

Authorities have also increased repression against student activists; several were convicted to prison terms or threatened with being barred from continuing their education, a punishment the government uses to curtail and punish peaceful student activism.

On May 24, the nongovernmental organization (NGO) Imam Ali's Popular Student Relief Society (IAPSRS) posted on its Twitter account that the Branch 28 court of appeals upheld a March 2021 sentence shutting the group. The IAPSRS is one of the most prominent Iranian NGOs working on poverty reduction, child marriage, and the death penalty for children.

Branch 55 of the International Relations Court at Shahid Beheshti Judicial Complex ordered the dissolution of the group, accepting the Interior Ministry's assessment that IAPSRS had "deviated" from its original mission and "insulted religious beliefs." The court cited "questioning Islamic rulings" and "promoting falsehood by publishing statements against the Islamic Republic of Iran" as evidence of "deviation."

Authorities have disrupted mobile and internet connections to quash protest movements. In May, authorities imposed a near-total shutdown of mobile and home broadband data in some cities in Khuzestan Province, amid reported street protests against a potential hike in the price of bread.

Authorities also heavily disrupted internet access in large parts of the country and blocked or periodically disrupted access to social media and messaging platforms after countrywide protests began in September following Amini's death. The Iranian parliament has also moved to ratify the general outlines of the draconian "Regulatory System for Cyberspace Services Bill," which violates an array of human rights in Iran, including the right to freedom of expression and to privacy.

In October, a ranking Iranian judicial figure threatened legal action against two UK-based Persian news outlets, accusing them of inciting "terrorist acts" for their reports on the protests over Amini's death.

Human Rights Defenders and Civil Society Activists

Scores of human rights defenders remain behind bars while authorities continue to harass, arrest, and prosecute those seeking accountability and justice, including human rights lawyers Nasrin Sotoudeh, Mohamad Najafi, and Amirsalar Davoudi.

In the aftermath of protests related to Mahsa Amini's death, Iranian security apparatus arrested hundreds human rights defenders, students, women's rights activists, lawyers, journalists, and summoned and interrogated dozens of actors, athletes, and other public figures in connection to their expressed supports of the demands of the protestors.

In January, Branch 26 of Tehran's revolutionary court sentenced Narges Mohammadi, the rights defender, to six years in prison for "assembly and collusion to act against national security," and to two years in prison and 74 lashes for "acting against national security and disrupting public order." The summary trial was held behind closed doors, and she was denied access to a lawyer. Despite Mohammadi's announcement that she would comply with the summons to serve her latest sentence after being on a temporary release on medical grounds, security officers forcibly arrested her on April 12 at her home and returned her to Garchak Prison. She was still recovering from open-heart surgery at the end of February.

Seven members of the Persian Wildlife Heritage Foundation, a local NGO focused on preserving biodiversity, remained behind bars on the charge of "collaborating with the hostile state of the US." Iranian authorities have failed to produce any evidence to support their charges, nor have they investigated allegations of torture against them.

In June, Iranian authorities intensified their crackdown on civil society with a new wave of politically motivated arrests and sentences against journalists and activists, including Vida Rabani, Ahmad Reza Haeri, Amir Salar Davoudi, and Masoud Bastani. This was followed by the arrests of reformist critic, Mostafa

Tajzadeh, and two film directors, Mohammad Rasoulof and Mostafa Al-Ahmad, on July 9, 2022, followed on July 11 by another film director, Jafar Panahi.

According to HRANA, on July 12, authorities arrested at least seven family members of people killed during the bloody 2019 government crackdown on widespread protests. At time of writing, there was no information about charges against them.

On August 16, an appeals court upheld a decision issued against five human rights defenders charged with "establishing an illegal group" and "propaganda against the state" for attempting to hold the government accountable for its mismanagement of the Covid-19 crisis. Before their arrest, all seven rights defenders were preparing to file a complaint against the country's national task force against Covid-19. Articles 170 and 173 of the constitution protect every citizen's right to complain before a court when regulation of the government conflicts with laws or norms.

Due Process Rights, Fair Trial Standards, and Prison Conditions

Iranian courts, and particularly revolutionary courts, regularly fall far short of providing fair trials and use confessions likely obtained under torture as evidence in court. Authorities have failed to meaningfully investigate numerous allegations of torture against detainees and routinely restrict detainees' access to legal counsel, particularly during the initial investigation period. They have issued over 1,000 indictments in connection with widespread protests in September and November. As of November 14, at least 9 people had been charged with *moharabeh* ("enmity against God") or *isfad fil arz* ("corruption on earth"), both of which could carry the death penalty.

Authorities continue to endanger the lives of activists and rights defenders by continuing to imprison them and denying them access to immediate and sufficient medical care. In January, Bektash Abtin, a writer and poet, and Adel Kianpour, a prisoner in Ahvaz, died under unclear circumstances. In April, Mehdi Salehi, a prisoner on death row for his alleged role in 2017 and 2018 protests, died in prison and his family was pressured to bury him quickly. Amnesty International published a report documenting the apparent deliberate denial of access to medical care to more than 90 prisoners over the past 10 years.

The Islamic Revolutionary Guard Corps' (IRGC) Intelligence Organization continued to arrest Iranian dual and foreign nationals on vague charges such as "cooperating with a hostile state." The travel ban on Iranian-American Baker Namazi was dropped in October 2022 on medical grounds. Namazi's son, Siamak, who was sentenced in 2015 on vague espionage charges, received a furlough from Evin prison for a week.

Right to Life and Executions

Iran continues to be one of the world's leading implementers of the death penalty. This includes carrying out capital punishment of those convicted for crimes committed as children, as well as under vaguely defined national security charges and occasionally non-violent offenses.

Iranian law considers acts such as "insulting the prophet," "apostasy," same-sex relations, adultery, drinking alcohol, and certain non-violent drug-related offenses as crimes punishable by death. The law also prescribes the inhumane punishment of flogging for more than 100 offenses, including "disrupting public order," a charge that has been used to sentence individuals to flogging for their participation in protests.

According to rights groups, 306 executions have been documented since the Iranian New Year on March 21, 130 of them for drug-related charges and 151 of them based on the Islamic principle of qisas, or "retribution in kind" punishments. The United Nations special rapporteur on human rights in Iran, in his July 2022 report to the General Assembly, also raised concerns over the increase in drug-related executions. In September, families of prisoners on death row gathered outside prisons in Tehran and Karaj to peacefully protest what appeared to be a rise in the number of executions in the previous four months.

Women's Rights, Children's Rights, Sexual Orientation, and Gender Identity

On August 15, a new presidential decree sanctioned women for showing their hair on social media, with female government employees facing dismissal from their jobs if they have profile pictures without their *hijab*. In September, the secretary of Iran's Headquarters for Promoting Virtue and Preventing Vice announced plans to enforce dress codes through digital surveillance of public spaces..

On July 16, artist Sepideh Rashno was arrested for not complying with compulsory *hijab* laws. She later appeared on state TV apologizing while looking pale and unwell. HRA reported prior to the televised confession that Rashno was taken to the hospital for internal bleeding. Iranian authorities have a long record of coercing detainees into making false televised confessions.

Two months later came the death of Mahsa Amini, 22, sparking country-wide protests. Amini's death came two days after her arrest on the same charge that her *hijab* was "improper."

Women face discrimination in personal status matters related to marriage, divorce, inheritance, and decisions relating to children. Under the civil code, a husband has the right to choose the place of living and can prevent his wife from having certain occupations if he deems them against "family values." It also allows girls to marry at 13 and boys at age 15, as well as at younger ages if authorized by a judge. Under the Passports Law, a married woman may not obtain a passport or travel outside the country without the written permission of her husband, who can revoke such permission at any time.

While cases of femicide are increasingly reported in media and social media, Iran has no law on domestic violence to prevent abuse and protect survivors.

Under Iranian law, non-marital sex is criminalized with flogging if unmarried, or death if married, impacting women in particular as pregnancy serves as evidence of sexual relations and women who report sexual violence can find themselves prosecuted if authorities believe it to be consensual. Same-sex conduct is also punishable by flogging and, for men, the death penalty. Although Iran permits and subsidizes sex reassignment surgery for transgender people, no law prohibits discrimination against them.

In November 2021, Iran's parliament passed a population law that limited access to sexual and reproductive rights, including by outlawing sterilization and free distribution of contraceptives in the public healthcare system unless a pregnancy threatens a woman's health, and further limits already restricted access to safe abortion.

The law is part of a shift of Iran's population planning from providing family planning and access to contraception, once seen as a success story by international organizations, to increasing population growth by undermining women's access to sexual and reproductive health care.

Treatment of Minorities, Refugees, and Migrants

Iranian law denies freedom of religion to Baha'is and discriminates against them. Authorities continue to arrest and prosecute members of the Baha'i faith on vague national security charges and to close businesses owned by them. Iranian authorities also systematically refuse to allow Baha'is to register at public universities.

The government also discriminates against other religious minorities, including Sunni Muslims, and restricts cultural and political activities among the country's Azeri, Kurdish, Arab, and Baluch ethnic minorities. Minority activists are regularly arrested and prosecuted on arbitrary national security charges in trials that grossly fall short of international standards.

It appears that over the past year authorities have continued the crackdown against Kurdish political activists. On September 28, IRGC forces launched drone missile attacks against the bases of Kurdish opposition forces (Kurdistan Democratic Party of Iran or KDPI) in the Kurdistan Region of Iraq.

Decades of mismanagement and neglect in development policies have resulted in economic stagnation in areas inhabited by minorities such as Sistan-Baluchistan, Kurdistan, and Khuzestan. For years, Sistan-Baluchistan and Kurdistan have had some of the highest unemployment rates in the country. The government has also restricted the use of minorities' language and cultural activities.

Iran hosts a long-staying population of about 780,000 registered Afghan refugees and another estimated 2.1 million undocumented Afghans. The government of Iran is responsible for refugee registration and settlement. Following the Taliban takeover of Afghanistan in August 2021, Iranian border authorities have reportedly pushed back thousands of Afghan nationals to Afghanistan without any assessment of their individual needs for international protection.

Climate Change and Environmental Policies and Impact

As one of the world's top 10 emitters of greenhouse gases, Iran is contributing to the climate crisis, which is taking a mounting toll on human rights around the globe. Most of its emissions are from the energy sector: 88 percent of Iran's electricity comes from fossil fuels. Iran is the tenth largest producer of crude oil and the third largest producer of natural gas but also has significant renewable energy potential.

Energy costs are heavily subsidized, one of the factors leading to a high energy intensity per capita. Iran has taken few steps to reduce reliance on fossil fuels, regularly citing international sanctions as a barrier to transitioning towards cleaner energy. Iran is one of six countries that has not yet ratified the Paris Agreement.

There are longstanding concerns across Iran, and Khuzestan in particular, over mismanagement of water resources and pollution from oil development. For decades, environmental experts have warned that development projects in oil-rich Khuzestan, including the construction of hydroelectric dams, irrigation schemes, and water transfers to neighboring provinces are causing environmental harm and water shortages, affecting a range of rights.

Climate change is a serious threat to Iranian livelihoods, including from increased temperatures, more frequent and intense forest fires, dust storms, inland flooding, and sea level rise. In 2022, there were water protests in response to increased droughts and the government's mismanagement of water resources, which the authorities have responded to with arrests and violence. The increasing frequency and intensity of droughts is projected to continue diminishing agricultural productivity, compromising food security.

Key International Actors

Despite several rounds of indirect negotiations between Iran and the United States for a return to compliance with the 2015 Joint Comprehensive Plan of Action (JCPOA), the US has maintained its broad sectoral economic and financial sanctions on Iran.

Tehran continues to deny supporting the Houthi armed group in the Yemen conflict. The US has claimed Iran has offered significant "lethal" support.

On July 14, a Swedish court convicted an Iranian citizen of war crimes and murder for his role in the mass execution of political prisoners by Iranian authorities in 1988.

In September, Russia began using Iranian Shahed-136 loitering munitions in strikes on military bases and energy infrastructure inside Ukraine.

Following the protests, the US and European Union sanctioned several Iranian authorities and entities for serious human rights violations. On September 23, the US Department of Treasury issued a general license, updating, and expanding existing exemptions under US sanctions that would make it easier for technology companies to provide additional services that can help ensure safe communications for Iranian users.

On September 30, at the UN Human Rights Council, Chile delivered a joint statement on behalf of several countries urging Iran to conduct prompt, thorough, independent, impartial, and transparent investigations into the death of Mahsa Amini and to refrain from disproportionate use of force against peaceful protesters.

On November 24, the UN Human Rights Council held a special session, discussing Iranian authorities' use of excessive and lethal force against protesters.

In December, the UN General Assembly adopted a resolution that condemned Iran's human rights abuses, including the excessive use of force against protesters.

Iraq

After federal elections were held in October 2021, Iraq was marred in a protracted government-formation process for more than a year. The early elections were a key demand of protesters in a popular uprising in central and southern Iraq that forced the resignation of Iraq's government at the end of 2019.

Political dialogue and stalemate were occasionally broken by violent conflict between the most powerful political figures and blocs involved in negotiations, namely Muqtada al-Sadr and his movement, and the Coordination Framework parties. These groups clashed violently in Baghdad in fighting last August that left 30 people dead and tens more injured. In October, just over a year after the 2021 federal elections, political elites finally agreed on the appointment of Mohammed Shia al-Sudani as prime minister; he subsequently formed a cabinet.

In 2022, the Iraqi government under former Prime Minister Mustafa al-Kadhimi struggled to deliver on key demands made by protesters, leading to what the UNDP describes as a further breakdown in the social contract between rulers and ruled. In Erbil, Kurdistan Regional Government (KRG) authorities continued to threaten basic human rights and targeted civil society actors despite announcing a new five-year plan to address human rights issues in the Kurdistan Region of Iraq (KRI).

Uprising, Violence, and Accountability

In October 2019, hundreds of thousands of protesters took to the streets in central and southern Iraq demanding basic improvements to everyday life, including improved public services and employment opportunities, particularly among an expanding youth population. State security forces and armed groups affiliated with the state (including those that help comprise the Popular Mobilization Forces, or *al-hashd al-sha'abi*), opened fire on demonstrators and killed at least 487 protesters during the uprising.

Former Prime Minister Mustafa al-Kadhimi came into power in May 2020 promising legal accountability for the violence. In October 2020, he established a fact-finding committee to investigate the violence that occurred and those responsible. But between 2020 and October 2022, in the cases of killings, as-

WORLD REPORT 2023

sassinations, kidnappings, and injuries Human Rights Watch investigated, barely any of the legal complaints filed by families and individuals had progressed towards achieving justice.

In cases of killing, maiming, and disappearance of protesters investigated by Human Rights Watch, no legal accountability had been achieved, even for high-profile assassinations of activists such as Reham Yacoub in Basra in August 2020. In 2021, former Prime Minister al-Kadhimi touted the arrest of the alleged killer of well-known security analyst Hisham al-Hashimi, but the presiding judges in the case have on multiple occasions postponed the trial without arraigning the suspect.

The Iraqi government also promised compensation for those who had family members killed, and for those individuals injured while protesting. Human Rights Watch found that the government has succeeded in offering compensation, largely in the form of one-off payments for those killed, as well as monthly payments for families of those killed and some who have been injured. However, the compensation process has been slow and cumbersome for most seeking funds, with some injured having to wait more than two and a half years for compensation, and only receiving monies after hiring expensive lawyers to help process claims quicker. This compensation has no bearing on admission of guilt from the government or any state security personnel implicated in the violence.

Targeting of Government Critics

On February 3, a legal complaint was filed against a member of Iraq's High Commission for Human Rights (IHCHR), Dr Ali al-Bayati, because he sought to investigate allegations of torture of detainees—part of IHCHR's institutional mandate. Al-Bayati's legal case is one of many in which government critics and human rights advocates have been targeted with broadly defined defamation laws.

In the KRI, Kurdish authorities in 2022 used vaguely worded laws to target critics for expressing criticism and opinions they object to. In August, Kurdish authorities arrested dozens of journalists and activists in advance of planned protests called for by KRG critics. Three of those arrested and briefly detained were members of the Iraqi parliament. Similarly, in 2021, the Erbil Criminal Court sentenced three journalists and two activists to six years in prison after they were convicted in court proceedings marred by serious fair trial violations and political interference—a trend in the KRI dating back years.

Women's Rights

In addition to being targeted for playing a central role in the 2019-2020 protest movement, women continue to struggle against patriarchal norms embedded in Iraq's legal system. Some survivors of human trafficking are tried and convicted for prostitution. More generally, women survivors of gender-based violence have limited access to shelter or justice. While there are a small number of underground shelters for women in federal Iraq, run by local nongovernmental organizations, they are not widely supported, often criticized, and sometimes attacked by families and authorities as they do not consider them to be legal.

Women's rights groups remain committed to passing an anti-domestic violence law, but these efforts have stalled partly due to the prolonged government-formation process settled in October. Iraq's penal code enables impunity for male violence against women, including provisions that allow the husband to punish his wife, parents to discipline their children, and mitigated sentences for violent acts including murder for so-called honorable motives, or if a husband catches his wife or female relative in the act of adultery/sex outside marriage. The penal code also allows perpetrators of rape or sexual assault to escape prosecution or have their sentences quashed if they marry their victim.

Sexual Orientation and Gender Identity

Lesbian, gay, bisexual, and transgender (LGBT) people in Iraq experience systematic violent targeting because of their sexual orientation. This violence includes killings, abductions, torture, and sexual violence. The systematic, cyclical nature of this violence highlights a climate of impunity from which perpetrators of violence benefit.

This impunity is aided by a political context in which political elites with control of armed groups—some that are tied to the Popular Mobilization Forces, nominally under the authority of the prime minister—have authorized violent attacks against LGBT people. But Iraqi authorities have also targeted LGBT people using

HUMAN RIGHTS WATCH

"Everyone Wants Me Dead"
Killings, Abductions, Torture, and Sexual Violence Against LGBT People by Armed Groups in Iraq

a range of vague provisions in Iraq's penal code aimed at policing morals and public indecency and limiting freedom of expression.

On September 4, members of the Kurdistan Regional Government proposed a bill to the Kurdish Parliament that would punish any individual or group who advocates for the rights of LGBT people. A majority of Kurdish lawmakers signed onto the bill, which, if it were to become law, would penalize those who "promote" the rights of LGBT people with jail time and fines.

Civil Documentation

In September, seven aid groups found that nearly five years after the government declared victory over the extremist armed group Islamic State (also known as ISIS), up to 1 million Iraqis—displaced by the armed group's seizure of swaths of Iraqi territory and the battle to recapture them—remain unable to obtain basic civil documentation. The documents they cannot obtain include certificates of birth, marriage, and death, as well as Iraq's relatively new unified national identification card.

Such documents are essential for access to vital public services for displaced citizens, including monthly food disbursements and children's access to education. Difficulty accessing civil documentation is closely linked to persistent perceptions among Iraqi authorities and segments of the public that the displaced were or are affiliated with ISIS. Such perceptions often ignore the fact that most displaced persons fled their homes to avoid or escape the armed group's rule.

Repatriations from Northeast Syria

Iraqis make up a majority of the 66,000 Syrian and foreign detainees indefinitely and arbitrarily held as ISIS suspects and family members in camps and prisons in northeast Syria. As of September, an estimated 28,000 Iraqis, most of them women and children, were detained in camps while another 3,000 were held in prisons, all in life-threatening and often inhumane conditions. Iraq continues to slowly repatriate Iraqis from Syria, having accepted or helped bring home about 3,100 nationals in 2021 and 2022. For example, the government announced in June that it had repatriated nearly 500 families to Jadaa camp south of Mosul, and a month later said it was poised to repatriate another 150 families. Aid workers told Human Rights Watch that the repatriated children included more than 250 boys who had been held in a prison for adult males, all or most of them suffering from tuberculosis.

Yazidi Community

Human Rights Watch and other organizations documented a system of organized rape, sexual slavery, and forced marriage by ISIS forces of Yazidi women and girls. However, Human Rights Watch found no cases where an ISIS member has been prosecuted or convicted for those specific crimes, including where the crimes against them amounted to war crimes, crimes against humanity, or genocide against the Yazidis. Almost 3,000 Yezidi women and children remain missing following abductions by ISIS, but there has been no systematic effort by the Iraqi authorities to rescue them or ensure their return. Instead, families and Yazidi volunteers have largely driven all such rescue efforts.

In March 2021, the Iraqi parliament passed the Law on Yazidi Female Survivors. The law recognized as genocide many crimes committed by ISIS including kidnapping, sexual enslavement, forced marriage, pregnancy, and abortions forced upon women and girls who were Yazidi, Turkmen, Christian, or Shabak. The law provides for compensation for survivors, as well as measures for their rehabilitation and reintegration into society.

However, effective implementation of this law has yet to be achieved, in part because of the impasse over forming a new government and in part because of inadequate funding. In August, the United Nations International Organization for Migration (IOM) reported that more than 200,000 Yazidi survivors remained displaced from their homes.

Environmental and Health Alarm

Iraq is reportedly the fifth most vulnerable country to global warming and climate change. The impacts of rising temperatures, worsening droughts, and increasing number of sandstorms are exacerbated by political conditions. Poor governance, including water mismanagement, has contributed to the effects of the drought.

Meanwhile, Iraq's budget is dependent almost entirely on oil revenues. Oil output predictions suggest Iraq will deepen this dependency at a time when global activism around climate change and the push away from fossil fuels are growing. Increased oil output is also raising concerns around gas flaring in Iraq, the burning of gaseous byproducts that occurs during the oil production process. Worsening health conditions of residents living around gas flaring sites are raising questions for the Iraqi government and its partner oil companies about the persistence of this practice and who or what may be responsible.

Key International Actors

Two decades on from the US- and UK-led invasion of Iraq in March 2003, international actors continued to be implicated in human rights abuses in the country. In December 2021, the New York Times, examining the Pentagon's own records, found that the US military's bombing of Iraq in its fight against ISIS led to "the deaths of thousands of civilians, many of them children." The report corresponded with previous Human Rights Watch findings that the US failed to take adequate precautions to spare civilians while bombing purported ISIS targets.

Similarly, a Pax for Peace report published in April showed how residents of Hawija, in northern Iraq, continued to suffer from a June 2015 Dutch bombing of a munitions factory that killed at least 85 civilians and injured dozens more. Residents are demanding an apology, compensation, and a meaningful explanation of what occurred.

In May, the UK government sought to deport by chartered plane up to 30 Kurdish asylum seekers and refugees to the KRI, some of whom had been residing in the UK for more than 20 years. The UK government still deems Iraq so dangerous that it advises against all travel there, including the KRI. The UK government was ultimately forced to abandon its efforts at the eleventh hour in the face of safety concerns and widespread protest from rights groups in the UK and Iraq, and resistance from federal Iraqi authorities in Baghdad.

In July, an artillery attack on a water resort in Dohuk province killed 9 tourists and wounded at least 20 others. The attack was widely attributed to Turkey, suspected of targeting members of the Kurdistan Workers' Party (PKK), which Ankara calls a terrorist group. Turkey denied responsibility and placed blame on the PKK.

In September, Iranian drone and missile attacks targeting Iranian-Kurdish opposition groups based inside Iraq killed 13 people and injured many others. Human Rights Watch found some of the strikes, such as in Koya, east of Erbil, killed civilians. The attacks occurred weeks into mass protests inside Iran prompted by the death of Mahsa Amini on September 16, two days after Iran's "morality police" detained her for "improperly" wearing her hijab.

Israel and Palestine

Under a coalition government made up of a broad range of political parties and with Naftali Bennett and Yair Lapid as prime ministers, Israeli authorities doubled down on their severe repression of Palestinians. Israeli authorities' practices, undertaken as part of a policy to maintain the domination of Jewish Israelis over Palestinians, amount to the crimes against humanity of apartheid and persecution.

During three days of hostilities in August, Israeli forces launched scores of airstrikes, dropping explosive weapons with wide area effects in the densely populated Gaza, while the armed group Palestinian Islamic Jihad indiscriminately fired hundreds of rockets toward Israeli population centers. According to the UN Office for the Coordination of Humanitarian Affairs (OCHA), 49 Palestinians, including 17 children, were killed. Three hundred and sixty Palestinians and seventy Israelis were also injured during the escalation.

The August hostilities took place amid Israel's 15-year-long sweeping restrictions on the movement of people and goods in Gaza. Israel's closure policy, exacerbated by Egyptian restrictions on its border with Gaza, has deprived the more than 2 million Palestinians of Gaza, with rare exceptions, of their right to freedom of movement and opportunities to better their lives, severely limited their access to electricity, health care, and water, and devastated the economy. About 80 percent of Gaza's 2.1 million residents rely on humanitarian aid, according to the United Nations Relief and Works Agency for Palestine Refugees in the Near East (UNRWA).

In the West Bank, Israeli forces, following several attacks by Palestinians inside Israel in March, intensified their operations, killing 109 Palestinians as of October 24, according to OCHA, a 16-year-high. In May, renowned Al Jazeera journalist Shireen Abu Aqla was shot to death during an Israeli raid in the northern West Bank. Multiple independent investigations point to Israeli forces having killed her.

As of November 1, Israeli authorities also held 820 Palestinians in administrative detention without charge or trial based on secret evidence, the highest number since 2008, according to Israeli Prison Services figures.

Israeli authorities also continued to facilitate the transfer of Israeli citizens into settlements in the occupied West Bank—a war crime. According to the Israeli group Peace Now, the Bennett-Lapid government advanced plans for 7,292 housing units in settlements in the year between taking office and late June 2022, a 26 percent increase as compared to the annual average when Benjamin Netanyahu served as prime minister between 2012 and 2020.

According to OCHA, Israeli authorities also demolished 697 Palestinian homes and other structures in the West Bank, including East Jerusalem, in 2022, as of October 14, displacing 836 people. Most buildings were demolished for lacking building permits, which authorities make nearly impossible for Palestinians in these areas to obtain.

In May, Israel's High Court of Justice greenlighted the demolitions of the homes of more than 1,000 Palestinians in Masafer Yatta, in the southern West Bank, for being located in a firing zone for the Israeli army. The court said the military's power to declare closed military zones superseded international law.

In August, Israeli authorities raided the offices of, and issued closure orders against, seven prominent Palestinian civil society organizations, following their decision in 2021 to outlaw six of the groups by designating them "terrorist" organizations under Israeli law, and as "unlawful associations" under military law, which is applicable in the occupied West Bank.

Palestinian civil society also faced restrictions from the Fatah-dominated Palestinian Authority (PA) in the parts of the West Bank where it manages affairs and Hamas authorities in Gaza. The Palestinian statutory watchdog, the Independent Commission for Human Rights (ICHR), received 120 complaints of arbitrary arrests against the PA and 87 against Hamas; 106 complaints of torture and ill-treatment against the PA and 113 against Hamas; and 28 complaints against the PA for detention without trial or charge pursuant to orders from a regional governor between January and September 2022.

Benjamin Netanyahu's Likud Party and its allies won the majority of Knesset seats during November 1 elections, Israel's fifth election since 2019.

Gaza Strip

On August 5, Israeli authorities struck the home of an Islamic Jihad leader in Gaza without clear provocation, triggering three days of hostilities. Islamic Jihad indiscriminately fired over 1,100 rockets toward Israel, some of which misfired and landed inside Gaza. Israeli authorities pounded the densely populated Gaza with explosive weapons with wide area effects, carrying out 170 strikes, according to the Israel-based Meir Amit Intelligence and Terrorism Information Center. Beyond those killed and injured, the escalation resulted in damage to 2,000 Palestinian housing units, according to OCHA.

Between August 2 and 8, Israeli authorities sealed the crossings into Gaza, blocking residents in need of urgent medical care from getting treatment outside Gaza. The move also prevented the entry of fuel necessary to run Gaza's only power plant, causing it to shut down. Such measures that target Gaza's general civilian population amount to unlawful collective punishment.

Israeli Closure

For a 15th consecutive year, Israeli authorities blocked most of Gaza's population from traveling through the Erez Crossing, the only passenger crossing from Gaza into Israel through which Palestinians can travel to the West Bank and abroad. Israeli authorities often justify the closure, which came after Hamas seized political control over Gaza from the Fatah-led Palestinian Authority in June 2007, on security grounds. The closure policy, though, is not based on an individualized assessment of security risk; a generalized travel ban applies to all, except those whom Israeli authorities deem as presenting "exceptional humanitarian circumstances," mostly people needing vital medical treatment and their companions, as well as prominent businesspeople.

More than one-third of those seeking to travel for urgent medical care outside of Gaza were not approved in a timely manner during the first half of 2022, according to OCHA. The World Health Organization reported that 839 Palestinians in Gaza died between 2008 and 2021 while waiting for a response to their permit requests.

During the first nine months of 2022, about 1,060 Palestinians in Gaza exited via Erez each day, according to the Israeli rights group Gisha. The monthly average marks an increase as compared to recent years, largely driven by permits issued for Palestinians in Gaza to work in construction and agriculture, but remains less than 5 percent of the daily average of more than 24,000 before the beginning of the Second Intifada or Palestinian uprising in September 2000.

Gaza's exports during this period, mostly produce destined for the West Bank and Israel, averaged 504 truckloads per month, less than half the monthly average of 1,064 truckloads prior to the June 2007 tightening of the closure, according to Gisha. Authorities continue to severely restrict the entry of construction materials and other items they deem "dual-use" materials that could also be used for military purposes. The list of such items also includes X-ray and communications equipment, spare parts and batteries for assistive devices used by people with disabilities, and other vital civilian items.

The closure limits access to basic services. During the first nine months of 2022, families in Gaza on average had to make do without centrally provided electricity for about 12 hours a day, according to OCHA. Chronic prolonged power outages encumber many aspects of everyday life, from heating and cooling and sewage treatment to health care and business, in particular for people with disabilities who rely on light to communicate using sign language or equipment powered by electricity, such as elevators or electric wheelchairs, to move. More than 97 percent of groundwater in Gaza, its only natural water source, is "unfit for human consumption," according to OCHA.

Egypt also restricts the movement of people and goods via its Rafah crossing with Gaza, at times fully sealing the crossing. In the first nine months of 2022, an average of 23,024 Palestinians crossed monthly in both directions, less than the monthly average of over 40,000 before the 2013 military coup in Egypt, according to Gisha.

According to a Save the Children report from June, four out of five of the children they interviewed in Gaza reported living with depression, grief, and fear after 15 years of closure.

Hamas authorities have blocked some women from traveling pursuant to regulations issued in February 2021 that allow male guardians to apply to courts to block unmarried women from leaving Gaza when such travel will cause "absolute harm," a broad term that allows men to restrict women's travel at will.

Hamas and Palestinian Armed Groups

In June, Hamas authorities published footage that appears to show Hisham al-Sayed, a Palestinian Bedouin citizen of Israel, held incommunicado for more than seven years after he entered Gaza. They provided no information about another Israeli citizen whom they have apparently held since 2014, Avera Magistu. Hamas' holding of both men, civilians with psychosocial disabilities, is unlawful.

In September, Hamas authorities executed five Palestinians, including two men accused of "collaboration" with Israel, following trials marred by due process violations. These were the first executions carried out in five years. Hamas authorities have carried out 33 executions in total since taking control in Gaza in June 2007. Courts in Gaza had, as of October 19, sentenced 24 people to death this year and 188 since June 2007, according to the Gaza-based Palestinian Center for Human Rights.

West Bank

In October, Israeli authorities implemented new guidelines that severely restrict the ability of foreign nationals to enter the West Bank to visit family, work, study, or teach.

Israeli Use of Force and Detentions

Israeli security forces increased the scale and number of military raids into Palestinian communities in the West Bank in April, following several attacks by Palestinians inside Israel in March. In April, then-Prime Minister Bennett declared that there would be "no restrictions" on Israeli forces' actions. As of October 24, Israeli forces killed 109 Palestinians in the West Bank, including at least 27 children, according to OCHA. Those killed include Palestinians alleged to have attacked Israelis, journalists, workers crossing through openings in the separation barrier (the Israeli army has in recent years tacitly approved of Palestinians passing through the barrier), and bystanders, including 44-year-old Ghada Sabatin, an unarmed mother of six gunned down at a checkpoint.

Israeli authorities have rarely held accountable security forces who used excessive force or settlers who attacked Palestinians. Even in the high-profile killing of Shireen Abu Aqla and the clearly-documented violent assault of her funeral procession, Israeli authorities, while acknowledging that an Israeli soldier likely killed her, said it was accidental and that there would be no criminal probe into the matter.

Israeli settlers killed two Palestinians, wounded 161, and caused property damage in 368 incidents, as of September 12, according to OCHA. Between 2005 and 2021, Israeli police closed 92 percent of investigations against settlers who attacked Palestinians without an indictment filed, according to the Israeli rights group Yesh Din.

As of October 8, Palestinians killed one Israeli settler and wounded 44 in the West Bank, according to OCHA.

While applying Israeli civil law to settlers, Israeli authorities govern West Bank Palestinians, excluding Jerusalem residents, under harsh military law. In so doing, they deny them basic due process and try them in military courts with a nearly 100 percent conviction rate. The Israeli newspaper Haaretz reported in August that Israeli courts had not granted a single petition to cancel an administrative detention order in 2022 and the Israeli organization Association for Civil Rights is not aware of any case of it not having done so.

As of October 1, Israel held 4,623 Palestinians in custody for "security" offenses, according to Israeli Prison Services figures. As of October 10, Israeli authorities detained 190 Palestinian children, according to the Palestinian prisoner rights group Addameer. Israel incarcerates many Palestinians from the Occupied Palestinian Territory (OPT) inside Israel, complicating family visits and violating international humanitarian law's prohibition against their transfer outside occupied territory.

In March, Israeli authorities arrested Salah Hamouri, a French-Palestinian human rights defender, and placed him in administrative detention, where he remained at time of writing. In October 2021, they removed his residency status based on "breach[ing] allegiance" to Israel, an unlawful move that could trigger his expulsion from his native Jerusalem.

In August, Khalil Awawdeh ended a nearly six-month-long hunger strike against his months-long administrative detention after Israeli authorities agreed to release him in October. Israeli authorities, though, did not release him in October and he remained in detention as of November 10.

In August, Israeli authorities sentenced Gaza aid worker Mohammad al-Halabi to 12 years in prison, after holding him for six years before and during his trial, for allegedly diverting millions of dollars to Palestinian armed groups. His trial was marred by severe due process violations, including keeping secret much of the supposed evidence against him. Audits by donor governments and independent firms hired by World Vision, Halabi's employer, found no wrongdoing.

In August, Israeli authorities held Nasser Nawaja, a field researcher for the Israeli rights group B'Tselem, incommunicado for more than 12 hours, accusing him of "causing trouble."

More than 1,300 complaints of torture, including of painful shackling, sleep deprivation, and exposure to extreme temperatures, have been filed with Israel's Justice Ministry since 2001, resulting in two criminal investigations and no indictments, according to the Israeli rights group, the Public Committee Against Torture. The group Military Court Watch reported that 74 out of 100 Palestinian children interviewed in 2022 said they were physically abused in detention by Israeli forces, and 42 percent were subjected to solitary confinement.

As of September 14, Israeli authorities held the bodies of 106 Palestinians killed since 2015 in what they consider security incidents, as leverage to secure Hamas's release of the bodies of two Israeli soldiers presumed killed in 2014 hostilities, as authorities have acknowledged, according to the Jerusalem Legal Aid and Human Rights Center.

Settlements and Home Demolitions

Israeli authorities provide security, infrastructure, and services for about 700,000 settlers in the West Bank, including East Jerusalem.

The difficulty in obtaining Israeli building permits in East Jerusalem and the 60 percent of the West Bank under Israel's exclusive control (Area C) has driven Palestinians to build structures that are at constant risk of demolition or confiscation for being unauthorized, including dozens of schools. Entire Palestinian communities in areas like the South Hebron Hills find themselves at high risk of displacement. International law prohibits an occupying power from destroying property unless "absolutely necessary" for "military operations."

In March, the Israeli High Court ruled that four families in the East Jerusalem neighborhood of Sheikh Jarrah could temporarily remain in their homes, as the Justice Ministry evaluates ownership of the land. Israeli settler organizations have sought in Sheikh Jarrah and Silwan, another East Jerusalem neighborhood, to take possession of Palestinian homes and evict their long-term residents. They have done so under a discriminatory law, upheld by Israeli courts, that allow these groups to pursue claims for land they claim Jews owned in East Jerusalem before 1948. Palestinians, including Sheikh Jarrah residents facing displacement, are barred under Israeli law from reclaiming property they owned in what became Israel, and from which they fled in 1948.

Freedom of Movement

Israeli authorities continued to require Palestinian ID holders with rare exceptions to hold difficult-to-obtain, time-limited permits to enter Israel and large parts of the West Bank, including East Jerusalem. B'Tselem describes this as "an arbitrary, entirely non-transparent bureaucratic system" where "many applications are denied without explanation, with no real avenue for appeal."

Israeli authorities, as of June 2020, maintained nearly 600 checkpoints and other permanent obstacles within the West Bank, in addition to nearly 1,500 ad-hoc "flying" checkpoints erected between April 2019 and March 2020, according to OCHA. Israeli forces routinely turn away or delay and humiliate Palestinians at checkpoints without explanation, while permitting largely unfettered movement to Israeli settlers.

Israel continued construction of the separation barrier. Authorities began building the barrier more than two decades ago, ostensibly for security reasons, but 85 percent of it falls within the West Bank rather than along the Green Line separating Israeli from Palestinian territory. In so doing, the barrier carves off nearly 10 percent of the West Bank, cuts off thousands of Palestinians from their agricultural lands and isolates 11,000 Palestinians who live on the western side of the barrier but are not allowed to travel to Israel and whose ability to cross the barrier to access their property and basic services are highly restricted.

Palestinian Authority

More than a year after PA security forces beat to death prominent activist and critic Nizar Banat in June 2021 while he was in custody and rounded up scores demanding justice for his death, no one has been held to account. Prosecutors brought charges against 14 security officers, but critics say the authorities are moving too slowly and are biased.

PA personal status laws discriminated against women, including in relation to marriage, divorce, custody of children, and inheritance. Palestine has no comprehensive domestic violence law. The PA has long been considering a draft family protection law, but women's rights groups have raised concerns that it does not go far enough to prevent abuse and protect survivors.

In the summer, several social and cultural events in the West Bank were canceled following threats against organizers. The Palestinian rights group al-Haq called on the PA to better protect these spaces and investigate threats against such activities.

Israel

In March, a series of attacks by Palestinians, including a shooting in Hadera and B'nei Barak and a stabbing and car-ramming in Beersheva, killed 9 Israeli civilians and 2 police officers.

The Knesset reinstated in March a temporary order that bars, with few exceptions, the granting of long-term legal status inside Israel to Palestinians from the West Bank and Gaza who marry Israeli citizens or residents. Such a restriction, which has been in place since 2003, does not exist for spouses of virtually any other nationality.

In July, the Israeli High Court upheld a 2008 law allowing Israeli authorities to revoke a person's citizenship based on "breach of loyalty."

Israeli authorities continued to systematically deny asylum claims of the roughly 28,000 African, largely Eritrean and Sudanese, asylum seekers in the country, while allowing in thousands of Ukrainian refugees. Over the years, the government has imposed restrictions on their movement, work permits, and access to health care and to education to pressure asylum seekers to leave.

Key International Actors

US President Biden visited Israel and Palestine in July. The administration has largely failed to speak out about human rights abuses, including Israel's outlawing of prominent Palestinian civil society groups. The administration, though, did condemn and launch an investigation into Shireen Abu Aqla's killing. In March, the US Congress authorized $1 billion in funding for Israel's Iron Dome air defense system, supplementing the annual $3.7 billion in security assistance the US provides the country.

Nine European Union states in July said they received "no substantial information" that justified Israel's designations of Palestinian civil society groups as "terrorist organizations" and "unlawful associations," and would continue their financial support to them.

The EU continued to condemn Israel's settlement policy. The EU's main focus remained to attempt to revamp the "peace process;" while acknowledging some human rights abuses, it has not imposed meaningful consequences for those abuses. In October, the EU-Israel Association Council convened for the first time in a decade, despite escalating Israeli repression.

The International Criminal Court (ICC) prosecutor's Palestine investigation remained ongoing.

In September, a human rights due diligence exercise commissioned by Meta, the parent company of Facebook and Instagram, of its Israel and Palestine content moderation in May 2021 found that the company censored social media posts by Palestinians and their supporters, including on human rights abuses.

Italy

The September election of a coalition government led by Giorgia Meloni of the hard-right, nationalist Brothers of Italy raised serious concerns about more abusive migration policies and restrictions on reproductive rights. Italy continued to support Libya to intercept boats and return migrants and asylum seekers to abuse in that country, while often delaying disembarkations in Italy of people from nongovernmental organization (NGO) rescue ships.

Authorities' failure to include racist motivation when addressing such crimes as the brutal July killing of a Nigerian street vendor or the 2020 killing of a Black Italian man, for which four men were convicted, raised concerns. Poverty levels remain at a record high, harming people's rights. Significant barriers to accessing abortion, including high rates of conscientious objection, remained. The European Commission called for continuing efforts to ensure judicial independence and efficiency, while noting shrinking civil society space.

Migrants and Asylum Seekers

The positive treatment of Ukrainians in Italy contrasted with abusive policies and practices affecting others seeking protection or safety.

By the end of July, almost 150,000 people coming from Ukraine had been granted temporary protection; and approximately 27,500 Ukrainian students were enrolled in Italian schools by the beginning of June. While the government allocated funds for nongovernmental small-scale accommodation programs for Ukrainian refugees and created 8,000 more places in the national asylum and refugee reception system, refugee rights organizations expressed concern that asylum seekers and refugees from other nationalities were being displaced to make space for the new arrivals.

The police, who process all initial asylum claims, prevented asylum seekers from countries other than Ukraine from lodging claims, leaving hundreds homeless and destitute.

In July, the Italian government renewed funding for Libya for migration controls despite the finding that same month by the UN Fact-Finding Mission to Libya that migrants and refugees are exposed to risk of crimes against humanity in Libya. At this writing, the agreement between Italy and Libya on migration cooperation was expected to automatically renew in February 2023 for three years.

According to government statistics, more than 85,000 people reached Italy, including 9,930 unaccompanied children, by sea by the end of October, a significant increase over 2021. The continued failure to ensure adequate facilities and swift transfers meant the reception center on Lampedusa was periodically overwhelmed.

Italian authorities allowed NGO rescue ships to disembark, usually after some delay, but also often held NGO ships in port, inhibiting rescue efforts. In August, the Court of Justice of the European Union ruled in a case brought by the rescue organization Sea-Watch that holding ships is legitimate only if the state can demonstrate there is a "clear risk" to safety, health, or the environment. According to the think tank ISPI, between August 2021-August 2022, only 14 percent of people disembarked in Italy were rescued by NGOs.

The trial of 21 people from three rescue organizations on charges of aiding and abetting unauthorized immigration was expected to reopen in late 2022, after the court suspended the proceedings in June citing procedural errors on the part of the prosecutor's office.

About 28 months after a flawed program was launched to provide residency permits to undocumented migrants working in agriculture, domestic work, and home care, only 61 percent of the roughly 207,800 applications had led to a positive response as of December 2022, with tens of thousands of applications still pending (roughly the 20 percent).

The former mayor of Riace, Domenico Lucano, had an appeal pending at time of writing against his September 2021 sentence to over 13 years in prison on charges of abetting irregular immigration and irregularities in an otherwise celebrated integration program for asylum seekers.

In May, a court acquitted the president and two members of Baobab Experience, a nongovernmental association helping needy migrants in Rome, of aiding and abetting unauthorized immigration for having helped nine migrants buy bus tickets to travel from Rome to Ventimiglia.

Discrimination and Intolerance

In July, a court sentenced two brothers to life in prison and two others to over 20 years in prison for the brutal beating to death in September 2020 of 21-year-old Willy Monteiro Duarte, a Black Italian, in a town on the outskirts of Rome. The men were not charged with the aggravating circumstance of racial bias. Also in July, an Italian man beat and strangled in broad daylight a Nigerian street vendor as onlookers failed to intervene. The police and prosecutor quickly ruled out racist motivation for the killing, prompting criticism.

In May, the Democratic Party reintroduced a bill, passed in the Chamber of Deputies in 2020 but rejected by the Senate last year, to make incitement to violence or discrimination "based on sex, gender, sexual orientation or gender identity" a crime. The bill would broaden existing law on bias crimes in Italy, increase funding for victim support, and institute a national day against prejudice based on sexual orientation or gender identity. The recently elected coalition government is composed of political parties that have long opposed the bill.

The Labor Ministry presented in March new guidelines to foster access to quality and sustainable jobs for people with disabilities in keeping with its commitments under the EU Strategy for the Rights of Persons with Disabilities 2021-2030.

Poverty and Inequality

The Covid-19 pandemic dramatically increased the number of people experiencing absolute poverty in Italy. In 2021, about 5.6 million people, including nearly one-third of all non-national residents, were unable to buy goods and services essential to achieve a minimally acceptable standard of living as defined by the Italian government.

An estimated 22 percent of people living in Italy are at risk of food poverty or are food insecure. Exacerbating existing issues with social exclusion and equitable distribution of resources, the prices for groceries and unprocessed foods increased by 8.2 percent between June 2021 and June 2022.

In May 2022, the government approved a package of measures to counter the impacts of price inflation, including increasing income-based subsidies for domestic gas and electricity and providing families earning less than €35,000 annum a one-time €200 stimulus payment.

Almost one third of women and over one third of foreigners were employed in "non-standard" work with fewer rights protections.

At its periodic review of Italy's record in late September, the UN Committee on Economic, Social, and Cultural Rights expressed concerns about the limited enjoyment of rights by migrants, asylum seekers, and refugees; the punitive approach taken towards workers in the informal economy; and exploitative practices in the agriculture, construction, and garment and textile industries especially of migrant workers, including undocumented migrants. The Committee also expressed concerns about persistent rates of high poverty, the adequacy of the old-age pension system and unemployment benefits, and the rights of disadvantaged and marginalized groups to food security, housing, and protection from discrimination.

Women's Rights

The Interior Ministry reported that 79 women were killed by relatives or people they knew in the first ten months of the year, 46 of them by a partner or ex-partner.

In April, the European Court of Human Rights condemned Italy for failing to sufficiently protect a woman and her children from domestic violence despite repeated complaints. The woman's partner stabbed their one-year-old boy to death and gravely injured her in September 2018. The case illustrates the ongoing problems that women who experience domestic violence have obtaining protection from the authorities in practice.

Despite abortion being legal in Italy, and a recent survey finding 73 percent of Italians support access to abortion, there remain multiple barriers to abortion, including large numbers of medical professionals invoking conscientious objection, and lack of an enforced requirement that persons in need of an abortion be referred to another provider.

Latest data from the Health Ministry, published in June with respect to 2020, showed that 64.6 percent of gynecologists and 44.6 percent of anesthesiologists in Italy refuse to perform abortions. Access to medical abortions—using prescription drugs to end safely a pregnancy—also varied significantly among regions of the country, with a national average of 35 percent across procedures.

After formal ratification at the end of 2021, the International Labour Organization convention on violence and harassment in employment is scheduled to enter into force in October.

Children's Rights

The Education Ministry did not act on reports that the products it authorized for education during the pandemic surveilled or had the capacity to surveil children online, outside school hours, and deep into their private lives. One EdTech product transmitted children's personal data to advertising technology companies, enabling these companies to track and target children across the internet.

Rule of Law

In June, Parliament adopted reforms to restructure the justice system. In its July European rule of law report, the European Commission noted that implementing legislation would need to include provisions to ensure judicial independence in line with European standards, and the need for continuing efforts to improve efficiency and reduce notoriously lengthy proceedings. The report notes the continuing lack of an independent national human rights institute and the narrow civic space, in particular for groups working with migrants.

A March Interior Ministry decree significantly limits access under freedom of information procedures to documents relating to migration and border policies, including cooperation agreements with third countries, for broad reasons of nationality security, defense, and protection of international relations.

Environment and Human Rights

Parliament amended the constitution in March to include protection of the environment, biodiversity, and ecosystems as a fundamental principle, and to place responsibility on private enterprise to avoid harm to health or the environment.

In July, the UN special rapporteur on the implications for human rights of the environmentally sound management and disposal of hazardous substances and wastes called on Italy to take steps to protect people from exposure to toxic substances and speed up remediation processes, stop exporting pesticides banned from use in the EU, and make a drastic change in its approach to waste management.

Japan

Japan is a liberal democracy with an active civil society. In July, two days before an upper house election, former Prime Minister Shinzo Abe was shot and killed during a campaign rally in Nara Prefecture. The suspect, Tetsuya Yamagami, was reportedly motivated by his family's financial difficulties caused by the Unification Church, as well as problematic ties between Abe and the religious group. On July 10, the ruling Liberal Democratic Party (LDP) won a majority of seats in Japan's upper house election.

Japan has no laws prohibiting racial, ethnic, or religious discrimination, or discrimination based on sexual orientation or gender identity. Japan does not have a national human rights institution.

Refugees

Japan's asylum and refugee determination system remains strongly oriented against granting refugee status. In 2021, the Justice Ministry received 2,413 applications for refugee status, but recognized only 74 people as refugees, and categorized 580 people, 498 from Myanmar, as needing humanitarian assistance, allowing them to stay in Japan. Applications for refugee status in 2021 decreased by 88 percent from 2017, when nearly 20,000 applications were filed.

Unusually, since Russia's invasion of Ukraine in February, Japan had accepted 2,035 people from Ukraine as "evacuees" as of October 19. In August 2022, the Justice Ministry announced it also granted refugee status to 133 people fleeing Afghanistan after the Taliban took power in August 2021.

Death Penalty

In December 2021, Japan executed three prisoners on death row. In July, Japan executed another prisoner, with 106 prisoners remaining on death row as of July 26. Concerns have long been raised about death-row inmates being notified of their execution only on the day it takes place and having inadequate access to legal counsel, among others.

Women's Rights

The revised article 731 of the Civil Code went into effect in April, raising the minimum age that girls can get married from 16 to 18 with parental permission, effectively ending child marriage.

In a series of court rulings from early to late 2022, the Tokyo District Court ordered universities to compensate people who had sued the school for damages caused by discriminatory admission policies. The lawsuits began after several medical schools were found to be discriminating against women and repeat applicants in 2018. Japan has an Equal Employment Opportunity Law between men and women, but it only applies to the area of employment.

Children's Rights

In June, Japan passed the Child Basic Act, the country's first national law for the rights of the child, based on the Convention on the Rights of the Child. In June, Japan revised the Child Welfare Act. The revisions included a measure to address financial incentives for institutionalization of children without parental care, and introduction of mandatory judicial review for determining whether a child should be removed from their family, for which the United Nations Committee on the Rights of the Child has urged Japan at the latest country reports review.

The Education Ministry failed to act following reports that the online learning products it had authorized for children's education during the Covid-19 pandemic infringed on children's rights. Nine out of the 10 products reviewed by Human Rights Watch surveilled or had the capacity to surveil children online. Seven of these products transmitted children's personal data to advertising technology companies, enabling these companies to track and target children across the internet.

Sexual Orientation and Gender Identity

Despite a significant public campaign, the Diet did not pass non-discrimination legislation that would protect lesbian, gay, bisexual, and transgender (LGBT) people. Japan's national government does not recognize same-sex relationships, but municipal and prefecture-level authorities representing more than half of the country's population including Tokyo have begun to issue "marriage" certificates, which have no legal effect, to same-sex couples. The government still requires sterilization surgeries before transgender people can be legally recognized according to their gender identity. In November 2021, the Supreme Court ruled for the first time that a prohibition to have any underage children, (a discriminatory requirement in the "Gender Identity Disorder Special Cases Act" for a transgender person to be legally recognized), is constitutional.

Criminal Justice

Japan's "hostage" justice system holds criminal suspects for long periods in harsh conditions to coerce confessions. In May 2022, the Justice Ministry started to review the implementation of the 2016 Criminal Procedure Code revisions, which introduced mandatory video and audio recording of interrogations in some criminal cases.

In June, Japan amended its penal code, replacing "imprisonment with labor" and "imprisonment" with "imprisonment … which allows the enforcement of necessary work and guidance." Additionally, Japan lacks alternative measures to imprisonment even for people who committed non-violent crimes and use drugs, have mental health conditions, are pregnant, or have children.

Climate Change and Policy Impacts

Japan is among the top 10 emitters of greenhouse gases responsible for the climate crisis. In October 2021, Japan updated its Nationally Determined Contribution (NDC) to the Paris Agreement, aiming to cut emissions to net zero by 2050 and reducing its greenhouse gas emissions by 46 percent by 2030, earning it an "almost sufficient" rating for its "Domestic Target" from the Climate Action Tracker.

In October 2021, Japan adopted a new Basic Energy Plan that stated Japan would aim to reduce coal to 19 percent of energy use by 2030, just a 13 percent reduction from current levels, and increase renewable energy to between 36 and 38 percent. In May, Japan joined fellow members of the G7 in committing to end international financing in fossil fuels by the end of 2022, although the commitment included a significant loophole that allows for investments in the gas sector.

On July 28, Japan voted in favor of a United Nations General Assembly resolution recognizing a clean, healthy, and sustainable environment as a human right. Japan abstained in October 2021 when the resolution was passed at the UN Human Rights Council.

In the summer, Japan experienced its most severe heat wave on record, and Tokyo broke a record for the number of days of severe heat in a year by mid-summer.

Business and Human Rights

In September, Japan's Ministry of Economy, Trade and Industry released "Guidelines on Respect for Human Rights in Responsible Supply Chains," the first set of guidelines in Japan outlining human rights due diligence responsibilities for Japanese companies. While this could be a much-needed tool, these non-binding guidelines should be significantly strengthened and do not substitute for binding legislation. Japan should adopt robust legislation to regulate how companies respect human rights and environmental standards in their own operations and global value chains.

Foreign Policy

Japan officially states that "the promotion and protection of all human rights is a legitimate interest of the international community," and "grave violations of human rights need to be addressed in cooperation with the international community."

In September, Japan announced it will suspend accepting new officers and cadets from the Myanmar military for training, citing the Myanmar junta's execution of four pro-democracy activists as a major factor in its decision. After the February 1, 2021 military coup, Japan accepted eight military personnel for training. Prior to Japan's announcement, research by Human Rights Watch has previously located Japan-trained officers at Myanmar military bases where units have been implicated in serious abuses.

In response to the Chinese government's abuses in Xinjiang and Hong Kong, Japan refrained from sending ministers to the 2022 Beijing Winter Olympics. Just days before the opening ceremony, Japanese lawmakers passed a Diet resolution highlighting human rights issues in Xinjiang, Tibet, Inner Mongolia, and Hong Kong. Specifically, the February 1 resolution calls for the "monitoring of serious human rights situations in cooperation with the international community," and "implementation of comprehensive relief measures."

Japan has not endorsed the Safe Schools Declaration, an intergovernmental commitment aiming to strengthen the prevention of, and response to, attacks on students, teachers, schools, and universities during war.

Jordan

In 2022, Jordanian authorities removed regulations and safety measures taken in response to the Covid-19 pandemic but did not rescind a state of emergency declared in March 2020, granting the prime minister sweeping powers to rule by decree.

In early 2022, Jordanian lawmakers amended the country's electoral and political parties laws and enacted constitutional amendments in line with the recommendations issued by the Royal Committee to Modernize the Political System convened by Jordan's King Abdullah II in 2021. The recommendations emphasized the need for "full respect for human rights and the creation of a safe space for fundamental freedoms that would enable political participation," but the new legislation maintained vague provisions that can be used by authorities to constrain political parties.

Freedom of Expression

Jordanian law criminalizes speech deemed critical of the king, foreign countries, government officials and institutions, Islam and Christianity, and defamatory speech. In September, Human Rights Watch issued a report documenting how Jordanian authorities are using vague and overly broad criminal laws to suppress free speech and other freedoms. In 2020, the number of cases relating to these charges almost doubled from the previous year, according to the annual reports from the National Center for Human Rights (NCHR).

On March 8, Jordanian authorities briefly detained Daoud Kuttab, a prominent Palestinian-American journalist and director general of the Amman-based Community Media Network, following a complaint about an article posted in 2019 about the detention of an investor. The day before, authorities arrested journalist Taghreed al-Rishq apparently over a tweet in which she criticized a pro-government journalist.

Jordanian authorities further curtailed press freedom in 2022 by issuing arbitrary press gag orders prohibiting reporting on important local developments, including all local reporting around the shooting to death of a woman college student in June. Jordanian press outlets did not report on revelations in February that the king opened Swiss bank accounts in 2011 into which were transferred millions of dollars.

Freedom of Association and Assembly

Under the Public Gatherings Law amended in March 2011, Jordan did not require government permission to hold public meetings or demonstrations, but authorities continued to require organizations and venues to obtain permission from the Interior Ministry or General Intelligence Department to host events.

Several Jordanian laws restrict freedom of association, including the Labor Law of 1966, which limits the ability to freely form trade unions, and the Associations Law of 2008, which regulates the formation and operation of nongovernmental groups. Jordanian authorities impose onerous pre-approval restrictions on the receipt of foreign funding by nongovernmental groups (NGOs).

In late 2019, Jordanian authorities created a centralized committee under the Prime Minister's Office to study and decide foreign funding approval requests, but representatives of donor states and local NGOs told Human Rights Watch in 2022 that the committee has done little if anything to ease the restrictions. In September 2022, the Community Media Network, a local NGO, filed a complaint with the NCHR over authorities' arbitrary rejection of a 25,000 Jordanian Dinar (US$35,200) grant from the German development agency to produce a campaign to raise awareness about recycling.

Refugees and Migrants

By late 2022, over 670,000 people from Syria had sought refuge in Jordan, according to the United Nations High Commissioner for Refugees (UNHCR). Over 85 percent of Syrians lived outside refugee camps in rented accommodation.

According to the UNHCR, Jordan also hosted asylum seekers and refugees from other countries in 2022, including 65,854 Iraqis, 12,934 Yemenis, 5,579 Sudanese, 651 Somalis, and 1,379 from other countries. Authorities continued to enforce a January 2019 decision banning the UNHCR from registering as asylum seekers individuals who officially entered the country for the purposes of medical treatment, study, tourism, or work, effectively barring recognition of non-Syrians as refugees and leaving many without UNHCR documentation or access to services.

Authorities continued to implement the Jordan Compact, the 2016 agreement between the Jordanian government and donor countries, which aimed to improve the livelihoods of Syrian refugees by granting new legal work opportunities and improving the education sector. By early 2022, labor authorities had issued or renewed at least 252,000 work permits for Syrians since 2016, although many of these were renewals. The UNHCR reported in January that authorities issued 62,000 work permits for Syrians in 2021 alone. Most professions remained closed to non-Jordanians, and many Syrians continued to work in the informal sector without labor protections.

The roughly 230,000 school-age Syrian refugees in Jordan face multiple obstacles to education that are most acute for children ages 12 and older, including poverty-driven child labor and child marriage, lack of affordable school transportation, government policies that limit access to education, and lack of inclusive education and accommodation for children with disabilities.

Only a quarter of secondary-school-age Syrian refugee children in Jordan were enrolled in school. Non-Syrians refugees and asylum seekers were in many cases prevented from enrolling their children in school in 2022. Children without official identification numbers were unable to access online learning platforms during Covid-19 school closures.

Jordan hosted an estimated 80,000 migrant domestic workers in 2022, mostly from the Philippines, Sri Lanka, and Indonesia. NGOs repeatedly referred domestic workers who had suffered multiple abuses to labor ministry investigators. Abuses included wage theft, unsafe working conditions, long working hours without rest, passport and document confiscation, and physical, verbal, and sexual abuse.

Women's and Girls' Rights

Jordan's personal status code remains discriminatory, despite amendments in 2019. Women need the permission of a male guardian to marry for the first time, and marriages between Muslim women and non-Muslim men are not recognized. Women cannot travel abroad with their children, as men can, without the permission of their child's father, other male guardian, or a judge. While women can travel outside the country without needing permission, authorities sometimes comply with requests from male guardians to bar their unmarried adult daughters, wives, and children from leaving the country. Authorities also arrest women reported as "absent" for fleeing their home by their male guardians under the Crime Prevention Law.

Article 98 of Jordan's penal code, amended in 2017, states that the "fit of fury" defense does not allow mitigated sentences for perpetrators of crimes "against women," but judges continued to impose mitigated sentences under article 99 if family members of victims did not support prosecutions of their male family members. Article 340 of the penal code also allows a man to receive a reduced sentence if he kills or attacks his wife or any of his female relatives in the alleged act of committing adultery or in an "unlawful bed."

Such discriminatory laws leave women exposed to violence. Similarly, the penal code and Juveniles Act do not prohibit corporal punishment and allow parents to punish children in accordance with "general norms."

In July, women protested outside Parliament for improved legislation to combat gender-based violence and transparent accountability measures for the perpetrators of violence against women. The protests followed a series of public killings of women including the stabbing of a woman by her husband outside a courthouse in Karak and the fatal shooting by a man of 21-year-old student at her university campus in Amman.

Article 9 of Jordan's Nationality Law does not allow Jordanian women married to non-Jordanian spouses to pass on their nationality to their spouse and children. In 2014, authorities issued a cabinet decision purporting to ease restrictions on access to key economic and social rights for non-citizen children of Jordanian women, but the measures fell short of expectations. Non-citizen children of Jordanian women no longer require work permits for employment, but many professions in Jordan remained closed to non-Jordanians.

Sexual Orientation and Gender Identity

Jordan has no laws that explicitly criminalize same-sex relations. The penal code includes vague "immorality" provisions that are used to target sexual and gender minorities. Jordanian law does not prohibit discrimination based on sexual orientation and gender identity.

State actors in Jordan have undermined lesbian, gay, bisexual, and transgender (LGBT) people's right to privacy with digital targeting, namely entrapment on social media and dating applications, online harassment and "outing," online extortion, monitoring social media, and reliance on illegitimately obtained digital evidence in prosecutions. Human Rights Watch documented cases where security forces have used digital targeting, based on "immorality" provisions and the Cybercrime Law, to entrap LGBT people, arbitrarily arrest and detain them based on digital evidence found on their personal devices, censor content related to gender and sexuality online, and intimidate LGBT rights activists.

Jordan summarily deports foreign nationals found to be HIV-positive, and LGBT people living with HIV have reported facing stigma and discrimination by medical professionals and employers, without any legal recourse.

Criminal Justice

Jordan remains one of the few countries in the world that still allow imprisoning people for debt, which is prohibited under international law. In 2022, the parliament passed amendments to the main law that mandates debt imprisonment. While the amendments were an improvement, they fell short of ending the practice entirely. As of April 1, at least 148,000 people were wanted for prison terms for unpaid debts, according to the Justice Ministry. Human Rights Watch has documented how, in the absence of an adequate social security net, tens of thousands of Jordanians took out loans to cover basic necessities only to end up in prison or wanted for failure to repay.

As of November, authorities had not carried out any executions in 2022.

Local governors continued to use provisions of the Crime Prevention Law of 1954 to place individuals in administrative detention for up to one year, in circumvention of the Criminal Procedure Law. Jordan's NNCHR reported in late 2021 that 21,322 persons were administratively detained in 2020, some for longer than one year, marking a dramatic decrease from 37,853 administrative detentions in 2019.

Penal code amendments that came into effect in June included articles that criminalized attempts to commit suicide or express intent to commit suicide and statements that seek to instill fear in people.

Key International Actors

In September 2022, the US and Jordan signed a new memorandum of understanding under which the US committed to providing Jordan with $1.45 billion per year in US bilateral foreign assistance from 2023 through 2029.

Normalization efforts between Jordan and Syria continued in 2022, but ongoing border issues including rampant drug smuggling from Syria hampered a broader rapprochement.

Jordan is a member of the Saudi Arabia and United Arab Emirates-led coalition fighting Houthi forces in Yemen, which has committed numerous violations of international human rights and humanitarian law in Yemen.

Kazakhstan

Anti-government protests rocked Kazakhstan in January, setting off a cascade of human rights violations by authorities, including disproportionate use of force against protesters, arbitrary arrest and imprisonment, and ill-treatment and torture of detainees. Kazakhstan has rejected calls for an independent investigation with external experts into the events. Following the protests, President Kasym-Jomart Tokayev secured his hold on power, and on November 20 was re-elected to a new seven-year term in snap presidential elections.

Meanwhile, longstanding rights abuses persisted. Authorities cracked down on government critics and continued to impose heavy restrictions on the rights to peaceful protest, freedom of speech, and freedom of religion. Domestic violence and torture continued with impunity. Kazakhstan voted on constitutional amendments on June 5 in a national referendum. Changes included strengthening the status of the human rights commissioner and establishing a constitutional court.

Presidential Elections

Kazakhstan held early presidential elections on November 20 after President Tokayev in mid-September signed off on an additional amendment to the constitution introducing a one-time seven-year term limit on presidential office. The OSCE/ODHIR election monitoring mission concluded that the elections were "lacking competitiveness...and underlined the need for further reforms." No election in Kazakhstan has ever been deemed free and fair by independent international election monitors.

Excessive Use of Force

Authorities used lethal force in responding to protests and violence in January. At least 232 people, including 19 security force members, died in the violence. Human Rights Watch documented how Kazakh security forces used excessive force on at least four occasions between January 4 and 6, resulting in 10 people being shot dead, as well as lethal force against protesters and rioters who posed no immediate threat. To date, only one law enforcement officer involved in the lethal response to the January violence has been prosecuted.

Accountability and Justice

In response to the January events, President Tokayev replaced his government, declared a state of emergency, and requested military help from the Collective Security Treaty Organisation, a six-country regional military alliance including Russia. On January 7, he ordered troops to "shoot to kill without warning." On January 11, nine top United Nations human rights experts called on Kazakhstan to ensure "independent and human rights-based investigations of State use of force against protesters."

In mid-August, the Prosecutor General's Office said there were over 5,300 criminal investigations into the violence. Kazakh authorities have rejected calls by international human rights bodies and others to carry out an independent investigation involving international experts.

Torture

Hundreds of people detained in connection with the January events have alleged ill-treatment or torture, and at least six people have died in pretrial detention centers, according to official figures. Azamat Batyrbaev, a protester from Taldykorgan, claimed police beat him and burned him with a hot iron after he was detained. While authorities initiated 234 criminal cases on allegations of torture, as of this writing, only eight police officers have been put on trial on charges of torture.

Civil Society

Authorities arrested the unregistered Democratic Party head Zhanbolat Mamay in February in connection with the January events, and later brought criminal charges of insulting a law enforcement officer and disseminating knowingly false information. In June, he was additionally charged with disseminating false information and organizing mass riots during the January protests. On November 2, Mamay was transferred to house arrest one week after the latter two charges were requalified and dropped respectively. Several other activists have been targeted with politically motivated charges in connection with the January events, including Aidar Baisagatov in Ust-Kamenogorsk, Moldabai Sadibekov in Shymkent, and Darkhan Ualiyev in Almaty.

Police arrested Artyom Sochnev, an environmental activist from Stepnogorsk on January 4 on charges of "inciting social discord" for recording a live video blog about the protests. In July, authorities dropped the charges.

Ermek Narymbaev, an activist who fled Kazakhstan in 2016 after he was convicted of "inciting national discord" was arrested on February 6 while reentering Kazakhstan. He was then transferred to a prison colony to serve out his 2016 sentence.

At least 10 political opposition activists were criminally charged or convicted in 2022 for alleged membership in banned so-called "extremist" groups, a violation of their right to freedom of expression and association.

Freedom of Assembly

The right to peaceful assembly continues to be heavily restricted and policed. People who try to peacefully protest are detained, fined, or sentenced to short-term custodial sentences.

On January 2, hundreds of people in Zhanaozen, western Kazakhstan, began to protest increased energy prices. The protests spread quickly across the country, with the focus widening to broader economic and political issues. On January 4, law enforcement forcibly dispersed peaceful protests in Almaty, and then rioters and some protesters attacked security forces and public buildings and looted shops.

Ethnic Kazakhs whose loved ones are detained or disappeared in China continued to intermittently protest outside the Chinese consulate in Almaty in 2022. Several faced intimidation and short-term detention before Xi Jinping's visit to Kazakhstan in September.

Freedom of Expression

Media workers continued to face harassment, arrest, physical attack, and prosecution. Media freedom watchdogs, including Reporters Without Borders and Adilsoz, reported that security forces shot at some journalists and detained and arrested others while they were reporting on the January violence.

On January 6 media worker Diasken Baytibaev was wounded by live fire, and his driver, Muratkhan Bazarbayev, was fatally shot. Uralskaya Nedelya journalist Lukpan Akhmedyarov, Daryn Nursapak of Altay News, Bakhyt Smyagul of the newspaper Bukpa, and Nurzhan Baimuldin of the media outlet Kokshetau-Asia all spent between 5 and 15 days in administrative detention after trying to report on the events.

The Organization for Security and Co-operation in Europe (OSCE) Representative on Freedom of the Media Teresa Ribeiro on January 12 called for "safe working conditions for journalists," and "a restoration of internet access" after reports of government interference in journalists' reporting efforts.

Kazakhstan's Supreme Court on July 19 acquitted Seitkazy and Aset Mataev, journalists who in 2016 were sentenced to six and five years in prison, respectively, on spurious embezzlement charges.

Labor Rights

In June, Kazakhstan underwent special review by the Committee on the Application of Standards for violations of the International Labour Organization's Freedom of Association and Protection of the Right to Organise Convention. The committee noted "the long-standing and persistent nature of the issues," published an extensive list of conclusions and recommendations, and requested the government develop a time-bound action plan to implement the conclusions.

Authorities continued to ignore a May 2021 UN Working Group on Arbitrary Detention decision calling for the immediate release of labor activist Erzhan Elshibaev, who remains in prison. On September 29, he was sentenced to an additional seven-year prison sentence on charges of disobeying and inciting others to disobey prison administration.

Violence against Women and Girls

Although authorities acknowledge domestic violence is a serious problem, impunity remains the norm. The Kazakh government failed to allocate sufficient resources to ensure that police and service providers can identify, prevent, and adequately respond to domestic violence. Law makers took no action to review a draft domestic violence law that was suspended in 2021.

Almaty city authorities allowed activists to gather at a March 8 Women's Day rally but denied permission for a march.

Kazakhstan has repatriated over 670 women and children from detention camps for ISIS suspects and their families in northeast Syria. Human Rights Watch research found that many children are in school and reintegrating successfully, but that families are often unable to obtain birth certificates or death certificates for the fathers of children who were killed in Syria. Without death certificates, families are not eligible for certain social benefits, and without birth certificates, children may be denied educational services.

Disability Rights

A new law, "On Improving the Quality of Life of Persons with Disabilities," signed by the president on June 29, introduces some technical improvements for people with disabilities, including replacing the stigmatizing term "invalid" with "person with disabilities." An obligatory medical exam and other barriers continue to obstruct children's access to inclusive education. Authorities have not meaningfully addressed the isolation, violence, neglect, physical restraint, and overmedication that children with disabilities can face in segregated special schools or residential institutions.

Sexual Orientation and Gender Identity

Kazakhstan does not provide for legal protection against discrimination based on sexual orientation or gender identity. The process for changing one's legally recognized gender remains invasive and humiliating.

Freedom of Religion

The right to freedom of religion is curtailed, with mandatory registration requirements for religious groups and strict restrictions on religious literature. On July 19, a court in southern Kazakhstan sentenced Anatoli Zernichenko to seven years in prison for posting online Muslim texts that authorities claimed "promoted terrorism." Pope Francis visited Kazakhstan in mid-September and commended the government for abolishing the death penalty.

Poverty and Inequality

The rigid eligibility criteria and means tests of Kazakhstan's main social assistance program, Targeted Social Assistance, has excluded many people from accessing social security. Low-income families also face stigma and discrimination when trying to access state benefits.

Key International Actors

Kazakhstan began its three-year term on the UN Human Rights Council in January.

Multiple international actors expressed concern about the January violence and called on authorities to ensure an impartial and independent investigation into the events, including the European Union, the United States, and Switzerland. The European Parliament on January 19 issued a strongly worded resolution on the situation in Kazakhstan calling for a proper international investigation into the human rights violations committed in January.

In June, United Nations Deputy Secretary-General Amina Mohammed travelled to Astana where she met with President Tokayev and civil society organizations working to combat gender-based violence.

On August 22, a delegation of the European Parliament's Subcommittee on Human Rights conducted a three-day fact-finding visit to Kazakhstan, where they highlighted the need for a "transparent, comprehensive and fair investigation into January 2022 events" and called on authorities to stop harassing political and civil society activists, and to release Zhanbolat Mamay.

EU President Charles Michel called Kazakhstan a "crucial partner" after his meeting with President Tokayev in Astana on October 27, and reiterated the EU's call for a "full, fair and transparent investigation into the events of January."

Kenya

William Samoei Ruto and his deputy, Rigathi Gachagua, won Kenya's closely contested August 9 presidential election, after the Supreme Court rejected an opposition challenge. Ruto was deputy to outgoing Kenyan President Uhuru Kenyatta since March 2013, but Kenyatta openly supported his former rival and Ruto's challenger, Raila Odinga.

Despite disputes over the tallying of the presidential votes, resulting in tense moments and brief street protests, when the electoral commission declared Ruto winner, the entire electoral process was not as violent as in many previous elections. Kenya failed to ensure accountability for security forces abuses, including use of excessive force during violence in the previous elections. There was misappropriation of funds meant for the Covid-19 response.

Lack of Accountability for Misused Covid-19 Relief Funds

Kenyan authorities have yet to hold to account those implicated in the misuse of funds meant for households most affected by the Covid-19 pandemic. In August 2020, investigators recommended the prosecution of at least 15 top government officials and business people over the alleged misuse of millions of dollars meant for buying Covid-19 medical supplies.

Kenya's Ethics and Anti-Corruption Commission uncovered evidence of tenders being allegedly allocated to politically connected individuals and businesses. Following public outcry and media reports, the Kenyan government ordered an investigation into huge sums meant for medical supplies. The Kenyan government received around 200 billion Kenyan shillings (US$ 1.6 million) in donor aid and grants to support Kenya's response to the Covid-19 pandemic.

In July 2021, a Human Rights Watch report found that the Covid-19 crisis devastated many lives and livelihoods when Kenyan authorities imposed stringent control measures, including curfews, stay at home directives, and other restrictions on movement.

Thousands of people lost their only sources of income, with businesses closing and sole breadwinners of households losing jobs. Thousands of families suffered or faced the threat of starvation and eviction due to non-payment of rent.

Although the government created a cash transfer program to cushion households in informal settlements in the capital, Nairobi, the program was undermined by serious irregularities. It lacked transparency, failed to adhere to laid down criteria, and in some instances was characterized by favoritism and cronyism. Although the program was designed to pay beneficiaries weekly transfers for 35 weeks, the frequency and duration of the transfers varied widely, with some just receiving the transfer a handful of times.

President Uhuru Kenyatta promised accountability for all the Covid-19 funds, but at time of writing, no one has been charged or convicted over misuse of the funds.

Security Forces Conduct

In April, a report of the Missing Voices Group, a coalition of 15 Kenyan and international human rights groups, including Human Rights Watch, implicated Kenyan police in disappearances and extrajudicial killings.

The report documents 219 cases of police killings and enforced disappearances in 2021 alone. Out of these, 187 cases were of police killings, and 32 of enforced disappearances. Of the 32 cases of enforced disappearances, two of the victims were later found alive following public outcry. Four of those who had been disappeared by Kenyan security forces were found dead slightly over a day later. The whereabouts of 30 people remain unknown.

The report implicates Pangani Police officers in the extrajudicial killings of at least 30 people, most of who had last been seen in the custody of the police officers from the station. This is not the first time Pangani police station has been in the spotlight over human rights abuses.

In February 2020, Human Rights Watch research implicated officers from the same police station in the killings of at least two people in Nairobi's Mathare settlements. Witnesses told Human Rights Watch how police from Pangani Station had shot dead Peter Irungu, 19, and Brian Mung'aru, 20, while the two young men were kneeling and pleading with police to spare their lives.

Failure to Investigate Bodies Dumped in River

Kenyan authorities have failed to investigate and ensure accountability for bodies being dumped in River Yala, western Kenya. In March, residents of Yala, Siaya county, western Kenya, raised alarm over bodies apparently dumped by unidentified people in the Yala River at night. They told media that they had retrieved bodies from the river almost daily between July 2021 and January 2022, but police in the area had ignored the reports. In March, several human rights activists from Nairobi and Mombasa joined the residents to retrieve the bodies, and by mid-May had found more than 30. Some of the bodies were of people who had, according to reports in Kenyan media, long been missing, including that of an officer of the Kenya Wildlife Service, Francis Oyaro, who had been missing for months.

The bodies were taken to the Yala sub-county mortuary, where pathologists took samples for testing to identify them, but police did little to investigate the deaths. A Nairobi-based activists' protection organization said that some of the community leaders who had been at the forefront of bringing the issue to public attention were threatened by people who identified themselves as police. Despite public criticism and demands for accountability on these issues, the residents of Yala retrieved seven more bodies from the river towards the end of September 2022.

Disability Rights

Men, women, and children with real or perceived psychosocial disabilities continue to be shackled—chained or locked in small, confined spaces—in Kenya due to inadequate support and mental health services, and prevalent stigma. Human Rights Watch found at least 60 men, women, and children with real or perceived psychosocial disabilities chained, hidden from view, in the compound of the Coptic Church Mamboleo in Kisumu city in western Kenya. Kenyan authorities have done little to investigate state and private institutions housing people with mental health conditions.

Children's Rights

In July, Kenya adopted an amended Children's Act, enshrining a constitutional protection and harmonizing national law with numerous obligations in the African Charter on the Rights and Welfare of the Child.

The Education Ministry failed to act following reports that it had built and offered an unsafe online learning product for children's use during the Covid-19 pandemic. This product was found transmitting children's personal data to an advertising technology company, enabling the company to track and target children across the internet.

Sexual Orientation and Gender Identity

At least one person was arrested in July over the killing of Sheila Adhiambo Lumumba, a 25-year-old Kenyan non-binary lesbian. Lumumba was sexually assaulted and brutally murdered in their home in Karatina, north of Nairobi. Kenya's penal code criminalizes same-sex act between consenting adults. Article 162 punishes "carnal knowledge against the order of nature" with up to 14 years in prison, and Article 165 makes "indecent practices between males" punishable with up to five years in prison.

Intersex children are recognized and protected against discrimination in the Children's Act, 2022.

Refugee Rights

Kenyan authorities continued to undermine the rights of refugees by threatening repeatedly to shut down the two main refugee camps in northern Kenya, Dadaab and Kakuma, and force the refugees and asylum seekers back to their countries. In March 2021, the Kenyan government issued a 14-day ultimatum to the United Nations refugee agency (UNHCR) to develop a plan for closing Kakuma and Dadaab refugee camps.

In April 2021, UNHCR presented the government with "sustainable rights-based measures" to address the refugees' longstanding displacement—including voluntary repatriation, third country departures, and alternative stay options in Kenya. Kenyan authorities later extended the deadline for the camp closure to

June 30, 2022. However, government officials said nothing on June 30, and the new administration in place since August 2022 remained silent on the issue. The uncertainty caused significant anxiety among refugees and asylum seekers in the camps. Many are from Somalia and South Sudan, which face ongoing security challenges.

The government did not provide any justification for its latest attempt to shut down the camps. Authorities had previously threatened in 2016 and 2019 to close the Dadaab camp on grounds that it allegedly harbored members of the Somalia-based Islamist armed group Al-Shabab, though they never provided evidence to support the allegation, and no one from the camp had been prosecuted for links with terrorism as of September.

Toward the end of 2021, Kenya signed into law a new Refugee Act, which promises greater freedoms and rights for refugees, including better access to education and employment. While a positive step, the law provides for greater work and movement opportunities for refugees from East African Community countries than others, such as Somalians, who make up over 50 percent of Kenya's refugee population. Parliament had not passed a regulatory framework for the new law as of mid-2022.

Key International Actors

Kenya's general election attracted the interest of key partners both regionally and globally. President Ruto's inauguration ceremony was attended by heads of state from the East Africa region and representatives from partner countries in Europe, the United States, and Israel. Kenya is the economic powerhouse in East Africa.

Trial proceedings before the International Criminal Court on charges of witness tampering in the court's long-dismissed case against Ruto stemming from the 2007-2008 post-election violence were halted after the defendant, Paul Gicheru, was found dead at his home in Nairobi in September 2022.

Kosovo

There was slow progress on accountability for war time abuses. Tensions flared after Kosovo authorities ordered that ethnic Serbs in the north may not enter Kosovo with Serbian issued IDs or license plates. Ethnic Serbs raised barricades close to the border in protest, and Kosovo authorities kept border crossings closed until barricades were lifted. Journalists continued to face attacks, harassment, and threats with a poor state response.

Accountability for War Crimes

Four war crimes cases were pending before the Hague-based international Specialist Chambers for Kosovo against eight former members of the Kosovo Liberation Army (KLA), including former Kosovo President Hashim Thaci. Charges relate to crimes committed during the 1998-1999 war in Kosovo. In May, the Chambers added additional war crimes charges against Thaci and three other former KLA members for detaining 12 persons without due process in Budakovo, southern Kosovo, between July 1998 and September 1998 and April 28-29, 1999.

The Chambers in June extended detention of Hashim Thaci and former parliamentary speaker Kadri Veseli, citing concerns with witness tampering and a risk of absconding. The trial of former KLA commander Salih Mustafa heard closing arguments in September. A verdict was expected by the end of 2022. Mustafa is accused of the murder of civilians, torture, and arbitrary detention and was the first war crimes suspect arrested and transferred to the Specialist Chambers.

In September, the Pristina Basic Court found Kosovo Serb Svetomir Bacevic guilty of war crimes for having mistreated an older ethnic Albanian woman in Peja in 1998. Bacevic was sentenced to five years' imprisonment.

In March, the Kosovo Special Prosecution filed an indictment charging an ethnic Albanian man holding Serbian citizenship with war crimes in the village of Izbica in March 1999. The suspect, alongside unidentified members of Serbian police and military, is charged with participation in the execution of 130 people.

Asylum Seekers and Displaced Persons

Between January and August, the Kosovo Ministry of Internal Affairs registered 301 forced returns to Kosovo, the majority from Germany; 38 were children. Of those forcibly returned, 6 were Roma, 13 Ashkali, and rest ethnic Albanian. During the same reporting period, the ministry registered 28 voluntary returns to Kosovo. The ministry said it had no data on the ethnicity of those who voluntarily returned. By mid-August, Kosovo had registered five asylum seekers from Ukraine.

Freedom of Media

Between January and August, the Association of Journalists of Kosovo registered 22 cases of attacks, threats and intimidation against journalists and media outlets. The association reported that in most cases journalists face harassment, threats, and intimidation on social media platforms. According to the association, criminal investigations move slowly when they are initiated.

In February, Prindon Sadriu, husband of Kosovo's president's and a high ranking official in the Ministry of Foreign Affairs, in a Facebook post labelled journalists and media in Kosovo as "a joint criminal enterprise." In March, the prime minister's chief of staff, Luan Dualipi, in a Facebook post, connected Kosovo's media to "criminal businesses" and called on citizens to boycott them. Such statements risk undermining public confidence in media and creating a hostile environment for journalists.

Women's Rights

Domestic violence survivors continue to face obstacles to obtaining protection, including few prosecutions and failure by judges to issue restraining orders against abusers, and reduced sentences in cases of the murder of women by their husbands, according to the Kosovo Women's Network.

The August gang rape of an 11-year-old girl in a public park in Pristina triggered large demonstrations across the country, protesting poor state response to violence and sexual violence against women and girls. At time of writing, five suspects, including three under 18, were in custody and investigations were pending.

The 2018 mechanism set up to provide financial compensation for the estimated 20,000 wartime survivors of sexual violence continued to have limited reach. Shame and fear of stigma prevent some victims from seeking compensation.

Sexual Orientation and Gender Identity

The Centre for Equality and Liberty, a civil society organization that works for lesbian, gay, bisexual, and transgender (LGBT) people in Kosovo, recorded five cases of threats and attacks against LGBT people in Kosovo, four of which relate to violence by family members or partners against transgender persons. The center expressed concerns about anti-LGBT statements by private and public figures, particularly on social media.

In March, the Kosovo parliament rejected legislation aimed at allowing same-sex civil partnerships.

Kosovo Pride was held in June without any major incidents.

Accountability for International Institutions

No progress was made in financially compensating members of the Roma, Ashkali, and Balkan Egyptian communities who were victims of lead poisoning in now-closed camps for displaced persons run by the United Nations Mission in Kosovo (UNMIK). A 2016 report by the Human Rights Advisory Panel (HRAP), an independent body established to investigate complaints of abuses by UNMIK, recommended that the United Nations pay individual compensation and apologize to victims. To date, the UN has done neither. Only one state has contributed to the voluntary UN trust fund set up for community assistance project set up in 2017.

Key International Actors

In July, US Secretary of State Anthony Blinken met with President Vjosa Osmani and Prime Minister Albin Kurti in Washington DC, stressing the importance of normalizing relations between Kosovo and Serbia. In September, Kosovo was one of 18 countries surrounding Ukraine to receive US military aid ($2.2billion total) as a result of being "potentially at risk of future Russian aggression."

Following her June country mission to Kosovo, Council of Europe Commissioner for Human Rights Dunja Mijatovic raised issues regarding the safety of journalists and obstacles to their work. The commissioner also noted concerns with access to education for women and protection of survivors of domestic violence.

In a statement in May, the EU ambassador to Kosovo flagged concerns regarding public smear campaigns, threats, and physical attacks on journalists in Kosovo and called on authorities to improve their response to such attacks.

In a July resolution on Kosovo, the European Parliament condemned political pressure against journalists and expressed concern at high level of domestic and gender-based violence and lack of implementation of legal protections for LGBT people.

The October European Union Commission progress report on Kosovo noted slow and inefficient administration of justice prone to undue political influence. It also noted outstanding concerns with public smear campaigns, threats, and attacks against journalists, as well as the need to ensure gender equality in practice, and stressed the need for further measures to protect the rights of minorities, in particular Roma, Ashkali, and Balkan Egyptians.

Kuwait

Kuwait's political system is in turmoil. The fourth cabinet since the formation of the parliament in 2020 resigned in April, and Emir Jaber al-Ahmad al-Sabah dissolved the National Assembly in June. New elections were held on September 29.

Authorities continue to restrict freedom of speech and peaceful assembly and prosecute activists and others, using several provisions of the penal code, and national security and cybercrime laws. In November, Kuwait executed seven individuals, the first executions since 2017.

Authorities further restricted women's rights while failing to tackle discrimination and violence against women.

Bidun, a community of stateless people, face discrimination from authorities, who severely suppress the community's efforts to realize their rights.

Freedom of Expression and Assembly

The penal code, national security law, print and publication law, and cybercrime law all criminalize various aspects of free expression, including speech deemed insulting to Islamic principles, the emir, jurists, and members of the public prosecution. These laws also prohibit comments "causing harm to the relationships between Kuwait and other Arab and friendly states," and publishing secret government documents, with no exception for the public interest. Authorities, particularly in the State Security and public prosecution office, routinely use these provisions to summon, detain or prosecute activists and dissidents.

In a case that drew widespread criticism, in December 2021, the public prosecutor's office brought charges against Dr. Safaa Zaman, the Kuwait Association for Information Security president, following her televised comments about the risk of storing citizens' and residents' data on servers outside the country, particularly in Egypt. On March 22, the court of first instance acquitted her of the charges, a ruling upheld by the Court of Appeal.

Authorities also use Article 12 of the 1979 Public Gatherings Law, which bars non-Kuwaitis from participating in public gatherings, to arrest and sometimes deport migrants or Bidun individuals who participate in protests.

On August 31, authorities from the Ministry of Interior arrested at least 14 Bidun activists in relation to their participation in a demonstration on August 26. They were subsequently released on bail. On June 12, the *Arab Times* reported that Kuwait intended to deport "expats" who demonstrated against two leaders of the India BJP party.

Women's Rights, Sexual Orientation, and Gender Identity

Kuwait's personal status laws discriminate against women in matters of marriage, divorce, and child custody, including by requiring women to have male guardian permission to marry and by stripping them of spousal maintenance from their husband if they refuse to live with their husbands "without justification." Women can only apply to the courts for a divorce on limited grounds, while men can divorce without any restrictions. Kuwaiti women married to non-Kuwaitis cannot pass Kuwaiti citizenship to their children or spouses on an equal basis with Kuwaiti men.

Despite outrage at shocking killings of women in public in recent years, Kuwait's penal code continues to allow impunity for men who commit violence against women. Article 153 allows men who kill their wives, daughters, sisters, or mothers upon finding them in the act of extra-marital sex to receive a reduced sentence of a maximum of three years in prison or a fine. Article 182 also allows an abductor who uses force, threats, or deception with the intention to kill, harm, rape, prostitute or extort the victim to avoid punishment if he marries the victim with the permission of her guardian. In January, after consulting with religious authorities, the all-male parliament dropped a legal amendment that would have repealed Article 153.

In February, women protested the backsliding on women's rights including new restrictions such as male guardianship rules over women. Authorities allowed women to join Kuwait's army, but in January stipulated that they can only do so if they obtain their guardian's or husband's permission, wear a hijab, and work only in medical and support positions. They are also banned from carrying weapons and will only be enrolled when necessary to fill required vacancies. In February, authorities banned a desert wellness yoga retreat because lawmakers complained that women conducting yoga positions in public was "dangerous." The previous year they had closed a gym for hosting women's dance classes.

The National Assembly passed a domestic violence law in 2020 that includes some penalties to combat domestic violence and provides some assistance for survivors, but the lack of implementation of these measures to protect women and girls against violence remains significant, including that the authorities have still not established shelters for survivors or other services as required under the law. The penal code criminalizes adultery with up to five years in prison and a fine, and article 193 punishes consensual same-sex relations between men by up to seven years in prison.

In a positive step, on February 16, the Constitutional Court ruled unconstitutional a 2007 penal code provision, Article 198, that prohibited "imitating the opposite sex." The law had been used against transgender people, who faced imprisonment or a fine.

Authorities continue to crack down on LGBT symbols. On June 3, authorities summoned the US chargé d'affaires after the US Embassy posted a picture on Twitter of the rainbow flag on June 1 to mark the start of Pride Month. On June 25, the Kuwait Times reported that Kuwaiti authorities confiscated items at a phone accessory shop with rainbow flag colors, referring to the colors as "immoral expressions."

Stateless People and Migrant Rights

The Bidun are a group of about 100,000 stateless people who claim Kuwaiti nationality, dating back to the foundation of the state in 1961. The government rejects their claims and refers to them as "illegal residents," creating obstacles for Bidun to obtaining civil documentation, receive social services, and access their rights to health, education, and work.

The Central System for the Remedy of Situations of Illegal Residents, the administrative body in charge of Bidun affairs, has been issuing temporary ID cards since 2011. These cards often state the cardholder possesses Iraqi, Saudi, Iranian, or other citizenship, but it is unclear how the agency determined this and what due process procedures are available for Bidun to challenge the determinations.

In recent years there have been several reports of Bidun youth dying of suicide, activists claim, due to their difficult living conditions and lack of legal status.

Except for those whose fathers or grandfathers occupy certain public sector jobs, such as in the military and Ministry of Health or Education, and those whose mothers have Kuwaiti nationality, Bidun children are barred from free public schools. While certain charitable funds help with expenses, they do not cover all costs. During the Covid-19 school shutdowns, Bidun children reportedly had more difficulty accessing devices for online education.

Two-thirds of Kuwait's population is comprised of migrant workers, who remain vulnerable to abuse, largely due to the *kafala* (sponsorship) system which ties migrants' visas to their employers and requires that migrants get their employers' consent to leave employment or change jobs. Minor reforms to *kafala*, previously introduced, have yet to be extended to migrant domestic workers. Over the last year, no additional legal reforms were introduced to end the abusive *kafala* system.

Migrant domestic workers face additional forms of abuse, including being forcibly confined in their employers' homes, and verbal, physical and sexual abuse. While government shelters and complaint procedures exist for victims, there are serious barriers to accessing them, particularly for abuses like owed or delayed wages.

Climate Change Policies and Impacts

As one of the world's hottest and most water-stressed countries, Kuwait is acutely vulnerable to the impacts of climate change. As the world's seventh-largest exporter of crude oil, the country has the sixth-highest greenhouse gas emissions per capita globally. The increasing frequency and intensity of heat waves, decreased precipitation, and rising sea levels pose risks to the right to health, life, water, and housing, especially of low-income migrant workers and the Bidun who are already marginalized.

Key International Actors

Kuwait has a bilateral defense cooperation agreement with the United States, and the US uses military bases in the country. Kuwait is a member of the Saudi-led coalition conducting military operations in Yemen. On August 14, Kuwait named its first ambassador to Tehran, six years after severing ties in support of Saudi Arabia's decision to cut diplomatic ties with Iran.

Kyrgyzstan

Despite promises to uphold human rights and freedoms, Kyrgyz authorities restricted critical voices and civil society throughout the year. There was a proposal to re-initiate the highly problematic draft "foreign agents" law along with harassment and smear campaigns against nongovernmental organizations (NGOs) and human rights defenders. Press freedom came under siege with a spate of criminal cases against independent journalists, bloggers, and media.

An overly broad law penalizing "false" information was applied twice without judicial oversight. In March, a blanket protest ban was introduced in Bishkek and extended until December. Custodial deaths remain a serious concern in Kyrgyzstan's penal system. An effective and independent investigation into the death in custody of human rights defender Azimjon Askarov two years ago has yet to be completed. Measures put in place to protect women and girls have yet to end impunity for domestic violence, which is still the norm.

New Parliament

Kyrgyz citizens voted on a new parliament on November 28, 2021, following elections that monitors from the Organization for Security and Co-operation in Europe (OSCE) found to be competitive, albeit marred by limitations on civil and political rights, as well as significant procedural problems, during the vote counting. Widely considered to have been significantly weakened after the constitutional reform of 2021, the parliament was reduced from 120 to 90 members and stripped of some of its powers, making it dependent and vulnerable to pressure by the president, who now has the power to change election laws, as well as to initiate criminal investigations into members of parliament.

In August, President Sadyr Japarov signed a decree on the "Convocation of People's Kurultai"—a traditional people's council with delegates from all regions of the country. Members of the parliament have protested the decree, as it circumvented the requirement for the parliament to pass a law on the issue. Parliament rejected such a law in May.

Civil Society

In February, a member of the parliament suggested reconsideration of the previously rejected "foreign agents" draft law, arguing that foreign-funded NGOs are interfering with the work of the government. The suggestion was accepted by the parliament's speaker for consideration. Both NGOs and independently funded media could be subjected to negative labeling that affects their legitimate activities.

In August, Karakol City Court acquitted Kamil Ruziev, head of the human rights NGO Ventus, of charges of forgery brought against him in 2020 by the State Committee on National Security (GKNB) in apparent retaliation for his efforts to bring to justice security service officers allegedly engaged in torture and other human rights violations against detainees. The prosecutor immediately appealed the decision.

In October, more than 20 people were detained and further placed in pretrial detention for two months after publicly disagreeing with the impending transfer of the Kempir-Abad dam to Uzbekistan as part of a broader demarcation deal with the neighboring country. Those detained included activists, human rights defenders, bloggers, and politicians.

Freedom of Expression

In June and August, the Kyrgyz Ministry of Culture, the government agency responsible for implementing the widely criticized law on false information, blocked websites of two media outlets without judicial oversight. The website of *ResPublica* newspaper was blocked for two months in June, as was the website of the information agency 24.kg in August, based on complaints by private individuals regarding information published there. The website of 24.kg has been subsequently unblocked. In October, the ministry blocked the website of Azattyk Media for two months over a video on the Kyrgyzstan-Tajikistan border that cited Tajik authorities.

In March, Kyrgyz police raided the office of the privately owned opposition media channel Next TV and detained the outlet's director, Taalaibek Duishenbiev, for the channel's reposting of an article from a Ukrainian media that suggested Kyrgyzstan would provide military assistance to Russia for its invasion of Ukraine.

The channel was instructed to qualify the post as "extremist." In September, Duishenbiev was convicted of incitement of interethnic hatred and initially sentenced to five years of imprisonment, but his sentence was later commuted to a three-year probation that includes limitation on his movement.

In January, Kyrgyz police raided the office of Temirov Live, an independent investigative journalism outlet, detaining the channel's principal investigator, Bolot Temirov, on charges of drug possession. The journalist and his colleagues claim the drugs were planted on him during the raid. Weeks before the raid, Temirov and his team had published an investigation into the GKNB's leader, Kamchibek Tashiev, which implicated Tashiev in an alleged corruption scheme involving the export of state-produced fuel. In September, Temirov was acquitted on the drugs charges but, in response to an appeal by the prosecution, in November Bishkek city court ruled to expel Temirov, and he was deported to Russia.

Freedom of Assembly

In March, a blanket protest ban was introduced in the central district of Bishkek, which was later expanded to all districts of the capital. The ban was later extended until December. The decision was never made public; it became known after several activists were detained for protesting Russia's invasion of Ukraine. Since then, any public display of symbols of either Ukraine or Russia has also been subjected to fines. The authorities provided an alternate, remote location for protests.

In March, the police detained several human rights defenders and activists Aziza Abdirasulova, Dinara Oshurakhunova, Ondurush Toktonasyrov, and Nurbek Toktakunov who were protesting Russia's invasion of Ukraine, charging them with hooliganism and disobeying police orders.

Deaths in Custody

In June, the deaths in custody of political analyst Marat Kazakpaev and banker Bakyt Asanbaev were widely criticized and raised concerns over neglect and mistreatment. Both were in GKNB's pretrial detention on separate charges. Kazakpaev died after several months of concern over his worsening health condition.

Asanbaev was found hanged in his cell. A joint government-public investigative commission concluded that it was a "tragic coincidence."

The National Center for Torture Prevention, Kyrgyzstan's national prevention mechanism on torture, in June reported that over the past three years, at least 151 known cases of deaths have occurred in Kyrgyzstan's detention centers and prisons. Shortly after the center published its report, the UN Human Rights Office expressed concern at a proposal by deputy head of the cabinet, Edil Baisalov, to dissolve the center and transfer its powers to the office of the ombudsman of Kyrgyzstan. At time of writing, no further action on the proposal has been taken.

Human rights defender Azimjon Askarov, wrongfully imprisoned in 2010, had also died in custody in 2020 after being medically neglected. In September 2021, the GKNB was tasked with re-opening an earlier investigation into his death. The investigation has yet to be concluded.

Violence against Women and Girls

Although Kyrgyzstan has taken important steps in recent years to tackle domestic violence, the rewriting of laws that occurred as part of the legal inventory instigated in 2021, following adoption of the new constitution, and reforms in the Criminal and Criminal-Procedural Codes, have largely undone these steps.

Cases of violence against women and girls remain underreported and survivors face multiple barriers to accessing services and justice, such as insufficient shelters and other essential services, dismissive response by authorities, stigma, and attitudes that perpetuate harmful stereotypes and practices, including by police, judicial officials, and government and religious leaders. Of great concern is the culture of impunity for violence against women and girls that appears to be widespread both among the public and law enforcement circles.

In August, three men, two of whom are police officers, were convicted of the multiple rape and sexual abuse of a 13-year-old girl in a case that caused huge public outcry including because of concerns that the police officers were being shielded from accountability. The police officers were sentenced to 15 years. In October, a fourth accused in the case was sentenced to eight years.

Disability Rights

Although a May 2022 presidential decree increased the monthly social benefit payments to adults and children with disabilities, Kyrgyz authorities have largely ignored their human rights commitments to people with disabilities. A governmental council established to implement the Convention on the Rights of Persons with Disabilities failed to meet even once in 2022. There is a lack of affordable rehabilitation centers and there have been reports that families have to pay bribes to get a disability certificate—a prerequisite for receiving benefit payments—due to corruption within the system. An NGO-led pilot project integrating elements of inclusive education is currently implemented in 23 schools, focusing on modifying the school program to accommodate the needs of children with disabilities.

Torture

According to statistics from the Kyrgyz National Center for Torture Prevention, 1,422 complaints of torture were received in the first eight months of 2022. The center also reports that in 2021, more than 76 percent of those perpetrating torture and ill-treatment were police officers. Impunity for torture and ill-treatment remains the norm in pretrial detention centers, prisons, and closed institutions. Human rights defenders report that police officers incriminated in torture cases rarely receive penalties, cases are often quickly closed, and many police officers are acquitted.

Conflict at the Kyrgyzstan-Tajikistan Border

In September, a four-day border clash between Kyrgyz and Tajik border guards injured 206 people and killed at least 62 people, including a 15-year-old girl who was reportedly hit by a shell fragment. At least one school was attacked and burned by Tajik-affiliated forces. To date there has been no impartial investigation by authorities of either country into whether its military violated the laws of war during a similar 2-day conflict in 2021 conflict, in which over 40 people died.

Key International Actors

In April, the UN Working Group on discrimination against women and girls expressed concern at the end of a country visit about the increase in the number of gender-based violence cases and the continued impunity for perpetrators of violence against girls and women. The Working Group urged Kyrgyzstan to accelerate prompt and adequate investigation of all cases of violence against women and girls, and to provide the survivors access to redress.

In June, the UN special rapporteur on extreme poverty urged the authorities to invest more in pre-primary education, improve the quality of schools, and strengthen its social protection system for persons in poverty, as well as tackle the problem of corruption.

In September, during its annual Human Rights Dialogue with the Kyrgyz Republic, the European Union expressed concern over the shrinking space for civil society and the implementation of the law on false information. The EU also flagged its concerns on reports of deaths in detention and over the absence of a transparent investigation into the death in detention of human rights defender Azimjon Askarov.

In November, the UN Human Rights Committee voiced concern about reports of government pressure on human rights defenders, lawyers, politicians, journalists, and others for expressing their opinions, particularly those critical of the government, including the criminal prosecution of bloggers and journalists.

Lebanon

Lebanon entered the fourth year of a crippling economic crisis that has had disastrous consequences for rights and pushed over 80 percent of the population into poverty. Marginalized communities, including refugees, people with disabilities, children, older people, migrant workers, and LGBT people, have been disproportionately impacted. The crisis has had a devastating impact on the provision of public services, and in particular education, security, and health.

The Lebanese government and the International Monetary Fund reached a staff-level agreement for a program worth about US$3 billion over 46 months, contingent on key reforms that the political establishment has been stalling and obstructing.

In May, Lebanon held the first parliamentary elections since the October 2019 mass protests, which were marked by serious violations, including vote buying, violence and incitement, and abuse of power by political parties. Lebanon's established political parties failed to make any public commitments to strengthen human rights' protections. While 13 independent reformist candidates won seats, the election did not result in any meaningful shift in the political status quo.

Lebanon's president and prime minister failed to agree on a new government since the outgoing cabinet's mandate expired after the elections in May. Michel Aoun's presidential term came to an end on October 31, but parliamentarians have yet to elect a new president.

The political establishment continued to obstruct the domestic investigation into the Beirut blast in August 2020, which killed more than 220 people and injured more than 7,000.

Decades of corruption and mismanagement in the electricity sector have led to its unraveling, with the state unable to provide more than two to three hours of electricity per day.

Justice and Accountability

More than two years have passed since the catastrophic explosion in Beirut's port on August 4, 2020, which also devastated half the capital and caused extensive property damage, yet no one has been held accountable.

Human Rights Watch's review of hundreds of pages of official documents strongly suggests that some government officials were aware that the presence of ammonium nitrate in the port could result in a fatal disaster and tacitly accepted the risk to human life. This amounts to a violation of the right to life under international human rights law.

Yet, the political establishment has continued to obstruct and delay the domestic investigation. Politicians implicated in the explosion have filed over 25 requests to dismiss the chief investigator, Judge Tarek Bitar, and other judges involved in the case, resulting in multiple suspensions of the probe. The latest series of legal challenges filed against Judge Bitar have resulted in the suspension of the investigation since December 23, 2021.

In September, the justice minister and Higher Judicial Council agreed to nominate an alternate judge to "work on urgent and necessary matters" in the case, in a move that legal experts and judges have claimed is illegal.

Families of the victims, rights groups, and UN human rights experts have called for a UN Human Rights Council-mandated international, independent fact-finding mission into the explosion. However, no country has yet put forward such a resolution amid claims that they are waiting for France's "green light."

The Beirut blast case has clearly illustrated the Lebanese judiciary's lack of independence and susceptibility to political interference. A draft law that aims to bolster the judiciary's independence has been stalled in parliament since 2018, and the amendments that parliamentarians have made to the draft weaken many of its provisions.

In addition, Human Rights Watch found multiple failures, gross negligence, and procedural violations in four politically sensitive murder investigations in the past two years, including the assassination of prominent intellectual and Hezbollah critic Lokman Slim, reflecting that generous donor funding and training to Lebanon's security forces and judiciary have not resulted in the rule of law.

Financial and Economic Crisis

According to the World Bank, the Lebanese crisis ranks among the "most severe crises episodes globally since the mid-nineteenth century," and is the product of three decades of deliberate, reckless fiscal and monetary policy.

The currency has lost more than 95 percent of its pre-crisis value. This rapid devaluation, as well as supply-chain bottlenecks and fuel shortages have caused food prices to increase dramatically by 483 percent in January 2022 compared to the year before, and remaining high at 332 percent as of June 2022. As the Central Bank ran out of foreign reserves and lifted subsidies on the import of most vital goods, prices for electricity, water, and gas skyrocketed, increasing by 595 percent between June 2021 and June 2022. The price hikes turned utilities essential for business, health, and food into a luxury many people can afford only in limited quantities, if at all.

A nationally representative survey conducted by Human Rights Watch between November 2021 and January 2022 found that the median household reported a monthly income of just US$122. Seventy percent of households said they had difficulty making ends meet or were always behind on basic expenses, and 22 percent said that they sometimes or often did not have enough to eat in the past month.

While the crisis has impacted most people, the special rapporteur on extreme poverty found that women, children, migrant workers, Syrian and Palestinian refugees, and people with disabilities are particularly affected.

The crisis has had a devastating impact on the provision of public services. Schools have been struggling to operate amid resignations and strikes by teachers, electricity and internet cuts, and inflation. Public schools for hundreds of thousands of Lebanese and Syrian students have largely been closed for the last three years.

The healthcare sector is crumbling amid the migration of thousands of doctors and nurses from Lebanon, a shortage in medicines and medical supplies, and electricity cuts. The National Social Security Fund (NSSF), the largest employment-based provider of social services, is almost bankrupt and has not been reimbursing subscribers for their medical bills.

Despite increased support from donor states, Lebanese army soldiers, whose real wages have fallen from $900 to less than $50 a month, have received minimal pay increases and have had to take on extra jobs or quit. Within Lebanon's Internal Security Forces, desertions, inability to reach duty stations due to fuel costs, and the need to reduce shifts to allow members to do other work, has reduced their ability to meet security needs.

Lebanon's social protection system suffers from large coverage gaps and is chronically under-funded. Since the financial crisis, Lebanon has only introduced one new social assistance program, the Emergency Social Safety Net Project (ESSN), financed by the World Bank, to provide cash transfers to 150,000 households during 2022.

As the crisis deepened, many have resorted to dangerous migration routes towards Europe by sea. In April, a boat carrying around 80 Lebanese, Syrians, and Palestinians sank off the coast of Tripoli following its interception by the Lebanese army navy. Only 48 survivors were rescued.

Electricity Crisis

Decades of corruption and mismanagement have crippled the electricity sector, with the state unable to provide more than two to three hours of electricity daily. While widespread blackouts affect everyone living in Lebanon, the crisis has exacerbated inequality in the country.

A Human Rights Watch survey found that the average household had generator bills that accounted for 44 percent of monthly income. The disparities between income levels are huge. For those in the bottom quintile who accessed a generator, their generator bills consumed 88 percent of their monthly income, on average, compared to 21 percent for the top quintile.

The lack of reliable and continuous electricity has impacted people's right to electricity, an adequate standard of living, including food, medical care and water, and access to education, health, and livelihoods.

Abuses by Security Forces

Despite parliament passing an anti-torture law in 2017, torture by security forces persists, judicial authorities continue to ignore the law's provisions, and accountability for torture remains elusive.

In September, a Syrian refugee died in the custody of State Security as a result of torture. Several officers were arrested and are being tried in military courts, which lack independence.

Torture complaints filed by protesters in 2020 have not moved forward in the courts.

In 2019, Lebanon's Council of Ministers appointed the five members of the national preventative mechanism against torture, but it has still not allocated funding for the mechanism.

In October 2021, members of the Lebanese army used unlawful force during a demonstration that Hezbollah and its allies called for to demand the removal of the judge leading the Beirut Blast investigation. Although the army admitted that an officer who used live fire in contravention to orders was under investigation, there has not yet been a verdict in the case.

Freedom of Expression

Journalists, media workers, and activists in Lebanon are silenced by private actors and government authorities using criminal insult and defamation laws, often for criticizing government policies and corruption.

The broad jurisdiction of the military courts is particularly used to silence and punish any peaceful dissent or criticism of the security agencies. In June 2022, Shaden Fakih, a well-known comedian, was convicted by the military court for allegedly tarnishing the reputation of the Internal Security Forces after she posted a skit on her Instagram page.

Women's Rights

Women continue to face discrimination under 15 distinct religion-based personal status laws. Discrimination includes inequality in access to divorce, child custody, and inheritance, and property rights. Unlike men, Lebanese women cannot pass on their nationality to foreign husbands and children.

A growing number of femicide and domestic violence cases have underscored the need for a stronger implementation of Lebanon's family violence law.

Migrant Workers

Tens of thousands migrant domestic workers, primarily from Africa and Southeast Asia, reside in Lebanon and their status is regulated by a restrictive and abusive regime of laws, regulations, and customary practices known as the kafala (sponsorship) system.

Attempts to dismantle the kafala system have been blocked, including by recruitment agencies, many of whom are accused of subjecting workers to abuse, forced labour, and human trafficking.

Sexual Orientation and Gender Identity

LGBT people face systemic discrimination in Lebanon and continue to be disproportionally affected by the economic crisis. Transgender women in Lebanon face systemic violence and discrimination in accessing basic services, including employment, health care, and housing.

Article 534 of the penal code punishes "any sexual intercourse contrary to the order of nature" with up to one year in prison, but a district court of appeal ruled in 2018 that consensual same-sex conduct is not unlawful.

Lebanese authorities have repeatedly interfered with human rights events related to gender and sexuality. In June, Lebanese authorities unlawfully banned peaceful gatherings of LGBT people. Rights groups have appealed the decision.

Refugees

Lebanon hosts nearly 900,000 registered Syrian refugees, and the government estimates another 500,000 live in the country informally. Only 16 percent of Syrian refugees have legal residency, making most of them vulnerable to harassment, arrest, detention, and deportation. It is estimated that nine out of ten Syrian refugees live in extreme poverty.

Lebanese authorities are making plans to return refugees, even though Syrians who return face grave abuses and persecution at the hands of the Syrian government and affiliated militias.

In addition, there are approximately 174,000 Palestinian refugees living in Lebanon, where they continue to face restrictions, including on their right to work and own property.

Legacy of Past Wars and Conflicts

The independent national commission established in 2020 to investigate the fate of the estimated 17,000 Lebanese kidnapped or disappeared during the country's civil war from 1975 to 1990 has yet to be allocated a budget and headquarters to operate from.

In March, the Appeals Chamber of the Special Tribunal for Lebanon reversed the acquittal of Hezbollah agents Hassan Merhi and Hussein Oneissi, convicting them in absentia of being co-perpetrators in the assassination of former Lebanese Prime Minister Rafik al-Hariri in 2005.

Key International Actors

Syria, Iran, Saudi Arabia, and other regional powers exert their influence in Lebanon through local political allies and proxies.

Lebanon's maritime border dispute with Israel escalated over the summer after a ship began setting up an Israeli drilling platform in the Karish field, a disputed area rich in natural gas and oil. On October 11, Lebanon and Israel reached a historic agreement demarcating the disputed maritime border after years of US-mediated negotiations.

The UN Security Council extended the United Nations Interim Force in Lebanon UNIFIL's mandate in south Lebanon until 31 August 2023.

Lebanese security agencies continue to receive assistance from a range of international donors, including the United States, European Union, United Kingdom, France, and Saudi Arabia.

In July, the European Union extended its targeted sanctions framework aimed at targeting those hampering the formation of a government or reform efforts. At time of writing, no individual or entity had been sanctioned.

Libya

Armed groups aligned with the two rival authorities, the Tripoli-based Government of National Unity (GNU) and the Government of National Stability (GNS) based in the east, clashed in Tripoli and its environs after GNS forces attempted to take control of the capital. The fighting resulted in the deaths and injuries of hundreds, including civilians, the destruction of civilian infrastructure, the contamination of civilian neighborhoods with landmines and unexploded ordnance, and displacement.

Hundreds of people, including civilians, remain missing since the 2019-2020 conflict in Tripoli and its environs. Authorities continued to find mass graves and unmarked individual graves with dozens of bodies in the western town of Tarhouna and the coastal town of Sirte.

Authorities and armed groups cracked down on civil society activists and journalists while invoking draconian laws.

Migrants, asylum seekers, and refugees faced arbitrary detention, ill-treatment, sexual assault, forced labor, and extortion by groups linked with the GNU's Interior Ministry, members of armed groups, smugglers, and traffickers.

Political Process and Elections

Political talks facilitated by the United Nations Mission to Libya (UNSMIL) failed to produce presidential and legislative elections slated for December 2021. The talks collapsed in 2022. In January, the House of Representatives appointed Fathi Bashagha as the prime minister-designate in parallel to the existing GNU. Bashagha, allied with Khalifa Hiftar from the Libyan Arab Armed Forces (LAAF), formed the GNS in March and took control of government institutions in the east and south of the country. Forces allied with the GNS clashed with GNU supporters between May and August but were unable to control Tripoli.

The LAAF remained in control of Sirte and eastern Libya, and most of the southern region and did not actively participate in the August fighting in the capital.

The UN-facilitated political negotiations in April, May, and June, in Cairo, Egypt, failed to reach an agreement on the legislative and constitutional basis for national elections.

After a nine-month hiatus, in September, the UN secretary-general appointed former Senegalese Minister Abdoulaye Bathily as special representative and head of UNSMIL in Libya.

Libya remains without a permanent constitution, with only the 2011 constituent covenant in force. A draft constitution proposed by the elected Libyan Constitution Drafting Assembly in July 2017 has yet to be put to a national referendum.

The Supreme Court in Tripoli reconvened its constitutional chamber in August, after six years of shutdown. In September, the speaker of parliament appointed a new chief justice of the Supreme Court, despite initial refusal by the incumbent president of the court to depart his post.

Armed Conflict and War Crimes

The formation of the GNS triggered fighting in Tripoli and its environs as of May. August saw the heaviest fighting since the October 2020 ceasefire agreement and a shift in the balance of power between armed groups in Tripoli. Forces allied with the GNS attacked GNU positions in Tripoli, resulting in the killing of 32 people, including four civilians, and the wounding of 159 people, including civilians, according to the Libyan Ministry of Health.

The fighting also damaged critical infrastructure in Tripoli including power plants, which affected the provision of electricity according to the General Electricity Company of Libya, and four healthcare facilities, according to the Ministry of Health. The ministry also said its staff evacuated 64 families caught in the line of fire.

Armed groups from the LAAF in August temporarily imposed restrictions on civilian movements in Qasr Bouhadi, a town 20 kilometers south of Sirte, including restrictions on access to healthcare and education due to undefined "security operations," according to the UN. Armed groups reportedly broke into homes and arrested people, prompting the UN to call on armed groups to release all those "arbitrarily detained," without specifying the number.

In August, the General Authority for the Search and Identification of Missing Persons removed unidentified human remains from two unmarked grave sites in Sirte. Throughout the year they also continued to uncover unmarked individual and mass graves in Tarhouna, where hundreds went missing between 2014-2020 under Al-Kani militia control. The General Prosecutor's Office in Tripoli said in August that authorities had identified 120 out of 259 bodies extracted from graves in Tarhouna and announced that they had opened 280 criminal cases into unlawful killings, torture, enforced disappearances, armed robbery, and kidnappings in the town, 10 of which had been referred to trial. The office also said it had issued 376 arrest warrants, including 10 international warrants, and that 20 individuals were in provisional detention.

The Tarek Bin Ziyad Brigade of the LAAF in January arbitrarily arrested at least 50 residents of the eastern city of Derna following the escape of five detainees from Derna's Garnada high-security prison. The brigade recaptured all five detainees within a week. Those arrested were mostly unrelated to the five, and as of October, there was no confirmation if they had all been released.

Turkish and other military forces as well as thousands of foreign fighters from Chad, Sudan, Syria, and elsewhere, and members of private security companies including the Wagner Group, remained in Libya despite pledges during the two Berlin conferences on Libya in 2020 and 2021 to remove foreign fighters.

The UN Sanctions Committee's Panel of Experts report from May found foreign fighters and private military companies were continuing to pose a serious threat to security in Libya and that the arms embargo was being violated with impunity. Since the establishment by the UN Security Council of the Libya Sanctions regime in 2011 pursuant to Resolution 1970, no one has been held accountable for arms embargo violations.

Prohibited landmines and booby traps as well as abandoned and unexploded ordnance (UXO) in Libya continued to kill and maim civilians and deminers. Since the end of the 2019-2020 conflict at least 130 people, mostly civilians, have been killed by mines and UXO, according to the Libyan Mine Action Center.

Judicial System and Detainees

Libya's criminal justice system remained weak. Where prosecutions took place, there were serious due process concerns and military courts continued to try civilians. Judges, prosecutors, and lawyers remained at risk of harassment and attack by armed groups.

Libya's Justice Ministry holds thousands of detainees, including women and children, in at least 27 prisons nominally under its control. In his briefing to the Security Council on October 24, Abdoulaye Bathily said that the Libyan Justice Ministry as of October 1 held nearly 11,000 convicted individuals, including 55 women. Nearly 6,000 more, including 113 women, were held in pretrial detention, many of whom had no access to judicial review. He said 135 juveniles were also detained. According to Bathily, this represents a 40 percent increase since August 2021.

Armed groups held thousands of others in irregular detention facilities. Prisons in Libya are marked by inhumane conditions such as severe overcrowding, ill-treatment, and torture.

In June, the Tripoli Appeals Court referred a case against dozens of defendants allegedly implicated in the 1996 Abu Salim Prison massacre, when authorities killed over 1,200 inmates, to the military prosecution citing lack of jurisdiction. Most defendants have been held since 2011, including Abdullah Al-Senussi, former intelligence chief under Gaddafi.

International Justice and the ICC

The International Criminal Court's (ICC) prosecutor continued his investigation in Libya.

In June, ICC judges terminated proceedings against LAAF commander Mahmoud El-Werfalli following notification of his death. El-Werfalli was wanted for the war crime of murder related to several incidents in and around Benghazi between June 2016 and January 2018. In September, the court's judges also terminated proceedings against Al-Tuhamy Khaled following notification of his death. Khaled was the former head of the Internal Security Agency under Muammar

Gaddafi and was wanted for war crimes and crimes against humanity committed between February and August 2011.

Saif al-Islam Gaddafi, wanted by the ICC since 2011, remains a fugitive and Libya remains under legal obligation to surrender him to the Hague.

In June, the ICC deputy prosecutor visited Tripoli and Tarhouna and met with authorities, including the general and military prosecutors, but as of November 3, no new investigations had been announced.

A United States federal judge in the state of Virginia ruled in July 2022 that Khalifa Hiftar should compensate the Libyan families that sued him in the United States for allegedly ordering the torture and unlawful killing of their relatives in Libya. As of October 25, the case remained under appeal.

The Human Rights Council in July renewed by consensus the mandate of the independent Fact-Finding Mission on Libya for a "final non-extendable" period of nine months.

Death Penalty

The death penalty is stipulated in over 30 articles in Libya's penal code, including for acts of speech and association. No death sentences have been carried out since 2010, but military and civilian courts continued to impose them.

Misrata's Court of Appeals of the First Criminal Circuit in September sentenced Diaa el-Din Ahmed Miftah Balaou to death for "insisting on apostasy from the Islamic religion" after he "refused to repent and abandon his ideas," in a case brought against him in 2019. As of September 26, the sentence was not yet final, as under Libyan law the Supreme Court automatically reviews all death sentences.

Freedom of Assembly and Association

Libya's penal code stipulates severe punishments, including the death penalty, for establishing "unlawful" associations and prohibits Libyans from joining or establishing international organizations without government permission.

Presidential Decree 286 on regulating nongovernmental organizations, passed in 2019, includes burdensome registration requirements and stringent regulations on funding and notification ahead of attending events. The Tripoli-based Commission of Civil Society, tasked with registering and approving civic organizations, has sweeping powers to inspect documents and cancel the registration and work permits of domestic and foreign organizations.

LAAF forces continued to prevent local and international human rights organizations from accessing eastern Libya.

Freedom of Speech and Expression

The Internal Security Agency in Tripoli arrested between November 2021 and March 2022 nine men and posted apparently-forced confessions on social media. The men were accused of "atheist, areligious, secular and feminist" activities, according to the UN Mission to Libya (UNSMIL). As of October 25, they were held in different detention facilities in Tripoli, including Mitiga Prison controlled by the armed group linked with the Interior Ministry Rapid Deterrence Force, and Al-Jdeidah Prison controlled at least nominally by the Justice Ministry. The general prosecutor had started proceedings against four of them as co-defendants. It was unclear when proceedings would start against the other five. Since these arrests, several Libyan grassroots movements, including the Tanweer Movement, were dissolved as members went into hiding or fled overseas fearing persecution.

In March, Internal Security Apparatus in the eastern town of Ajdabiya, affiliated with the LAAF, released Mansour Mohamed Atti al-Maghribi, a civic activist and head of the Red Crescent Society in Ajdabiya, without charge after 10 months of arbitrary detention.

Some provisions in Libyan laws unduly restrict freedom of speech and expression, including criminal penalties for insulting religion and the death penalty for promoting theories or principles that aim to overthrow the political, social, or economic system. The 2021 Cybercrime Law contains overbroad provisions and draconian punishments, including fines and imprisonment that could violate freedom of speech.

Women's Rights, Sexual Orientation, Gender Identity

Libya does not have a domestic violence law that sets out measures to prevent domestic violence, punish abusers, and protect survivors. The penal code allows for a reduced sentence for a man who kills or injures his wife or another female relative because he suspects her of extramarital sexual relations. It also allows rapists to escape prosecution if they marry their victims.

Libya's Family Code discriminates against women with respect to marriage, divorce, and inheritance. The 2010 nationality law also discriminates against women allowing only Libyan men, but not women, to pass on Libyan nationality to their children and requiring women to get authorities' permission before marrying a non-Libyan man. In October, the GNU issued a decision ostensibly expanding the rights of non-citizen children of Libyan women, including visa-free entry into Libya and access to education and healthcare, but fell short of granting women full equal rights including the right to pass on the Libyan nationality to their children.

The penal code prohibits all sexual acts outside marriage, including consensual same-sex relations, and punishes them with flogging and up to five years in prison.

Internally Displaced Persons

As of June, the International Organization for Migration (IOM) estimated there were 143,419 internally displaced people in Libya.

Among them are thousands of former residents of the town of Tawergha, who were driven out by anti-Gaddafi groups from Misrata in 2011 and have been unable to return due to massive and deliberate destruction of the town and the scarcity of public services there.

Migrants, Refugees, and Asylum Seekers

The IOM recorded 1,295 people dead and missing along the Central Mediterranean migration route in 2022 as of October 25.

Also as of October, there were 667,440 migrants in Libya according to the IOM, 43,000 of whom are registered asylum seekers and refugees according to the UN refugee agency, UNHCR.

On October 7, the burned bodies of 15 people believed to be migrants were found near a boat in the town of Sabratha on the western coast after fighting by rival armed groups involved in trafficking there, according to UNSMIL. The Interior Ministry pledged to investigate the incident.

The bodies of at least 20 people—18 Chadian migrants and two Libyans—were recovered on June 28 in the Libyan desert near the Chadian border, according to the IOM, quoting the Libyan Ambulance and Emergency Services. The individuals reportedly died of dehydration.

The European Union continued to collaborate with abusive Libyan Coast Guard forces, providing material and technical support and aerial surveillance to intercept and return thousands of people to Libya. As of August, Libyan forces intercepted or rescued 16,506 people and returned them to abusive conditions in Libya, according to the IOM.

Migrants, asylum seekers, and refugees were arbitrarily detained in inhumane conditions in facilities run by the GNU's Interior Ministry and were held with smugglers and traffickers, where they were subjected to forced labor, torture, ill-treatment, extortion, and sexual assault.

Malaysia

Under then-Prime Minister Ismail Sabri Yaakob, who assumed office in August 2021, the Malaysian government aggressively cracked down on free speech and peaceful protests, harassing, intimidating, and arbitrarily arresting activists and critics of the government. Authorities frequently use hateful rhetoric against refugees and migrants, as well as lesbian, gay, bisexual, and transgender (LGBT) people to paint these populations as threats to the country's security and identity.

Prime Minister Ismail dissolved parliament on October 10, setting the stage for the country's 15th general elections on November 19. The tightly contested elections led to a hung parliament and a week of tension, which ended when Malaysia's king named Anwar Ibrahim as the country's 10th prime minister on November 24. The new parliament opened on December 19, passing a confidence motion for Anwar, who had spent three decades in the opposition and 10 years in prison on politically motivated charges.

In August, the Federal Court, the country's highest court, rejected the final appeal of former Prime Minister Najib Razak, sending him to prison for 12 years for his involvement in the embezzlement of billions of dollars from the state-owned investment fund 1Malaysia Development Berhad (1MDB).

Freedom of Expression and Assembly

The government uses a range of broad and vaguely worded laws to prosecute critical speech, including the 1948 Sedition Act and section 233 of the 1998 Communications and Multimedia Act (CMA).

Graphic artist Fahmi Reza faced several investigations and arrests for his political satire. In February, he was charged twice under CMA section 233 for posters shared on social media caricaturing authorities. He was discharged but not acquitted in one of the cases in August. In April, he was arrested under CMA section 233 and the Sedition Act in relation to a cartoon depicting a monkey in clothing similar to that worn by Malaysia's royalty.

In July, Siti Nuramira Abdullah was charged with causing religious disharmony under penal code section 298A for an open mic comedy performance that was deemed offensive to Islam, during which she had removed her headscarf and baju kurung, a traditional dress. Her boyfriend was charged under CMA section 233 for allegedly uploading the video. Authorities revoked the comedy club's license and permanently blacklisted its owners from registering any other businesses.

Police have targeted people participating in peaceful protests. In January, dozens of people involved in a series of protests calling for the suspension of the head of the anti-corruption commission were called in for police questioning, including four members of parliament.

Police questioned three members of the nongovernmental organization (NGO) Lawyers for Liberty in April after they held a protest outside the Singapore embassy over the Singapore government's scheduled execution of a Malaysian man with an intellectual disability. The police also investigated members of the Malaysian Bar Council for holding a candlelight vigil on the eve of the execution.

In June, authorities blocked 300 lawyers from marching to parliament to present a memorandum calling on the government to protect judicial independence. The police asserted that the lawyers did not have a police permit for the march, even though a permit is no longer required under Malaysia's Peaceful Assembly Act.

In July, police blocked students and political activists from marching to Independence Square to protest rising living costs. Police opened an investigation into the demonstration and issued summons for 30 protesters.

Media freedom also suffered over the past year. In March, a seven-judge panel of the Federal Court dismissed online news portal Malaysiakini's application for review of the court's 2021 finding of contempt of court against the outlet over five online comments posted by readers.

Police Abuse and Impunity

Police routinely torture suspects in custody with impunity. The standard of care for detainees is problematic, with reports of deaths from treatable illnesses. At least 20 detainees had died in police custody centers during the year.

In July, the government took a major step backward on police accountability by pushing a bill through parliament to create a toothless Independent Police Complaints Commission. The new commission will have no powers of search and seizure, limited powers to compel production of evidence, and no ability to hold hearings.

Refugees, Asylum Seekers, and Trafficking Victims

Malaysia is not a party to the 1951 Refugee Convention. About 185,000 refugees and asylum seekers—the majority from Myanmar, including over 100,000 ethnic Rohingya Muslims—are registered with the United Nations refugee agency (UNHCR) but are not granted legal status. They are unable to work or enroll in government schools, forcing many into situations of exploitation and abuse.

The government has denied UNHCR access to immigration detention centers since August 2019, leaving the agency unable to assess whether those in detention are entitled to protection. The director-general of immigration reported in April that over 17,500 asylum seekers were being held in 21 immigration detention centers nationwide, including more than 1,500 children.

From June through October, the immigration department deported over 1,700 Myanmar nationals, including military defectors, without assessing their asylum claims or other protection needs.

In April, over 500 Rohingya refugees escaped from a detention center. Six of them, including two children, were killed crossing a road while fleeing. According to the home minister, the Rohingya had been in detention for more than two years.

Conditions in immigration detention facilities are dire. According to a report by a coalition of Indonesian NGOs, at least 149 Indonesians died in Malaysia's detention centers between January 2021 and June 2022.

In July, the government initiated a registration scheme, Tracking Refugees Information System (TRIS), requiring all refugees and asylum seekers to register for biometric ID cards. The home minister announced the cards would be recognized as refugees' sole IDs rather than the UNHCR cards. The system is run by a private for-profit company chaired by the former head of the country's police intelligence services.

In September, the national security council director-general proposed shutting down UNHCR's presence in Malaysia in order to manage refugees "without foreign interference."

Freedom of Religion

Malaysia restricts the rights of followers of any branches of Islam other than Sunni, with those following Shia or other branches subject to arrest for deviancy. In June, the religious affairs minister warned Muslims not to participate in a Japanese festival on the grounds that it contained elements of other religions.

Criminal Justice

The government announced plans to abolish the mandatory death penalty in June. In October, amendments were tabled in parliament to do so but failed to pass prior to the dissolution of parliament ahead of the general elections.

Malaysia detains individuals without trial under restrictive laws. Both the 1959 Prevention of Crime Act (POCA) and the 2015 Prevention of Terrorism Act give government-appointed boards the authority to impose detention without trial for up to two years, renewable indefinitely; to order electronic monitoring; and to impose other significant restrictions on freedom of movement and association. In April, the Federal Court voided POCA's exclusion of judicial review of the grounds for detention.

In July, parliament voted to extend for another five years the provision in the Security Offenses (Special Measures) Act, or SOSMA, that allows for preventive detention of up to 28 days without judicial review, after the extension was originally voted down in March.

Sexual Orientation and Gender Identity

State-sponsored discrimination against LGBT people remains pervasive in Malaysia, including the funding of conversion practices that seek to change people's sexual orientation or gender identity.

HUMAN RIGHTS WATCH

"I Don't Want to Change Myself"

Anti-LGBT Conversion Practices, Discrimination, and Violence in Malaysia

HUMAN RIGHTS WATCH

justice For sisters

Federal law punishes "carnal knowledge against the order of nature," interpreted as adult consensual same-sex conduct, with up to 20 years in prison and mandatory whipping. State and federal territory Sharia (Islamic) laws criminalize both same-sex activity and gender nonconformity, resulting in frequent arrests of transgender people.

In March, Google removed a "conversion therapy" app produced by the government in 2016 from its Play store.

In June, Malaysia banned the Disney movie "Lightyear" after the company refused to comply with an order from the Film Censorship Board that it cut scenes "promoting the LGBT lifestyle," including a same-sex kiss. In July, the movie "Thor: Love and Thunder" was likewise banned after Disney refused to make requested cuts of "LGBT elements."

Women's Rights

In August, the Court of Appeal overturned a 2021 High Court ruling that granted automatic entitlement to Malaysian citizenship to children born overseas to Malaysian mothers and foreign fathers. The decision reinstates a discriminatory practice in which women are denied equal rights as men to confer citizenship to their spouses and children.

In April, a Sharia court ordered Member of Parliament Maria Chin Abdullah to be jailed for seven days on contempt charges for having criticized the court's sentencing of a woman to jail for rescheduling her ex-husband's visitation dates with their children in 2019. Maria Chin Abdullah stated at the time that women are discriminated against under the Sharia system. Her challenge of the court's proceedings was ongoing at time of writing. The woman, Emilia Hanafi, served her 7-day prison sentence in June-July.

Children's Rights

Malaysia continues to permit child marriage under both civil and Islamic law. Girls ages 16 and 17 can marry with the permission of their state's chief minister. For Muslims, most state Islamic laws set a minimum age of 16 for girls and 18 for boys, in violation of Malaysia's obligations under international human rights law, but also permit marriages below those ages, with no apparent minimum, with the permission of a Sharia court.

In March, the minister of women, family and community development stated in parliament that the government did not intend to ban child marriage.

Environment

In March, construction started on the Nenggiri hydropower project in Kelantan, despite concerns from Indigenous communities. An Orang Asli group in Kelantan is protesting the dam, stating it will threaten their homes and ancestral land, livelihoods, culture, and identity, and access to clean water and food, and that affected communities did not receive adequate compensation.

The Sabah state government has maintained secrecy over a carbon trading deal that would hand management of 4.9 million acres of tropical forest to Singapore-based Hoch Standard for up to 200 years. Authorities did not engage in any consultative process with Indigenous or other communities that would be affected. Details surrounding a separate carbon trade deal in Sabah, launched in 2021 but only announced publicly in August 2022, are similarly opaque.

In January, authorities cracked down on people criticizing the government's role in severe flash floods that took place in December 2021, which many blamed on rampant logging. Fahmi Reza was summoned by police regarding a poster he made modifying the coat of arms of Pahang, which was heavily flooded, with a tree and two axes. The police also summoned for questioning a journalist from *Free Malaysia Today* over a report critical of the government's response to the floods.

Key International Actors

Malaysia has been very critical of the failure of the Association of Southeast Asian Nations (ASEAN) to make any progress addressing the crisis in Myanmar. Foreign Minister Saifuddin Abdullah urged the bloc to formally engage with the opposition National Unity Government.

Maldives

The government led by President Ibrahim Mohamed Solih pledged to tackle corruption and advance human rights, but in reality, failed to bring essential reforms to the justice system.

The influence of Islamist extremist groups and political leaders remained pervasive within the government, police, and the judiciary. Authorities bent to pressure from these groups, as well as from the Muslim fundamentalist Adhaalath Party—a member of the ruling coalition—by rolling back fundamental rights, including freedom of speech and assembly, and the rights of lesbian, gay, bisexual, and transgender (LGBT) people, and of women.

Despite the Maldivian government's commitment to reaching net-zero emissions by 2030, authorities did not adequately enforce environmental laws and continued to prioritize development projects over the protection of local communities and the environment.

Based on findings of the government-appointed Commission on Deaths and Enforced Disappearances, police arrested three men in connection with the 2014 disappearance of Ahmed Rilwan, an outspoken journalist who uncovered political corruption, and the 2017 fatal stabbing of Yameen Rasheed, a blogger and government critic. Previously, political interference, police cover-ups, and judicial misconduct undermined investigations and prosecutions of those responsible for these and other attacks on civil society activists.

Freedom of Speech, Freedom of Expression and Assembly

Islamist political organizations and political leaders incited hatred and violence, including on social media, against individuals and civil society groups who sought to counter religious and violent extremism and promote individual freedoms. They targeted human rights defenders, women's rights and LGBT rights activists, journalists, and bloggers. The failure of the government to provide accountability in these cases has meant that gangs, powerful religious groups, and their political patrons increasingly exercise a chilling effect on free speech in the country.

In June, Islamist extremists disrupted a gathering of 150 people, including diplomats and government officers, at an International Yoga Day event in the capital, Male. They deemed the event heretical, a celebration of idolatry or polytheism. Authorities arrested six people connected to the incident. The following month, the Adhaalath Party decreed the practice of yoga forbidden, stating that no Muslim should engage in it.

The government rebuffed efforts to amend the Freedom of Assembly Act and continued to use it to block protests. The law requires protesters to seek permission from the police, and protest only in designated areas. In May, civil society activists petitioned the High Court, seeking a repeal of these provisions.

Authorities prosecuted four men for their involvement in the May 2021 bomb attack targeting parliament speaker and former President Mohamed Nasheed. Nasheed's supporters claimed that the main conspirators are unlikely to be held to account. His opponents accused him of being a *laadheenee*, or "enemy of Islam." Nasheed has expressed fears that his life is still in danger.

Freedom of Media

In June, the Maldivian parliament enacted legislation that allows the courts to force journalists and media outlets to reveal their sources. Local journalists and media rights organizations campaigned against the new Evidence Act, claiming that it risked seriously undermining press freedom in the country. Although he ratified the Evidence Act in July, two months later, President Solih said that his government would amend the law to address concerns raised by journalists.

Women's and Girls' Rights

Women remained severely underrepresented in the Maldives' judiciary, parliament, and local governing bodies, particularly in higher-ranking stations and positions. Women represent a mere 4.6 percent of the national parliament.

The government has not taken steps to address gender-based violence, which often goes unreported.

The UN Working Group on discrimination against women and girls, invited by the government, visited the Maldives in September to evaluate its progress in

WORLD REPORT 2023

HUMAN RIGHTS WATCH

"I Could Have Been Next"
Stymied Reforms in the Maldives

achieving gender equality and eliminating discrimination against women and girls. In its report, the UN Working Group applauded the Maldives government for its strong commitments to advancing gender equality.

Nevertheless, despite noting some positive steps, the report highlighted the continued subordination of women due to pervasive societal norms, gender-stereotyping, and religious conservatism. Significant shortcomings remain relating to the effective implementation of legal protections and barriers to remedy for women, particularly regarding gender-based violence.

Sexual Orientation and Gender Identity

In July, police arrested three men for allegedly engaging in consensual same-sex relations with a Bangladeshi national who was also arrested. Another three men were arrested in connection with the case in September. The Bangladeshi national was sentenced to seven months in prison in August after he pleaded guilty; 40 additional charges were filed against him in September.

Among those arrested was the prominent lawyer, Ahmed Nazim Abdul Sattar, the younger brother of Parliament speaker and former President Mohamed Nasheed. He was sentenced to three months and 26 days in home confinement on September 15, after having pleaded guilty to the charge of engaging in homosexual relations.

The police said they were investigating 38 individuals who they believe have engaged in same-sex relations with the Bangladeshi national.

The Maldivian penal code criminalizes adult, consensual same-sex sexual conduct. Punishment can include imprisonment of up to eight years and 100 lashes and applies to men and women. Same-sex marriage is outlawed and punishable by up to a year in prison. Extremist groups in the Maldives use social media to harass, target and threaten those who promote the rights of LGBT people.

Climate Change

The Maldives is one of the world's most vulnerable countries to the impacts of climate change, including sea-level rise and extreme weather events, as over 80 percent of the country is less than one meter above mean sea level. The government's nationally determined contribution (NDC) to the Paris Agreement, updated in 2020, aims to reach net-zero emissions by 2030, but requires international support to reach this goal.

The Solih government has acknowledged increased threats from climate change, yet it has failed to adequately enforce environmental protection laws and launched developmental projects that risk environmental harm, including land reclamation—something the ruling party criticized while in opposition.

To adapt to rising sea levels and support tourism, the government commissioned the Addu Development project to create new land in Addu City by dredging sand from nearby lagoons. But civil society groups, including the citizen-led environmental group Save Maldives, have called on the government to cancel the project based on the project's environmental impact assessment, which found the project could harm people, local tourism, and the environment.

Transparency and public awareness surrounding development projects in the country remains limited, with affected communities, civil society, and the general public largely excluded.

Key International Actors

Governments announced strategic and developments partnerships with the Maldives but failed to publicly call for human rights improvements.

In August, President Solih visited New Delhi for the third time since coming into office and reaffirmed his government's commitment to the "India First' policy." India is aiding the Greater Male Connectivity Project—the largest-ever infrastructure project in the Maldives.

In February, the government of Australia established a permanent diplomatic presence in the Maldives and agreed to collaborate on climate change, security in the Indian Ocean region, and drug rehabilitation.

On March 12, 2022, the Maldivian government signed an agreement with the United States Agency for International Development (USAID) to strengthen the country's economic and democratic governance and bolster inclusive and sustainable development.

Mali

Human rights deteriorated dramatically in Mali in 2022 as attacks against civilians by Islamist armed groups and killings of suspects by pro-government forces during counterterrorism operations surged. The government increasingly cracked down on media and opposition voices, narrowing civic space. The mounting abuses occurred amid a background of an ongoing political crisis and significant tension with Mali's diplomatic partners, anchored in Mali's decision to employ the Wagner Group, a private military security contractor with apparent links to the Russian government.

The transitional government that came to power in a 2021 coup—the second military overthrow in less than a year—undermined efforts to investigate the mounting allegations of atrocities by state actors. Impunity for past and ongoing abuses by all armed groups persisted.

Little progress was made in restoring state authority and services, including the judiciary. The humanitarian situation worsened as a result of global food shortages, the effects of climate change, and, for part of the year, regional economic sanctions stemming from the political crisis. The number of internally displaced people increased from 2021, bringing the total to over 422,000.

The engagement of the Wagner Group, and the mounting allegations of summary executions and other abuses by them, intensified tensions with other military partners, particularly France, which ended a decade-long military operation in Mali in August. Likewise, Mali's relationship with the United Nations and neighboring West African countries deteriorated throughout the year, increasing Mali's political isolation.

Political Crisis and Abuses of Civil and Political Rights

In June, the transitional government shortened the timeline for a return to democratic rule from five to two years, until March 2024. A new electoral law allowed for members of the ruling junta to run in future elections provided they resign or retire from security posts six months prior to voting.

Threats, harassment, and expulsions of journalists and bloggers created a climate of fear and self-censorship, especially regarding alleged security force abuses. In February, Malian authorities expelled *Jeune Afrique* reporter Benjamin Roger, and in March, they suspended Radio France International and France 24 from operating in the country after both outlets reported on security force abuses. In July, the authorities detained an online commentator, Alhassane Tangara, after a pro-government group denounced him on Facebook. On November 3, authorities suspended a Malian news channel, *Joliba TV News*, citing "serious and repeated breaches and violations of the substantive provisions of the code of ethics for journalists."

Authorities detained several critics of the government, holding some for months without trial, including several who were arrested on trumped-up charges and tortured in 2021.

In January, security forces arrested and held for six months Dr. Étienne Fakaba Sissoko, a professor of economics, for alleged "subversive" speech after he criticized government appointments. The leader of the African Solidarity for Democracy and Independence (*Solidarité Africaine pour la Démocratie et l'Indépendance*, SADI) party, Dr. Oumar Mariko, reportedly left the country after he was detained in December 2021 and later threatened with further detention for denouncing army abuses.

On May 16, security officials detained seven military personnel on charges of plotting a coup. At time of writing, the authorities had not provided any information about their whereabouts, raising concerns about their enforced disappearance.

Atrocities by Islamist Armed Groups

During 2022, various Islamist armed groups aligned with the Islamic State in the Greater Sahara (ISGS) and Al-Qaeda expanded their attacks into southwestern Mali and to the capital, Bamako, killing hundreds of civilians, as well as scores of UN peacekeepers and government security force members.

On January 16, Islamist fighters executed four ethnic Dogon men after removing them from a convoy of traders near the town of Douentza.

Since March, fighters from ISGS have allegedly killed hundreds of civilians, most of them adult men, in attacks on villages in the Gao and Menaka regions, bordering Niger. Most of the victims were ethnic Daoussahak, a Tuareg sub-group.

On June 18 and 19, fighters linked to Al-Qaeda allegedly killed over 120 people from Dianwali, Deguessago, and Diallassagou villages in Mopti region.

At least 72 people, nearly one-third of them civilians, were killed by improvised explosive devices (IEDs) allegedly planted by Islamist armed groups nationwide in 2022, mostly in Mopti region.

In areas under their control, Islamist armed groups downed telecommunication towers, imposed zakat (religious tax), and implemented Sharia (Islamic) law and punishments via courts that did not adhere to fair trial standards. These groups also contributed to food insecurity by attacking those who did not conform to their vision of Islamic law, including by looting livestock and besieging villages.

The French journalist Olivier Dubois, kidnapped in Gao region on April 8, 2021, was still being held hostage by Al-Qaeda-affiliated Jamaa Nusrat al-Islam wal-Muslimin (JNIM) at time of writing.

Abuses by State Security Forces

Malian and allied foreign security forces were implicated in hundreds of unlawful killings of suspects and civilians, mostly during large counterterrorism operations in the Mopti and Ségou regions.

In March, Malian and allied security forces allegedly summarily executed over 300 men in custody, including suspected Islamist fighters, in Moura, central Mali. The incident was the worst single atrocity in Mali's decade-long armed conflict between government forces and Islamist armed groups.

On March 3, the bodies of 35 men, many blindfolded and most with bullet wounds, were found in Danguèrè Wotoro hamlet, Ségou region. The men had previously been detained in the Diabaly army camp, according to witnesses. Around March 5, Malian and foreign soldiers believed to be from the Wagner Group killed 33 men, including 29 Mauritanians, near Robinet El Ataye village, Ségou region. On April 19, Malian and allied foreign soldiers allegedly killed at least 50 civilians in Hombori, Mopti region, and on September 18, over 35 villagers in Gouni, Mopti region.

On January 27, soldiers executed 14 Dogon civilians in Tonou village in apparent retaliation after an army vehicle hit an IED. On December 31, 2021, during an operation in Boudjiguiré in Koulikoro region, Malian soldiers detained and later executed at least 13 men. Mali and foreign soldiers allegedly raped several women during counterterrorism operations.

There was little progress in investigations opened by the government into several of these incidents, and the authorities barred UN human rights investigators access to the locations of the abuses.

Violations of Children's Rights

The UN reported that scores of children were killed or maimed by armed groups in Mali in 2022. Armed groups also recruited and used over 300 children as child soldiers. As of October 2022, insecurity forced the closure of 1,950 schools, leaving more than 519,300 children out of school.

Accountability for Abuses

Authorities made some progress in terrorism-related cases, but not for large-scale atrocities implicating ethnic militias and government soldiers. Hundreds of people were detained for extended periods awaiting court trials.

The government pursued corruption cases linked to the fraudulent purchase of military hardware and equipment during the administration of the late President Ibrahim Boubacar Keita, who was ousted in a 2020 coup.

There was no effort to implement the recommendations of the UN International Commission of Inquiry into war crimes committed by Malian security forces and crimes against humanity by Islamist armed groups and ethnic militias between 2012 and 2018.

The International Criminal Court continued the trial of a former Islamist commander on charges of war crimes and crimes against humanity, including rape and sexual slavery committed in 2012-2013.

Key International Actors

The deployment in late 2021 of the Russian Wagner Group, described by the Malian government as "military trainers," and subsequent allegations of atrocities against them and Malian security forces, brought sharp condemnation from Mali's foreign partners including the United States, France, Germany, the European Union, and the United Kingdom.

Russia took the lead in providing significant military assistance in counterterrorism efforts, while Mali's relations with France deteriorated. In January, Mali expelled the French ambassador after France's foreign minister questioned the legitimacy of the transitional government.

Strained relations between the EU and Mali over rights abuses and Mali's partnership with the Wagner Group led to a significant reduction in the EU Training Mission in Mali (EUTM) and the EU Capacity Building Mission (EUCAP).

In February, France announced the end of its nine-year counterterrorism operation, which, at its peak, had over 5,000 troops. It completed the withdrawal in August, a month after Task Force Takuba, the 900-strong European counterterrorism special forces, left the country.

In February, the EU imposed a travel ban and asset freeze on five members of the transitional government. The US froze military assistance to the Malian government in October 2020 pending free and fair elections. In November, France suspended development assistance to the country.

In June, after the transitional government shortened the timeline for elections from five to two years, the Economic Community of West Africa States (ECOWAS) lifted the economic and financial sanctions it had imposed in January. At time of writing, Mali remained suspended from the ECOWAS and the African Union.

In June, Mali withdrew from the G5 Sahel, a 5,000-strong regional counterterrorism force launched in 2017, in protest after being passed over for the rotating presidency of the organization. The G5 Sahel also includes Burkina Faso, Chad, Mauritania, and Niger. The EU expressed regret at Mali's decision.

In April, the UN Human Rights Council renewed the mandate of the UN independent expert on Mali for another year. In July, the UN Security Council extended the mandate of UN peacekeepers, the UN Multidimensional Integrated Stabilization

Mission in Mali (MINUSMA). In August, it renewed the Mali Panel of Experts, which monitors the 2017 travel bans and asset freezes imposed on individuals obstructing implementation of a 2015 peace agreement.

Throughout the year, Malian authorities imposed operational constraints including no-fly zones on MINUSMA, obstructed investigations into alleged human rights abuses by state security forces, hindering MINUSMA's ability to fulfil its mandate and straining relationships with troop-contributing countries. In July, Malian authorities arrested 49 Ivorian soldiers working for a MINUSMA contractor and days later expelled the UN spokesperson for comments made about their arrests. The soldiers were charged in August with "undermining state security."

Mexico

Since the beginning of the "war" on organized crime in 2006, rates of violent crime have skyrocketed in Mexico, reaching historic highs under the administration of current President Andrés Manuel López Obrador, who took office in December 2018. Although authorities often blame this violence on criminal groups, most crimes are not investigated and those responsible are never identified or prosecuted.

Since 2007, successive governments have deployed the military domestically to fight organized crime and conduct law enforcement tasks. Soldiers, police, and prosecutors have committed serious, widespread human rights violations, including torture, enforced disappearances, and extrajudicial killings, with near total impunity. Efforts to reform police and prosecutors' offices have been ineffective. Congress, controlled by López Obrador's party, disbanded the Federal Police in 2019. It formally transferred police functions to the Ministry of Defense in 2022.

Thousands of people continue to disappear every year. Over 105,000 were officially considered missing as of September. Most disappeared after 2006.

Mexico is one of the deadliest countries in the world for journalists and human rights defenders.

President López Obrador has collaborated with the US government in anti-immigration policies aimed at preventing migrants from travelling through Mexico to reach the United States.

Violence and Impunity

Levels of violent crime have reached historic highs under President López Obrador. The homicide rate was 28 homicides per 100,000 in 2021.

Around 90 percent of crimes are never reported, a third of reported crimes are never investigated, and just under 16 percent of investigations are "resolved," (either in court, through mediation, or through some form of compensation), meaning authorities resolved just over 1 percent of all crimes committed in 2021, according to the national statistics agency.

Criminal Justice System

Police, prosecutors, and soldiers commonly use torture to obtain confessions, and engage in other abuses against those accused of crimes. The justice system regularly fails to ensure due process.

Judges are legally required to order pretrial detention for those accused of many offenses, without evaluating the circumstances of the case, violating international human rights standards. Around 85 percent of those sent to prison in 2020 had not been convicted of any crime, according to an analysis of official data by human rights organization Intersecta. Congress, controlled by López Obrador's party, expanded the list of crimes requiring mandatory pretrial detention in 2019.

Prisons are notoriously unsanitary and overcrowded. Prosecutors continue to use arraigo detention, a mechanism allowing them to obtain judicial authorization to detain anyone for up to 40 days without charge, in violation of international human rights standards.

Torture

Torture is widely practiced by police, prosecutors, and soldiers to obtain confessions and extract information. In the most recent survey of incarcerated people conducted by Mexico's national statistics office in July 2021, nearly half of respondents said that, after they were detained, police or soldiers had subjected them to physical abuse. Among those who had confessed to a crime, 38 percent said they did so only because authorities had beaten or threatened them.

The use of evidence obtained through torture in criminal trials is prohibited. However, many defendants face barriers and delays to proving they were tortured, limiting the effectiveness of the prohibition. A 2017 law required the attorney general to create a registry to track torture complaints. As of September 2022, the registry had yet to be created.

Military Abuses

Soldiers and marines have been deployed for law enforcement and to fight organized crime for decades, leading to widespread human rights violations. From

2007 through September 2022, the army killed 5,335 civilians, according to government data. Since 2018, the number of human rights commission complaints against the Army and National Guard has steadily increased. In 2021, the commission received 940 such complaints, the highest number in eight years.

President López Obrador has greatly expanded the budget, autonomy, and responsibilies of the armed forces, deploying them for hundreds of tasks traditionally conducted by civilian authorities, such as law enforcement, customs enforcement, controlling irregular immigration, running social programs, and administering public works projects. The military can legally detain civilians, take charge of crime scenes, and preserve evidence. Charging the military with these tasks has in the past contributed to human rights abuses.

In October, an investigation by human rights groups and journalists reported that the military had purchased the spyware Pegasus in 2019 and used it to illegally spy on human rights defenders, journalists, and opposition party politicians despite promises by President López Obrador that the government no longer spied on civilians.

Abuses by members of the military against civilians are supposed to be prosecuted in civilian, not military, courts, but those responsible are rarely brought to justice. In 2022, Congress passed a reform to ensure that soldiers assigned to carry out civilian policing activities are subject to the Military Code of Justice rather than to civilian law.

Emails obtained by journalists as part of "Guacamaya Leaks" suggest senior military officials have obstructed the investigation of abuses possibly committed by soldiers and that the secretary of defense may have pressured civilian authorities not to pursue an investigation into an army officer implicated in the Ayotzinapa case.

As of September, there were seven cases before the Supreme Court, filed by human rights groups and opposition parties, challenging the use of the military for law enforcement as unconstitutional.

Disappearances

At least 105,000 people are missing in Mexico, according to official statistics. Authorities believe the true number is likely higher. Nearly 90,000 of them have disappeared since the beginning of the "war" on organized crime in 2006. Thousands continue to disappear every year. More than 36,000 have disappeared since President López Obrador took office.

Authorities believe many of the disappeared have been buried in common graves by state and local officials after forensic services declared them "unidentified" or "unclaimed." From 2006 to 2020, at least 50,000 bodies passed through the custody of state and local forensic medical services without being properly identified, according to freedom of information requests by activists. Others may have been killed and buried in hidden graves by police, the military, or criminal groups. From 2006 to 2021, authorities reported having found at least 4,000 such graves across the country.

When families report disappearances, prosecutors and police rarely investigate. Families of the disappeared have formed more than 130 "search collectives" to investigate disappearances, including, frequently, by digging up mass graves.

In 2019, a well-respected human rights defender was appointed to head the government's National Search Commission (CNB). Since then, the CNB has taken steps to update the official missing persons' registry by requesting information from state and local officials and it has created an online platform to report disappearances anonymously and show real-time numbers of those disappeared, excluding personally identifying information. It has also begun creating a series of Human Identification Centers to exhume bodies from mass graves and attempt to identify them using the registry.

In April, the United Nations Committee on Enforced Disappearances presented the report on its visit to Mexico—its first visit to any country. The committee criticized Mexican officials for their "passive attitude" towards disappearances and expressed concern over "near total impunity" for these crimes. At the time the report was released, just 36 people had been convicted for involvement in enforced disappearances.

Attacks on Journalists and Human Rights Defenders

Journalists and human rights defenders—particularly those who criticize public officials or expose the work of criminal cartels—often face attacks, harassment, and surveillance by government authorities and criminal groups.

Mexico is one of the most dangerous countries in the world for journalists. From January to September 2022, 15 journalists were killed. In the first half of 2022, Article 19 recorded 331 threats, attacks, or other forms of aggression against journalists. Many journalists self-censor.

Authorities routinely fail to investigate crimes against journalists adequately. The federal Special Prosecutor's Office to investigate crimes against journalists had opened 1,552 investigations and obtained 32 convictions, including seven for homicide, from its creation in 2010 through September 2022. The vast majority of convictions have been obtained since the current special prosecutor was appointed in 2017.

Mexico is also one of the most dangerous countries in the world for human rights defenders. In the first six months of 2022, 12 human rights defenders were killed, according to the human rights groups Comité Cerezo. As with journalists, violence against human rights defenders is rarely investigated or prosecuted.

In 2012, the federal government established the Protection Mechanism for Human Rights Defenders and Journalists, which provides bodyguards, armored cars, and panic buttons, and helps beneficiaries temporarily relocate in response to serious threats. The mechanism lacks sufficient staff and funding and struggles to coordinate with state and local officials, leaving it sometimes unable to meet protection needs. Eight journalists and two human rights defenders have been killed under the program's protection, seven of them since President López Obrador took office.

Women's and Girls' Rights

A wave of states legalized abortion in 2022. As of November, eleven states allowed abortion for any reason up to at least 12 weeks of pregnancy. All states allow abortion in cases of rape. Despite legalization, people continue to face many barriers when trying to access abortion.

The Supreme Court ruled in 2021 that absolute criminalization of abortion is unconstitutional, and that people should not be criminally prosecuted for undergoing the procedure; that state governments do not have the authority to legislate that life begins at conception; and that medical staff's right to conscientiously object to performing abortions is subject to limits.

In 2021, the government reported around 3,700 killings of women, a quarter of which were considered femicides—killings of women because of their gender. Women's rights groups say femicide is likely under-reported.

Mexico officially ratified the International Labour Organization Convention on Violence and Harassment (C190) in July 2022. The treaty obligates Mexico to provide comprehensive protections to ensure a world of work free from violence and harassment, including gender-based violence and sexual harassment.

Migrants and Asylum Seekers

Criminal cartels, common criminals, and sometimes police and migration officials prey upon people migrating through Mexico, although crimes against migrants are rarely reported, investigated, or punished.

President López Obrador has intensified efforts to prevent migrants from traveling through Mexico to reach the US. He has deployed nearly 30,000 soldiers for immigration enforcement.

Soldiers and immigration agents operate immigration checkpoints throughout the country. Often, they target Black, brown, or Indigenous people. In May, the Supreme Court ruled these checkpoints unconstitutional, saying they disproportionately affect Indigenous and Afro-Mexican people.

Mexico detained more than 307,000 migrants in 2021—the highest number ever. Mexico's immigration detention centers are notoriously overcrowded and unsanitary. Staff there often pressure migrants to agree to "assisted return" to their countries and discourage them from applying for asylum even when they say their life could be in danger if sent back.

The López Obrador administration has imposed stricter visa rules and other new entry requirements on travelers from Venezuela, Ecuador, Brazil, and Colombia. News media reported the US had pressed the administration to tighten entry requirements and prevent migrants from flying through Mexico to reach the US. Since the visa requirement for Venezuelans was put in place in January, the number making the dangerous trip through the Darien Gap, between Colombia and Panama, has skyrocketed.

Mexico's asylum system is severely overstretched. Since 2013, the number of new applications has nearly doubled every year, but funding has not kept pace. Mexico's refugee agency relies heavily on funding and other support from the Office of the UN High Commissioner for Refugees (UNHCR). Mexico received more than 130,000 asylum applications in 2022, a record high and the third highest number in the world in 2021, according to UNHCR, but processed just 40,000, including many from previous years. From January to September 2022, it received more than 86,000 applications.

Sexual Orientation and Gender Identity

A wave of states voted to legalize same-sex marriage in 2022. As of November, it was available in all 32 states. In five states (Nuevo León, Aguascalientes, Chiapas, Chihuahua, and Guanajuato), the governor has decided officials should perform same-sex marriages although the state legislature has not reformed the civil code to recognize the practice.

Twenty states have passed laws creating a procedure permitting transgender people to change their names and gender markers on birth certificates through a simple administrative process. In 2019, the Mexican Supreme Court issued a landmark ruling with clear guidelines on legal gender recognition, holding that it must be an administrative process that "meets the standards of privacy, simplicity, expeditiousness, and adequate protection of gender identity" set by the Inter-American Court of Human Rights. In March, the court expanded the right to legal gender recognition to include children and adolescents.

Disability Rights

Under the López Obrador administration, serious gaps remain in protecting the rights of people with disabilities. They lack access to justice, education, legal standing, legal capacity, protection from domestic violence, and informed consent in health decisions. In 2019, Human Rights Watch documented cases of state-run hospitals and private individuals who shackled people with disabilities. Women with disabilities suffer disproportionate violence.

In many states, people with disabilities have no choice but to depend on their families for assistance or to live in institutions, which is inconsistent with their right to live independently and be included in the community under the Convention on the Rights of Persons with Disabilities (CRPD).

In October 2021, following a CRPD committee recommendation, the government publicly apologized to a man with intellectual and psychosocial disabilities who had been imprisoned for four years after a judge had found him unfit to stand trial.

In 2021 the Supreme Court ruled that guardianship was unconstitutional, but federal and state legislatures still need to legislate to ensure legal capacity and supported decision-making for people with disabilities.

In May, Congress passed amendments to the General Health Act prohibiting forced psychiatric treatment and any restraints, including shackling. The reform mandates community-based services and conversion of psychiatric hospitals to general hospitals.

Climate Policy and Impacts

As one of the world's top 15 emitters of greenhouse gases, Mexico is contributing to the climate crisis that is taking a growing toll on human rights around the globe. In 2021, a judge annulled the López Obrador administration's climate action plan because it did not increase emissions reductions targets in violation of Mexican law. In November 2022, the government announced its intention to present a new more ambitious plan.

The López Obrador administration attempted to reform the constitution to favor the distribution of energy from state-owned fossil-fuel power plants over renewable energy providers, but Congress rejected his proposal in April. In parallel, it has pursued a policy of investment in fossil fuels, acquiring an oil refinery in the US and fast-tracking the construction of another in Dos Bocas, Tabasco. In 2022, more than 70 percent of the federal budget under "climate change mitigation and adaptation effects" was allocated to the transport infrastructure of fossil gas.

Key International Actors and Foreign Policy

Mexico's foreign policy regarding human rights under the López Obrador administration has been based on the principle of "non-intervention." In June 2021, Mexico criticized other countries in the region that had condemned the jailing of critics and opposition candidates in Nicaragua, saying that they were intervening in Nicaragua's internal affairs.

In June 2020, Mexico was elected as a non-permanent member of the UN Security Council for 2021 to 2022. Mexico highlighted that one of its priorities on the council would be the protection of children. Mexico endorsed the Safe Schools Declaration in May 2021.

In October 2020, Mexico was re-elected to the UN Human Rights Council. Mexico did not support a decision to discuss a report by the UN High Commissioner for Human Rights on possible crimes against humanity in Xinjiang, China, nor a resolution to renew the independent fact-finding mission to investigate possible crimes against humanity in Venezuela.

In 2020, Mexico appointed itself as one of 23 "Champion countries" of the Global Compact for Safe, Orderly and Regular Migration.

Morocco and Western Sahara

Moroccan authorities stepped up their harassment of activists and critics and continued to detain and subject dissidents, journalists, bloggers, and human rights defenders to unfair trials. Laws restricting individual freedoms remained in effect, including laws that discriminate against women and lesbian, gay, bisexual, and transgender (LGBT) persons. Western Sahara remained a taboo issue, with draconian laws used by prosecutors to punish even peaceful advocacy for self-determination.

Criminal Justice System

According to the Code of Penal Procedure, a defendant has the right to contact a lawyer after 24 hours in police custody, extendable to 36 hours, but no automatic right to have a lawyer present during police interrogations. Police have for many years used coercive tactics to pressure detainees to sign self-incriminating statements, which judges have used for convictions.

Once cases progress to the trial phase, higher profile dissidents in particular face other due process violations including prolonged pretrial detentions, inability to access court files, coercion of individuals to testify in favor of the prosecution, and the lack of notification of trial sessions that have resulted in convictions in absentia.

Freedom of Association and Assembly

Authorities continued to impede the work of the Moroccan Association for Human Rights (AMDH), the country's largest independent human rights group. As of January 13, authorities declined to process the administrative formalities for 74 of 99 AMDH local branches, impeding their ability to open new bank accounts or rent spaces, according to AMDH. The AMDH also reported that other civic groups were also affected by the authorities' denial of legal status or refusal to complete administrative procedures, including groups that work on violence against women and youth groups.

Freedom of Expression and Human Rights Defenders

Morocco's penal code punishes with prison and fines nonviolent speech offenses, including "causing harm" to Islam or the monarchy, and "inciting against" Morocco's "territorial integrity," a reference to its claim to Western Sahara. While the Press and Publication Code does not provide prison as a punishment, journalists, activists, and bloggers on social media have been prosecuted under the penal code for their critical, nonviolent speech.

Moroccan authorities have also prosecuted high-profile journalists and activists for non-speech crimes since the mid-2010s. Critics have been prosecuted in unfair trials for serious crimes such as money laundering, espionage, rape, sexual assault, and human trafficking. Among the tactics to muzzle dissent, authorities have resorted to unfair trial proceedings, digital and camera surveillance, harassment campaigns by media close to the royal court known as the Makhzen, physical surveillance, aggression and intimidation, and targeting of relatives of activists.

On July 21, the Wadi Zem First Instance Court sentenced Said Amara, head of the Wadi Zem AMDH branch, to seven months in prison (of which four months were a suspended sentence) and a 6,000 Dirham (US$545) fine for "insulting an employee in the course of his duty," in reference to an alleged altercation between him and a police commander in Wadi Zem. According to AMDH, the court did not permit testimonies by witnesses summoned by the defense. Amara was released on September 7.

The same court sentenced blogger Fatima Karim on August 15 to two years in prison for allegedly publicly insulting Islam through posts on her Facebook page.

A court in Rabat in January 2021 sentenced in absentia Maati Monjib, a historian and free speech activist, together with six co-defendants, to one year in prison for "receiving funds from a foreign organization in order to undermine Morocco's internal security," for a complaint brought against him in 2015. At the time of his conviction, he was being held in pretrial detention on separate embezzlement charges, but authorities did not transfer him to the court session where his other case was being heard. As of September 26, both cases remained ongoing. In 2021 authorities imposed a travel ban and an asset freeze on him.

WORLD REPORT 2023

The al-Hoceima Appeals Court on June 16 upheld a four-year prison sentence imposed by the al-Hoceima Court of First Instance against social media commentator Rabie al-Ablaq for disrespecting the king. The court doubled the fine imposed by the lower court from 20,000 to 40,000 Dirhams (around US$3,640). The allegations against al-Ablaq, who was active in the social justice street protest movement Hirak in Morocco's Rif region, were based on two videos posted on Facebook and YouTube in which al-Ablaq addressed the king in a casual tone and contrasted his personal wealth to Morocco's widespread poverty.

A Rabat court of first instance in February sentenced Mohamed Ziane, a lawyer and former minister, to three years in prison on charges including offending officials and institutions, defamation, and "spreading false information about a woman because of her gender." Other charges included "participation in adultery," "sexual harassment," and "participation in misbehavior destined to provide a bad example to children." Ziane appealed the decision and remained provisionally free. As of September 19, the appeals proceedings had not started.

Ziane has been targeted by authorities since 2017, when he publicly criticized statements and decisions on security matters by the government during the Hirak protests, and when he took on as lead lawyer the case of Hirak top leader Nasser Zefzafi, who was prosecuted alongside 52 other protest leaders for "harming the state's internal security" and "rebellion."

Amnesty International's Security Lab found in March that two phones of Aminatou Haidar, an award-winning human rights defender from Western Sahara, were targeted and infected by the Pegasus spyware between 2018 and 2021. Pegasus, developed and sold by the Israel-based company NSO Group, becomes a powerful surveillance tool once installed on a phone by gaining complete access to the camera, calls, media, microphone, email, text messages, and other functions. Pegasus spyware has been used against human rights activists, journalists, opposition figures, politicians, and diplomats, including in Morocco.

Western Sahara

The United Nations-sponsored process of negotiations between Morocco and the Polisario Front, the movement that seeks self-determination for Moroccan-controlled Western Sahara, remained stalled. The UN has classified Western Sahara as a non-self-governing territory. A 1991 ceasefire agreement between the Polisario Front and Morocco failed to bring about a referendum on self-determination, and in November 2020, the Polisario Front said it ended the ceasefire.

Moroccan authorities systematically prevent gatherings supporting Sahrawi self-determination and obstruct the work of some local human rights groups, including by blocking their legal registration.

Nineteen Sahrawi men remained in prison after they were convicted in unfair trials in 2013 and 2017 for the killing of 11 security force members, who died during clashes in 2010 when authorities forcibly dismantled a protest encampment in Western Sahara's Gdeim Izik. In June, 18 of them filed a complaint against the Moroccan government with the United Nations Working Group on Arbitrary Detention, alleging acts of torture and political repression.

Women's and Girls' Rights

The Family Code discriminates against women regarding inheritance and in decisions concerning children after divorce if the woman remarries. The code sets 18 as the minimum age of marriage but allows judges to grant "exemptions" to marry girls aged 15 to 18 at the request of their families.

While Morocco's 2018 Violence against Women law criminalized some forms of domestic violence, established prevention measures, and provided new protections for survivors, it required survivors to file for criminal prosecution in order to obtain protection, which few can do. It also did not set out the duties of police, prosecutors, and investigative judges in domestic violence cases, or fund women's shelters. The penal code exempts corporal punishment of children from penalty if it causes only "light harm."

Morocco's law does not explicitly criminalize marital rape, and women who report rape can find themselves prosecuted instead for engaging in sexual intercourse outside of marriage if authorities do not believe them. Pregnant girls and adolescent mothers, who are exposed to criminal punishment if unmarried, would not be expected to stay in school.

In September, women protested calling for legalizing abortion after a 14-year-old girl was reported to have died following a clandestine abortion. Abortion is illegal in Morocco and is punishable by up to five years in prison, except in cases when the woman's health is in danger.

Sexual Orientation and Gender Identity

Consensual sex between adults who are not married to one another is punishable by up to one year in prison. Moroccan law also criminalizes what it refers to as acts of "sexual deviancy" between members of the same sex. Article 489 of the penal code punishes same-sex relations with prison terms of up to three years and fines of up to 1,000 dirhams ($91).

In a memorandum published in October 2019, the National Human Rights Council, a state-appointed body, recommended decriminalizing consensual sex between non-married adults. More than 25 NGOs expressed support for the recommendation. The Moroccan government did not act upon it.

Refugees and Asylum Seekers

The government has yet to approve a draft of Morocco's first law on the right to asylum, introduced in 2013. A 2003 migration law remained in effect, with provisions criminalizing irregular entry that failed to provide an exception for refugees and asylum seekers. Civic groups reported that authorities continued to arbitrarily detain migrants in ad-hoc detention facilities, followed by forced relocations or expulsions. According to the Mixed Migration Center, arrests of migrants and refugees by authorities increased in mid-2022 in Laâyoune, Western Sahara, with people detained in unhygienic conditions before expulsion to remote desert locations, including near the Morocco-Algeria border.

In June, at least 23 African men died at the Spain-Morocco border in Mellila. The incident occurred as around 2,000 people—migrants and asylum seekers, including many from Sudan, South Sudan, and Chad—attempted to enter Spain by climbing the high chain-link fences surrounding Melilla, one of two Spanish enclaves in North Africa. Video and photographs from the incident show Moroccan security forces using excessive force, including beatings, and Spanish Guardia Civil launching teargas at men clinging to the fences. Moroccan courts sentenced dozens of migrants to prison in connection with the June incident for a slew of offenses, including human smuggling, illegal entry into Morocco, and violence against law enforcement. As of September 19, the Spanish authorities had yet to publish the results of an investigation announced by the state attorney general in June. – attempted to enter Spain by climbing the high chain-link fences surrounding Melilla, one of two Spanish enclaves in North Africa. Video and photographs from the incident show Moroccan security forces using excessive force, including beatings, and Spanish Guardia Civil launching teargas at men clinging to the fences. Moroccan courts sentenced dozens of migrants to prison in connection with the June incident for a slew of offenses including human smuggling, illegal entry into Morocco, and violence against law enforcement. As of September 19, the Spanish authorities had yet to publish the results of an investigation announced by the State Attorney General in June.

Yidiresi Aishan (also known as Idris Hasan), a Uyghur activist, remained under threat of extradition from Morocco to China since his July 2021 arrest upon arrival in Morocco from Turkey. Authorities in Morocco arrested him based on an Interpol red notice, issued at China's request, "for belonging to a terrorist organization." Extraditing Hasan would violate Morocco's international obligations to not forcibly return anyone to a country where they would risk persecution and torture.

… HUMAN RIGHTS WATCH

Mozambique

The humanitarian situation in Mozambique worsened in 2022 amid ongoing attacks by an Islamic State (ISIS)-linked group locally known as "Mashababos" or Al-Shabab. Mozambican forces, with the support of troops from Rwanda and the Southern African Development Community (SADC) regional force, have significantly increased their presence in the region and recovered areas previously under the control of the insurgents.

The situation remained volatile in 2022, with fighting shifting to southern areas of Cabo Delgado and northern areas of Nampula province that had not experienced attacks before.

Government security forces across the country continued to use force and arbitrary detentions to restrict people's right to peacefully protest. Press freedom came under pressure as new laws limiting freedom of expression and the work of journalists and were debated or passed in the national parliament. The European Union approved additional military support for the SADC mission to Mozambique (SAMIM). Mozambique was elected as a non-permanent member of the United Nations Security Council for a two-year membership starting on January 2023.

Violence in Northern Mozambique

The humanitarian situation in northern Mozambique worsened as attacks by an Islamic State (ISIS)-linked group, known locally as Al-Shabab or "Mashababos" led to a spike in abductions and destruction of homes by the armed group. The violence has displaced thousands of people, and by the end of August, more than 946,000 were internally displaced in northern Mozambique after fleeing their homes in Cabo Delgado province.

In early March, local Al-Shabab fighters reportedly killed at least 15 civilians in the villages of Mbuidi, Malamba, and Nangōmba, in Nangade district, Cabo Delgado province.

In June, the group staged a series of attacks in Ancuabe district, 45 kilometers from the provincial capital, Pemba, an area previously considered safe, killing at

427

least seven people, four of whom they beheaded, and forcing thousands to flee their homes. Several people who fled the attacks told Human Rights Watch that hundreds of children had gone missing, as they fled separate ways from their parents, neighbors, and family members.

In September, the ISIS-linked group claimed responsibility for attacks on several villages in northern Mozambique, including two in Nampula province. Several witnesses told Human Rights Watch that armed men burned homes, a school, and a church in the Catholic Comboni Mission in the town of Chipene in Nampula. Many civilians were killed, including an Italian nun.

Right to Peaceful Protest

State security forces used lethal force and arbitrary arrest and detention to limit people's right to peaceful protest across the country.

In January, a group of women activists led by Observatorio da Mulher (Women Observatory) opened a formal complaint with the Attorney's General Office against police officers who in December 2021 forcibly broke up a peaceful protest against gender-based violence. During the protest, which was organized as part of the 16 Days of Activism to End Violence Against Women campaign, police arbitrarily arrested at least 17 women, who were released on the same day. As of September 2022, the case was still under investigation.

In April, during a session in parliament, the minister of interior, Arsenia Massingue, pledged to punish police officers who unlawfully prevented the right to peaceful protest. Despite the minister's comments, members of the security forces continued with impunity to prevent peaceful protests.

In August, police used live bullets to disperse hundreds of unarmed market traders in Gondola, Manica province, who were demanding better work conditions. At least three people were injured and 21 arrested. Also in August, police used tear gas to disperse a crowd at the Maputo fish market, where mostly women were protesting lack of compensation for being transferred from the old to the new market.

Freedom of Media and Expression

Press freedom was under pressure as new laws limiting the work of journalists and freedom of expression were debated or passed in the national parliament.

Lawmakers continued to hold public hearings on the proposed drafts of a new media law and a new broadcasting law that were introduced in 2021, which local and international groups said would "criminalize the work of journalists."

The draft law bans rebroadcasting of foreign political shows, and limits the number of correspondents from international broadcasters and other foreign media to two per outlet. The draft law also includes a provision that limits the right of journalists to defend themselves in cases of defamation against the president. At time of writing, parliament had not scheduled a date for the final debate and approval of the draft laws.

In May, parliament approved a new counterterrorism law with a clause stating that anyone intentionally spreading false information about a terrorist act can be punished with a prison term of 8 to 12 years. The law also includes prison terms of between 12 and 16 years for anyone who publishes "classified information."

The media rights group MISA-Mozambique urged parliament to amend the law, saying that "criminalizing the publication of classified information punished journalists and ordinary citizens, rather than the officials who failed in their duty to safeguard state secrets." Despite growing opposition from local and international media rights groups, the law was published in the government gazette in July.

Unresolved Kidnappings

Police officers continued to be implicated in cases of kidnappings for ransom across the country. In May, the Mozambican Criminal Investigation Service (Sernic) announced the arrest of three members of a gang of kidnappers, two of whom were members of the national police force, and one a Sernic agent.

In April, Attorney-General Beatriz Buchili denounced police complicity in cases of kidnappings in Mozambique in her annual report on the country's state of justice. She claimed the involvement of some "members of the police, lawyers, magistrates, and other figures in the judiciary creates fragilities in investigating these cases." In February, President Filipe Nyusi said it was unacceptable that police stations had been transformed "into breeding grounds for kidnappers."

In May, the National Police chief, Bernardino Rafael, announced that of out the six cases of kidnapping of businesspeople or their relatives reported in the first quarter of 2022, only one was resolved, after the family paid an undisclosed amount of ransom.

In May alone, two cases of kidnapping were reported in the capital, Maputo. One of the cases involved the son of a businessman who was kidnapped near his house in a well- secured area, close to the president's office.

In July, a businessman and owner of a hotel in Maputo was kidnapped by unknown men in front of his house, which is located between both the houses of the national police chief and the head of the State Information and Security Service (SISE).

Key International Partners

International partners continued to respond to requests from the Mozambican government to support in its military operations against Islamist armed groups in northern Mozambique.

In April, the United States government named Mozambique a priority country for the US Strategy to Prevent Conflict and Promote Stability. The US Strategy aims to support a locally led approach to address the causes of conflict and strengthen the foundation of stability. In July, the US Congress sent a bipartisan delegation to Mozambique, and in August, the US House of Representatives passed a resolution calling on the Mozambique government to protect its civilians and restore security in Cabo Delgado.

In June, the SAMIM began implementing the Peace Building Support initiatives in the northern part of the country. The program was designed to enhance social protection mechanisms, law and order, humanitarian assistance and capacity building initiatives in areas under attack from armed groups.

Also in June, Mozambique was elected as a non-permanent member of the United Nations Security Council. During the two-year term starting on January 1,

2023, President Nyusi said Mozambique would contribute to building peace in the world, advocating dialogue and multilateralism.

In September, the European Union approved about US$15 million in additional military support for the SAMIM, in Cabo Delgado, under the bloc's European Peace Facility. Also in September, during a visit to the country, EU High Representative Josep Borrell announced that Rwandan troops in Mozambique would receive EU financial support. Borrell referenced the need for a multifaceted approach and to respect human rights and international humanitarian law to successfully fight terrorism, but did not call for accountability for abuses committed by security forces.

Myanmar

Since staging a coup on February 1, 2021, the Myanmar military has carried out a brutal nationwide crackdown on millions of people opposed to its rule. The junta security forces have carried out mass killings, arbitrary arrests, torture, sexual violence, and other abuses that amount to crimes against humanity. Freedom of speech and assembly face severe restrictions.

Expanded military operations have resulted in numerous war crimes against ethnic minority populations in Kachin, Karen, Karenni, and Shan States. The military has also committed abuses including using "scorched earth" tactics, burning villages in Magway and Sagaing regions. The Myanmar military has long defied international calls for accountability, including for atrocity crimes committed against the Rohingya and other ethnic minorities. The junta's ineptitude and mismanagement of the country's economy since the coup has heightened the suffering of the population and entrenched a climate of fear and insecurity.

Torture, Political Executions, Deaths in Custody

Since the coup, junta authorities have arbitrarily arrested more than 16,000 pro-democracy supporters. Many former detainees alleged torture or other ill-treatment, such as sexual violence, during their detention. One journalist recounted after his release that guards raped and beat him in detention.

Myanmar's military and police are responsible for scores of deaths in custody. Human Rights Watch documented in detail the deaths of six detained activists that involved apparent torture or the denial of adequate medical care. At least 273 people have died in police or military custody in police stations, military interrogation centers, and prisons since the coup, according to the United Nations Office of the High Commission for Human Rights (OHCHR). The military junta has carried out grossly unfair trials in closed courts to impose lengthy and often harsh sentences. By November 2022, the junta's security forces killed at least 2,400 persons, according to the nongovernmental Assistance Association for Political Prisoners.

The junta brought multiple charges against Aung San Suu Kyi, the leader of the ousted National League for Democracy party, including for corruption, incitement, and breaching the Official Secrets Act. In September, three of her deposed cabinet ministers—Soe Win, Sett Aung and Kyaw Win—and Australian economic adviser Sean Turnell were convicted under the Official Secrets Act and each sentenced to three years' imprisonment. Earlier that month, Aung San Suu Kyi and former President Win Myint were each sentenced to three years and hard labor under electoral fraud charges. The multiple convictions meant Aung San Suu Kyi faces more than 23 years in prison.

In November, the junta announced the release of up to 6,000 prisoners as part of a National Day amnesty. These included several individuals arbitrarily detained, including Australian professor Sean Turnell, former United Kingdom ambassador to Myanmar Vicky Bowman and her husband Htein Linn, Japanese filmmaker Toru Kubota, and American botanist Kyaw Htay Oo.

In July, the junta executed four men—the country's first death sentences carried out in more than 30 years. The men were former opposition lawmaker Phyo Zeya Thaw, prominent activist Kyaw Min Yu, known as "Ko Jimmy," Hla Myo Aung, and Aung Thura Zaw, all of whom were convicted after closed trials that fell far short of international standards.

War Crimes and Other Atrocities

The military's indiscriminate use of artillery and airstrikes has killed and injured numerous civilians, damaged villages, including schools, and forced thousands to flee. Blocks to mobile internet data and networks are ongoing in many parts of the country where anti-junta opposition has resulted in clashes between the Myanmar military and pro-democracy armed groups.

On September 16, military helicopters fired rockets and machine guns before an infantry attack on a school in Let Yet Kone, Sagaing Region, killing at least 13 people, including seven children. UN Secretary-General Antonio Guterres "strongly" condemned the attack, saying, "Attacks on schools and hospitals in contravention of international humanitarian law also constitute one of the six grave violations against children in times of armed conflict strongly condemned by the Security Council."

A separate airstrike the same day in Moebye, Shan State, on an internally displaced person's (IDP) camp killed four people, including two children.

On October 23, the military carried out an airstrike on a music concert in Hpakant, Kachin State, organized by the opposition Kachin Independence Organization (KIO) to commemorate the ethnic organization's 62nd anniversary, in an apparent violation of the laws of war. The attack killed at least 80 people and injured over 100. Junta forces subsequently blocked access to medical care for those harmed.

OHCHR reported that military operations destroyed up to 30,000 civilian infrastructures, including schools in Magway and Sagaing Regions, as well as in Kachin, Shan, Karen, and Karenni States. The OHCHR said that since the coup, at least 382 children have been killed; there were 266 other reported deaths following raids and arrests in villages, and another 111 reported cases where victims were burned alive or after extrajudicial killings, in apparent attempts to destroy evidence of crimes.

In July, Amnesty International reported that the military's use of banned landmines in Karenni State amounted to war crimes. The human rights organization Fortify Rights also reported that attacks on civilians in Karenni State constituted war crimes.

In July, a tenuous ceasefire between the ethnic Arakan Army and the Myanmar military ended, resulting in months of renewed fighting, civilian deaths, and forced mass displacements along the border of Rakhine and Chin States, with reports of shelling falling into Bangladesh.

Displaced Populations and Aid

The conflicts in Myanmar have displaced nearly 1 million people internally since the coup, with an additional 70,000 fleeing to neighboring countries. The junta has blocked desperately needed humanitarian aid from reaching millions of displaced people and others at risk, part of its longstanding "four cuts" strategy designed to isolate and terrorize civilian populations. In areas of armed conflict, including in the southeast and northwest, the junta's obstruction of humanitarian assistance violates international humanitarian law.

Security forces imposed new travel restrictions on humanitarian workers, blocked access roads and aid convoys, destroyed non-military supplies, attacked aid workers, and shut down telecommunications services. The military has also attacked health facilities and medical workers, in violation of international law. Military forces have seized food deliveries and medical supplies en route to displacement sites and arrested people suspected of supporting aid efforts.

In September, following increased fighting between the Arakan Army and military, junta authorities banned UN and international nongovernmental organizations from six townships in Rakhine State and shut down all junta-controlled boats and public transportation serving those townships.

The requisite travel authorization process for humanitarian staff has grown even more erratic and constrained. Local frontline aid workers operate amid grave insecurity, at regular risk of harassment and detention at checkpoints as well as landmines and shelling in civilian areas and displacement sites.

In May, the Association of Southeast Asian Nations (ASEAN) Coordinating Centre for Humanitarian Assistance (AHA Centre) and UN Office for the Coordination of Humanitarian Affairs (OCHA) met with junta officials regarding the ASEAN Humanitarian Assistance Delivery Arrangement Framework, raising concerns that ASEAN and UN aid operations would be further weaponized by junta authorities, without the involvement of local groups or the opposition.

Disrupted supply chains, increasing prices and scarcity of goods, and loss of access to agricultural livelihoods have compounded food shortages around the country. The Myanmar kyat has faced extreme volatility since the coup, contributing to food crises for displaced and conflict-affected populations, as well as in urban and peri-urban areas. An estimated 11 million people are facing acute food insecurity, according to the UN. The junta imposed new banking regulations in September requiring aid recipients to present ID cards to receive cash assistance.

Persecution of Rohingya

About 600,000 Rohingya are effectively restricted to living in Rakhine State, subject to systematic abuses that amount to the crimes against humanity of apartheid, persecution, and deprivation of liberty.

The junta has imposed new movement restrictions and aid blockages on Rohingya camps and villages, including a ban in September on UN and international nongovernmental operations, increasing water scarcity, food shortages, disease, and malnutrition. In April, with the monsoon season looming, the UN reported new junta restrictions on infrastructure projects in the camps, leaving 28,000 Rohingya in unfit longhouses requiring urgent repair, many that "pose life-threatening risks to the inhabitants and other residents."

The frequency of Rohingya arrests for "unauthorized travel" increased. At time of writing, security forces had detained more than 1,300 Rohingya, hundreds of them children, commonly en route to Malaysia. Many have been sentenced to the maximum penalty of five years in prison.

About 135,000 Rohingya and Kaman Muslims have been held arbitrarily and indefinitely in detention camps for 10 years. The junta continued carrying out its problematic "camp closure" process, which entails replacing temporary longhouses with permanent structures built on top of or near the existing sites, further entrenching segregation and denying Rohingya the right to return to their pre-2012 homes. In August, junta authorities visited camps in Sittwe to collect demographic data and measure plots of land.

Junta authorities have continued rolling out the National Verification Card process as part of its Pan Khin (Flowerbed Project) "citizenship scrutiny" exercise, coercing Rohingya to accept IDs that mark them as foreigners in their own country.

The breakdown of the informal ceasefire between the Myanmar military and Arakan Army and growing struggle for political control has put Rohingya and Rakhine civilians at serious risk of injury, arrest, and displacement.

Michelle Bachelet, then-UN high commissioner for human rights, announced in August following a visit to the Rohingya refugee camps in Bangladesh that "the current situation across the border means that the conditions are not right for returns."

Shrinking Civic Space and Legal Challenges

Under junta chief Sr. Gen. Min Aung Hlaing, the junta has persistently squeezed civic space and targeted activists for persecution and arrest. On September 20, the junta warned that social media endorsement such as "liking" or "sharing" opponents' content could result in a prison sentence of up to 10 years.

Lawyers are increasing harassed by junta authorities when defending political and criminal cases. Closed courts and a lack of due process are just some of the challenges they face. The junta has sought to legitimize its power by arbitrarily changing laws, appointing junta-aligned judges, and arresting lawyers for defending junta opponents.

A law enacted in March formally brought the police under armed forces control, requiring police officers to comply with all military orders, including taking part in military operations.

Sexual Orientation and Gender Identity

Myanmar's penal code punishes "carnal intercourse against the order of nature" with up to 10 years in prison and a fine. Under the military junta, lesbian, gay, bisexual, and transgender (LGBT) people have been particularly likely to be targeted with sexual violence in custody.

Since the coup, women have also reported sexual violence and other forms of gendered harassment and humiliation from police and military officials.

Key International Actors

In February, the International Court of Justice heard Myanmar's four preliminary objections to the case brought by Gambia under the international Genocide Convention regarding Myanmar's alleged genocide against the Rohingya. In July, the court rejected the objections, allowing the case to proceed on the merits. Myanmar has until April 2023 to file its counter-memorial. The United Kingdom, Netherlands, Canada, and Germany have announced plans to support the case through formal interventions.

In March, the United States formally determined that the Myanmar military's atrocities against the Rohingya amount to genocide and crimes against humanity. At the International Criminal Court (ICC), the prosecutor continued his office's investigation into alleged crimes against humanity, based on the completion of these crimes in Bangladesh, an ICC member, following the 2017 atrocities against the Rohingya.

The UN-backed Independent Investigative Mechanism for Myanmar (IIMM), mandated to build case files for criminal prosecution of individuals responsible for serious crimes, reported in July that it had collected and analyzed evidence that "reinforces the Mechanism's assessment … that crimes against humanity continue to be systematically committed in Myanmar."

The US, UK, Canada, and European Union imposed further sanctions on individuals and entities linked to the junta. In February, the EU imposed sanctions on junta-controlled businesses, including the Myanmar Oil and Gas Enterprise (MOGE), the only government entity to do so thus far. In April, the BURMA Act passed the US House of Representatives, directing US President Joe Biden to sanction individuals who undermine stability and democracy in Myanmar, which now requires passage by the Senate.

In July, French company TotalEnergies withdrew from Myanmar, where it had operated the largest oil and gas field since the 1990s. The exit granted an increased stake in the project to the remaining partners—MOGE, US-based Chevron, and Thai-based PTTEP, with PTTEP stepping in as operator. Other companies, including Chevron, Woodside, Mitsubishi, Petronas, and ENEOS, announced plans to withdraw at least partially from operations in Myanmar.

Telenor, the Norway-based telecoms company, exited the country in March. The other major foreign telecoms company, Qatar-based Ooredoo, announced the sale of its Myanmar operations in September.

The European Parliament adopted two resolutions condemning ongoing abuses by the junta and urging tougher actions by the European Union. The March resolution recognized the opposition National Unity Government (NUG), Committee Representing Pyidaungsu Hluttaw (CRPH), and National Unity Consultative Council (NUCC) "as the only legitimate representatives of the democratic wishes of the people of Myanmar."

Myanmar continued to defy the "five-point consensus" of ASEAN. The bloc continued to bar junta representatives from high-level meetings, noting at the August Foreign Ministers' Meeting that they were "deeply disappointed by the limited progress in and lack of commitment of the Nay Pyi Taw authorities."

In September, Min Aung Hlaing met with Russian President Vladimir Putin in Moscow. Russia has become the junta's closest ally and main supplier of arms since the coup.

In December, the UN Security Council adopted a UK-drafted resolution denouncing the Myanmar military's rights violations since the coup, in the first Security Council resolution on Myanmar since the country's independence in 1948. All Security Council members voted for the resolution, except for China, India, and Russia, which abstained.

The UN Human Rights Council adopted an EU-led resolution on Myanmar in March and a resolution on the Rohingya led by the Organisation of Islamic Cooperation (OIC) in July. The General Assembly adopted a resolution on Myanmar in November.

Nepal

Following years of delay, the government drafted a law to advance the transitional justice process. Although the bill proposed some positive steps, victims and rights activists said that it hindered accountability for some serious crimes and does not meet Nepal's international legal obligations. The bill was not adopted before parliament was dissolved in September, ahead of the elections.

Violations by the police and army, including cases of alleged extrajudicial killings and custodial deaths resulting from torture, were rarely investigated, and alleged perpetrators are almost never held to account.

In July, after public protests, parliament extended the statute of limitations for filing rape allegations from one year to two years for adult victims, and three years for children after they turn 18. Activists said that the statute of limitations remains among several obstacles to justice. Members of marginalized communities, including Dalits, are disproportionately affected by sexual violence and have particular difficulty accessing justice.

In March, breaking from its normal practice of abstaining from country resolutions, Nepal joined 141 members at the United Nations General Assembly to vote against the Russian invasion of Ukraine, but in October—as a member of the Human Rights Council—voted against a resolution to debate violations committed by the Chinese government in Xinjiang.

In November, Nepal held elections to the federal parliament and seven provincial assemblies for the second time since a federal constitution was promulgated in 2015, resulting in a hung parliament.

Transitional Justice

In August, the government tabled a bill to amend the 2014 Transitional Justice Law, which had been struck down by the Supreme Court in 2015. The failure of successive governments to amend the law is a key reason that there has been no progress in delivering justice and accountability for conflict-era violations since a 10-year Maoist insurgency ended in 2006. The bill was drafted following only brief consultations with victims' groups and civil society.

Nepal has two transitional justice commissions, the Truth and Reconciliation Commission and the Commission of Investigation on Enforced Disappeared Persons. The two commissions have received over 60,000 complaints from victims but have failed to complete a single investigation.

The new bill had some positive aspects, including on the right to reparation and interim relief for victims who were left out of earlier programs. It would prevent amnesty for certain categories of violations and would establish a special court to hear cases recommended by the transitional justice commissions. It would also guarantee the right of the families of victims of enforced disappearance to their relative's property. The bill would mandate the transitional justice commissions to study the root causes and impact of the conflict and recommend institutional reforms.

However, it also contained provisions that would hinder accountability, making it difficult or impossible to prosecute those responsible for serious violations including war crimes and crimes against humanity. Other provisions that violate international law include limitations on the right to appeal. It was not brought to a vote before parliament was dissolved on September 17.

Rule of Law

Authorities failed to end impunity for ongoing abuses by the security forces. Deaths caused by excessive or unnecessary force while policing protests, as well as deaths in custody and allegations of torture, are rarely if ever credibly investigated, nor are perpetrators brought to justice.

On May 18, a 20-year-old Dalit man, Sundar Harijan, died in Rolpa jail in western Nepal. According to authorities, his death was a suicide. Harijan had been convicted of theft of mobile phones while still a minor but was sent to an adult jail. He had been due for release in 2020 but was transferred to Rolpa, where at the time of his death he was serving the sentence of another man, convicted of offences related to organized crime, who had been released in his place. An initial government inquiry led by a committee of prison staff absolved all officials. A subsequent Home Ministry investigation, part of which was obtained by Human Rights Watch, implicated prison officials in swapping the two men's identities and indicated that there may be suspicious circumstances in Harijan's death. However, the report was not published, and no action was announced.

On June 6, an 18-year-old woman, Nabina Tharu, in Bardiya district was killed when police used tear gas and live ammunition against villagers who had blocked a highway to demand the government do more to protect them from wild animals from a nearby national park. The government responded by appointing an investigative committee, composed of police and officials from the Department of National Parks, and no action is known to have followed.

Women's and Girls' Rights

A series of rape allegations led to protests and calls to address widespread sexual violence in Nepal. Official statistics show that the number of recorded rapes had risen in recent years. The victims disproportionately belong to marginalized social groups, including Dalits.

In June, hundreds of protesters gathered outside the prime minister's office and elsewhere around the country after a 24-year-old woman used social media to describe how she had been drugged, raped, filmed, and then blackmailed eight years earlier. Nepal's rape law contained a statute of limitations that prevented allegations over one year old from being filed with police. Parliament's decision to extend the statute of limitations to either two or three years, depending on the age of the victim, still denies access to justice in countless cases.

Victims of conflict-related sexual violence perpetrated during Nepal's 1996-2006 civil war are among those affected by the statute of limitations, which is not addressed by the new transitional justice bill. No perpetrators have been brought to justice. In May, the government announced that it would provide interim relief, but the program has not yet been designed or implemented.

A new citizenship act was passed by parliament in September, but President Bidya Bhandari refused to endorse it. If it becomes the law, the act could provide citizenship documents to thousands of people who were previously excluded. However, it still contains provisions that discriminate against women by making it harder for them to pass Nepali citizenship to their children than for men.

Children's Rights

In May, Human Rights Watch found that Nepal's Education Ministry had violated children's right to privacy and other rights through the education technology (EdTech) products it had authorized for children's education during the pandemic. One of these products, YouTube, collected and transmitted children's personal data to the advertising arm of its parent company, enabling both to track and target children across the internet for advertising purposes.

Sexual Orientation and Gender Identity

Nepal has a mixed record on lesbian, gay, bisexual, and transgender rights. In some ways, its legal progress has been exemplary for the region, but implementation has proven inconsistent. In 2007, the Supreme Court called for legal recognition of transgender people based solely on their self-identification, but some authorities continue to demand proof of surgeries. The court also mandated a study on equal marriage rights for same-sex couples, but the 2018 criminal code only recognizes marriages between men and women. In recent years LGBT rights activists have filed a series of writ petitions at the Supreme Court challenging the government's failure to uphold the rights of transgender people in practice, but the cases have all faced delays at the court.

Key International Actors

Nepal is a participant in the Chinese government's "Belt and Road Initiative," although there have been delays in implementing any of the proposed projects. Nepal continues to restrict free assembly and expression rights of its Tibetan community under pressure from Chinese authorities.

There was controversy over Nepal's decision to join a United States development program, the Millennium Challenge Corporation, which was seen by some as harmful to the country's relationship with China.

Nepal's donors, including European bilateral donors and UN agencies, continued to fund programs to support respect for human rights, police reform, access to justice, and respect for the rule of law, but were hesitant to press the government to advance transitional justice or end impunity for abuses by security forces.

Nicaragua

The government of President Daniel Ortega and his wife, Vice-President Rosario Murillo, deepened its systematic repression against critics, journalists, and human rights defenders. Dozens of people arbitrarily detained remain behind bars.

Since taking office in 2007, the government has dismantled all institutional checks on presidential power. Amid repression of critics and political opponents, President Ortega was elected, in 2021, to a fourth consecutive term.

The government closed over 2,000 nongovernmental organizations (NGOs) in 2022 and intensified its crackdown against members of the Catholic Church.

Abuses by the National Police and armed pro-government groups during a brutal 2018 crackdown that left over 300 protesters and bystanders dead remain unpunished.

Persistent problems include a total abortion ban and severe restrictions on freedom of expression and association.

Arbitrary Prosecution of Critics

As of September 2022, 209 people perceived as government critics remained in detention, according to local rights groups, including many who were arrested in the context of the 2021 elections.

Critics have been charged with undermining national integrity, propagating false news, laundering money, and related crimes. In many cases, they have been held incommunicado for weeks or months at El Chipote detention facility, some in prolonged solitary confinement. On the limited occasions when visits have been allowed, detainees have reported to family members abusive conditions, including repeated interrogations, inadequate medical attention, and insufficient food.

From February through May 2022, 50 government critics, including seven presidential candidates in the 2021 elections, received sentences of up to 13 years in prison and were disqualified from holding public office. Criminal proceedings were based on bogus charges and violated basic due process rights.

Hugo Torres, 73, a government critic, who was a guerrilla fighter in the 1970s revolution that first brought Ortega to power, died in detention in February 2022. Torres had been arbitrarily arrested in June 2021 and reportedly held in inhumane conditions, and incommunicado for prolonged periods.

In August 2022, police arbitrarily arrested Bishop Rolando Álvarez, an outspoken critic, along with five priests, two seminarians, and one cameraman, after holding them hostage at the episcopal curia of Matagalpa for two weeks. The police accused Álvarez of "acts of hatred" and "destabilizing the state." Authorities sent him to house arrest. The others are currently being held in detention. A judge granted prosecutors' requests to hold them 90 days in detention without charges.

In October, police arbitrarily detained Bishop Enrique Martínez Gamboa. He remained in detention at time of writing.

Freedom of Expression, Association

Human rights defenders, journalists and critics are targets of death threats, assault, intimidation, harassment, surveillance, online defamation campaigns, and arbitrary detention and prosecution.

Police frequently station themselves outside critics' homes, preventing them from leaving, in what in many cases amounts to arbitrary arrest. Those harassed are unable to visit friends and family, attend meetings, go to work, or participate in protests, religious events, or political activities. Some have been arrested repeatedly—sometimes abused in detention—for periods ranging from several days to several months.

Six journalists detained in the context of the 2021 elections were convicted of spreading "fake news," money laundering, and undermining national integrity, in 2022, and sentenced to up to 13 years in prison.

Police detained two La Prensa workers in July 2022, and a judge granted prosecutors' requests to hold them in detention for 90 days without charge. La Prensa then reported that an unspecified number of its reporters, editors, and photographers had left Nicaragua, citing constant police harassment. Since 2018, 200 journalists have reportedly gone into exile. La Prensa ended its newspaper's print edition in August 2021, when the Customs Authority withheld newsprint it had imported.

Authorities closed over 2,000 NGOs in 2022, including women's, religious, international aid, and medical groups. Many of these closures are based on abusive legislation, including a "foreign agents" law, passed 2020. At least 70 more were closed from 2018 through 2021. They also canceled the legal status of 18 universities, between December 2021 and February 2022, stranding thousands of students.

In August 2022, authorities closed at least 17 radio stations, including some run by the Catholic Church, citing, for example, lack of operating permits.

In September 2022, authorities suspended CNN's Spanish-language service from all cable channels in the country.

Legislators have passed several laws that severely restrict freedom of expression and association and have used them to forcibly close hundreds of non-profits, universities, and media outlets and to arbitrarily detain and prosecute journalists and human rights defenders.

In April 2022, the National Assembly passed a "Regulation and Control of Non-Profit Organizations" law that allows the Interior Ministry to ask legislators to cancel the legal status of groups that "promote campaigns to destabilize the country." Authorities can also seize the assets of associations that commit "unlawful acts," violate "public order," or hinder the Interior Ministry's "control and surveillance."

In 2020, authorities passed a cybercrime law that criminalizes a wide range of online communications, including by punishing with sentences of up to five years the "publication" or "dissemination" of "false" or "distorted" information on the internet that is "likely to spread anxiety, anguish or fear." The same year a "Foreign Agents" law was enacted, which allows cancellation of the legal status of organizations that obtain foreign funds for activities that "interfere in Nicaragua's internal affairs."

Right to Vote and Run for Office

Legislation passed between October 2020 and February 2021 has been used to deter critical speech, inhibit opposition participation in elections, and keep critics in prison without bringing formal charges.

After the National Assembly appointed Supreme Electoral Council (CSE) members loyal to President Ortega in 2021, the CSE stripped the main opposition parties' registration.

In July 2022, authorities dismissed five elected opposition mayors, de facto, citing their party's lack of registration, and appointed government party members to replace them.

Indigenous Peoples' Rights

Indigenous and Afro-descendant people face discrimination, reflected in poverty rates, precarious living conditions, and persistent violence.

Investigations into homicides and attacks related to territorial disputes in the Mayangna Sauni As Territory have stalled, the UN Office of the High Commissioner for Human Rights (OHCHR) reported in 2022.

Impunity for 2018 Crackdown

Police, in coordination with armed pro-government groups, repressed massive anti-government protests in 2018, killing at least 328 people, injuring some 2,000, and detaining hundreds. Authorities reported that 21 police officers were killed in the context of demonstrations.

Many protesters were detained for months, subjected to torture and other ill-treatment including electric shocks, severe beatings, fingernail removal, asphyxiation, and rape. Serious violations of due process and other rights also marred prosecutions against protesters.

No police officer has been convicted in connection with these abuses.

Women's and Girls' Sexual and Reproductive Rights

Nicaragua has, since 2006, prohibited abortion under all circumstances, even when a pregnancy is life-threatening or results from rape or incest. Those who have abortions face prison sentences up to two years; medical professionals who perform them, up to six years. The ban forces those confronting unwanted pregnancies to seek illegal and unsafe abortions, risking their health and lives.

Rates of domestic abuse, violence against women, and femicide, defined as a man's murder of a woman "in the public or private sphere," increased from August 2019 to December 2020, OHCHR reported.

The government did not publish figures on femicides and other forms of violence against women in 2022. A local human rights organization reported 46 femicides between January and October 2022.

Nicaraguan Asylum Seekers

Between April 2018 and March 2022, 200,000 citizens fled Nicaragua, the UN High Commissioner for Refugees reported.

The United States Border Patrol apprehended 164,600 Nicaraguans from January to September 2022, up from 50,000 in all of 2021 and only a few thousand in years prior. Many others fled to Costa Rica, Mexico, Panama, and Europe.

Key International Actors

In March 2022, the United Nations Human Rights Council established a group of human rights experts with a one-year mandate to investigate human rights violations committed in Nicaragua since April 2018.

No international monitoring bodies have been allowed to enter the country since 2018, when authorities expelled the Inter-American Commission on Human Rights (IACHR)'s Special Monitoring Mechanism for Nicaragua (MESENI), the IACHR-appointed Interdisciplinary Group of Independent Experts (GIEI), and OHCHR.

Also in March, authorities expelled Apostolic Nuncio to Nicaragua Monsignor Waldemar Stanisław Sommertag. In July, authorities cancelled the legal registration and expelled the Missionaries of Charity Association of the Order of St. Teresa of Calcutta. In August, after the police arrested Bishop Rolando Álvarez, Pope Francis said that he was "following closely, with concern and sorrow, the situation in Nicaragua."

In September 2022, OHCHR reported a "deterioration of the human rights crisis," saying the government continued "silencing critical and dissenting voices" and was "drastically reducing civic space."

In November 2021, Nicaragua announced its withdrawal from the Organization of American States (OAS). The OAS General Assembly and Permanent Council had said that the 2021 elections were not free nor fair, and that Nicaragua had violated its commitments under the Inter-American Democratic Charter. In April 2022, the Ortega government said the withdrawal was "completed," seized the OAS office in the country; and revoked the credentials of OAS representatives; however, the OAS says that the OAS Charter remains in effect in Nicaragua until the end of 2023, requiring Nicaragua's compliance with obligations under the Inter-American System.

The US sanctioned additional Nicaraguan officials and the state mining company, bringing to 53 the individuals and entities sanctioned, as of September, under the Global Magnitsky Act of 2016, the Nicaraguan Human Rights and Corruption Act of 2018, and other US laws and executive orders. In October 2022, the US Department of State imposed visa restrictions on over 500 Nicaraguans and the Department of the Treasury's Office of Foreign Assets Control imposed sanctions on the Nicaraguan mining authority, the General Directorate of Mines (DGM).

In November 2021, the US enacted a law to monitor, report on, and address corruption by the Ortega government and human rights abuses by Nicaraguan security forces.

In September 2022, the European Parliament denounced the "deterioration" of the rule of law and "escalation" of repression against the Catholic Church.

Also in September, the Ortega government expelled the European Union envoy to Nicaragua days after the EU delegation to the UN called for the restoration of democracy and the freeing of political prisoners. The government also severed diplomatic relations with the Netherlands after it cited concerns with human rights violations and deteriorating democratic institutions in Nicaragua when cancelling funding for a hospital project.

The EU maintains sanctions on 21 individuals and three state-linked entities in Nicaragua. They were renewed in October for a one-year period. The United Kingdom has sanctioned 13 individuals implicated in human rights violations, and Canada has sanctioned 35.

Nigeria

Political tensions were high as Nigeria prepared for 2023 general elections that will usher in a new president. The elections are set to take place amid worsening insecurity and threats from multiple armed groups.

The brutal killing of 40 worshippers in a church in southwest Ondo State by gunmen and spates of attacks by Islamist and other armed groups within proximity of Nigeria's seat of government in Abuja signaled critical levels of insecurity in 2022.

Boko Haram and its splinter factions, including the Islamic State West Africa Province (ISWAP), continued to carry out attacks in the northeast and expanded their activities beyond the region. ISWAP carried out a high-profile attack on a prison in Kuje within the Federal Capital Territory (FCT) that allowed hundreds of prisoners to escape, and was linked to other incidents including the church killings and an attack on a train from Abuja to Kaduna in which eight people were killed and 72 kidnapped.

In January, Nigerian authorities officially categorized criminal groups operating in the northwest as terrorists. The groups, popularly known as "bandits," emerged following years of conflict between nomadic herdsmen and farming communities. In 2022, bandits carried out kidnappings for ransom, killings, rape, and looting across communities in the region. The Abuja-based Center for Democracy and Development stated in April that over 100 bandit groups with an average of 30 members each operate with military grade weapons in largely ungoverned spaces in the northwest.

Gunmen agitating for the secession of the southeast region continued killings of residents and government officials in the region.

Nigerian authorities responding to the security threats across the country were also implicated in abuses.

Violence in the Northwest

Bandit groups continued to carry out widespread killings, kidnappings, and looting across several states in Nigeria's northwest region, while the military responded with airstrikes.

In January, many people were killed and displaced in an attack by bandits on villages in Anka and Bukkuyum districts in Zamfara State. This reportedly came a week after the Nigerian military killed about 100 bandits during airstrikes targeting bandits' camps. In February, a military airstrike targeting bandits killed seven children in the Maradi region of the Republic of Niger which borders the northwestern Sokoto, Zamfara, and Katsina States in Nigeria.

An August report by a committee set up by the Zamfara State government to review the security situation in the state revealed that 4,983 women were widowed, 25,050 children were orphaned, and 190,340 people were displaced between 2011 and 2019. The report added that over 3 billion naira (US$6.8 million) was paid to bandits as ransom for 3,672 people abducted during this period.

Separatist Agitations in the Southeast

The trial of Nnamdi Kanu, leader of the Indigenous People of Biafra (IPOB) group agitating for the secession of southeast Nigeria, on treason and terrorism-related charges was delayed by preliminary proceedings including two bail applications that the court denied. The judge also struck out eight of fifteen charges filed against Kanu for failing to disclose any valid offenses. In October, Kanu was discharged and acquitted of the remaining charges by Nigeria's Court of Appeal but remained in custody following a further appeal to the Supreme Court by the government to challenge this decision.

Citizens in the southeast continue to observe, to varying extents, a "sit-at-home" order introduced by IPOB in August 2021 as a means of pressuring the government to release Kanu. The order requires citizens in southeastern states to stay at home and public places to stay closed on Mondays and any other day that is announced, including days Kanu is set to appear in court. Gunmen seeking to enforce the order have killed, maimed, and destroyed properties of citizens in

HUMAN RIGHTS WATCH

HUMAN RIGHTS WATCH

"Those Who Returned Are Suffering"
Impact of Camp Shutdowns on People Displaced by Boko Haram Conflict in Nigeria

the region. IPOB has denounced the activities of the gunmen and stated that they have since suspended the sit-at-home order.

Security forces and vigilantes opposing the separatists have also been implicated in abuses including extrajudicial killings in the region.

Nigerian media reported that over 287 people were killed in the southeast between January and May 2022.

Boko Haram Conflict

Following the reported death of Boko Haram leader Abubakar Shekau in June during a clash with fighters of the ISWAP breakaway faction, both groups continued fighting in 2022.

ISWAP claimed responsibility for an attack on a prison in Kuje, 40 kilometers from Abuja, the capital. About 900 inmates were freed during the attack, including over 60 Boko Haram members, though authorities said some were recaptured. Security analysts highlighted the involvement of Ansaru, a rising Al Qaeda-backed splinter faction of Boko Haram, in the attack. In August, a leaked memo to President Muhammadu Buhari from the Kaduna State governor warned that Ansaru had formed a permanent operational base in Kaduna State near the Federal Capital Territory and was consolidating its grip on local communities in the state by running a parallel government.

ISWAP was also linked to a March attack on a Kaduna-bound train from Abuja. Eight people were killed and 72 kidnapped during the attack. By October, all kidnapped victims regained their freedom under different circumstances.

In Borno State, the epicenter of the Boko Haram conflict, the government continued to shut down camps for internally displaced persons in Maiduguri, the state capital. The closures cut off aid for thousands of displaced persons and compelled them to leave the camps without consultation, adequate information, or sustainable alternatives to ensure their safety and ability to support themselves in communities where they were forced to resettle or return.

Accountability for Serious Crimes

In April, International Criminal Court Prosecutor Karim Kahn made his first visit to Nigeria following his predecessor's closing of the preliminary examination of the situation in the country.

In December 2020, the ICC Prosecutor's Office had concluded that a full investigation was warranted after finding reasonable basis to believe that Boko Haram and its breakaway factions, as well as the Nigerian security forces, committed war crimes and crimes against humanity. During his visit, Khan highlighted the need for such crimes to be addressed through domestic proceedings, failing which the ICC will take them up, and agreed with Nigerian authorities on next steps with timelines to inform any future decision he will make on the situation.

Domestic trials for hundreds of Boko Haram suspects remained postponed since 2018.

More than a year after a 2021 judicial panel report implicated security forces in the killing of protesters in Lagos in 2020, Nigerian authorities have made no effort to ensure justice and accountability.

In September, some victims of human rights abuses by the defunct Special Anti-Robbery Squad and other units of the Nigerian Police were paid compensation following proceedings led by the National Human Rights Commission.

Freedom of Expression and Media

In May, a female college student, Deborah Samuel, was murdered by a mob in northwestern Sokoto State after being accused of blasphemy against the Prophet Mohammed. Efforts by the authorities to identify and arrest suspects were met with protests, which further stoked religious tensions across the predominantly Muslim state.

Although the Nigerian Constitution guarantees the right to freedom of expression, thought, and conscience, its criminal law categorizes insult to religion as an offense and Sharia (Islamic law), applicable in 12 northern states including Sokoto, criminalizes blasphemy.

In January, Nigerian authorities lifted a ban on Twitter, imposed on June 2021, that restricted access to the social media platform after it deleted President

Buhari's tweets for violating its policies. In June, the Economic Community of West African States (ECOWAS) Court found that the Twitter ban violated the rights of Nigerians, including the rights to freedom of expression and access to information and the media.

In August, Nigeria's National Broadcasting Commission imposed a fine of 5 million naira (about US$11, 500) on four television companies for broadcasting documentaries on the banditry crisis in the northwest, including a BBC Africa Eye documentary titled, "Bandits Warlords of Zamfara," claiming that the documentaries glorified terrorism. The broadcast authority also suspended operations of 52 state and private broadcast stations for failure to pay license renewal fees. Civil society groups challenged the suspension, prompting a court to restrain the broadcast authority from revoking the station's licenses pending its determination of the case.

Sexual Orientation and Gender Identity

In April, a federal legislator introduced an amendment to the Same Sex Marriage Prohibition Act (2013) which would outlaw cross dressing and make it punishable with six months jail term or a fine of 500,000 naira (US$1,160). The proposed amendment will undergo several readings before it is debated and voted upon by legislators. Nigerian law criminalizes same-sex conduct as well as public displays of same-sex amorous relationships, same-sex marriages, and the registration of gay clubs, societies, and organizations.

Women's Rights

In March, lawmakers rejected proposed amendments to the Nigerian Constitution aimed at fostering women's rights and political participation. The proposed amendments seek to grant citizenship to foreign husbands of Nigerian women, a right already granted to Nigerian men with foreign wives, and the inclusion of affirmative actions to ensure more women can participate in leadership. The rejection of the proposed amendments sparked protests following which lawmakers promised to reconsider them.

In September, Nigeria ratified the International Labour Organization (ILO) Violence and Harassment Convention (C190), making it the first country in West

Africa and the eighth country in the world to do so. The treaty obligates Nigeria to provide comprehensive protections to ensure a world of work free from violence and harassment, including gender-based violence and sexual harassment.

Children's Rights

According to a United Nations report released in June, Boko Haram affiliated groups and splinter factions, including ISWAP, abducted at least 211 children and recruited at least 63 children, including 54 girls, between January and December 2021. At least 88 children were killed or maimed by parties to the conflict, and 53 girls were raped or subjected to sexual violence, including forced marriage. A minimum of 15 schools were attacked, 12 of these by ISWAP and over 45 children alleged to be associated with armed groups were detained by the military.

In September, Nigeria signed a handover protocol with the UN agreeing that children taken into military custody on suspicion of involvement with Boko Haram should be transferred within seven days to civilian authorities for reintegration.

In September, the UN Educational, Scientific and Cultural Organization (UNESCO) estimated that Nigeria has 20.2 million out of school children, one of the three highest in the world along with India and Pakistan.

A June report by the United Nations International Children's Emergency Fund (UNICEF) stated that over 23 million girls were married before age 18. In 2021, Human Rights Watch found child marriage in Nigeria to be prevalent both in states that had adopted the Child Rights Act, which sets the age of marriage at 18, and in states that had yet to adopt the law.

The Education Ministry failed to act following reports that it had recommended unsafe online learning products for children during the Covid-19 pandemic. All seven products surveilled or had the capacity to surveil children online, outside school hours, and deep into their private lives.

Disability Rights

Nigeria has yet to enact a legal ban on chaining of people with mental health conditions and psychosocial disabilities as a path towards ending the horrific practice across the country. Accessing human rights-respecting and community-based mental health care and psychosocial support continues to be difficult for most Nigerians.

Poverty and Inequality

Nigeria's food inflation reached 22 percent in July, causing severe hardship as families struggled to afford food.

In June, the federal government announced that 2 million households are benefiting from its Conditional Cash Transfer (CCT) program.

Over 95 million Nigerians are living in poverty on about US$1.90 a day according to estimates by the World Bank. Human Rights Watch research in 2021 found Nigeria lacks a functional social protection system to protect citizens from economic shocks. It also found that ad-hoc initiatives such as the CCT program failed to protect people's right to an adequate standard of living during the Covid-19 pandemic.

Key International Actors

In April, the United States government approved the $997 million sale of 12 AH-1Z attack helicopters and related military equipment to the Nigerian government, which it had suspended in 2021 due to human rights concerns. US authorities said the new sale will include training for the Nigerian military to minimize civilian harm in air operations. In July, an Intercept report revealed possible US involvement in 2017 Nigerian military airstrikes, which the Nigerian authorities said were intended to hit Boko Haram targets but instead killed over 160 displaced persons, most of them children, in a camp in Rann, Borno State.

Foreign Policy

President Buhari condemned the January military coup in Burkina Faso and supported efforts by ECOWAS and the African Union to restore constitutional order in Burkina Faso and other countries on the continent where recent coups have taken place.

In April, Nigeria abstained from voting on a UN General Assembly resolution to suspend Russia from the UN Human Rights Council over allegations of gross human rights violations arising from its invasion in Ukraine. In March, Nigeria voted in favor of another General Assembly resolution highlighting the humanitarian consequences of Russia's military offensive in Ukraine.

North Korea

The Democratic People's Republic of Korea (DPRK, North Korea) remains one of the most repressive countries in the world. Ruled by third-generation authoritarian leader Kim Jong Un, the government responded to the Covid-19 pandemic with deepened isolation and repression, increased ideological control, and by maintaining fearful obedience of the population by using threats of torture, extrajudicial executions, wrongful imprisonment, enforced disappearances, and forced hard labor.

The government does not tolerate pluralism, bans independent media, civil society organizations, and trade unions, and systematically denies all basic liberties, including freedom of expression, peaceful assembly, association, and freedom of religion and belief. North Korean authorities routinely send perceived opponents of the government to secretive political prison camps (kwanliso) in remote regions where they face torture and other ill-treatment, starvation rations, and forced labor. Collective punishment is also used to silence dissent.

The government systematically extracts forced, unpaid labor from its citizens to build infrastructure and conduct other government-ordered campaigns and public work projects. The government fails to protect the rights of numerous at-risk groups, including women, children, and people with disabilities.

In 2022, the North Korean government maintained extreme and unnecessary measures under the pretext of protecting against the spread of Covid-19, which isolated the country ever further by keeping its borders closed, restricting foreign trade to minimal levels, and limiting travel and distribution of food and other products within the country.

The North Korean government failed to protect economic rights, resulting in violations of the right to health, food, and access to an adequate standard of living in 2022. The impact of the nearly three-year-long Covid-19 nationwide country lockdown intensified as the country was hit by major droughts in May, and flooding in July and August. Meanwhile, in May, North Korea imposed more severe lockdowns across the country after it announced North Korea's first official Covid-19 case. The government continued to prioritize weapons' development and conducted a record number of over 30 missile tests between January and October.

Freedom of Movement

Moving from one province to another, or traveling abroad without prior approval, is illegal in North Korea and such restrictions were strictly enforced during the year, causing serious hardship. The government maintained heightened enforcement of a ban on "illegal" travel to China with border buffer zones set up in August 2020, which extend one to two kilometers from the northern border and operated continuously in 2022.

Border guards are under orders to "unconditionally shoot" on sight anyone entering or leaving without permission. There were several reports of border guards shooting North Koreans trying to leave the country, some resulting in death.

During the year, almost all international travel remained banned. In January, North Korea restarted cross-border rail trade and opened a "disinfection center" at Uiju, North Pyongan province, constructed in March-April 2021, where product quarantines lasted up to three months. It stopped it after a Covid-19 outbreak in Dandong in April and restarted it in September.

Official trade continued at minimal levels and unofficial trade has largely ceased. All international staff of United Nations agencies and nongovernmental organizations have departed the country, and very few diplomats remain.

The government maintained enhanced restrictions on domestic travel because of Covid-19, with strict requirements for travel permits for those allowed to move. Authorities maintained increased road checkpoints, blocked inter-district movements, and enhanced enforcement to prevent "illegal" travel. These measures severely hurt people's livelihoods and their ability to access food, medicines, and other essential goods, resulting in food insecurity and other serious problems.

Activist networks in China and South Korea that help North Koreans flee their country and transit China to a safe third country said they face major obstacles because of increased numbers of random checks on roads in China and greater surveillance.

Many North Koreans in China remained hidden in safe houses for months as the Chinese government sought to detain North Korean refugees and return them to North Korea, violating China's obligations as a state party to the UN Refugee Convention. North Koreans fleeing into China should be protected as refugees sur place because of the certainty of punishment on return because they left without permission.

North Korean law states that leaving the country without permission is a crime of "treachery against the nation," punishable by death. The 2014 UN Commission of Inquiry (COI) on human rights in the DPRK found those forcibly returned by the Chinese government face crimes against humanity in North Korea. Very few North Koreans are escaping the country. Just over 1,000 North Koreans fled to the south in 2019, but only 42 reached South Korea between January and September 2022.

Right to Health

North Korea has a largely impoverished and malnourished population that is almost entirely unvaccinated against Covid-19. In December 2021, COVAX—an international initiative created in April 2020 to procure and distribute vaccines to low- and middle-income countries—allocated 8.12 million doses of Covid-19 vaccines for distribution in North Korea. By April, following North Korea's unresponsiveness to introduce vaccines, COVAX reallocated those doses to other countries, so they could be used before they expired. North Korea was one of the only two countries in the world that had not yet started a vaccination program by that time.

In May, North Korea announced its first official Covid-19 case, when Kim Jong Un suffered a high fever after being in contact with a frontline worker with Covid-19 in a pharmacy visit in May, according to North Korean official media reports. In July, North Korea issued a decree threatening with the death penalty those "stealing or selling emergency medicines, ... fake or faulty medicines."

In May, North Korea reportedly received Covid-19 related aid from the Chinese government, but North Korea did not respond to offers of vaccines from the US, South Korea, and Russia. In August, Kim Jong Un declared victory over the Covid-19 outbreak, dropped its mask mandate and resumed normal public activities.

Yet, in September, Kim Jong Un called on his country to start a vaccination program, over a year-and-a-half after other countries started vaccinating their populations. Vaccinations reportedly started being administered in the northern border city of Sinuiju, and the port city of Nampo, in August.

Freedom of Expression and Information

The North Korean government does not permit freedom of thought, opinion, expression, or information. All media is strictly controlled. Accessing phones, computers, televisions, radios, or media content that is not sanctioned by the government is illegal and considered "anti-socialist behavior" to be severely punished. The government regularly cracks down on those viewing or accessing unsanctioned media. It also jams Chinese mobile phone services at the border, and targets for arrest those communicating with people outside of the country or connecting outsiders to people inside the country.

As concerns over possible unrest increased due to people's suffering during lockdowns, North Korea ramped-up ideological campaigns and restricted access to unofficial, unsanctioned information. In a letter in January, Kim Jong Un addressed farmers about the country's "critical food problems," but focused on asking farmers to stop selling products on the black market and to deal with deep-rooted anti-socialist behavior. Media outlets with contacts inside the country reported crackdowns on authorized cell phones at border regions, and further tightening controls over unsanctioned mobile phones and computers.

Forced Labor

The North Korean government routinely and systematically requires forced, uncompensated labor from much of its population to sustain its economy. The government's forced labor demands target women and children through the Women's Union or schools, workers at state-owned enterprises or deployed abroad, detainees in short-term hard labor detention centers (rodong dallyeondae), and prisoners at long-term ordinary prison camps (kyohwaso) and political prison camps (kwanliso).

At some point in their lives, a significant majority of North Koreans must perform unpaid hard labor, often justified by the state as "portrayals of loyalty" to the government. Since punishment for crimes in North Korea is arbitrary, depending on a person's record of loyalty, personal connections, and capacity to pay bribes, refusal of a government order to work as a "volunteer" can result in severe punishment, including torture and imprisonment.

North Korea remains one of only seven UN member states that has not joined the International Labour Organization.

At-Risk Groups

North Korea uses songbun, a socio-political classification system that in its creation grouped people into "loyal," "wavering," or "hostile" classes, and justifies discriminating against lower classed people in employment, residence, or schooling.

Women and girls in North Korea also suffer a range of sexual and gender-based abuses, in addition to violations suffered by the general population. These include widespread gender discrimination, sexual and gender-based violence, and constant exposure to stereotyped gender roles.

Key International Actors

North Korea has ratified six human rights treaties, but there is no evidence the government will effectively implement the treaties or any other human rights instruments. The 2014 COI report concluded that government officials are responsible for crimes against humanity. It recommended the UN Security Council refer the situation to the International Criminal Court.

On December 16, 2021, the UN General Assembly adopted a resolution by consensus condemning human rights in North Korea. On April 1, 2022, the UN Human Rights Council adopted by consensus a resolution on North Korean human rights.

The US government currently imposes human rights-related sanctions on North Korean government entities, as well as on Kim Jong Un and on several other top officials. In December 2021, the European Union extended human rights-related sanctions on two top government officials and the country's top public prosecutor's office. In April, the European Parliament passed a resolution on human rights in North Korea, which stressed the importance of accountability for past and ongoing crimes against humanity.

Japan continues to demand the return of 12 Japanese citizens whom North Korea abducted in the 1970s and 1980s. Some Japanese civil society groups allege the number of abductees is much higher.

Pakistan

Pakistan is exceedingly vulnerable to climate change and faces rates of warming considerably above the global average, making extreme climate events more frequent and intense. In March and April, an extreme heat wave in South Asia featured some of the hottest recorded temperatures in the country's modern history and led to spikes in maternal mortality and deaths of older people. In August, Pakistan experienced devastating floods covering over one-third of the country, killing over 1,000 people, displacing more than 30 million, and causing billions of dollars in damage. These crises came as Pakistan faced deepening political and economic crises and skyrocketing food and fuel prices.

In early April, Prime Minister Imran Khan, facing a vote of no-confidence after losing the support of most of the parliament, attempted to dissolve the national assembly. The action was declared unconstitutional by the Supreme Court. The parliament subsequently removed Imran Khan as prime minister on April 10. In October, Imran Khan was disqualified by the Election Commission of Pakistan from his parliamentary seat for non-declaration of assets.

Throughout the year, the government continued to control media and curtail dissent. Authorities harassed and at times detained journalists and other members of civil society for criticizing government officials and policies. Violent attacks on members of the media also continued.

Women, religious minorities, and transgender people continued to face violence, discrimination, and persecution, with authorities failing to provide adequate protection or hold perpetrators to account. The government continued to do little to hold law enforcement agencies accountable for torture and other serious abuses.

Attacks by Islamist militants, notably the Tehrik-i-Taliban Pakistan, targeting law enforcement officials and religious minorities killed dozens of people.

Freedom of Expression, Attacks on Civil Society Groups

Government threats and attacks on media continued to contribute to a climate of fear among journalists and civil society groups, with many resorting to self-censorship. Authorities have pressured or threatened media outlets not to criticize government institutions or the judiciary. In several cases in 2022, government regulatory agencies blocked cable operators and television channels that aired critical programs.

Pakistan's sedition law, based on a colonial-era British provision, is vague and overly broad and has often been used against political opponents and journalists. Shahbaz Gill, a senior official with the opposition party Pakistan Tehrik-i-Insaaf (PTI), was arrested in Islamabad in August on charges of sedition and incitement to mutiny after he said on a television program that junior military officers should not follow orders that are against public opinion. Gill was subsequently released on bail.

In May, journalists Sami Abraham, Arshad Sharif, Sabir Shakir, and Imran Riaz Khan were charged with abetment of mutiny and publication of statements causing public mischief by criticizing state institutions and the army in their journalistic work and unspecified social media posts. In October, Arshad Sharif was killed by the police in Kenya. Sharif had left Pakistan citing threats to his life.

Several journalists suffered violent attacks and threats in 2022. In April, members of

political party, Pakistan Tehrik-I-Insaf assaulted Khawar Mughal in Lahore. Also, in April, Gharida Farooqi, a renowned television journalist was subject to threats of rape.

Nongovernmental organizations (NGOs) reported intimidation, harassment, and surveillance by government authorities. The government used the "Regulation of INGOs in Pakistan" policy to impede the registration and functioning of international humanitarian and human rights groups.

Freedom of Religion and Belief

The Pakistani government did not amend or repeal blasphemy law provisions that have provided a pretext for violence against religious minorities and have left them vulnerable to arbitrary arrest and prosecution. The death penalty is mandatory for blasphemy, and dozens of people remained on death row as of late 2021.

Members of the Ahmadiyya religious community continue to be a major target for prosecutions under blasphemy laws, as well as specific anti-Ahmadi laws. Militant groups and the Islamist political party Tehreek-e-Labbaik (TLP) accuse Ahmadis of "posing as Muslims." The Pakistan penal code also treats "posing as Muslims" as a criminal offense.

In January, an anti-cybercrime court sentenced Aneeqa Atiq, a woman, to death for sharing "blasphemous content" on WhatsApp. In February, Mushtaq Ahmed, who had a psychosocial disability, was stoned to death by a mob for allegedly desecrating the Quran, in Khanewal, Punjab.

In March, a 21-year-old woman in Dera Ismail Khan, Khyber-Pakhtunkhwa province was killed by three women who accused her of blasphemy. According to the police investigation, the suspects claimed that a 13-year-old female relative of theirs found out in "a dream" that the victim had committed blasphemy.

In August, authorities in Punjab brought a blasphemy charge against Waqar Satti, a journalist, for posting a video on Twitter.

According to a Pakistani human rights organization, the Centre for Social Justice, at least 1,855 people have been charged under Pakistan's blasphemy laws between 1987 and February 2021.

Abuses against Women and Girls

Violence against women and girls—including rape, murder, acid attacks, domestic violence, and forced and child marriage—remained widespread. Human rights defenders estimate that roughly 1,000 women are killed in so-called honor killings every year.

The UN Children's Fund, UNICEF, estimates that 18.9 million girls in Pakistan marry before the age of 18, and 4.6 million before 15. Married girls are often forced into dangerous pregnancies at a young age and pregnancies that are too closely spaced. Women from religious minority communities remain particularly vulnerable to forced marriage. The government did little to stop child and forced marriages.

Among those millions severely affected by floods were at least 650,000 pregnant women and girls, 73,000 of whom were near their due date. According to the

United Nations Population Fund (UNFPA) many of the affected women lacked access to the healthcare facilities and support they needed to deliver their children safely.

Even before the 2022 floods, Pakistani women faced numerous reproductive health challenges and had one of the highest maternal mortality ratios in South Asia.

In January, Pakistan appointed Justice Ayesha Malik, the first ever female Supreme Court judge.

In January, Pakistan's parliament passed a bill strengthening protections for women in the workplace against violence and harassment. The law expanded the definition of the workplace to encompass both formal and informal workplaces, bringing it closer to the definition set out in the 2019 International Labour Organization (ILO) Violence and Harassment Convention (C190), which Pakistan has not ratified.

Children's Rights

More than 400 children were killed in the floods, and many more injured. UNICEF reported that at least 3.4 million children needed urgent humanitarian assistance and were at increased risk of waterborne diseases, drowning, and malnutrition. Most of the approximately 16 million affected children were without homes, lacked access to safe drinking water, and had to live in unsanitary conditions.

The situation was exacerbated by the fact that the 72 worst-hit districts in Pakistan already had high levels of poverty and impaired growth and development among children. The floods also fully or partially destroyed more than 18,000 schools. The hardest-hit province, Sindh, had nearly 16,000 schools destroyed alone. Another 5,500 schools were used to house families displaced by the floods.

Even before the floods, over 5 million primary school-age children in Pakistan were out of school, most of them girls. Human Rights Watch research found that girls miss school for reasons including lack of schools, costs associated with studying, child marriage, child labor, and gender discrimination. School closures to protect against the spread of Covid-19 affected almost 45 million students; Pakistan's poor internet connectivity and the difficulty many families face affording internet service and devices hampered online learning.

Child sexual abuse remains common. The children's rights organization Sahil reported an average of over 12 daily cases of child sexual abuse across Pakistan for the first six months of 2022. The real figures are likely to be significantly higher due to underreporting.

Terrorism, Counterterrorism and Law Enforcement Abuses

Tehrik-Taliban Pakistan (TTP), Al-Qaeda, Balochistan Liberation Army (BLA) and their affiliates claimed responsibility for carrying out suicide bombings and other attacks against security personnel and civilians that caused hundreds of deaths and injuries during the year.

Pakistan law enforcement agencies were responsible for grave human rights violations, including detention without charge and extrajudicial killings. Pakistan failed to enact a law criminalizing torture, despite Pakistan's international obligation to do so as a party to the Convention against Torture.

Pakistan has more than 3831 prisoners on death row, one of the world's largest populations facing execution. At least 516 individuals have been executed since Pakistan lifted the moratorium on the death penalty in December 2014. Those on death row are often from the most marginalized sections of society.

In June, Islamabad High Court in a landmark decision held that, "When there is sufficient evidence to conclude that it is, prima facie, a case of enforced disappearance then it becomes an obligation of the State and all its organs to trace the disappeared citizen." However, the government failed to take any significant measures to implement the decision.

Sexual Orientation and Gender Identity

Pakistan's penal code continued to criminalize same-sex sexual conduct, placing men who have sex with men and transgender people at risk of police abuse, and other violence and discrimination.

Transgender women in Pakistan, particularly in the Khyber-Pakhtunkhwa province, remained under threat of attack and at least seven transgender women were killed in the province in 2022. In September, protests by religious groups against a 2018 transgender rights law caused lawmakers to consider revising it, threatening the rights protections it enshrines.

Key International Actors

In August, the International Monetary Fund (IMF) decided to revive a stalled loan program approved in July 2019 and disburse nearly US$1.17 billion to reduce some burdens of the economic crisis on Pakistan's population. The IMF had earlier conditioned the loan program on austerity measures, including removing electricity and fuel subsidies and imposing a fuel tax that added to inflation and further burdened many Pakistanis' ability to realize their economic rights.

In September, MEPs from the European Parliament's Subcommittee on Human Rights (DROI) visited Pakistan. The delegation focused on the human rights situation as part of the final round of EU monitoring of Pakistan's preferential trade access to the EU market under the "GSP+" scheme for 2014-2033 and its preparations for an application to the next GSP system to be determined in 2024. The delegation urged Pakistan to undertake timely reforms and legislative changes on human rights issues with determined and structured action, including the quick adoption of laws against torture and enforced disappearance, and to substantially reduce the number of crimes carrying the death penalty.

In September, Pakistan Foreign Minister Bilawal Bhutto demanded "climate justice" from the world. Also, in September, a draft paper by the United Nations Development Programme (UNDP) proposed that Pakistan's creditors should consider allowing debt relief so Pakistan can prioritize financing its disaster response over repayment of loans.

Pakistani and Chinese governments deepened extensive economic and political ties in 2022, and work continued on the China-Pakistan Economic Corridor, a project consisting of construction of roads, railways, and energy pipelines.

In September, US Secretary of State Antony Blinken met Foreign Minister, Bilawal Bhutto Zardari to commemorate the 75th anniversary of US-Pakistan relations noting:r "We've had our differences; that's no secret. But we share a common objective: a more stable, a more peaceful, and free future for all of Afghanistan and for those across the broader region." USAID Administrator Samantha Power visited Pakistan as part of a flood relief effort that brought $56 million in assistance. Earlier in the year, former Prime Minister Imran Khan alleged US involvement in his removal from office calling it a US-backed "regime change" operation in connivance with the then Pakistani opposition parties and referring to a "cipher" as evidence. The US denied these allegations..

Papua New Guinea

Although a resource-rich country, almost 40 percent of Papua New Guinea's (PNG) population lives in poverty. The Covid-19 pandemic highlighted ongoing challenges with economic mismanagement and a severely under-resourced health care system. Weak implementation of laws on violence against women and children fosters a culture of impunity. In January, PNG's parliament voted to repeal the death penalty, 30 years after it was reintroduced.

In August, James Marape was sworn in for a second term as prime minister following an election marred by violence, delays, and electoral irregularities, including the burning of ballot boxes by frustrated voters not on the common roll in East Sepik and Hela. The PNG government sent extra security personnel to the Highlands in response to tribal fighting during the election period, after armed men killed at least 18 people in an attack in Enga Province. Thousands of people fled the violence, which also caused damage to schools and hospitals. The United Nations condemned the escalation of violence, calling for an investigation and prosecution of perpetrators. Police investigated 15 candidates for election-related violence in Enga; at time of writing, the candidates were on the run. In September, the UN estimated that 89,000 people had been displaced by violence in Papua New Guinea's Highlands since May.

Over 1,000 people were displaced by violence in Goroka town in September that followed the killing of the chief executive officer of PNG Ports Corporation in September.

Pressures on media freedom continued. In February, the head of news and current affairs at EMTV was suspended and later sacked, reportedly on the orders of a government minister, after the news team ran stories about an Australian businessman operating in PNG facing criminal charges.

Women's and Girl's Rights

PNG remains one of the most dangerous places to be a woman or girl. Over 1.5 million people experience gender-based violence each year. In April, a special parliamentary committee tabled its final report on measures to prevent violence against women and girls, recommending that PNG's parliament establish a permanent committee on gender-based violence.

In February 2022, parliament passed legislation to strengthen criminal penalties for "sorcery"-related violence, which continues. In July, following the death of a prominent businessman, nine women in Enga Province were accused of "sorcery" by members of the businessman's tribe and were splashed with petrol, burned, and assaulted vaginally with hot iron rods. Police rescued five of the women, but assailants killed four. Perpetrators of "sorcery"-related violence are rarely prosecuted. At time of writing, it appeared that no arrests had been made in the case, although the police commander said key suspects would be arrested soon.

PNG laws designed to protect women and children, including the Lukautim Pikinini (Child Welfare) Act 2015 and the Family Protection Act 2013, are rarely enforced. Initiatives such as Family Sexual and Violence Units within the police force remain limited. A dire lack of services for survivors of gender-based violence compounds the problem.

PNG has one of the highest maternal mortality rates in the world. More than 2,000 women and girls die in childbirth in PNG each year; their deaths are largely preventable. The risk of maternal death is increased by limited access to hospitals, with more than 80 percent of the population living outside urban centers.

Two women won parliamentary seats in the national election, returning women to the PNG parliament for the first time in five years.

Children's Rights

PNG has an underfunded health system. One in thirteen children die each year, mostly from preventable diseases.

Although school attendance rates for children have improved, the United Nations Children's Fund, UNICEF, estimates that a quarter of primary and secondary school-aged children do not attend school, especially girls. Just 15 percent of children have had their birth officially registered, with undocumented children more vulnerable to trafficking and exploitation.

Police Abuse

Police in PNG have a long record of violence with impunity, including against children. During the national election, police allegedly shot dead a 22-year-old woman holding her baby when they fired into the crowd at a polling booth in Port Moresby. Police said they were investigating the incident, but at time of writing it was unclear whether any investigation had commenced.

PNG police are severely understaffed, chronically underfunded, and often lack resources such as petrol, stationery, and vehicles. Police were ill-equipped to prevent outbreaks of violence during the national election.

Asylum Seekers and Refugees

At time of writing, less than 100 refugees and asylum seekers transferred there by the Australian government since 2013, remained in PNG. The Australian government withdrew from offshore processing in PNG at the end of 2022. New Zealand has agreed to work with UNHCR on referrals from PNG.

Refugees and asylum seekers in PNG continued to endure violence and harassment, with little protection from authorities. Medical facilities have proven unable to cope with the complex medical needs of asylum seekers, particularly their mental health needs.

Land and Environmental Rights

Mining contributes 10 percent of gross domestic product, but is a key driver of environmental and human rights harms.

In February, the Bougainville government agreed with local landowners to re-open the Panguna copper and gold mine in the autonomous region of Bougainville. The mine closed in 1989 due to community anger at environmental damage and inequitable profits, leading to a decade-long conflict between the central government and rebels in Bougainville. The mine's former operator, Rio Tinto, in 2021 agreed to fund an independent environmental and human rights impact assessment of the mine, following a 2020 complaint about the mine's impact on communities' health and environment.

While contributing very little to global emissions that are driving the climate crisis, coastal and island communities in PNG are facing serious climate impacts as sea-level rise and coastal erosion limit access to food and water, and force residents to relocate. Carterets Islanders, some of the world's first communities displaced by the effects of climate change, are dependent on government food rations as rising sea levels and increased flooding destroy food crops.

In December 2021, parts of Papua New Guinea experienced a surge in king tides that flooded communities and displaced approximately 53,000 people. In May 2022, the International Organization for Migration delivered assistance in response to flooding induced by king tides in East Sepik, Manus, and the Autonomous Region of Bougainville.

Deforestation and forest degradation drive a significant portion of the country's emissions, though PNG committed to reducing emissions from these sources by 2030. According to Global Forest Watch, from 2020 to 2021, PNG lost around 88,000 thousand hectares of primary humid tropical forest. PNG has increased export of harvested timber in recent years, and struggles to regulate and manage logging companies.

Disability Rights

PNG has developed a national disability policy; however, the government has yet to pass comprehensive disability legislation.

In many cases, people with disabilities are unable to participate in community life or work because of lack of accessibility, stigma, and other barriers. Children with disabilities in PNG face abuse, discrimination, and a wide range of barriers to education. Access to mental health services and other support services are limited, and many people with psychosocial disabilities and their families often consider traditional healers to be their only option.

Sexual Orientation and Gender Identity

Same-sex relations are punishable by up to 14 years' imprisonment under PNG's criminal code. While there is little information on actual convictions, the law is sometimes used as a pretext by officials and employers to harass or extort money from gay and lesbian people in Papua New Guinea.

Right to Health

The fragile health system in PNG is underfunded and overwhelmed, with high rates of malaria and diabetes among its population of more than 8 million. PNG also has one of the highest rates of tuberculosis in the world, with an estimated 30,000 new cases per year. Critical resources have been diverted from tuberculosis to respond to Covid-19.

Key International Actors

Both the Chinese and Australian governments are vying for influence in the Pacific. Australia is the largest provider of aid and investment to PNG. For 2022-23, Australia will provide an estimated AU$479 million (US$320 million) in bilateral funding to Papua New Guinea, and an estimated AU$596 million (US$399 million) in official development assistance.

Australia and PNG have strong security ties. In August, PNG's Foreign Minister Justin Tkatchenko announced PNG is moving to negotiate a security treaty with Australia and potentially New Zealand. In 2022, Australia committed AU$580 million (US$396 million) to upgrade ports in PNG, and signed a Memorandum of Understanding with PNG to rebuild the country's air force.

The Chinese government also provides significant development and economic support to PNG. Beijing signed a security agreement with the Solomon Islands in March, but Beijing was unsuccessful in reaching a sweeping trade and security deal with 10 countries in the region, including PNG.

Chinese Foreign Minister Wang Yi visited PNG in June, prior to the national election. Days before the visit, the Chinese government released a position paper about its relations with Pacific countries that highlighted "mutual respect" and "common development" and focused on economic, technical, and social cooperation.

In March 2022, the Human Rights Council adopted the final outcome report on the Universal Periodic Review of PNG. In July, then-UN High Commissioner Michelle Bachelet wrote to PNG's foreign minister welcoming PNG's actions to repeal the death penalty and legislative steps to strengthen criminal penalties for sorcery-related violence, but expressed concern about the rights of women, girls, and LGBT people.

Peru

President Pedro Castillo decreed at least four states of emergency in 2022, suspending basic rights and deploying armed forces on streets and highways, supposedly to fight crime and respond to a strike. Peruvian rules for use of force by security forces do not comply with international standards.

The attorney general charged the president with corruption-related crimes. Prosecutors have accused him of obstructing corruption investigations.

Multiple members of Congress and the runner-up in the 2021 presidential election, Keiko Fujimori, are also under investigation on various criminal charges.

Congress replaced six of the seven members of the Constitutional Court in May through a selection process that lacked sufficient transparency.

Earlier in the year, the court issued several rulings that were inconsistent with international human rights standards, including on same-sex marriage, Indigenous rights, and justice for crimes against humanity.

Threats to freedom of expression and violence against women and defenders of environmental and Indigenous rights remain major concerns.

Judicial Independence and Rule of Law

As of September, prosecutors had opened six investigations into alleged corruption and other crimes against President Castillo, his relatives, and members of his administration. In October, the attorney general charged the president and two former cabinet members with belonging to a criminal organization, influence peddling and collusion.

The attorney general accused the administration, in August, of "constant obstruction" of investigations against the president. President Castillo called those investigations politically motivated.

In July, a former interior minister said the president dismissed him after he created a police unit to work with prosecutors investigating corruption in his administration. He was in office for two weeks.

In September, the head of the National Police Search Unit, who led a search in the presidential palace as part of a corruption investigation, was removed, a decision that the chief anti-corruption prosecutor viewed as retaliatory. In response to criticism, the administration reinstated him.

An obscure constitutional provision allows Congress to find the president "morally incapable" of governing and declare the presidency "vacated." In recent years, Congress has misused the provision, including, in 2020, to remove then-President Martín Vizcarra. Members have twice attempted to remove President Castillo by applying it. They were trying a third time, as of September 2022.

The congressional committee leading the selection process for Constitutional Court members did not apply consistent evaluation criteria or ensure sufficient transparency and civil-society participation. The committee presented the full Congress with six candidates for six vacancies, preventing it from making a genuine selection. Congress approved them in May. The replacement of a seventh member remained pending, as of October.

Public Security

Police used excessive force in Lima in 2020, during largely peaceful protests about the removal of President Vizcarra. Over 200 people were injured, and two protesters killed. The attorney general charged President Manuel Merino—the president of Congress who took over as President after Vizcarra's removal—and his prime minister and interior minister with involvement in abuses. A congressional subcommittee, in June 2022, blocked the prosecution after approving a flawed report that ignored solid evidence of human rights violations during the protests.

President Castillo issued disproportionate emergency decrees—in February, March, and April—suspending freedom of movement and assembly, permitting arbitrary home searches and arrests, and allowing deployment of the armed forces in Lima and neighboring Callao, supposedly to fight crime. An additional April decree suspended similar rights throughout the national road network, in response to a transportation workers strike. The states of emergency were no longer in effect as of September.

Congress passed a law in 2020 eliminating an explicit requirement that use of force be proportionate and granting police new protections against prosecution. Under Peru's use of force rules, the police and armed forces cannot be held criminally responsible for causing injuries or even death "when fulfilling their constitutional duty" and using their weapons "in accordance with regulations." In February 2022, the government approved state-of-emergency rules allowing police to request the armed forces to back them up, including by firing their weapons, when police "capacity," during any operation, is "overwhelmed."

In June 2022, then-Interior Minister Dimitri Senmache incorrectly told police officers that when "a criminal picks up a weapon, they lose the right to life."

Confronting Past Abuses

The Shining Path, other armed groups, or state agents killed or disappeared almost 70,000 people, Peru's Truth and Reconciliation Commission estimates, during an armed conflict from 1980 to 2000. The vast majority of those killed were low-income farmers; most spoke Indigenous languages.

Authorities have made slow progress in prosecuting abuses by government forces during the conflict. As of September 2022, courts had issued 50 convictions in 92 cases, Peruvian human rights groups reported.

Former President Alberto Fujimori (1990-2000) was sentenced in 2009 to 25 years in prison for crimes against humanity and corruption. In 2017, then-President Pedro Pablo Kuczynski granted him a humanitarian pardon on claims of illness. The Supreme Court, in 2018, reversed the pardon, but the Constitutional Court reinstated it in March 2022. The Inter-American Court of Human Rights then ordered Peru not to release Fujimori, and authorities, as of September, were abiding by that.

In March 2021, prosecutors charged Fujimori and three former health ministers with the forced sterilizations of thousands of mostly poor and Indigenous women during his presidency. The case remains pending.

In February 2022, the Constitutional Court upheld a 2013 decision that the 1986 killing, by Navy officers, of 113 detainees was not a crime against humanity. The ruling allows the statute of limitations to apply to the officers, which could lead to closing ongoing trials.

Freedom of Expression

Threats to freedom of expression remain a serious concern in Peru, as several journalists face prosecution for their work.

Peru's penal code punishes defamation with up to two years in prison, violating international standards. President Castillo's allies in Congress introduced a bill, in August, to increase the sentence to up to four years.

Charges of defamation have repeatedly been used to stifle reporting in the public interest in Peru, the Committee to Protect Journalists said.

Since late 2018, journalists Paola Ugaz and Pedro Salinas have faced criminal prosecution for alleged defamation and other offenses in several cases in connection with their reporting on sexual abuse scandals involving a Catholic lay organization. In five of seven cases, courts dismissed the case or complainants withdrew them.

Similarly, former presidential candidate César Acuña filed a criminal complaint against journalists Christopher Acosta and Daniel Yovera, and publisher Jerónimo Pimentel, for defamation, after they reported on accusations of corruption against Acuña. A judge sentenced Acosta and Pimentel to two years in prison and payment of over US$ 100,000 in damages. Acuña later dropped the complaint, and the convictions were annulled.

Women's and Girls' Rights

Gender-based violence is a significant problem. The Ministry of Women reported 136 femicides, defined as the killing of a woman in certain contexts, including domestic violence, in 2021—and 75 between January and August 2022.

Women and girls can legally access abortions only when a pregnancy threatens their life or health. In 2014, the Ministry of Health adopted technical guidelines for legal abortions, but many health service providers have failed to implement them, creating barriers to access. As of September, Congress was discussing a bill recognizing the "right to be born," which if approved, could become an additional obstacle to accessing a legal abortion.

Free distribution of emergency contraception pills has been subject to litigation since 2006. The pills have been distributed free of charge, pursuant to an injunction, since 2016. A ruling by the Constitutional Court on the constitutionality of free emergency contraception is pending.

In February, the UN Committee on the Elimination of Discrimination against Women urged Peru to fully decriminalize abortion and ensure effective investigations, prosecution, and punishment in gender-based violence cases.

Children's Rights

In June, Congress passed a law mandating shared custody of children between divorced or separated parents, as a general rule. Rights groups warned that it violates children's rights to safety, health, and well-being, and the rights of women, particularly those who are victims of domestic abuse.

In May, Congress passed a law granting parents' associations discretion to approve or reject educational materials. The law enables the restriction of comprehensive sexuality and gender education in schools. A lawsuit against it remained pending as of September.

Sexual Orientation and Gender Identity

During the 2021 campaign, President Castillo made disparaging comments about trans people and, once in office, appointed several ministers with a record of homophobic comments.

Same-sex couples are not allowed to marry or enter into civil unions. In 2021, certain courts recognized same-sex marriages contracted by Peruvians abroad. But in April 2022, the Constitutional Court ruled against recognizing any same-sex marriage abroad, by either Peruvians or foreigners.

An appeals court, in January, overturned a decision allowing trans Peruvians to change their name and gender marker on national identity documents. An appeal before the Constitutional Court remained pending as of September.

Environment and Indigenous Rights

At least seven environmental defenders, including six Indigenous people, were killed from January through September 2022. Their communities believe they were killed because of their defense of the environment.

In 2019, the Ministry of Justice established an inter-agency mechanism for protection of human rights defenders, but communities and rights groups complain it is ineffective.

Peru signed the Escazú Agreement, a treaty promoting access to information and the protection of environmental defenders, in 2018, but Congress voted against ratification in 2020. A congressional commission rejected ratification again in July 2022.

The right to free, prior, and informed consent of Indigenous people about measures and projects that affect them is enshrined in Peruvian law, and the country has ratified International Labor Organization Convention 169, which also protects this right. Yet, in March, the Constitutional Court dismissed the right of consultation of the Puno Chila Chambilla and Chila Pucara Indigenous communities, arguing that the right is not "fundamental" because it is not spelled out in the constitution.

In January, an oil tanker transferring crude oil to a refinery spilled at least 11,900 barrels in the ocean, Peru's government said. The spill reached at least 80 kilometers of coast, included protected areas, and affected the livelihoods of fishing and tourism workers, and other local residents, UN experts said.

Refugees and Migrants

As of June, the United Nations High Commissioner for Refugees reported more than 1.3 million Venezuelan migrants and asylum seekers in Peru. Peru had received more than 606,000 asylum requests from Venezuelans as of January, the Ombudsperson's Office said, and had granted asylum to 4,125—less than 1 percent.

President Castillo's government has acted increasingly hostile to Venezuelan migrants. In December 2021, the government tried to fly 41 undocumented migrants—none with criminal records in Peru—to Venezuela but failed to secure authorization to enter Venezuelan air space.

In August, President Castillo announced a program to expel migrants who "have come to commit crimes" in Peru.

A bill pending before Congress, as of September, would allow the government to limit the entry of foreigners for reasons of "national security, public health, internal order and public safety."

Philippines

The six-year term of President Rodrigo Duterte, which ended on June 30, was defined by the politics of threats and intimidation, thousands of extrajudicial killings of mostly impoverished Filipinos from urban areas, and serious damage to the country's democratic institutions. Since the inauguration of Ferdinand Marcos Jr. as president, the human rights situation has hardly changed.

The United Nations Office of the High Commissioner for Human Rights (OHCHR), in a September report that assessed the progress of the Philippines-UN Joint Program on Human Rights, which began in June 2021, laid out major human rights problems facing the country. Among these are the continued "harassment, threats, arrests, attacks, red-tagging against civil society actors, as well as the continued drug related killings by police." The report also noted that "access to justice for victims of human rights violations and abuses remained very limited."

President Marcos has sought to reassure the international community that he is committed to human rights. His officials, speaking before the United Nations Human Rights Council in October, highlighted several steps that they intended to take, while asserting that the human rights situation in the Philippines has improved. Human rights and civil society groups, however, debunked these claims with reports to the council of continuing human rights violations.

"Drug War" Killings

Soon after taking office on June 30, President Marcos stated he would continue the "war against drugs" initiated by his predecessor. While Marcos claimed his administration would do a "slightly different" anti-drug campaign by focusing on the rehabilitation of drug users, the unlawful use of force by the police and government agents continued. Monitoring by Dahas, a program run by the Third World Studies Center of the University of the Philippines, found that at least 90 people had been killed in what the center termed "drug-related violence" in the period since Marcos' inauguration and September 30.

The government reported that members of the Philippine National Police and the Philippine Drug Enforcement Agency killed 6,252 individuals during anti-drug operations from July 1, 2016, to May 31, 2022. After Marcos took office, the government stopped releasing these statistics. The official death toll does not include those killed by unidentified gunmen whom Human Rights Watch and other rights monitors have credible evidence to believe operate in cooperation with local police and officials. The OHCHR calculated in a 2020 report that the death toll was at least 8,663. Domestic human rights groups and the government appointed Philippines Commission on Human Rights state that the real figure of "drug war" killings is possibly triple the number reported in the OHCHR report.

The authorities have seriously investigated very few "drug war" killings. Only a handful of cases—12 out of thousands—are in varying stages of investigation by police or active review by prosecutors. To date, there is only one case, the video-recorded murder of 17-year-old student Kian delos Santos in August 2017, which resulted in the conviction of police officers.

"Red-Tagging" and Harassment of Activists

Government and military officials accused civil society groups of being supporters of communist New People's Army (NPA) insurgents, who have been waging a 53-year armed conflict across the Philippines. Such accusations made without evidence are part of what is commonly known in the Philippines as "red-tagging," which put the accused at heightened risk of attack by the security forces or unidentified gunmen. The military, police, and other national security forces have actively used social media to convey "red tagging" threats, and in several cases, those red-tagged persons were subsequently killed by unknown gunmen.

The government's National Task Force to End Local Communist Armed Conflict, which works closely with the military, police, and the president's office, accused numerous political activists of being members of the Communist Party or the NPA. Among those red-tagged by the task force is former Vice President Leni Robredo, who lost to Marcos in the recent presidential election. The task force has also red-tagged journalists, book publishers, and international nongovernmental groups (NGOs), including Oxfam.

In September, Judge Marlo Magdoza-Malagar, a judge of the Manila Regional Trial Court who had dismissed a case that sought to declare as "terrorist groups" the Communist Party of the Philippines and its armed wing, became a target of red-tagging, prompting lawyers' groups and even the Supreme Court to intervene. The court specifically demanded an explanation from former National Task Force spokesperson Lorraine Badoy why she should not be held in contempt.

Leaders and lawyers of peasant organizations and human rights groups who were red-tagged have been physically harmed by government security forces and vigilantes; several have been killed. Others were harassed, such as a group of nuns and peasant women who were charged with aiding "terrorist activities." In June, Clarita Carlos, the new chairperson of the National Security Council, publicly said that she did not favor red-tagging. Despite this declaration, the practice continued.

Attacks against Journalists

On October 3, unidentified gunmen fatally shot Percival Mabasa, a radio commentator in Las Pinas, a city in Metro Manila. Popularly known on-air and online as Percy Lapid, he was the second journalist killed since President Marcos took office. On September 18, a man stabbed radio broadcaster Renato Blanco to death in Negros Oriental in the central Philippines. Two other journalists were murdered in 2022, according to UNESCO. Federico Gempesaw, a radio commentator, was shot dead on June 29 in Cagayan de Oro City, while Jaynard Angeles, also a radio journalist, was killed on January 12 in Tacurong City, in the southern Philippines.

Apart from these killings, the harassment of journalists also persisted in the past year. In July, the government sought to silence journalists critical of the administration by shutting down websites Bulatlat and Pinoy Weekly, two alternative press publications. The National Security Council sought to close these two outlets because of alleged links to communist insurgency, a charge the editors and journalists denied.

During the year, the government used the cyber-libel law several times against journalists, columnists, critics of the government, and ordinary social media users. In August, police arrested activist and former member of parliament Walden Bello after a staff member in the office of Vice President Sara Duterte, the daughter of the former president, made allegations against him.

The Justice Department's Office of Cybercrime reported that 3,700 cyber-libel cases were filed as of May 2022. Of that number, 1,317 were filed in court while

1,131 were dismissed. Twelve cases ended in a conviction. Among those who have been convicted of cyber-libel is 2021 Nobel Peace Prize laureate Maria Ressa, the CEO of the news website Rappler.

Arbitrary Detention of Leila de Lima

Former Senator Leila de Lima, 62, one of the foremost critics of ex-President Duterte, remained in police detention since her arrest on trumped-up drug charges in 2017. De Lima faces unsubstantiated charges alleging that she received money from drug lords while serving as justice secretary. Her detention continues even though two key witnesses in the Philippine government's case against her have retracted their testimonies. Human Rights Watch believes the Duterte administration was retaliating against her for investigating extrajudicial killings under Duterte's anti-drug campaign.

Key International Actors

In September, the UN high commissioner for human rights released a report that highlighted prevailing rights violations and recommended continued monitoring and reporting to the council. Nevertheless, in October, the UN Human Rights Council failed to come up with a resolution to continue the council's scrutiny of the human rights situation in the Philippines. The UN human rights office, civil society organizations, and families of victims of abuses expressed their dire concerns about the situation in the Philippines.

The United Kingdom, Ireland, Norway, Australia, and the Netherlands have contributed to the UN-Philippines Joint Program designed to institutionalize human rights reforms in the Philippines.

In June, the prosecutor of the International Criminal Court (ICC) requested authorization from the court's judges to resume an investigation into possible crimes against humanity committed in the context of Duterte's "drug war." In November 2021, the Philippine government had requested a deferral of the ICC's probe under the principle of complementarity, claiming that it had begun its own investigations into cases of extrajudicial killings attributed to the police during "drug war" operations. The ICC prosecutor's office determined that the Philippine government failed to demonstrate it was taking steps to investigate several of the killings and hold perpetrators to account; it is now awaiting judicial review of its request to move forward with the investigation.

In February, the European Parliament adopted a resolution condemning the Philippine government's abuses and urging the European Commission to set "clear, public, time-bound benchmarks" for the Philippines to comply with its human rights obligations under the EU's GSP+ scheme, which is a condition for the country to keep its unilateral trade benefits. In March, EU officials visited the Philippines and urged "tangible and measurable progress" in that regard. Bilateral human rights discussions were again held in October.

The Philippines remains the biggest recipient of US foreign military assistance in the Asia-Pacific region, receiving a total of US$1.14 billion since 2015. In September, it was reported that the US government would be reprogramming $130 million in military aid it held back from Egypt and for new climate initiatives for Pacific Island nations, including the Philippines. US legislators have been calling for improved human rights compliance by Manila, particularly in the case of detained former Senator Leila de Lima.

Poland

Government attacks on judicial independence and rule of law remained a serious concern. Women's sexual and reproductive rights and activists continued to be under attack. Officials continued to use anti-LGBT rhetoric. Independent media outlets and journalists faced threats and obstacles in their reporting. While Poland admitted millions of people fleeing the war in Ukraine, unlawful pushbacks of migrants and asylum seekers from other parts of the world continued at the border with Belarus.

Judicial Independence

In its Rule of Law report published in July, the European Commission flagged that "serious concerns persist related to the independence of the Polish judiciary." The government continued to ignore calls to address the lack of independence and effectiveness of the Constitutional Tribunal.

In March, the Constitutional Tribunal confirmed a motion by Minister of Justice and Prosecutor General Zbigniew Ziobro stating that the way the European Court of Human Rights (ECtHR) had interpreted Article 6(1)—the right to a fair trial—of the European Convention on Human Rights was unconstitutional. In response, 27 former Polish Constitutional Tribunal judges in a public statement called out the tribunal's ruling, deeming it "another scandalous example of jurisprudence violating the Constitution."

Also in March, 94 active and former judges of Poland's Supreme Court called on Polish parliamentarians to fully implement judgments by the ECtHR and Court of Justice of the EU (CJEU) and scrap the politicized National Council of the Judiciary—the body responsible for nominating judges.

As a result of a 2021 CJEU ruling finding the Supreme Court's Disciplinary Chamber unlawful and incompatible with European Union standards, a bill passed by the Sejm in May abolished the chamber in its existing form, while retaining some its functions in a new Professional Liability Chamber at the Supreme Court.

The changes were largely cosmetic as they do not contain an obligation to reinstate unlawfully suspended judges and do not provide guarantees against influence by the executive for the functioning of an independent and impartial disciplinary system for judges. The changes failed to address the core issue of the continued appointment of judges to this new chamber in charge of disciplinary matters by the National Council of the Judiciary. Between June 2018 and June 2022, the Disciplinary Commissioner for Judges of Common Courts charged 127 judges with disciplinary offenses and filed indictments at lower courts in 38 cases. Courts delivered non-final sentences in 13 cases, among them two convictions.

The Supreme Court in June ruled that the country's National Council of the Judiciary is inconsistent with the constitution due to political interference. The government rejected claims that the council was under political control.

The European Commission in July took further steps in its infringement procedure on the violations of EU law by the Constitutional Tribunal and issued a reasoned opinion against Poland, saying that it "no longer meets the requirement of an independent and impartial tribunal previously established by law." It follows a 2021 ruling by the Constitutional Tribunal that found EU treaty provisions incompatible with the Polish constitution, thereby questioning supremacy of EU law and binding nature of CJEU rulings.

Freedom of Media

The government continued to interfere with the work of independent media outlets and journalists. Poland ranks 66, down from 64 in 2021, in the World Press Freedom Index of Reporters Without Borders. In its rule of law report, the European Commission stressed that the general environment for journalists continued to deteriorate and flagged concerns over restrictions on access to public information under the state of emergency.

Prior to lifting the state of emergency on its border with Belarus in July, authorities continued to prevent journalist from entering and reporting in the designated exclusion zone along the border with Belarus.

In two separate incidents in January, the adult children of two journalists, Wojciech Czuchnowski, a reporter at daily newspaper Gazeta Wyborcza, and Tomasz Lis, editor-in-chief at Newsweek Polska weekly, received death threats saying "we will kill you because you betray the motherland." Czuchnowski and Lis separately received similar threats. Both were known for reporting that was critical of the government. Police were investigating at time of writing.

In February, freelance journalist Pablo González was arrested by the Polish Security Services in Rzeszow close to the border with Ukraine, where he was reporting on the refugee crisis caused by Russia's invasion. He was accused of conducting illegal espionage on behalf of the Russian state. González's detention was twice extended by a Polish court. At time of writing, González remained in detention. Press freedom organizations raised concerns about the lack of evidence.

TVN24, a television station critical of the government, came under pressure in February after politicians from the United Right coalition tried to interfere with its editorial policy when three right-wing members of parliament were corrected by a TV-show host for making incorrect claims about rising energy prices. In addition, in a separate interview, Prime Minister Morawiecki the next day falsely accused TVN24's parent company of unpatriotic behavior by broadcasting Russian propaganda.

Sexual Orientation and Gender Identity

Government officials and aligned organizations continued to publicly smear lesbian, gay, bisexual, and transgender (LGBT) people.

The more than 90 regions and municipalities who declared themselves "LGBT Ideology Free" or adopted "charter of family rights" contribute to create a climate of fear among LGBT people. In February 2022, Parliament passed legislation granting government "educational welfare officers" authority to decide on types of extracurricular or educational activities in schools, and established a complex bureaucracy for approving or refusing activities—measures seen as a smoke screen to attack LGBT and reproductive rights. Poland's President vetoed the law in March 2022.

In a positive move in June, the Supreme Administrative Court ordered four municipalities to revoke their "LGBT Ideology Free" declaration as they were deemed discriminatory and pose a risk of violence against LGBT people.

Activists were subjected to SLAPP (strategic lawsuits against public participation) suits. SLAPPs are civil lawsuits intended to intimidate, censor, and silence critics by burdensome legal defense costs. In May, a lower court in Rzeszow rejected a case from the Niebylec commune against LGBT activist Bartosz Staszewski for alleged defamation over social media posts and media comments referring to the commune as an "LGBT Free-Zone." Niebylec was one of dozens of communities in Poland, which in 2019 passed a resolution to "stop LGBT ideology."

Women's Rights

Attacks on women's sexual and reproductive rights and women's rights activists continued.

Marta Lempart, a prominent women's rights activist, during the year had at least 10 lawsuits and charges filed against her because of her work. In total, Lempart has had over 100 lawsuits and charges filed against her for her work. In April, Justyna Wydrzynska, an activist with Abortion Without Borders, was charged with assisting someone to have an abortion and illegal "marketing" of medication for helping a domestic violence survivor access pills for a self-managed medication abortion. Wydrzynska's trial was postponed three times due to key witnesses failing to appear; at time of writing, the next hearing was scheduled for January 2023. In November, parliament voted to strip MP Joanna Scheuring-Wielgus of her immunity so that she can be charged with offending religious beliefs for holding a banner in church supporting women's right to abortion in October 2020.

Women's rights organizations reported an increase in women reaching out to seek information about sexual and reproductive health and access to abortion. Between October 2020, when the Constitutional Tribunal virtually banned access to legal abortions, and November 2022, at least five women died after being denied abortions despite facing pregnancy complications. In September, prosecutors in Katowice charged three doctors with endangering the life and health of a woman who died from sepsis after her water broke at 22 weeks but doctors did not terminate the pregnancy; two of the doctors in the case were also charged with manslaughter.

In June, the minister of health signed a regulation requiring Polish doctors to record pregnancies in a national database, which took effect in October.

Women's and reproductive rights groups have raised concerns that such sensitive health data could be misused by authorities to intimidate or prosecute women who, for instance, experience spontaneous miscarriages.

Migration and Asylum

By end of September, due to Russia's full-scale invasion of Ukraine in February, over 6 million refugees had crossed into Poland and over 1,391,000 were provided temporary protection under the EU Temporary Protection Directive. In the large numbers of people fleeing to Poland and ensuing chaotic circumstances at the border and collection points, women and girls were at particular risk of trafficking, exploitation, and gender-based violence due to security gaps and lack of prevention and response measures in the reception efforts in Poland. Women and girls fleeing the war in Ukraine also face difficulties accessing safe and legal abortion, as well as emergency contraception, due to Poland's highly restrictive laws.

While extending a warm welcome to most refugees fleeing Ukraine, unlawful pushbacks of migrants and asylum seekers from other countries to Belarus, sometimes violent, continued. In May, three local Polish border police commanders confirmed the practice of pushbacks. While a September 2021 state of emergency was lifted on July 1, 2022, in theory allowing access to the exclusionary zone close to the border, activists reported volunteers continued to be prosecuted on bogus human smuggling charges.

In two cases, in June and September, courts in Poland ruled the practice of pushbacks unlawful.

In July, Felipe González Morales, the UN special rapporteur on the situation for migrants, called on Polish authorities to halt pushbacks to Belarus.

Qatar

Qatar hosted the 2022 FIFA World Cup between November and December 2022. The tournament brought a new level of global scrutiny to the serious abuses that migrant workers face in the country. Authorities have introduced several labor reforms, especially since 2018, yet the benefits of these reforms were limited by their narrow scope, late introduction, and poor enforcement. Qatari laws continue to discriminate against women and lesbian, gay, bisexual, and transgender (LGBT) individuals.

Migrant Workers

Migrant workers in Qatar who helped to make the 2022 World Cup possible continued to face serious abuses, including unexplained deaths, injuries, unpaid wages, and exorbitant recruitment fees, despite labor reforms.

The benefits of these reforms and related initiatives have been limited. The Workers' Support and Insurance Fund became operational only in 2020, and based on data from Qatar's Ministry of Labour, the fund had compensated over 36,000 workers a total of 597,591,986 QAR (US$164 million) as of July 2022. Widespread wage abuses have persisted, and migrant workers have resorted to protests and strikes against wage delays, which are prohibited in Qatar, and for which authorities arrested and deported some workers.

Workers still struggled to change jobs easily. Several initiatives by the Supreme Committee, such as the Universal Reimbursement Scheme, in which workers are reimbursed recruitment fees, are promising, but as of July 2022, they applied to fewer than 50,000 workers of Qatar's migrant worker population of over 2 million.

Abusive elements of the *kafala* (sponsorship) system remained intact. In particular, "absconding," or leaving an employer without permission, remains a crime. Passport confiscations, high recruitment fees, and deceptive recruitment practices remain widespread and largely unpunished.

The World Cup highlighted unexplained migrant worker deaths in Qatar, but authorities have failed to make public any detailed or meaningful data about the number of deaths or their causes. Qatari authorities have also failed to investigate the causes of deaths of thousands of migrant workers, many of which are attributed to "natural causes" or "cardiac arrest," which are not deemed work-related. Under Qatar's labor law, only deaths considered work-related are compensated. In 2021, Qatar introduced new measures to increase protection from heat stress, including the prohibition of work when the wet-bulb globe temperature exceeds 32.1 degrees Celsius (89.7 degrees Fahrenheit), but does not go far enough to sufficiently protect workers.

Human Rights Watch, alongside other human rights groups and unions, launched the #PayUpFIFA campaign in May calling on FIFA and Qatar to fulfill their human rights responsibilities and obligations by providing remedy, including financial compensation, for abuses since 2010 such as deaths, injuries, unpaid wages, and exorbitant recruitment fees.

Women's Rights

Human Rights Watch documented how Qatari laws, regulations, and practices impose discriminatory male guardianship rules on women and harm women's abilities to make autonomous decisions about their lives and their rights. Women in Qatar must obtain permission from their male guardians to marry, pursue higher education on government scholarships, work in many government jobs, travel abroad until certain ages, and receive some forms of reproductive health care.

Unmarried Qatari women below 25 require their guardian's permission to travel outside Qatar, and men can petition a court to prohibit their wives and other female relatives' travel. Qatari women are also prohibited from events and bars serving alcohol, while unmarried Qatari women under 30 cannot check into some hotels.

Unmarried women who report sexual violence can be prosecuted for non-marital sex if authorities do not believe them with a penalty of up to seven years' imprisonment, as well as floggings if they are Muslim. Moreover, unmarried women who are pregnant or subjected to rape or other sexual violence are unable to receive necessary sexual and reproductive healthcare, as authorities require a marriage certificate for such access.

Qatar's Family Law also discriminates against women in marriage, divorce, legal responsibility for children, and inheritance. Women are required to obey their husbands and can lose their husband's financial support if they work or travel against their wishes. Men have a unilateral right to divorce; women must apply to the courts for divorce on limited grounds. Women are also denied the authority to act as their children's guardians, even when they are divorced and have primary legal responsibility for the children's residence and care.

Qatar's Family Law forbids husbands from hurting their wives physically or morally, and there are general criminal code provisions on assault. But there is no law on domestic violence or measures to protect survivors and prosecute their abusers. Qatar does not explicitly prohibit all corporal punishment of children by law.

In 2021 and 2022, Qatari women told Human Rights Watch that they were forced to return home or forcibly admitted to a psychiatric hospital after the authorities refused to support their wishes to live independently from their abusive families. Families can report women to the police for "absence" if they leave the home to reside elsewhere. The 2016 Mental Health Law allows for involuntary hospitalization, that is detention, including by male guardians or other Qatari authorities for three months, which is renewable, with no role given to the judiciary to review such detention.

While children and non-citizen spouses of Qatari men can obtain citizenship, children and non-citizen spouses of Qatari women can only obtain citizenship under narrow conditions, which is discriminatory.

Sexual Orientation and Gender Identity

Preventive Security Department Forces in Qatar arbitrarily arrest lesbian, gay, bisexual, and transgender (LGBT) people and subject them to ill-treatment in detention. Security forces pick people off the streets and in public places based solely on their gender expression, and unlawfully search their phones in detention.

Human Rights Watch documented recent cases of severe and repeated beatings and sexual harassment in police custody. Security officers also inflicted verbal abuse, extracted forced confessions, forced detainees to sign pledges that they would "cease immoral activity," and denied detainees access to legal counsel, family, and medical care. As a requirement for their release, security forces mandated that transgender women detainees attend conversion therapy sessions at a government-sponsored "behavioral support" center.

Qatar's penal code punishes consensual sexual relations between males above sixteen with up to seven years imprisonment (Article 285). It provides penalties between one- and three-years' imprisonment (Article 296) for any male who "instigates" or "entices" another male to "commit an act of sodomy or immorality." A penalty of 10 years' imprisonment (Article 288) is imposed on anyone who engages in consensual sexual relations with a person above sixteen, outside marriage, which could apply to consensual same-sex relations between women, men, or heterosexual partners.

Freedom of Expression

Qatar's penal code criminalizes criticizing the emir, insulting Qatar's flag, defaming religion, including blasphemy, and inciting "to overthrow the regime." Qatar's 2014 cybercrimes law provided for a maximum of three years in prison or a fine of 500,000 Qatari riyal (around US$137,325) for anyone convicted of spreading "false news" on the internet or for posting online content that "violates social values or principles," or "insults or slanders others," or both punishments. In January 2020, Qatar amended its penal code to impose up to five years in prison for spreading "rumors" or "false news" with ill intent or a fine of 100,000 Qatari riyal (around $27,465), or both.

Abdullah Ibhais, a former media and communications director for the Supreme Committee for Delivery and Legacy, was first arrested in November 2019. He is currently serving a three-year jail sentence after being convicted of bribery in April 2021. Ibhais claims he was subjected to a malicious prosecution in retaliation for his criticism of the handling of a migrant workers' strike in Qatar in August 2019.

Statelessness

Qatar's decision to arbitrarily strip families from the Ghufran clan of their citizenship since 1996 has left some members stateless and deprived of their rights to work, education, healthcare, marriage and starting a family, property ownership, and freedom of movement. Without valid identity documents, they face restrictions in accessing basic services and risk arbitrary detention. Those living in Qatar are denied government benefits afforded to Qatari citizens, including state jobs, food and energy subsidies, and free basic healthcare.

Climate Change Policy and Actions

As a significant greenhouse gas emitter, Qatar is contributing to the climate crisis, which is taking a growing toll on human rights around the globe. The country has the sixth-highest greenhouse gas emissions per capita globally, a considerable portion from air conditioning. Qatar has taken few steps to move away from the production and use of fossil fuels and is instead doubling down on producing liquified natural gas (LNG) for export. It has the world's third-largest reserves of fossil gas and is the second-largest exporter of fossil gas. Qatar updated its first Nationally Determined Contribution (NDC) in August 2021, a Paris Agreement-mandated, five-year national climate change action plan, announcing an emissions reduction target of 25 percent by 2030.

As one of the world's hottest countries, Qatar is particularly vulnerable to the impacts of climate change. Ninety-seven percent of Qatar's population lives along an exposed coastline, making them particularly vulnerable to both sea level rise and extreme weather events. Doha faced flash floods in July.

Key International Actors

Pressure on Qatar to expand liquefied natural gas has grown due to Russia's invasion of Ukraine, especially from Europe, which has looked to Qatar's LNG as an alternative to Russian energy. Qatar is holding talks with Germany, the United Kingdom, and France, among others, to boost gas supplies.

In November, the European Parliament urged FIFA and Qatar to compensate widespread abuses that migrant workers suffered while building the 2022 World Cup infrastructure and condemned the participation of European companies in such abuses.

Russian Federation

Russia's full-scale invasion of Ukraine on February 24 also marked the start of a new, all-out drive to eradicate public dissent in Russia. Russian authorities doubled down in their relentless attack against civic activism, independent journalism, and political dissent, in an apparent attempt to silence public opposition to the war, any criticism of the government, or any expression of social non-conformism.

Parliament adopted a broad range of new bills introducing war censorship with long prison sentences for "offences" such as referring to the armed conflict in Ukraine as a "war," criticizing the invasion, discussing the conduct of Russian armed forces, and reporting on war crimes by Russian military or Ukrainian civilian casualties.

In their conduct of the war in Ukraine, Russian forces have carried out indiscriminate bombing and shelling in civilian areas, torture, arbitrary detention, enforced disappearances, forcible transfers of civilians to other occupied Ukrainian territories or to Russia, and extrajudicial killings of civilians in areas under Russian occupation. Ukrainian civilians have also been forcibly enlisted into Russia's armed forces. For more information on Russian forces' violations of the laws of war in Ukraine, including potential war crimes and crimes against humanity, see Ukraine chapter.

In addition to being suspended from the United Nations Human Rights Council and leaving the Council of Europe, Russia at home adopted a "besieged fortress" mentality, amplifying its rhetoric of malevolent foreign influence, and adopted bills akin to the Soviet-era ban on foreign contacts. The scope of these new laws varies from drastic expansion of the "foreign agents" legislation to include individuals or organizations "under foreign influence," to branding political candidates as "affiliated with foreign agents," and introducing strict control over international academic cooperation programs. Authorities also continued to add more individuals and groups to the "foreign agents" registry and blacklist foreign organizations as "undesirable."

Russian authorities also proposed new, homophobic legislation and ramped up homophobic and anti-migrant rhetoric.

Two large waves of emigration from Russia took place in 2022—one immediately after February 24 and the other after the announcement of a general military draft of reservists in September.

In September, Yevgeny Prigozhin, a close associate of President Vladimir Putin, confirmed his role as founder and a leader of the Russian private military contractor group Wagner; in November, Wagner opened its first headquarters, in St Petersburg. UN experts, several governments, and Human Rights Watch research found evidence that Wagner forces have summarily executed, tortured, and beaten civilians in Central African Republic in 2019. In Mali, Human Rights Watch has documented the involvement of forces widely believed to be associated with the Wagner group in serious abuses during military operations. Wagner has also played a role in Russia's war against Ukraine since the February invasion.

In October, President Putin declared martial law in Russian-occupied areas of Ukraine and in parallel introduced varying "alert levels" in bordering regions of Russia, authorizing local governors to impose differing limitations on rights, in particular freedom of movement.

Freedom of Expression

On February 24, as thousands of Russians peacefully protested the war against Ukraine and numerous public figures condemned the invasion, Roskomnadzor (RKN), Russia's state media and communications regulator, warned mass media against disseminating "unverified" and "false" information, demanded that media referred to the war only as a "special military operation," and required that they use information only from official Defense Ministry briefings. RKN said that failure to comply would result in instant blocking of online resources and hefty fines.

Between February 28 and March 3, 2022, Russian authorities blocked access to at least eight Russian-language media sites.

On March 4, Russia's parliament expeditiously adopted, and President Putin signed, new laws that effectively outlawed anti-war speech and protest. The laws, which entered into force immediately, criminalize spreading information about the conduct of Russian armed forces that deviates from official information and discrediting them or calling for them to withdraw. The maximum penalty is 15 years' imprisonment. Two weeks later, amendments expanded these provisions to penalize "discrediting" any Russian state agencies abroad.

An exodus by independent Russian and foreign media outlets, which had started shortly after the invasion, continued after the laws' adoption, due to concerns for journalists' security. Several prominent outlets relocated outside Russia or switched to alternative platforms for broadcasting such as social media.

Authorities closed several other prominent independent outlets. Novaya Gazeta suspended operations in Russia on March 28, after two RKN warnings. In subsequent weeks, authorities blocked two new Novaya Gazeta online platforms, launched in the wake of the suspension, for "discrediting" and "false information." In August, they fined Novaya Gazeta 650,000 rubles (more than US$10,000) for alleged "media freedom violations," and in early September, a Russian court annulled the newspaper's printing license.

The first three criminal cases on the new charges were opened on March 16. The first accused was placed in pretrial detention. In October, Russian authorities announced that they had opened over 4,500 administrative offence cases and over 100 criminal cases on "discreditation" or "false information" about Russian Armed Forces. According to Russian human rights watchdogs, almost half of the criminal cases were against journalists, bloggers, or civic activists.

The charges proved a convenient tool against prominent opposition figures, such as Vladimir Kara-Murza and Ilya Yashin, both in pretrial detention since April and June respectively, for criticizing, among other things, Russian forces' attacks on civilians. In August, opposition politician and former Yekaterinburg Mayor Yevgeniy Roizman was charged with "discreditation" for using the term "invasion."

In July, Aleksey Gorinov, a deputy of a Moscow municipal council, received the harshest sentence to date, seven years' imprisonment, with a four-year ban on holding official positions, for delivering an anti-war speech during a council meeting.

In August, the Justice Ministry issued guidelines, clarifying that a factual statement should be qualified as "intentionally false information" and expressing negative opinions about the conduct of the military as "discrediting."

Hundreds more were prosecuted on these charges for a wide range of actions, including displaying or the wearing the yellow and blue colors of the Ukrainian flag holding peaceful protests, and displaying anything that hinted at pro-peace slogans.

The new law also criminalized any repeat offense of calling for sanctions against Russia, its nationals, or legal entities, punishable by up to three years in prison.

Russian authorities escalated their "foreign agents" branding campaign, based on the law which imposes this toxic label and burdensome labelling and reporting requirements on people and entities that accept any amount of foreign funding and engage in activism. They designated as "foreign agents" well-known public figures who were vocal in their opposition to the war, including opposition politicians, musicians, and bloggers.

In some cases, authorities used the notion of "indirect funding," where recipients were held responsible for funding sources of, for example, their contractor. Also in April, Russian authorities for the first time used the registry of individual foreign agents, adding dozens of activists, journalists, and prominent figures and claiming they were receiving unspecified funding from Ukraine. In July, Putin signed a new bill that drastically expands the notion of foreign agents by making it about undefined "foreign influence" rather than foreign funding.

Another law adopted in 2022 penalizes public calls "against national security," including public calls to impede the work of the security services.

Another law criminalizes "confidential cooperation with a foreign state, international or foreign organization," reminiscent of the Soviet-era ban on contacts with foreigners.

In September 2022, the Moscow City Court sentenced journalist Ivan Safronov to 22 years in a maximum-security prison and a hefty fine on high treason charges. The case materials were classified and trial was closed, but independent journalists who obtained the indictment concluded that the information he supposedly transferred to foreign intelligence could be obtained from open sources. Safronov's defense lawyers came under immense pressure from the authorities: two had to flee the country, another at time of writing was in custody for his social media comment about Russian armed forces.

In October, authorities charged Kara-Murza with treason for criticizing the Kremlin publicly while abroad; it was the first time they invoked a provision that equates "assistance to international or foreign organization" with treason.

A June law introduced administrative penalties for equating the USSR's leadership or military to those of Nazi Germany, denying the Soviet people's decisive role in Nazi Germany's defeat, or denying "the USSR's humanitarian mission" during the liberation of European countries. In August, a court sentenced opposition politician Leonid Gozman to the maximum penalty, 15 days' detention, on these charges for an old social media post, in which he stated that Stalin was worse than Hitler because he unleashed a total war on his own people. After 15 days authorities immediately re-arrested and sentenced him on the same charges to another 15 days for a similar 2013 social media post.

In September, a St. Petersburg court sentenced Igor Maltsev (aka Yegor Skorokhodov) to 44 months in prison on charges of hooliganism aggravated by "political hatred" for burning a wicker statue dressed in military uniform to protest the war.

Freedom of Assembly

Russian authorities continued to use Covid-19 as a pretext for blanket bans on public assemblies organized by civic and political activists and prosecuted organizers and participants for noncompliance, despite lifting almost all other pandemic-related restrictions. The pandemic also did not prevent the authorities from holding mass pro-government or state-sponsored events.

For over a month after February 24, demonstrators in different parts of Russia held mass protests against Russia's invasion of Ukraine. The authorities responded with mass detentions, police brutality, and criminalization of anti-war protests. They arrested over 15,000 protesters in the first month alone and opened thousands of administrative and hundreds of criminal cases against them.

In September 2022, a wave of protests sparked by the introduction of the draft ("mobilization") for military reservists took place in different regions of Russia, notably in regions whose population consists of ethnic minorities but who are overrepresented in draft numbers and were among the highest-ranking among military casualties. In Dagestan, where mass protests lasted several days, authorities violently dispersed protesters and opened at least 20 criminal cases against protesters for alleged violence against police.

Russian authorities continued to use criminal provisions envisaging up to five years in prison merely for repeated participation in entirely peaceful, albeit unauthorized public assemblies. In August 2022, a court in Kaliningrad sentenced Vadim Khairullin to one year in prison for attending a protest in support of imprisoned opposition politician Alexei Navalny. At time of writing, Kirill Ukraintsev remained in pretrial detention where he had been since April on the same charges, for labor rights protests.

Freedom of Association

In 2022, Russian authorities also doubled down on blacklisting organizations as "undesirable" and persecuting activists for alleged involvement with such organizations.

Under Russia's repressive "undesirables" laws, the General Prosecutor's Office can designate as "undesirable" any foreign or international organization that allegedly undermines Russia's security, defense, or constitutional order. The organization must then cease its activities in Russia. Russian citizens' continued involvement with them carries a criminal penalty.

In 2022, new amendments allowed Russian law enforcement to prosecute activists for anything they might have done abroad that could be qualified as affiliation with "undesirable" organizations.

In May, a court sentenced Mikhail Iosilevich to 20 months imprisonment for allegedly providing space at his café for Open Russia—blacklisted as "undesirable" in 2019—even though it was in fact organized by another group and Iosilevich had no connection to Open Russia. In July, Andrey Pivovarov, the former executive director of the Open Russia Civic Movement, was sentenced to four years' imprisonment on charges of leading an "undesirable organization."

Human Rights Defenders

In late December 2021, the Russian Supreme Court ordered the closure of Memorial, Russia's most prominent human rights organization, in liquation proceedings against its two key entities, International Memorial Society and Memorial Human Rights Center. The proceedings had been initiated by prosecutors over alleged violations of the "foreign agents" law. The liquidation was finalized in February 2022, when the Supreme Court rejected their respective appeals.

Also, in late December 2021, Russian authorities blocked the website of OVD-Info, a human rights watchdog focusing on freedom of assembly.

In April 2022, Russian authorities revoked the registration of 15 foreign NGOs and foundations, forcing them to shut their offices in Russia, including Human Rights Watch and Amnesty International.

Torture, Ill-Treatment in Custody, Police Accountability

In July 2022, parliament adopted a law that explicitly introduced the notion of torture and provides for a penalty higher than other charges that had previously been used for cases that fit the international definition of torture, including in the context of coercion of confessions.

Nevertheless, ill-treatment, including torture, by law enforcement officials persisted.

On September 26 police arrested and beat Artyom Kamardin for public recitation of his anti-war poetry.

In September 2022, anti-fascist activist Yury Neznamov, detained on allegations of plotting a terrorist attack on a power plant, stated that he was electrocuted and waterboarded by Federal Security Service officers to coerce a confession.

In March, police at several precincts beat and used other physical violence against numerous anti-war protesters in custody. In September, three women anti-war protesters who had been tortured in Moscow police stations at that time, managed to identify their abusers, but authorities did not investigate.

Penitentiary administrations repeatedly placed Navalny and Yuri Dmitriyev, a researcher and rights advocate, in punishment cells known for their poor conditions. Both are serving lengthy prison sentences on politically motivated charges. From August to October, Navalny was sent to a punishment cell six times, Dmitriyev three times in less than a month, for minor "violations" of prison rules.

Chechnya

Chechen authorities under governor Ramzan Kadyrov continued to ruthlessly quash all forms of dissent. In December, Chechen security agents rounded up, subjected to ill-treatment and kept in incommunicado detention, dozens of family members of five Chechen bloggers and activists, who live abroad and criticized Kadyrov online. They forced the families to "apologize" and publicly dissociate themselves from their exiled relatives.

1ADAT, an anti-Kadyrov social media channel, was one of the key targets. In January, Chechen police abducted Zarema Mussaeva, the mother of 1ADAT's supposed administrator, Ibrahim Yangulbaev, and human rights lawyer Abubakar Yangulbaev, and forcibly brought her from Nizhny Novgorod to Chechnya, where she remained in detention at time of writing on bogus criminal charges.

In August, media reported on the extrajudicial execution of 19-year-old Salman Tepsurkayev dating back to September 2020, days after his abduction. Tepsurkayev moderated the Telegram channel 1ADAT, which routinely features Chechen dissident voices, including those critical of Kadyrov. Authorities have not opened an investigation into his disappearance or alleged torture and killing.

Kadyrov became a major official spokesman glorifying abusive warfare in Ukraine and in October he called for the "razing of Ukrainian cities to the ground." He organized the deployment of several thousand Chechen servicemen to Ukraine; human rights organizations reported complaints from Chechnya's residents about forced recruitment of their family members.

In November 2021, the European Court of Human Rights ruled in favor of Luisa Tapayeva, a divorced Chechen woman seeking to reunite with her four daughters. In Chechnya and other parts of the North Caucuses, local authorities enforce local customs that treat children as the property of their father and paternal family, which makes it difficult for single mothers to gain custody.

Counterterrorism and Counter-Extremism

In March 2022, authorities designated Meta, the new company name for Facebook, an extremist organization and blocked the use of Facebook and Instagram, another Meta-owed platform, for anti-war speech.

Lilia Chanysheva, the former head of Navalny's team in Ufa, remained in detention since her November 2021 arrest on unsubstantiated charges of leading an extremist group. In May 2022, Navalny was indicted on the same charges. In January, Russian authorities added Chanysheva, Navalny, and some of his aides and allies in exile to the registry of terrorists and extremists.

In 2022, dozens were fined on charges of displaying "extremist" symbols for social media posts that included or mentioned symbols of Navalny's "Smart Voting" electoral project, displayed the logo of the Foundation Against Corruption, or showed old photos taken with Navalny. The number of such cases in Moscow spiked in summer of 2022, apparently linked to the autumn municipal elections. Extremism-related convictions preclude candidates from running.

In October, Russian authorities charged Navalny and his supporters Chanysheva, Volkov, and Zhdanov with "propagating terrorism, publicly calling for extremism, financing extremist activities and "rehabilitating Nazism."

In late September, prosecutors started issuing bloggers warnings about "attracting users" on Facebook and Instagram, alleging that this may be considered as "extremist" activity. In October, they warned users against placing ads on these platforms.

In June, Tatarstan's Supreme Court ruled to ban as "extremist" the All-Tatar Public Center. In 2021 the Justice Ministry had suspended the center's activities on allegations of "ethnic enmity."

Russian courts sentenced at least 20 persons to 11 to 18 years in prison on politically motivated charges of membership of Hizb-ut-Tahrir (HuT), a pan-Islamist movement that seeks to establish a caliphate but denounces violence to achieve that goal. At least another 13 persons were detained on the same charges and also face lengthy prison terms. Russia banned HuT as a terrorist organization in 2003.

Police continued to raid houses and open new criminal cases against Jehovah's Witnesses, banned as "extremist" in Russia since 2017. In 2022, at least 84 Jehovah's Witnesses were sentenced to up to 7 years in prison, and 68 were behind bars awaiting trial.

Several people were indicted for supposed affiliation with Nurdzhular, a group of followers of the late Turkish theologian Said Nursi that Russia banned as extremist in 2008, even though it has no history of incitement or violence.

Environment, Climate Change, and Human Rights

As one of the world's top 10 emitters of greenhouse gases, Russia is contributing to the climate crisis that is taking a mounting toll on human rights around the globe. It is also the third largest producer of fossil fuels and a top gas exporter. The Climate Action Tracker rates Russia's climate action plan as "critically insufficient" to meet the Paris Agreement goal to limit global warming to 1.5°C above pre-industrial levels.

Watchdogs continued to report physical attacks, harassment, intimidation, and prosecution of grassroot activists and environmental groups.

Massive forest fires again raged in different parts of Russia and by late September nearly 4 million hectares of forests burned, over half of them in Siberia and Russia's Far Eastern region. Almost half of Russia's forests were explicitly excluded from fire-fighting measures, according to Greenpeace.

In September 2022, a group of environmental activists lodged the first ever "climate lawsuit" against the government in the Supreme Court, demanding radical reduction of Russia's greenhouse gas emissions.

Right to Asylum, Prohibition of Refoulement, Migration

Russian authorities facilitated forcible returns of North Korean workers who tried to escape strict surveillance by North Korean officials and apply for asylum.

In September 2021, Russian authorities adopted a law on simplified naturalization of foreigners who serve in the Russian military and started to actively lure and coerce migrants to join the Russian military, presumably to fight in Ukraine, and even opened a military recruitment office inside the migrant processing center in Moscow. In response, three Central Asian republics publicly warned their nationals of criminal liability for mercenary activities.

In one incident captured on camera, police harassed migrant workers from Central Asia, demanding that they go to the draft office and fight for Russia.

Domestic Violence, Sexual Orientation and Gender Identity

The government continued its trajectory of anti-lesbian, gay, bisexual, and transgender (LGBT) discrimination.

In February, a St. Petersburg court ruled in favor of the Justice Ministry's lawsuit to close Sphere Foundation, the legal entity used by Russian LGBT Network to receive funds and implement various efforts to support LGBT people.

In July, a court in Komsomolsk-na-Amure acquitted Yulia Tsvetkova, an artist and LGBT and women's rights activist, in an absurd, politically motivated criminal pornography case related to her activism, after 31 months of investigation and trial. Her appeal was pending at time of writing.

In October, a bill submitted by an MP from the ruling United Russia party that would extend to adults the existing ban on "gay propaganda" among children passed the first parliamentary reading. RKN supported the bill, stating that the "popularization of deviant relations does not fit with our society's traditional values" and that "such information ... is dangerous for the entire society."

A bill submitted to parliament in September would ban information about voluntary childlessness, which its authors consider "foreign ideology that forms destructive social behavior... [and] contradicts Russia's traditional family values and state policy."

Five years after the decriminalization of some forms of domestic violence, legislation to strengthen protections against and penalties for domestic abuse remains stalled. Groups report increasing numbers of women seeking assistance but continued underreporting to authorities as inadequate police and judicial response persists.

Rights to Freedom of Expression and Privacy Online

Over the past year, Russian government continued restricting access to popular censorship circumvention tools such as Virtual Private Network (VPN) services and anonymizers, further undermining the ability of people in Russia to access arbitrarily blocked information.

Authorities fined technology companies for their failure to comply with overbroad state laws that censored online content. In March 2022, the Russian government restricted access to Facebook on the grounds that the platform was spreading "discrimination against Russian media," and to Twitter on the grounds that the platform was "spreading false information" about the war in Ukraine. Later that month, authorities blocked Instagram in response to the company's changes to its violent speech policies.

Russian authorities expanded their control over people's biometric data, including by collecting such data from banks, and using facial recognition technology to surveil and persecute activists. activists.

In July 2022, a new law was adopted allowing Russian authorities to extrajudicially close mass media outlets and block online content for disseminating "false information" about the conduct of Russian Armed Forces or other state bodies abroad or for disseminating calls for sanctions on Russia. The bill also envisaged liability for reprinting or reposting of such materials.

The Education Ministry failed to act following reports that it had recommended unsafe online learning products for children's use during the Covid-19 pandemic, which transmitted children's personal data to advertising technology companies.

Key International Actors *(see also Ukraine chapter)*

From February 24, new international sanctions were imposed by the European Union, the US, the UK, Canada, and other governments against Russian individuals, companies, and other entities.

In October, the UN Human Rights Council adopted a resolution establishing a UN human rights monitoring mechanism on Russia (UN special rapporteur for Russia), for which international and Russian human rights groups had actively advocated.

In July, a group of UN human rights experts condemned Russian authorities' crackdown on civil society groups, human rights defenders, and media and urged the international community to redouble its efforts to support Russian civil society in the country and in exile.

In July, member states of the Organization for Security and Co-Operation in Europe (OSCE) invoked OSCE's Moscow mechanism to examine serious concerns about Russia's fulfilment of its human rights commitments. The rapporteur's report, published in September, found that increasing repression is "forcing nongovernmental organisations, anti-corruption activists, journalists ..., human rights defenders, lawyers and researchers to reduce or abandon their activities or to leave the country."

In July, the EU issued a statement on the 10th anniversary of the "foreign agent" law, strongly condemning the government's systematic attempts to instill fear and crack down on civil society and the democratic opposition.

In April, the United Nations General Assembly suspended Russia from the UN Human Rights Council over reports of "gross and systematic violations and abuses of human rights" in Ukraine. It also passed resolutions condemning Russia's invasion of and atrocities in Ukraine.

In March the Council of Europe's Committee of Ministers decided to expel Russia from the organization in connection with the invasion of Ukraine, one day after the Russian government notified the council of its withdrawal.

Several other international bodies and intergovernmental organizations have also suspended Russian membership, or expelled Russia altogether.

Rwanda

The ruling Rwandan Patriotic Front (RPF) party continued to wage a campaign against real and perceived opponents of the government. Critics, including internet bloggers and journalists, were arrested, threatened, and put on trial. Some said they were tortured in detention. The authorities rarely investigated enforced disappearances or suspicious deaths. Arbitrary detention and ill-treatment in unofficial detention facilities were common, especially around high-profile visits or large international events such as the June Commonwealth Heads of Government Meeting held in Kigali.

Abusive practices by Rwandan authorities stretched beyond the country's borders. In August, the United Nations Group of Experts on the Democratic Republic of Congo reported "solid evidence" of Rwandan forces fighting alongside and providing other support to the M23 armed group. Rwandan refugees and members of the diaspora reported being threatened and harassed by Rwandan government agents or their proxies. Human Rights Watch received information about several cases of Rwandan refugees being killed, disappeared, or arrested in suspicious circumstances, including in Mozambique and Uganda.

Political Space

Political space in Rwanda remains closed. Opposition parties face administrative obstacles to registration and political pressure to toe the government line. Over a dozen political opposition members are in prison. In many cases, they are being prosecuted or have been convicted on spurious grounds.

The trial of 10 people related to "Ingabire Day," an event scheduled for October 14, 2021, and organized by the unregistered opposition party Dalfa-Umurinzi to discuss, among other things, political repression in Rwanda, continued throughout 2022. At time of writing, eight party members were jailed in Mageragere prison, in Kigali, and one was in hiding. Théoneste Nsengimana, a journalist who was planning to cover the event and is being tried together with the group, is also jailed at the same prison.

The prosecution is basing its accusations on the group's decision to acquire *Blueprint for Revolution*, a book written by Srdja Popovic, the Serbian activist, and to follow a training organized by the author's organization, Canvas—the Center for Applied Non-Violent Actions and Strategies, established to advocate for nonviolent resistance in promoting human rights and democracy. Both the book and the training focus on peaceful strategies to resist authoritarianism, such as nonviolent protest, noncooperation, boycott, and mobilization.

The prosecution argued that discussions on distributing tracts saying that Rwandans are tired of being killed, kidnapped, beaten, and paying excessive taxes, and that Rwandans should be respected was an attempt to overthrow the government. The prosecution is seeking life sentences for eight out of the ten.

The trial of Christopher Kayumba, the former editor of *The Chronicles* newspaper, began in September. He was charged with rape and attempted rape, and the prosecution is seeking a 10-year sentence. He has requested that the trial, which is being held in Mageragere prison, be transferred to an open court. Kayumba was arrested in September 2021. He established a new political party, the Rwandese Platform for Democracy (RPD), in March 2021 and, shortly afterwards, his former houseworker accused him of raping her in 2012. Jean Bosco Nkusi, in charge of recruitment of mobilization for the RPD, was arrested in March 2021 and was convicted of fraud and of forming a criminal association and handed a 10-year sentence in April 2022.

The September 2021 conviction and 25-year sentence of critic and political opponent Paul Rusesabagina, on murder, membership in a terrorist group, and other charges, after a flawed trial, was upheld on appeal in April. Rusesabagina was forcibly disappeared and unlawfully returned to Rwanda in August 2020.

Freedom of Expression

At time of writing, several journalists and commentators were behind bars in Rwanda. In some cases, they were arrested for speaking out about security force abuses, including unlawful and arbitrary detention, torture and extrajudicial killings, or for criticizing the ruling RPF and its human rights record. Allegations that the authorities beat or otherwise ill-treat political prisoners are common in Rwanda.

The trial of three journalists working for the YouTube channel Iwacu TV concluded on July 15, 2022. Damascene Mutuyimana, Shadrack Niyonsenga, and Jean Baptiste Nshimiyima were arrested in October 2018, and charged with spreading false information with the intention of creating a hostile international opinion of Rwanda, publishing unoriginal statements or pictures, and inciting insurrection, according to the Committee to Protect Journalists. Prosecutors sought a 22 year and 5 months sentence. On October 5, they were acquitted and released.

On May 30, a detained commentator popular on YouTube, Aimable Karasira, told a judge that he was tortured in detention and denied medical treatment. In a July 7 court appearance, he said he had been punished for talking about how he was treated in detention and beaten again. Karasira is on trial for "genocide denial and justification, and divisionism." He has spoken about losing family members both to Hutu extremists and to the RPF during and after the 1994 genocide.

Karasira said that the prison authorities were inflicting the same treatment on the YouTube journalist Dieudonné Niyonsenga—alias "Cyuma Hassan"— and Christopher Kayumba. Niyonsenga was convicted of forgery, impersonating journalists, and hindering public works and sentenced to seven years in 2021 after reporting on the impact of the Covid-19 guidelines on vulnerable populations.

In September 2021, the prosecution appealed the 15-year sentence handed to Yvonne Idamange, a Tutsi online commentator and genocide survivor who has criticized the Covid-19 lockdown and the government-organized genocide commemorations. The prosecution is seeking a 30-year sentence.

Refugees and Asylum Seekers

In April, the United Kingdom and Rwandan governments announced the signing of a new Asylum Partnership Agreement, under which the UK plans to expel to Rwanda people seeking asylum in the UK through "irregular" routes. Under the agreement, asylum seekers sent to Rwanda would be processed under Rwanda's asylum system and, if recognized as refugees, granted refugee status there, with Rwanda otherwise handling rejected claims. The plan, which is an abrogation of the UK's international responsibilities and obligations to asylum seekers and refugees, was challenged in a UK court.

Attacks and threats by Rwandan government agents or their proxies on Rwandan refugees living abroad, including in Uganda, Mozambique, South Africa, and Kenya, continued. The victims have tended to be political opponents or critics of the Rwandan government or of President Paul Kagame. In his September 2022 annual report, the UN secretary-general highlighted the case of harassment and threats against Noël Zihabamwe, a Rwandan refugee living in Australia, and persons in Rwanda associated with him, following his engagement with the UN Working Group on Enforced and Involuntary Disappearances.

Sexual Orientation and Gender Identity

Rwanda is one of a few countries in East Africa that does not criminalize consensual same-sex relations, and the government's policies are generally seen as progressive. However, in practice, lesbian, gay, bisexual, and transgender (LGBT) people have faced stigma as a result of their sexual orientation and gender identity. Human Rights Watch received information that Rwanda rejected asylum claims from individuals persecuted for their sexual orientation or gender identity in their home country.

International Justice

Almost three decades after the 1994 genocide, a significant number of people responsible for the genocide, including former high-level government officials and other key figures, have been brought to justice.

On September 29, the trial of Félicien Kabuga, one of the alleged masterminds of the genocide, began in The Hague at the International Residual Mechanism for Criminal Tribunals. Kabuga was first indicted by the International Criminal Tribunal for Rwanda in 1997 and arrested in France in May 2020.

In recent years, the Rwandan government has requested or signed extradition treaties with dozens of countries in an attempt to have remaining genocide suspects returned for trial in Rwanda, although there are persistent concerns about failure to uphold fair trial standards in domestic atrocity trials. In April, Swedish authorities extradited to Kigali Jean Paul Micomyiza, whom they arrested in November 2020 following an indictment by Rwandan prosecution.

Key International Actors

Despite concerns about human rights violations related to the meeting, including the arbitrary detention and ill-treatment of poor and marginalized people to "clear" the streets of Kigali, the Commonwealth Heads of Government Meeting went ahead in June. Journalists reported being blocked from entering the country and prevented from working independently. During the meeting, schools were shut down and prison visits suspended—ostensibly for a "hygiene activities" and an awareness campaign.

Senator Robert Menendez, chairman of the United States Senate Foreign Relations Committee, said on July 20 that he would place a hold on US security assistance to Rwanda in Congress over concerns about its human rights record and its role in the conflict in Congo. In a letter to US Secretary of State Antony Blinken, Menendez asked for a comprehensive review of US policy toward Rwanda.

Blinken traveled to Rwanda in August to raise the case of Rusesabagina, who was living in the US when he travelled from the US to Dubai, United Arab Emirates, where he was forcibly disappeared. He also raised concerns about Rwanda's support for the M23 rebellion in eastern Congo.

Saudi Arabia

Authorities conducted arrests of peaceful dissidents, public intellectuals, and human rights activists and sentenced people to decades-long prison terms for posting on social media. Abusive practices in detention centers, including torture and mistreatment, prolonged arbitrary detention, and asset confiscation without any clear legal process, remain pervasive.

Announced legal reforms are severely undermined by widespread repression under de facto ruler Crown Prince Mohammed bin Salman, known as MBS. On March 12, Saudi authorities executed 81 men, the largest mass execution in decades, despite recent promises to curtail its use of the death penalty.

A series of attacks by the Saudi and United Arab Emirate-led coalition in Yemen killed at least 80 people in January.

Construction is underway for NEOM, a US$500 billion mega-city development project in Tabuk province. Human rights organizations have documented violations by Saudi authorities, including forced evictions, against the Huwaitat community to make room for construction. In July, Saudi authorities announced plans for "The Line," a vertically layered city within NEOM that will heavily utilize artificial intelligence and "human-machine interface" technology, raising concerns about the use of digital technology to surveil future residents.

Authorities launder their reputation, stained by a deplorable human rights record, through funding lavish sports and entertainment institutions, figures, and events.

Freedom of Expression, Association, and Belief

Dozens of Saudi human rights defenders and activists continued to serve long prison sentences for criticizing authorities or advocating for political and rights reforms. Blogger, activist, and 2015 Sakharov Prize winner Raif Badawi remains under a travel ban despite completing his unjust 10-year prison sentence in March.

Women's rights defenders including Loujain al-Hathloul, Nassimah al-Sadah, and Samar Badawi also remain banned from travel and under suspended prison sentences, allowing the authorities to return them to prison for any perceived criminal activity. Human rights activist Mohammed al-Rabea, aid worker Abdulrahman al-Sadhan, and human rights lawyer Waleed Abu al-Khair remained in prison on charges that relate to peaceful expression or activism.

Saudi authorities increasingly target Saudi and non-Saudi social media users for peaceful expression online and punish them with decades-long sentences. On August 9, an appeals court sentenced Salma al-Shehab, a Saudi doctoral student at the University of Leeds in the United Kingdom, to 34 years in prison for "disrupt[ing] the order and fabric of society," apparently based solely on her Twitter activity. That same day, Saudi courts sentenced Nourah bin Saeed al-Qahtani to a lengthy 45 years in prison for "using the internet to tear the [country's] social fabric."

In September, Saudi prosecutors summoned US citizen Carly Morris for "disrupt[tion] of the public order," seemingly in connection to an ongoing investigation into her social media activity. In April, Morris published a series of tweets about her inability to travel outside Saudi Arabia with her eight-year-old daughter and access important documents for her.

Dual US-Saudi citizen Salah al-Haidar, detained between May 2019 and February 2021, remains on trial on charges related to his peaceful criticism of the Saudi government on social media.

The Saudi government is notorious for repressing public dissent and has a well-established record of attempting to infiltrate technology platforms and use advanced cyber surveillance technology to spy on dissidents.

Yemen Airstrikes and Conflict

The Saudi and UAE-led coalition carried out three attacks in Yemen in January 2022 in apparent violation of the laws of war that resulted in at least 80 apparently civilian deaths, including three children, and 156 injuries, including two children. The coalition attacks were in apparent retaliation for Houthi attacks on the United Arab Emirates' Abu Dhabi National Oil Company and the Abu Dhabi international airport on January 17.

On October 2, Hans Grundberg, the United Nations special envoy for Yemen, announced that the nationwide ceasefire in place since April 2022 had expired after warring parties failed to extend and expand its terms.

The Yemen Data Project reported in January that coalition airstrikes increased by 43 percent in the months immediately following the UN Human Rights Council's failure to pass the resolution to renew the mandate of the UN Group of Eminent International and Regional Experts on Yemen, the only international, independent body that had been investigating abuses by all parties to the conflict in Yemen.

The United Nations Development Programme estimates the protracted conflict in Yemen has killed over 377,000 people directly or indirectly since 2015. Key causes of death include inadequate food, health care, and infrastructure. Warring parties have targeted civilian objects, including homes, hospitals, schools, and bridges, internally displacing more than 4 million people.

Criminal Justice

Saudi Arabia has no written laws concerning sexual orientation or gender identity, but judges use principles of uncodified Islamic law to sanction people suspected of committing sexual relations outside marriage, including adultery, and extramarital and homosexual sex. If individuals are engaging in such relationships online, judges and prosecutors utilize vague provisions of the country's anti-cybercrime law that criminalize online activity impinging on "public order, religious values, public morals, and privacy."

On March 12, authorities executed 81 people, including 41 people from the Shia community, in the country's largest mass execution in decades. While the Interior Ministry claimed they were executed for crimes including murder and links to foreign terrorist groups, rampant and systemic abuses in the criminal justice system suggest it is highly unlikely that any of the men received a fair trial. Only three of the 41 Shia men had been convicted on murder charges.

Despite statements by Saudi Arabia's Human Rights Commission claiming that no one in Saudi Arabia will be executed for a crime committed as a child, the provision does not apply to *qisas*, retributive justice offenses usually for murder, or *hudud*, serious crimes defined under the country's interpretation of Islamic law that carry specific penalties. Abdullah al-Huwaiti, who was 14 at the time of his alleged crime and whose previous death penalty conviction was overturned by the Saudi Supreme Court on the basis of a false confession and insufficient evidence, was sentenced to death again on March 2 by a lower criminal court.

Human Rights Watch reported in March on 10 Nubian Egyptians unjustly and arbitrarily detained on speech, association, and terrorism charges, seemingly in reprisal for expressing their cultural heritage. The Specialized Criminal Court brought charges against them in September 2021.

At least four detained Muslim Uyghurs, including one 13-year-old girl, remained at imminent risk of deportation from Saudi Arabia to China, where they would be at serious risk of arbitrary detention and torture.

Migrants and Migrant Workers

Migrant workers routinely report abuse and exploitation. Authorities continue to impose one of the most restrictive and abusive *kafala* (visa sponsorship) systems in the region, which despite recent reforms remains largely unchanged. It gives employers excessive power over migrant workers' mobility and legal status in the country and underpins their vulnerability to a wide range of abuses—from passport confiscation to delayed wages—which can amount to forced labor.

In January, Human Rights Watch reported on the horrific detention conditions of thousands of ethnic Tigrayan people deported between December 2020 and September 2021 from Saudi Arabia to Ethiopia. Interviewees uniformly described horrendous conditions in formal and informal detention centers in the Saudi Arabian cities of Abha, Hadda, Jizan, and Jeddah. They described severely cramped, unsanitary detention conditions and physical abuse by guards. Upon return to Ethiopia, deportees were arbitrarily arrested, mistreated, and forcibly disappeared.

The BBC reported on Kenyan domestic worker Diana Chepkemoi, 24, who returned from Saudi Arabia to Kenya in September and said her employer told her she was "bought" and that "anything" could be done to her. The Kenyan foreign ministry reported that 89 Kenyans—more than half of them female domestic workers—died in Saudi Arabia between 2020 and 2021 under suspicious circumstances. In most cases, Saudi authorities identified the cause of death as non-work related and failed to investigate further.

Saudi Arabia's economy relies heavily on migrant workers. Over 6.3 million migrants fill mostly manual, clerical, and service jobs in Saudi Arabia, constituting more than 80 percent of the private sector workforce. Saudi Arabia carries out regular arrests and deportations of undocumented migrant workers, including major arrest campaigns in November 2013 and August 2017. Many workers become undocumented through no fault of their own because employers can report migrant workers, sometimes falsely, for "absconding" or when they flee abuse. Migrants are denied the right to contest their detention and deportation.

Women's Rights

Despite some reforms, authorities continue to implement a male guardianship system requiring women to obtain male guardian permission to get married, leave prison, or obtain some forms of sexual and reproductive healthcare. Husbands reportedly can withhold consent if a woman seeks higher education abroad.

In March, Saudi lawmakers passed the country's first codified personal status law. However, despite Saudi authorities' promises for a "comprehensive" and "progressive" personal status law, the law entrenches discriminatory provisions on women in marriage, divorce, inheritance, and decisions relating to children. Rather than dismantling it, the law instead codifies male guardianship and sets out provisions that can facilitate and excuse domestic violence including sexual abuse in marriage.

Women are required to have their male guardian's permission in order to marry. Once married, women are required to then obey their husband in a "reasonable manner." Articles 42 and 55 together state a husband's financial support is specifically made contingent on a wife's "obedience" to the husband, and she can lose her right to such support if she refuses without a "legitimate excuse" to have sex with him, move to or live in the marital home, or travel with him. Article 42(3) states that neither spouse may abstain from sexual relations or cohabitation with the other without the other spouse's consent, implying a marital right to intercourse.

Article 9 declares the legal age of marriage as 18 but allows courts to authorize the marriage of a child under 18 if they have reached puberty and if it can be proved that the marriage provides an "established benefit" to the child.

While men can unilaterally divorce women, women can only petition a court to dissolve their marriage contract on limited grounds and must "establish harm" as a prerequisite. The law does not specify what constitutes "harm" or what evidence can be submitted to support a case, leaving room for judges' discretion in interpretation and enforcement.

Elements of the male guardianship system that remain in practice can prevent a divorced woman from financial independence. For example, a man can funnel post-divorce financial support payments to his ex-wife through her male relative if she lives with her family post-divorce, denying her direct access to the payments.

Under the Saudi Personal Status Law, fathers are the default guardians of their children. Even if the authorities order the children to live with their mothers, women have limited authority over their children's lives and cannot act as guardians of children unless a court appoints them. The 2016 and 2019 legal amendments allowing mothers with primary custody of their children to apply for passports, provide travel permission, and obtain important documents for their children without a male guardian are seemingly inconsistently applied.

Climate Change Policies and Impacts

By its own admission, Saudi Arabia is "particularly vulnerable" to climate change as an "arid country with a harsh climate and sensitive ecosystem." Water scarcity is common in Saudi Arabia, most land is non-arable, and average rainfall is low. Yet Saudi Arabia remains one of the world's leading exporters of fossil fuels.

Key International Actors

The United States provides logistical and intelligence support to Saudi-led coalition forces in Yemen and billions of dollars' worth of weapons. Remnants of a bomb used in the January Saudi-led coalition attack on a Yemeni detention facility were identified as part of the Paveway laser guidance kit produced by the US defense contractor Raytheon. In August, the US State Department approved a US$3.05 billion sale of 300 Patriot surface-to-air missiles to Saudi Arabia. Human Rights Watch has documented the coalition's use of US-manufactured weapons in at least 22 apparently unlawful attacks under the laws of war to date.

French President Emmanuel Macron hosted MBS for a meeting at the Elysée Palace in Paris in July. In June, three rights groups filed a criminal complaint with a court in Paris against French arms companies Dassault Aviation, Thales, and MBDA France for their role in supplying the Saudi-led coalition with weapons used in alleged war crimes in Yemen.

Global reliance on fossil fuels increases the risk that the US and European Union governments' engagement with Saudi Arabia directly and indirectly contribute to rights abuses. In July, US President Joe Biden visited MBS in Jeddah, a move allegedly motivated by a desire to lower global fuel prices but which did not translate into a public request on the matter nor significantly increase Organization of the Petroleum Exporting Countries Plus (OPEC+) oil output, in which Saudi Arabia is a key decision-maker in the oil market cartel. According to US officials, US-Saudi partnership could lead to the expansion of 5G and 6G mobile networks and possible new military facilities in Saudi Arabia.

Former UK Prime Minister Boris Johnson visited Riyadh in March to encourage Saudi oil production and emphasized this in public calls in July.

In June, EU ministers approved the European Commission's plan for a "strategic partnership with Gulf." The strategy largely overlooks human rights, leaving the issue to yearly, largely fruitless, human rights dialogues, and focuses almost solely on strengthening bilateral political and economic ties.

Serbia

Independent journalists continued to face intimidation, threats, and violence. War crimes prosecutions remained slow, inefficient, and marred by delays. A pan-European pride parade in Belgrade took place with police protection, despite authorities having banned it, underscoring the precarious situation for lesbian, gay, bisexual, and transgender (LGBT) people in Serbia.

Freedom of Media

Journalists critical of the government continued to face threats and attacks, with inadequate state response.

Between January and late August, the Independent Journalists' Association of Serbia (NUNS) registered two physical attacks, three attacks on property, and 26 cases of intimidation and threats, including five bomb threats, against journalists and media outlets.

In June, unidentified assailants threw stones at a Bulgarian TV crew covering a story on alleged pollution at a mine in Serbia, close to the Bulgarian border. Police were investigating the attack at time of writing.

In April, deputy editor-in-chief for news website Autonomija, Dinko Gruhonjic, received a message on Facebook threatening to kill and sexually assault him, his wife, and his children in response to an article he had written criticizing Serbia's response to the war in Ukraine, just one among the many regular threats he receives. An investigation into the threat by the Belgrade Prosecution Office was pending investigation at time of writing.

Also in April, N1TV broadcaster and daily newspaper Danas received death threats via emails, messaging apps, and social media sites, threatening to "slaughter" employees of the outlets, referring to them as American mercenaries. It is unclear what prompted the threats. An investigation by the Belgrade Prosecution Office was pending at time of writing.

Following a March article profiling a Ukrainian refugee who had fled to Serbia, Danas journalist Miljko Stojanovic received multiple threats on social media, including threats of physical violence and "disfiguring" him. Police in March detained one suspect, but no charges had been brought at time of writing.

Pro-government media continued smear campaigns against independent journalists and outlets in connection with reporting critical of the government.

Accountability for War Crimes

Between January and August, the War Crimes Prosecutor's Office launched seven new investigations against war crimes suspects. As of August, 16 cases against 39 defendants were pending before Serbian courts. Ongoing proceedings were marred by significant delays and postponements.

In February, the Appeals Court in Belgrade overturned the guilty verdict of former Bosnian Serb army soldier, Dalibor Krstovic, who in May 2021 was found guilty and sentenced to nine years' imprisonment for raping a woman prisoner detained in an elementary school in BiH town of Kalinovik in August 1992. The Appeals Court ordered a retrial.

In April, following a retrial, the Belgrade Higher Court, found former Bosnian Serb policeman Milorad Jovanovic guilty of torturing non-Serbian civilian prisoners, leading to one death. Jovanovic was sentenced to nine years imprisonment.

The first trial in Serbia for war crimes in Srebrenica was yet again delayed in July when a defense lawyer asked to be removed from proceedings. Seven Bosnian Serb former police officers resident in Serbia are charged with the killing of more than 1,300 Bosniak civilians in July 1995. An eighth suspect was excused from trial in February 2021, due to health problems. The trial has been postponed over 20 times since it began in December 2016 with the accused claiming to have poor health or simply failing to appear at hearings without sanction.

In May, proceedings against four former Bosnian Serb soldiers charged with the 1993 Strpci train massacre in BiH was delayed, as one of the defendants cited health concerns, prompting the Belgrade Higher Court to postpone proceedings.

Refugees, Asylum Seekers and Migrants.

Between January and August, Serbia registered 2,653 asylum seekers, a 21 percent decrease from the same period in 2021, but only allowed 251 asylum applications to be lodged.

The asylum system remained flawed, with difficulties for asylum seekers accessing procedures, low recognition rates, and long delays. Between January and August, Serbia granted refugee status to two people and subsidiary protection to nine. Serbia granted temporary protection to 817 people, almost exclusively from Ukraine.

By end of September, 61 unaccompanied migrant children were registered with Serbian authorities. Serbia lacks formal age assessment procedures for unaccompanied children, putting older children at risk of being treated as adults instead of receiving special protection.

Sexual Orientation and Gender Identity

Between January and September, Da Se Zna! recorded 30 incidents of hate motivated incidents against LGBT people, including 10 physical attacks. One of the incidents involved two police officers who allegedly assaulted a gay man in a bathroom in Belgrade in May. Investigations into the cases were pending at time of writing.

Authorities sought to cancel the September 17 pan-European Europride march in Belgrade, citing security concerns and the tensions with Kosovo as reasons. The move triggered international criticism including by EU Equality Commissioner Helen Dalli, Council of Europe Commissioner of Human Rights Dunja Mijatovic, and members of the European Parliament, who travelled to Belgrade to support the event. Organizers submitted notification of new limited route to the police, received reassurances from Prime Minister Ana Brnabic, and the march took place. Seven participants were attacked after the march. Investigations into the attacks were pending at time of writing.

On August 12, a man entered the Belgrade Pride Info Center, destroyed furniture and threatened staff. Police arrested the man on the scene and a criminal investigation was pending at time of writing. It was the 13th attack on the Center since 2018. Right wing religious and political groups have pressured the ministry of education to ban "LGBT topics" in the school curriculum.

People with Disabilities

The number of people with disabilities living in institutions increased since 2021. In three of the six institutions for children with disabilities, children continued to be housed with unrelated adults, which puts them at a higher risk of violence and abuse. Mainstream education for children with disabilities remained limited, with the vast majority of those in institutions continuing to be segregated into separate schools for children with disabilities or not given opportunities for education at all.

Key International Actors

Following a July visit to Serbia, Organization for Security and Co-operation in Europe Representative on Freedom of the Media, Teresa Ribeiro, stressed the need for more concerted action to ensure a safe, free, and pluralistic media landscape in Serbia.

In an April statement following Serbia's parliamentary and presidential elections, European Union Representative Josep Borrel and EU enlargement commissioner, Oliver Varhelyi, encouraged Serbia to show concrete results on the rule of law, accelerate reforms on the independence of the judiciary, and improve media freedom and war crimes accountability.

The October EU Commission progress report on Serbia said further efforts were needed to improve cooperation between civil society and the government as verbal attacks and smear campaigns against civil society organizations continued. The report also expressed the need to strengthen human rights institutions by allocating sufficient funds and human resources. The report stated that threats and violence against journalists remained a concern.

In July, the European Parliament supported Serbia's future membership in the EU but condemned restrictions to media freedom and independence, and harassment of journalists and civil society.

Singapore

The Singapore government uses draconian criminal laws and civil defamation suits to harass and prosecute critical voices, including activists, bloggers, and journalists. There is little freedom of assembly. In 2022, after a two-year halt, Singapore resumed executions of death row prisoners, despite widespread international condemnation. On November 29, Singapore's parliament voted to repeal the colonial-era law criminalizing sexual relations between men. However, there are still no legal protections against discrimination on the basis of sexual orientation or gender identity.

Freedom of Assembly and Expression

The Hostile Information Campaigns provisions of the overbroad and ambiguous Foreign Interference (Counter-Measures) Act (FICA) went into effect on July 7. The law gives sweeping powers to the home minister to require removal or disabling of online content, publication of mandatory messages drafted by the government, banning of apps from being downloaded in Singapore, and disclosure of information by internet and social media companies. The minister's authority under the law is reinforced by severe criminal penalties and judicial review is limited to only procedural matters.

The government can also designate individuals as "politically significant persons" who can be required to follow strict limits on receiving funding and disclose all links with foreigners. The law's broad language encompasses a wide range of ordinary activities by civil society activists, academics, and journalists who engage with non-Singaporeans.

The government maintains strict restrictions on the right to peaceful assembly through the Public Order Act (POA), requiring a police permit for any "cause-related" assembly if it is held in a public place, or in a private venue if members of the public are invited. The definition of an "assembly" is extremely broad, and those who fail to obtain the required permits face criminal charges.

The Public Order Act provides the police commissioner with authority to reject any permit application for an assembly or procession "directed towards a political end" if any foreigner is involved.

Attacks on Human Rights Defenders

Singapore's restrictive laws are frequently used against activists and media critical of the government. On February 25, activist Jolovan Wham was sentenced to a fine of S$3,000 (US$2,100), or 15 days in prison in lieu of the fine, under the Public Order Act. The "assembly" for which he was convicted consisted of posing for a photo outside the courthouse while holding a sign calling for charges against journalist Terry Xu to be dropped. On September 9, a High Court judge dismissed his appeal. However, on March 3, the Attorney General's Office withdrew charges of unlawful assembly against Wham for an earlier instance in which he stood in public holding a sign with a "smiley face."

In April, Terry Xu, editor of The Online Citizen, a news website shut down by the government in 2021, received a jail sentence for criminal defamation related to a letter to the editor published by the outlet. The author was sentenced to three months and three weeks in jail.

In June, police called in for questioning activists Kirsten Han and Rocky Howe about a four-person vigil in March outside Changi Prison, and a photograph taken outside the prison in April. The vigil was held the night of Abdul Kahar Othman's execution, and the photograph was taken two nights before Nagaenthran Dharmalingam's hanging. They are being investigated for violating the Public Order Act. Han potentially faces a fine of up to S$5,000 (US$3,500) and imprisonment for up to six months under Criminal Procedure Code section 39 for refusing to surrender passwords to her social media accounts.

Criminal Justice System

The death penalty is mandated for many drug offenses and certain other crimes. However, under provisions introduced in 2012, judges have some discretion to bypass the mandatory penalty and sentence low-level offenders to life in prison and caning. There is little transparency on the timing of executions, which often take place with short notice.

After a two-year hiatus in executions, authorities have issued 14 execution notices since November 2021. After a two-year hiatus in executions, authorities have issued 14 execution notices since November 2021. In 2022 Singapore executed 11 people, including Nagaenthran Dharmalingam, a Malaysian man with an intellectual disability. In April, the authorities issued an execution notice to Malaysian Dachinmurty Kataiah, even though he had a pending civil claim against the attorney-general over the unauthorized disclosure of his personal letters. The Court of Appeal granted a stay of execution, noting that it appeared Datchinmurthy had been "singled out" for execution.

Lawyers defending inmates on death row have faced harassment and punitive cost orders, obstructing inmates' access to legal counsel and right to a fair trial.

Use of corporal punishment is common in Singapore. For medically fit males ages 16 to 50, caning is mandatory for a wide range of crimes. Such caning constitutes torture under international law.

Sexual Orientation and Gender Identity

On November 29, Singapore's parliament voted to repeal section 377A of the criminal code, outlawing sexual relations between two male persons. On the same day, the parliament passed constitutional amendments to prevent future legal challenges to the current definition of marriage as being between one man and one woman, effectively blocking any challenges relating to the definition of marriage from being brought to court. There are no legal protections against discrimination on the basis of sexual orientation or gender identity. Singapore precludes LGBT groups from registering and operating legally.

In May, Parliament passed the Adoption of Children Act, which limits eligibility to adopt children to couples whose marriage would be recognized in Singapore, precluding adoption by same-sex couples. The minister for Social and Family Development reiterated in parliament that the government, as a matter of public policy, "does not support the formation of same-sex family units."

Migrant Workers and Labor Exploitation

Foreign migrant workers face labor rights abuses and exploitation through exorbitant debts owed to recruitment agents, non-payment of wages, restrictions on movement, confiscation of passports, and sometimes physical and sexual violence. Foreign women employed as domestic workers are particularly vulnerable to violence.

Migrants' work permits are tied to a particular employer, making workers extremely vulnerable to intimidation and exploitation. Foreign domestic workers, who are covered by the Employment of Foreign Manpower Act rather than the Employment Act, are excluded from many key labor protections, such as limits on daily work hours and sick leave and annual leave protections.

Many migrant workers in Singapore are housed in crowded dormitories. Under regulations put in place in June 2020 and in effect until June 2022, migrant workers needed an "exit pass" from their employer to leave their dormitory. Now they are still required to get a "visit pass" to go to four popular locations in Singapore on Sundays or public holidays.

In June, the Ministry of Manpower declined to renew the work permit of Zakir Hossain Khokan, who had been working in Singapore for 19 years, claiming that his Facebook post from October 2021 about the treatment of migrant workers was "false" and that he had "overstayed his welcome."

Key International Actors

Singapore is a regional hub for international business and maintains good political and economic relations with both China and the United States, which considers the city-state a key security ally.

Somalia

In May, after a controversial and delayed electoral process, former President Hassan Sheikh Mohamud was elected as Somalia's president. The prolonged electoral process stalled critical rights reforms.

In 2022, the country faced a devastating food crisis following four consecutive below-average rainy seasons. Some 6.7 million people (41 percent of the population) faced extreme hunger, with the United Nations warning that 300,000 people will likely face famine in the final quarter of the year. Over half of the country's children were reported to be suffering acute malnutrition.

Individuals with long track records of abuse continue to be appointed into positions of authority. In August, the new cabinet of ministers included Muktar Robow, who had played a leadership role in the Islamist armed group Al-Shabab. Robow had been under house arrest for over three years without trial under the previous administration. In September, Puntland's president appointed as advisor Gen. Mohamed Said Hersi "Morgan," the commander of the Somali army, who under former President Siad Barre led the destruction of Hargeisa in the early phases of the country's civil war, and later was implicated in war crimes in southern Somalia.

Federal and regional authorities throughout Somalia repeatedly harassed, arbitrarily arrested, and attacked journalists. On October 8, the federal Information Ministry released a directive that "prohibited dissemination of extremism ideology messages, both from traditional media broadcasts and social media." On October 11, the intelligence services detained, and the prosecution later charged, prominent and widely respected media rights advocate and freelance journalist, Abdalle Ahmed Mumin, whose organization had raised concerns that the directive could restrict free speech.

The government did not move forward with the establishment of a National Human Rights Commission, or the planned review of the outdated criminal code, pending since the previous administration. Upon returning to office, President Hassan Sheikh committed to finalizing judicial reforms.

In Somaliland, authorities clamped down on free expression and association, with security forces reportedly using excessive and lethal force during demonstrations against alleged plans to postpone the November presidential elections.

Attacks on Civilians

By November, the UN had recorded at least 613 civilian deaths and 948 injuries. The majority were killed during targeted and indiscriminate Al-Shabab attacks using improvised explosive devices (IEDs), suicide bombings, and shelling, as well as targeted killings. These attacks increased during the electoral process, notably in February and March, and again after President Hassan Sheikh took up office, following an uptick in government-led and clan militia offensives against Al-Shabab.

On October 29, Al-Shabab conducted double car bombings at the Ministry of Education in the center of Mogadishu, killing at least 121 people and injuring hundreds. On March 23, Al-Shabab claimed responsibility for a complex attack on the Beledweyne regional headquarters ahead of elections there, killing at least 48 people, including a female parliamentarian, and injuring over 100. Al-Shabab continued to conduct targeted killings. In January, former journalist and government spokesperson, Mohamed Ibrahim Moalimu, survived an attack, claimed by Al-Shabab, on his car.

In November 2021, Uganda held a court martial in Mogadishu to try soldiers from its AMISOM troops implicated in the August 2021 killing of seven civilians around Golweyn, Lower Shabelle, following an ambush by Al-Shabab fighters. The court sentenced two of the soldiers to death and three to life sentences.

The Somali government did not hand over Al-Shabab cases from military to civilian courts. Authorities throughout the country carried out executions, many following military court proceedings that did not meet international fair trial standards.

Al-Shabab members continued to execute individuals it accused of working with or spying for the government and foreign forces, often after convicting them in unjust trials.

Outcomes remain unknown of the federal and regional investigations into the May 2020 massacre of seven health workers and a pharmacist in the village of Gololey, Balcad District, reportedly by government security forces.

Displacement and Access to Humanitarian Assistance

Somalia faced its fifth consecutive below-average rainy season. Ongoing conflict and insecurity, along with extreme weather patterns—increasing in intensity and frequency due to climate change—compounded by food-price hikes, exacerbated communities' existing vulnerabilities. Somalia is heavily dependent on food imports, with up to 90 percent of its wheat supply usually from Russia and Ukraine.

Three million livestock died in 2022 because of droughts, heavily impacting pastoralist and agro-pastoralist communities' access to basic needs. In September, the UN warned that famine would occur in Baidoa, including among people displaced there, and Burhakaba districts in Bay region, in the last quarter of the year.

According to the Norwegian Refugee Council and the UN refugee agency (UNHCR), by August, 1 million people had been internally displaced since the drought began in January 2021, including more than 800,000 in 2022 alone.

Humanitarian agencies continued to face serious access challenges due to conflict, targeted attacks on aid workers, generalized violence, and restrictions imposed by parties to the conflict, including arbitrary taxation and bureaucratic hurdles. Media reported that United States counterterrorism legislation was hampering certain aid agencies' access to those in greatest need in Al-Shabab controlled areas. Al-Shabab continued to impose blockades on some government-controlled towns, notably the town of Hudur, and occasionally attacked civilians who broke them.

Sexual Violence

The UN continued to report incidents of conflict-related sexual and gender-based violence, including of girls, in which the victims were often killed. Sexual violence against displaced women and girls is well documented and humanitarian actors warned enhanced protection measures are needed, including legal and policing reforms as well as improved humanitarian responses.

Key legal reforms stalled, including progressive federal sexual violence legislation. The Somali criminal code classifies sexual violence as an "offense against modesty and sexual honor" rather than a violation of bodily integrity; it also punishes same-sex relations. The independent expert on the situation of human rights in Somalia reported that the clan system continues to deal with sexual violence cases in proceedings that fail to protect the rights of survivors.

Abuses against Children

Children continue to bear a heavy toll of ongoing insecurity, conflict, drought, and lack of key reforms in the country. All Somali parties to the conflict committed serious abuses against children, including killings, maiming, the recruitment and use of child soldiers, and attacks on schools.

Somali federal and regional security forces unlawfully detained children, notably for alleged ties with armed groups, undermining government commitments to treat children primarily as victims. Puntland once again sentenced child offenders to death and long prison sentences for their alleged involvement with armed groups. The government failed to enact legislation codifying the Convention on the Rights of the Child or introduce child rights compliant justice measures with children continuing to be detained alongside adults.

The drought had a devastating impact on children's access to education. Media reported that children dropped out of school because their parents could no longer finance their schooling.

Somaliland

Authorities in Somaliland continued to restrict free expression, media, and association.

On August 11, security forces reportedly used excessive force to clamp down on protests against perceived plans to delay presidential elections, with an estimated five people killed and 100 detained. Government officials accused protesters of violence. The internet was temporarily shut down on the day of the protests.

In April, several journalists were detained while covering violence in the Hargeisa central prison, with two of them initially sentenced to 16 months' imprisonment but later released.

In July, the authorities suspended the BBC, accusing it of "undermining the credibility of the Somaliland State." In September, the Ministry of Information revoked the license of CBA TV, a private station covering news on the Horn.

Key International Actors

Somalia was elected to the UN Human Rights Council in October 2021 in a non-competitive slate.

In February, the International Monetary Fund (IMF) told media that funding under the Heavily Indebted Poor Countries Initiative could be postponed if the electoral process was not completed by May. In June, following the selection of the new president, the IMF disbursed US$350 million. In July, the European Union resumed budget support and disbursed €13.5 million ($13.8 million) to the federal government. The EU committed €120 million ($125 million) to support the military component of the African Union Mission in Somalia/African Union Transition Mission in Somalia (AMISOM/ ATMIS), with funding primarily covering troop allowances.

Following the selection of President Hassan Sheikh, the US resumed military operations in Somalia. In May, media reported that the Biden administration would send around 500 special operations troops back to Somalia with the authority to target suspected Al-Shabab leaders, and in September that authority was used to target an Al-Shabab leader.

US drone strikes increased in the second half of the year. Since the start of contemporary US military operations in Somalia in 2007, the Pentagon has not provided compensation to any civilian victims of unlawful US airstrikes or their family members.

While the year started with a severe shortage in humanitarian funding, the response plan was 71 percent funded by October following significant donor mobilization, notably by the US.

South Africa

South Africa struggled to realize economic and social rights, due to increasing inequality and unemployment, exacerbated by the Covid-19 pandemic and corruption. The high- profile trial of former president, Jacob Zuma for fraud, corruption, money laundering and racketeering continued to suffer delays, with the trial being postponed to early 2023. The country has failed to take concrete steps to address environmental pollution and the dangers posed by toxic wastes to people living close to abandoned mines and dams.

The government's efforts to curb xenophobic violence has yet to yield tangible improvement in the protection of migrants. Anti-foreigner groups perpetuate the unsubstantiated notion that foreigners are responsible for unemployment and crimes in the country. Women and members of the lesbian, gay, bisexual, trans and intersex (LGBTI) community continue to face abuses, including murder, assault, and harassment.

Right to a Healthy Environment

On March 18, the High Court of South Africa in Pretoria issued a landmark judgment declaring that Mpumalanga province's unsafe level of air pollution is in breach of the residents' right to an environment that is not harmful to their health and well-being. This is according to section 24(a) of the Constitution, as well as other relevant sections of the constitution. The court then ordered the government to clean up the environment in the province.

A combination of poor governance and unethical business practices has left many communities living in the shadow of thousands of abandoned mines that litter South Africa. Abandoned coal mines pose grave safety and health risks to local communities, polluting critical water sources and arable land, and endanger the safety and lives of people, including children, who return to the unsafe mines in the hopes of eking out an income.

The Jagersfontein dam, in the Free State province, containing toxic mine waste that can cause long term environmental damage and health risks, collapsed on September 11, killing at least one person, injuring at least 35 others, and resulting in four people missing. According to media reports, sewage works were destroyed, leaving raw sewage flowing untreated into water sources, together with toxic mine waste.

Rule of Law

Zuma's corruption trial has suffered frequent delays. One of the reasons for the delays was caused by his appeal in June to the Constitutional Court against the Supreme Court's dismissal of his special plea to remove the lead state prosecutor, Billy Downer, whom he accused of lacking independence and impartiality. The Pietermaritzburg High Court was supposed to resume the trial of the case on October 17 but postponed the trial to January 2023 to allow the presiding judge to consider whether he should still be on the case.

Zuma has also started a private prosecution against Downer and journalist Karyn Maughan, for allegedly publishing documents containing his medical information in possession of the National Prosecuting Authority, without the permission of the National Director of Public Prosecutions.

Police Conduct

Members of the South African Police Services continue to violate rights with little accountability. On July 5, the court acquitted four police officers of killing Mthokozisi Ntumba, a bystander shot and killed during student protests at the University of Witwatersrand on March 10, 2021. In August the Independent Police Investigative Directorate announced an investigation into an incident captured on video footage of police officers assaulting an unnamed man in the Western Cape.

Women's Rights

In January, the government passed new laws, namely the Criminal Law (Sexual Offences and Related Matters) Amendment Act, the Criminal and Related Matters Amendment Act, the Domestic Violence Amendment Act, and the Criminal Law (Forensics Procedures) Amendment Act, to strengthen efforts to address the disturbingly high number of gender-based violence cases in the country. Despite these efforts, Police Minister Bheki Cele reported that between April and June,

855 women were killed, and over 11,855 cases of gender-based violence against women were reported, including 9,516 cases of rape.

Sexual Orientation and Gender Identity

South Africa's 2019 National Action Plan to combat Racism, Racial Discrimination, Xenophobia and Related Intolerance (NAP), recognizes the need to prevent discrimination and prejudice against LGBTI persons, in line with its constitutional goals of equality and non-discrimination. The National Intervention Strategy, adopted in 2014, and reviewed in 2019, considers the Gender-Based Violence and Femicide National Strategic Plan to ensure that the protection and advancement of LGBTI rights are adequately funded by the government.

In a letter to Human Rights Watch in February, Deputy Minister of Justice and Constitutional Development John Jeffery stated that the National Task Team on Gender and Sexual Orientation-based Violence Perpetrated against Lesbian, Gay, Bisexual, Transgender and Intersex Persons has established, among other initiatives, a Rapid Response Team, which monitors, and tracks hate crimes. The Minister reiterated the South African government's commitment to ensure that the Act is an intersectional, collaborated response to end discrimination, violence, hate, and bias crimes on the grounds of sexual orientation, gender identity, gender expression, and sex characteristics in the country.

Throughout 2022, LGBTI persons continued to face violence, including killings, sexual assault, harassment, and discrimination. The 2022 national census failed to recognize gender diversity by including a gender question that provides respondents with only two options: male or female.

In June 22, a Pretoria Magistrate court sentenced a man to 25 years for the murder of a lesbian woman who rejected his advances in 2021. In August, two men and a child were sentenced to 20- and 10-years' imprisonment respectively, for gang raping a gay man in 2017.

Children's Rights

Between 2021 and mid-2022, 400,000 to 500,000 children dropped out of school in South Africa, bringing the total number of out of school children to

750,000, according to the United Nations Children's Fund (UNICEF). Teenage pregnancy was identified as one of the reasons why children drop out of school in the country. Over half-a-million children with disabilities are excluded from education. On September 21, the South African Constitutional Court declared the Copyright Act unconstitutional because it did not include exceptions that would allow for the reproduction and adaptation of literary materials to meet the needs of persons who had a visual or print disability.

In November 2021, South Africa adopted the Policy on Prevention and Management of Learner Pregnancy in Schools, which recognizes students' right to continue in school during and after their pregnancy. Approximately 33 percent of girls do not return to school after falling pregnant. Since January, schools are compelled to report pregnancies under the age of 16, the age of consent, and as such any sexual activity below that age is statutory rape.

Xenophobia

Amid the economic downturn and unemployment fueled by Covid-19 restrictions, many foreign nationals in South Africa faced xenophobic violence. Vigilante groups such as "Operation Dudula" and "Put South Africa First", conducted door-to-door searches for undocumented foreign nationals, whom they blame for South Africa's high crime and unemployment rates.

In April, an anti-migrant mob killed a 43-year-old Zimbabwean national in Diepsloot, Johannesburg: in June, another mob set fire to the Yeoville market in Johannesburg, where mostly migrant shopkeepers rented stalls; and in September, a group of South Africans burned the homes of two migrant men in Plettenberg Bay, Western Cape.

Xenophobic sentiments in the country were further reinforced by prominent political figures such as Julius Malema, a member of parliament and leader of the Economic Freedom Fighters party. In January 2022, Malema visited restaurants in Johannesburg's Mall of Africa to assess the ratio of South African to foreign nationals employed by businesses there.

In April, acting resident coordinator of the United Nations in South Africa, Dr. Ayodele Odusola, raised concern about xenophobic violence in the country. In July, UN experts condemned the violence and called for accountability against xenophobia, racism and hate speech that was harming migrants, refugees, and asylum seekers.

Despite its strong legal and human rights framework on refugees and asylum seekers, South Africa's asylum management system continued to fail many in need of protection. The UN refugee agency (UNHCR) estimated that South Africa hosted over 240,000 refugees and asylum seekers as of April 2022. However, many others remained undocumented. Refugees and asylum seekers continued to face enormous challenges in applying for asylum and obtaining or renewing documentation.

In mid-2022, some government refugee reception offices reopened for the first time since their 2020 closure. However, many refugees and asylum seekers faced language, access, or technical barriers to using the online systemfor applications or permit renewals. Despite the government's extensions of permit renewal deadlines several times between 2020 and 2022, the ongoing barriers to registration and documentation caused asylum seekers and refugees to face risks of evictions, police harassment, and deportation, as well as difficulties opening or maintaining bank accounts, accessing basic services, and enrolling their children in school.   and documentation caused asylum seekers and refugees to face risks of evictions, police harassment, and deportation, as well as difficulties in opening or maintaining bank accounts, accessing basic services, and enrolling their children in school.

Climate Change Impacts and Policy

South Africa is among the top 20 emitters of greenhouse gases—and the top emitter in Africa. It is also among the world's top 10 coal producers and fourth biggest exporter, contributing to the climate crisis that is taking a growing toll on human rights around the globe. Although South Africa has included renewable energy in its energy mix, it continues to heavily rely on coal for 70 percent of energy demand, and the government has declared that this will be the case for the foreseeable future.

In the September 2021 update to its Nationally Determined Contribution (NDC), a Paris Agreement-mandated five-year national climate change action plan, the government announced plans for increasing yet still insufficient emission reduc-

HUMAN RIGHTS WATCH

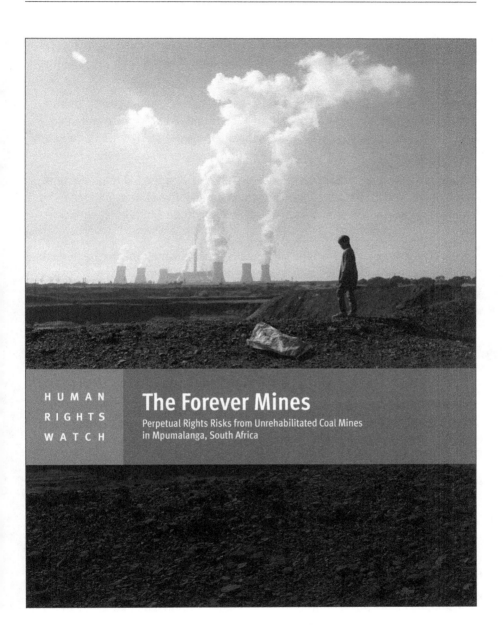

The Forever Mines
Perpetual Rights Risks from Unrehabilitated Coal Mines in Mpumalanga, South Africa

tions and a plan to reach net zero by 2050 giving the country an insufficient rating by the Climate Action Tracker, and independent scientific analysis that tracks government climate action.

In November 2021, at COP26 (Conference of the Parties) in Glasgow, Scotland, the United States, United Kingdom, European Union, French, and German governments announced that they would set aside $8.5 billion in funding for South Africa to assist with a more rapid and just transition from coal power.

In February, the government introduced the Climate Change Bill to parliament. The bill seeks to "enable the development of an effective climate change response and a long-term transition to a low-carbon and climate-resilient economy."

As a water-scarce country, South Africa is particularly vulnerable to the impacts of climate change. Extreme weather events have become more intense because of climate change, such as flooding in the Eastern Cape in January. In April more floods occurred in both KwaZulu-Natal and in the Eastern Cape that killed 448 people, displaced over 40,000 people and destroyed more than 12,000 homes, according to the UN.

Foreign Policy

In March, South Africa presented a draft resolution on the humanitarian situation in Ukraine to the UN General Assembly, which was criticized for not calling out Russia for its aggression but instead broadly mentioned "parties to the conflict." The country abstained from a UNGA vote, in April, to suspend Russia from the UN Human Rights Council.

President Cyril Ramaphosa raised objections to a draft Countering Malign Russian Activities in Africa Bill which was passed by the US House of Representatives in April and was pending before the Senate at time of writing. The bill seeks to sanction Africans doing business with Russian entities under US sanctions.

In February, South Africa extended by three months the deployment of 1,495 soldiers as part of its contribution to the Southern African Development Community (SADC) Mission in Mozambique, which the SADC authorized in July 2021 to support Mozambique's military operation against armed Islamist fighters in its Cabo Delgado province.

South Korea

While the Republic of Korea (South Korea) broadly respects the rights of its citizens, there are significant human rights concerns, especially regarding lesbian, gay, bisexual, and transgender (LGBT) people, women, migrants, racial minorities, older people, and people with disabilities. Before former President Moon Jae-in left office in May, his administration failed to pass a comprehensive anti-discrimination law to provide protection for these groups, despite strong public support for the draft law.

South Korea's public health measures to limit the spread of Covid-19 raised serious privacy concerns when the government announced it would test AI facial recognition technology to track the spread of the disease.

In August, large-scale flooding in Seoul disproportionately affected low-income residents living in semi-basement apartments (*banjiha*), bringing greater attention to prevailing economic inequalities in the country.

Women's Rights

Discrimination against women and girls is pervasive. In May, the candidate of the People Power Party, Yoon Suk-yeol, won the presidencye. His campaign included appeals to anti-feminist male voters that included blaming feminism for the decline in birthrate (which now hovers around 0.81, the lowest in the world), pledging to abolish the Ministry of Gender Equality and Family (which promotes women's rights and combats domestic violence), promising to enhance punishments for false accusations of sexual violence, and claiming there is no systemic gender discrimination in South Korea. At time of writing, the government was still discussing how to carry out the abolition of the Ministry of Gender Equality and Family.

The Economist magazine's "Glass Ceiling Index," which assesses women's educational attainment, women in managerial positions, and number of female parliamentarians, gives South Korea the lowest rank among Organization for Economic Co-operation and Development (OECD) member countries. The survey found that women earn 38 percent less than their male counterparts and that the country has the highest proportion of women working temporary jobs in the OECD.

The government continues to struggle to address rampant problems with digital sex crimes. In December 2021, new legislation passed by the National Assembly went into effect. This legislation, collectively known as the "Anti-Nth Room" laws, is an attempt to combat an uptick in digital sex crimes by strengthening punishments against offenders and holding internet service providers responsible for illegal content distributed on their systems. However, sex crime chat rooms remain hard to regulate, and in September, reports surfaced of new Telegram chat rooms, similar to the Nth Room, which were circulating pornographic deepfake content. The government has failed to take steps beyond the criminal legal system to address digital sex crimes, such as prevention through education and changing social norms, providing civil remedies, and expanding services for people targeted by digital sex crimes.

While the Constitutional Court of Korea decriminalized abortion in 2021, the National Assembly has yet to pass legislation to clarify how and where South Korean women can obtain legal abortions. The lack of legislation on abortion hinders providers and compromises women's right to health care.

Freedom of Expression

Though South Korea has a free press and a lively civil society, the government and large corporations use the country's criminal defamation laws to limit scrutiny of their actions. Convictions for criminal defamation are based only on whether what was said is in "the public interest," not its verity, and can result in up to seven years' imprisonment and a fine.

On September 15, the Constitutional Court started a review, following 11 petitions filed by individuals and district courts, of the National Security Act, which aims to ensure state security but has been used to criminalize positive comments about North Korea or dissemination of materials alleged to be North Korean propaganda. The law imposes significant restrictions on South Koreans' right to access information about North Korea. It also criminalizes acts to join, praise, or induce others to join an unclearly defined "anti-government organization," a broad term that is not defined in the law.

Children's Rights

The Education Ministry failed to act following reports that it had recommended unsafe online learning products for children's use during the Covid-19 pandemic. These products, two of which were built by the government, transmitted children's personal data to advertising technology companies, enabling them to track and target children across the internet for advertising purposes.

Sexual Orientation and Gender Identity

Discrimination against LGBT people remains pervasive in South Korea. In July, Seoul celebrated its first LGBT Pride parade in three years, which was attended by an estimated 13,000 people. An additional 15,000 anti-LGBT protesters also showed up to protest the marchers.

In the district elections held in Seoul in June, Cha Hae-young, a 35-year-old bisexual politician and LGBT rights activist, became the first openly LGBT elected official in South Korea.

In April, the Supreme Court of Korea overturned the military convictions of two gay soldiers who had been prosecuted for same-sex conduct under Article 92-6 of the Military Criminal Act. Although the court did not rule the provision unconstitutional, its decision set a precedent that should protect other soldiers who engage in same-sex activity.

In January, a South Korean court ruled against a gay couple who had registered for spousal health insurance benefits, asserting that there was no legal justification for expanding the definition of marriage to include same-sex partnerships.

Policy on Human Rights in North Korea

Since taking office, Yoon has strengthened the government's promotion of human rights in North Korea. In July, South Korea appointed Lee Shin-hwa to the long vacant position of special ambassador for North Korean human rights. Yoon's administration pledged to formally establish the North Korean Human Rights Foundation, an important institution created through the passage of the North Korean Human Rights Act of 2016. However, at time of writing, the government had yet to do so.

In June, prosecutors opened an investigation into the forced repatriation of two North Korean fisherman who had been apprehended off the coast of South Korea in 2019. The two men, whose identities were revealed by lawmakers in September, faced torture, forced labor, and possible execution when they were involuntarily returned without fair process.

In May, after North Korea officially announced a Covid-19 outbreak, Yoon stated that South Korea was prepared to send humanitarian aid to North Korea, including medicine and Covid-19 vaccines, and in September, his administration proposed a meeting with North Korean officials to discuss the possibility of reunions of families separated by the Korean War.

Workers' Rights

South Korea's ratifications of three core conventions of the International Labour Organization (ILO) — No. 29 on forced labor, No. 87 on freedom of association, and No. 98 on the right to organize and collective bargaining—entered into force in April.

However, the government has not ratified Convention No. 190, which requires ratifying states to implement measures to end harassment and violence in the workplace. According to the result of a survey conducted by Gapjil 119, a hotline that offers legal advice to workers facing harassment, nearly 29 percent of South Korean workers face abuse at work. However, there has been a growing social movement against employers' abuse of power, verbal and physical bullying, and failing to pay workers on time.

In September, the National Assembly debated a bill that would limit employers from seeking damages for losses incurred during strikes.

Key International Actors

South Korea provided more than $560 million annually in foreign aid primarily to countries around the world via the Korea International Cooperation Agency (KOICA) but did little to raise human rights issues publicly or privately in foreign policy or development aid consultations despite pledges by Yoon in his inaugural speech to protect freedom and human rights.

South Korea is a major diplomatic ally of the United States. Economically, its largest trading partner is China, which purchases more than 25 percent of South Korea's exports. However, in October, South Korea supported an initiative at the UN Human Rights Council to discuss a report by the UN High Commissioner for Human Rights on possible crimes against humanity in the Xinjiang region of China. The same month, South Korea also co-sponsored the annual resolution at the United Nations General Assembly condemning North Korean human rights violations, which it had been unwilling to sponsor since 2019. Under Yoon, South Korea has moved to repair relations with Japan that frayed significantly during the rule of former President Moon.

South Sudan

In 2022, South Sudanese confronted another year of violence, hunger, and stark challenges. Conflict persisted. Violence between armed groups in Upper Nile, southern Central Equatoria and southern Unity states resulted in displacements and serious abuses, some of which may qualify as war crimes or crimes against humanity. Conflict related sexual violence continued. Intercommunal and intersectional violence persisted in most parts of the country, with killings, displacement, looting, and destruction of property.

Meanwhile, the authorities threatened, harassed, and arbitrarily detained critics, journalists, protesters, and human rights activists for long periods without trial.

The country experienced its worst humanitarian crisis since independence, with the United Nations office for the Coordination of Humanitarian Affairs (OCHA) reporting that at least 7.7 million were food insecure. The agency attributed this to conflict, chronic underdevelopment, and severe weather conditions. Over 2.2 million people were internally displaced, in addition to over 2.3 million who had fled the country.

Parties to the 2018 Revitalized Agreement on the Resolution of Conflict in South Sudan agreed to extend the transitional period by 24 months from February 2023 when it should have concluded.

Attacks Against Civilians and Aid Operations

Between February and May, armed youth supported by government forces attacked civilians in Sudan People's Liberation Army in Opposition (SPLA/IO)-held territories in Leer, Koch, and Mayendit counties. In September, the United Nations Mission in South Sudan (UNMISS) issued a report concluding that at least 44,000 people were displaced, 173 unarmed civilians killed, 131 women raped, or gang raped, and at least 12 people sustained serious injuries.

The UNMISS findings were consistent with Human Rights Watch research on attacks in Leer county, which found similar patterns of abuses, including attacks against children, older people, and people with disabilities. Looting and destruction of food stocks, cattle, and humanitarian aid particularly exacerbated the dire food situation, leaving civilians at risk of starvation.

Ceasefire monitors in South Sudan documented similar patterns of abuses between January and May, implicating the South Sudan People's Defense Forces (SSPDF) supported by armed youth militias in attacks against unarmed civilians in territories controlled by the SPLA/IO in Upper Nile such as Maban, Longechuk, and Maiwut.

In February, President Salva Kiir signed separate peace deals with breakaway factions of the SPLM/A-IO known as Kitgwang led by Gen. Johnson Olony and Gen. Simon Gatwech Duel, which among other things, guaranteed them amnesty and allowed their forces to be integrated into the national army.

In July, violence broke out between Kitgwang, supported by government forces, and SPLA/IO in Upper Nile state, causing humanitarian crisis in the area. In August and September, violence within the Kitgwang faction and with the SPLA/IO in Tonga and Panyikang led to serious human rights abuses and displacement of thousands of people.

The government's counter-insurgency campaign against the National Salvation Front rebel group in Central and Western Equatoria states continued. Both sides committed abuses, including sexual violence, unlawful killings, and abductions of civilians.

Attacks against aid operations by armed groups and government forces persisted with no known investigations or prosecutions of perpetrators, all of whom were South Sudanese, were killed by armed groups in 2022.

Children and Armed Conflict

Recruitment and use of children by armed groups persisted. In March, a report by ceasefire monitors documented forced recruitment of children as young as 13 by SSPDF in Unity and Lakes states. A similar report in July implicated Cpt. Philip Khamis in recruiting children into National Security Service in Tambura, Western Equatoria state.

A UN report on children and armed conflict confirmed the recruitment and use of 129 children, of which 30 percent are below the age of 15, as combatants, bodyguards, and cooks by various groups, including the SSPDF, SPLM/A-IO, the South Sudan National Police Service, the South Sudan Opposition Alliance (SSOA), the National Salvation Front (NAS), forces loyal to Gen. James Nando, and forces loyal to Gen. Moses Lukujo.

Intercommunal Violence

In July, a UN report attributed more than 60 percent of civilian deaths in South Sudan to intercommunal violence and community-based militias.

Between April and June, UNMISS documented 117 civilian deaths and 35 injured from renewed intercommunal fighting between the Dinka Twic Mayardit and Dinka Ngok communities in the Abyei Administrative Area, intra-communal clashes in Greater Tonj, as well as attacks by armed Dinka and armed Nuer Youth on communities in Tonj North County.

Civic Space and Rule of Law

Authorities continued to restrict free expression, and freedom of association and assembly. Authorities have arbitrarily detained critics, human rights defenders, and journalists.

In October, the government started its trial of Abraham Chol Maketh, a clergy member arrested in July 2021 for predicting the South Sudanese government would be overthrown that month, and Kuel Aguer Kuel, a politician, arrested in August 2021 for links with an "anti-government movement." Human Rights Watch called for the independence of the judiciary to be respected.

Their detention and prosecution are part of a larger pattern of unlawful detentions, which exposes persistent weaknesses and challenges in the criminal justice system, including political interference from other branches of the government.

On August 7, the police and National Security Service agents detained seven people in KonyoKonyo market in Juba. They were protesting the rising cost of living. The security agents shot at protesters, injuring one person in the leg, and beat others with sticks and gun butts. The police arrested Diing Magot, a freelance journalist with Voice of America, who was interviewing protesters at

Konyokonyo and unlawfully detained her for eight days in the Malakia police station.

Legislative Developments

In May, parliament passed the amendment to the Political Parties Act 2012, despite a boycott by the SPLM-IO Party. The act contains a restrictive provision requiring a political party to have at least 500 members in at least eight of the nation's 10 states.

In September, the ministry of justice and constitutional affairs launched a cybercrimes court and appointed a special prosecutor to investigate and prosecute crimes committed online pursuant to the Cybercrimes and Computer Misuse Provisional Order issued by President Kiir in December 2021. The order, which gives the prosecution broad powers to arrest, search and seize, contains overly vague definitions of the terms "computer misuse," "terrorism," "indecent content," and "offensive communication;" and could be used to target and silence political critics and dissidents and restrict rights to privacy, freedom of expression, and access to information.

In September, the Lakes state government passed the Customary Law and Public Order Bill 2022 into law which outlawed child and forced marriage in that state.

At time of writing, review of the National Security Service Amendment Bill was pending. The bill limits, but does not eliminate, the agency's powers of arrest and detention. The bill was referred to the presidency in April 2021 for resolution but in August 2022 the presidency referred it to the ministry of justice for further guidance.

South Sudan criminalizes consensual same sex relations with up to 10 years in prison and forms of gender expression with up to one year.

Key International Actors

In March, the UN Security Council renewed the mandate of UNMISS for another year. That same month, the UN Human Rights Council, following a close vote, renewed the mandate of the Commission on Human Rights in South Sudan for another year.

In March, President Kiir ordered the release of a report written by the NSS and UK based law firm 9BR Chambers on the eruption of conflict in 2013 and 2016. The report, stood by the claim that an attempted coup by Riek Machar and other politicians was the cause of the 2013 and 2016 conflicts despite the African Union Commission of Inquiry and UN bodies finding no evidence of this.

In May, the UN Security Council renewed the arms embargo, travel ban, and assets freeze imposed on South Sudan for another year, and extended the mandate of the panel of experts until July 2023. The resolution requires South Sudan to achieve key progress on five benchmarks set out in resolution 2577(2021), upon which it shall review the arms embargo measures.

On July 15, the US cut off funding to the South Sudan peace process monitoring mechanism, citing lack of progress and political will to implement critical reforms. Also, for the first time, the US did not grant a waiver for South Sudan under the Child Soldiers Prevention Act; this resulted in the US holding back US$18 million to the UN peacekeeping force.

Impunity remained widespread, with only a handful of cases of security forces being tried for crimes against civilians in front of military court or in civilian trials.

The African Union Commission (AUC) has responsibility under the 2018 peace agreement to establish the Hybrid Court for South Sudan, but it failed to move ahead with the court's creation or press for greater action by South Sudanese authorities to establish the court together with the AU Commission.

Spain

Spain's pushback policy contributed to the deaths of migrants at its land and sea borders. Poverty increased during the year as inflation rose, particularly affecting food and energy prices. A landmark new law on rape and sexual consent was an improvement given weaknesses in Spanish legislation. Evictions of renters and mortgage-holders continued, despite an extension of a pandemic-related moratorium for people who could demonstrate socioeconomic vulnerability. Thousands of people living in an informal settlement near Madrid entered a third year without electricity.

Asylum and Migration

According to the United Nations refugee agency, UNHCR, by late October at least 25,389 people had arrived irregularly by sea to Spain's mainland and the Canary Islands, while 1,720 arrived by land. The lack of safe and legal routes continued to cause harm and death. Caminando Fronteras, a migrant rights group, estimated that 978 people had died at sea trying to cross by boat from Africa to Spain during the first half of the year, with about four in five of the deaths on the Atlantic route.

On June 24, at least 23 African men died during an attempt by as many as 2,000 people to enter Spanish territory by scaling a fence that separates the enclave of Melilla from Moroccan territory. The causes of death have not been definitively ascertained. Footage of the event showed Moroccan police beating people scaling the fence and Spanish police using tear gas and working with their Moroccan counterparts to send people back over the border. Dozens of migrants and police forces on both sides of the border were injured. Spanish authorities subsequently confirmed that they had summarily returned people to Morocco. Investigative journalists published findings in November that one migrant died on Spanish territory, and that his body was yet to be returned to his family.

In May, Spain ignored UNHCR concerns about the risk of torture and deported a 32-year-old Algerian asylum seeker who had been convicted of criminal offenses in Algeria. In May, the human rights ombudsperson reminded authorities that people from Morocco were entitled to seek international protection at the Temporary Stay Center for Foreigners in Melilla, from which they were being turned away.

An October ruling by the Constitutional Tribunal, in a case brought by a Moroccan man who arrived by boat in the Canary Islands in November 2020 and whom authorities tried to deport the next month, criticized police for failing to ensure his access to legal representation on arrival. The tribunal also drew attention to repeated failure by the police in this case and others to ensure proper judicial oversight of migration detention.

By late October, Spain had granted temporary protection to more than 150,000 people fleeing the conflict in Ukraine, including Ukrainian nationals, stateless people, and their dependents; Ukrainians already in Spain with and without regular status and unable to return home; and third country nationals previously living in Ukraine and unable to return to their country of origin.

By June, Spain had provided work and residence permits to 9,300 young people aged 16 to 23 who had either come to Spain as unaccompanied children or had been in state care, using a regularization program established in late 2021. The measure was focused on ensuring regulated access to the labor market, initially in agriculture, but increasingly in hospitality, manufacturing, and commerce.

Poverty and Inequality

Official data published in June found that 27.8 percent of the population was "at risk of poverty or social exclusion" in the country in 2021. This represented a small increase from the previous year, which equates to 397,000 more people, according to a leading anti-poverty nongovernmental organization. More than half (54 percent) of single-parent households, largely women-led, were at risk of poverty.

Governmental efforts, including furlough payments and additional social transfers, to blunt the economic impact of the Covid-19 pandemic may have helped slow this increase, as the percentage of the population in severe social and material deprivation decreased marginally over this period. However, official data from 2021 showed that many households were already facing an increasing cost of living, as the percentage of households struggling with housing and energy costs increased.

HUMAN RIGHTS WATCH

HUMAN RIGHTS WATCH

"We Can't Live Like This"
Spain's Failure to Protect Rights Amid Rising Pandemic-Linked Poverty

Price inflation increased by 10.5 percent between August 2021 and August 2022, reaching the highest level since the current official measure began in 1994 and exacerbating concerns about increasing poverty. By September, certain staple foods were between 25 and 40 percent more expensive than the previous year.

In May, the country's main food bank network predicted that demand would rise by a fifth by the year's end, driven by the pressures of inflation on people living on low incomes.

The government adopted reforms to the Minimum Vital Income (IMV) program, established in May 2020, to reduce high rejection rates, improve the flawed eligibility calculation method, and ensure faster processing of applications for the social assistance program. Although the government raised IMV support levels at the start of the year, including specific additional payments for single-parent households and people with disabilities, the increases were rapidly outpaced by inflation. The program also retained arbitrary criteria, which continued to exclude most people aged between 18 and 22, and people without one year's continuous legal residence.

In June, the government extended to the end of the year a moratorium on evictions of people who could demonstrate "social and economic vulnerability," a measure introduced in 2020 to mitigate the impact the Covid-19 pandemic. However, despite this move, housing rights activists raised concerns about the adequacy of the law's definition of "vulnerability" as evictions continued to be enforced, with 11,000 taking place in the first three months of the year.

A government draft law that would introduce the statutory concept of "affordable housing" and seek to remedy a system-wide lack of public housing was pending in Parliament at time of writing.

At time of writing, an estimated 4,000 people, including more than 1,800 children, living in parts of Cañada Real, an informal settlement in greater Madrid, were entering a third year without electricity. Residents raised concerns about dealing with extreme weather, and the impact on children's access to education and hygiene. Residents filed suit in September asking for an investigation into the move by authorities and energy providers to cut off utilities in October 2020. In October, in an admissibility decision relating to a separate complaint brought by residents of Cañada Real, the European Committee of Social Rights directed the government to take immediate measures to ensure sufficient electricity to the settlement or offer suitable alternative accommodation to residents.

Gender-Based Violence and Sexual Abuse

In August, Parliament approved long-awaited legislation on rape and sexual consent. The new "Yes Means Yes" law clarifies that consent cannot be inferred from passivity, silence, or by default, and attempts to close a loophole in which rape of children could be tried as a lower offense of "sexual abuse" where violence and intimidation are not proven. Activists raised concerns that certain recategorization of crimes under the new law reduces minimum sentences for some sexual crimes, which can also have retrospective application

Official figures published in March and June showed that complaints to the authorities of gender-based violence increased during the prior year and the first three months of 2022. The figures also showed that judicial authorities were using new powers from 2021 to suspend visitation rights in cases of suspected domestic violence.

In July, the human rights ombudsperson's new service for victims of clerical sexual abuse began its work, and by late September reported that it had attended to 230 victims, most of whom are men. The ombudsperson's investigation—the first of its kind in Spain—is in progress.

Right to Health

In July, the UN CEDAW held that Spanish health authorities had in 2012 violated the rights of a woman known as NAE by forcing her to have a premature induction of labor and cesarean delivery without her consent, thereby subjecting her to obstetric violence. The committee recommended that the state provide reparations to NAE, ensure an improved approach to free, prior, and informed consent in the context of reproductive health, and greater respect for patients' rights when dealing with complaints in the judicial system.

The government announced draft legislation in May to allow women workers to take three days of paid leave per month for severe period pain and proposing to remove the three-day waiting period for access to abortion and a parental requirement for girls aged 16 and 17 to access abortion.

Surveillance and Right to Privacy

In April, digital rights researchers based in Canada published findings that the phones of at least 65 people, including Catalan and Basque pro-independence politicians, lawyers, and civil society activists, had been infected with spyware. Later reports suggested the National Intelligence Center (CNI) was responsible for the hack. The human rights ombudsman's investigation into the affair concluded that the CNI's actions had been in line with existing law but encouraged an assessment of whether the legislation governing surveillance was adequate.

In May, the government dismissed the director of the National Intelligence Centre (CNI) after further reports of spyware attacks. The prime minister announced legislation proposing a restructuring and change in oversight of the CNI, and a change in the official secrets law. Cybersecurity experts and human rights groups were critical of whether the steps taken were sufficient to address the lack of oversight.

Discrimination and Intolerance

A March report, produced by two nongovernmental organizations and financed by the Equality Ministry, documented widespread discrimination by real estate agents and private landlords based on racial, ethnic, or national origin. The same report also found that people of minority racial or ethnic background made up 90 percent of inhabitants of informal settlements.

Equal treatment and anti-discrimination legislation, which became law in July, modified existing hate-crime legislation to include anti-gypsyism (anti-gitanismo) and aporofobia (fear of the poor) as prosecutable motives in criminal law.

In September, the government sought to expedite a draft law with provisions on gender recognition based on self-identification for transgender and non-binary people, including children. The lower house of parliament's rejected a similar proposed legislation the previous year. The September draft law also proposed improvements to protections from discrimination for lesbian, gay, bisexual, and transgender (LGBT) people.

Sri Lanka

An economic crisis caused acute shortages of essential goods including fuel and medicines, electricity cuts, spiraling price inflation, and desperate hardship for millions of people, jeopardizing their rights to health, education, and an adequate standard of living. Women and girls were particularly affected.

The crisis sparked several months of widespread protests against the government of President Gotabaya Rajapaksa, alleging misgovernance and corruption and calling for his removal from office. In July, after protesters overran the president's official residence and other government buildings, Rajapaksa fled the country and resigned. He was replaced by his party's nominee, Ranil Wickremesinghe, who had previously been prime minister several times.

Wickremesinghe launched a crackdown on dissent, using the security forces to attack and disperse peaceful protesters, carrying out dozens of arrests including under the draconian Prevention of Terrorism Act.

Both the Rajapaksa and Wickremesinghe administrations blocked efforts at accountability for violations committed during and after Sri Lanka's civil war. The victims of past abuses, as well as human rights defenders and other civil society activists, faced harassment, intimidation, and surveillance by state security agencies.

Accountability and Justice

The government opposed efforts to advance accountability for violations of international law committed during and after Sri Lanka's civil war, from 1983 to 2009, between the government and the separatist Liberation Tigers of Tamil Elam (LTTE).

Former President Gotabaya Rajapaksa had pursued policies that are hostile to the Tamil and Muslim communities, while using the security forces to intimidate and suppress human rights activists and the families of victims of enforced disappearance. In August, Mothers of the Disappeared, a group campaigning to know the fate of missing loved ones, marked 2,000 days of continuous activism.

Wickremesinghe took office pledging to uphold rights but refused to join efforts of the United Nations Human Rights Council to advance accountability.

The UN high commissioner for human rights, in her September 2022 report, found that the Sri Lankan government "had still not presented a credible new roadmap on transitional justice.... Instead, accountability processes for past crimes were obstructed, perpetrators granted Presidential pardon and the Office on Missing Persons and the Office for Reparations ... have failed to achieve the tangible results expected by victims and other stakeholders."

On October 6, the Human Rights Council adopted a resolution extending the mandate of a UN project to collect and analyze evidence of conflict-era violations for use in future prosecutions, and mandating enhanced UN monitoring of the rights situation.

Economic and Social Rights

Sri Lanka had high levels of public debt and, especially following tax cuts introduced by the Rajapaksa administration in 2019, one of the lowest levels of taxation in the world. Dwindling foreign reserves led to difficulties financing essential imports, including fuel, food, and medicine. In May, Sri Lanka defaulted on its foreign debts, accelerating an economic crisis that disastrously impacted living standards. In June, the United Nations warned that 5.7 million people "require immediate humanitarian assistance."

Sri Lanka's principal social protection program, Samurdhi, purports to make cash payments to very low-income households. The World Bank reported in 2021 that "less than half of the poor were beneficiaries of Samurdhi, and benefit amounts remain largely inadequate."

In the 2022 budget, the Defense Ministry received the highest allocation at 373 billion rupees (then US$1.86 billion), an increase from the previous year, amounting to 15 percent of total expenditure. The Health Ministry was allocated less than half that, a decrease from the previous year, despite the Covid-19 pandemic.

The Rajapaksa administration repeatedly acted to block financial transparency and accountability for alleged corruption by weakening independent institutions and by intervening to prevent investigations and prosecutions in high-profile cases. Numerous prominent corruption cases were withdrawn or dismissed by the courts.

A 2020 amendment to the constitution had undermined the independence of institutions responsible for defending human rights and the rule of law, including the judiciary, the Human Rights Commission, the National Audit Office, and the Commission to Investigate Allegations of Bribery or Corruption. Although Wickremesinghe promulgated a further amendment, these measures fell short of reversing those changes.

On September 1, Sri Lanka agreed to a bailout plan with the International Monetary Fund (IMF). According to the IMF, the proposed program will include measures to increase social protection coverage and address corruption. However, the detailed contents of the proposed program had not been published at time of writing, and it cannot be implemented until a debt restructuring agreement is reached with Sri Lanka's international creditors.

Freedom of Peaceful Assembly

The widespread economic hardship generated a protest movement in which large numbers of people from all walks of life participated. Protesters raised a wide variety of demands, including accountability for human rights abuses. The most prominent demands included that President Rajapaksa should resign, and that a new government should adopt constitutional reforms and address corruption.

For several months, protesters occupied a site outside the presidential secretariat in central Colombo, and at the height of the protests in July they briefly occupied the secretariat and the official residences of the president and prime minister.

President Gotabaya Rajapaksa declared a state of emergency on April 1, then imposed a 36-hour curfew and blocked social media in an attempt to curb protests. The state of emergency lasted five days. On several occasions, police used unnecessary or excessive force, including on April 19, when they fired on protesters in Rambukkana, near Kandy in central Sri Lanka. One person was killed and at least 14 wounded.

On May 6, the government reimposed a state of emergency. On May 9, government supporters attacked peaceful anti-government protest sites in Colombo. Following the attack there were numerous violent incidents in Colombo and elsewhere, including clashes between government supporters and anti-government protesters, and attacks on the property of ruling party politicians. Over 150 people were injured and at least five died in different incidents. Prime Minister Mahinda Rajapaksa resigned the same day, and the president appointed Ranil Wickremesinghe to replace him three days later.

On July 9, protesters overran the president's official residence in Colombo. President Gotabaya Rajapaksa fled the country that evening, and later resigned. Ranil Wickremesinghe became acting president and was later elected president by members of parliament and inaugurated on July 21.

On July 18, Wickremesinghe proclaimed a third state of emergency, and on July 21 issued an order to "call out with effect from July 22, 2022, all the members of the Armed Forces .... for the maintenance of public order." In the early hours of July 22, Sri Lankan security forces forcibly dispersed people at a peaceful protest site and assaulted protesters in central Colombo, injuring more than 50 people and arresting at least 9 others. .... for the maintenance of public order."

The police subsequently targeted perceived protest leaders for arrest and detention, making dozens of arrests. Following a protest on August 18, three student activists were detained under the Prevention of Terrorism Act (PTA). On September 23, the government invoked the Official Secrets Act to declare areas of central Colombo "high security zones," inside which public gatherings required prior written permission from the police, before revoking the order one week later," inside which public gatherings required prior written permission from the police, before revoking the order one week later.

Human Rights Defenders

The authorities continued to target civil society groups, including human rights defenders and the families of victims of past violations. The UN high commissioner for human rights reported that activists are "regularly visited in their offices or homes or called by the police for inquiries," while in the north and east,

HUMAN RIGHTS WATCH

HUMAN RIGHTS WATCH

"In a Legal Black Hole"
Sri Lanka's Failure to Reform the Prevention of Terrorism Act

"[o]rganisations report being unable to work without surveillance" and must "get approval from the [government] district secretariat for any activity."

Counterterrorism Laws

Following years of campaigning by Sri Lankan activists, as well as diplomatic pressure from the European Union and others, the government amended the Prevention of Terrorism Act in March. Since its introduction as a "temporary" measure in 1979, the law has been used to enable abuses including torture and prolonged arbitrary detention, targeting minorities in particular.

Even as amended, the law still allows the government to detain anyone for up to a year without charge, without producing any evidence, and without the possibility of bail. The amendments do not provide meaningful safeguards against torture, instead encouraging it by allowing convictions based on confessions to a police officer. Following the amendment, the law still does not meet any of the five "necessary prerequisites" set out in December 2021 by seven UN human rights experts for meeting Sri Lanka's international human rights obligations.

Despite promising to observe a moratorium on the use of the law, authorities in August detained three student activists who participated in a demonstration under the PTA. The government said it would replace the law but failed to hold consultations to ensure a rights-respecting framework.

Women's and Girls' Rights

The Muslim Marriage and Divorce Act (MMDA), which governs marriage in the Muslim community, contains numerous provisions that violate the rights of Muslim women and girls, including by allowing child marriage without setting any minimum age. The act stipulates that only men can be judges of the Qazi (family) court, makes it easier for men than for women to obtain a divorce, and does not require a woman or girl's consent to be recorded before the registration of her marriage. Furthermore, the penal code permits what would otherwise constitute statutory rape, in cases of child marriage that are permitted under the MMDA, by providing that a man having sexual relations with a girl under the age of 16 years commits rape unless she is above the age of 12 and is his wife.

For decades, campaigners have called for the MMDA to be amended. In 2021, the cabinet approved reforms to the act that Muslim women's rights activists welcomed. However, they were not presented to parliament and the process appeared to have been derailed.

Sri Lanka has among the most restrictive abortion laws in the world, imposing long prison sentences for all abortions with exceptions only for saving a woman's life. On March 8, 2022, then-Justice Minister Ali Sabry called for parliament to consider legalizing abortion in cases of rape. However, the government failed to bring new legislation.

Sexual Orientation and Gender Identity

The penal code prohibits "carnal intercourse against the order of nature" and "any act of gross indecency." These provisions are widely understood to criminalize consensual same-sex activity. Another provision, which prohibits "cheating by personation," is used by police to target transgender people, while the 1841 Vagrants Ordinance contains overbroad and vague provisions that are used to target transgender women and women suspected to be sex workers.

The states of emergency that were repeatedly imposed during 2022 included provisions to increase the criminal penalties imposed for violating these laws. In March, the UN Committee on the Elimination of Discrimination against Women issued a decision calling for decriminalization of consensual same-sex relations.

Key International Actors

The rivalry between China and other powers to assert strategic influence in the region partly forms the context for Sri Lanka's international relations. Key actors include India, the United States, and Japan, which along with Australia are members of the Quadrilateral Security Dialogue, known as the Quad, aimed at countering China. Economic assistance provided to Sri Lanka has partly been viewed by states through the lens of this rivalry.

On September 1, Sri Lanka reached a staff-level agreement with the International Monetary Fund. However, it cannot be implemented until a debt restructuring agreement is reached with foreign creditors. Private investors hold around half of Sri Lanka's debt, while major bilateral creditors include China, Japan, and India. The debt negotiations are therefore complicated by strategic considerations. USAID Administrator Samantha Power traveled to Sri Lanka in September and noted US concerns about governance regarding obtaining IMF resources. She called on Sri Lankan authorities to implement reforms to "enlist the trust and confidence of Sri Lankans who are waiting to see the change that they feel they were promised."

The European Union is an important trading partner that has leverage over Sri Lanka through its GSP+ program, which grants the country tariff-free access to the EU market in exchange for Sri Lanka's obligation to comply with human rights and labor rights conventions. The EU urged Sri Lanka to replace the PTA, and to meanwhile reduce its use and release PTA prisoners detained without charges. Throughout the protests, the EU delivered humanitarian assistance and urged authorities to respect human rights and undertake structural reforms. to respect human rights and undertake structural reforms.

The UN Human Rights Council resolution on Sri Lanka was led by a core group including the United Kingdom, United States, Canada, Germany, and Malawi.

Sudan

Since the October 25, 2021 coup, protest groups that took to the streets faced repression from heavily deployed security forces.

As of September, at least 117 people had been killed and nearly 6,000 injured by state security forces since the October 25 coup in connection with repression of the protests. Security forces also unlawfully detained, forcibly disappeared, and committed sexual and gender-based violence against individuals perceived to be active in the protest movement.

Though the state of emergency imposed following the coup was lifted on May 29, 2022, abuses justified under it have continued, including arbitrary arrests of protesters.

The international response to the coup, including by the previously established "Troika" (United States, United Kingdom, and Norway), has been muted. The United Nations Integrated Mission to Support Transition in Sudan (UNITAMS), the African Union (AU), and Inter-Governmental Authority on Development (IGAD) in May established a tripartite mechanism to facilitate a political dialogue between various actors, including the military. Protest groups rejected the mechanism, saying it sidelined their demands.

In September, the steering committee of the Sudan Bar Association concluded discussions around a draft transitional constitution.

The International Criminal Court's (ICC) trial of Ali Kosheib, or Kushayb, former Janjaweed leader, began in April. He is charged with 31 counts of war crimes and crimes against humanity allegedly committed in Darfur. The ICC prosecutor expects to complete presenting his case against Kushayb in early 2023.

Given the political instability created by the coup, ongoing protests, and suspended international funds, Sudan's economy continued to deteriorate. This impacted an array of social and economic rights, including access to basic health care. Price hikes, particularly on food, linked in part to the conflict in Ukraine, has resulted in further economic hardships. The United Nations (UN) World Food Program (WFP) warned that 40 percent of the population may slip into food insecurity.

Conflict, Abuses in Darfur, and Blue Nile

In Darfur, the site of widespread abuses for almost two decades, attacks against civilians continued. In West Darfur, a renewed cycle of violence since December 2021 left hundreds dead, thousands displaced, hundreds of civilian homes scorched, and property looted.

Between December 5 and 7, 2021, armed groups from Arab tribes attacked the Kereneik locality in West Darfur, including a displaced persons' camp in the area, leaving 44 dead and at least 15,000 displaced.

In April, there was another large-scale attack on Kereneik locality, which affected at least 16 nearby villages. Over 160 people were killed and 98,000 displaced according to local authorities. Survivors of the attack said armed Arabs, joined by members of the Rapid Support Forces (RSF), launched the attack which also resulted in significant property damage, including through arson.

In Blue Nile, that borders Ethiopia and is governed by Sudan People's Liberation Army/Movement-North (SPLA/M-North), clashes which occurred between the Hausa and Birta ethnic groups left over 100 people dead, and caused a massive displacement in the region.

Ongoing Crackdown on Protesters

Protests against the coup and for a new civilian transition continued throughout the year, primarily in Khartoum but also in other cities such as Atbara, in River Nile state in northern Sudan, and Wad Madani, in the central region.

The junta deployed a range of security forces, primarily from the Central Reserve Police (CRP) and anti-riot police, but on occasion military units, to suppress the protests.

In efforts to suppress protests since the coup, security forces have killed at least 117 people, including 23 children. They have regularly resorted to excessive use of force, including lethal force. On November 17, 2021, security forces violently dispersed protests in Khartoum's Bahri area, killing 16 people, the deadliest day since the beginning of the coup. On January 17, security forces used live ammunition, killing seven protesters. The use of lethal force by security forces continued throughout the year, with eight protesters killed on June 30 in Khartoum.

In addition to live ammunition, security forces also unlawfully used tear gas canisters, stun grenades, and rubber bullets, causing severe physical harm.

Security forces also targeted hospitals and medical care providers. Several hospitals in Khartoum were raided by security forces, arresting wounded protesters, and disrupting provision of medical care.

Unlawful Detention, Arrest, and Ill-Treatment

Security forces, notably from the Criminal Investigative Directorate (CID), have unlawfully detained hundreds, many of whom are active or perceived by the authorities to be active in the protest movement and forcibly disappeared scores. Security forces have ill-treated detained protesters and threatened women protesters with sexual violence. In December 2021, the UN reported receiving at least 13 reports of cases of rape and gang rape of female protesters by security forces.

Security forces have also ill-treated children, including allegedly stripping them naked and partially shaving their heads.

Authorities have detained hundreds in prisons in Khartoum under vague emergency orders without judicial or prosecutorial oversight. Following the lifting of the state of emergency on May 29, the UN said a total of 171 detainees in connection to the protests were released. Detaining authorities have also violated due process, including denying lawyers and families' access to detainees.

In May, several Forces of Freedom and Change (FFC) leaders were released from prison after being charged with financial related offenses.

On January 14, seven people were arrested in connection with the killing of a CRP commander at a protest the day before. Four have since been released. However, Mohamed Adam, then 17; Ahmed al-Fatih ("al-Nannah"); and Mohamed el-Fatih remained in detention at time of writing. Lawyers said the three have been tortured and been forced to deliver false confessions. The three appeared in court on May 28 but the trial was postponed after the court ordered a medical examination into the allegation of torture.

Accountability

There have been no meaningful domestic steps toward accountability for abuses committed against protesters since the coup, or for prior abuses including the June 3, 2019 massacre, or decades of war crimes and crimes against humanity committed against civilians in Darfur, Blue Nile, and South Kordofan. Days after seven protesters were killed on January 17, al-Burhan ordered an investigation into the killings and for findings to be submitted within 72 hours. To date, no findings have been made public.

On April 5, the ICC held its first Darfur trial of Ali Kosheib, or Kushayb. Proceedings are ongoing. In August, the ICC prosecutor visited three internally displaced people's (IDP) camps in Central and South Darfur, and, for the first time, briefed the UN Security Council from the site of a situation country, warning against "a false dawn" after "a backwards step on cooperation" from the Sudanese authorities in the previous months.

Right to Education

Sudan's penal code criminalizes sex outside of marriage. As a result, unmarried pregnant girls and adolescent mothers may face criminal punishments, and often do not manage to stay in school.

Sexual Orientation and Gender Identity

Individuals accused of "homosexual sex" face between five years and life imprisonment, depending on the number of prior convictions.

Refugees and Migrants

Sudan hosted more than 1.1 million refugees and asylum seekers during 2021, most of whom were South Sudanese. While the government maintains an open border policy for refugees, protection gaps undermine their liberty, safety, and dignity. Some lack access to registration, documentation, and public services. Sudan's encampment policy imposes movement restrictions by requiring asylum seekers and refugees to stay in designated camps. Outside camps, some refugees and asylum seekers were subjected to arrest, detention, harassment, or extortion.

Key International Actors

In November 2021, the UN High Commissioner for Human Rights designated Adama Dieng as Sudan's independent expert, mandated to report on human rights abuses following the coup. Dieng traveled to Sudan in February 2022 and again in June 2022.

As international funding remained suspended following the coup, the deputy head of the Sovereign Council, Mohamed Hamdan Dagalo ("Hemedti"), headed to Moscow for meetings with Russian officials to discuss economic relationships among other issues. The visit aimed at deepening ties with Russia which faced western sanctions as result of its invasion of Ukraine.

On March 21, the United States (US) Department of the Treasury's Office of Foreign Assets Control (OFAC) designated the Sudan Central Reserve Police (CRP) for serious human rights abuses. In July, the US House of Representatives passed a Congress approved resolution that condemned the coup and called on the administration to identify leaders of the coup for potential targeted sanctions. No steps have so far been taken by the US government against individuals for their role in repression in Sudan. In August, the first US ambassador in 25 years, John Godfrey, arrived in Khartoum to assume duties.

Sudan's regional and international partners supported a tripartite mechanism, composed of UNITAMS, AU, and IGAD. The mechanism has facilitated a series of talks with various actors, but resistance committees and other protest groups boycotted the process. Meanwhile, the US, UK, Saudi Arabia, and United Arab Emirates (UAE) (known as the "Quad") have also sought to facilitate talks between different stakeholders.

International actors, including the World Bank and United States Agency for International Development (USAID), suspended assistance to Sudan shortly after the coup. Sudan lost access to around US$4 billion pledged by international actors that was dedicated to support multiple projects, including agriculture, energy, as well as direct budget support.

In June, Paris Club countries suspended Sudan's debt removal process. The decision, triggered by the coup and failure to fulfil agreed conditions, was a setback to efforts by the ousted government to write off over $23 billion of debt.

The World Food Program announced in July that they received $100 million from the World Bank for food and cash transfers to over two million people, including internally displaced people. The WFP already warned that almost 40 percent of the population could slide into hunger by September.

Border clashes between Sudan and Ethiopia continued to be reported. In June, Sudan accused Ethiopia of capturing and killing seven soldiers and a civilian.

Syria

In 2022, civilians in Syria faced another year of grave abuses and severe hardship, perpetuated by the Syrian government and other parties to the conflict and compounded by the worst economic and humanitarian crisis the country has faced since the start of the conflict in 2011. In September, the chair of the United Nations Independent International Commission of Inquiry (COI) on Syria warned that the country may again return to "larger-scale fighting."

In June, the UN Human Rights Office announced that more than 306,000 civilians were killed in Syria between March 1, 2011, and March 31, 2021. As of August, the Syrian Network for Human Rights declared that around 111,000 people remain disappeared, most at the hands of the Syrian government.

Although Syria remains unsafe, refugee hosting countries like Turkey and Lebanon began advocating for large-scale returns of Syrian refugees in 2022.

Government-Held Areas (Central, West, and Southwest Syria)

Syrian security forces and government-affiliated militias continue to arbitrarily detain, disappear, and mistreat people across the country, including children, people with disabilities and older people, and returnees and individuals in retaken areas who have signed so-called reconciliation agreements. Authorities also continued to unlawfully confiscate property and restrict access to areas of origin for returning Syrians.

On March 30, the Syrian government passed a law criminalizing torture and assigning a penalty ranging from three years' imprisonment up to the death penalty where the torture results in death or involves rape. The law also prohibited any authority from ordering torture and invalidated any evidence gathered through torture. However, according to the COI's September 2022 report, "torture and ill-treatment in detention remained systematic, including in Sednaya prison and in several detention facilities operated by Syrian intelligence."

On April 18, Syrian President Bashar al-Assad ratified a new cybercrimes law aimed at curbing the "misuse of technology," and combatting "cybercrime" in the face of new technologies. The new law introduced harsh punishments for vaguely defined crimes, including "cybercrimes" that target public officials and government employees.

On April 30, a general amnesty granted by al-Assad for "Syrian citizens detained on 'terrorism-related' crimes,'" was carried out haphazardly and without transparency and led to the documented release of only a small number of detainees. Thousands remain disappeared, many since 2011, with no information on their whereabouts.

On April 27, footage of executions by Syrian Military Intelligence of at least 41 individuals in 2013 in the Damascus neighborhood of Tadamon was published in the media. On September 16, Agence France Presse (AFP) reported on what former prisoners called the "salt rooms," primitive mortuaries inside Syria's prisons designed to preserve bodies in the absence of refrigerated morgues.

Northwest Syria

Northwest Syria is home to more than 4.1 million civilians, at least half of whom have been displaced at least once since the start of the conflict. Civilians in these areas are effectively trapped, lacking resources to relocate, unable to cross into Turkey, and fearing persecution if they attempt to relocate to government-held areas.

In Idlib and western Aleppo, indiscriminate attacks by Syrian-Russian military forces on civilians and critical civilian infrastructure persisted in 2022. One Russian air attack on Idlib on July 22 killed seven civilians, including four children from one family, according to the Syrian Network for Human Rights. Since the beginning of Russia's military intervention in Syria in 2015, and by March 2022, the civilian harm monitor Airwars estimated that Russian actions across the country had killed almost 25,000 civilians.

At the same time, according to the COI, Hay'et Tahrir al-Sham (HTS), the dominant anti-government armed group, continued to raid and arbitrarily detain activists, humanitarian workers, and civilians voicing critical opinions. The report also documented continued monopolization of the fuel market and other services as well as confiscation of property at the hands of the Al-Qaeda-affiliated armed group.

Northeast Syria

In May, Turkish President Recep Tayyip Erdoğan threatened to launch what would be Turkey's fourth military incursion into northeast Syria since 2016 aimed at driving out the Kurdish-led, United States-backed Syrian Democratic Forces (SDF) from areas it controls south of Turkey's border. While at the time of writing no full-scale invasion of the targeted areas had taken place, air raids by Turkish forces and mutual bombardment by Turkish-backed local armed groups and the SDF intensified. The Biden Administration has stated that the 900 US troops currently on the ground in Syria would remain for the time being. After the US withdrawal from Afghanistan in 2021, this represents one of the US's largest troop deployments in an active war zone.

Turkey last invaded and occupied parts of northeast Syria in October 2019, where it remains in control. In Turkish-occupied territories, Turkey and local Syrian factions continued to abuse civilians' rights and restrict their freedoms with impunity. Most of northeast Syria remains under the control of the Kurdish-led Autonomous Administration.

Following the territorial defeat of the Islamic State in 2019, about 66,000 men, women, and children (suspected former ISIS members and their families) remained arbitrarily and unlawfully detained in life-threatening, degrading, and often inhuman conditions by the SDF in northeast Syria. They include nearly 43,000 foreigners—about 60 percent of them children from nearly 60 countries who have been held for more than three years without ever being brought before a court. Fewer than three dozen countries are known to have repatriated or helped bring home any of their nationals, and most of these have allowed only a limited number to return.

An ISIS attack on al-Sina'a prison in Hasakeh city on January 20 triggered a 10-day battle that drew in US and UK forces to fight alongside the SDF, left more than 500 dead and displaced at least 45,000 residents, according to the UN. At time of writing, authorities in northeast Syrian had still not provided a breakdown of how many boys imprisoned in al-Sina'a were missing or dead. During military operations to recapture ISIS attackers and detainees who had escaped the prison, dozens of private buildings housing more than 140 families were destroyed, apparently by the SDF. At the time of writing, the SDF had not provided affected residents with any compensation or plans for reconstruction or alternative housing.

The SDF has also carried out mass arrest campaigns against civilians including activists, journalists, and teachers. In late July 2022, amid heightened tensions with Turkey, the SDF reportedly arrested at least 16 activists and media workers. According to the Syrian Network for Human Rights, the arrests were carried out under the pretext of "espionage."

Economic Crisis and Rights Implications

Syrians faced the worst economic crisis since the conflict began in 2011, brought on by the prolonged nature of the armed conflict, economic crises in neighboring Turkey and Lebanon, the Covid-19 pandemic, sanctions, a severe drought, and the economic consequences of the war in the Ukraine.

In 2022, 90 percent of Syrians lived below the poverty line and at least 12 million Syrians out of an estimated remaining population of around 16 million were food insecure, according to the World Food Programme (WFP). More than 600,000 children were chronically malnourished. Access to shelter, healthcare, electricity, education, public transportation, water, and sanitation have all worsened dramatically since the conflict began. People across the country were facing fuel shortages and rising food prices.

In February, the government announced the exclusion of some 600,000 families from its subsidies program, which includes gas and heating fuels, bread, and other basic commodities such as flour and sugar. The move triggered protests in the southern governorate Suwaida and public criticism online.

In September, a deadly cholera outbreak spread across northern Syria leading to fears that it may spread to the rest of Syria and the region more broadly.

Obstacles to Humanitarian Aid and Reconstruction

At least 14.6 million Syrians needed humanitarian aid across Syria in 2022, an increase of 1.2 million from 2021, according to the UN Office for the Coordination of Humanitarian Affairs (OCHA).

Millions in northeast and northwest Syria relied on the cross-border flow of food, medicine, and other lifesaving assistance, including the Covid-19 vaccine. Aid workers told Human Rights Watch that non-UN agencies had nowhere near the UN's capacity to buy supplies and transport them into the northwest. They said that shutting down UN aid supplies and ending UN funding, as Russia has repeatedly threatened to do with its UN Security Council veto, would deny aid to millions of people.

Non-UN aid groups in northeast Syria said they have been unable to bring in enough aid, particularly for health care, since the UN was forced to stop its cross-border operations between Iraq and Syria in January 2020.

In July 2022, Russia vetoed a UN Security Council resolution that would have renewed authorization for a full year for the only remaining cross-border humanitarian aid operation through the Bab al-Hawa crossing from Turkey to northwest Syria, without Damascus's backing. Instead, the Security Council agreed to extend this critical lifeline for only six months, meaning it would expire in January 2023 in the middle of winter, when needs are greatest. At time of writing, it was unclear if Russia will agree to another renewal of the mandate.

The Syrian government continued to impose severe restrictions on the delivery of humanitarian aid in government-held areas of Syria and elsewhere in the country and to divert aid to punish those who express dissent. A lack of sufficient safeguards in procurement practices by UN agencies providing aid in Syria has resulted in a serious risk of financing abusive entities.

Women's Rights

Women in government held areas continued to face discrimination in relation to marriage, divorce, responsibility over children, and inheritance under the Personal Status Law. A woman loses her right to financial maintenance from her husband if she refuses to live with her husband in the marital home without a "legitimate excuse" or if she works outside the marital home without her husband's permission. While authorities amended the law in 2019, removing some references to "disobedience" by women to their husbands, the law still punishes women for some acts of disobedience relating to mobility.

Authorities in 2020 repealed Article 548 of the penal code, which allowed men to receive reduced sentences if they injured or killed their wives or immediate female relatives on finding them engaging in an "illegitimate" sexual act. However, other articles remain that could allow men to receive reduced sentences for violence against women. The penal code also criminalizes adultery in a manner that discriminates against women and provides a longer prison sentence for adultery for women than men.

Sexual Orientation and Gender Identity

Syrian state and non-state actors have subjected men, boys, transgender women, and nonbinary people to sexual violence during the Syrian conflict, resulting in severe physical and mental health consequences. Under Article 520 of the Syrian penal code, "unnatural sexual intercourse" is punishable by up to three years in prison.

Displacement Crisis

The displacement crisis remains one of the most dire and protracted consequences of the war. Since the start of the armed conflict in 2011, 12.3 million have been forced to flee the country, according to OCHA, with 6.7 million currently internally displaced across the country.

In Turkey, opposition politicians have made speeches that fuel anti-refugee sentiment and suggest that Syrians should be returned to war-torn Syria. President Erdogan's coalition government has responded with pledges to resettle Syrians in Turkish-occupied areas of northern Syria. Against this backdrop of anti-refugee sentiment, Turkey is unlawfully deporting hundreds of Syrian men and some boys to northern Syria.

In Lebanon, the caretaker minister of displaced, Issam Charafeddine, announced in July a government plan to begin returning 15,000 Syrian refugees to Syria a month. In September, Lebanon's caretaker prime minister tasked Abbas Ibrahim, head of General Security, the agency responsible for the exit and entry of foreigners that has carried out forcible deportations of Syrians in the past, with negotiating the "voluntary and safe" return of Syrian refugees to Damascus.

WORLD REPORT 2023

In July, it appeared that Denmark's controversial move to designate parts of Syria "safe," thereby opening the door for the potential return of hundreds of Syrian refugees, was discredited when the Netherlands Council of State ruled that Syrian asylum seekers in the Netherlands cannot be automatically transferred to Denmark. Despite Denmark's designation, most European Union member states, the EU itself, and UN High Commissioner for Refugees, maintain that Syria is not safe for refugee returns.

Returnees to Syria continue to face a host of human rights violations, including arbitrary detention, torture, forced disappearances, and abuse by Syrian authorities. Returning refugees also face extreme economic hardship, unable to afford basic food items. Most find their homes either totally or partially destroyed and are unable to afford the costs of renovation. The Syrian government provides no assistance in repairing homes.

At least 2.4 million of the 6.1 million school-age children in Syria are out of school, and 1 in 3 schools is damaged, destroyed, or used for military or other purposes. Children with disabilities across Syria faced myriad abuses, such as greater risks during attacks and a lack of access to the basic support services they need, including health care, assistive devices, and education. Despite billions of dollars in aid, humanitarian operations in Syria have failed to sufficiently identify and address the rights and needs of children with various types of disabilities.

International Accountability Efforts

On January 13, 2022, a German court convicted and sentenced Anwar R., a former member of Syria's General Intelligence Directorate, for crimes against humanity. He is the most senior former Syrian government official to be held accountable for serious crimes in Syria.

Earlier in February 2021, the same court sentenced Eyad A., another former Syrian intelligence official, to four and a half years in prison for aiding and abetting crimes against humanity.

A second trial in Germany involving allegations of torture and murder by state agents during Syria's decade-long brutal armed conflict started on January 19.

The International Impartial and Independent Mechanism (IIIM), an evidence-gathering body established by the UN General Assembly in December 2016, continued to gather and preserve evidence for future criminal prosecutions.

The Investigation and Identification Team of the Organisation for the Prohibition of Chemical Weapons in The Hague continues to investigate responsibility for the use of chemical weapons in the Syrian conflict. The team has confirmed that Syrian government forces used chemical weapons on multiple occasions.

Key International Actors

The UN-led peace process, including the constitutional committee, made no progress in 2022. Russia, Turkey, the United States, and Iran continue to provide military and financial support to warring factions and to shield them from accountability.

Israel has increasingly and frequently conducted aerial strikes in Syria, including on military targets of the Syrian government's allies Iran and Hezbollah, a powerful Shiite political party and armed group. Such strikes targeted both Aleppo and Damascus airports in 2022. An Israeli attack on Damascus International Airport on June 10 disrupted the delivery of UN aid supplies for about two weeks, the UN said. The US-led Global Coalition to Defeat ISIS continues to fund the SDF and support its operations against ISIS.

In the UN Security Council, the US, and some European Council members have pushed for the reinstatement of the full humanitarian cross-border mechanism. Russia has continued to use its veto power to block expansion of the cross-border aid mandate back to its original four crossing points. At time of writing, there was only one crossing authorized by the Security Council.

Individuals credibly implicated in atrocity crimes, entities within or affiliated to the Syrian government, and ISIS continue to be under robust sanctions by the United States, European Union, and the United Kingdom, in addition to a few sector-wide sanctions that may have had a direct or indirect negative impact on people's rights, especially those who are most vulnerable.

Tajikistan

The government of Tajikistan intensified its crackdown on human rights and fundamental freedoms in 2022, violently repressing peaceful gatherings in the Gorno Badakshan Autonomous Oblast (GBAO) and using trumped-up charges against human rights defenders in retaliation for their professional activities.

The crackdown in GBAO was sparked by demonstrations against persecution of the Pamiri ethnic minority by regional and national authorities. Journalists and bloggers outside GBAO were targeted for their coverage of the events and the "anti-terrorist" special operation in GBAO that followed in June, as well as for critical reportage of the government.

Dozens of members and leaders of banned opposition parties remain behind bars on politically motivated charges. Domestic violence against women and girls remains prevalent. Tajikistan also engaged in a military conflict with the neighboring Kyrgyzstan, with dozens of civilians killed and hundreds injured.

Crisis in Gorno-Badakshan Autonomous Region

Between November 2021 and June 2022, at least 40 people were killed as a result of actions by security forces in GBAO to quash protests by the region's population over perceived harassment and persecution.

Tajik authorities labeled the protests "illegal," alleging they were organized by criminal groups with connections to terrorist organizations. Media reported that police on at least one occasion violently dispersed protesters using rubber bullets and teargas with military support deployed from the capital, Dushanbe. In the military's subsequent "anti-terrorism operation" at least 46 people were arrested, and hundreds more face charges or have been brought to trial for participation in the protests.

Since 2012, the region has seen regular violent stand-offs between the population and the military, and continued harassment and persecution of the Pamiri—a distinct ethnic and religious minority that populates GBAO.

Civil Society

In May, a human rights defender and journalist from GBAO and ethnic Pamiri, Ulfatkhonim Mamadshoeva, was detained on charges of organizing the May protests, alleging it was an attempt to overthrow the constitutional order. Soon after her detention, Mamadshoeva was seen in a broadcast on state television, where she appeared to admit to organizing the protests and apologized for causing distress to residents of GBAO. While the interview was clearly recorded while in detention, the exact circumstances in which it was filmed are unclear. In December Mamadshoeva was sentenced to 21 years of imprisonment.

In May, at least 13 members of "Commission 44," an independent group established in GBAO in 2021 to investigate the November protests, were detained and interrogated. Seven members were subsequently released, but in June, two received lengthy prison terms of 18 years on charges of organizing a criminal association and receiving financial assistance from abroad.

In July, a Tajik internet activist Shodruz Akhrorov, who was deported from Russia in March for allegedly violating residence rules, was sentenced by a Dushanbe court to six years in prison on charges of "calling for extremism via the internet." Akhrorov published videos critical of the lack of support for Tajik migrant workers in Russia on the part of Tajik authorities.

Freedom of Expression

Authorities continued to severely restrict freedom of expression online and offline, prosecuting journalists, bloggers, and activists for expressing their views and for independent reporting. In contrast to recent years the charges applied have included "extremism," "terrorism," and "calls to violent change to constitutional order," all of which come with extremely long prison sentences. There is heavy media censorship and persecution of the few independent media outlets.

Journalists and activists covering the protests in GBAO in particular were targeted, among them independent journalists Khushom Gulom and Ulfatkhonim Mamadshoeva, who were detained without due process, and have in December been sentenced to 8 and 21 years of imprisonment. Four journalists from Radio Ozodi and Current Time media outlets were attacked after interviewing Mamadshoeva, with unidentified attackers stealing their equipment and mobile phones, severely beating and threatening to kill one of them. After receiving a warning from the Prosecutor General's Office, an independent media outlet, Asia Plus, announced it would no longer cover the events in GBAO; it was threatened with closure for alleged "one-sided" coverage of the protests.

Two bloggers, Daleri Imomali and Abdullo Ghurbati, known for their critical coverage of state institutions and investigative journalism pieces covering the rest of Tajikistan, were detained in June and at time of writing remained behind bars. They are charged with "participation in activities of banned political parties and organizations" under Article 307 of the Criminal Code. Official representatives of the two banned partiess—Islamic Revival Party of Tajikistan (IRPT)and Group 24—refuted this accusation.

Radio Ozodi, the Tajik service of RFE/RL, is restricted in its professional activities by the refusal of the Foreign Ministry to issue long-term accreditation to its journalists, contrary to the terms of Tajik legislation on media accreditation.

Journalists who run the independent Azda TV in exile report ongoing pressure on their relatives in Tajikistan by the Tajik security services, including threats of criminal cases and to limit their freedom to leave the country.

Kidnappings and Forced Disappearances

The use of renditions targeting Pamiri diaspora leaders in Russia increased between November 2021 and August 2022 with at least 7 activists forcibly disappeared and kidnapped to Tajikistan, including two ethnic Pamiris with Russian citizenship. All later re-appeared in Tajikistan, some making televised speeches in which they said they had returned to Tajikistan voluntarily. A diaspora group has raised concerns authorities may have tortured and otherwise abused them in detention.

Political Prisoners, Prison Conditions, and Torture

Leaders and members of the banned IRPT previously imprisoned to long or life prison sentences remain behind bars despite continued international calls for their release. One of the founders of IRPT, 80-year-old Zubaydullo Rozik, was placed in special punishment cells twice for providing religious education to other prisoners, which is illegal in Tajik prisons.

Tajik prisons continue to be ill-equipped and overcrowded, with prisoners routinely facing ill-treatment, despite an ongoing prison reform. There has been no genuine investigation and no accountability for the November 2018 and May 2019 prison riots in Khujand and Vahdat that resulted in the deaths of at least 50 prisoners and five prison guards in circumstances that remain unclear, and the deaths in July 2019 of 14 prisoners by poisoning during a prison transfer.

As of September, at least 16 of the 70 detainees from the May protests in GBAO had received prison sentences ranging from 8 years to life sentences following closed trials. Many of them have complained to their relatives of torture and ill-treatment while in pretrial detention, according to a Pamiri news service.

Conflict at the Kyrgyzstan-Tajikistan Border

In September, Tajikistan engaged in a miliary conflict with Kyrgyzstan, resulting in the deaths of at least 18 civilians in Tajikistan, including at least 3 children. At least one school was damaged by fire during the conflict. Authorities reported scores of civilian homes had been burned, however no reports were available on how many people may have been internally displaced. Tajik authorities also claimed that Kyrgyz forces allegedly fired on an ambulance traveling not far from Isfara, near the Kyrgyz border, killing five members of a family, including two children, who were inside the vehicle. There has been no investigation and no accountability for civilian deaths in the April 2021 conflict between Kyrgyzstan and Tajikistan.

Domestic Violence

Domestic violence in Tajikistan remained prevalent, and the authorities have failed to effectively implement a 2013 law on the prevention of violence in the family. While the law offers some protection to survivors, it does not criminalize domestic violence or marital rape and does not include provisions for survivors to adequate support and protection.

Social stigma, economic dependence, impunity for perpetrators, lack of accessibility to protection measures for women with disabilities, including shelters, and insufficient number of shelters pose serious barriers for survivors' access to help, especially in rural areas. The Committee on Women and Family Affairs said that one of the main causes of suicide among women is domestic violence, as reported in the media.

Anti-Discrimination Legislation

Anti-discrimination legislation was passed by both the lower and upper chambers of Tajikistan's parliament in June and July respectively, introducing into law concepts such as direct and indirect discrimination, sexual harassment, and segregation on a discriminatory basis. The law tasks the Ombudsman's Office as the authorized body responsible for implementation of the law, including conducting anti-discrimination assessments of future draft laws. However, the law excludes "sexual orientation" and "gender identity" as protected categories, although these concepts were included in the initial draft.

Key International Actors

In March at the 49th session of the UN Human Rights Council, UN High Commissioner for Human Rights Michelle Bachelet noted the ongoing practice of suppressing political dissent in Tajikistan, and the widespread atmosphere of fear and repression in GBAO.

In May, the European Union delegation in Tajikistan jointly with the embassies of France, Germany, the United Kingdom, and the United States expressed its concern about the violent clashes in GBAO.

In July, the European Parliament condemned the intimidation and harassment of journalists and human rights defenders in Tajikistan, including those working on GBAO, and called on the Tajik authorities to set up an effective and independent investigation into the violent clashes in GBAO.

In September, the acting UN high commissioner for human rights mentioned the crisis in GBAO, raising concern over harassment of human rights defenders and journalists, some of whom are facing up to 25 years or life term prison sentences for their activism.

Tanzania

President Samia Suluhu Hassan's government lifted the ban on newspapers, ended a decades-long prohibition on pregnant students and adolescent mothers attending school, and released a political opposition leader from detention. However, the government continued arresting opposition supporters. Authorities have yet to conduct meaningful investigations into serious abuses that marred the 2020 elections and have not reformed the raft of legislation restricting the right to freedom of expression. The government forcibly relocated pastoral Maasai communities, despite protests by community members, local groups, and the international community.

Freedom of Expression and Media

Despite taking some positive steps by lifting the ban on some publications, media continued to face severe restrictions.

On February 10, the minister for information lifted the ban on *Mseto, Mawio, Mwanahalisi,* and *Tanzania Daima* newspapers, which had been imposed for publishing articles critical of late President John Magufuli. Since 2015, authorities had regularly revoked the licenses of newspapers for publishing material critical of the government, often citing the 2016 Media Services Act.

On July 1, the Tanzania Communications Regulatory Authority (TCRA) suspended online media outlet DarMpya for failing to renew its license, following the publication's coverage of a June 17 protest in Dar es Salaam against alleged interference by Kenya during the government's relocation of pastoralist Maasai communities in northern Tanzania. Local media reported that DarMpya changed its name to ZamaMpya in August after TCRA did not approve its application to renew its license.

The whereabouts of the investigative journalist Azory Gwanda, who was picked up from his home in Kibiti by unidentified people in November 2017 while investigating serious alleged human rights violations, remain unknown. The authorities have not conducted meaningful investigations into his forced disappearance despite calls by local activists and media.

Government Opponents

On March 4, the authorities released Freeman Mbowe, chairperson of the Chadema political party, Tanzania's main opposition party, after he spent more than seven months in pretrial detention on terrorism charges. Police arrested Mbowe and 11 other party members on July 22, in Mwanza, where they were due to hold a conference to discuss reforms to the country's constitution, which the party said gives too much power to the president.

On May 25, police in Manyara arrested and detained for several hours 20 members of Chadema's youth wing at a meeting on constitutional reforms. Chadema alleged in a statement that the police beat some of the youth leaders while they were in detention.

Children's Rights

On March 8, the Tanzanian government and the World Bank published their agreement to restructure Tanzania's Secondary Education Quality Improvement Program, pledged new measures to effectively end a school ban against students who are pregnant or are mothers, and ensure their right to education. The government pledged to forbid "involuntary pregnancy testing," which had been mandatory in most secondary schools and is used to expel pregnant students. These reforms remained outstanding at time of writing.

The Education Act still allows for students to be expelled if they are married or if they commit "an offense against morality," which has been used in the past to expel students who are pregnant, married, or are mothers.

On September 15, the African Committee of Experts on the Rights and Welfare of the Child found that Tanzania violated pregnant girls and adolescent mothers' right s to education, health, privacy, and their best interests through mandatory pregnancy testing at schools, and subsequent expulsion of pregnant and married girls.

The government has also not outlawed child marriage despite a 2016 High Court decision to amend the Marriage Act to raise the legal age of marriage to 18 for girls and boys.

Land Rights

Following longstanding land disputes in the northern Arusha region, in mid-2022 the government pushed ahead with its involuntary and forcible relocation of pastoral Maasai communities from a designated game-controlled area in Ngorongoro, despite protests by community members, widespread international criticism, and a 2018 court injunction against the evictions. United Nations human rights experts warned that the government's actions could amount to forced evictions and arbitrary displacement, prohibited under international law.

Tanzanian authorities threatened to arrest and "hold accountable" people that protested the relocation. Authorities also announced plans for a 10-day special operation to remove all "illegal immigrants" following allegations that pastoralists from Kenya had illegally crossed the border to occupy the area. Maasai people inhabit both Kenya and Tanzania.

The authorities threatened and arrested people for commenting on the relocation exercise and on June 10, security forces shot at and fired tear gas at protesting community members. Police arrested and later charged 23 community members for the killing of policeman Garlius Mwita on June 10.

Sexual Orientation and Gender Identity

The authorities continue to use the Sexual Offenses Special Provisions Act of 1998 to punish consensual adult same-sex conduct by up to life imprisonment, while the authorities continue to restrict organizations working to promote the rights and health off lesbian, gay, bisexual, and transgender (LGBT) people.

On September 11, the minister of information, Nape Nnauye, said that people found to be distributing materials depicting same-sex relations online would face "strict action." The 2020 Electronic and Postal Communications (Online Content) Regulations) prohibit "promoting homosexuality," which could include conducting LGBT rights advocacy. Violators may be fined or sentenced from one to up to five years in prison.

Thailand

The government of Prime Minister Gen. Prayut Chan-ocha continued to restrict fundamental rights, particularly freedom of expression and assembly, and prosecuted human rights and democracy activists, community advocates, environmental defenders, and critics of the monarchy. Government promises to fulfill Thailand's human rights obligations and end impunity for abuses remained largely unfulfilled.

Restrictions on Freedom of Expression, Assembly

As of September, the Thai Lawyers for Human Rights reported that at least 1,860 people had been prosecuted since mid-July 2020 for exercising freedom of expression and assembly.

Since the government ordered the nationwide enforcement of the Emergency Decree on Public Administration in Emergency Situation in March 2020 to control the spread of Covid-19, at least 1,469 people have been prosecuted under this draconian law—primarily for taking part in democracy protests. Police and prosecutors have leveled charges such as violating social distancing measures, curfew restrictions, and other disease control measures. Most of these criminal cases were not dropped after the government lifted the emergency measures on October 1.

In November 2020, Prime Minister Prayut ordered authorities to use all laws against democracy protesters, bringing back lèse-majesté (insulting the monarchy) prosecution under article 112 of the penal code after a three-year hiatus. Authorities have since charged at least 215 people under Article 112 in relation to various activities undertaken at democracy protests or comments made on social media. In addition, making critical or offensive comments about the monarchy is also a serious criminal offense under the Computer-Related Crime Act. Authorities have also charged some political activists with sedition under Article 116 of the penal code.

Authorities held outspoken critics of the monarchy—including Tantawan Tuatulanon, Netiporn Sanesangkhom, Nutthanit Duangmusit, and Sophon Surariddhidhamrong—in pretrial detention for months in lèse-majesté cases. These activists were released on bail only after agreeing to restrictive conditions, such as full or partial house arrest, wearing tracking devices, being banned from criticizing the monarchy and taking part in political rallies, and not being allowed to leave Thailand.

Officials enforced similar bail conditions on several leaders and members of pro-democracy groups, including Arnon Nampha, Parit Chiwarak, Jatupat Boonpattararaksa, Panupong Jadnok, and Chonticha Chaengrew. As of October, at least 10 dissidents remained in pretrial detention for participating in democracy protests or committing acts that authorities considered to be insulting or offensive to the monarchy. At time of writing, some of them had already been locked up for over 200 days.

Judicial interpretation of lèse-majesté offenses seems to vary according to interpretations by different courts, making convictions arbitrary and sometimes going beyond what is stipulated in the law. In September, the Bangkok South Criminal Court sentenced Jatuporn Sae-Ung to three years in prison on lèse-majesté charges for wearing a Thai national dress at a democracy protest in a context that authorities claimed was done to mock Queen Suthida.

The momentum of the youth-led democracy uprising, widely known for its iconic three-finger salute, was seriously disrupted by the government's criminal prosecutions, violent crackdowns, and pervasive surveillance and harassment of protesters. Democracy protests briefly returned to the street in October in response to the Constitutional Court's ruling on September 30 that permitted Prime Minister Prayut to remain in office, after opposition parties submitted a petition challenging that he had stayed longer as prime minister than the eight years allowed by the constitution.

Torture and Enforced Disappearances

On August 24, the House of Representatives approved and passed the Prevention and Suppression of Torture and Enforced Disappearance Bill. The law will become effective 120 days after the government announcement in the royal gazette on October 24.

Torture and enforced disappearance have long been problems in Thailand. Most reported cases have not been resolved, and hardly anyone has been punished.

Human Rights Watch documented numerous cases related to counterinsurgency operations in Thailand's southern border provinces, in which police and military personnel tortured ethnic Malay Muslims in custody. There are also credible reports of torture being used as a form of punishment of military conscripts. During the five years of military rule after the 2014 coup, many people taken into incommunicado military custody alleged that they were tortured or otherwise ill-treated while being detained and interrogated by soldiers.

In addition, police and military units often carried out anti-drug operations without effective safeguards against torture and other abuses. In August 2021, police officers tortured to death a suspected drug trafficker in Nakhon Sawan province. Authorities arrested the commanding officer and six of his subordinates. In June, the Central Criminal Court for Corruption and Misconduct Cases sentenced them to death (later reduced to life imprisonment) on murder charges.

In August, the Attorney General's Office indicted four park officials accused of abducting and murdering ethnic Karen activist Porlajee "Billy" Rakchongcharoen in April 2014. The charges include illegal confinement, premeditated murder, and concealing the victim's body.

Since 1980, the UN Working Group on Enforced or Involuntary Disappearances has recorded 76 cases of enforced disappearance in Thailand, including the prominent Muslim lawyer Somchai Neelapaijit in March 2004. In recent years, at least nine dissidents who fled persecution in Thailand were forcibly disappeared in neighboring countries. In September 2021, the Working Group raised concerns in its annual report about enforced disappearances in the context of transnational transfers between Thailand and neighboring countries.

Thailand is a state party to the Convention against Torture and Other Cruel, Inhuman or Degrading Treatment or Punishment and also signed, but did not ratify, the International Convention for the Protection of All Persons from Enforced Disappearance.

Human Rights Defenders, Repressive NGO Law

The government has failed to fulfill its obligation to ensure human rights defenders can carry out their work in a safe and enabling environment.

Police made no progress in investigating violent attacks in 2019 targeting prominent democracy activists Sirawith Seritiwat, Anurak Jeantawanich, and Ekachai Hongkangwan.

Democracy activists and human rights defenders in Bangkok and other provinces reported being intimidated by officials to stop them from organizing or participating in protests, especially during the visits by cabinet ministers or members of the royal family.

Cover-up actions and shoddy police work continued to hamper the efforts to prosecute soldiers who shot dead ethnic Lahu activist Chaiyaphum Pasae in March 2017 in Chiang Mai province.

Despite the adoption of Thailand's National Action Plan on Business and Human Rights in 2019, Thai authorities failed to protect human rights defenders from reprisals and end the abusive use of strategic lawsuits against public participation (SLAPP). Former National Human Rights Commissioner and Magsaysay Award winner Angkhana Neelapaijit is one of the many activists hit with such retaliatory lawsuits.

The Global Alliance of National Human Rights Institutions restored the National Human Rights Commission of Thailand to A status in March. The current members of the commission have become more active in responding to human rights-related issues from political and civil rights to economic, social, and cultural rights.

The controversial Operations of Not-for-Profit Organizations Bill, which was approved in principle by the government in February 2021, faced strong domestic and international opposition because of the choking and controlling effects the draft law would have on all civil society organizations. The law also included broad restrictions on foreign funding for nongovernmental organizations (NGOs). After massive international criticism and a growing national campaign against the draft law, the government sent it back for further revisions to be done in an unspecified timetable by the Ministry of Social Development and Human Security.

Lack of Accountability for State-Sponsored Abuses

Despite overwhelming evidence that soldiers were responsible for most casualties during the 2010 political confrontations with the United Front for Democracy Against Dictatorship, known as the "Red Shirts," which left at least 99 dead and more than 2,000 injured, no military personnel or government officials from the administration of then-Prime Minister Abhisit Vejjajiva have been charged.

The government also has failed to pursue criminal investigations of extrajudicial killings related to anti-drug operations, especially the more than 2,800 killings that accompanied then-Prime Minister Thaksin Shinawatra's "war on drugs" in 2003.

Violence and Abuses in Southern Border Provinces

The armed conflict in Thailand's Pattani, Yala, Narathiwat, and Songkhla provinces, which has resulted in more than 7,000 deaths since January 2004, subsided in the first half of 2022 due partly to the announcement by the Thai military and Barisan Revolusi Nasional (BRN) to reduce violence during Ramadan. BRN leaders later criticized the government for lacking commitment and taking advantage of the situation to raid insurgent strongholds.

Since August, insurgent attacks of military targets and civilians increased despite ongoing dialogues between representatives of the government and BRN.

The government has failed to prosecute members of its security forces responsible for torture, unlawful killings, and other abuses of ethnic Malay Muslims. In many cases, authorities provided financial compensation to victims or their families in exchange for their agreement not to speak out against the security forces, and not file criminal cases against officials.

Thailand has not endorsed the Safe Schools Declaration, which outlines a set of commitments to strengthen the protection of students, teachers, schools, and universities from the worst effects of armed conflict.

BRN, meanwhile, continued to recruit children for insurgent activities in 2022.

Refugees, Asylum Seekers, and Migrant Workers

Thailand is not a party to the 1951 Refugee Convention or its 1967 protocol. The authorities continued to treat asylum seekers as illegal migrants subject to arrest and deportation.

In September, immigration officials denied Thaw Nandar Aung, also known as Han Lay, democracy activist and former Myanmar beauty pageant winner, entry at Bangkok's Suvarnabhumi Airport, raising concerns that she would be deported to Myanmar and could face harsh punishment for opposing the military junta. After intense international pressure, the government allowed her to resettle to Canada as a refugee. However, Thai officials' frequent arrests and threats to deport Myanmar human rights and democracy activists and dissidents on the Thai-Myanmar border means the possibility of forced return of asylum seekers and refugees is a constant threat.

Authorities have made no progress in investigating the apparent enforced disappearance of exiled dissidents from Vietnam and Laos in Bangkok.

The government refused to let the UN refugee agency conduct status determinations for Lao Hmong, ethnic Rohingya and Uighurs, and people from Myanmar and North Korea. More than 50 Uighurs and several hundred Rohingya remain in indefinite detention in squalid conditions in immigration lockups.

Despite government-instituted reforms in the fishing industry, many migrant workers faced forced labor, remain in debt bondage to recruiters, cannot change employers, and receive sub-minimum wages that are paid months late.

The government has failed to adequately protect internationally recognized worker rights, such as the right to freedom of association and collective bargaining. Union busting continued in industrial areas, and union leaders faced harassment and dismissal by hostile employers. Migrant workers of all nationalities are barred by provisions in the Labor Relations Act 1975 from organizing and establishing labor unions or serving as a government recognized labor union leader.

Gender Inequality

While Thailand enacted the Gender Equality Act in 2015, implementation remains problematic. Most cases filed under the act feature discrimination against transgender people, who face barriers to health care, education, and employment because Thailand lacks a legal gender recognition procedure. There has been little progress in the parliamentary review of the Life Partnership Bill and the Equal Marriage Bill. If enacted, these draft laws could pave the way towards recognizing the fundamental dignity of same-sex couples and providing them with important legal protections.

Key International Actors

The US, European Union and its member states, and other like-minded countries raised concerns about the government's plan to introduce the NGO Law, as well as other major human rights issues. These countries have also been instrumental in providing protection for refugees, who are often arrested by the authorities and are at risk of refoulement.

In September, the EU and Thailand finalized their Partnership and Cooperation Agreement; negotiations stalled in 2014 after the military takeover and resumed in 2021.

Despite unresolved concerns raised by the member states and rights groups during the UN third cycle Universal Periodic Review (UPR) of Thailand in November 2022—such as torture, enforced disappearance, freedom of expression, association and peaceful assembly, refugees, death penalty, and impunity for state-sponsored rights abuses—and poor records on rights issues at regional and international levels, the government announced in September its intention to stand for election to the UN Human Rights Council for the 2025-2027 term.

Tunisia

In 2022, serious human rights violations continued, including restrictions on free speech, violence against women, and arbitrary restrictions under the country's state of emergency. Authorities have taken a range of repressive measures against opponents, critics, and political figures, including assigning them to fixed residences, imposing travel bans, and prosecuting them—sometimes in military courts—for public criticism of the president, security forces, or other officials. President Kais Saied's July 2021 power grab has weakened government institutions designed to check presidential powers and stunted the country's democratic transition.

In September 2021, President Saied suspended most of the 2014 constitution and granted himself almost unlimited power to rule by decree. He used this authority to consolidate power in 2022 by introducing a series of regressive reforms and undermining the independence of the judiciary. After suspending parliament in July 2021, Saied dissolved it completely in March 2022 after parliamentarians tried to meet online to protest his exceptional measures.

President Saied maintained his declared political roadmap by holding a constitutional referendum on July 25 and early legislative elections on December 17. However, the constitutional reform process has been opaque and was boycotted by a large part of the opposition and civil society. The new constitution, which was approved on July 26, granted almost unchecked powers to the president without strong protections for human rights.

Constitutional Reform

President Saied ordered a national referendum to take place on July 25 on a new draft constitution to replace the 2014 constitution. Saied's proposed constitution was drafted by a panel whose members the president named himself and who worked behind closed doors, soliciting little if any input from others. The draft was published only three weeks prior to the referendum, leaving virtually no time for public debate.

The new constitution was approved on July 26 by 94.6 percent of eligible voters, based on a turnout of only 30.5 percent. It came into force on August 17 after the final results were announced.

The new constitution establishes a presidential system similar to what Tunisia had prior to the 2011 uprising, and concentrates powers in the presidency. It creates a second chamber alongside the Assembly of Representatives of the People, consisting of people elected by members of the regional and district councils instead of by universal suffrage. The text drastically scales back the role of the Parliament compared to the country's post-revolutionary constitution.

The new constitution enumerates many rights but eviscerates the checks and balances needed to protect them. It doesn't fully ensure the independence of the judiciary and the Constitutional Court that Tunisia has yet to establish.

On September 22, the African Court of Human and Peoples' Rights issued a significant ruling stating the exceptional measures taken by Saied were disproportionate. The court ordered the abrogation of several decrees, including the one suspending most of the 2014 constitution, and ordered the establishment of the Constitutional Court within two years.

Judicial Independence

On February 12, Saied dissolved the High Judicial Council (HJC) in a move that compromised the judiciary's independence from the executive. The HJC was Tunisia's highest judicial body and oversaw judicial appointments, discipline, and career progression of magistrates. President Saied replaced the HJC with a temporary body partly appointed by the president and granted himself powers to intervene in the appointment, career tracks, and dismissal of judges and prosecutors.

Tunisian judges went on strike for four weeks to oppose the decree dissolving the HJC. The new constitution, which came into force in August, deprives judges of the right to strike.

On June 1, Saied issued a decree that further undermined the independence of the judiciary by giving the president the authority to summarily dismiss magistrates. Under the same decree, he sacked 57 magistrates, accusing them of corruption and obstructing investigations.

On August 10, the administrative court of Tunis suspended the president's decision with respect to 49 of the 57 magistrates and ordered their reinstatement. The authorities have not yet acted on the court's ruling.

Elections

President Saied dismantled a number of national institutions, including the independent electoral commission (Instance Supérieure Indépendante pour les Elections) that he restructured only three months before the referendum vote. On April 21, Saied issued a decree which changed the composition of the body, giving himself the right to intervene in the nomination of all its members.

Three months before the legislative elections, Saied amended the electoral law without any public consultation or debate. Decree 2022-55, issued on September 15, reduces the members of the assembly from 217 to 161 and allows voters to cast ballots for individual candidates instead of party lists, a change intended to diminish political parties' influence, according to observers. The new law no longer imposes the principle of gender parity to ensure equal participation of women.

Backsliding on Freedoms

Tunisia has seen significant regression in freedom of expression and the press. The authorities have harassed, arrested, and prosecuted activists, journalists, political opponents, and social media users for speech offenses, including for criticizing President Saied, the security forces, or the army. Some were tried in military courts.

Lawyer Abderezzak Kilani, a former government minister and head of the National Bar Association, was jailed on March 2 and tried by a military court on charges including "disturbing the public order," and "insulting public officials" in connection with a verbal exchange he had with security forces while trying to visit a client.

On June 11, journalist Salah Attia was arrested and subsequently tried by a military court on charges of "accusing a public official of illegal acts related to his functions without proof," "denigrating the army," and "knowingly disturbing others via public telecommunications networks." His prosecution was related to comments he made on the Al Jazeera TV channel related to President Saied and the Tunisian army. On August 16, Attia was sentenced to three months in prison.

According to the National Syndicate of Tunisian Journalists (SNJT), harassment and detention of journalists in connection with their work have increased over the past year, and access to information has become more difficult. In 2022, Tunisia fell in the Reporters Without Borders press freedom index from 73rd to 94th place.

On September 16, President Saied issued a new decree on combating crimes related to information and communication systems that could severely curtail freedoms of expression and the press and the right to privacy. Producing, promoting, or publishing "false news or rumors" is now punishable under Article 24 of the decree by up to five years in prison, and up to 10 years if deemed to target public officials.

Security forces periodically prevented demonstrations by blocking access to certain locations and used excessive force to disperse demonstrators, including on January 14, during the anniversary of the 2011 revolution when authorities banned public gatherings on health grounds, and on July 22, during a protest opposing the constitutional referendum.

Since Saied's power grab, authorities have imposed dozens of arbitrary travel bans without judicial oversight, restricting people's freedom of movement. In June and July, former parliamentarians Saida Ounissi and Jamila Ksiksi were prevented from leaving Tunisia.

Women's Rights

President Saied has done little to advance women's rights. While his 2021 appointment of a female prime minister, Najla Bouden, is a first in North Africa, Saied has granted her little to no political autonomy.

Tunisian law continues to discriminate against women in inheritance rights. In 2018, former President Beji Caid Essebsi introduced a bill to parliament to set equality in inheritance rights as the default, but it was never adopted. President Saied has expressed his firm opposition to the reform of inheritance laws.

Tunisia lacks a policy that protects pregnant girls' right to education, leading to irregular enforcement of their education rights when school officials impose arbitrary restrictions.

Despite the 2017 violence against women law, which set out new support services, prevention, and protection mechanisms for survivors, there are numerous shortcomings in the law's implementation, particularly in the way the police and judiciary address complaints of domestic violence. The insufficiency of state funding for the law's implementation is a critical gap, as well as the lack of shelters for women who have nowhere to turn.

President Saied's dissolution of parliament has precluded the body from debating or adopting any legislation that could secure or expand women's rights.

Retaining some of the 2014 constitution's provisions, the 2022 constitution stipulates women and men are "equal in rights and duties and are equal before the law without any discrimination," and commits the state to take measures to eliminate violence against women. However, the 2022 constitution introduced a new provision stipulating "Tunisia is part of the Islamic Umma [community/nation]" and making the realization of the purposes of Islam a responsibility of the state (article 5). Such provisions could be used to justify curbs on rights, notably women's, based on religious precepts' interpretations, as other states in the region have also done.

Sexual Orientation and Gender Identity

Article 230 of the penal code punishes consensual same-sex conduct between both men and women with up to three years in prison.

State actors in Tunisia have undermined lesbian, gay, bisexual, and transgender (LGBT) people's right to privacy with digital targeting, namely online harassment and "outing," and monitoring social media. Authorities sometimes rely on illegitimately-obtained digital evidence in prosecutions. Human Rights Watch documented cases where government digital targeting has resulted in crackdowns on LGBT organizing, as well as arbitrary arrests. As a result of online harassment, LGBT people reported being forced to change their residence and phone numbers, delete their social media accounts, flee the country for risk of persecution, and suffer severe mental health consequences.

HUMAN RIGHTS WATCH

"So What If He Hit You?"
Addressing Domestic Violence in Tunisia

Turkey

President Recep Tayyip Erdoğan's authoritarian government regularly targeted perceived government critics and political opponents and exerted strong control over the media and judiciary in the long run-up to parliamentary and presidential elections that will take place in the first half of 2023. The deepening economic crisis saw the official annual inflation rate rise to 85 percent in October. In October, a government-sponsored law came into force that criminalizes the dissemination of "false information," tightens control over social media companies and online news websites, and gives authorities further powers to censor independent journalism and restrict the right to information.

Freedom of Expression, Association, and Assembly

Print media and private television channels are mostly owned by companies with close government links, which is reflected in the content of their news coverage. Independent media in Turkey operate mainly via online platforms, with authorities regularly ordering removal of critical content and prosecuting journalists, most severely under Turkey's Anti-Terror Law. At time of writing, at least 65 journalists and media workers were in pretrial detention or serving prison sentences for terrorism offenses because of their journalistic work or association with media.

After their June arrest in Diyarbakir, 16 Kurdish journalists working for various Kurdish media platforms were placed in pretrial detention on suspicion of "membership of a terrorist organization," a widely abused charge. In October, nine more Kurdish journalists were arrested and placed in pretrial detention in various cities. At time of writing, they remained in detention.

The government enforced an August 2019 regulation requiring media companies streaming online news coverage and digital streaming platforms to obtain licenses from the government-aligned broadcasting watchdog, the Radio and Television Supreme Council (RTÜK). The council has regularly imposed arbitrary fines and temporary suspensions of broadcasting on the few television channels critical of the government. Online media platforms Voice of America and Deutsche Welle chose not to apply for licenses from the council on the grounds that it would result in them being subject to similar disproportionate sanctions and censorship; on June 30, an Ankara court blocked access to both media outlets from Turkey at the request of the council. Both platforms at time of writing were blocked in Turkey by court order.

Of particular concern in the period before the 2023 elections was the government's October package of legal amendments tightening control over online news sites and social media companies by compelling them to comply with government content removal requests or face bandwidth reduction (internet throttling), and introducing the vague and widely drawn offence of "disseminating false information," punishable with a one- to three-year prison sentence. Thousands of people every year already face arrest and prosecution for their social media posts, typically charged with defamation, insulting the president, fomenting hatred, or spreading terrorist propaganda.

Provincial authorities regularly ban protests and assemblies of constituencies critical of the government. For example, they banned a women's rights rally in Istanbul on March 8. Turkey's longest lasting peaceful assembly, the Saturday Mothers/People, relatives of people subjected to enforced disappearances by state actors since the 1980s, has been banned for over four years from the central Istanbul location where it has been held since 1995.

Women's Rights

Turkey's 2021 withdrawal from the Council of Europe Convention on Preventing and Combating Violence against Women and Domestic Violence, known as the Istanbul Convention, continued to be vocally opposed by women's rights groups in Turkey. In July, in response to multiple legal challenges brought by women's groups and opposition political parties, Turkey's highest administrative court issued a controversial decision finding that the withdrawal from the convention by presidential decree had been lawful. In July, the UN Committee for the Elimination of Discrimination against Women (CEDAW) called on the government to reverse its decision, noting that its withdrawal "further weakens protections for women." Following a visit to Turkey, the United Nations special rapporteur on violence against women said that, in addition to eroding protections, withdrawal from the convention "emboldened perpetrators" and increased women's risk of violence.

WORLD REPORT 2023

Challenges in providing effective protection to women in Turkey who report domestic violence are reflected in the high number of murders of women, with the Interior Ministry reporting that of 307 women killed in 2021, 38 had received protection orders from police and courts. The CEDAW Committee called on Turkey to ensure adherence to protection orders, including by holding authorities accountable for failure to enforce orders or register domestic violence complaints.

Human Rights Defenders

On April 25, an Istanbul court sentenced human rights defender Osman Kavala to life imprisonment on the charge of attempting to overthrow the government, and 7 co-defendants to 18-year prison sentences for allegedly aiding and abetting. The case centered on the baseless charge that Kavala organized the lawful and overwhelmingly peaceful 2013 Istanbul Gezi Park protests that spread across Turkey. Kavala has been arbitrarily detained since November 2017 and, at the verdict, the court ordered the immediate arrest of the co-defendants, six of whom were incarcerated at time of writing. President Erdoğan has made repeated public speeches against Kavala throughout the trial and the case demonstrates the high level of political control over Turkey's courts.

The convictions of Kavala and the others, which are under appeal, flagrantly disregard the Council of Europe's February 2022 decision to trigger infringement proceedings against Turkey for flouting a 2019 European Court of Human Rights (ECtHR) judgment ordering Kavala's immediate release on grounds of insufficient evidence. In July, in response to the infringement process, the ECtHR ruled that Turkey has violated the European Convention on Human Rights through noncompliance with judgments.

The authorities continued to use terrorism and defamation charges to harass rights defenders, and to violate their right to assembly. In October, an Ankara court placed Şebnem Korur Fincancı, the head of Turkey's Medical Association and a rights defender, in pretrial detention pending investigation on suspicion of spreading terrorist propaganda for comments she made in a TV broadcast calling for an investigation into allegations that the Turkish military had used chemical weapons against the armed Kurdistan Workers' Party (PKK).

In November, the Court of Cassation issued its decision overturning the 2020 convictions of Taner Kılıç, former chair of Amnesty International Turkey, and three others. Kılıç was convicted on bogus charges of membership of a terrorist organization and the three others for aiding and abetting terrorism because of their participation in a human rights education workshop. The ECtHR ruled in May 2022 that Kilic had been arbitrarily detained and his freedom of expression violated.

Torture and Ill-Treatment in Custody

Allegations of torture and ill-treatment in police custody and prison over the past six years have rarely been subject to effective investigations or the prosecution of perpetrators. There are also regular reports of ill-treatment, including severe beatings and cruel, inhuman, and degrading treatment, and over-crowding in removal centers where foreign nationals including asylum seekers and migrants are subject to administrative detention pending deportation procedures.

There was no indication that authorities had opened any investigation into military personnel for the torture of Osman Şiban and Servet Turgut, two Kurdish men detained by the army in their village in the southeast in September 2020, taken away in a helicopter, and later found by their families seriously injured in hospital. Turgut died of his injuries. Şiban is facing trial on charges of "membership of a terrorist organization" for allegedly aiding members of the PKK in his village. Four journalists in the southeastern city of Van who were themselves arrested after reporting on the men's arrest and torture were, in January 2022, acquitted of "membership of a terrorist organization" having spent six months in pretrial detention.

Following a visit to Turkey, the UN Sub-Committee on the Prevention of Torture in September flagged concerns about the exercise of fundamental rights and guarantees during the first hours of detention, which are of paramount importance for the prevention of torture and ill-treatment, and on the situation of migrants in removal centers.

Kurdish Conflict and Crackdown on Opposition

While clashes between the military and the PKK have greatly decreased in rural areas of Turkey's eastern and southeastern regions, Turkey has concentrated its military campaign against the PKK, including with drone strikes in the Kurdistan Region of Iraq where PKK bases are located, and increasingly in northeast Syria against the Kurdish-led, US- and UK-backed Syrian Democratic Forces (SDF). In May, President Erdoğan threatened to launch what would be Turkey's fourth military incursion into northeast Syria against the SDF controlling the area since 2016. At time of writing, no full-scale invasion of the targeted areas had taken place. In Turkish-occupied territories of northeast Syria, Turkey and its local Syrian proxies continued to abuse civilians' rights and restrict their freedoms with impunity.

While Turkey blamed the PKK for a July 20 attack on a tourist resort in Zakho in the Kurdistan Region of Iraq, killing nine Iraqi tourists, both the Kurdistan Regional Government and Baghdad blamed the Turkish military. Turkish authorities also accused the PKK of a November 13 bomb attack in central Istanbul that killed six civilians and injured scores more, although the group denied involvement.

With the ruling coalition persisting in its campaign of criminalizing the opposition Peoples' Democratic Party (HDP) which has 56 seats in parliament, scores of former HDP members of parliament and mayors are held as remand prisoners or are serving sentences after being convicted of terrorism offenses because of their legitimate non-violent political activities, speeches, and social media postings. Among them are jailed former co-chairs Selahattin Demirtaş and Figen Yüksekdağ, in prison since November 4, 2016, despite a 2020 ECtHR judgment ordering Demirtas's immediate release. A closure case against the HDP was pending before the Constitutional Court.

Refugees, Asylum Seekers, and Migrants

Turkey continues to host the world's largest number of refugees, around 3.6 million from Syria granted temporary protection status, and over 320,000 from Afghanistan, Iraq, and other non-European countries whom the Turkish govern-

WORLD REPORT 2023

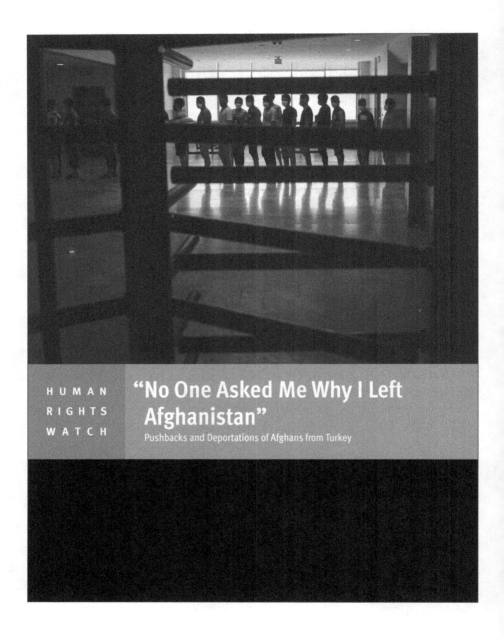

ment mostly deems irregular migrants and in a relatively few cases "conditional refugees."

With opposition politicians increasingly fuelling anti-refugee sentiment by advocating for the return of Syrians to war-torn Syria, President Erdoğan has responded with pledges to resettle Syrians in Turkish-occupied areas of northern Syria. Hundreds of Syrian men and some boys were unlawfully deported to northern Syria, often by being detained and coerced into signing voluntary return forms.

Afghans, many of whom had fled Afghanistan after the August 2021 Taliban takeover, were often unable to register asylum applications and were deported. Pushbacks of Afghans at Turkey's border with Iran were also reported.

Sexual Orientation and Gender Identity

The Erdoğan government demonstrated increasing readiness to endorse anti-lesbian, gay, bisexual, and transgender (LGBT) hate speech fomenting societal polarization in the year before 2023 presidential and parliamentary elections. The interior minister made public speeches including content that was directly anti-LGBT at least five times. The eighth successive ban on the Istanbul Pride week events in June was matched with an unprecedented number of police arrests of those who attempted to assemble, with 372 kept in custody for many hours before being released. In September, the state broadcasting watchdog RTÜK endorsed for public broadcast a video privately produced to advertise an anti-LGBT platform's event taking place in Istanbul. The video described LGBT people as a virus and destructive of families.

Climate Change, Environment and Human Rights

Turkey is a growing contributor to the climate crisis, which is taking a mounting toll on human rights around the world. In 2021, Turkey ratified the Paris Agreement, yet its climate policies and commitments are "critically insufficient" to meet global goals to limit global warming to 1.5°C above pre-industrial levels, according to the Climate Action Tracker. The government has committed to reaching net zero emissions by 2053, yet new coal power plants threaten this goal.

Turkey is a major importer of plastic waste from the European Union. Plastics are made from fossil fuels and toxic additives and emit significant amounts of greenhouse gas, contributing to the climate crisis. The government has failed to adequately implement its environmental and occupational health laws and regulations, increasing the negative impacts of pollution from plastic recycling on workers and local communities. Air pollutants and toxins emitted from recycling affect workers, including children, and people living near recycling facilities.

Key International Actors

Russia's full-scale invasion of Ukraine in February contributed to a humanitarian, energy, and food security crisis for the region and for countries around the world dependent on gas and grain. The conflict has increased Turkey's international prominence. In July, Turkey assisted the UN in brokering a deal with Russia and Ukraine to provide a passage for grain shipments through Russian-blockaded Ukrainian ports.

Behind a renewal of tensions with Greece focused on the alleged militarization of Greek islands close to Turkey lies an entrenched dispute over maritime boundaries, the status of Cyprus, and access to gas reserves in the east Mediterranean. The dispute also serves domestic nationalist political agendas in the year before Turkey's elections. The European Union's decision-making European Council in its June conclusions renewed a call for Turkey "to fully respect international law, to de-escalate tensions in the interest of regional stability."

The EU provides financial support to Turkey for hosting refugees in return for restrictions on entry of refugees and migrants to the EU. Though still formally a candidate for EU accession, the process is at a standstill. The EU included Turkey in its statement on situations that require the UN Human Rights Council's attention, stressing the "continued deterioration of respect for the rule of law and human rights."

In its report on Turkey in October, the European Commission stressed that "[i]n the absence of an effective checks and balances mechanism, the democratic accountability of the executive branch continues to be limited to elections," and pointed to the continuing "deterioration of human and fundamental rights."

HUMAN RIGHTS WATCH

HUMAN RIGHTS WATCH

"It's as If They're Poisoning Us"
The Health Impacts of Plastic Recycling in Turkey

As a NATO member, Turkey in May threatened to veto Sweden and Finland's expedited NATO membership bid that followed Russia's invasion of Ukraine. Turkey demanded that the two countries take bolder steps to prosecute terrorism, end arms embargoes on Turkey, and extradite to Turkey individuals charged under the country's Anti-Terror Law. At time of writing, although Turkey had lifted its veto, it had not ratified the membership accession.

Turkmenistan

A change in leadership in Turkmenistan in 2022 did not lead to improvements in its human rights record. The country remained one of the most closed and repressive in the world.

The government tolerates no political pluralism, independent media, or nongovernmental organizations (NGOs). Authorities jail perceived opponents and government critics. The fate and whereabouts of dozens of victims of enforced disappearances remain unknown. The government failed to adequately address a worsening food security crisis. Freedom of movement is subject to substantial restrictions.

Elections and Cult of Personality

On March 12, Serdar Berdymukhamedov won presidential elections after his father, Gurbaguly, resigned the presidency. The eight other candidates aligned themselves with Berdymukhamedovs' policies. The Organization for Security and Co-operation in Europe (OSCE) did not monitor the vote due to lack of "political pluralism."

Authorities routinely compel people to attend state events involving the president and his family. The Turkmen Initiative for Human Rights (TIHR), a Vienna-based group, reported that in June, hundreds sought medical help and dozens were hospitalized after they were mobilized to participate in an outdoor event for Gurbanguly Berdymukhamedov's jubilee in 47 degree Celsius (116.6 degrees Fahrenheit) heat.

Covid-19

While the government continued to deny any Covid-19 cases in the country, in October 2021, a source in Turkmenistan's healthcare system told Radio Azatlyk, the Turkmen-language service of the US government-funded Radio Liberty, that about 25,000 people had died from coronavirus-like symptoms. Authorities used Covid-19 as a pretext to keep the county's borders closed at least through May for nearly all travel, and for several months restricted domestic travel to and from at least two regions.

In April, Azatlyk reported that healthcare facilities lacked medicine and Covid-19 tests to adequately treat patients.

Poverty and Food Insecurity

Due to lack of reliable data of adequate quality, statistics regarding poverty rates, food security, and income in Turkmenistan are unreliable or nonexistent.

However, public reporting indicates that authorities' denial and inaction to address a worsening economic crisis and increasing poverty have significantly exacerbated food security. The availability for subsidized food staples has continued to shrink while prices have continued to rise.

Bread shortages in state stores continued. Independent media outlets documented shoppers queueing for hours to access subsidized bread.

In April, Azatlyk reported that police in Ashgabat threatened to jail people for 15 days for purchasing more bread than they are allotted under an uncodified rationing system. In February, police briefly detained customers for this and threatened to fine them for repeat violations.

In January, Azatlyk reported that police in Ashgabat threatened to prosecute residents, mostly pensioners, after they had complained to the Trade Ministry about getting shortchanged on their subsidized food.

Civil Society

Turkmen government tolerates no independent civic activism, systematically harasses and intimidates activists, including in exile, retaliates against their relatives, and severely punishes any peaceful dissent. NGOs are outlawed unless registered and no international human rights organizations have access to the country.

In April, TIHR reported that police and security officers threatened people with whom TIHR correspondent Soltan Achilova had spoken with "serious problems," and forced them to stop communicating with her.

The Turkmenistan Helsinki Foundation (THF), a human rights organization in exile, reported that on August 16, in Istanbul, Turkey, six men, allegedly consulate employees, beat five Turkmen activists in the courtyard of the Turkmen consulate, inflicting head injuries on one of them. The activists, whom consular staff admitted onto the premises, were attempting to deliver an open letter to President Berdymukhamedov regarding the dire situation many Turkmen migrants face abroad.

In February, a 62-year-old woman lost consciousness at an Ashgabat police station and was hospitalized after officers screamed at and frightened her, pressuring her to convince her son, Rozgeldy Choliev, who lives in exile, to return to Turkmenistan and stop criticizing the government.

In May, TIHR learned that Agadjuma Bayramov, who was arrested in 2016 and sentenced to six years on trumped-up charges in retaliation for interviews he had given to Azatlyk, had been released. According to TIHR, since Bayramov's release authorities have repeatedly prevented him from undertaking any domestic travel and ordered his family and relatives to cease communicating with him. In June, Bayramov went to Ashgabat to visit his sons, but police detained and escorted him back to his village in Mary province. In November he was allowed to visit relatives also living in Mary province.

In August, Rights and Freedoms of Turkmen Citizens, a Prague-based group, reported that security services had made threats against its social media editor, who lives outside the country.

Freedom of Media and Information

Authorities strictly monitor access to information. The state owns or controls all print and electronic media. Social networks and messaging apps are blocked. The country remained closed to independent foreign and Turkmen media outlets.

Although Turkmen law does not outlaw Virtual Private Networks (VPNs), it bans "uncertified" encryption programs and criminalizes "deliberately providing illegal services that provide technical programs" online, for which the penalty is imprisonment for up to seven years.

Independent media reported that authorities continued to intermittently block access to the internet and the Virtual Private Networks (VPNs). Azatlyk described full or partial internet disruptions and blocking of VPNs in late 2021 and in five non-consecutive months of 2022. In July, it reported that authorities across the country threatened to imprison information technology specialists who provided VPN installation services.

In February, Azatlyk reported that police interrogated citizens suspected of using VPNs and threatened them with criminal prosecution. In January Ashgabat authorities reportedly inspected mobile phones of students of one of the capital's engineering schools, threatened them with expulsion for accessing social media and the websites of "banned" outlets.

Cloudfare Radar, a US-based internet infrastructure provider, reported in mid-April "near complete internet shutdown" in Turkmenistan for almost two days.

Turkmen.news reported in February that authorities started to block entire subnets, which facilitate more efficient network traffic, of providers providing virtual/dedicated server services. In September, it reported that the blocking of subnets continued and access to IMO messenger, and a Behance platform, popular among artists, had been jammed.

Freedom of Movement

Turkmenistan's government continued to arbitrarily deny its citizens' right to freedom of movement. Foreign and domestic travel is heavily restricted and monitored.

In April, Azatlyk reported that police in Ashgabat conducted mass raids against domestic migrant workers, detained, and beat them, with one man sustaining a fractured jaw. In January, authorities expelled from Ashgabat and Akhal province nearly 250 internal migrant workers from Lebap region because they lacked "special permits" from regional administration and migration authorities.

The government continued to refuse to renew expiring passports for many Turkmen citizens residing abroad, exposing them to the risk of a range of human rights violations.

In September, Turkey, following the Turkmen government's request, abolished the visa exemption regulation for Turkmen nationals, placing many Turkmen migrant workers at risk of deportation.

Political Prisoners, Enforced Disappearances, Torture

The Turkmen government subjects individuals who have fallen out of favor with authorities to lengthy prison sentences following unfair and closed trials. The exact number of individuals imprisoned on what appear to be politically motivated charges is unknown. Dozens have disappeared in the country's prison system, some for as long as 20 years. Authorities barred their families from any contact with their loved ones and refused to provide them with information about their fate or whereabouts. Torture is widespread in Turkmen prisons.

According to Prove They Are Alive, an international campaign dedicated to ending enforced disappearances in Turkmenistan, an estimated 162 people have been forcibly disappeared in Turkmen prisons. At least 27 of them died in prison in solitary confinement. The terms of nearly three dozen have expired or were scheduled to expire in 2022, but their fate and whereabouts remain unknown.

On December 10, authorities released Pygambergeldy Allaberdyev, a lawyer sentenced to six-year prison term in September 2020 on bogus charges for alleged connections with activists abroad. In May, the United Nations Working Group on Arbitrary Detention had found Allaberdyev's detention to be arbitrary and called for his immediate release.

Numerous others continued to serve out prison sentences on bogus, politically motivated, charges. These included 26-year-old Nurgeldy Khalykov, a Turkmen.news freelance correspondent, sentenced in 2020 to four years on fabricated fraud charges. The outlet stated that every time it flagged Khalykov's case, authorities retaliated by placing him in solitary confinement.

They also included Mansur Mengelov, an activist for Baloch minority rights, sentenced to 22 years imprisonment in an unfair trial in 2012; Khursanai Ismatullaeva, a doctor sentenced in 2021 on bogus fraud charges; activist Murad Dushemov, sentenced in 2021 to four years for publicly demanding access to information about the Covid-19; YouTube blogger Murat Ovezov, sentenced in 2020 to five years on bogus fraud charges for openly expressing his critical views online; and Seryozha Babaniyazov, sentenced to two years in 2021 on bogus pornography charges, in retaliation for posting leaflets criticizing corruption in Balkanabat.

Political dissident Gulgeldy Annaniyazov remained on a five-year term of forced internal exile, after his 11-year sentence on politically motivated charges ended in March 2019.

Key International Actors

Deputy Secretary-General of the United Nations Amina J. Mohammed, during her June trip to Turkmenistan, discussed the "inviolability of human rights, gender equality and empowerment of women and girls" with senior government officials, including Berdymukhamedov.

European Union Special Representative (EUSR) for Central Asia Ambassador Terhi Hakala visited Turkmenistan in December 2021, and in May 2022 and met with Berdymukhamedov. She did not publicly raise rights abuses. In its statement on the International Day of the Victims of Enforced Disappearances, the EU flagged its concern about the fate of people subjected to enforced disappearances and urged the authorities to acknowledge and eradicate the problem.

In April, the United States Commission on International Religious Freedom recommended the redesignation of Turkmenistan as a "country of particular concern" for "systematic and egregious" religious freedom violations, as well as the use of targeted sanctions on responsible government agencies and officials. In July, the US State Department's human trafficking report in 2022 again placed Turkmenistan in the lowest category, "Tier 3," citing a "government policy or pattern of forced labor."

In September, the US mission to the OSCE during the Warsaw Human Dimension Conference made critical comments about the presidential election and noted that it "resulted in a dynastic transfer of power."

In November 2021, members of US Congress wrote a letter to then-President Bedymukhamedov calling for release of several "political prisoners," including Halykov, Ismatullaeva, and Annaniyazov.

The World Bank, for the second consecutive year, excluded Turkmenistan from its annual report due to the lack of reliable data.

In February, World Trade Organization (WTO) members approved opening accession talks with Turkmenistan.

Uganda

Authorities in Uganda, as in previous years, failed to hold security forces accountable for serious human rights abuses. The police and the military, which were implicated in serious rights violations around the 2021 general elections, continued to restrict rights to freedom of expression and assembly, especially for government critics and political opposition. The authorities placed restrictions on civil society organizations, media, and online communication, as state agents routinely harassed and intimidated journalists.

Conduct of Security Forces

In December 2021, Uganda sent Uganda People's Defence Force (UPDF) soldiers into eastern Democratic Republic of Congo as part of a joint operation with the Congolese army in an assault on the Allied Democratic Forces (ADF) rebel group. The government claimed the ADF was responsible for the November 16, 2021, suicide bombings in Kampala that killed four people and wounded 37.

UPDF soldiers and police in April killed at least 11 people as part of a disarmament operation that began in March.

Freedom of Expression and Assembly

Authorities clamped down on journalists and government critics and placed further restrictions on social media.

On December 28, 2021, military officers broke into the home of government critic and satirical writer, Kakwenza Rukirabashaija, beat him, and took him to an unknown location where they detained him for 14 days. Police later charged Rukirabashaija with "offensive communication" over earlier tweets critical of President Yoweri Museveni and his son, Muhoozi Kainerugaba. On February 9, Rukirabashaija fled Uganda to seek treatment for the injuries he sustained from beatings in detention. Two days before he fled the country, a Kampala court turned down his application to have his passport returned.

On February 22, a security official kicked freelance journalist, Lawrence Kitatta, as he covered an opposition protest in Kampala outside the home of Anita

WORLD REPORT 2023

Among, the then deputy speaker of parliament. Kitatta told the Committee to Protect Journalists (CPJ) he was forced into hiding and unable to work for days due to fear. He said he was tailed at an office at which he worked by unknown people suspected to be government security officers.

On March 10, a group of armed police and military officers raided the offices of The Alternative DigiTalk, an online television station, in Kampala, arrested nine staff members, and confiscated their equipment. On March 15 and 16, seven of the nine were released on police bond, while Norman Tumuhimbise and Faridah Bikobere were remanded at Luzira prison and later charged with cyberstalking and offensive communication "to disturb the peace and quiet of the President of Uganda." The charges resulted from their sharing excerpts of Tumuhimbise's two books that are critical of President Museveni. On March 21, police released Tumuhimbise and Bikobere on bail.

On September 8, parliament amended the 2011 Computer Misuse Act, further restricting freedom of expression online. According to the new law, a "person who uses social media to publish, distribute or share information, prohibited under the laws of Uganda or using disguised or false identity, commits an offence," and would be subjected to either a fine of 16 million Uganda shillings (around US$4,200), five years in jail, or both.

On October 4, police arrested nine university students protesting the building of the East Africa Crude Oil Pipeline (EACOP) through Uganda, outside the European Union offices in Kampala, and charged them with being a "common nuisance." The nine were released on bail on October 10.

Attacks on Civil Society Groups

On May 10, the Ugandan High Court overturned the suspension of Chapter Four, a legal aid organization. On August 10, 2021, the National Bureau for Non-governmental Organizations indefinitely suspended 54 civil society groups, including Chapter Four, on a range of grounds, including allegedly operating with expired permits. The bureau accused Chapter Four of failing to file annual returns and audited books of accounts.

On June 22, President Museveni announced the restoration of the Democratic Governance Facility, an EU fund for nongovernmental organizations, on condition that the government is included in its decision-making on the disbursement of funds to Ugandan organizations. The president suspended the fund in 2021.

Arrest and Harassment of Opposition Leaders and Supporters

On May 23, police arrested Kizza Besigye, an opposition politician and leader of the Red Card Front movement, at a rally in Kampala protesting the government's handling of increases in fuel prices and other basic commodities. On May 25, authorities charged Besigye with inciting violence and granted him a 30 million Uganda shillings (about $8,100) cash bail. Besigye refused to pay because he considered it excessive and politically motivated. Two weeks later, on June 6, authorities released Besigye after the High Court reduced the cash bail to three million Uganda shillings ($810). On June 12, police arrested Besigye again at a rally in Kampala and charged him with inciting violence. A court initially denied, but later granted, his bail application; Besigye was released on bail on July 1.

On May 30, police arrested six other opposition leaders, including parliamentarian Anna Adek; Doreen Nyanjura, the deputy mayor of Kampala; and four activists, Wokuri Mudanda, Susan Nanyojo, Mariam Kizito, and Alice Amony, as they protested the continued detention of Besigye, but later released them on bail.

On May 25, soldiers raided the offices of the Forum for Democratic Change (FDC), an opposition political party, assaulted its officials, stole money, confiscated documents, and arrested at least two of them. This was on the eve of the by-election in Omoro County in Northern Uganda, which was triggered by the death of Jacob Oulanyah, the former area parliamentarian. The next day, security officers arrested several other supporters of FDC and other opposition parties.

A year after their arrests, opposition parliamentarians Mohammad Ssegirinya and Allan Ssewanyana of the National Unity Platform remained in detention without trial. On September 24 and 27, 2021, armed men presumed to be government security officers arbitrarily re-arrested both Ssewanyana and Ssegirinya after they were separately granted bail on murder and terrorism-related charges and released from prison, bundled them into unmarked vehicles, and drove them to unknown destinations. On September 28, 2021, police presented them at court in Masaka, where they were charged with new murder charges and remanded.

Land Rights

Ugandan media reported that between June 2 and 5, violent clashes between unknown people and residents occurred in the northern village of Apaa that left six people dead, three critically injured, and over 200 houses burned. The area has been plagued by a decade-long dispute between the government and the communities during which authorities have forcibly evicted Apaa residents, claiming the area is part of wildlife and forestry reserves. Security officers have burned homes, beat people, and looted property during the evictions. Officials blocked access to Apaa for outsiders for three years, closed a health center and market serving the area, and excluded residents from participating in the 2021 general elections.

Sexual Orientation and Gender Identity

Uganda's penal code punishes "carnal knowledge" between people of the same gender with up to life in prison. On August 3, Uganda's National Bureau for NGOs banned Sexual Minorities Uganda (SMUG), a prominent lesbian, gay, bisexual, and transgender (LGBT) rights organization, for not having officially registered with it. SMUG's director told Human Rights Watch that the registration bureau refused to approve SMUG's name, a requirement for registration, because the name of the organization makes it clear that it supports rights and wellbeing of LGBT people. SMUG had provided education on sexuality and advocated for health services for LGBT people since 2004.

Accountability for International Crimes

Reparation proceedings continued before the International Criminal Court (ICC) in the case of Dominic Ongwen, a former commander of the Lord's Resistance Army (LRA). Ongwen was convicted in 2021 of war crimes and crimes against humanity; an appeal is pending. Joseph Kony, the LRA's founding leader and the only living remaining ICC suspect of LRA crimes, remains a fugitive.

Uganda's International Crimes Division continued its trial, which has dragged on for 13 years, against LRA commander Thomas Kwoyelo. At time of writing, the most recent hearing was in June. Kwoyelo has been in prison since he was captured by Ugandan forces in 2009.

Wider accountability for crimes committed during the 25-year conflict in northern Uganda, including abuses by the Ugandan armed forces during the conflict, remains limited. The Ugandan army has said that soldiers who committed abuses have been prosecuted and convicted but has not provided details of such cases.

Children's Rights

Uganda's teenage pregnancy rate stands at 25 percent—the highest in East Africa. One in four Ugandan girls and women ages 15-19 have given birth before turning 18, and 34 percent of girls are married before the age of 18. Uganda maintains a "re-entry" policy framework that specifies that girls may return to school after giving birth, but presents additional barriers and conditions for return. Regulations state that girls are required to go on mandatory maternity leave when they are three months' pregnant. They are only allowed to resume schooling after one year, when their child is at least six months old, regardless of their personal situation.

In June, the government adopted its second five-year National Strategy to End Child Marriage and Teenage Pregnancy, pledging key measures to end both, including enforcing compulsory education of all children for at least 11 years, and facilitating adolescent mothers' return to school.

Ukraine

Russia's full-scale invasion of Ukraine on February 24 and the ensuing war had a disastrous impact on civilians, civilian property, and energy infrastructure, and overshadowed all other human rights concerns in the country. Russian forces committed a litany of violations of international humanitarian law, including indiscriminate and disproportionate bombing and shelling of civilian areas that hit homes, healthcare, and educational facilities. In areas they occupied, Russian or Russian-affiliated forces committed apparent war crimes, including torture, summary executions, sexual violence, and enforced disappearances. Those who attempted to flee areas of fighting faced terrifying ordeals and numerous obstacles; in some cases, Russian forces forcibly transferred significant numbers of Ukrainians to Russia or Russian-occupied areas of Ukraine and subjected many to abusive security screenings.

As of mid-November 2022, the United Nations Human Rights Monitoring Mission in Ukraine (HRMMU) had verified at least 6,700 civilian deaths and more than 10,000 wounded since the start of the conflict and believed the actual figures were higher. At time writing, more than 14.5 million civilians had been displaced by the war: according to the UN Office for the Coordination of Humanitarian Affairs (OCHA), there were 6.5 million internally displaced in Ukraine, 5 million had fled to European countries, and another 2.8 million went to Russia and Belarus.

In September, Russian President Vladimir Putin claimed Donetska, Luhanska, Khersonska, and Zaporizka regions, which Russian forces partially occupied, as part of Russia. The claim had no legal value. Russian forces, in areas of these regions under their control, staged referenda on joining Russia and in some cases forced residents to vote at gunpoint.

Information about Ukrainian forces violating the laws of war by mistreatment, and apparent summary executions, of prisoners of war, which would be a war crime, also emerged.

Indiscriminate and Disproportionate Russian Attacks

Russian forces carried out numerous attacks that killed and wounded thousands of civilians. Some of these attacks were unlawful under international humanitarian law, including because they were indiscriminate or disproportionate in their effects on civilians.

In early March, after effectively encircling the northeastern city of Chernihiv, Russian forces killed at least 98 civilians and wounded at least 123 others in eight attacks on the city. In one of the deadliest, on March 3, Russian forces dropped several unguided aerial bombs on an apartment building complex, killing at least 47 civilians. On March 16, Russian forces attacked a bread line outside a supermarket that killed at least 17, and conducted two other attacks that damaged two hospitals. There were Ukrainian military targets in the vicinity of some of these attacks, but Human Rights Watch found at least four of the eight attacks to be unlawful. Attacks in the area diminished once Ukrainian forces re-took the region at the end of March.

During its three-month siege of Mariupol, Russian forces used explosive weapons with wide area effects, razed the urban landscape, and killed and injured untold numbers of civilians. In one attack, on March 16, Russian aircraft dropped bombs on the Donetsk Regional Theater in Mariupol, causing the roof and two main walls to collapse. At the time of the attack, hundreds of civilians were sheltering in the theater, which was also a center for the distribution of medicine, food, and water to civilians. An investigation by Amnesty International concluded that the strike killed at least a dozen people and likely many more, and seriously injured many others. Russian forces took full control of the city on May 20.

On June 27, Russian forces launched a missile which struck a busy shopping center in Kremenchuk, central Ukraine. The attack killed at least 18 civilians and wounded dozens of others. The impact crater from a Russian missile strike that hit minutes later and the blast damage to the adjacent shopping center, as examined by Human Rights Watch, were consistent with the detonation of warheads weighing nearly 1,000 kilograms with large, high-explosive payloads.

A Kharkiv regional official said that over a thousand civilians were killed in strikes in Kharkiv region as of August. Human Rights Watch documented numerous unlawful attacks by Russian forces in Kharkiv, including the use of explosive weapons with wide area effects in densely populated residential neighborhoods. On March 9, Russian forces dropped a large air-delivered munition on an apartment building in Izium city, killing 51 civilians, most of whom were sheltering in the basement. At the time of the attack, there was ongoing fighting for control of the Izium's city center, but multiple witnesses told Human Rights Watch that there were no Ukrainian forces in the building at the time of the attack. Human Rights Watch documented eight unlawful attacks that took place in Kharkiv in May and June, just a fraction of all the attacks reported in the region during that period. The eight attacks killed 12 civilians, wounded 26 others, and damaged five hospital buildings.

Attacks Damaging Hospitals

Russian forces carried out multiple attacks, including with cluster munitions, which damaged healthcare facilities in several regions, without regard for the special protection afforded such facilities under the laws of war. Since February 24, 2022, the World Health Organization reported more than 700 attacks on healthcare facilities, personnel, and transport vehicles, killing and injuring more than 200 people. As of November 29, the Health Ministry reported that "144 objects of medical infrastructure" had been destroyed and 1013 more were damaged.

On March 17, while Chernihiv city was encircled by Russian forces, Human Rights Watch documented how at least one Uragan rocket dispersed submunitions over a medical complex containing the Chernihiv Regional Children's Hospital. According to local officials, the submunitions killed 14 civilians and injured 24.

In Derhachi, a town outside Kharkiv city, Russian forces launched at least three attacks hitting different buildings of the main hospital between March and May.

On June 26, an expended rocket motor and tail section of an Uragan cluster munition rocket hit the Kharkiv Region's Clinical Trauma Hospital, piercing the roof and causing damage to the sixth and seventh floors. Hospital officials reported that the medical complex had been hit by attacks on at least four previous occasions.

WORLD REPORT 2023

Attacks On, and Military Use of, Schools

Many schools were damaged or destroyed by Russian attacks. According to a September 21 situation report by the UN Office for the Coordination of Humanitarian Affairs, the Ukrainian Ministry of Education and Science reported that more than 300 education facilities had been destroyed since the war began. Both Russian and Ukrainian forces at times used schools for military purposes, leading to their coming under attack by the opposing force.

Russian Killings of Fleeing Civilians and Attack on a Humanitarian Convoy

Russian forces fired on civilian vehicles in multiple incidents, including targeted attacks on civilians trying to flee hostilities, without any apparent effort to verify whether the occupants were civilians. In Kyiv and Chernihiv regions, Human Rights Watch documented three separate incidents in which Russian forces fired on civilian vehicles between late February and early March, killing six civilians and wounding three. In one of these cases, Russian soldiers pulled a man from a van and summarily executed him.

On March 6, Russian forces repeatedly bombarded an intersection just outside Irpin, six kilometers from Kyiv, where hundreds of civilians were trying to flee the Russian military's advance. At least eight civilians, including two children, were reportedly killed in the bombardment.

On September 30, a Russian forces' missile strike hit a convoy in Zaporizhzhia as it was moving from Ukraine-controlled to Russia-occupied territory to deliver humanitarian aid. The attack killed at least 26 civilians and wounded over 50.

Cluster Munitions

Hundreds of Russian cluster munition attacks were documented, reported, or alleged in at least 10 of Ukraine's 24 regions, killing an estimated 689 civilians between February and July 2022. Human Rights Watch documented Russian forces' use of cluster munitions in Chernihiv, Kharkiv, Mykolaiv, and Donetsk regions.

Human Rights Watch documented Russian forces' use of cluster munitions in attacks on populated areas of Mykolaiv on March 7, 11, and 13 which killed civilians and damaged homes, businesses, and civilian vehicles. The attack on March 13 killed nine people who were reportedly waiting in line at a cash machine.

On April 8, a Tochka-U short-range ballistic missile equipped with a cluster munition warhead hit the Kramatorsk train station and dispersed 50 9N24 submunitions over the tracks, station, and parking lot. Evidence points to Russia being responsible for the attack which killed 61 civilians and injured over 100 more as they were awaiting evacuation trains or assisting with the evacuation itself, making it one of the single deadliest incidents for civilians since Russia's full-scale invasion began.

Ukrainian forces also used cluster munitions on several occasions. *The New York Times* reported that Ukrainian forces used Uragan cluster munition rockets in an attack on Husarivka in Kharkiv region on March 6 or 7, when the village was under Russian control. From May to early September, Ukrainian forces repeatedly attacked the city of Izium and surrounding areas, while they were under Russian control, with cluster munitions. On May 9, two civilians were killed and four others were injured when several submunitions detonated around their building, which was in a residential area in the south of Izium. Russian forces were located fewer than 150 meters away.

Cluster munitions are banned by the 2008 Convention on Cluster Munitions, which has been ratified by 110 states. Neither Russia nor Ukraine is a party to the convention.

Landmines

The use of antipersonnel landmines in Ukraine has been extensive since February 24. Human Rights Watch has documented the use of eight types.

In the city of Bucha, 30 kilometers north of Kyiv, following Russian forces' month-long occupation, the Ukrainian government's demining unit found a total of 20 victim-activated booby traps and antipersonnel mines, including two bodies with devices placed on them.

Ukrainian deminers also located and cleared numerous antipersonnel mines, including hand grenades with tripwires, in Kharkiv region, following Russian forces' retreat early September.

Human Rights Watch spoke to over 100 witnesses about the presence of landmines and observed remnants in numerous neighborhoods in Izium and on the city's outskirts following the retreat of Russian forces in early September. Healthcare workers present in Izium during this time said that they treated dozens of civilian casualties. One said that the total number of civilian casualties was nearly 50, including at least five children. They said most of the traumatic amputations of lower limbs they performed during that period were due to injuries consistent with personnel landmine blasts. The head of the Ukrainian demining operation in Izium told Human Rights Watch that, from September 15 to 30, they had deactivated or destroyed thousands of PFM-1 variant mines and that there were so many they stopped keeping track.

Ukraine signed the 1997 Mine Ban Treaty in 1999 and became a state party in 2006. Russia has not joined it.

Attacks on Energy Infrastructure

Starting in October, Russian forces repeatedly launched missile and drone strikes on energy and other infrastructure throughout Ukraine, leading to power cuts and leaving millions periodically without heat, electricity, water-generating capacity, and other vital services ahead of the cold winter months. The attacks killed at least 77 civilians and injured nearly 300. The attacks appeared designed primarily to instill terror among the population and make life untenable for them.

Impacts on People with Disabilities

UN bodies expressed concerns on the situation of people with disabilities caught up in the conflict, including children and adults with disabilities living in residential institutions. The Committee on the Rights of Persons with Disabilities noted reports of people with disabilities being abandoned or trapped in their homes or institutions, with no access to support services. UN human rights experts also noted the disproportionate impact of the conflict on children with disabilities, including those evacuated from institutions in conflict zones to other areas of Ukraine or abroad.

Migrants

In the early months of the invasion, Ukraine continued to arbitrarily hold migrants and asylum seekers in detention in several sites across the country, including near the front lines in Mykolaiv. Ukrainian authorities eventually released or relocated most migrants to safer areas.

Russian Forces' Abuses During Occupation

Russian forces committed apparent war crimes and potential crimes against humanity in occupied areas of Ukraine, including ill treatment, torture, arbitrary detention, and the forcible disappearance of civilians and members of the Ukrainian armed forces. Some detained individuals were summarily executed, with their bodies showing signs of torture.

Russian forces tortured and unlawfully detained many civilians and held them for days and weeks in inhumane and degrading conditions in makeshift facilities such as pits, basements, boiler rooms, and factories. In March, in the northeastern town of Yahidne, Russian forces held over 350 villagers, including at least 70 children, for 28 days in a damp, cold, and dirty school basement. Ten older people died during that time.

When Russian forces detained civilians, they routinely refused to acknowledge the detentions or to provide information about the detainees' whereabouts, constituting enforced disappearances in violation of international law. The HRMMU documented 407 cases of enforced disappearances between late February and July in areas controlled by Russian or Russian-affiliated forces.

Human Rights Watch documented seven cases in the Kyiv and Chernihiv regions in which Russian soldiers beat detainees, used electric shocks, or carried out mock executions to coerce them to provide information. In the Kharkiv region, Human Rights Watch documented the cases of 14 men and one woman in Izium who were arbitrarily detained and tortured during the six-month period when Russian forces occupied the area. Survivors described being subjected to electric shock, waterboarding, severe beatings, threats at gunpoint, and being forced to hold stress positions for extended periods.

Human Rights Watch documented 42 cases occurring between March and July in which Russian forces forcibly disappeared civilians or otherwise held them arbitrarily, in some cases incommunicado, in the occupied areas of Khersonska and Zaporizka regions. Many were tortured, including through prolonged beatings and in some cases electric shocks; some were blindfolded and handcuffed for the duration of their detention. Except for one case, Russian forces did not tell families where their loved ones were held or provide other information on their fates.

In June, the HRMMU reported that Russian forces transferred "an unknown number" of civilians it had detained in Ukraine to the Russian Federation and other locations under their control, where they were "held in penal institutions, often together with prisoners of war."

Human Rights Watch documented the detention of 10 civilians, including one woman, by Russian forces in the Kyiv region between February 26 and late March who apparently forcibly transferred them to detention facilities in Russia's Kursk and Bryansk regions. This constitutes a war crime. Families told Human Rights Watch that they learned about the men's locations only from former prisoners and had still not received any confirmation of the detentions from Russian authorities.

Russian forces summarily executed civilians and others who had last been seen in the custody of Russian forces; their bodies often showed signs of abuse. On February 27, in the village of Staryi Bykiv in Chernihiv, Russian forces rounded up six men from three different families, took them to the end of the village, and summarily executed them.

During the Russian occupation of Bucha from March 4 to 31, Russian forces appear to have committed numerous summary executions, among other abuses. After Russian forces withdrew, local officials reported finding 458 bodies scattered throughout the town, the vast majority civilians. Approximately 50 of the bodies had hands tied and showed signs of torture, strongly suggesting that they had been detained and then summarily executed.

In Izium, in Kharkivska region, Russian forces and others operating under their command executed at least three men they detained, dumping their bodies in the forest, only to be found four months later.

Conflict-Related Sexual Violence

Both the UN Commission of Inquiry, established in March by the UN Human Rights Council, and the HRMMU reported sexual and other gender-based violence. In September, the HRMMU reported that it had documented 43 incidents, including 30 cases of forced nudity, rape, and gang rape, committed by Russian forces in homes or communities in areas under Russian control or occupation as well as in detention settings. The HRMMU report also included 2 cases of forced nudity and threats of sexual violence committed by Ukrainian armed forces or law enforcement and 11 cases of forced public stripping by civilians or by territorial defense forces.

Women, including older women, and girls constituted the majority of reported victims.

Human Rights Watch documented two cases in which Russian forces raped Ukrainian women, one in which they raped a girl, and a fourth in which a doctor who had treated the survivor provided information about the assault. In one of the cases, which took place on March 13, a Russian soldier repeatedly raped a woman sheltering with her family at a school in Kharkiv region. The woman told Human Rights Watch that he also beat her and cut her face, neck, and hair.

Survivors of sexual violence face significant challenges in accessing critical services, including time-sensitive medical care. Active hostilities, occupation, displacement, and destruction or unavailability of medical services and supplies hindered survivors' access to essential medical, psychosocial, legal, and socioeconomic support services. Stigma, shame, and fear of reprisals also deterred survivors from reporting sexual violence or seeking help.

Forcible Transfers and the Filtration Process

Russian officials told Ukrainian civilians fleeing hostilities in the Mariupol area that they could not go to Ukrainian-controlled areas but had to go to Russia or other areas of Ukraine occupied by Russia. Civilians who had their own cars or the means to hire one could evade this. However, for others fleeing who did not have such means, Russian and Russian-affiliated officials transported them to Russia or Russian-occupied areas in organized mass transfers, often against

HUMAN RIGHTS WATCH

"We Had No Choice"
"Filtration" and the Crime of Forcibly Transferring Ukrainian Civilians to Russia

WORLD REPORT 2023

their will or in a context where they had no meaningful choice, which constitutes a war crime.

Russian and Russian-affiliated authorities also subjected thousands of Ukrainian citizens trying to flee hostilities to compulsory, punitive, and abusive security screening known as "filtration." As part of the filtration process, Russian authorities collected vast amounts of information, including civilians' biometric data. Those who "failed" the filtration process, apparently due to their suspected ties to the Ukrainian military or to nationalist groups, were presumably detained in Russian-controlled regions.

Abuses against Prisoners of War

Prisoners of war (POWs) on both sides have been ill-treated, tortured, and in some cases apparently summarily executed. In November 2022, the United Nations Office of the High Commissioner for Human Rights stated that it had identified "patterns of torture and ill-treatment of [Ukrainian] POWs held by the Russian Federation (including by affiliated armed groups)," including through beatings, electric shocks, mock executions, and "placement in a hotbox or a stress position."

There is no indication, according to OHCHR, of Russian authorities holding any investigations into these abuses that resulted in prosecutions.

OHCHR documented episodes of torture and ill-treatment of Russian POWs held by Ukrainian forces, upon capture and during internment, including beatings upon entry to places of internment and forced kneeling for extended periods. OHCHR noted investigations by Ukrainian authorities into two extrajudicial executions of POWs, but that it had "not seen progress in these proceedings."

On July 29, according to the HRMMU, several dozen Ukrainian POWs were killed and over 100 wounded at the detention facility in Olenivka, in Russian-controlled Donetsk. Many of the prisoners had surrendered after the fall of Mariupol to Russian forces in mid-May. The United Nations secretary-general established a fact-finding mission to investigate, but at time of writing, no independent investigators had been allowed access to the prison. According to media reports, beatings and torture of prisoners at the facility had been commonplace.

On March 27, Russian forces captured three members of Kherson's Territorial Defense Forces and repeatedly tortured them. The body of one was found, while a second died two months after capture from injuries inflicted in detention. The third man was still suffering from injuries due to torture when interviewed by Human Rights Watch in July.

Both Russian and Ukrainian authorities have also broadcast images and details of captured prisoners of war, thereby exposing them to public curiosity, in violation of the Geneva Conventions.

On April 2 and 4, Russia broadcast programs on state television showing Ukrainian POWs in Russian custody in Sevastopol. A March 26 report by the HRMMU noted the existence of "a large number of videos" showing Ukrainian POWs being insulted, intimidated, and interrogated immediately after capture.

Ukraine's State Security Service (SBU) and Interior Ministry also posted hundreds of photos and videos on its social media accounts and on a website apparently run by the Interior Ministry of captured Russian soldiers, often with their passports and identification documents. Many of the Russian POWs appeared to be under duress; some of the soldiers were blindfolded, gagged, or masked. On March 27, videos posted online showed Ukrainian forces abusing captured Russian fighters, including shooting three of them in the leg. The incident apparently took place in a village near Kharkiv. A video posted on March 28 by a Ukrainian journalist shows three charred bodies at the same location, but the identity of the bodies and the circumstances surrounding the deaths remained unclear at this writing.

Legislative Developments

Ukraine has yet to ratify the International Criminal Court's (ICC) founding treaty but has accepted the court's jurisdiction over alleged crimes committed on its territory since November 2013.

On June 20, Ukraine's parliament approved ratification of the Council of Europe Convention on Preventing and Combating Domestic Violence and Violence against Women, known as the Istanbul Convention. For more than a decade, women's rights groups had been advocating for this step to combat violence against women and girls.

On August 30, Ukraine's parliament passed on first reading a media bill that threatens press freedom. It would expand the powers of the National Council of Television and Radio Broadcasting, the state broadcasting regulator, allowing it to, among other things, block online media without a court order.

Key International Actors

As part of an unprecedented response to Russia's full-scale invasion of Ukraine, multilateral organizations and foreign governments swiftly engaged a range of accountability mechanisms and tools, underscoring the importance of accountability for serious crimes.

On March 2, the ICC prosecutor opened an investigation into alleged serious crimes in Ukraine following a request by a group of ICC member countries to do so. Judicial officials in countries across Europe have also opened criminal investigations using their national laws to examine serious crimes committed in Ukraine.

On March 4, the UN Human Rights Council established an Independent International Commission of Inquiry to investigate human rights and humanitarian law violations associated with the war; the commission was tasked with collecting, analyzing, and consolidating evidence of violations, including identifying those responsible where possible with a view to ensuring accountability.

On October 18, the commission published its first report, based on investigations in four regions, finding "an array of war crimes, violations of human rights and international humanitarian law have been committed in Ukraine." The commission found that Russian forces were responsible for "the vast majority of the violations identified" and that Ukrainian forces ... committed international humanitarian law violations in some cases, including two incidents that qualify as war crimes."

On March 25, the European Agency for Criminal Justice Cooperation supported the establishment of a "joint investigation team" (JIT) to facilitate cooperation among a number of countries' criminal investigations on Ukraine, as well as the ICC. The countries participating in the JIT are Lithuania, Poland, Ukraine, Estonia, Latvia, Slovakia, and Romania.

To support the Ukrainian authorities' criminal investigations, many governments, including those of the United States, the United Kingdom, and the European Union, have offered Ukraine evidentiary, technical, and operational assistance to bolster its judicial capacity. Meanwhile, domestic and international civil society groups have been vigorously working to document violations as they occur.

At time of writing, it remained unclear how these accountability mechanisms would be coordinated, although multiple efforts were underway to ensure synergies among various initiatives.

The United Nations Security Council held public discussions on violations in Ukraine, including environmental and humanitarian concerns related to Russia's occupation of the nuclear power plant at Zaporizhzhia. On April 27, the Security Council held an informal meeting and, on September 22, convened a ministerial-level meeting, both focused on accountability for serious crimes in Ukraine.

The United Nations Security Council held public discussions of Russian violations in Ukraine, including environmental and humanitarian concerns related to Russia's occupation of the nuclear power plant at Zaporizhzhia. On April 28, the Security Council held an Arria-Formula meeting, and on September 22, the Security Council convened a ministerial-level meeting; both focused on accountability for war crimes in Ukraine.

The Security Council, has, however, failed to take any substantive action due to Russia's veto power. The day after Russia's invasion of Ukraine, the Security Council considered a resolution ordering Russia to halt the invasion and withdraw its troops from Ukraine. According to the United Nations Charter, as a party to the conflict, Russia should have abstained from the vote. However, Russia cast the lone veto, killing the resolution. None of the other four veto powers criticized Russia for that apparent violation of the charter. Shortly after, Security Council members referred the situation in Ukraine to the General Assembly, though the Security Council continues to periodically discuss the conflict.

The General Assembly, by contrast, passed four resolutions condemning Russia's invasion of Ukraine and Russian violations, including one that suspended Russia's membership in the Human Rights Council. In response to the suspension, Russia announced its withdrawal from the Human Rights Council. UN Secretary-General Antonio Guterres spoke out repeatedly on Russian violations and, while on a visit to Russia and Ukraine in April, urged Moscow to cooperate with the ICC.

Forty-five member states of the Organization for Security and Co-operation in Europe (OSCE) invoked the Moscow Mechanism on two occasions (March 13 and June 2), allowing the organization to deploy a mission of experts to Ukraine. In its July 14 report, the mission found a "clear pattern of serious violations of [international humanitarian law] attributable mostly to Russian armed forces," and pointed to indiscriminate attacks against civilians, as well as signs of torture and ill-treatment of killed civilians, as evidence that Russia had violated international law.

United Arab Emirates

In 2022, United Arab Emirates (UAE) authorities introduced amendments to a wide range of laws yet continued an alarming campaign of repression and censorship against dissidents.

The UAE has expanded its surveillance capabilities, both online and through drone surveillance in public spaces. UAE authorities continue to block representatives of international human rights organizations and United Nations experts from conducting in-country research and visiting prisons and detention facilities. Local news sites exercise self-censorship, and journalists face tremendous limitations in their work. Expo 2020 took place in Dubai from October 1, 2021, to March 31, 2022, after it was postponed due to Covid-19.

Freedom of Expression, Association, and Assembly

Scores of activists, academics, and lawyers are serving lengthy sentences in UAE prisons following unfair trials on vague and broad charges that violate their rights to free expression and association.

Ahmed Mansoor, a leading Emirati human rights defender, remained imprisoned in an isolation cell for a sixth year. Details of UAE authorities' persecution of Mansoor emerged in 2021, revealing grave violations of his rights that demonstrated the State Security Agency's unchecked powers to commit abuses. In July 2021, a private letter he wrote detailing his mistreatment in detention leaked to regional media, sparking renewed concern over his well-being and possible retaliation. An informed source reported that after the letter's publication, authorities retaliated by moving Mansour to a smaller and more isolated cell, denied him access to critical medical care, and confiscated his reading glasses.

Prominent academic Nasser bin-Ghaith, serving 10 years on charges stemming from criticism of UAE and Egyptian authorities, and university professor and human rights lawyer Mohammed al-Roken, serving 10 years following his conviction alongside 68 other people in the grossly unfair "UAE 94" trial, also remained in prison. Several of those convicted in the UAE 94 trial remain in detention despite completing their sentences.

Authorities released on health grounds Michael Bryan Smith, a UK national, in October 2021 after he spent more than 10 years in prison, despite being pardoned in 2014. Authorities denied him and other prisoners living with HIV regular and uninterrupted access to critical medication and adequate healthcare throughout his detention.

In late 2021, authorities designated four self-exiled dissidents of the UAE94 group—Hamad al-Shamsi, Mohammed Saqr al-Zaabi, Ahmed al-Shaiba al-Nuaimi, and Saeed al-Tenaiji—as "terrorists" under the country's vague and arbitrary counterterrorism law. The designation immediately led to asset freezes, property confiscations, and the criminalization of communications with them by their UAE-based relatives.

The UAE deploys some of the world's most advanced surveillance technologies to pervasively monitor public spaces, internet activity, and even individuals' phones and computers, in violation of their right to privacy, freedom of expression, association, and other rights. Websites, blogs, chat rooms, and social media platforms are also heavily monitored and curtailed. The authorities block and censor content online that they perceive to be critical of the UAE's rulers, its government, its policies, and any topic, whether social or political, that authorities may deem sensitive.

The December 2021 amendments to the penal code and Cybercrime Law further curtailed space for dissent. Article 174 of the penal code stipulates a minimum prison sentence of five years and a minimum fine of 100,000 dirhams (US$27,225) if the act takes place in "writing, speech, drawing or by statement or using any means of technology or through the media." Two new provisions may directly affect the work of journalists based in the UAE. Article 178 provides for sentences of three to 15 years in prison for anyone who, without a license from the appropriate authorities, collects "information, data, objects, documents, designs, statistics or anything else for the purpose of handing them over to a foreign country or group or organization or entity, whatever its name or form, or to someone who works in its interest." The Cybercrime Law contains an entirely new section entitled, "Spreading Rumors and False News."

The Associated Press reported that during Expo 2020, officials repeatedly tried to force visiting journalists to sign forms that implied they could face criminal prosecution for not following their instructions on site.

Migrant Workers

The UAE's *kafala* (sponsorship) system ties migrant workers' visas to their employers, preventing them from changing or leaving employers without permission. Those who left their employers without permission faced punishment for "absconding," including fines, arrest, detention, and deportation, all without any due process guarantees. Many low-paid migrant workers were acutely vulnerable to forced labor. Research by Equidem documented forced labor practices, illegal recruitment fees, withholding of wages and benefits, and a lack of access to grievance mechanisms for the majority of the migrant workers engaged on projects at Expo 2020.

A new labor law, adopted in November 2021, came into force in February 2022, along with executive regulations for its enforcement. The changes include allowing for flexible, temporary, part time, and remote work, as well as explicit language prohibiting sexual harassment and discrimination. It also allows workers to change employers within their probationary period.

Domestic workers who face a range of abuses were still excluded from the labor law. While a 2017 law on domestic workers guarantees some labor rights, it is weaker than the labor law and falls short of international standards.

Climate Change Policies and Impacts

As one of the world's top 10 crude oil producers, the UAE heavily contributes to the climate crisis. The UAE has taken some positive steps to reduce emissions, including by increasing renewable energy capacity and removing some fossil fuel subsidies. Yet it maintains plans for significant fossil fuel use and production, both for export and domestic purposes. The UAE's 2020 update to its national climate action plan, which pledges to reduce emissions by 23.5 percent by 2030, is "highly insufficient" to meet the Paris Agreement's goal to limit global warming to 1.5 Celsius above pre-industrial levels. The UAE is scheduled to host COP28, the international climate change conference, in November 2023.

The UAE is particularly vulnerable to the impacts of climate change including from extreme heat, increased droughts, and sea level rise. Eighty-five percent of its population lives along coastlines, which are just several meters above sea level.

Women's and Children's Rights

The December 2021 penal code reintroduced the criminalization of consensual nonmarital sex, which had been dropped from the older law as part of amendments introduced in 2020. Unmarried couples who have a child face no less than two years in prison unless they marry and register their child, or they acknowledge the child and obtain a birth certificate and other official documents. Unmarried pregnant women face difficulties accessing prenatal health care and registering their children.

Under the Federal Personal Status Law, a woman needs a male guardian's permission to marry. A married woman can lose her right to spousal maintenance from her husband if she refuses to have sexual relations with her husband without a lawful excuse. Men can unilaterally divorce their wives, whereas a woman must apply for a court order to obtain a divorce.

The UAE's 2019 domestic violence law has some positive provisions, including protection orders. However, it defines domestic violence in a way that allows wide judicial discretion on what constitutes abuse by male guardians against their wives, female relatives, and children. It also prioritizes reconciliation over safety for the victim as it requires proposing "conciliation" between the victim and the abuser before any criminal action is pursued.

The UAE's nationality law automatically guarantees UAE citizenship to children of Emirati men but not to children born to Emirati mothers and foreign fathers.

The government did not take steps to fulfil its 2018 commitment at its UN Universal Periodic Review to ban corporal punishment of children in all settings.

Sexual Orientation and Gender Identity

The 2021 penal code criminalizes sodomy with an adult male. It also continues to criminalize vaguely defined acts allowing authorities to arrest people for a wide range of behaviors, including public displays of affection, gender nonconforming expressions, and campaigns promoting the rights of lesbian, gay, bisexual, and transgender (LGBT) people.

Article 411 of the penal code criminalizes a "flagrant indecent act" and any saying or act that offends public morals, with a punishment of a prison sentence or a fine of Dh1,000 to Dh100,000 ($270-$27,000). If it is a repeated offense, the punishment is at least three months' imprisonment and a fine of Dh10,000 to Dh200,000 ($2,700-$54,000).

The UAE's federal penal code punishes "any male disguised in female apparel and enters in this disguise a place reserved for women or where entry is forbidden, at that time, for other than women" with one year's imprisonment, a fine of up to Dh10,000 ($2,700), or both. In practice, transgender women have been arrested under this law even in mixed-gender spaces.

In June, the government pressured Amazon to restrict items and search results related to LGBT people, symbols, and issues on its website in the United Arab Emirates.

Key International Actors

As a party to the armed conflict in Yemen, the United States provided logistical and intelligence support to Saudi and UAE-led coalition forces. An internal report from the US Government Accountability Office (GAO) found serious gaps in US government oversight of how arms sold to Saudi Arabia and the UAE are being used.

United Kingdom

The UK government in 2022 adopted laws that violate rights and proposed significantly weakening human rights protections in domestic law. The government signed an agreement to transfer asylum seekers who arrived irregularly in the United Kingdom to Rwanda, putting them at risk. Rising food, rents, and energy prices, and inadequate social protections threatened the rights of people on the lowest incomes, including to food and housing. The government failed to take meaningful steps to address institutional racism including in policing. Although the UK government worked with partners to press other states failing to uphold their human rights obligations, it did not consistently prioritize human rights in its foreign policy agenda and undermined international standards.

Rule of Law and Human Rights

Four laws adopted in a single week in April raised grave human rights concerns: an immigration law that dismantles key aspects of existing asylum and refugee protections, replacing them with a discriminatory system; a police law that restricts and increases penalties for protests; an election law requiring voter identification, likely to create disenfranchisement based on race, ethnicity and socioeconomic status, and reducing the independence of electoral oversight; and a law limiting people's rights to judicially review social security, and immigration tribunal decisions.

In June, following a flawed consultation process, the government announced legislation to repeal the Human Rights Act, which incorporates the European Convention on Human Rights into domestic law, replacing it with a weaker Bill of Rights. The proposals sought to diminish the influence of the European Court of Human Rights on domestic courts, to reduce public authorities' obligations to protect rights, and to limit the responsibility of the UK authorities to protect rights outside UK borders. The proposed legislation attracted widespread criticism, including from domestic civil society groups, United Nations experts, and the Council of Europe's commissioner for human rights. At time of writing, the status of the plans was unclear following changes to the prime minister and cabinet ministers in September and October.

Asylum and Migration

In April, the UK and Rwandan governments signed an agreement, allowing migrants and asylum seekers arriving by irregular means into the UK to be sent to Rwanda where their cases would be determined, undermining the refugee protection system. In June, the European Court of Human Rights issued three decisions temporarily halting the UK's plans for the first such transfer flight. The plan's legality was subject to a court challenge at time of writing.

The Nationality and Borders Act, enacted in April, discriminates against and criminalizes those seeking asylum through irregular routes, provides for pushbacks at sea and offshore processing, and increases powers to strip citizenship. It was roundly criticized by the UN Refugee Agency, UN experts, and more than 200 domestic civil society groups.

The UK continued to lack a time limit on immigration detention.

Right to Social Security, Adequate Standard of Living

People with lower incomes were particularly hard hit by a cost-of-living crisis precipitated by sharp increases in energy and food prices, and slow government efforts to mitigate these impacts. Inflation reached a four decade high of 10.1 percent in July, with single-parent households (overwhelmingly women-led), households led by a Black, Bangladeshi or Pakistani person, and single pensioners worst affected. A study projected that inflation would reverse the modest decrease in child poverty recorded the previous year.

Restrictive social security policies continued to negatively impact the right to an adequate standard of living, to food, and to housing for families with children and other recipients of social security support, including many people in paid employment. An overall cap on the amount of social security support a household can receive affected 123,000 families, while a cap on social security payments to larger families affected around 400,000 households and 1.4 million children.

A below inflation increase in social security support levels in April's budget and a failure to reverse a 2021 cut to the main social security program left people who rely on social security worse off in real terms. The government refused to review disability-linked benefits, ignoring a July recommendation made by a parliamentary committee.

Right to Food

The country's largest food bank network, the Trussell Trust, said in March that it had distributed 2.1 million emergency food parcels to people in need, an 81 per cent increase since 2017. The Independent Food Aid Network reported in October that 91 percent of its member organizations had experienced an increase in demand since July, and that one in four was reducing the size of food parcels because their supplies had been affected.

Official data on food security published in March showed single-parent households, households led by Black people, and people in social housing were more likely to be food insecure.

Survey data gathered by the Food Foundation showed that nearly one in 25 adults now reported that they or someone in their household had gone a whole day without eating. People with disabilities and people receiving social security support were nearly four times more likely to be food insecure.

Right to Safe and Adequate Housing

Homelessness numbers rose, after pandemic mitigation measures such as eviction bans and increased support to house rough sleepers ended. Data from England and Scotland showed the end of the eviction ban in June 2021 and reduced support networks contributed to increasing homelessness. Data from England, published in July, showed that "no fault evictions," a legal provision allowing a private landlord to evict a tenant without providing a reason, had increased dramatically during 2022. In response, the government published a consultation paper in June, which proposed ending the "no fault" loophole, among other measures that could better protect housing rights.

Local authorities in England, particularly in Greater London, continued to over-rely on substandard "temporary accommodation," including over the medium- to long-term, to address the shelter needs of people who would otherwise be

WORLD REPORT 2023

"I Want Us to Live Like Humans Again"
Families in Temporary Accommodation in London, UK

completely unhoused. The overreliance on temporary accommodation is in part exacerbated by cuts to affordable housing programs.

An official inquiry into the June 2017 Grenfell Tower fire that killed 71 people concluded its public hearings and began preparing its final report. The government passed building safety legislation in April, and fire safety regulations for high rise residential buildings in May, implementing many recommendations from the inquiry's first phase, including greater oversight of building safety during planning, making landlords responsible for replacing dangerous cladding, and greater retrospective liability where homes are found to be unfit for habitation. However, the government refused to include a legal requirement for people with disabilities living in high-rise buildings to have personal evacuation plans, prompting strong criticism and legal action considering the deaths of 15 of the Grenfell Tower's 37 residents with disabilities in the fire.

Conflict-Related Abuses

Legislation relating to killings during the conflict in Northern Ireland continued to make its way through parliament. Rights groups and the Council of Europe's Commissioner of Human Rights raised serious concerns, particularly about proposals for a conditional amnesty for killings, and the inadequacy of a proposed review mechanism to satisfy human rights obligations to investigate killings.

Legislation introduced in June to replace the Human Rights Act would ban all human rights claims relating to UK armed forces acting overseas, including abuse by soldiers, and by soldiers trying to enforce their human rights. The bill was suspended following the appointment of a new prime minister in September.

Women's Rights

In July, the UK ratified the Istanbul Convention, but did so with reservations that exclude from protection migrant women who depend on their abuser—leaving them without access to crucial support and a pathway to escape violence—and limit the possibilities of prosecution for violence committed outside UK territory. The convention took effect on November 1.

Women and girls in Northern Ireland continue to face significant obstacles and variation between hospital trusts in accessing abortion services.

In August, Scottish legislation came into force requiring local authorities and education providers to ensure availability of free products to manage menstruation for all.

Racism and Ethnic Discrimination

An April government policy paper on race and ethnic disparities, asserting that institutional racism had disappeared, received widespread criticism from anti-discrimination groups.

During the year, multiple reports evidenced the negative impact of institutional racism in various areas of life, including at work (particularly for women of color), in pre-natal and maternity care, the broader medical system, sport, policing, and mental health detention.

The independent police oversight mechanism for England and Wales published recommendations in April for police to address the disproportionately discriminatory use of "stop and search" powers, citing data that Black people were seven times more likely to be stopped and searched than white people.

In April, Parliament approved new anti-trespass powers specifically linked to informal settlements, likely to negatively impact Roma, Gypsy, and Traveller people.

Sexual Orientation and Gender Identity

The UK dropped from 10th to 14th in ILGA's 2020 European ranking reflecting the negative climate for transgender people, with trans and non-binary people continuing to face an often-hostile environment in the media and public debate, as well as inadequate legal protections.

An independent review into health services related to gender identity for children and young people in England published an interim report in February, indicating a need to improve the quality of care and increase capacity.

In March, Scotland's authorities proposed legislation to make it easier to obtain legal gender recognition without the medical diagnosis and two-year wait required elsewhere in the UK. UK national government plans to reform gender recognition are stalled.

Covid-19

A public inquiry into the UK authorities' handling of the Covid-19 pandemic began preliminary public hearings in October. The inquiry is tasked with identifying lessons learned to inform future pandemic responses. At time of writing, more than 200,000 people had died of Covid in the UK.200,000 people have died of Covid in the UK.

Climate

The United Kingdom is among the top 20 emitters of the greenhouse gases responsible for the climate crisis, which is taking a growing toll on human rights around the globe.

Prior to hosting the 2021 UN climate conference, the UK embraced ambitious emissions reduction targets—through its national climate plan commitment to reduce emissions by 68 percent by 2030 compared to 1990 levels, and a legislated target to reach a 78 percent reduction by 2035 compared to 1990 levels. According to the Climate Action Tracker, the UK's 2030 target is aligned with the Paris Agreement goal to limit global warming to 1.5°C above pre-industrial levels.

However, current programs are not on track to reach net-zero targets. The UK still produces over 40 percent of its electricity from gas, despite significant renewable energy potential. The reliance of UK homes on gas for heating and insufficient government programs to increase energy-efficiency measures are exacerbating the climate crisis and putting the right to an adequate standard of living at risk for millions of low-income people.

In July, temperatures in the UK exceeded 40°C for the first time on record, leading to a surge in hospitalizations and fires. Scientists calculated the July heatwave was made at least 10 times more likely by climate change. According to the UK's climate advisory body, the UK's climate adaptation efforts have not kept pace with the country's increasing climate risks, including risks of heat-related health impacts and climate impacts on infrastructure and food security.

More than a year after a regulation was adopted by Parliament to restrict imports of agricultural commodities linked to illegal deforestation or the violations of laws pertaining to the ownership or use of land, the government is yet to determine essential aspects of the legislation's implementation such as enforcement mechanisms and the commodities that are covered. Results from a public consultation, which were released in June, show overwhelming support from the public for the legislation to be implemented promptly and ambitiously.

Foreign Policy

The UK has shown its commitment to addressing several key issues, including taking concerted action with partners to press states failing to uphold their human rights obligations. However, in the face of competing policy interests, the UK has failed to consistently prioritize human rights in its foreign policy agenda and undermined international standards.

The UK continued to take coordinated action in response to violations committed by the military junta in Myanmar. In 2022, it sanctioned 6 individuals and 12 entities, and joined its G7 partners in condemning the junta's executions of 4 pro-democracy activists. In August, the UK took an important step to tackle impunity by announcing its intention to intervene in The Gambia's case before the International Court of Justice alleging Myanmar's atrocities against the Rohingya violated the Genocide Convention. As penholder on Myanmar at the UN Security Council, the UK proposed a resolution responding to abuses stemming from the February 1, 2021 military coup.

The UK continued to lead in seeking to hold the Chinese government accountable for its ongoing violations and crimes. It consistently pressed China to grant the UN high commissioner for human rights full and unfettered access to Xinjiang, and called on UN member states to, at minimum, debate the Commissioner's long-awaited report on Xinjiang. The UK also joined the G7 in underscoring its grave concerns with the erosion of civil and political rights in Hong Kong; but has not yet sanctioned implicated officials.

The UK responded robustly to Russia's February 2022 invasion of Ukraine, supporting accountability efforts, including mobilizing countries to refer the situation to the International Criminal Court prosecutor for investigation, imposing sanctions, and establishing a Ukraine Family Scheme and Homes for Ukraine scheme. However, it failed to waive visa requirements for those fleeing Ukraine and replicate the schemes for Afghans. The resettlement schemes for Afghans are still not functioning properly, with many at-risk Afghans unable to find safety in the UK.

The April agreement between the UK and Rwanda allows the UK to expel people there, despite most never having set foot in Rwanda and it not being a safe third country for asylum seeker transfers. In June, the UK prime minister attended the Commonwealth Heads of Government Meeting in Rwanda and failed to publicly raise any human rights concerns.

Through its Gulf Strategy Fund, the UK provides support and funding to several regimes involved in egregious human rights violations, including Bahrain.

The UK played a largely positive role at the Human Rights Council, including leading on Sri Lanka, tabling a resolution ensuring continued reporting on Sudan, supporting the establishment of a commission of inquiry to investigate abuses in Ukraine, a special rapporteur on the human rights situation in Russia and a group of experts on Nicaragua, and joining a statement on China. It supported a resolution on women and girls in Afghanistan and renewal of the independent expert on sexual orientation and gender identity. However, it continues to oppose the Commission of Inquiry on the Occupied Palestinian Territory and Israel, and voted against the resolution on racism, racial discrimination, and xenophobia.

The UK played an obstructionist role at the World Trade Organization on a proposed waiver of intellectual property rules for the Covid-19 response. The text adopted in June 2022 failed to address barriers to increasing Covid-19 vaccine production and excluded tests and treatments.

WORLD REPORT 2023

United States

The United States made some progress implementing more rights-respecting policies. It enacted a law, the Inflation Reduction Act, which advances the right to health and takes steps to address the climate crisis. However, officials need to take bolder steps to dismantle the systemic racism baked into many US institutions and structures; meet the challenges posed by climate change, threats to democracy domestically and abroad, and health crises like the Covid-19 pandemic; and ensure respect for rights. Entrenched, unequal power structures—largely based on racism, white supremacy, and economic inequality—are barriers to meaningful change.

The administration of US President Joe Biden promised reforms to harsh and abusive border policies, but many have been delayed. On top of migrant status, race and ethnicity are primary factors predicting who is subjected to harsh immigration policies such as expulsion, detention, deportation, and extreme anti-asylum policies. Despite pockets of criminal legal system reform, many authorities continue to raise alarmist and often unfounded claims about rising crime to pursue policies that rely primarily on law enforcement and punishment instead of addressing underlying needs, such as improving access to housing, health, voluntary mental health services, and educational opportunities.

Those experiencing abuses increasingly struggle to find relief in the US court system, including before the US Supreme Court, which has increasingly issued rulings undermining rights protections, like the 2022 ruling undoing constitutional protections for abortion access.

Racial Justice

Direct financial assistance and relief measures in response to the Covid-19 pandemic helped to ease economic conditions temporarily, but racial disparities persist in access to adequate health care, water, education, employment, and housing.

Despite unprecedented support in Congress and significant movement on reparations initiatives at the state and local levels, the federal government failed to

WORLD REPORT 2023

"If I Wasn't Poor, I Wouldn't Be Unfit"
The Family Separation Crisis in the US Child Welfare System

HUMAN RIGHTS WATCH | ACLU

create a commission to study the legacy of enslavement and develop reparations proposals.

In light of Congress's inaction, racial justice advocates urged the Biden administration to create such a commission by executive order by Juneteenth 2022. In August 2022, the United Nations Committee on the Elimination of Racial Discrimination (CERD) concluded that the US had failed to implement international anti-racism legal standards. Among other recommendations, the UN CERD urged the US, for the first time, to establish a commission to study and develop reparations proposals.

In May, a Tulsa, Oklahoma, county judge denied in part a motion to dismiss made by the city of Tulsa and other defendants as part of a lawsuit brought on behalf of survivors and descendants of the 1921 Tulsa race massacre for damages and continuing harm stemming from it. The denial is the first time a case for reparations for the massacre has made it past the motion to dismiss stage and will enable the last three known survivors of the massacre, all over 100 years old, to have the merits of their case heard in court.

Following the violent insurrection at the US Capitol on January 6, 2021, networks of white supremacists and far-right extremists have expanded and broadened their presence online. Marginalized communities fear for their safety amid a continued rise in reported hate crimes in the first half of 2022, including shootings motivated by white supremacist ideology.

Poverty and Inequality

Income inequality increased in 2021, driven primarily by pre-tax and transfer declines in low-wage and working-class incomes. But pandemic-related social spending contributed to the national poverty rate falling that year. Stimulus payments, an expanded Child Tax Credit, and more generous unemployment insurance kept millions of adults out of poverty and nearly halved child poverty, which fell to an all-time low.

But this historic reduction in poverty is reversing. Many of the programs that brought relief were temporary and have since ended, and the US government has failed to enact more permanent structural reforms. For example, the government's failure to renew the Child Tax Credit, which expired in December 2021, pushed 3.7 million children into poverty.

By the beginning of 2022, wealth concentration in the US was near its highest level in more than 40 years, as the top 1 percent of households owned roughly one-third of all private wealth.

Black, Latinx, and Native American households continue to have poverty rates more than double that of non-Latinx white households, emphasizing persistent race- and ethnicity-based disparities in income, wealth, debt, and employment.

Price inflation undermined access to basic commodities and services essential for rights, including food, housing, and health care.

Criminal Legal System

Despite gradual reductions in incarceration rates since 2009, the US continues to have the world's highest reported incarceration rate, with nearly 2 million people held in state and federal jails and prisons on any given day, and millions more on parole and probation.

Black and brown people remain vastly over-represented in jails and prisons, many of which failed to provide sufficient protections against Covid-19 infection. Reported data seven months after the rollout of vaccines showed that just over half had been vaccinated. More than 600,000 people in US prisons have contracted the virus and over 2,900 have died from it. Many jurisdictions reduced incarceration in response to the pandemic, but detained populations began returning to their pre-pandemic numbers in 2021 even as Delta variant cases surged.

Despite widespread calls for systemic reform during the summer of 2020, especially to reduce over-reliance on policing and address societal problems with investment in supportive services, few jurisdictions have enacted meaningful measures. Some localities have made efforts to deploy mental health care professionals instead of police in appropriate circumstances; some have funded non-law enforcement violence interrupters. However, police budgets overall have not shrunk. Congress has not even passed the weak reforms proposed in the federal Justice in Policing Act.

In 2022, less than half of US police departments provided data on their use of force, necessitating nongovernmental data collection and analysis. In 2022 alone, police killed over 400 people. On a per capita basis, police kill Black people at three times the rate they kill white people.

Children in the Criminal, Youth and Family Court Systems

Despite a 73 percent drop in child arrests since the mid-1990s, a high number of children continue to be incarcerated each year, with over 240,000 instances of detention documented in 2019, a March report by the Sentencing Project showed. There was a 9 percent increase between 2010 and 2019 in the likelihood of detention, which grew even more common for Black, Latinx, and Asian/Pacific Islander children, while holding steady for white and Indigenous children.

Slow progress continues towards ending life without parole sentences for children. According to the Campaign for the Fair Sentencing of Youth, 32 states have no child serving the sentence or have banned it for children.

Child welfare systems in the US too often respond to circumstances of poverty with punishment, charging families with neglect and removing children from their parents instead of providing support to help keep families together, a joint Human Rights Watch and American Civil Liberties Union report released in November documented. Every three minutes a child is removed from their home and placed in the foster system. Black and Indigenous people and those living in poverty are disproportionately affected.

Drug Policy

Drug overdose deaths continued to rise according to the latest available data, with more than 107,000 deaths reported in the US from December 2020 to December 2021, roughly a 15 percent increase over the prior year. Overdose deaths increased significantly among Black and Indigenous populations, by 44 and 39 percent, respectively.

The Biden administration included investments in harm reduction approaches that offer those using drugs health-centered care and access to voluntary treat-

WORLD REPORT 2023

ment, as part of its inaugural 2022 National Drug Control Strategy, the first time a US administration has done so. However, these investments were small compared to others and the administration and states continue to rely to a significant degree on criminalization to solve issues associated with problematic drug use, even though harm reduction strategies are proven to be more effective.

In October, Biden announced that he would pardon thousands of people convicted of simple marijuana possession in the federal system and order a review of how marijuana is treated under federal law. The pardon excluded non-citizens, even though marijuana convictions often trigger deportation, causing devastating harm to many people with strong links to the United States.

Rights of Non-Citizens

The Biden administration continued to arbitrarily expel thousands of people entering the US through the southern border, without respecting their right to seek asylum, under the abusive Title 42 policy. Since the policy was introduced in March 2020, those expelled included thousands of children, including at least 7,500 under age 4. Haitians, Africans, Guatemalans, Salvadorans, and people of many other countries and regions have been expelled. The administration planned to terminate the policy in May, but a federal judge blocked it from doing so.

In October, the administration decided to apply Title 42 to Venezuelans. The administration also continued to force non-Mexicans to wait for their asylum hearings in dangerous Mexican cities under its inherently problematic Migrant Protection Protocols, commonly known as "Remain in Mexico," including asylum seekers at particular risk of harm who were entitled to exceptions, such as people, and people living with disabilities, HIV, or other chronic health conditions. After a June 30 Supreme Court ruling, the administration finally ended the Remain in Mexico program, but it used procedures that violated some asylum seekers' due process rights.

The administration closed some immigration detention centers and ended some "zero tolerance" policies put in place by former President Donald Trump; however, as of September, about 25,000 non-citizens were still being detained. The administration continued to increase its use of electronic monitoring devices and other methods of surveillance of immigrants as it released more than 300,000 non-citizens from immigration detention. Human Rights Watch has found many methods of electronic surveillance used by the US to be abusive and unnecessary and called for a ban on ankle monitors and any devices that provide continuous location tracking.

State officials from Texas, Arizona, and Florida bused and flew migrants from the southwestern border to cities in distant states without regard for the likely location of their relatives or court hearings. Texas Governor Greg Abbott continued targeting suspected migrants for arrest and incarceration under Operation Lone Star, a discriminatory and abusive $4 billion border policy.

The Department of Homeland Security announced designations or extensions of Temporary Protected Status for Afghanistan, Cameroon, Ethiopia, Myanmar, South Sudan, Sudan, Syria, Ukraine, and Venezuela—protecting people in the US originating from these countries from deportation for a set period. As of October, US authorities had not remedied abuses Human Rights Watch documented in February against scores of Cameroonian asylum seekers.

Health and Human Rights

In 2022, over 230,000 people in the US died from Covid-19. In September, President Biden declared the Covid-19 pandemic "over," despite nearly 3,000 people dying from the virus that week. Biden's statements reflect ongoing inconsistency in the US' response to the Covid-19 pandemic. Throughout 2022, the US Centers for Disease Control and Prevention changed the parameters of its Covid-19 cautions while rolling back protections, sending a worrying signal that a leading health authority is not prioritizing the protection of marginalized groups from illness and death.

Soaring prices and inadequate health insurance have created a crisis of unaffordable medicine in the US, which undermines the right to health, drives people into financial distress and debt, and disproportionately affects socially and economically marginalized people. Despite its shortcomings, the US government's passage of the Inflation Reduction Act will advance the right to health for millions of people by lowering drug costs for people over 65, and make private health insurance more affordable for people with low and middle-incomes.

HUMAN RIGHTS WATCH

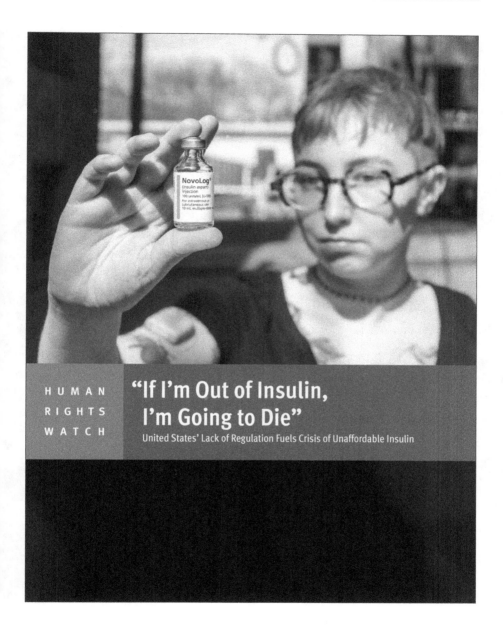

HUMAN RIGHTS WATCH

"If I'm Out of Insulin, I'm Going to Die"

United States' Lack of Regulation Fuels Crisis of Unaffordable Insulin

WORLD REPORT 2023

Voting Rights

Democratic institutions and election administrators contended with baseless claims of election fraud. Several states passed laws that sought to limit who may vote and which votes are counted, opened the door to partisan actors interfering with elections, and potentially enabled criminal prosecutions of election administrators. These restrictions on the right to vote disproportionately impact Black, Indigenous, and Latinx individuals.

In December, the US Supreme Court heard arguments in *Moore v. Harper,* a case that threatened to cut off avenues of recourse for voting rights violations connected to electoral districting. Conversely, several states expanded voter protection, including initiatives to increase voting by mail, to protect election workers, and to ease voter registration.

Soon after election day, the Organization for Security and Co-operation in Europe's international observation mission reported that the November 8 elections "were competitive and professionally managed," but noted that "efforts to undermine voters' trust in the electoral process by baselessly questioning its integrity can result in systemic challenges."

Climate Change Policy and Impacts

The US is currently the world's second-largest greenhouse gas emitter and the country that has most contributed to the climate crisis.

In August, the US enacted the Inflation Reduction Act, the most significant single piece of legislation the country has passed to address the climate crisis. The act sets the country on track to meet its commitment to cut greenhouse gas emissions in half by 2030, but this target is not sufficient to meet the Paris Agreement goal of limiting global warming to 1.5°C above pre-industrial levels. Further, the Inflation Reduction Act provides considerable support to the fossil fuel industry, putting people at the front lines of fossil fuel production and those already harmed by climate change at further risk.

In June, the US Supreme Court limited the Environmental Protection Agency's ability to restrict greenhouse gas emissions from power plants.

In the US, heat waves, hurricanes, wildfires, and other extreme weather events linked to climate change disproportionately impacted people with low incomes as well as Black, Indigenous, and other people of color, exacerbating existing structural inequities. Authorities have not adequately protected at-risk populations—including pregnant people, people with disabilities, and older people—from foreseeable impacts.

Women's and Girls' Rights

In June, the Supreme Court, in *Dobbs v. Jackson Women's Health Organization*, overturned the 50-year constitutional guarantee of abortion access. More than half of all US states are poised to ban abortion and at time of writing, 18 states had already criminalized or restricted abortion.

Following the ruling, President Biden issued two executive orders to safeguard access to reproductive healthcare services. He also established an interagency Task Force on Reproductive Health Care Access to coordinate efforts across the federal government to protect access to reproductive rights.

In its Concluding Observations, the UN CERD raised concerns about the impact of systemic racism, along with intersecting factors including gender and race, on the ability of women and girls to access comprehensive sexual and reproductive health services without discrimination. Lack of access to health insurance and care contributed to higher rates of maternal and cervical cancer deaths than in comparable countries, with Black women dying at higher rates than others.

Harmful laws in the majority of US states force young people under 18 to involve a parent in their abortion decision or go to court to receive a judicial bypass.

Disability and Older People's Rights

As of September, 157,898 out of 1,045,904 Covid-19 deaths were recorded in long-term residential facilities, where only just over half of residents were up to date with vaccines. In March, in his first State of the Union Address, President Biden pledged to reduce the use of chemical restraints—the misuse of medications to control behavior—in nursing homes, address staff shortages and inadequate training, improve sub-standard services, and increase accountability. In August, the Centers for Medicare and Medicaid Services continued to allow nursing homes to employ uncertified staff.

In September, over opposition from disability, racial justice, peer-led, and other groups, including Human Rights Watch, California put into place a measure that allows family members, police, outreach workers, and others, to involuntarily refer people to the jurisdiction of a newly established, deceptively named "CARE Court" system. The involuntary referral can result in an order from a judge exerting power over fundamental areas of a person's life, including medication, housing, and other services and support, in contravention of the right to informed consent, health, and legal capacity.

Sexual Orientation and Gender Identity

Lawmakers in US states introduced more than 150 bills targeting transgender people, particularly transgender children, threatening their rights and health. Indiana, South Dakota, and eight other states enacted laws prohibiting trans children from participating in sports consistent with their gender identity. Alabama and Oklahoma passed laws barring trans children from using bathrooms that correspond with their gender identity. In 2022, 20 states introduced "Don't Say Gay or Trans" bills, which restrict discussions of sexual orientation or gender identity in schools; Alabama and Florida enacted them.

Officials in Texas attempted to criminalize gender-affirming care. While Texas's orders were blocked by a state judge, Arizona and Alabama passed legislation banning gender-affirming care for trans youth. Nine states continue to explicitly exclude gender-affirming care from Medicaid coverage. continue to explicitly exclude gender-affirming care from Medicaid coverage.

Trans people and healthcare providers who provide gender-affirming care continue to face high levels of violence and harassment; an increasing trend of online anti-LGBT rhetoric in 2022 resulted in serious offline consequences.

Growing anti-LGBT legislation and sentiment is particularly concerning following the overturning of Roe v. Wade, which has rendered LGBT parental rights, same-sex marriage, and consensual same-sex conduct vulnerable targets. In response, the House of Representatives passed the Respect for Marriage Act which would require federal and state governments to recognize legally performed same-sex marriages. At time of writing, the bill has not been voted on in the Senate.

Foreign Policy

The United States responded to the Russian invasion of Ukraine in February by imposing unprecedented sanctions on Russian authorities, other individuals, and entities and sending over $18 billion in military equipment to Ukraine. Facts about how the weapons are being used and by whom are severely lacking.

In March, the US launched a $320 million European Democratic Resilience Initiative aimed, in part, at defending the human rights of people in Ukraine and neighboring states. In April, the US led efforts that suspended Russia from the UN Human Rights Council (HRC). The Ukraine conflict spurred renewed attention to justice mechanisms, with Congressional interest in cooperating with the International Criminal Court (ICC) and creating jurisdiction in the US for war crimes committed abroad regardless of the alleged perpetrator's or victim's nationality.

In January, the US began a three-year term on the HRC. In September, the US and allies proposed a debate there on a report by the UN high commissioner for human rights describing the Chinese government's targeting of Turkic Muslims in Xinjiang as apparent crimes against humanity. In June, entry into force of the United States Uyghur Forced Labor Prevention Act established a rebuttable presumption that goods from Xinjiang are made from forced labor and should be banned. The US also engaged in a diplomatic boycott of the 2022 Winter Olympics hosted by Beijing.

In March, Secretary of State Anthony Blinken formally determined that the Myanmar military's abuses against ethnic Rohingya Muslims constituted genocide. Blinken has not made any determination on the abuses committed in Ethiopia's Tigray region despite calls from Congressional leadership to do so.

The Biden administration released three strategies to address conditions that often lead to rights abuses: a new conflict prevention and stability effort; a strategy to "anticipate, prevent, and respond" to mass violence; and a Strategy on Countering Corruption that supports civil society in exposing corruption.

After withdrawing from Afghanistan in 2021, the US created Operation Allies Welcome to resettle Afghans including those who worked for the US government. In September, it refocused the program on certain categories of Afghans abroad who lack visa options.

After the Taliban takeover, the US revoked the credentials of the Afghan Central Bank, thereby cutting it off from the international banking system, citing illegitimate rule and ongoing rights abuses. In February, President Biden blocked $7 billion of Afghanistan's reserves and, in September, moved half of those monies to a new fund to address growing famine concerns. In July, the US killed Al-Qaeda leader Ayman al-Zawahiri in a drone strike in Kabul.

In August, Blinken launched a strategy for sub-Saharan Africa prioritizing partnership and democratic values. While in Rwanda, Blinken raised concerns about Rwandan support for the M23 armed group in eastern Democratic Republic of Congo, political repression, and the flawed trial and detention of US resident Paul Rusesabagina.

Despite new authority to sanction persons or entities responsible for rights abuses in northern Ethiopia, the US made no designations in 2022. In January, the US terminated Ethiopia's trade privileges under the African Growth Opportunity Act (AGOA) over gross human rights violations by the government and other warring parties in northern Ethiopia. In Sudan, the Biden administration sanctioned a militarized police unit for serious human rights abuses on protesters since the coup on October 25, 2021, but took no further action against individuals or Sudanese authorities for the abuses.

The US sold arms and provided security assistance to countries with poor human rights records including Egypt, Israel, and Saudi Arabia. Egypt receives $1.3 billion annually, though President Biden withheld $130 million of a possible $300 million that Congress conditioned on human rights progress in 2021. Senator Patrick Leahy blocked an additional $75 million to Egypt, citing "insufficient progress" on treatment of political prisoners. The US sells more military equipment to Saudi Arabia than to any other country and gives the Philippines the most military grants and loans in Asia, despite both governments' well-documented abuses. Nigeria receives significant US military assistance though its security forces commit abuses.

Broad US sanctions on Iran remain, though the US issued a general license that will allow technology companies to provide communications services to Iranians more freely. The US Department of State publicly condemned the death in September of Mahsa (Jina) Amini, which sparked mass protests throughout Iran, and imposed sanctions on Iran's Morality Police and others.

The Biden administration condemned the killing of Palestinian-American journalist Shireen Abu Aqla, who was shot while covering an Israeli army raid in the West Bank city of Jenin on May 11. Multiple independent investigations, including by the *Washington Post*, CNN, and the UN Office of the High Commissioner for Human Rights found that an Israeli soldier likely killed her. In November, the FBI launched an investigation into her death. Israel acknowledged in September that Abu Aqla was probably shot by an Israeli soldier but said that, if so, the killing was accidental and that it would not participate in the US probe.

The US failed to condemn Israeli authorities for raiding and issuing closure orders for the offices of seven prominent Palestinian civil society organizations in August, after also failing to condemn Israeli authorities' outlawing of six of the groups last year.

In June, the US announced a policy that prohibits US production and acquisition of antipersonnel landmines as well as their use and stockpiling outside of the Korean Peninsula. The move largely aligns US policy with the 1997 Mine Ban Treaty, which the US has not joined. The US did not review its policy on cluster munitions which are prohibited by the 2008 Convention on Cluster Munitions.

In October, the US tightened frameworks governing counterterrorism strikes. The classified rules reportedly restrict strikes to known individuals and when there is "near certainty" that no civilians are present. The policy reverses President Trump's more relaxed policy but maintains problematic operations outside of recognized armed conflicts. In January, following an investigation by *The New York Times* and criticism from others about civilian harm as a result of US operations, the Pentagon launched a plan to address inadequacies in investigations and casualty response, though gaps remain including on accountability for civilian casualties.

President Biden pledged to close the US military prison at Guantanamo Bay but 36 foreign Muslim men remain, most detained for more than two decades without charge or trial. Prosecutions of five Guantanamo detainees charged in the attacks of September 11, 2001, were stalled in flawed military commissions. The defendants were in talks to drop the death penalty in exchange for guilty pleas with life sentences.

Uzbekistan

Stalled legal reforms, continued restrictions on freedom of speech, and authorities' heavy-handed response to protests in the autonomous region of Karakalpakstan contributed to the further decline of Uzbekistan's human rights record in 2022. Authorities targeted outspoken and critical bloggers with criminal charges, and obstructed the work of independent human rights groups. Consensual same-sex relations between men remained criminalized. Impunity for domestic violence, ill-treatment, and torture is the norm.

An alliance of nongovernmental organizations (NGOs), trade unions, and business associations found no evidence of systemic forced labor in Uzbekistan's 2021 cotton harvest, and in March announced an end to the long-standing international boycott of Uzbekistan's cotton.

In June, the government published proposed constitutional amendments, including a provision that would enable the president to remain in office for another two seven-year terms. Uzbekistan's political system remains authoritarian.

Conduct of Police and Security Forces

At least 21 people were killed and over 270 were injured in early July in Uzbekistan's autonomous region of Karakalpakstan, following protests over proposed constitutional amendments that began on July 1 in Nukus, the regional capital. Then-United Nations (UN) High Commissioner for Human Rights Michelle Bachelet on July 5 called on authorities to "immediately open a transparent and independent investigation." United States and European Union officials also called for an investigation.

Human Rights Watch found that law enforcement officers used excessive force in response to the largely peaceful demonstrations in Karakalpakstan, leading to serious injuries and unlawful deaths of multiple participants. Police initially detained more than 500 people, including the activist, Dauletmurat Tazhimuratov, who had first called for protests. It is not known how many people remain in detention at time of writing.

Criminal Justice, Torture

A serious lack of accountability for torture and ill-treatment persists. Following the Karakalpakstan violence, media reported allegations of ill-treatment and torture of some detainees and interference with detainees' access to lawyers and family members. On July 15, the Uzbek government established a commission headed by Uzbekistan's Ombudswoman to investigate human rights violations, but its composition means it is not independent of government influence.

Review of the draft criminal code, which retains many rights-violating articles, stalled throughout 2022.

Authorities continued to ignore a May 2021 opinion issued by the UN Working Group on Arbitrary Detention calling for the immediate release of Kadyr Yusupov, a former diplomat imprisoned in January 2020 for five-and-a-half years on charges of treason. In December 2021, Yusupov was transferred to an open prison.

Freedom of Speech

Authorities continued to imprison bloggers in 2022, as respect for speech and media freedoms further declined. Journalists faced harassment and prosecution. Defamation and insult, including insulting the president, remain criminal offenses. On January 21, a Tashkent court convicted the blogger Miraziz Bazarov on criminal slander charges and imposed restrictions on his freedom of movement for three years. In April, the Supreme Court upheld the blogger Otobek Sattoriy's six-and-a-half-year prison sentence on dubious extortion charges.

On January 26, the Muslim blogger and government critic Fazilhoja Arifhojaev was sentenced to seven-and-a-half years in prison on charges of threatening public security for reposting and commenting on a social media post about whether a Muslim should congratulate non-Muslims on their religious holidays. His sentence was upheld on appeal.

On February 3, a Khorezm court sentenced Sobirjon Babaniyazov to three years in prison for insulting the president online. Valijon Kalonov, a 52-year-old government critic from Jizzakh who had called for a boycott of the 2021 presidential elections, is being held in a psychiatric hospital in the Samarkand region, after a court ruled in December 2021 he should undergo compulsory psychiatric treatment.

On July 1, police arrested the Karakalpak journalist Lolagul Kallykhanova on accusations of encroaching public safety after she publicly spoke out against proposed constitutional amendments. At time of writing, she remained in detention.

Uzbek authorities appeared to have disrupted internet access in Karakalpakstan starting June 27, with a complete shutdown from July 1. Internet Outage Detection and Analysis, a network traffic measurement tool, reported that the internet in Karakalpakstan was intermittently cut from July 1 to 3.

Civil Society

Uzbek authorities hinder the work of independent NGOs with excessive and burdensome registration requirements. Authorities made no effort in 2022 to pass the stalled draft NGO code, but on June 16 passed a decree requiring local NGOs that receive foreign funding cooperate with a state-appointed national partner, ensuring state control over project implementation. Agzam Turgunov, founder of the independent rights group Human Rights House, submitted his tenth application for registration in October 2022, and at time of writing was awaiting response.

Uzbek authorities persisted in their refusal to restore full legal status and rights to more than 50 people, including human rights defenders, who, since 2016, had been released from prison after having served politically motivated sentences.

Freedom of Religion

Muslims who practice their faith outside state controls continued to be targeted by authorities with spurious religious and extremism-related criminal charges. Authorities also persisted in forcing some Muslim men to shave off their beards.

In July, a Bukhara court sentenced Bobirjon Tukhtamurodov to 5 years and 1 month imprisonment for participating in a banned religious organization. Other Muslims, including Oybek Khamidov, Khasan Abdirakhimov, and Alimardon

Sultonov, were imprisoned on extremism related criminal charges in 2022. According to Forum18, an international religious freedom watchdog, citing a communication by the Tashkent police, two dozen Muslims were arrested in February on extremism related charges.

In September, the US Commission on International Religious Freedom (USCIRF) recommended in its annual report that Uzbekistan be placed on the United States' special watch list for violators of religious freedom. USCIRF reported that the Uzbek security agents pressured rights defenders not to meet with them during an April visit to Uzbekistan.

Women's Rights

Domestic violence remains largely unaddressed in Uzbekistan. In its February conclusions on Uzbekistan, the UN Committee on the Elimination of Discrimination against Women noted concern about the "high incidence of gender-based violence against women" and called on the government to explicitly criminalize domestic violence, effectively investigate and punish perpetrators, and strengthen victim services and protection, amongst other recommendations.

On June 21, UNICEF representative in Uzbekistan Munir Mammadzade expressed concern over violence perpetrated against women and children, which it deemed commonplace, and called for an end to impunity and access to improved protection and family support services.

Sexual Orientation and Gender Identity

Gay and bisexual men in Uzbekistan continue to face threats and extortion by both police and non-state actors, as well as arbitrary detention, prosecution, and up to three years' imprisonment under Article 120 of the criminal code. According to the National Centre for Human Rights, a government body, 25 of 36 people convicted in 2021 under Article 120 are serving prison sentences.

In late August, the Internal Affairs Ministry proposed a new law requiring compulsory medical examinations of so-called "dangerous groups," namely men who have sex with men, sex workers, and drug users, to test for HIV.

Counterterrorism and "Extremism"

In March, reporting on her visit to Uzbekistan that concluded in December 2021, the UN Special Rapporteur for Protecting Human Rights while Countering Terrorism Fionnuala Ní Aoláin found that Uzbekistan's "broad and vaguely defined" definitions of terrorism and extremism impinge on fundamental rights. She expressed "deep concern" about fair trial guarantees and the use of so-called "expert" evidence in counterterrorism and extremism cases.

Separately, she commended the Uzbek government for repatriating more than 500 nationals from northeast Syria, Iraq, and Afghanistan. Most are women and children who are family members of Islamic State (ISIS) suspects. Human Rights Watch surveys with parents, teachers, and social workers of repatriated children found that many of the children are attending school and reintegrating quite well.

Forced Labor

On March 10, the Cotton Campaign announced that its monitors observed no systemic forced labor in the 2021 cotton harvest in Uzbekistan, although individual cases of forced labor and some coercion and interference by local authorities persisted. As a result, the campaign ended a 11-year-old pledge by over 330 international companies not to use Uzbek cotton in their products. The lack of independent trade unions and NGOs to monitor labor rights violations undermines the progress Uzbekistan has made so far.

Key International Actors

Following its February 2022 review of Uzbekistan, the UN Committee on Economic, Social and Cultural Rights expressed concern about the inability of civil society organizations to operate freely, and the intimidation, harassment, violence, and stigma against lesbian, gay, bisexual, transgender, and intersex people in Uzbekistan, among other concerns.

On her visit to Uzbekistan in June, UN Deputy Secretary-General Amina Mohammed commended Uzbekistan's president on the country's reform path. According to the UN, human rights were among the topics Mohammed raised during the visit.

In March, European officials conducted a monitoring visit to review Uzbekistan's progress fulfilling its obligations under the Generalised Scheme of Preferences (GSP+) unilateral trade preferences, a schemed conditioned on the ratification and implementation of core human rights treaties. The officials addressed human rights and rule of law concerns, paying particular attention to "registration of NGOs and Trade Unions and anti-discrimination."

During its Human Rights Dialogue with Uzbekistan in March, the EU raised concerns on freedom of expression, freedom of assembly, registration of NGOs, and anti-discrimination, and called for prompt investigations of attacks against bloggers and protesters. On July 6, the EU and Uzbekistan formally concluded negotiations for a new Enhanced Partnership and Cooperation Agreement, which provides for cooperation on human rights and fundamental freedoms, among others.

Venezuela

In November 2021, the International Criminal Court (ICC) prosecutor Karim Khan opened an investigation into possible crimes against humanity in Venezuela. In 2020, the United Nations Fact-Finding Mission (FFM) had found sufficient grounds to believe crimes against humanity have been committed as part of a state policy to repress opponents.

The UN Office of the High Commissioner for Human Rights (OHCHR), which has a presence in Venezuela, lost access in 2022 to detention centers where political prisoners are held.

Judicial authorities have participated or been complicit in the abuses, serving as a mechanism of repression.

Venezuela faces a severe humanitarian emergency, with millions unable to access adequate health care and nutrition.

Authorities harass and persecute journalists, human rights defenders, and civil society organizations. Persistent concerns include brutal policing practices, lack of protection for Indigenous people, and poor prison conditions.

An exodus of some 7.1 million Venezuelans represents one of the largest migration crises in the world.

A 2022 report by a European Union electoral observation mission laid out concrete recommendations to pave the way to free and fair elections.

Negotiations, that were stalled since October 2021, resumed in November.

Persecution of Political Opponents, Arrests, and Torture

The government has jailed political opponents and disqualified them from running for office. As of October, the Penal Forum, a network of pro-bono defense lawyers, reported 245 political prisoners.

At least 114 political prisoners have spent more than three years in pretrial detention, despite time limits included in a recent Criminal Code reform. Approximately 875 of the 15,770 civilians arbitrarily arrested from 2014 through June 2022 have been prosecuted in military courts, the Penal Forum reported.

While some detainees have been released or transferred from Bolivarian National Intelligence Service (SEBIN) facilities to prisons, new critics have been subject to arbitrary detention.

OHCHR continued receiving complaints of torture, ill-treatment, and incommunicado detentions in 2022.

Security forces and colectivos—pro-government armed groups—have repeatedly attacked demonstrations since 2014, including with violent raids, brutal beatings and point-blank range shootings.

According to official sources consulted by OHCHR, the Attorney General's Office recorded 235 complaints of human rights violations involving deprivation of liberty, from May 2021 through April 2022, including 20 in terrorism-related charges.

OHCHR and the UN Working Group on Arbitrary Detentions, reported persistent challenges to ensuring the rights to liberty and fair trials. There are also delays in implementing judicial release orders.

In September, the UN FFM reported that crimes committed by intelligence services, on orders of high-level authorities, including Nicolás Maduro, were part of a deliberate policy to repress government opponents. The mission again described these as crimes against humanity.

Alleged Extrajudicial Killings

Agents of the Special Action Forces (FAES) and other police and military units have killed and tortured with impunity in low-income communities, including during security raids called "Operations To Liberate the People."

Between 2016 and 2019, security forces alleged "resistance to authority" in more than 19,000 killings. Evidence showed many were extrajudicial killings. OHCHR documented continuing patterns of such killings in marginalized neighborhoods but reported a significant reduction in number in 2022.

Armed Groups

Armed groups—including the National Liberation Army (ELN), Patriotic Forces of National Liberation (FPLN), and groups that emerged from the Revolutionary Armed Forces of Colombia (FARC)—operate mostly in border states, establishing and brutally enforcing curfews and regulations governing everyday activities.

On January 1, 2022, clashes broke out between the Joint Eastern Command—a coalition of dissident groups that emerged from the demobilized FARC—and ELN guerrillas, over control of territory in Colombia's Arauca state and Venezuela's Apure state. Both groups committed abuses including killings; forced displacement; and forced recruitment, including of children.

Venezuelan security agents have conducted joint operations with ELN fighters and have been complicit in their abuses.

Judicial Independence, Impunity for Abuses

The judiciary stopped functioning as an independent branch of government in 2004.

There has been no meaningful justice for crimes committed with knowledge or acquiescence of high-level authorities.

Judicial authorities have been complicit in abuses, the FFM reported in 2021, including by issuing retrospective warrants for illegal arrests, ordering pre-trial detention routinely, upholding detentions based on flimsy evidence, and failing to protect victims of torture.

Venezuela's National Assembly, controlled by supporters of Nicolás Maduro, revised the Organic Law of the Supreme Court of Justice in January, requiring an entirely new Supreme Court, which plays a critical role in appointing and removing lower court judges, of 20 justices—down from 32. The selection process, was not independent. Although Venezuela's constitution allows only one 12-year term, justices who had failed to act as a check on executive power were reappointed for longer.

Indigenous Rights and Mining

Authorities reportedly failed to consult residents before creating a special mining zone in 2016, which encompasses 14 Indigenous territories. Mining is one of the main drivers of deforestation and water pollution, contributing to diseases including malaria. SOS Orinoco and the media outlet Correo del Caroní reported that people from Indigenous communities close to mines are experiencing severe poisoning from the mercury used to separate gold from impurities. Some have been forcibly displaced.

Authorities have failed to protect Indigenous populations from violence, forced labor, and sexual exploitation. Human Rights Watch has documented horrific abuses—amputations, shootings, and killings—by groups controlling illegal gold mines in southern Venezuela, operating with government acquiescence.

On March 20, a clash between the Bolivarian National Armed Forces (FANB) and a remote Yanomami Indigenous community in Amazon State left four Indigenous people dead. Authorities held incommunicado at a Caracas military hospital for more than three months a 16-year-old who had been shot and was seriously injured. OHCHR urged a proper investigation, including of the incident's "underlying causes." Lawyers said investigations are stalled.

The UN FFM in September referred to abuses by security forces and armed groups, including the ELN, against people in mining areas.

Several Indigenous leaders have been threatened or attacked by state and non-state actors. In June, Virgilio Trujillo, an Indigenous leader who opposed illegal mining in the Uwottuja community and had received death threats, was shot dead.

Disability Rights

In May the Committee on the Rights of Persons with Disabilities concluded there is no law or mechanism to combat and punish discrimination against people with disabilities and a non-inclusive education model. There is a need to ensure accessibility, access to justice, and remove restrictions on legal capacity.

Sexual Orientation and Gender Identity

Venezuela has no comprehensive civil legislation protecting people from discrimination on the grounds of sexual orientation and gender identity, apart from specific provisions in the Labor Code and the housing law. There are no legal protections for same-sex couples.

The Military Code of Justice punishes consensual same-sex conduct by service personnel with up to three years in prison and dismissal. Following a challenge by the group Venezuela Igualitaria, the Supreme Court of Justice has announced that it will review the provision.

Women's Rights

Abortion is criminalized in Venezuela except when the life of the pregnant woman is at risk.

According to a study by HumVenezuela, an independent platform by civil society organizations monitoring the humanitarian emergency, sexual and reproductive health services for women suffer from a loss of capacity. By March, there was a 61.7 percent shortage of contraceptives and 55.8 percent of pregnant women were "unable to receive adequate obstetric care."

In September, the UN FFM documented that women and girls have reported sexual violence by FANB agents working at checkpoints and armed actors controlling mining areas.

Right to Vote

In February, the European Union mission that monitored 2021 elections issued a final report describing serious obstacles to voting and running for office, including arbitrary disqualification of government opponents seeking to run, partisan use of state resources, unequal access to media and social media, blocking of websites, and lack of judicial independence and respect for the rule of law. Such conditions, they said, undermined the election's fairness and transparency.

Presidential elections are scheduled for 2024, legislative and regional elections for 2025.

Humanitarian Emergency

The 2022-2023 UN Humanitarian Response Plan for Venezuela estimates that there are 5.2 million people in need of support in areas such as health, food security and water, sanitation, and hygiene.

HumVenezuela said in March that most Venezuelans face difficulties in accessing food, with 10.9 million undernourished or chronically hungry. Some 4.3 million are deprived of food, sometimes going days without eating.

The collapse of Venezuela's health system has allowed a resurgence of vaccine-preventable and infectious diseases. Barriers to performing transplants are reportedly resulting in hundreds of deaths. As of March, some 8.4 million gravely ill people were having trouble obtaining medical services, and more than 9 million people needing medications and healthcare supplies could not afford them. Power and water outages at healthcare centers—and emigration of healthcare workers—were further weakening operational capacity.

The government has not published official epidemiological data since 2017.

Lack of access to basic services aggravates the humanitarian crisis. Access to drinking water and sanitation declined from 2021 to 2022, HumVenezuela reported, leaving some 4.4 people in dire need of drinking water and 1.3 million people in dire need of basic sanitation services.

Refugee Crisis

Some 7.1 million Venezuelans have fled the country since 2014, the Inter-Agency Coordination Platform for Refugees and Migrants from Venezuela (R4V) reports, some 5.9 million to Latin American and Caribbean countries.

While many neighboring governments welcome them, lack of a coordinated regional strategy leaves thousands stranded in inadequate conditions or unable to obtain refugee status or other legal protection, forcing them to head north. Xenophobia remains a significant challenge.

New visa restrictions have prevented Venezuelans from flying to Mexico and Central American countries, significantly increasing the number struggling through a dangerous jungle on the Darien Gap, along the Colombia–Panama border. over

107,000 Venezuelans crossed the gap between January and September, compared to around 1,500 in 2021. They face egregious abuses, including sexual violence.

As of May, some 76,000 Venezuelans had obtained Temporary Protected Status in the United States. In July, the US extended protection for them through March 10, 2024.

On October 12, the US and Mexican governments announced that Venezuelans crossing the border irregularly would be expelled to Mexico without the chance to seek asylum. A new program will allow some Venezuelans to apply to travel to the US by plane. Requirements to apply to the program are often difficult to fulfil.

Freedom of Expression

Authorities have stigmatized, harassed and repressed the media, closing dissenting outlets. Fear of reprisals makes self-censorship a serious problem.

Authorities use the vague 2017 Law Against Hatred—under which publishing "messages of intolerance and hatred" is punishable by imprisonment of up to 20 years—to restrict anti-government speech.

In February, internet service providers blocked media websites, including of Efecto Cocuyo, Crónica Uno, and El Nacional, the watchdog VeSinFiltro reported. The Inter-American Commission on Human Rights' (IACHR) Office of the Special Rapporteur for Freedom of Expression, in July, reported increased censorship through deliberate blocking digital platforms and cuts in Internet service.

Human Rights Defenders

Venezuelan authorities harass and persecute human rights defenders and civil society organizations addressing the human rights and humanitarian emergencies.

Javier Tarazona, from the group Fundaredes, remained in prison, as of writing. He was arbitrarily detained in July 2021, after exposing links between Venezuelan security forces and armed groups.

Several organizations and the IACHR expressed concerns that an international cooperation bill introduced in the National Assembly in May could enable arbitrary cancelations of organizations' legal status for promoting or participating in activities contrary to government interests.

On June 28, authorities dismissed charges brought in 2021 against five workers of the humanitarian group Azul Positivo.

In September, two intelligence officers visited the offices of the human rights organization Provea, which was hosting a press conference with family members of union workers arrested in July.

Prison Conditions

Corruption, weak security, deteriorating infrastructure, overcrowding, insufficient staffing, and improperly trained guards allow armed gangs effectively to control detainees.

The Venezuelan Observatory of Prisons (OVP) estimates around 54 percent of detainees are being held pretrial.

The OVP estimates 7,792 people died in prison between 1999 and 2021. Low-quality hygiene and medical services and lack of access to clean water and sufficient, nutritious food contribute to hunger and disease. In the past four years, deaths from malnutrition and tuberculosis exceeded violent deaths, according to OVP.

Key International Actors

In October, the UN Human Rights Council extended the FFM's mandate for an additional two years. In a September report, it concluded high level authorities were responsible for a deliberate policy to repress opponents and the Venezuelan government "colluded" with "criminal groups" in the Arco Minero region.

During a visit to Venezuela in March, the ICC prosecutor announced he would establish an in-country office in Caracas. On April 15, Venezuelan authorities asked him to defer his investigation into possible crimes against humanity, asserting their "genuine will" to investigate cases domestically. On April 20, Khan notified

ICC judges of Venezuela's request, indicating he would ask them to reject it and allow him to continue his probe.

The UN high commissioner for human rights updated the Human Rights Council, in March, on continuing abuses, including challenges to due process, restriction of civic space, and arbitrary detentions. In June, she called for independent investigations and accountability, reparations for victims and families, strengthening judicial independence, and separation of powers. She mentioned persistent challenges to the full realization of economic, social, and cultural rights.

The UN's World Food Program, which gained permission from the Maduro government in 2021 to supply food to young children, had by August 2022 delivered meals to 210,000 beneficiaries in 1,700 schools across seven states. Representatives expect the program to reach 1.5 million people by the end of the 2022-2023 school year.

The R4V Platform called for US$1.79 billion to assist 8.4 million people in the region, including Venezuelan migrants, Colombian returnees, and host communities. As of October, only 16.8 percent of the plan was funded.

The 2022-2023 UN Humanitarian Response Plan for Venezuela called for $795 million to assist 5.2 million of the most vulnerable Venezuelans. As of October, $130.7 million was raised, covering 16.4 percent of the plan.

In October, Venezuela failed in its bid to be re-elected as a member of the UN Human Rights Council.

Several governments and institutions retain targeted sanctions against Venezuelan officials implicated in human rights abuses and corruption.

Newly elected Colombian President Gustavo Petro announced Colombia would reopen its border with Venezuela and appointed an ambassador, who took office in Caracas on August 29. Argentina also announced its intention to reestablish diplomatic relations in April.

In March and June, the United States sent official delegations to Caracas for the first time in years for conversations apparently prompted by an interest in accessing Venezuelan oil. In June, President Biden offered his support to Juan Guaido--whom the US acknowledges as the interim President of Venezuela- and reaffirmed the US willingness to calibrate sanctions policy based on the outcomes of negotiations. During a congressional hearing on Venezuela, Assistant Secretary of State for Western Hemisphere Affairs Brian Nichols [right?] warned of additional sanctions if negotiations do not restart. The US eased oil sanctions the same day negotiations resumed in November.

In October, Venezuela released seven US citizens wrongfully detained, in exchange for the release of two nephews of Nicolas Maduro's wife who were detained in the US on drug smuggling charges.

In November the Venezuelan government and opposition signed an agreement to increase the humanitarian aid reaching Venezuelan people

.

Vietnam

Vietnam systematically suppresses basic civil and political rights. The government, under the dictatorial one-party rule of the Communist Party of Vietnam (CPV), severely restricts the rights to freedom of expression, association, peaceful assembly, movement, and religion.

Government prohibitions remain in place on independent labor unions, human rights organizations, and political parties. People trying to establish organizations or workers' groups outside approved government structures face harassment, intimidation, and retaliation from the authorities. Authorities require approval for public gatherings, and systematically refuse permission for meetings, marches, or public gatherings they deem to be politically unacceptable.

A decree issued on August 31 restricts international nongovernmental organizations (NGOs) operating in Vietnam from doing anything against "national interests, laws, national defense, security, social order and safety" and "social ethics, national fine customs and practices, national traditions, identity or great national unity" of Vietnam. No definitions of these terms are provided in the decree, but groups deemed to violate these provisions will be shut down.

Authorities blocked access to sensitive political websites and social media pages, and pressured social media and telecommunications companies to remove or restrict content critical of the government or the ruling party.

Critics of the government face police intimidation, harassment, restricted movement, arbitrary arrest and detention, and imprisonment after unfair trials. Police regularly hold political detainees for months without access to legal counsel and subject them to abusive interrogations. Party-controlled courts sentence bloggers and activists to long prison sentences on bogus national security charges.

In March, Vietnam lifted all Covid-19 requirements for both domestic and international travel, but it continued to restrict freedom of movement for rights activists, dissidents, and government critics.

In October, Vietnam was elected to the United Nations Human Rights Council for the 2023-2025 term despite concerns about rights abuses.

Freedom of Expression, Opinion, and Speech

Political dissidents and human rights activists face systematic harassment, intimidation, arbitrary arrest, abuses in custody, and imprisonment.

Vietnam currently holds more than 160 people in prison for peacefully exercising their basic civil and political rights. During the first nine months of 2022, the courts convicted at least 27 people for voicing criticism of the government, and campaigning on human rights, environment, or democracy causes, and sentenced them to long prison sentences. They included citizen journalist Le Van Dung and democracy activist Dinh Van Hai.

In August, a court in Hanoi rejected the appeals of prominent blogger Pham Doan Trang, and land rights activists Trinh Ba Phuong and Nguyen Thi Tam. At time of writing, police were holding at least 14 other people in pretrial detention on politically motivated charges, including human rights defenders Nguyen Thuy Hanh, Nguyen Lan Thang, Bui Van Thuan, and Bui Tuan Lam.

In 2022, Vietnam stepped up its repression of NGO activists. Courts convicted journalist Mai Phan Loi, environmental lawyer Dang Dinh Bach, and environmental defender Nguy Thi Khanh on politically motivated charges of alleged tax evasion and sent them to prison. Nguy Thi Khanh is a 2018 winner of the internationally prestigious Goldman Environmental Prize, honoring grassroots environmental activists.

Freedom of Media, Access to Information

The government prohibits independent or privately owned media outlets, and imposes strict control over radio and television stations, and print publications. Authorities block access to websites, frequently shut down blogs, and require internet service providers to remove content or social media accounts deemed politically unacceptable.

In October, a new decree went into effect that requires technology companies to open physical offices in country and to store users' data in Vietnam. This highly problematic decree will give the government greater ability to pressure companies and is likely to lead to violations of the rights to freedom of expression, association, and privacy. US business groups sent a letter of complaint regarding

HUMAN RIGHTS WATCH

HUMAN RIGHTS WATCH

"Locked Inside Our Home"
Movement Restrictions on Rights Activists in Vietnam

these new requirements to Prime Minister Pham Minh Chinh. It is unclear if he responded to them.

Freedom of Movement

The government routinely violates the right to freedom of movement and other basic rights by subjecting activists, dissidents, human rights defenders, and others to indefinite house arrest, harassment, and other forms of detention. Authorities frequently detain activists just long enough to prevent them attending public protests, trials of fellow activists, meetings with foreign diplomats, and other human rights-related events.

Security agents keep people under house arrest by stationing plainclothes security agents outside homes, using padlocks to lock people inside, erecting roadblocks and other barriers to prevent people from leaving their homes and others from entering, mobilizing neighborhood thugs to intimidate people into staying home, and even applying very strong adhesives—such as "superglue"—on homeowner's locks.

The Vietnam government also systematically blocks rights activists, bloggers, dissidents, and their family members from domestic and international travel, including by stopping them at checkpoints, airports and border gates, and denying passports or other documents that would allow them to leave or enter the country.

In February, Human Rights Watch published a report, "'Locked Inside Our Home': Movement Restrictions on Rights Activists in Vietnam," detailing Vietnam's systemic and severe restrictions on freedom of movement between 2004 and 2021.

In March, security agents prevented eight democracy supporters from attending an event in Hanoi in support of Ukraine. In August, police prohibited human rights lawyer Vo An Don and his family from leaving Vietnam for the United States, citing national security.

Freedom of Religion

The government restricts religious practice through legislation, registration requirements, and surveillance. Religious groups must get approval from, and register with, the government and operate under government-controlled management boards. While authorities allow government-affiliated churches and pagodas to hold worship services, they ban religious activities that they arbitrarily deem to be contrary to the "national interest," "public order," or "national unity," including many ordinary types of religious functions.

Police monitor, harass, and sometimes violently crack down on religious groups operating outside government-controlled institutions. Unrecognized religious groups—including Cao Dai, Hoa Hao, Christian, and Buddhist groups—face constant surveillance, harassment, and intimidation. Followers of independent religious groups are subject to public criticism, forced renunciation of faith, detention, interrogation, torture, and imprisonment. As of September 2021, Vietnam acknowledged that it had not officially recognized about 140 religious groups with approximately 1 million followers.

Children's Rights

Violence against children, including sexual abuse, is pervasive in Vietnam, including at home and in schools. Numerous media reports have described cases of guardians, teachers, or government caregivers engaging in sexual abuse, beating children, or hitting them with sticks.

Women's Rights

In April, poet Da Thao Phuong publicly accused a former colleague of raping her 23 years ago and explained how the case was hushed up. The case spread quickly over social media, inspiring hopes that it would serve as a springboard for growth of a #MeToo movement in Vietnam, but there was little follow up and the authorities took no action.

Sexual Orientation and Gender Identity

In recent years, the Vietnamese government has taken modest strides to recognize the rights of lesbian, gay, bisexual, and transgender (LGBT) people, including by removing prohibitions on same-sex relationships and legal gender change.

In August, Vietnam's Ministry of Health officially confirmed that same-sex attraction and being transgender are not mental health conditions, and issued orders to hospitals and health providers to end discriminatory and abusive treatment of LGBT people.

Key International Actors

Vietnam tried to balance its relationships with China, its largest trade partner, and the United States, its second largest trade partner. On both the issues of Russia's invasion of Ukraine and US-China tension in the region, Vietnam proclaimed that it would not take sides.

Vietnam repeatedly voiced protests against China's military drills and increasing militarization on the disputed sea.

In March, Vietnam abstained from a vote at the United Nations General Assembly on passage of a resolution calling on Russia to end its military offensive in Ukraine and denouncing Russia's violations of international humanitarian and human rights law. In October, Vietnam again abstained from a vote to condemn Russia's unlawful annexations in Ukraine. In 2022, Vietnam celebrated the 10th anniversary of the establishment of a comprehensive strategic partnership with Russia.

In May, Prime Minister Pham Minh Chinh attended the US-Association of Southeast Asian Nations Summit in Washington DC and met President Joe Biden at the White House. Ahead of the Summit, US legislators pressed Biden to raise human rights concerns with Pham Minh Chinh. While Biden did not publicly raise the issues, it is unclear if he mentioned them in private.

The European Union issued some statements of concern around intensifying repression in Vietnam and held fruitless human rights consultations with the government. In September, Bernd Lange, chairman of the European Parliament's Committee on International Trade, visited Vietnam. EU claims that the conclusion of a bilateral free trade agreement in 2020 would contribute to more freedom and open space for civil society in Vietnam proved wrong; the bloc had yet to make any use of the supposedly stronger leverage to address human rights abuses by Hanoi that the deal allegedly provides.

Australia's bilateral relationship with Vietnam continues to grow, even as an Australian citizen, Chau Van Kham, remained in prison in Vietnam for his alleged involvement in an overseas political party declared unlawful by the Vietnamese government.

Japan remains the most important bilateral donor to Vietnam. In May, Japan Prime Minister Fumio Kishida visited Vietnam, and in September, Vietnam President Nguyen Xuan Phuc visited Japan. As in previous years, Japan failed to use its economic leverage to publicly urge Vietnam to improve its human rights record.

Yemen

On April 1, the United Nations announced that it had brokered a two-month truce agreement between the Houthi armed group and the Saudi and United Arab Emirates-led coalition. While the truce was renewed for an additional two months on June 2 and August 2, on October 2, parties to the conflict failed to renew the temporary ceasefire. While the truce was in effect, violations and abuses persisted in Yemen, including unlawful attacks that killed civilians; restrictions on freedom of movement and humanitarian access to and from Taizz, Yemen's third-largest city; arbitrary detention; and forced internal displacement.

After more than seven years, the protracted conflict in Yemen has led to one of the world's largest humanitarian crises, with more than 20 million Yemenis in need of assistance and suffering from inadequate food, health care, and infrastructure. The conflict has included unlawful attacks against civilian objects such as homes, hospitals, schools, and bridges, which were carried out deliberately and indiscriminately. Fighting has internally displaced more than 4 million people from their homes. There has been virtually no accountability for violations committed by parties to the conflict. Food insecurity, already on the rise, was further exacerbated by Russia's war on Ukraine.

Unlawful Attacks

In late January 2022, the Saudi and UAE-led coalition carried out three attacks in Sanaa, Hodeidah, and Saada in apparent violation of the laws of war that resulted in at least 80 apparently civilian deaths, including three children, and 156 injuries, including two children. The coalition attacks were in apparent retaliation for Houthi attacks on the UAE on January 17.

On January 17, coalition airstrikes destroyed two residential buildings and killed Houthi Brig. Gen. Abdullah al-Junid and nine other people, including two women, who a survivor and two other witnesses said were civilians. Nine other civilians were also injured, including three women.

On January 20, a coalition airstrike hit a telecommunication building in Hodeidah, destroying it, in an apparently disproportionate attack targeting critical infrastructure. Internet monitoring tools reported that from approximately 1:00 a.m. on January 21 until January 25 there was a near-total internet blackout in

Yemen. The attack killed five civilians who were nearby, including three children, and injured 20 others, including two children, according to relatives of victims.

On January 21, coalition airstrikes targeted a Houthi-controlled detention facility in Saada governorate. A photograph of a remnant from one of the munitions used in the attack included markings indicating that it was a laser-guided missile kit manufactured by the US defense contractor Raytheon. The Saudi and United Arab Emirates-led coalition stated that the attack was on a military facility. However, Mwatana for Human Rights and Human Rights Watch found no evidence to support that claim. Houthi forces guarding the facility also shot at detainees trying to flee, killing and injuring dozens.

Despite the truce, on July 23, the Houthis apparently shelled a residential neighborhood in Taizz, killing one child and wounding 11 others who were reportedly playing at the time. The UN special envoy condemned the attack.

Children and Armed Conflict

Yemen's protracted armed conflict and humanitarian crisis severely impact children: 13 million children in Yemen need humanitarian assistance, 2 million are internally displaced, and more than 10,200 children have been killed or maimed, according to UNICEF. Education and health services for children have been disrupted by damage to schools and hospitals caused by fighting. Yemen's laws explicitly permit corporal punishment of children in the home.

The Houthis and the Saudi and UAE-led coalition have committed serious violations against children throughout the war. Indiscriminate attacks have destroyed schools and hospitals and killed or injured thousands of children. The Houthis have recruited thousands of children as soldiers and pro-government Yemeni forces have also deployed children into combat.

In the last week of July, 38 children were killed or injured by the parties to the conflict, the highest number of child casualties in one week since early 2020, according to Save the Children.

In April, the Houthis signed an action plan with the United Nations to strengthen protection of children, and pledging to end recruitment and use of children as soldiers, killing and maiming of children, and attacks against schools and hospitals.

Landmines

Casualties as a result of landmines and unexploded ordinance rose, despite the truce agreement. In July, UN Special Envoy Hans Grundberg said that civilian casualties from landmines rose because "civilians moved through areas that were previously inaccessible due to fighting before the truce."

Save the Children found that landmines and unexploded ordnance were the largest killers of children since the start of the truce agreement. More than 42 children were apparently killed and injured by landmines and unexploded munitions between April and the end of June.

From mid-2019 to early August 2022, Yemeni Landmine Records documented 426 civilian deaths as a result of mines, including improvised explosive devices, and unexploded ordnance. Houthi forces have used antipersonnel landmines in violation of the 1997 Mine Ban Treaty, to which Yemen is a party, and the Saudi Arabia-led coalition has used internationally banned cluster munitions.

Arbitrary Detentions, Torture, and Enforced Disappearances

All parties to the conflict, including Houthi forces, the Yemeni government, the UAE, Saudi Arabia, and various UAE and Saudi-backed Yemeni armed groups have arbitrarily arrested, forcibly disappeared, tortured, and ill-treated people across Yemen. Hundreds of Yemenis have been detained at official and unofficial detention centers across the country.

On August 6, security forces apparently affiliated with the Southern Transitional Council (STC), a secessionist organization in southern Yemen, detained Yemeni journalist Ahmed Maher from his home in the southern port city of Aden, according to the Committee to Protect Journalists. On September 4, the STC released a video of Maher bearing signs of possible torture and ill-treatment, during which he confessed to assassinations and other serious crimes.

Amnesty International reported that detained journalist Tawfiq Al Mansouri was denied urgently needed medical care in detention. The Houthis detained Al Mansouri in 2015 and have been denying his requests for a hospital transfer since 2020.

Blocking and Impeding Humanitarian Access

The Houthis and the Yemeni government impose unnecessary restrictions and regulations on humanitarian organizations and aid projects, creating lengthy delays.

On May 16, the first commercial flight in six years departed Sanaa, as part of the UN-backed truce which included an agreement to reopen Sanaa International Airport for commercial flights. By mid-August, more than 15,000 passengers had traveled to and from Sanaa on 31 round-trip flights.

Despite UN efforts, there was little progress on opening the roads in and around Taizz, Yemen's third-largest city. Houthi forces continued to close the vital roads, violating freedom of movement and further contributing to the already grave humanitarian crisis in Taizz. The main roads in and out of the city of Taizz have been closed since 2015 by Houthi forces, severely restricting freedom of movement for civilians and impeding the flow of essential goods, medicine, and humanitarian access to the city's residents.

The two-month truce, which started April 2, included a provision for the special envoy for Yemen, Hans Grundberg, to "invite the parties to a meeting to agree on opening roads in Taiz and other governorates to facilitate the movement of civilian men, women, and children." On July 3, the Office of the Special Envoy shared plans for a phased reopening of the roads in Taizz to help alleviate civilian suffering. But the Houthi authorities rejected the proposal, prompting rare criticism by the European Union delegation to Yemen, which said that "the EU deeply regrets a rejection by the Houthis of the latest proposal."

On July 26, hundreds of Yemenis took to the streets in Taizz to protest the Houthi authorities' refusal to open the main roads.

Environment and Human Rights

On June 13, the UN announced that salvage operations for the FSO Safer, a supertanker moored off the coast of Hodeida, could not begin due to insufficient funding, and opened a US$20 million crowdfunding campaign to make up the funding gap. The Safer has been stranded without maintenance off Yemen's coast since 2015 and holds an estimated 1.14 million barrels of light crude oil.

The FSO Safer could explode or rupture at any time, threatening an environmental and humanitarian catastrophe, according to the United Nations.

The Houthi authorities, who control Hodeida, signed a memorandum of understanding with the UN on March 5 agreeing to facilitate a two-stage UN-coordinated plan to prevent the Safer from exploding or breaking apart. On September 21, the UN announced it had raised sufficient funds to begin a four-month-long operation to transfer oil from the Safer to a secure vessel. Following this first step, a second stage will involve installing a replacement vessel within 18 months. A total of $115 million is required for both stages.

Right to Food

More than half of Yemen's population faces food insecurity, which was further exacerbated by the conflict in Ukraine. Ukraine and Russia were leading exporters of agricultural products to Yemen and disruptions related to the war worsened already-rising food prices and deepened poverty. Before the war, Yemen imported at least 27 percent of its wheat from Ukraine and 8 percent from Russia.

According to the International Rescue Committee, skyrocketing food prices in recent years have left more than half the population in need of food assistance, while the sharp depreciation of the Yemeni rial has made imported food, oil, and other necessities more expensive, and has dramatically reduced households' purchasing power.

Women's Rights, Sexual Orientation, and Gender Identity

Yemeni women face restrictions on movement in areas under Houthi control, where authorities require them to be accompanied by a mahram (male relative) in order to travel. The mahram requirement bars women from traveling without a male guardian or evidence of their written approval. Increased Houthi restrictions related to the mahram requirement have prevented Yemeni women from working, especially those who must travel, according to Amnesty International. These restrictions also apply to Yemeni female humanitarian workers, which has made it more difficult for women to conduct fieldwork and has impacted access to aid for Yemeni women and girls.

Yemen's penal code prohibits same-sex relations. Article 264 punishes anal sex with 100 lashes and one year in prison if participants are not married. If married, the same article prescribes death by stoning. Article 268 punishes sex between women with up to three years in prison.

Abuses against Migrants

Migrants in Yemen face severe human rights violations along the journey from Somalia, Ethiopia, and Djibouti to Saudi Arabia in search of work, with many held in inhumane conditions without adequate access to basic services and food.

According to the International Organization for Migration (IOM), between April and June 2022, over 11,000 migrants arrived in Yemen from Djibouti and Somalia after dangerous boat journeys. The IOM estimates that over 43,000 migrants are stranded throughout Yemen.

Key International Actors

On April 7, President Abdo Rabbu Mansour Hadi transferred his presidential authority to an eight-member presidential leadership council with Rashad al-Alimi, a politician, as the council president. The council is backed by Saudi Arabia and the UAE, while Houthi forces continued to receive support from Iran.

Arms sales to Saudi Arabia, the UAE, and other coalition members continued from Western countries including the United States, the United Kingdom, France, Germany, Italy, Canada, and others.

An internal report by the US Government Accountability Office (GAO) found serious gaps in US government oversight of how arms sold to Saudi Arabia and the United Arab Emirates (UAE) are being used.

Since the UN Human Rights Council narrowly voted to end the Group of Eminent Experts on Yemen's mandate in October 2021, there has been no alternative mechanism to monitor the human rights situation in Yemen and ensure accountability for abuses.

In April, international donors pledged $1.6 billion to the humanitarian response for lifesaving humanitarian assistance and protection services, which is $2.7 billion less than the $4.3 billion needed for humanitarian programming.

Zimbabwe

The human rights climate in Zimbabwe deteriorated in 2022 without the government taking any meaningful steps to uphold rights and ensure justice for serious past abuses primarily committed by state security forces. There has been little progress on investigations into abductions, torture, arbitrary arrests, and other abuses against opposition politicians and activists. The government has yet to pass the Independent Complaints Commission Bill to establish an independent complaint mechanism—as provided by Zimbabwe's Constitution—to receive and investigate public complaints against the security services.

Repression of civil society organizations and activists continued unabated in 2022. In November 2021, the government proposed a bill to amend the Private Voluntary Organizations (PVO) Act to further restrict the operations of non-governmental organizations (NGOs). The government said the amendment is aimed at curbing terrorism financing and money laundering to comply with the Financial Action Taskforce (FATF) recommendations. There are, however, concerns that its passage would seriously threaten the right to freedom of association in the country.

The Cyber and Data Protection Act of 2021 has further undermined the rights of Zimbabweans, including civil society groups and human rights defenders. In February and March 2022, the authorities slowed down the internet significantly, with disruptions, during rallies and demonstrations by opposition parties and their supporters.

Section 73 of the Criminal Law (Codification and Reform) Amendment Act, 2006 (Criminal Law Code), which punishes consensual same-sex conduct between men with up to one year in prison, a fine or both, contributes to stigma and discrimination against lesbian, gay, bisexual, and transgender (LGBT) people.

Lack of Accountability for Abuses

Authorities often arbitrarily arrested, harassed, and prosecuted critics of the ruling party through lengthy detentions and trials.

Notable critic and author, Tsitsi Dangarembga, and another protester, Julie Barnes, have faced a prolonged trial since their arrest in July 2020 during an anti-government protest on charges of public incitement to violence, breach of peace, and bigotry. On September 29, the Harare Magistrate court gave them a six-month suspended jail sentence and a fine for participating in a public gathering with the intent to incite violence and for breaking Covid-19 protocols.

The Movement for Democratic Change (MDC) Alliance members, Cecilia Chimbiri, Netsai Marova, and a member of parliament, Joanna Mamombe, were in court 61 times between January and May 2022, facing charges of faking their own abduction. The authorities are prosecuting the three women for reporting that in May 2020 they were abducted from police custody by suspected state security agents, assaulted and sexually abused, then dumped in Bindura, 80 kilometers from Harare, the capital. They were accused of taking part in a protest against the government during the Covid-19 lockdown.

Failure to investigate these women's reports of assault and sexual abuse violates the country's obligation to ensure access to justice and effective remedies in cases of human rights violations under international and African regional human rights law.

More than four years after the Motlanthe Commission of Inquiry's into the 2018 post-election violence, no steps have been taken to implement its recommendations This includes ensuring justice for the six people killed and 35 injured by government security forces.

Rights to Food, Water, and Sanitation

The World Bank ranked Zimbabwe second out of 177 countries for food price inflation between April to July 2022, which has contributed to deteriorating food security. As of August 2022, the World Food Program estimates that between 30 and 38 percent of the rural population is food insecure. This is despite the minister of agriculture stating that Zimbabwe would attain food security by 2022 through agricultural transformation. Climate change—which has exacerbated floods, cyclones, and droughts—the Covid-19 pandemic, and the war in Ukraine have led to a food crisis in the country. climate change exacerbating floods, cyclones, and droughts. the Covid-19 pandemic, as well as the ongoing war in Ukraine have led to a food crisis in the country.

While the government has introduced several action plans to address the growing food insecurity in the country, such as the National Nutrition Strategy and the National Policy on Drought Management, there has been no effective implementation of farming projects, allegedly due to corruption, poor policy implementation, and lack of coordination among the ruling and opposition political parties.

Many parts of Zimbabwe continue to face a water crisis, with some places in Harare going without safe water for years, and residents turning to potentially contaminated wells and boreholes. Human Rights Watch research shows that neighboring towns like Chitungwiza, Ruwa, Epworth, and Norton draw water from Harare's water system, which is reportedly contaminated with algae and toxic substances linked to incidents of water-borne diseases in those locations.

In 2022, according to media reports, water supplies varied from erratic to non-existent in some parts of Harare, following a reduction in water production at Morton Jaffray Water Treatment Waterworks. The country's second largest city, Bulawayo, has faced similar water shortages. In March, Bulawayo authorities introduced 20-hour day water rationing due to poor rainfall.

Access to safe water has also remained a challenge in rural areas with some areas being more affected than others due to a lack of reliable water sources, such as dams and boreholes.

The government has taken some positive steps to address the crisis, including setting aside US$5.3 million for a critical Harare water treatment project. There are, however, delays in disbursing the funds, exposing residents to further risks. The lingering water crisis has affected the rights of Zimbabweans under section 77 of the 2013 constitution, which provides for the right to safe, clean, and potable water.

Forced Evictions

The government has continued to designate land for mining and commercial projects, without consulting affected communities. In 2022, about 50 families in Nyamakope village, in the district of Mutoko, alleged that a Chinese mining company told them that they would have to leave their homes and land that fell within the mining area licensed to the company by the government. According to media reports some families were given $2,500 as compensation, an amount considered meagre since it does not allow them to secure new housing and did not consider their relationship with their ancestral land.

On January 20, a Zimbabwean civil society group flagged concerns about Chinese mining projects in the country and the threats of displacement faced by affected local communities. In response to rising concerns, the Chamber of Chinese Enterprises in Zimbabwe called on the Zimbabwean government to "avoid granting projects with demolition disputes, environmental risks, and cultural conflicts to Chinese enterprise."

Children's Rights

In May, in the case of *Kawenda v Minister of Justice, Legal and Parliamentary Affairs & Others*, the Constitutional Court declared the Criminal Law Code provisions that set the age of consent to sexual intercourse at 16 years as inconsistent with section 81(1) of the 2013 constitution, which defines a child as anyone under 18 years. Parliament in March passed the Child Marriage Bill, which, if signed into law, will establish the age of legal and customary law marriages or a civil partnership as 18 years.

Key International Actors

In December 2021, four United Nations special rapporteurs on the rights to freedom of peaceful assembly and the right to freedom of association, the promotion and protection of the right to freedom of opinion and expression, the situation of human rights defenders, and on the promotion and protection of human rights and fundamental freedoms while countering terrorism, released joint comments and expressed concerns about the grave consequences of Zimbabwe's Private Voluntary Organizations Amendment Bill "for the exercise of civil and political rights, including the right to freedom of association of Private Voluntary Organizations in Zimbabwe."

In February, the European Union renewed sanctions on Zimbabwe citing continued intimidation of political opposition and other government critics, as well as the restriction of the democratic and civic space through the Data Protection Act and the proposed PVO Amendment Bill.

The United Kingdom added Zimbabwe Defense Industries in February to the list of designated persons on targeted sanctions for being involved in the commission of serious human rights violations in Zimbabwe.

In March, the United States also extended its sanctions on Zimbabwe for another year, stating that human rights violations and violent crackdowns on the opposition continued amid President Emerson Mnangagwa's failed promises to introduce political reforms six years after replacing the late President Robert Mugabe.

Senegalese President Macky Sall, chairperson of the African Union, and Alena Douhan, the UN special rapporteur on the negative impact of unilateral and coercive measures on the enjoyment of human rights, in May and August respectively called for the lifting of sanctions, claiming they adversely impact living conditions and human rights of Zimbabweans at a time of crisis.

CPSIA information can be obtained
at www.ICGtesting.com
Printed in the USA
JSHW032049020223
37106JS00002B/10